Problem Solving and Structured Programming in
FORTRAN 77

FOURTH EDITION

Problem Solving and Structured Programming in

FORTRAN 77

FOURTH EDITION

Elliot B. Koffman
Frank L. Friedman

Temple University

Addison-Wesley Publishing Company, Inc.
Reading, Massachusetts   Menlo Park, California   New York
Don Mills, Ontario   Wokingham, England   Amsterdam   Bonn
Sydney   Singapore   Tokyo   Madrid   San Juan

Keith Wollman, Sponsoring Editor
Bette J. Aaronson, Production Supervisor
Nancy Benjamin, Production Editor
Joyce Cameron Weston, Text and Cover Design
Roy Logan, Manufacturing Supervisor

Library of Congress Cataloging-in-Publication Data

Koffman, Elliot B.
    Problem solving and structured programming in
FORTRAN 77.

    1. FORTRAN 77 (Computer program language).
2. Structured programming.   I. Friedman, Frank L.
II. Title.
QA76.73.F25K64   1990   005.26   89-18494
ISBN 0-201-51216-5

To our families
Caryn, Richard, Deborah, and Robin Koffman
and
Martha, Shelley, and Dara Friedman

Preface

This is a textbook for a first course in problem solving and programming methods using the FORTRAN language. It assumes no prior knowledge of computers or programming. A course in high-school algebra is sufficient mathematics background for most of the material in this textbook, except for sections of the last chapter. In other chapters, examples that require more mathematical background are clearly marked.

The most significant change in this edition is a substantial increase in the number of engineering and science examples, including at least one new case study in each chapter. We have also retained most of the general examples. The net result is a textbook that can be used either in a FORTRAN course for engineering and science majors or in an introductory programming course for a general audience.

Problem Solving, Structured Programming, and Modularization

The first edition of this textbook was published in 1977, the same year that FORTRAN 77 became the standard version of the FORTRAN language. The first edition pioneered the teaching of problem solving and structured programming in a FORTRAN course, a tradition that has continued in successive editions.

Problem solving continues to be emphasized in this edition. Chapter 2 contains a new section on the art and science of problem solving, which includes a discussion of the engineering and scientific method.

This edition has an increased emphasis on modular programming, which is an important component of structured programming. Chapter 4 introduces the use of library functions; Chapter 5 is a new chapter on user-defined functions and subroutines. In this edition, we discuss both kinds of FORTRAN subprograms before coverage of arrays (Chapter 6). This allow us to use subprograms in many of the program examples that manipulate arrays.

Organization of the Book

The first seven chapters represent the core of the book and should be studied by all students. Students in a general course should skip many of the engineering examples; students in a predominately engineering or science section may skip some of the business-oriented case studies.

Chapter 1 provides an overview of computer hardware and software, including an expanded introduction to the history of computers. It contains an introduction to FORTRAN statements and data types, and the use of FORTRAN in different programming environments. It also introduces the essentials of using files, so that students can write programs that access data files prepared by their instructor or send their program results to an output file.

Chapter 2 describes problem solving, algorithm refinement, and decisions in programs. The chapter begins by discussing problem solving in engineering and science followed by a general discussion of problem solving and algorithm refinement. It also shows how to write conditions and implement decisions in FORTRAN using the IF statement. The chapter covers all aspects of the use of the IF statement, including the Block IF form for implementing decisions with multiple alternatives.

Chapter 3 describes two control structures for implementing loops: the DO loop and the WHILE loop. As in earlier editions, we include the WHILE loop because we believe students should know how to use this control structure, which is fundamental to structured programming. Even though the WHILE loop is not part of the FORTRAN 77 standard, it is provided as an optional feature in many versions of FORTRAN 77 and will be included in the new FORTRAN standard (FORTRAN 8X). For those who do not have access to this control structure, we show how to implement it in standard FORTRAN 77.

Chapter 4 provides additional details on FORTRAN data types, including the use of library functions in expressions. The chapter also introduces the FORMAT statement.

Chapter 5 is a new chapter on subprograms. The chapter covers both function and subroutine subprograms. It introduces preconditions and postconditions as part of a function's documentation. It also shows how to use structure charts to document the flow of control and data between the main program and its subprograms.

Chapter 6 introduces the array, focusing on one-dimensional arrays. Chapter 7 covers advanced features of arrays, including multidimensional arrays, searching an array, and sorting an array. The chapter also discusses additional subprogram concepts, including COMMON storage and the SAVE statement. The chapter ends with a discussion of random number generation and computer simulation.

The remaining chapters cover advanced material. These chapters do not have to be studied in any particular order. If time permits, instructors in classes with a general audience should concentrate on Chapters 8 and 9, which cover additional features of formatting, file processing, and string manipulation. Instructors in classes with science and engineering students should spend more time on Chapters 10 and 11, which cover graphing, computer-aided design, and numerical methods.

FORTRAN Versions and Computers

The text uses FORTRAN 77 as its language of instruction rather than FORTRAN 8X. The reason for this choice is the current widespread availability of FORTRAN 77 compilers. At the time of publication of this book, FORTRAN 8X was still awaiting final approval so there were no FORTRAN 8X compilers. As mentioned earlier, we have included one important new control structure from FORTRAN

8X, the WHILE loop. Appendix D summarizes many of the important features of FORTRAN 8X.

The text is not oriented toward any specific computer. Chapter 1 discusses booting a personal computer and logging onto a timeshared computer. Most of the examples are written as interactive programs, which is the most prevalent mode of programming today. All of the new programs have been tested on an IBM-compatible personal computer using Microsoft FORTRAN 77. Appendix C describes how to use this popular compiler for microcomputers.

Pedagogical Features

We employ many pedagogical features to enhance the usefulness of this book as a teaching tool. Some of these features are discussed below.

End of Section Exercises: Most sections end with a number of self-check exercises. These include exercises that require analysis of program segments as well as short programming exercises. Answers to these exercises appear in the back of the book.

End of Chapter Exercises and Projects: Each chapter ends with a set of quick-check exercises with answers. There are also chapter review exercises whose solutions appear in the back of the book. Finally, there is a set of programming projects whose solutions appear in the instructor's manual.

Examples and Case Studies: The book contains a large number and variety of programming examples. Whenever possible, examples contain complete programs or subprograms rather than incomplete program fragments. There are also substantial case studies that help a student integrate and apply concepts studied over several chapters.

Syntax Display Boxes: The syntax displays describe the syntax and semantics of each new FORTRAN feature and also provide examples.

Program Style Displays: The program style displays discuss issues of good programming style.

Error Discussions and Chapter Reviews: Each chapter ends with a discussion of common programming errors. A chapter review includes a table of new FORTRAN statements.

Appendices and Supplements

A reference table of FORTRAN statements appears on the inside covers of the book. There are appendices on FORTRAN Library Functions and Character Sets. Also, there is an appendix on MS-DOS and the Microsoft FORTRAN 77 compiler and one covering FORTRAN 8X.

Supplements include an instructor's manual, transparency masters, and a program disk with all the programs that appear in the book. Use the reference numbers below to order these supplements from your Addison-Wesley sales representative.

Instructor's Manual: 1-201-51217-3
Transparency Masters: 1-201-52147-4
Program Disk: 1-201-51218-1

We are very grateful to Thomas Cunningham at Indiana University of Pennsylvania for his work on producing the instructor's manual.

Acknowledgments

Many people participated in the development of this book. Professors Bart Childs and Glen Williams, and Mr. Mitch Fincher of Texas A & M University carefully reviewed the previous edition and provided many suggestions for improvement. They also prepared a host of engineering examples, exercises, case studies, and programming projects for inclusion in the book. Their help was invaluable in increasing the number of engineering and science applications presented.

The principal reviewers were most essential in suggesting improvements and finding errors. The principal reviewers include: Professor James Allert, University of Minnesota; Walter Brainerd, UNICOMP; Professor William H. Dodge, Rensselaer Polytechnic University; Professor George J. Dudas, Pennsylvania State University, Behrend College; Professor Sundaresan Jayaraman, Georgia Institute of Technology; Professor Richard A. Lejk, University of North Carolina at Charlotte; Professor Ernie Rilki, William Rainer Harper College; Abolfazl Sirjani, IBM; Professor Conrad L. White, Northern Illinois University.

We would also like to acknowledge the contribution of Professor Richard Epstein of George Washington University. Professor Epstein provided the original draft of much of the material in Chapters 10 and 11.

The personnel at Addison-Wesley responsible for the production of this book worked diligently to meet a very demanding schedule. The sponsoring editor, Keith Wollman, was closely involved in all phases of the manuscript preparation and provided much help and guidance. His assistant, Debbie Lafferty, did an excellent job of coordinating the reviewing process. Bette Aaronson supervised the design and production of the book, while Nancy Benjamin coordinated the conversion of the manuscript to a finished book.

E.B.K.
F.L.F.

Contents

6. Arrays   284

7. More Arrays and Subprograms   338

11. ▬▬▬ Introduction to Numerical Methods   527

Application Areas

Engineering/Science
Converting inches to centimeters, 20
Heat loss and pressure loss formulas, 40
Parallel resistance, 59
Testing column safety, 83
Computing compass bearing, 101
Physics of falling bodies, 121, 145
Temperature conversion, 137
Computing radiation levels, 161
Hydrostatic pressure, 176
Engineering properties of lumber, 176
Theory of relativity, 190
Shooting an arrow through a window, 193
Flow of water through a pipe, 215, 233
Computing maximum tensile loads, 221, 265
Radioactive decay, 232
Image enhancement, 346
Simulation and random numbers, 374
Movement of radioactive particles, 393
The game of Life, 394
Survey of land boundaries, 427
Wind chill factor, 449
Parametric equations, 508
Contour plots, 511, 515
Computer-aided design, 520
Interference pattern, 526

Business
Value of coin collection, 33
Payroll computations, 30, 43, 78, 89, 129
Price of concrete, 91
Savings certificate interest, 146, 231
Balancing a checkbook, 156
Mortgage interest, 231, 399
Computing electric company bills, 282
Processing time cards, 283
Budget categories, 322
Airline reservations, 393
Inventory control, 395
Bookstore inventory, 420, 438
Merging mailing lists, 422

Mathematics and Statistics
Area and circumference of a circle, 69
Average of measurements, 125
Computing value of e, 138
Powers of 2, 144
Square root approximation, 175
Roots of a quadratic equation, 191
Factorial function, 236
Combinations of r items from n items, 240
Rounding a number, 244
Prime numbers, 251
Area of a triangle, 280
Average value and standard deviation, 292
Area of a polygon, 310
Plotting a function, 319, 498
Adding matrixes, 345
Estimating pi, 376
Dot product of arrays, 392
Trigonometric functions, 452
Roots of equations, 528
Newton's method, 536
Vector and matrix operations, 537, 539
Linear equations, 543
Linear regression and correlation, 553
Numerical integration, 561

General
Smallest of three numbers, 81
Sum of integers, 117, 133
Counting down, 134
Worm attacks apple, 140
Product of non-zero values, 151, 154
Guessing a number in an interval, 200
Registering voters, 217
Sorting, 268
Largest value in a list, 304
Tic-tac-toe display, 341
Course enrollment, 343
Searching an array, 355
Sorting an array, 357
Student grading, 360
Cryptogram generator, 474
Syntax analysis, 477
Text editor, 481

1. Introduction to Computers and Programming

I N THIS chapter, we introduce computers and computer programming. We begin with a brief history of computers and a description of the major components of a computer, including memory, central processor, input devices, and output devices. We also discuss how information is represented in a computer and how it is manipulated.

Following this introduction, we begin a discussion of the main topics of this book: problem solving, programming, and FORTRAN. We first discuss problem solving with a computer. Then languages for computer programming are described. Finally, some simple computer operations are presented along with some short FORTRAN programs that demonstrate these operations. The FORTRAN programs contain statements for reading and displaying information and for performing simple computations.

Also described are the steps involved in creating a FORTRAN program and the roles performed by special programs that are part of a computer system. These programs include the operating system, compiler, editor, and loader.

1.1   Electronic Computers Then and Now

It is difficult to live in today's society without having some contact with computers. Computers are used to provide instructional material in schools, print transcripts, send out bills, reserve airline and concert tickets, play games, and even help authors write books.

However, it wasn't always this way. Just a short time ago, computers were fairly mysterious devices that only a small percentage of our population knew much about. Computer "know-how" turned around when advances in solid-state electronics led to large reductions in the size and cost of electronic computers. Today, a personal computer (see Fig. 1.1), which costs less than $3000 and sits on a desk, has as much computational power as one that 10 years ago would cost more than $100,000 and would fill a 9' × 12' room. This price reduction is even more remarkable when we consider the effects of inflation over the last decade.

If we take the literal definition for a *computer* as a device for counting or computing, then the abacus might be considered the first computer. However, the first electronic digital computer was designed in the late 1930s by Dr. John Atanasoff at Iowa State University. Atanasoff designed his computer to perform mathematical computations for graduate students.

The first large-scale, general-purpose electronic digital computer, called the ENIAC, was built in 1946 at the University of Pennsylvania with funding supplied by the U.S. Army. The ENIAC was used for computing ballistics

Figure 1.1. *IBM Personal Computer*

tables, for weather prediction, and for atomic energy calculations. The ENIAC weighed 30 tons and occupied a 30′ × 50′ space (see Fig. 1.2).

Although we are often led to believe otherwise, computers cannot think! They are basically devices for performing computations at incredible speeds (more than one million operations per second) and with great accuracy. However, in order to accomplish anything useful, a computer must be *programmed*, or given a sequence of explicit instructions (the *program*) to carry out.

To program the ENIAC it was necessary to connect hundreds of wires and arrange thousands of switches in a certain way. In 1946, Dr. John von Neumann of Princeton University proposed the concept of a *stored program computer* in which the instructions of a program would be stored in computer memory rather than be set by wires and switches. Since the contents of computer memory can be easily changed, it would not be nearly as difficult to reprogram this computer to perform different tasks as it was to reprogram the ENIAC. Von Neumann's design is the basis of the digital computer as we know it today.

Brief History of Computers

Table 1.1 lists some of the important milestones along the path from the abacus to modern-day electronic computers. We often use the term *first gener-*

Figure 1.2. *The ENIAC Computer (Photo Courtesy of Sperry Corporation)*

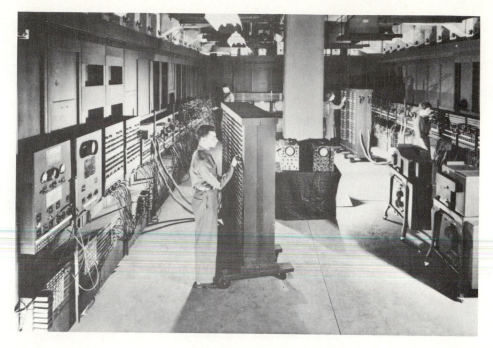

ation to refer to electronic computers that used vacuum tubes (1939–1958). The *second generation* began in 1958 with the changeover to transistors. The *third generation* began in 1964 with the introduction of integrated circuits. The *fourth generation* began in 1975 with the advent of large-scale integration.

Categories of Computers

Modern-day computers are classified according to their size and speed. The three major categories of computers are microcomputers, minicomputers, and mainframes.

Many of you have seen or used *microcomputers* such as the IBM PC (see Fig. 1.1) or the Macintosh computer (see Fig. 1.3). Microcomputers are also called personal computers or desktop computers because they are used by one person at a time and are small enough to fit on a desk. The largest microcomputers, called *workstations* (see Fig. 1.4), are commonly used by engineers to produce engineering drawings and to assist in the design and development of new products.

Minicomputers are the next larger variety of computers. They generally operate at faster speeds than microcomputers and can store larger quantities of information. Minicomputers can serve several different users simultaneously.

Table 1.1. *Milestones in Computer Development*

DATE	EVENT
2000 BC	The abacus is first used for computations.
1642 AD	Blaise Pascal creates a mechanical adding machine for tax computations. It is unreliable.
1670	Gottfried von Leibniz creates a more reliable adding machine, which adds, subtracts, multiplies, divides, and calculates square roots.
1842	Charles Babbage designs an analytical engine to perform general calculations automatically. Ada Augusta (a.k.a. Lady Lovelace) is a programmer for this machine.
1890	Herman Hollerith designs a system to record census data. The information is stored as holes on cards which are interpreted by machines with electrical sensors. Hollerith starts a company that will eventually become IBM.
1939	John Atanasoff, with graduate student Clifford Berry, designs and builds the first electronic digital computer. His project was funded by a grant for $650.
1946	J. Presper Eckert and John Mauchly design and build the ENIAC computer. It used 18,000 vacuum tubes and cost $500,000 to build.
1946	John von Neumann proposes that a program be stored in a computer in the same way that data are stored. His proposal (called "von Neumann architecture") is the basis of modern computers.
1951	Eckert and Mauchly build the first general-purpose commercial computer, the UNIVAC.
1957	John Backus and his team at IBM complete the first FORTRAN compiler.
1958	The first computer to use the transistor as a switching device, the IBM 7090, is introduced.
1958	Seymour Cray builds the first fully transistorized computer, the CDC 1604, for Control Data Corporation.
1964	The first computer using integrated circuits, the IBM 360, is announced.
1975	The first microcomputer, the Altair, is introduced.
1975	The first supercomputer, the Cray-1, is announced.
1976	Digital Equipment Corporation introduces its popular minicomputer, the VAX 11/780.
1977	Steve Wozniak and Steve Jobs found Apple Computer.
1978	Dan Bricklin and Bob Frankston develop the first electronic spreadsheet, called VisiCalc, for the Apple computer.
1981	IBM introduces the IBM PC.
1981	Apollo Computer ships the first Domain workstation.
1982	Sun Microsystem introduces its first workstation, the Sun 100.

Figure 1.3. *Macintosh Computer with Mouse*

Figure 1.4. *SUN Microsystems SPARCstation 370 (Photo Courtesy of Sun Microsystems, Inc.)*

A small- or medium-size company might use a minicomputer to perform payroll computations and to keep track of its inventory. Engineers often use minicomputers to control a chemical plant or a production process.

The largest computers are called *mainframes*. A large company would have one or more mainframes at its central computing facility. Mainframes are often used as "number crunchers" to generate solutions to systems of equations that characterize an engineering or scientific problem. A mainframe can solve in seconds equations that might take hours to solve on a minicomputer or even days on a microcomputer. The largest mainframes are called *supercomputers* and are used to solve the most complex systems of equations.

In the late 1950s, mainframe computers could perform only fifty instructions per second. Now it is not uncommon to have much smaller workstations that can perform over twenty million instructions per second. Obviously, there have been tremendous changes in the speed and size of computers in a relatively short time.

1.2 ▬▬▬ Components of a Computer

Despite large variations in cost, size, and capabilities, modern computers are remarkably similar in a number of ways. Basically, a computer consists of the components shown in Fig. 1.5. The arrows connecting the components show the direction of information flow.

All information that is to be processed by a computer must first be entered into the computer's *main memory* via an *input device*. The information in main memory is manipulated by the *central processor,* and the results of this manipulation are stored in main memory. Information in main memory can be displayed through an *output device. Secondary memory* is often used for storing large quantities of information in a semipermanent form. These components and their interaction are described in more detail in the following sections.

Main Memory   Main memory is used for storing information and programs. All types of information—numbers, names, lists, and even pictures—may be represented and stored in main memory.

Picture the memory of a computer as an ordered sequence of storage locations called *memory cells*. To be able to store and *retrieve* (access) information, we must have some way to identify the individual memory cells. To accomplish this, each memory cell has associated with it a unique *address* that indicates its relative position in memory. Figure 1.6 shows a computer memory consisting of 1000 memory cells with addresses 0 through 999. Almost all

Figure 1.5. *Components of a Computer*

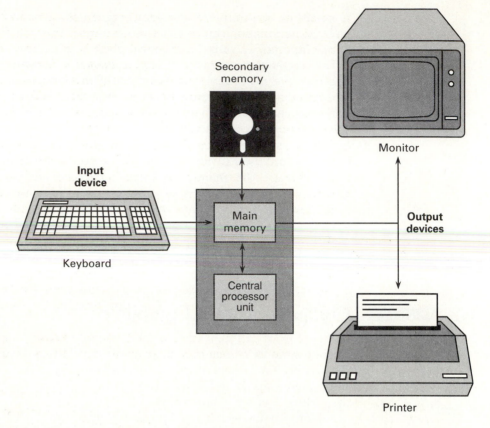

Figure 1.6. *A Computer Memory with 1000 Cells*

Memory

Address	Contents
0	−27.2
1	354
2	0.005
3	−26
4	H
⋮	⋮
998	X
999	75.62

large-scale computers have memories consisting of millions of individual cells. Most personal computers have less than one million memory cells.

The information stored in a memory cell is called the *contents* of a memory cell. Every memory cell always contains some information, although we may have no idea what that information is. Whenever new information is placed in a memory cell, any information already there is destroyed and cannot be retrieved. In Fig. 1.6, the contents of memory cell 3 is the number −26, and the contents of memory cell 4 is the letter H.

The memory cells shown in Fig. 1.6 are actually aggregates, or collections, of smaller units called *bytes*. A byte is the amount of storage required to store a single character. The number of bytes in a memory cell varies from computer to computer. A byte is an aggregate of even smaller units of storage called *bits*, which are single binary digits (0 or 1). There are generally eight bits to a byte.

Each value stored in memory is represented by a particular pattern of zeros and ones. To store a value, the computer sets each bit of a selected memory cell to 0 or 1, thereby destroying what was previously in that bit. To retrieve a value from a memory cell, the computer copies the pattern of zeros and ones stored in that cell to another storage area, the *memory buffer register*, where the bit pattern can be processed. The copy operation does not destroy the bit pattern currently in that memory cell.

The process just described is the same regardless of the kind of information—character, number, or program instruction—stored in a memory cell.

Central Processor Unit

The *central processor unit* (CPU) performs the actual processing or manipulation of information stored in memory. The CPU can retrieve information from memory. This information may be either data or instructions for manipulating data. It can also store the results of these manipulations back in memory for later use.

The CPU control unit coordinates all activities of the computer. It determines which operations should be carried out and in what order; it then transmits coordinating control signals to the computer components.

The CPU also performs a variety of arithmetic operations, including addition, subtraction, multiplication, and division. These arithmetic operations are performed on data that are stored in main memory; the computational results are then saved in memory. A typical CPU can perform an arithmetic operation in about a millionth of a second. The CPU also consists of electronic circuitry to compare information and to make decisions based on the results of the comparison.

Input and Output Devices

Input/output devices enable us to communicate with the computer. Specifically, we must be able to enter data for a computation into memory. Later, the computational results that are stored in memory can be displayed.

Most of you will be using a *keyboard* as an input device and a *monitor* or *display screen* as an output device. A computer keyboard resembles a typewriter keyboard except that it has some extra keys for performing special functions. On the keyboard shown in Fig. 1.7, the two columns of keys on the left (labeled F1 through F10) are *function keys*. The function performed by pressing one of these keys depends on the program that is executing.

A monitor is similar to a television screen. Some monitors have *graphics capability*, which enables the output to be displayed as a two-dimensional graph or picture.

Another common input device is a *mouse* (see Fig. 1.3). A mouse is used to move an electronic pointer called the *cursor* around the display screen. The computer user can select an operation pictured on the screen by clicking a button when the mouse is over that item.

If you are using a personal computer, the keyboard and/or monitor may be built into the computer or connected to it by cables. If you are using a minicomputer or mainframe, the keyboard and monitor together comprise a computer *terminal* (see Fig. 1.8); the terminal is connected to the computer by cables or via telephone lines.

The only problem with using a monitor as an output device is that there is no written record of the computation. Once the image disappears from the monitor screen, it is lost. If you want *hard-copy output*, then you have to send your computational results to an output device called a *printer* (see Fig. 1.9).

Secondary Memory

Most computers have a limited amount of main memory. Consequently, *secondary memory* provides additional data-storage capability on most computer

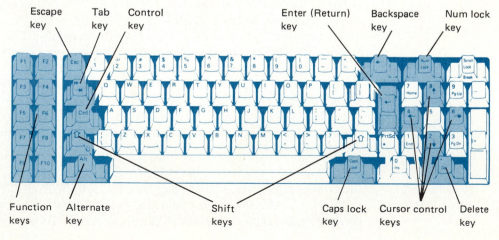

Figure 1.7. *Keyboard for the IBM PC/XT*

Escape key   Tab key   Control key   Enter (Return) key   Backspace key   Num lock key

Function keys   Alternate key   Shift keys   Caps lock key   Cursor control keys   Delete key

Figure 1.8. *A Computer Terminal*

Figure 1.9. *A Printer*

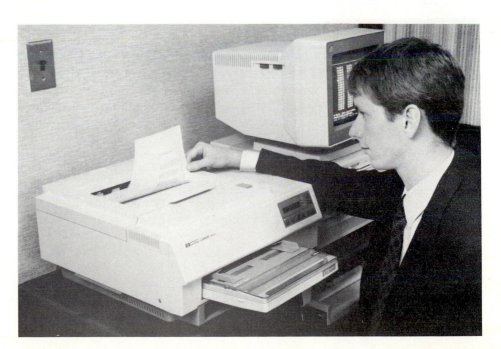

Figure 1.10. *Inserting a Floppy Disk into a Disk Drive*

systems. For example, a *disk drive,* which stores data on a disk, is a common secondary storage device for today's personal computers (Fig. 1.10).

There are two kinds of disks: *hard disks* and *floppy disks.* A computer may have one or more drives of each kind. A hard disk normally cannot be removed from its drive, so the storage area on a hard disk is often shared by all the users of a computer. However, each computer user may have his or her own floppy disks that can be inserted into a disk drive as needed. Hard disks can store much more data than can floppy disks and operate much more quickly, but they are also much more expensive.

Many types of information can be stored on disk, for example, a computer program, payroll data from a business, or data from earthquake seismic readings taken by a research center. Each of these collections of information is called a *file.* You must give a file a unique name when you first store it on a disk, so that you can retrieve that file at a later date.

Comparison of Main and Secondary Memory

Main memory is much faster and more expensive than secondary memory. The CPU can manipulate only data that are in main memory; therefore, data in secondary memory must be transferred to main memory before processing. Data in main memory are *volatile* and disappear when you switch off the computer. Data in secondary memory are *permanent* and do not disappear when the computer is switched off.

1. What are the contents of memory cells 0 and 999 in Fig. 1.6? What memory cells contain the letter X and the fraction 0.005?
2. Explain the purpose of main memory, the central processor, and the disk drive and disk? What input and output devices will be used with your computer?

1.3 ▬▬▬ Problem Solving and Programming

We mentioned earlier that a computer cannot think; therefore, in order to get it to do any useful work, it must be provided with a *program,* or a list of instructions to be carried out by the computer. Programming a computer is a lot more involved than simply writing a list of instructions. Problem solving is an important component of programming. Before we can write a program to solve a particular problem, we must consider carefully all aspects of the problem and then organize its solution.

If you are like most programming students, you will probably spend a great deal of time initially at the computer terminal entering your programs. You will spend more time later removing the errors that inevitably will be present in your programs. Following the steps described below should help you minimize the time and effort spent in programming.

It is tempting to rush to the computer terminal and start entering your program as soon as you have some idea of how to write it. You should resist this temptation and instead think carefully about the problem and its solution before writing any program instructions. When you have a solution in mind, you should plan it out on paper and modify it if necessary before writing the program.

Once the program is written on paper, you should *desk check* your solution by "executing" it much as the computer would. You should carefully determine the result of each instruction using sample data that are easy to manipulate (e.g., small whole numbers). You should compare these results with what would be expected and make any necessary corrections to the program when the results are incorrect. Only then should you go to the computer terminal and start to enter the program. Experience has shown that a few extra minutes spent evaluating the proposed solution in this way often saves hours of frustration later. The process you should follow is shown in Fig. 1.11.

Figure 1.11. *A Problem-Solving and Programming Strategy*

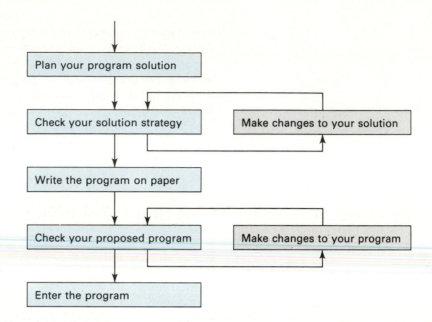

In this text, we will stress a methodology for problem solving that we have found useful in helping students to learn to program. We will teach a technique called *structured programming* that should enable you to write programs that are relatively easy to read and understand, that contain fewer initial errors, and that are easy to maintain and modify in the future.

1.4 Programming Languages

Languages used for writing computer programs are called *programming languages*. There are many different programming languages, but most of them fall into three broad categories: machine, assembly, and high-level languages.

High-level languages are most often used by *programmers* (program writers). One reason for the popularity of high-level languages is that they are much easier to use than machine and assembly languages. Another reason is that a high-level language program is *portable*. This means that a high-level language program can be executed with little or no modification on many different types of computers. An assembly language or machine language program, on the other hand, may execute on only one type of computer.

Some common high-level languages are FORTRAN, BASIC, COBOL, Pascal, and C. Each of these languages was designed with a specific purpose in mind. FORTRAN is an acronym for FORmula TRANslation and its principal users have been engineers and scientists. BASIC (Beginners All-purpose Symbolic Instructional Code) was designed to be a language that could be easily learned and used by students. COBOL (COmmon Business Oriented Language) is used primarily for business data-processing operations. Pascal was designed as a language for teaching structured programming (more on this later). C combines the power of an assembly language with the ease of use and portability of a high-level language.

One of the most important features of high-level languages is that they allow us to write program statements that resemble English. We can reference data that are stored in memory using descriptive names (e.g., NAME, RATE, RADIUS, WEIGHT) rather than numeric memory-cell addresses. We can also describe operations that we would like performed using familiar symbols. For example, in several high-level languages, the statement

```
PRICE = COST + PROFIT
```

means add COST to PROFIT and store the result in PRICE.

We can also use descriptive names to reference data in assembly language; however, we must specify the operations to be performed on the data more explicitly. The high-level language statement above might be written as

```
LOAD  COST
ADD   PROFIT
STORE PRICE
```

in an assembly language.

Machine language is the native tongue of a computer. Each machine language instruction is a *binary string* (string of 0's and 1's) that specifies an operation and the memory cells involved in the operation. The assembly language statements above might be written as

```
0010 0000 0000 0100
0100 0000 0000 0101
0011 0000 0000 0110
```

in a machine language. Obviously, what is easiest for a computer to understand is most difficult for a person and vice versa.

A computer can execute only programs that are in machine language. Consequently, a high-level language program must first be translated into machine language. This process is described in the next section.

SELF-CHECK EXERCISE FOR SECTION 1.4

1. What do you think the high-level language statements below mean?

```
X = A + B + C
X = Y / Z
D = C − B + A
```

1.5 ▬▬▬ Processing a High-Level Language Program

Before it can be processed, a high-level language program must be entered at the terminal. The program will be stored in secondary memory (usually a disk) as a file called the *source file* (see Fig. 1.12). The programmer uses an *editor program* to enter the program and to save it as a source file.

Once the source file is saved, it must be translated into machine language. A *compiler* program processes the source file and attempts to translate each statement. Often, one or more statements in the source file will contain a *syntax error*. This means that these statements do not correspond exactly to the syntax (grammar) of the high-level language. In this case, the compiler will cause some error messages to be displayed.

At this point, you can make changes to your source file and have the compiler process it again. If there are no more errors, the compiler will create an *object file*, which is your program translated into machine language. The object file is generally stored in secondary memory. The *linker* program combines the object file with any additional object files (for example, programs for input and output) that may be needed into a *load file*. Finally, the *loader* program places the load file into main memory, ready for execution. The editor, compiler, linker, and loader programs are part of your computer system. This process is shown in Fig. 1.12.

Executing a Program

To execute a program, the CPU must examine each program instruction in main memory and send out the command signals required to carry out the instruction. Normally, the instructions are executed in sequence; however, as we will see later, it is possible to have the CPU skip over some instructions or execute some instructions more than once.

During execution, data may be entered into memory and manipulated in some specified way. Then, the result of this data manipulation will be displayed.

Figure 1.13 shows the effect of executing a simple payroll program stored in memory. The first step of the program requires entering data for a single employee into memory. In step 2, the employee data are manipulated by the central processor as directed by the program, and the results of computations are stored in memory. In the final step, the computational results may be displayed as payroll reports or employee payroll checks. An example of a program that does this is provided later in the chapter.

SELF-CHECK EXERCISES FOR SECTION 1.5

1. What is the difference between the source file, the object file, and the load file? Which do you create and which does the compiler create? Which one is processed by the loader? Which file is processed by the linker?
2. What is a syntax error? Where would a syntax error be found?

Figure 1.12. *Preparing a Program for Execution*

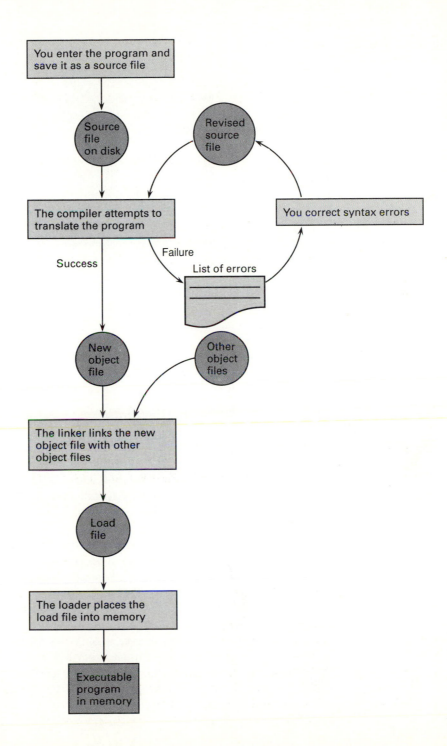

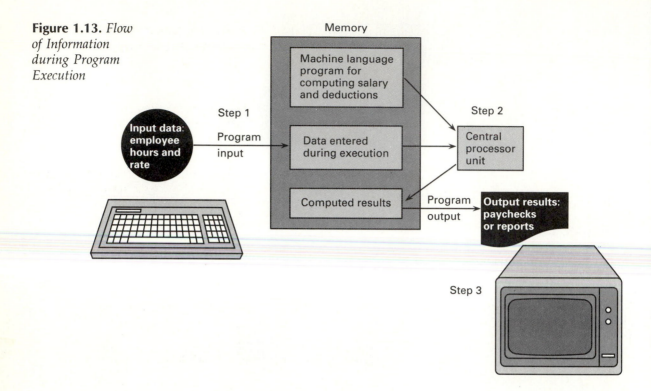

Figure 1.13. *Flow of Information during Program Execution*

1.6 ▬▬▬ Introduction to FORTRAN

FORTRAN was first used in 1957 and was the first high-level programming language. It was originally used primarily for scientific computation but has evolved over the years into a language for many different kinds of programming applications. More recent versions of FORTRAN have been designed to facilitate writing *structured programs*—programs that are relatively easy to read, understand, and keep in good working order.

A *language standard*, which describes all FORTRAN language statements and specifies their syntax, ensures that a FORTRAN program written on one computer will execute on another computer. As this edition of the text is being written, the FORTRAN standards committee is busy defining a new standard version of FORTRAN, called FORTRAN 8X. We expect the new standard to be approved by 1990; however, it most likely will not be widely available during the lifetime of this edition. For that reason, we use FORTRAN 77 (approved in 1978) as the language of instruction in this text. Appendix D describes the new features found in FORTRAN 8X.

The rest of this chapter will provide a brief introduction to FORTRAN. Statements for reading data, performing simple computations, displaying results, and writing files will be described.

Two Sample Programs

Before beginning our in-depth study of FORTRAN, we will examine two short programs. Don't worry about understanding the details of these programs yet; they will all be explained later.

EXAMPLE 1.1

Figure 1.14 contains a FORTRAN program (last line is END) followed by a sample execution of that program. The information entered by the program user is in color in the sample execution.

Figure 1.14. *Printing a Welcoming Message*

```
        PROGRAM HELLO
        CHARACTER *10 NAME

        PRINT *, 'Enter your name (in quotes) and press return.'
        READ *, NAME

        PRINT *, 'Hello ', NAME
        PRINT *, 'We hope you enjoy studying FORTRAN!'

        STOP
        END

Enter your name (in quotes) and press return.
'Bob'
Hello Bob
We hope you enjoy studying FORTRAN!
```

The statement

```
        PROGRAM HELLO
```

identifies HELLO as the name of this program. The statement

```
        CHARACTER *10 NAME
```

identifies a memory cell (called NAME) that will be used to store the program user's name. Each program statement starting with PRINT * causes a line of output to be displayed on the screen during program execution. The first PRINT * statement generates the first output line, which asks the program user to enter a name.

The statement

```
READ *, NAME
```

reads the characters Bob (entered by the program user) into the memory cell NAME. The next statement

```
PRINT *, 'Hello ', NAME
```

displays these characters after the message *string* 'Hello '.
The lines

```
STOP
END
```

terminate program execution and indicate the end of the program.   ∎

EXAMPLE 1.2   The program in Fig. 1.15 converts inches to centimeters. The statements

```
REAL CPERIN
PARAMETER (CPERIN = 2.54)
```

define a memory cell, CPERIN, whose value is a constant, 2.54.

Figure 1.15. *Converting Inches to Centimeters*

```
PROGRAM CONVRT
REAL CPERIN
PARAMETER (CPERIN = 2.54)
REAL INCHES, CENT

PRINT *, 'Enter a length in inches'
READ *, INCHES

CENT = CPERIN * INCHES
PRINT *, 'That equals ', CENT, ' centimeters.'

STOP
END


Enter a length in inches
30.0
That equals    76.20000 centimeters.
```

The number of inches to be converted is read into the memory cell INCHES by the statement

```
READ *, INCHES
```

The statement

```
CENT = CPERIN * INCHES
```

computes the equivalent length in centimeters by multiplying the length in inches by 2.54 (the number of centimeters per inch); the product is stored in memory cell CENT.

The statement

```
PRINT *, 'That equals ', CENT, ' centimeters.'
```

displays a message string, the value of CENT, and a second message string. ■

One of the nicest things about FORTRAN is that it lets us write program statements that resemble English. At this point, you probably can read and understand the sample programs, even though you may not know how to write your own programs.

Each of the statements in the preceding programs satisfies the FORTRAN syntax that pertains to that statement type. If the program statements that you enter do not follow this syntax, they may not be translated. The following sections provide a detailed explanation of the statements seen so far.

Declaring Variables and Parameters

How do we tell FORTRAN what *symbolic names* will be used to name data in a program? One way is the *type declaration statement*. The *type declaration*

```
CHARACTER *10 NAME
```

in Fig. 1.14 associates NAME with a memory cell that will be used to store up to ten characters of data. The type declaration

```
REAL INCHES, CENT
```

in Fig. 1.15 gives the names of two memory cells that will be used to reference data items that are real numbers (e.g., 30.0).

Symbolic names that appear in type declarations are called *variables*. Variables are used in a program for storing input data items and computational results. The words REAL, INTEGER, CHARACTER *10 that begin a type declaration statement tell FORTRAN what type of data (e.g., a real number, an integer, a string of characters) will be stored in the variable. The *data types* REAL, INTEGER, and CHARACTER will be discussed in more detail in Section 1.9.

The *parameter statement*

```
PARAMETER (CPERIN = 2.54)
```

specifies that the symbolic name CPERIN will be used as the name of the constant 2.54. Symbolic names that appear in a PARAMETER statement are called *parameters*. The type of a parameter (e.g., REAL) should be declared in a type declaration statement that precedes the PARAMETER statement.

Only data values that never change or change very rarely (e.g., the number of centimeters per inch is always 2.54) should be associated with a symbolic name that is a parameter. It is illegal to attempt to change the value of a parameter in a FORTRAN program.

You have quite a bit of freedom in selecting symbolic names that are used in a FORTRAN program. The syntactic rules are shown below.

Rules for FORTRAN Symbolic Names

1. A symbolic name must always begin with an uppercase letter (A–Z).
2. A symbolic name must consist of uppercase letters (A–Z) or digits only.
3. A symbolic name must consist of one to six characters.

Some valid and invalid symbolic names are listed below.

Valid Symbolic Names

    LET1, LET2, INCHES, CENT, CPERIN, HELLO

Invalid Symbolic Names

    1LET, TWO*FOUR, JOE'S, CENTPERINCH

The statements introduced in this section are summarized in the following displays. Each display describes the syntax of the statement and provides examples and an interpretation of the statement. Each of the elements in italics is described in the interpretation section.

Program Statement

SYNTAX: PROGRAM *programname*

EXAMPLES: PROGRAM HELLO
           PROGRAM INCENT

INTERPRETATION: The PROGRAM statement is the first statement of a FORTRAN program. It identifies the name, *programname*, of the program; *programname* must follow the syntax rules for a FORTRAN symbolic name.

NOTES: The PROGRAM statement is not required in FORTRAN 77, but we recommend that you use it to name each FORTRAN program. You also should use *programname* in the name given to the source file containing that program. On many systems, the source file name should have the form *programname*.FOR. The *extension* part of the file name, .FOR, identifies the source file as a FORTRAN program. Following this convention will help you remember which source file contains a particular FORTRAN program.

Type Declaration

SYNTAX: REAL *variable-list*
           INTEGER *variable-list*
           CHARACTER **length variable-list*
           LOGICAL *variable-list*

EXAMPLES: REAL X, Y, Z
          INTEGER COUNT
          CHARACTER *10 NAME
          LOGICAL DEBUG

INTERPRETATION: A memory cell is allocated for each symbolic name in the *variable-list*. The type of data (REAL, INTEGER, CHARACTER, LOGICAL) to be stored in each variable (or parameter) is specified at the beginning of the statement. Commas are used to separate the symbolic names in the *variable-list*. If the type is CHARACTER, the *length* of the character data item is specified as an integer value after the symbol *.

PARAMETER Statement

SYNTAX: PARAMETER (*parameter-list*)

EXAMPLES: PARAMETER (PI = 3.141593)
          PARAMETER (CPERIN = 2.54, FMONTH = 'JANUARY')

INTERPRETATION: The *parameter-list* consists of one or more parameter definitions separated by commas. Each parameter definition has the form

   parameter = value

where *parameter* becomes the symbolic name of the constant represented by *value*. A *parameter* cannot be redefined by any subsequent program statements. The type of each *parameter* should be declared first.

Program Style

Choosing Symbolic Names

It is very important to pick meaningful symbolic names to make your program easier to read and understand. For example, SALARY would be a good name for a variable used to store a person's salary; the identifiers S and BAGEL would be bad choices.

If you mistype a symbolic name, the compiler may or may not detect this as a syntax error. Sometimes mistyped names wind up looking like other variable names. For this reason, avoid picking names that are very similar to each other. Also, names that are almost the same can cause quite a bit of confusion.

Many compilers permit long symbolic names (more than six characters) that may include lowercase characters. On these compilers, you could associate the constant 2.54 with the name CentPerInch instead of with the six-letter name CPERIN used in Fig. 1.15. Your instructor may prefer that you do this to enhance program readability. However, keep in mind that this is not standard and reduces program portability.

Program Style

Separate Declaration of Parameters and Variables

In Fig. 1.15, the data type of CPERIN is declared in a separate type declaration statement before variables INCHES and CENT are declared. Also, the value associated with CPERIN is defined before the variables are declared. We will follow the practice of declaring parameters and variables in separate type declarations throughout the text. We will also declare and define parameters first. The reason for this is that parameters may appear in subsequent variable declaration statements. We will see examples of this later in the text.

Assignment Statements

One of the main functions of a computer is to perform arithmetic computations. In this section, we will see how to specify computations using the *assignment statement*.

The assignment statement

```
CENT = CPERIN * INCHES
```

in Fig. 1.15 is used to assign a value to the variable CENT. In this case, CENT is being assigned the result of the multiplication (∗ means multiply) of the parameter CPERIN by the variable INCHES. Valid information must be stored in both CPERIN and INCHES before the assignment statement is executed. As shown in Fig. 1.16, only the value of CENT is affected by the assignment statement; CPERIN and INCHES retain their original values.

Figure 1.16. *Effect of CENT = CPERIN * INCHES*

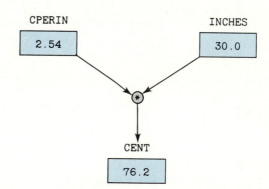

The symbol = is the *assignment operator* in FORTRAN and should be pronounced "gets" or "is assigned the value of" rather than "equals." The general form of the assignment statement is shown in the next display.

Assignment Statement (Arithmetic)

SYNTAX: *result = expression*

EXAMPLE: Z = Y + X − 3

INTERPRETATION: The variable specified by *result* is assigned the value of *expression*. The previous value of *result* is destroyed. The expression can be a single variable, parameter, or constant, or involve variables, parameters, constants, and the arithmetic operators listed in Table 1.2.

Table 1.2. *FORTRAN Arithmetic Operators*

ARITHMETIC OPERATOR	MEANING
**	exponentiation (e.g., X ** 2 is X^2)
*	multiplication
/	division
+	addition
−	subtraction

EXAMPLE 1.3

In FORTRAN, you can write assignment statements of the form

        SUM = SUM + ITEM

where the variable SUM is used on both sides of the assignment operator. This is obviously not an algebraic equation, but it illustrates something that is often done in programming. This statement instructs the computer to add the current value of the variable SUM to the value of ITEM; the result is then stored back into SUM. The previous value of SUM is lost in the process, as illustrated in Fig. 1.17; however, the value of ITEM is unchanged.   ∎

Figure 1.17. *Effect of SUM = SUM + ITEM*

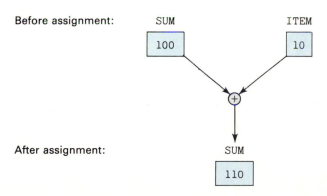

EXAMPLE 1.4

Assignment statements can also be written with an expression part that consists of a single variable or value. The statement

```
NEWX = X
```

instructs the computer to *copy* the value of X into NEWX. The statement

```
NEWX = -X
```

instructs the computer to get the value of X, *negate* that value, and store the result in NEWX (e.g., if X is 3.5, NEWX becomes -3.5). Neither of the preceding assignment statements changes the value of X.   ∎

The READ Statement

Data cannot be manipulated by a computer unless it is first stored in main memory. There are three ways to place a data value in memory: associate it with a parameter, assign it to a variable, or read it into memory. If we wish to be able to store different data values each time a program is run, then the data must be read in as the program is executing.

The READ statement

```
READ *, INCHES
```

is used in Fig. 1.15 to read a real number into the variable INCHES. This statement causes the number entered at the terminal to be stored in the variable INCHES. The *cursor* (a moving place marker) indicates the current position on the screen. As you type each character, it appears on the screen and the cursor advances to the next screen position. After typing a number, the program user should press the key labeled *return* or *enter*. The effect of this READ statement is shown in Fig. 1.18.

Figure 1.18. *Effect of READ *, INCHES*

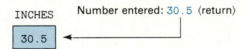

The READ statement in Fig. 1.14 reads a person's name. Each time the program is run, a different person's name (up to ten characters in length) may be read into variable NAME by the READ statement

```
READ *, NAME
```

The characters read into NAME must be surrounded by single quotes or apostrophes. Figure 1.19 shows the effect of this statement when the character data item 'Bob' is entered. As shown in Fig. 1.19, only the characters inside the apostrophes are stored, not the apostrophes.

Figure 1.19. *Effect of READ *, NAME*

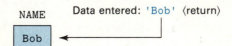

Sometimes a single READ statement is used to read more than one data item. In this case, the program user should leave at least one space between data items. Figure 1.20 shows the effect of the statement

        READ *, NAME, AGE

assuming that AGE is declared as a type INTEGER variable.

Figure 1.20. *Effect of READ *, NAME, AGE*

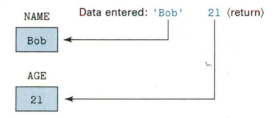

How do we know when to enter the input data and what data to enter? Your program should print a prompting message (as explained in the next section) to inform the program user what data should be entered and when.

READ Statement

SYNTAX: READ *, *input-list*

EXAMPLES: READ *, INCHES
           READ *, NAME, AGE

INTERPRETATION: Data are entered into each variable specified in the *input-list*. Commas are used to separate the variable names in the *input-list*. When a READ statement is executed, program execution is suspended until the required data items are entered and ⟨return⟩ is pressed. There must be one data item for each variable in the *input-list*, and the order of the data must correspond to the order of the variables in the *input-list*. At least one space should be left between data items.

The PRINT Statement

To see the results of a program execution, we must have some way of specifying what variable values should be displayed. In Fig. 1.15, the statement

        PRINT *, 'That equals ', CENT, ' centimeters.'

causes the line

        That equals   76.20000 centimeters.

to be displayed. There are actually three separate items printed by this statement: the character string 'That equals ', the value of the real variable CENT, and the string ' centimeters.'. A *character string* (or *string*) is a sequence of characters enclosed in single quotes or apostrophes. When a PRINT statement is executed, the characters enclosed in quotes are printed but the quotes are not.

In Fig. 1.14, the statement

```
PRINT *, 'Hello ', NAME
```

causes the line

```
Hello Bob
```

to be printed. In this case, the value of variable NAME is printed after the string 'Hello '.

Finally, the statements

```
PRINT *, 'Enter your name and press return.'
PRINT *, 'Enter a length in inches.'
```

are used to display *prompts* or *prompting messages* in Figs. 1.14 and 1.15, respectively. A prompting message is a string that is displayed just before a READ statement is executed to prompt the program user to enter data. The prompt may describe the format of the data expected. It is important to precede each READ statement with a PRINT statement that displays a prompt; otherwise, the program user may have no idea that the program has stopped executing or what data to enter.

The PRINT Statement

SYNTAX: PRINT *, *output-list*

EXAMPLE: PRINT *, 'Age is ', AGE

INTERPRETATION: The value of each variable or constant is printed in the order in which it appears in *output-list*. A string is printed without the quotes. The cursor advances to the start of the next line after the entire output line is displayed.

STOP and END

After the program computations are performed and the output results are displayed, program execution should be halted. The statement

```
STOP
```

halts program execution.

The last statement in every FORTRAN program is

```
END
```

The END statement marks the end of the FORTRAN source program during translation; the translation phase terminates when the END statement is processed by the compiler. If the STOP statement is omitted, program execution terminates when the END statement is reached.

**STOP
Statement**

SYNTAX: STOP

INTERPRETATION: Terminates the execution of a running program.

**END
Statement**

SYNTAX: END

INTERPRETATION: Indicates the end of a program unit during translation.

**SELF-CHECK
EXERCISES FOR
SECTION 1.6**

1. Which of the following symbolic names are legal?

   ```
   END    READLN   BILL    PROGRAM   SUE'S    RATE    OPERATE   START
   BEGIN   CONST   XYZ123   123XYZ   THISISALONGONE   Y=Z
   ```

2. Correct the syntax errors in the program below and rewrite it. What does each statement of your corrected program do? What is printed?

   ```
   REAL *, X, Y, X
   15.0 = Y;    Z = -Y + 3.5
   Y + Z = X
   PRINT *, x; Y; z
   STOP
   END
   ```

3. Write the PRINT statement that causes the line

   ```
   The value of X is _____ pounds.
   ```

   to be printed where the value assigned to variable X is inserted in the blank space.

4. Which are valid FORTRAN statements?

   ```
   a. X + Y = Z
   b. Z = X +* Y
   c. PROGRAM FORTRN
   d. PROGRAM FORTRN.FOR
   e. READ *, X, Y
   f. PRINT *, X, Y
   g. READ *, X, 3.14159
   h. PRINT *, X, 3.14159
   i. REAL (PI = 3.14159)
   j. PARAMETER (PI = 3.14159)
   ```

1.7 ▬▬▬▬ FORTRAN Programs

In the preceding sections, we described seven kinds of FORTRAN statements: the type declaration and the PARAMETER, assignment, READ, PRINT, STOP, and END statements. They will appear in most of the programs that you write.

Linear Programs

In this section, we will show you some more examples of FORTRAN programs. All the programs in this chapter are called *linear* programs because the program statements are executed in linear order or sequence.

EXAMPLE 1.5

A new program is shown in Fig. 1.21. This program computes an employee's gross pay and net pay using the algebraic formulas

gross pay = hours worked × hourly rate
net pay = gross pay − tax amount

These formulas are written as the FORTRAN assignment statements

```
GROSS = HOURS * RATE
NET = GROSS - TAX
```

Figure 1.21. *Payroll Program*

```
      PROGRAM MYPAY
      REAL TAX
      PARAMETER (TAX = 25.00)
      REAL HOURS, RATE, GROSS, NET

      PRINT *, 'Enter hours worked'
      READ *, HOURS
      PRINT *, 'Enter hourly rate'
      READ *, RATE

      GROSS = HOURS * RATE
      NET = GROSS - TAX

      PRINT *, 'Gross pay is $', GROSS
      PRINT *, 'Net pay is $', NET

      STOP
      END

Enter hours worked
15
Enter hourly rate
3.35
Gross pay is $    50.250000
Net pay is $    25.250000
```

in the payroll program shown in Fig. 1.21. New values of HOURS and RATE are read each time the program is executed; a constant TAX of $25.00 is always deducted.

This program first reads the data representing hours worked and hourly rate and then computes gross pay as their product. Next, it computes net pay by deducting a constant tax amount of 25.00. Finally, it displays the computed values of gross pay and net pay.   ■

Program Style

Use of Blank Space and Lowercase Letters

Program style is a very important consideration in programming. A program that "looks good" is easier to read and understand than a sloppy program. Most programs will be examined or studied by someone else. In the real world, only about 25 percent of the time spent on a particular program is spent on its original design or coding; the remaining 75 percent is spent on maintenance (i.e., updating and modifying the program). It makes everyone's job easier if a program is neatly stated and its meaning is clear from the beginning.

The consistent and careful use of blank spaces can significantly enhance the style of a program. Beyond column 6 of a line, blanks are ignored by the compiler and may be inserted as desired to improve the style and appearance of a program. As shown in Fig. 1.21, we will always leave a blank space after a comma and before and after arithmetic operators such as *, −, =. Blanks inside strings are not ignored and are used to make program output more readable. We also use blank lines to separate sections of the program.

The standard FORTRAN character set does not include lowercase letters. However, most compilers permit lowercase letters to be used inside strings in FORTRAN programs. The use of lowercase in prompting messages and strings that are displayed makes the program output easier to read. Consequently, we will use lowercase in strings even though this use is not standard. Check whether your FORTRAN compiler allows lowercase before following this practice.

These measures are taken for the sole purpose of improving the style and, hence, the clarity of the program. They have no effect whatever on the meaning of the program as far as the computer is concerned; however, they do make it easier for humans to read and understand the program and its output.

Programs in Memory

It is worthwhile to pause for a moment and look at the payroll program in memory. Fig. 1.22a shows the payroll program loaded in memory and the program data area before execution of the program body. The question mark in memory cells HOURS, RATE, GROSS, and NET indicates that these variables are *undefined* (value unknown) before program execution begins. During program execution, the data values 40.0 and 4.50 are read into the variables HOURS and RATE, respectively. After the assignment statements shown earlier are used to compute values for GROSS and NET, all variables are defined as shown in Fig. 1.22b.

Figure 1.22: *Memory Before and After Execution of a Program*

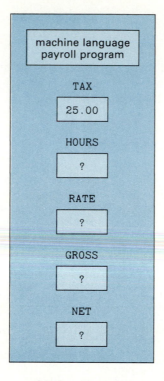

a) before execution   b) after execution

Additional Examples

The next program illustrates the use of type INTEGER data in FORTRAN. In FORTRAN, an integer value is a number without a decimal point; a type INTEGER variable is used to store an integer value.

EXAMPLE 1.6

The program in Fig. 1.23 determines the value of a small collection of coins (nickels and pennies only). The variables are declared to be type INTEGER since it is impossible to have 2.5 coins.

The assignment statement

```
CENTS = 5 * NICKEL + PENNY
```

computes the value in cents of the collection of coins in the obvious way. The two PRINT statements

```
PRINT *, 'You have ', COINS, ' coins.'
PRINT *, 'Their value is ', CENTS, ' cents.'
```

each cause an integer value to be printed between two strings. ∎

Figure 1.23. *Computing Integer Values*

```
      PROGRAM CHANGE
      INTEGER NICKEL, PENNY, COINS, CENTS

      PRINT *, 'How many nickels do you have?'
      READ *, NICKEL
      PRINT *, 'How many pennies do you have?'
      READ *, PENNY

      COINS = NICKEL + PENNY
      CENTS = 5 * NICKEL + PENNY

      PRINT *, 'You have ', COINS, ' coins.'
      PRINT *, 'Their value is ', CENTS, ' cents.'

      STOP
      END

How many nickels do you have?
3
How many pennies do you have?
2
You have             5 coins.
Their value is            17 cents.
```

EXAMPLE 1.7

The program in Fig. 1.24 computes the average speed travelled on a trip and also the gas mileage. It uses the two formulas

speed = distance / time
mileage = distance / gallons

The input data consist of the trip distance and time and the number of gallons of gasoline used.

The statement

    PRINT *

is a PRINT statement without an output list; it causes a blank line to be displayed in the middle of the program output. ∎

Rules for Positioning Statements

As you type in FORTRAN programs, make sure that you begin each new statement on a separate line. Furthermore, do not begin a FORTRAN statement before column 7. Make sure you press the space bar at least six times before you type in the statement. On some systems, pressing the tab key will advance you to column 7.

Figure 1.24. *Trip Speed and Gas Mileage Computations*

```
      PROGRAM TRIP
      REAL SPEED, TIME, DISTNC, MILAGE, GALLON

      PRINT *, 'Enter distance in miles:'
      READ *, DISTNC
      PRINT *, 'Enter time of trip in hours:'
      READ *, TIME

      SPEED = DISTNC / TIME

      PRINT *, 'Average speed in MPH was ', SPEED
      PRINT *

      PRINT *, 'Enter gallons used:'
      READ *, GALLON

      MILAGE = DISTNC / GALLON
      PRINT *, 'Miles per gallon was ', MILAGE

      STOP
      END

Enter distance in miles:
100
Enter time of trip in hours:
1.5
Average speed in MPH was    66.66666

Enter gallons used:
25
Miles per gallon was    4.000000
```

Another constraint is that column 72 is the last column on a line that may be used in a FORTRAN statement. Any characters typed beyond column 72 may be ignored by the FORTRAN compiler.

You can continue a long FORTRAN statement on the next line by placing any symbol other than blank or zero in column 6 of the next line. We recommend that you use the symbol + in column 6 of a line to indicate that it is a continuation of the previous line. In the following statement, the symbol + in column 6 indicates that the output list for the PRINT statement is continued on the second line:

```
    PRINT *, 'The distance travelled in miles is',
   +        DISTNC
```

Column 1 can be used as either a *comment designator* or a *statement label*. If a line contains C or * in column 1, FORTRAN assumes that the line is a comment and does not attempt to translate or execute that line.

```
C This line contains a C in column 1 and is ignored.
* So is this one.
```

If FORTRAN does not find C or * in column 1, but does find a number anywhere in columns 1 through 5, it assumes the rest of the line is a regular FORTRAN statement and that the number in columns 1 through 5 is the statement label (an integer). For example, the following line has the label 10:

```
10 PRINT *, 'This PRINT statement has label 10'
```

We will discuss comments and labels later. The FORTRAN rules for column use are summarized in Table 1.3.

Table 1.3. *Use of Columns in* FOR-*TRAN*

COLUMN	USE
1	C or * indicates that the line is a comment.
1–5	May contain the statement label.
6	Any character except a blank or a zero marks the line as a continuation of the previous line.
7–72	Contains the FORTRAN statement.
73–	May be ignored by the compiler (system dependent).

1.8 ▌ Introduction to Data Types and Expressions

So far in this chapter, we have written programs that manipulate numeric data and character data. We will review the properties of these *data types* next.

Two types of numeric data were manipulated: REAL and INTEGER. We used the arithmetic operators +, −, *, / and the assignment operator = to manipulate these data. In addition to these operators, the exponentiation operator ** can also be used with numeric data (e.g., x^2 can be written as X**2 in FOR-TRAN).

The basic distinction between the numeric data types is that type REAL variables may be used to store data containing a decimal point and a fractional part, whereas type INTEGER variables can store only integer values. For this reason, type INTEGER variables are more limited in their use; they are often used to represent a count of items (e.g., a count of coins).

A real number is represented as a string of digits containing a decimal point. A real number may also be written in FORTRAN scientific notation. In scientific notation, a real number begins with an integer or real value followed by the letter E and an integer (possibly preceded by a sign). Examples of real numbers are shown in Table 1.4.

Table 1.4. *Some Real Numbers*

3.14159	
−0.005	
+12345.0	
−15.0E−04	(value of -15.0×10^{-4} or -0.0015)
−2.345E2	(value of -2.345×10^2 or -234.5)
1.2E+6	(value of 1.2×10^6 or 1200000)
1.15E−3	(value of 1.15×10^{-3} or 0.00115)

As shown by the last real number in Table 1.4, 1.15E−3 means the same as 1.15×10^{-3} where the *exponent* −3 causes the decimal point to be moved left three digits. A positive exponent causes the decimal point to be moved to the right; the + sign may be omitted when the exponent is positive.

The third data type discussed in this chapter is type CHARACTER. Character data are always enclosed in apostrophes (e.g., 'A') when written in a FORTRAN statement. Apostrophes are also used when character data are entered at a terminal. The blank character (' ') is denoted by pressing the space bar between a pair of apostrophe characters.

EXAMPLE 1.8

The program in Fig. 1.25 reads one character into each of three separate CHARACTER variables and prints them in reverse order enclosed in asterisks.

Figure 1.25. *Program for Example 1.8*

```
      PROGRAM INITAL
      CHARACTER *1 BORDER
      PARAMETER (BORDER = '*')
      CHARACTER *1 FIRST, SECOND, THIRD

      PRINT *, 'Enter 3 characters with each character in quotes'
      READ *, FIRST, SECOND, THIRD

      PRINT *, BORDER, THIRD, SECOND, FIRST, BORDER

      STOP
      END

Enter 3 characters with each character in quotes
'E' 'B' 'K'
*KBE*
```

The character value '*' is associated with the parameter BORDER. Each character entered at the terminal is stored in a variable of type CHARACTER *1.

The PRINT statement

```
PRINT *, BORDER, THIRD, SECOND, FIRST, BORDER
```

prints five character values. As shown in the program output, each character value is printed in a single print position. The order in which the characters are displayed is the reverse of the order in which they are read. ∎

The fourth FORTRAN data type that we will discuss in this text is type LOGICAL. There are only two values associated with this data type and they are written as .TRUE. and .FALSE.. The statements

```
LOGICAL CLOUDY
CLOUDY = .TRUE.
```

declare a type LOGICAL variable named CLOUDY and assign the LOGICAL value TRUE. to this variable.

Evaluating Expressions

Thus far, most of the expressions we have used in programs have been relatively simple. To write more complicated expressions correctly, we must know the FORTRAN rules for evaluating expressions. For example, in the expression A + B * C, is * performed before + or vice versa? Is the expression X / Y * Z evaluated as (X / Y) * Z or as X / (Y * Z)?

Fortunately, FORTRAN follows the normal rules of algebra in evaluating expressions. Two expressions with multiple operators are:

```
1.8 * CELSUS + 32.0
(SALARY − 5000.00) * 0.20 + 1425.0
```

In both cases, the multiplication is performed before the addition. The use of parentheses in the second expression causes the subtraction to be done first. The rules for expression evaluation in FORTRAN are described below.

Rules for Expression Evaluation

- (a) All parenthesized subexpressions are evaluated first. Nested parenthesized subexpressions are evaluated inside out, with the innermost subexpression evaluated first.
- (b) *Operator precedence:* Operators in the same subexpression are evaluated in the following order:

**	first
*, /	next
+, −	last

■ (c) *Left associative:* Operators in the same subexpression and at the same precedence level (such as + and –) are evaluated left to right. The only exception to this rule is that consecutive exponentiation operators are evaluated right to left (e.g., X ** Y ** 2 is evaluated as X ** (Y **2)).

EXAMPLE 1.9

The formula for the area of a circle, $A = \pi \times r^2$, is written in FORTRAN as

        AREA = PI * RADIUS ** 2

where PI is the parameter 3.14159. The *evaluation tree* for this formula is shown in Fig. 1.26. In this tree, the arrows connect each operand with its operator. The order of operator evaluation is shown by the number to the left of each operator; the rules that apply are shown to the right. ■

Figure 1.26. *Evaluation Tree for AREA = PI * RADIUS ** 2*

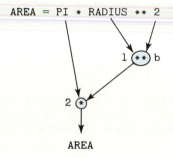

EXAMPLE 1.10

The formula for the average velocity, v, of a particle traveling on a line between points p_1 and p_2 in time t_1 to t_2 is

$$v = \frac{p_2 - p_1}{t_2 - t_1}$$

This formula is written and evaluated in FORTRAN as shown in Fig. 1.27. ■

Figure 1.27. *Evaluation Tree for V = (P2 − P1)/(T2 − T1)*

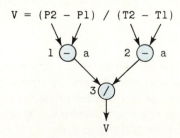

Inserting parentheses in an expression affects the order of operator evaluation. You should use parentheses freely to clarify the order of evaluation.

EXAMPLE 1.11

Consider the expression

    Z - (A + B / 2.0) + W * Y

The parenthesized subexpression (A + B / 2.0) is evaluated first [rule (a)] beginning with B / 2.0 [rule (b)]. Once the value of B / 2.0 is determined, it can be added to A to obtain the value of (A + B / 2.0). Next, the multiplication operation is performed [rule (b)], and the value for W * Y is determined. Then the value of (A + B / 2.0) is subtracted from z [rule (c)], and finally this result is added to W * Y. The evaluation tree for this expression is shown in Fig. 1.28.

Figure 1.28. *Evaluation Tree for Z − (A + B / 2.0) + W * Y*

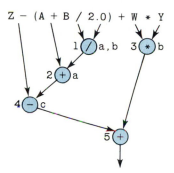

Writing Formulas in FORTRAN

There are two problem areas in writing a mathematical formula in FORTRAN; one concerns multiplication and the other concerns division. Multiplication can often be implied in a mathematical formula by writing the two items to be multiplied next to each other; for example, $a = bc$. In FORTRAN, however, the * operator must always be used to indicate multiplication, as in

    A = B * C

The other difficulty arises in formulas involving division. We normally write the numerator and denominator on separate lines:

$$m = \frac{y - b}{x - a}$$

In FORTRAN, all assignment statements must be written on one line; consequently parentheses are often needed to separate the numerator from the denominator and to clearly indicate the order of evaluation of the operators in the expression. The formula above would be written as

    M = (Y − B) / (X − A)

EXAMPLE 1.12

This example illustrates how several mathematical formulas can be written in FORTRAN.

Mathematical Formula	FORTRAN *Expression*
a. $b^2 - 4ac$	B ** 2 - 4.0 * A * C
b. $a + b - c$	A + B - C
c. $\dfrac{a + b}{c + d}$	(A + B) / (C + D)
d. $\dfrac{1}{1 + x^2}$	1.0 / (1.0 + X ** 2)
e. $a \times -(b + c)$	A * (-(B + C))

The points illustrated are summarized next. ■

Rules for Writing FORTRAN Expressions

- Always specify multiplication explicitly by using the operator * where needed (see Example 1.12a).
- Use parentheses when required to control the order of operator evaluation (see Examples 1.12c and d).
- Never write two arithmetic operators in succession; they must be separated by an operand or parentheses (see Example 1.12e).
- Do not mix integer constants with real variables in expressions (called *mixed-mode expressions*). The only exception is using an integer constant as an exponent (see Examples 1.12a and d).

The next examples show how to write the FORTRAN forms of some formulas found in engineering problems.

EXAMPLE 1.13

The heat loss through a brick furnace wall in joules per second is expressed by the equation

$$q = \frac{kA(T_2 - T_1)}{L}$$

where T_2 is the inside temperature, T_1 is the outside temperature, L is the furnace wall thickness, A is the surface area affected, and k is the thermal conductivity constant. We implement this equation in FORTRAN as

```
Q = K * A * (T2 - T1) / L
```
■

EXAMPLE 1.14

The general equation for pressure loss due to pipe friction is

$$\Delta p = f \rho \frac{L}{D} \frac{v^2}{2}$$

where f is the friction factor, ρ is the density of fluid flowing in the pipe, L is pipe length, D is pipe diameter, and v is velocity. We implement this equation in FORTRAN as

```
DELTAP = F * RHO * (L / D) * (V ** 2 / 2.0)
```

EXAMPLE 1.15   The deflection of a cantilevered flat parallel spring is given by the equation

$$\delta = \frac{2}{3} \frac{sL^2}{Et}$$

where s is the tensile stress, E is the modulus of elasticity, L is the length, and t is the thickness of the spring. We implement this equation in FORTRAN as

```
DEFLEX = (2.0/3.0) * (S * L ** 2) / (E * T)
```

The preceding example used the subexpression

```
(2.0/3.0)
```

to represent the fraction 2/3. We did this because the result of dividing two integers in FORTRAN is always an integer (e.g., 2/3 is 0 in FORTRAN). We will explain this further in Section 4.1.

SELF-CHECK EXERCISES FOR SECTION 1.8

1. Identify the data type of each value below. Indicate which of these are invalid.

   15   'XYZ'   '*' $25.12   15.   −999   .TRUE.   'x'   "x"   '9'   '−5'

2. Let A, B, C, and X be the names of four type REAL variables and I, J, and K the names of three type INTEGER variables. Each of the statements below contains a violation of the rules for forming arithmetic expressions. Rewrite each statement so that it is consistent with these rules.

   a. X = 4.0 A * C   d. K = 3(I + J)
   b. A = AC   e. X = 5A / BC
   c. I = 2 * −J   f. I = 5J3

3. Implement the equations below in FORTRAN.
   a. Euler's formula for maximum buckling load on a long, slender column,

   $$Load = \frac{\pi^2 AE}{(l/r)^2}$$

   Where,
   Load is the largest safe load, pounds
   A is the cross-sectional Area, square inches
   E is the modulus of elasticity, pounds per square inch
   l is the effective length of column, inches
   r is the radius of column, inches

b. Pump Power Equation

$$Horse\ Power = \frac{QW(TDH)}{550\,E}$$

Where,
Q is the flow of water in cubic feet per second
W is the water density, 62.4 pounds per cubic foot
TDH is the Total Delivered Head in feet (pressure measurement)
E is the pump efficiency in %

c. Tool Cutting Speed

$$R = \frac{12C}{\pi d}$$

Where,
R is the spindle rpm
C is the cutting speed, feet per minute
d is the work diameter, inches

1.9 ▬▬▬ Introduction to Files and Batch Processing

Interactive Mode and Batch Mode

There are two basic modes of computer operation: *batch* and *interactive*. The programs that we have written so far are intended to be run in interactive mode. In this mode, the program user can interact with the program and enter data while the program is executing.

Interactive mode is most common today and is normally used on a personal computer or a larger *timeshared* computer. Timeshared computers enable many users to be connected by terminals to one central computer and to make simultaneous use of the central facilities.

In batch mode, the program user cannot interact with the program while it is executing. Consequently, all data must be prepared beforehand and typed into a data file in the sequence in which it will be read by the program. When the program executes, it accesses this data file, reads data as required, and writes the results to the display screen or to a separate output file. Normally, batch mode is used when there is a lot of data to process or when the program will take a long time to execute. In batch mode, the program user does not have to be present while the program executes.

Some instructors prefer to use batch mode for programming instruction. They can prepare a test data file for their students' programs. To demonstrate that a program works properly, the student must run it with the instructor's data file. Because the instructor may not be present to view the display screen when the program runs, the output results can be written to an output file, which can be either sent to a printer or copied onto the instructor's disk.

In this section, we will describe how to use data files and write output files in FORTRAN. However, we will continue to emphasize interactive programming in the rest of the text, so you may prefer to study this material later.

The OPEN Statement and Data Files

Example 1.16 shows how to access a data file from a batch program. We will discuss how to create data files in Section 1.10.

EXAMPLE 1.16

Figure 1.29 shows the payroll program rewritten as a batch program. The statements

```
READ (1, *) HOURS
READ (1, *) RATE
```

read the values of HOURS and RATE from the first line (HOURS) and the second line (RATE) of a data file. Each READ statement used with a data file must specify the *unit number* (in this case, 1) of the file being processed. The digit 1 and the

Figure 1.29. *Payroll Program Using a Data File*

```
PROGRAM MYPAY2
REAL TAX
PARAMETER (TAX = 25.00)
REAL HOURS, RATE, GROSS, NET

OPEN (UNIT = 1, FILE = 'PAYDATA', STATUS = 'OLD')

READ (1, *) HOURS
PRINT *, 'Hours worked are ', HOURS
READ (1, *) RATE
PRINT *, 'Hourly rate is $', RATE

GROSS = HOURS * RATE
NET = GROSS - TAX

PRINT *, 'Gross pay is $', GROSS
PRINT *, 'Net pay is $', NET

STOP
END
```

```
Hours worked are        15.00000
Hourly rate is         3.350000
Gross pay is $         50.25000
Net pay is $         25.25000
```

symbol * must appear in parentheses after the word READ. Note that there is no comma between the close parenthesis and the input list.

The OPEN statement

```
OPEN (UNIT = 1, FILE = 'PAYDATA', STATUS = 'OLD')
```

appears for the first time in Fig. 1.29. This statement precedes the first READ statement, and it associates unit number 1 with a data file named PAYDATA. The unit number must match the unit number appearing in the READ statement that processes the data file. On many systems the unit number is chosen arbitrarily, and we can use any integer that is not already associated with another data file or a system file. Ask your instructor about any restrictions that may apply to your system.

In the OPEN statement, the phrase

```
STATUS = 'OLD'
```

tells FORTRAN that file PAYDATA is an existing file that has previously been created and saved in secondary memory. For the sample run shown in Fig. 1.29, file PAYDATA must contain the two data values, one per line, as shown next:

File PAYDATA
```
15.0
3.35
```

In Fig. 1.29, there is a PRINT statement following each READ statement. The purpose of each PRINT statement is to *echo print* or display the data value just read, thereby showing the effect of the data-entry process. Because the program does not enter data interactively, you should not use PRINT statements that display prompting messages before the READ statements. ∎

READ Statement for a Data File

SYNTAX: READ (*unum*, *) *input list*

EXAMPLES: READ (3, *) HOURS
                READ (4, *) X, Y

INTERPRETATION: Data are entered into each variable specified in the *input list*. The data are taken from the next line of the file associated with the *unum*. This association is determined by an OPEN statement, which must execute before the READ statement. If there are not enough data items on the current line of the data file to satisfy the *input list*, data will be read from the next line of the file.

NOTES: Each time a READ statement executes, a new line of the data file is processed, starting with the first data item on that line. For this reason, any data items at the end of the previous line that were not processed by the previous READ statement will be skipped.

OPEN Statement

SYNTAX: OPEN (UNIT = *unum*, FILE = *fname*, STATUS = *fstat*)

EXAMPLE: OPEN (UNIT = 1, FILE = 'MYDATA', STATUS = 'OLD')
            OPEN (UNIT = 2, FILE = 'MYOUT', STATUS = 'NEW')

INTERPRETATION: The OPEN statement prepares a file for processing. It specifies the unit number, *unum*, associated with file *fname*. It also tells FORTRAN the status, *fstat*, of the file to be processed. The file specifier *unum* must be an integer not associated with another file. The file specifier *fstat* must be the string 'NEW' (for an output file) or 'OLD' (for an existing data file).

Unit Numbers for the Keyboard and Display Screen

On most FORTRAN systems, unit numbers 5 and 6 are preassigned. Generally, unit number 5 is associated with the keyboard and unit number 6 is associated with the display screen. If this is the case on your system, the statements

```
WRITE (6, *) 'Enter hours worked'
READ (5, *) HOURS
```

will display a prompt on the screen (unit 6) and then read the next data value typed on the keyboard (unit 5) into variable HOURS. (On some systems, unit number 6 is associated with the line printer instead of the display screen.)

You can also use the symbol * as a unit number to denote the *default* input device or output device. Normally, the default input device is the keyboard and the default output device is the screen. If this is the case, the statements

```
WRITE (*, *) 'Enter hours worked'
READ (*, *) HOURS
```

are equivalent to the ones above and to the simpler ones used earlier and listed below:

```
PRINT *, 'Enter hours worked'
READ *, HOURS
```

The WRITE Statement

The first WRITE statement in the preceding paragraph is used to write an output value on the file associated with unit number 6 (the screen). We can use the WRITE statement to write our program's output to a new file saved on disk instead of the screen. One reason for doing this is to have a permanent record of the program's output. The output displayed on the screen is only a temporary record that disappears as soon as the program is finished. We can display the information saved on the disk file as often as we want to, or we can print it.

EXAMPLE 1.17

The payroll program in Fig. 1.30 reads its data from data file PAYDATA and writes four lines of output to file OUT1. In the OPEN statement for file OUT1, the

Figure 1.30. *Using a Data File and an Output File*

```
       PROGRAM MYPAY3
       REAL TAX
       PARAMETER (TAX = 25.00)
       REAL HOURS, RATE, GROSS, NET

       OPEN (UNIT = 1, FILE = 'PAYDATA', STATUS = 'OLD')
       OPEN (UNIT = 2, FILE = 'OUT1', STATUS = 'NEW')

       READ (1, *) HOURS
       WRITE (2, *) 'Hours worked are ', HOURS
       READ (1, *) RATE
       WRITE (2, *) 'Hourly rate is $', RATE

       GROSS = HOURS * RATE
       NET = GROSS - TAX

       WRITE (2, *) 'Gross pay is $', GROSS
       WRITE (2, *) 'Net pay is $', NET
       PRINT *, 'Payroll program completed'

       STOP
       END

Payroll program completed
```

phrase

```
    STATUS = 'NEW'
```

specifies that file OUT1 is a new output file. The four WRITE statements write the four output lines shown at the bottom of Fig. 1.29 to output file OUT1 instead of the screen.

The PRINT statement

```
    PRINT *, 'Payroll program completed'
```

displays its output list (a string) on the screen, as shown in the sample run of Fig. 1.30. You could also do this using the WRITE statement

```
    WRITE (6, *) 'Payroll program completed'
```

We will say more about the READ and WRITE statements in chapters 4 and 8.

The WRITE Statement

SYNTAX: WRITE (*unum*, *) *output list*

EXAMPLES: WRITE (3, *) 'Hours is ', HOURS
            WRITE (4, *) X, Y, 'X is larger than Y'

INTERPRETATION: The value of each variable or constant in the *output list* is written to the file associated with unit number *unum*. A string is printed without the enclosing apostrophes. A new output line is started each time a WRITE statement executes.

Make sure you understand the differences between PRINT and WRITE. The output list for a PRINT statement appears after a comma. The output list for a WRITE statement appears after a close parenthesis. The PRINT statement always writes information on the default output device (usually the screen). The WRITE statement can be used to write information on the screen or in a file. The unit number specified in a WRITE statement determines where its output values will be sent.

SELF-CHECK EXERCISE FOR SECTION 1.9

1. Rewrite the trip program (see Fig. 1.24) as a batch program that uses a data file and an output file.

1.10   Using the Computer

After a program is written, it must be entered at the terminal. We discussed the process of entering and executing a program in Section 1.5 (see Fig. 1.12). The mechanics of doing this differ on each computer system; we will provide a general description of the process in this section.

Operating Systems

Some of you will be using a timeshared computer. Universities often use timeshared computers for instructional purposes. In a timeshare environment, many users are connected by terminals to one central computer, and all users share the central facilities.

Many of you will be using a personal computer, which is a smaller, desktop computer used by one individual at a time. Regardless of what type of computer you use, you will need to interact with a supervisory program, called the *operating system*, within the computer. In timeshared computers, the operating system allocates the central resources among many users. Some operating system tasks are

- validating user identification and account number
- making the editor, compiler, linker, or loader programs available
- allocating memory and processor time

- providing input and output facilities
- retrieving needed files
- saving new files

Even in smaller personal computers, the operating system must perform all but the first task.

Each computer has its own special *control language* for communicating with its operating system. We cannot really provide the details here, but we will discuss the general process next. Your instructor will provide the specific commands for your system.

Creating a Program or File

Before you can use a personal computer, you first need to boot up the computer. *Booting* a personal computer may involve inserting the operating system disk into the appropriate disk drive and switching on the computer. The operating system may prompt you for the date and time. Once booted, the operating system displays a prompt (for example, A>) to indicate that it is ready to accept commands. Figure 1.31 demonstrates booting an IBM Personal Computer using MS-DOS (the Microsoft™ Disk Operating System); the computer user enters the characters that are in color; the other characters are those that the operating system displays. (See Appendix C for more information on MS-DOS and the Microsoft FORTRAN compiler.)

Figure 1.31. *Booting a Personal Computer*

```
MS-DOS Version 3.3

Current date is Tue 1-01-1980
Enter new date: 4-05-89

Current time is 0:01:43.53
Enter new time: 10:30

A>
```

Before you can use a timeshared computer, you must *log on,* or *connect,* to the computer. To log on, you enter your account name and password (given to you by your instructor). For security reasons, your password is not displayed. Figure 1.32 demonstrates this process for the Digital Equipment Corporation VAX™ computer. The computer user enters the characters that are in color; the other characters are those that the operating system displays. The timeshared operating system shown (named VMS Version 4.5) displays the symbol $ as a prompt.

Figure 1.32. *Logging on to a Computer*

```
Username: Koffman
Password: Madaket

                    CIS Department Vax-11/780 VMS V5.1

        Last interactive login on Friday, 28-April-1989 10:20

$
```

Once you have booted your personal computer or logged on to a timeshared computer, you can begin to create your program. In most cases, you will use a special program called an *editor* to enter your FORTRAN program and save it in main memory. If you want a record of the program once it is entered, you must save it as a permanent file on disk; otherwise, your program disappears when your session with the editor is over. Follow these steps to create and save a program file or data file:

1. Log on to a timeshared computer or boot up a personal computer.
2. Access the editor program.
3. Indicate that you are creating a new file.
4. Enter each line of the program file or data file.
5. Name your file (if not named in step 3) and save it as a permanent file in secondary memory.
6. Exit from the editor.

Make sure you remember to perform step 5. The file created by the editor program is stored in main memory. Unless you save your editor file in secondary memory, it will be lost when you exit from the editor program.

Running the Program

Once you have created your program and you are satisfied that each line is entered correctly, you can attempt to compile, link, and load and execute it. On some systems you must give three separate commands; on other systems one command, such as RUN, initiates this sequence of operations.

If your program will not compile because it contains syntax errors, you must edit, or correct, the program. Follow these steps to correct and reexecute a program file:

1. Reaccess the editor program.
2. Access your program file.
3. Correct the statements containing syntax errors.
4. Save your edited program file.
5. Compile, link, load, and execute the new program file.

1.11 ▬▬ Common Programming Errors

One of the first things you will discover in writing programs is that a program rarely runs correctly the first time. Murphy's Law, "If something can go wrong, it will," seems to have been written with the computer programmer or programming student in mind. In fact, errors are so common that they have their own special name (*bugs*); the process of correcting them is called *debugging a program*. To alert you to potential problems, we will provide a section on common errors at the end of each chapter.

When an error is detected, an error message will be printed indicating that you have made a mistake and what the cause of the error might be. Unfortunately, error messages are often difficult to interpret and are sometimes misleading. However, as you gain experience, you will become more proficient at understanding them.

There are two basic categories of errors that occur: syntax errors and run-time, or execution, errors. Syntax errors are detected by the compiler as it attempts to translate your program. If a statement has a syntax error, it cannot be translated and your program will not be executed.

Run-time errors are detected by the computer during execution of a program. A run-time error occurs as a result of directing the computer to perform an illegal operation such as dividing a number by zero or manipulating undefined or invalid data. When a run-time error occurs, your program will stop execution and a diagnostic message will be printed that indicates the line where the error occurred. Sometimes the values of all variables will be printed as well.

Syntax Errors

Figure 1.33 shows a *compiler listing* of a payroll program with errors from the Digital Equipment Corporation VAX FORTRAN compiler. Line numbers are on the left, and each error message is shown directly beneath the line in error.

The program contains the following syntax errors:

- PARAMETER misspelled (line 3)
- missing * after PRINT (line 5)
- apostrophes used with READ statement (line 6)
- assignment statement with transposed variable and expression part (line 10)
- transposed comma and apostrophe in PRINT statement (line 11)
- missing apostrophe in PRINT statement (line 12)

Your compiler may display error messages that are different from the ones shown in Fig. 1.33. Some compilers list all error messages after the program or in a separate file altogether. If there are one or more errors, your compiler may be unable to translate your program and may not create an object file.

Figure 1.33. *Compiler Listing of a Program with Syntax Errors*

```
0001            PROGRAM MESSUP
0002            REAL TAX
0003            PARAMATER (TAX = 25.00)
%FORT-F-MISSDEL, Missing operator or delimiter symbol

0004            REAL HOURS, RATE, GROSS, NET
0005            PRINT, 'Enter hours worked'
%FORT-F-MISSVAR, Missing variable or constant
%FORT-F-IOINVFMT, Format specifier in error

0006            READ *, 'HOURS'
%FORT-F-IOINVLIST, Invalid I/O list element for input statement

0007            PRINT *, 'Enter hourly rate'
0008            READ *, RATE
0009            GROSS = HOURS * RATE
0010            GROSS - TAX = NET
%FORT-F-INVLEFSID, Left side of assignment must be variable or array
element

0011            PRINT *, 'Gross pay is $,' GROSS
%FORT-F-MISSDEL, Missing operator or delimiter symbol

0012            PRINT *, 'Net pay is $, NET
%FORT-E-MISSAPOS, Missing apostrophe in character constant

0013            STOP
0014            END
```

The error messages generated by a compiler do not always provide a clear indication of what is wrong. For example, in line 5 the actual error is due to a missing * after the word PRINT. The first error message gives no hint of this error. The second error message is a little better, but only if you understand that the symbol * serves as a *format specifier.*

One very common syntax error is caused by the improper use of apostrophes as *string delimiters.* Make sure you always use a single quote or apostrophe to begin and end a string; double quotes are not allowed. Also, check to see that your apostrophes are balanced, that is, make sure there are no missing or extra apostrophes in a string. If the apostrophe at the end is missing, the compiler will not be able to determine where the string stops (see line 12 in Fig. 1.33). Another common error is transposing a comma with an apostrophe in an output list (see line 11).

Another common error is misspelling a variable name. For example, if you misspell NET as NST in an assignment statement, FORTRAN will not tell you that you have an undeclared variable but will simply allocate a new variable named NST. If NST appears in the expression part, some FORTRAN compilers may warn you that NST was not defined before it was used. If NST appears on the left of an assignment (e.g., NST = . . .), there will be no warning and the expression value will be incorrectly assigned to NST, not NET, when the program executes.

Line-Positioning Errors

Sometimes errors are caused by lines that are too long or by lines that start in the wrong column. For example, if you start a line in column 6 instead of column 7, FORTRAN will assume that the new line is a continuation of the previous line. This will most likely cause a syntax error.

Lines that are too long can cause either syntax errors or run-time errors. For example, if the apostrophe at the end of a string appears after column 72, some FORTRAN compilers will ignore the apostrophe and display a missing-apostrophe syntax error.

If the name of a variable used in a long expression happens to begin in column 72, FORTRAN may ignore all but the first letter of that variable name. FORTRAN will assume that there is a new variable with a one-letter name and will allocate a memory cell for that variable (for example, variable W instead of variable WEIGHT). When evaluating the expression, FORTRAN will use whatever value happens to be stored in variable W instead of the value of variable WEIGHT. This may cause a run-time error or lead to incorrect program results.

Run-Time Errors

Run-time errors occur during program execution. When the computer detects a run-time error, it displays an error message and stops program execution at the statement in error.

Figure 1.34 shows a program with a run-time error. The program compiles successfully, but the assignment statement

```
Z = X / Y
```

attempts to divide a real value by zero (value of Y). This causes the computer

Figure 1.34. *Program with a Run-Time Error*

```
PROGRAM ERROR
REAL X, Y, Z
PRINT *, 'Enter X'
READ *, X
Y = 0.0
Z = X / Y
PRINT *, 'Z is ', Z
STOP
END


Program terminated at line 6
Attempted division by zero
```

to stop execution at line 6 and to display a message such as Attempted division by zero.

In Fig. 1.34, the computer displays an error message due to a run-time error. Although we don't like to see error messages, it is worse when errors occur with no indication that they exist. For example, a program may compute results that appear perfectly reasonable but that are, in fact, incorrect. We may have no idea that the program results are wrong and might use these results as the basis of an erroneous decision.

Be forewarned that such errors *can* happen—don't assume a result is correct just because it was generated by a computer. You should hand check all computational results using representative data to verify that the computed results are correct. You may not be able to do the computation with the same degree of accuracy as the computer, but you can derive approximate results for comparison purposes.

As we indicated earlier, debugging a program can be time-consuming. The best approach is to plan your programs carefully and desk check them beforehand to eliminate bugs before they occur. If you are not sure of the syntax for a particular statement, look it up in the text or in the glossary provided in this text. If you follow this approach, you will be much better off in the long run.

Other Kinds of Errors

Besides the errors mentioned above, you may encounter three other kinds of errors.

1. *Logic errors.* These are errors in the logic of your program, such as using the wrong variable name in an equation. These errors are difficult to detect and are usually found when the program generates strange-looking results. These errors are very common and very dangerous.
2. *System problems.* Even though your program may be perfect, it still may not run correctly because of problems with the computer system. Examples are when your program is writing an output file, but there is not sufficient room on the disk for the new file, or when the disk drive is malfunctioning. These types of problems are rare.
3. *Compiler problems.* Sometimes the FORTRAN compiler has bugs and cannot translate your program properly. Beginning programmers often blame their difficulties on a faulty compiler. Compiler errors are rare, however, and occur mostly with new compilers.

Chapter Review

The basic components of a computer were introduced. They are main memory and secondary memory, the central processor, and the input and output devices. A summary of important facts about computers that you should remember follows:

1. A memory cell is never empty, but its initial contents may be meaningless to your program.
2. The current contents of a memory cell are destroyed whenever new information is placed in that cell (via an assignment or a READ statement).
3. Programs must first be placed in the memory of the computer before they can be executed.
4. Data may not be manipulated by the computer without first being stored in memory.
5. A computer cannot think for itself; it must be instructed to perform a task in a precise and unambiguous manner, through a programming language.
6. Programming a computer can be fun—if you are patient, organized, and careful.

You also saw how to perform some fundamental operations using FORTRAN. You learned how to instruct the computer to read information into memory, perform some simple computations, and print the results of the computation. All of this was done using symbols (punctuation marks, variable names, and special operators such as *, −, and +) that are familiar, easy to remember, and easy to use. You do not have to know very much about your computer to understand and use FORTRAN.

In the remainder of the text, we will introduce more features of the FORTRAN language and provide rules for using these features. You must remember throughout that, unlike the rules of English, the rules of FORTRAN are precise and allow no exceptions. The compiler will be unable to translate FORTRAN instructions that violate these rules.

FORTRAN Statements

The FORTRAN statements introduced in this chapter are described in Table 1.5.

Table 1.5. *Summary of FORTRAN Statements*

STATEMENT	EFFECT
PARAMETER Statement	
PARAMETER (TAX = 25.00) PARAMETER (STAR = '*')	Associates the parameter TAX with the value 25.00 and the parameter STAR with the value '*'
Type Declaration	
REAL X, Y, Z INTEGER ME, IT	Allocates memory cells named X, Y, and Z for storage of real numbers and ME and IT for storage of integers
Assignment Statement	
DISTNC = SPEED * TIME	Assigns the product of SPEED and TIME as the value of DISTNC
READ Statement	
READ *, HOURS, RATE	Enters data into the variables HOURS and RATE
READ (1, *) X, Y	Reads a pair of data values from the file associated with unit number 1 into variables X and Y
PRINT Statement	
PRINT *, 'Net = ', NET PRINT *, X, Y	Displays the symbols Net = followed by the value of NET, then prints the values of X and Y on the next-line
OPEN statement	
OPEN (UNIT = 1, FILE = 'INDATA', + STATUS = 'OLD')	Associates the existing file named INDATA with unit number 1
WRITE Statement	
WRITE (2, *) 'X = ', X	Writes a line consisting of a string and the value of X to the file associated with unit number 2
STOP Statement	
STOP	Terminates program execution
END Statement	
END	Indicates the end of a program during translation and terminates program execution if STOP is missing

Quick-Check Exercises

1. What value is assigned to X by the following statement?

   ```
   X = 25.0 * 3.0 / 2.5
   ```

2. What value is assigned to X by the following statement, assuming X is 10.0?

   ```
   X = X - 20.0
   ```

3. Show the output line displayed when X is 3.456.

   ```
   PRINT *, 'The value of X is ', X
   ```

4. Show the output line when N is 345.

   ```
   PRINT *, 'The value of N is ', N
   ```

5. What data type would you use to represent the following items: number of children at school, a letter grade on an exam, the average number of school days absent each year?

6. What is the purpose of the PRINT statement used with a READ from the keyboard? Which statement executes first: READ or PRINT?

7. What is the purpose of the PRINT statement used with a READ from a data file? Which statement executes first: READ or PRINT?

8. If a READ statement is reading two numbers, what character separates the two numbers? What key is pressed after the second number is entered?

9. If a READ statement is reading a student's letter grade, what character is typed first?

10. How does the computer determine how many data values to enter when a READ statement executes?

11. How does the program user determine how many data values to enter when a READ statement executes?

12. The compiler listing shows what kind of errors (syntax or run-time)?

13. Indicate whether each characteristic that follows applies to secondary memory or main memory: used to store program files; used by the editor program for storage of a new file; provides temporary storage of data; provides relatively inexpensive storage; provides limited storage; accessed by the CPU during program execution.

Answers to Quick-Check Exercises

1. 30.0
2. −10.0
3. The value of X is   3.45600
4. The value of N is   345
5. INTEGER, CHARACTER *1, REAL
6. PRINT displays a prompt; PRINT is first.
7. PRINT echos the data value; READ is first.
8. a blank; the return or enter key

9. an apostrophe
10. It depends on the number of variables in the input list.
11. from reading the prompt
12. syntax errors
13. secondary, main, main, secondary, main, main

Review Questions

1. List at least three types of information stored in a computer.
2. List two functions of the CPU.
3. List two input devices, two output devices, and two secondary storage devices.
4. A computer can think.   T   F
5. List three categories of programming languages.
6. Give three advantages of programming in a high-level language such as FORTRAN.
7. What processes are needed to transform a high-level language program to a machine-language program ready for execution?
8. What are structured programs?
9. Check the variables that are syntactically correct:

```
INCOME  _____        TWO FOLD _____
1TIME   _____        C3PO     _____
CONST   _____        INCOME   _____
TOM'S   _____        R2DTWO   _____
```

10. What computer action is required by the statement below?

```
REAL CELL1
```

11. Write a program to read a five-character name and print the name out backward.
12. If the average size of a family is 2.8 and this value is stored in the variable FAMSIZ, provide the FORTRAN statement to display this fact in a readable way.
13. List four standard data types of FORTRAN.

Programming Projects

1. Write a program to convert a measurement in inches to centimeters and meters.

2. Write a program to convert a measurement in meters to inches and yards.

3. Write a program to convert a temperature in degrees Fahrenheit to degrees Celsius. Use the formula

$$Celsius = (5.0/9.0) \times (Fahrenheit - 32)$$

4. Write a program to read three data items into variables X, Y, and Z, then find and print their product and sum.

5. Write a program to read in the weight (in pounds) of an object, then compute and print its weight in kilograms and grams. (*Hint:* one pound is equal to 0.453592 kilograms or 453.59237 grams.)

6. Eight track stars entered the mile race at the Penn Relays. Write a program that will read in the race time in minutes (MINUTE) and seconds (SECOND) for each runner, then compute and print the speed in feet per second (FPS) and in meters per second (MPS). (*Hint:* There are 5,280 feet in one mile, and one kilometer equals 3,282 feet.) Test your program on each of the times below:

Minutes	Seconds
3	52.83
3	59.83
4	00.03
4	16.22

7. Write a program that prints your initials in large block letters. (*Hint:* Use a 6 × 6 grid for each letter and print six strings. Each string should consist of a row of asterisks interspersed with blanks.)

8. You are planning to rent a car to drive from Boston to Philadelphia. You want to be certain that you can make the trip on one tankful of gas. Write a program to read in the miles per gallon (MPG) and tank size (TNKSIZ) in gallons for a particular rental car, then print out the distance that can be traveled on one tank. Test your program for the following data:

Miles per Gallon	Tank Size (gallons)
10.0	15.0
40.5	20.0
22.5	12.0
10.0	9.0

9. A cyclist coasting on a level road slows from a speed of 10 miles per hour to 2.5 miles an hour in one minute. Write a computer program that calculates the cyclist's constant rate of acceleration and determines how long it will take the cyclist to come to rest, given an initial speed of 10 miles per hour. (*Hint:* Use the equation

$$a = (v_f - v_i)/t$$

where a is acceleration, t is time interval, v_i is initial velocity, and v_f is the final velocity.)

10. Write a program that reads the user's first and middle initials and then the first six letters of the user's last name. Blank characters should be entered if the user's last name has fewer than six letters. The user's name should then be displayed on the next line in the form last name, space, first initial, space, middle initial.

11. The diagram below shows two airline routes from Philadelphia to Dallas. Read each distance shown into a type INTEGER variable and then find the distance from Philadelphia to Dallas for each route.

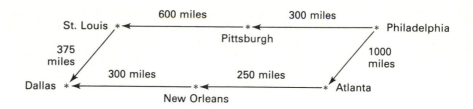

12. If a human heart beats on the average of once a second for 78 years, how many times does the heart beat in a life-time? (Use 365.25 for days in a year.) Rerun your program for a heart rate of 75 beats per minute.

13. In shopping for a new house, you must consider several factors. In this problem, the initial cost of the house, estimated annual fuel costs, and annual tax rate are available. Write a program that will determine the total cost after a five-year period for each set of house data below. You should be able to inspect your program output to determine the "best buy."

Initial House Cost	Annual Fuel Cost	Tax Rate
$67,000	$2,300	0.025
$62,000	$2,500	0.025
$75,000	$1,850	0.020

To calculate the house cost, add the initial cost to the fuel cost for five years, then add the taxes for five years. Taxes for one year are computed by multiplying the tax rate by the initial cost.

14. Write a program that will read in the diameter of a circle. The program will then calculate and print the radius, circumference, and area of the circle. Note that the radius of a circle is one-half the diameter, the circumference is π times the diameter, and the area is π times the radius squared.

15. Write a program that reads in the values of three resistors and calculates their total combined resistance. The three resistors are arranged in parallel as shown below:

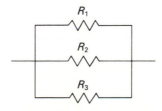

The formula for calculating the total resistance in this circuit is:

$$\frac{1}{\dfrac{1}{R_1} + \dfrac{1}{R_2} + \dfrac{1}{R_3}}$$

16. The Pythagorean theorem says that the sum of the squares of the sides of a right triangle is equal to the square of the hypotenuse. For example, if two sides of a right triangle are of lengths 3 and 4, then the hypotenuse is of length 5 ($3^2 + 4^2 = 5^2$). The three integers, 3, 4, and 5, together form a *pythagorean triple*. There is an infinite number of such triples. Given two positive integers, m and n, where $m > n$, a pythagorean triple can be generated by the following formulas:

$$side\ 1 = m^2 - n^2$$
$$side\ 2 = 2mn$$
$$hypotenuse = m^2 + n^2$$

Write a program that reads in values for m and n and calculates the pythagorean triple generated according to the formulas above.

17. A manufacturer wishes to determine the cost of producing the top for a cylindrical container. The cost of each top will be COST dollars per square inch of the material needed to produce the top. The amount of material needed for each top is the area of the top, which is circular. Recall that the area of a circle is π times the radius squared. Write a program to read in the radius (RADIUS) of a top, the cost per square inch of the top (COST), and the number of tops to be produced (QUANT). Calculate the final cost of producing all the tops.

2. Solving Problems and Making Decisions

THE ABILITY to solve problems is an essential component of programming. In this chapter, we focus on a variety of strategies that are useful for solving problems. Problem-solving strategies such as divide and conquer, stepwise refinement, solution by analogy, and solution by generalization will be illustrated.

The division of a problem into smaller subproblems will be discussed. We will see how to represent the list of steps in a solution strategy as an algorithm and how to implement an algorithm as a program. We will discuss how to hand simulate or trace the execution of an algorithm or program to verify that it is correct.

The necessity for decision steps and repetition in a problem solution will be demonstrated. The IF statement will be introduced as a way to specify decisions in a program. Relational operators will be used to describe conditions that evaluate to true or false.

2.1 ▬▬ The Art and Science of Problem Solving

You must be able to solve problems to succeed in academics or in the real world. Problem-solving ability is a combination of art and science. The art of problem solving is the transformation of an English description of a problem into a form that permits a mechanical solution. A relatively straightforward example of this process is transforming an algebra word problem into a set of algebraic equations, which can then be solved for one or more unknowns.

In the real world, this process is more difficult because problem descriptions are often incomplete, imprecise, or ambiguous. The successful problem solver must be able to ask the right questions in order to clarify the problem and obtain any information missing from the problem statement (called *problem specification*). Next, the problem solver must analyze the problem and attempt to extract its essential features, identifying what is provided (the problem inputs) and what is required (problem outputs). The problem solver must also be able to determine whether there are any constraints or simplifying assumptions that can be applied to facilitate the problem solution. Often, we cannot solve the most general case of a problem but must make some realistic assumptions that limit or constrain the problem so that it can be solved.

The science part of problem solving involves knowledge of the problem environment, knowledge of the formulas or equations that characterize the environment, and the ability to apply and manipulate those formulas. Using this knowledge, the problem solver can develop a series of steps whose successful completion will lead to the problem solution. Once the solution is obtained, the problem solver must verify its accuracy by comparing the computed results with observed results.

The Engineering and Scientific Method

Engineers and scientists are problem solvers. As part of the problem-solving process, they must follow the problem-analysis steps described below.[1]

1. **Recognize and understand the problem.** Perhaps the most difficult part of problem solving is developing the ability to recognize and define the problem precisely. If the problem is not totally defined, you must study the problem carefully, eliminate the things that are unimportant, and zero in on the root problem.
2. **Accumulate facts.** Ascertain all pertinent physical facts, such as sizes, temperatures, voltages, weights, and costs. Some problems require that steps 1 and 2 be done simultaneously.
3. **Select appropriate theory or principle.** Select appropriate theories or scientific principles that apply to the problem solution. Understand and identify limits or constraints that apply.
4. **Make necessary assumptions.** Perfect solutions do not exist to real problems. Simplifications need to be made if problems are to be solved. Make sure your simplifications do not significantly affect the accuracy of the solution.
5. **Solve the problem.** If steps 3 and 4 result in a set of mathematical equations (model), you can solve the problem by applying mathematical theory, a trial-and-error solution, or some form of graphical solution.
6. **Verify and check results.** In engineering practice, the work is not finished merely because a solution has been obtained. It must be checked to ensure that it is mathematically correct and that units have been properly specified.

Solving Programming Problems

The engineering and scientific method can be adapted to solve programming problems as well. The basic steps involved in solving a programming problem are listed next.

1. **Recognize and understand the problem.** Same as step 1 in the engineering and scientific method.
2. **Determine the problem inputs and the problem outputs.** Identify what information is supplied as problem data and what results should be computed and displayed.
3. **Develop an algorithm.** Formulate a list of steps that must be followed to derive the desired problem outputs.

---

[1] Adapted with permission from Arvid Eide, et al., *Engineering Fundamentals and Problem Solving*, 2d ed. (New York: McGraw-Hill, 1986).

4. **Select appropriate theory or principle.** Identify any formulas that may be needed in the list of algorithm steps developed in step 3.
5. **Write the program.** Implement the algorithm as a program that satisfies the syntax rules of FORTRAN.
6. **Verify and check results.** Just because a program runs and generates results does not necessarily mean that the program is correct. Test the program by comparing its results to hand calculations for several different sets of test data.

We will illustrate the application of these steps in Section 2.3 and the rest of this text. But first we will discuss how to perform step 3—develop an algorithm.

2.2 Representing and Refining Algorithms

Divide and Conquer

One of the most fundamental methods of problem solving is to break a large problem into several smaller *subproblems*. This enables us to solve a large problem one step at a time, rather than to provide the entire solution at once. This technique is often called *divide and conquer*.

As an example, let us assume it is the year 2000 and we have a household robot (named Robbie) to help with some simple chores. We would like Robbie to serve us our breakfast. Unfortunately, Robbie is an early production model, and to get Robbie to perform even the simplest task, we must provide the robot with a detailed list of instructions.

Case Study: Robbie Serving Breakfast

Problem

Robbie is at point R (for Robbie) in Fig. 2.1. We want Robbie to retrieve our favorite box of cereal (point C) and bring it to the table (point T) in the next

Figure 2.1. *Robbie Serving Breakfast*

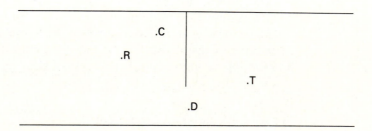

Case Study: Robbie Serving Breakfast, continued

room. The positions of these points and an additional point D (described later) are shown in Fig. 2.1.

Design Overview

We can accomplish our goal by having Robbie perform the four steps listed below.

Initial Algorithm

1. Move from point R to point C.
2. Retrieve the cereal box at point C.
3. Move from point C to point T.
4. Place the cereal box on the table at point T.

Solving these four subproblems will give us the solution to the original problem.

Algorithm Refinements

We can attack each subproblem independently. To solve any of these problems, we must have an idea of the basic operations that Robbie can perform. We will assume that Robbie can rotate or turn to face any direction, move straight ahead, and grasp and release specified objects. Given this information, we can see that subproblems 2 and 4 are basic operations, provided Robbie is in the correct position. Therefore, we will concentrate on moving Robbie into position (subproblems 1 and 3).

In solving the first subproblem

1. Move from point R to point C.

we must allow for the fact that Robbie can move in only one direction at a time, and that direction is straight ahead. Consequently, the steps required to solve subproblem 1 are

1.1 Turn to face point C.
1.2 Move from point R to point C.

Step 3 may be solved in a similar way. However, since Robbie cannot walk through walls, the steps for solving subproblem 3 might be

3.1 Turn to face the doorway (point D) between the rooms.
3.2 Move from point C to point D.
3.3 Turn to face point T.
3.4 Move from point D to point T.

Case Study: Robbie Serving Breakfast, continued

To summarize the events so far, we divided the original problem of getting Robbie to bring our breakfast cereal to the table into four subproblems, all of which can be solved independently. Two of these subproblems were broken down into even smaller subproblems.

The complete list of steps required to solve our problem is shown below. The process of adding detail to a solution algorithm (e.g., rewriting step 1 as steps 1.1 and 1.2) is called *stepwise refinement*.

Final Algorithm

1. Move from point R to point C.
   1.1 Turn to face point C.
   1.2 Move from point R to point C.
2. Retrieve the cereal box at point C.
3. Move from point C to point T.
   3.1 Turn to face the doorway (point D) between the rooms.
   3.2 Move from point C to point D.
   3.3 Turn to face point T.
   3.4 Move from point D to point T.
4. Place the cereal box on the table at point T.

Algorithms in Everyday Life

Algorithms are not unique to the study of robots or computer programming. You have probably been using algorithms to solve problems without being aware of it.

Case Study: Changing a Flat Tire

Problem

You are driving a car with two friends and suddenly get a flat tire. Fortunately, there is a spare tire and a jack in the trunk.

Design Overview

After pulling over to the side of the road, you decide to subdivide the problem of changing a tire into the subproblems below.

Case Study: Changing a Flat Tire, continued

Initial Algorithm

1. Get the jack out and jack up the car.
2. Loosen the lug nuts from the flat tire and remove it.
3. Get the spare tire, place it on the wheel, and tighten the lug nuts.
4. Lower the car.
5. Secure the jack and flat tire in the trunk.

Algorithm Refinements

Since these steps are relatively independent, you decide to assign subproblem 1 to friend A, subproblem 2 to friend B, subproblem 3 to yourself, and so on. If friend A has used a jack before, then the whole process should proceed smoothly; however, if friend A does not know how to use a jack, it might be necessary to refine step 1 further.

Step 1 Refinement

1.1 Get the jack from the trunk.
1.2 Place the jack under the car near the tire that is flat.
1.3 Insert the jack handle in the jack.
1.4 Place a block of wood against one of the other tires to keep the car from rolling.
1.5 Jack up the car until there is enough room for the spare tire.

Step 1.4 requires a bit of decision making on your friend's part. The actual placement of the block of wood depends on whether the car is facing uphill or downhill, as described next.

Step 1.4 Refinement

1.4.1 If the car is facing uphill, then place the block of wood in back of a tire that is not flat; if the car is facing downhill, then place the block of wood in front of a tire that is not flat.

Finally, step 1.5 involves a repetitive action: moving the jack handle until there is sufficient room to put on the spare tire. Often, people stop when the car is high enough to remove the flat tire, forgetting that an inflated tire requires more room. It may take a few attempts to complete step 1.5.

Step 1.5 Refinement

1.5.1 Move the jack handle repeatedly until the car is high enough off the ground that the spare tire can be put on the wheel.

The previous examples illustrate the algorithm-refinement process. Throughout the rest of this chapter (and the text), we will discuss computer problem solving, and we will see that the principles discussed here carry over. Pertinent concepts from this section include

- dividing a problem into subproblems
- solving each subproblem separately
- refining an algorithm step to provide solution detail
- decision making in an algorithm step
- repetition of an algorithm step

2.3 Problem Solving Illustrated

In this section, we will apply the problem-solving method described at the end of Section 2.1 to a programming problem. The first step is to recognize and understand the problem.

Understanding the Problem

An important skill in human communication is the ability to listen carefully. Often, we are too busy thinking of what our response will be to really hear what the other person is saying. This can lead to a lack of understanding between the speaker and the listener.

Many of us suffer from a similar difficulty when we attempt to solve problems that are presented either verbally or in writing. We do not pay close enough attention to the problem statement to determine what really is being asked; consequently, either we are unable to solve the stated problem or our problem solution is incorrect because it solves the wrong problem.

It is most important that you analyze a problem statement carefully before attempting to solve it. You should read each problem statement two or three times if necessary. The first time you read a problem, you should get a general idea of what is being asked. The second time you read it, you should try to answer these questions:

- What information should the solution provide?
- What data do I have to work with?

The answer to the first question will tell you the desired results, or the *problem outputs*. The answer to the second question will tell you what data are provided, or the *problem inputs*. It may be helpful to underline the phrases in the problem statement that identify the inputs and the outputs. Inputs are in italics and outputs are in boldface in the problem statement that follows.

Case Study: Finding the Area and Circumference of a Circle

Problem

Read in the *radius of a circle* and the *units of measurement* and compute and print the circle's **area** and **circumference**.

Design Overview

After identifying the problem inputs and outputs, we must determine the amount and type of memory required to store these data. Clearly, one memory cell each is required for the radius, the area, and the circumference of the circle. These memory cells should be type REAL, because the numeric values of these items can have fractional parts. A type CHARACTER memory cell can be used to hold the units of measurement. You must also choose meaningful variable names for those cells.

Data Requirements

Problem Inputs

the radius of a circle (REAL RADIUS)
the units of measurement (CHARACTER *12 UNITS)

Problem Outputs

the area of the circle (REAL AREA)
the circumference of the circle (REAL CIRCUM)

Once the problem inputs and outputs are known, the steps necessary to solve the problem should be listed. It is very important that you pay close attention to the order of the steps. The initial algorithm follows.

Initial Algorithm

1. Read the values of RADIUS and UNITS.
2. Find the area.
3. Find the circumference.
4. Print the values of the area and the circumference.

Algorithm Refinements

Next, we should refine any steps whose solution is not immediately obvious; for example, step 2 and step 3. Knowledge of the geometry of circles leads to the refinements below.

Case Study: Finding the Area and Circumference of a Circle, continued

Step 2 Refinement

2.1 Multiply the radius squared by the value of PI (3.141593).

Step 3 Refinement

3.1 Compute the product of 2, PI, and RADIUS.

Coding

Next, we must implement the algorithm as a program. This is done by first writing the declarations for the program using the problem input and output descriptions. Also, any additional variables or parameters introduced in the algorithm should be declared (e.g., the parameter PI). Then the algorithm steps should be written in FORTRAN. If an algorithm step is refined, then the refinement is implemented instead.

Following this procedure, we obtain the program shown in Fig. 2.2. Algorithm steps 1, 2.1, 3.1, and 4 are implemented in the program body; that is, following the declarations.

In Fig. 2.2, we introduced the variable UNITS and used it to store the units of measurement. The value of UNITS is simply read as a string enclosed in apostrophes and then echo printed in each PRINT statement that displays a result. For the time being, this is the only way that we will use character data.

We introduced the variable UNITS because the computer cannot keep track of the units associated with numbers by itself. It does not know (or care) whether the number 101.50 is in dollars, meters, or pounds. The programmer must make sure that each prompt describes the units required for an input variable (e.g., 'Enter the length (in meters)'). The programmer should also make sure that the program displays the correct units associated with all output values.

Figure 2.2. *Finding the Area and Circumference of a Circle*

```
      PROGRAM CIRCLE
C Finds and prints the area and circumference of a circle.
C The program user enters the circle radius and units of
C measurement.

C Declarations
      REAL PI
      PARAMETER (PI = 3.141593)
      REAL RADIUS, AREA, CIRCUM
      CHARACTER *12 UNITS
```

Case Study: Finding the Area and Circumference of a Circle, continued

```
C Read the value of RADIUS and UNITS
      PRINT *, 'Enter units (enclosed in apostrophes)'
      READ *, UNITS
      PRINT *, 'Enter radius (in ', UNITS, ')'
      READ *. RADIUS

C Find the area
      AREA = PI * RADIUS ** 2

C Find the circumference
      CIRCUM = 2.0 * PI * RADIUS

C Print the values of AREA and CIRCUM
      PRINT *, 'The area is ', AREA, ' square ', UNITS
      PRINT *, 'The circumference is ', CIRCUM, ' ', UNITS
      STOP
      END
Enter units (enclosed in apostrophes)
'centimeters'
Enter radius (in centimeters)
5.0
The area is       78.53976 square centimeters
The circumference is       31.41593 centimeters
```

Testing

The sample output shown in Fig. 2.2 provides a good test of the solution because it is relatively easy to compute the area and circumference by hand for a radius value of 5.0. The radius squared is 25.0, so the value of the area appears correct. The circumference should be ten times PI, which is also an easy number to compute by hand. It would be useful to try another test involving a radius of 1.0 and a different unit of measurement.

SELF-CHECK EXERCISES FOR SECTION 2.3

1. Describe the problem inputs, outputs, and algorithm for computing the sum and average of three numbers.
2. Describe the problem inputs, outputs, and algorithm for this problem: Compute the discounted price for an item given the list price and the percentage of the discount.

2.4 ▬▬▬ Comments and Documentation

The program in Fig. 2.2 contains some English phrases on lines that begin with the letter C. These phrases, called *comments*, are used to make the program easier to understand by describing the purpose of the program (the first comment line) and the purpose of each program step (the other comments). Comments are an important part of the *documentation* of a program because they help others read and follow the program; however, they are ignored by the compiler and are not translated into machine language. The syntax and use of comments are described in the next displays.

Comment

> SYNTAX: C *comment*
>   * *comment*
>
> EXAMPLE: C This is a comment
>   * So is this
>
> INTERPRETATION: The C (or *) in column 1 indicates that the current line is a *comment*. Comments are listed with the program but are otherwise ignored by the FORTRAN compiler. Lowercase is permitted in comments. A blank line is also considered a comment.

Program Style

> *Using Comments and Blank Lines*
>
> Blank lines and comments can make a program more readable. Blank lines separate a program into sections, and comments describe the purpose of each program section. Generally, there will be one comment in the program for each major algorithm step.
>
> A comment within the program should summarize what the step does rather than simply restate the step in English. For example, the comment
>
> ```
> C Find the area
>       AREA = PI * RADIUS ** 2
> ```
>
> is more descriptive and, hence, preferable to
>
> ```
> C Multiply the radius squared times PI
>       AREA = PI * RADIUS ** 2
> ```
>
> Each program should begin with a series of comments that specify
>
> - the programmer's name
> - the date of the current version
> - a brief description of what the program does
> - a description of the program inputs and outputs
> - a list of any program variables and what they represent
>
> Although space considerations prevent us from doing this in the text, we strongly recommend that you follow this practice. The program in Fig. 2.2 could begin with the following comments:

```
C Finds and prints the area and circumference of a circle.
C The program user enters the circle radius and units of
C measurement.

C Programmer:  Ethan Waldman
C Date: July 15, 1990
C Instructor:  Dr. F. Tran

C Data Requirements
C    Inputs:  RADIUS - the radius of a circle
C             UNITS - the units of measurement
C    Outputs: AREA - the area of a circle
C             CIRCUM - The circumference of a circle
```

2.5 ▬▬▬ Decision Steps, Conditions, and IF Statements

In the algorithms illustrated so far, each step is executed exactly once in the order in which it appears. However, most programs are not that simple. Instead, they require the use of *decision steps* to instruct the computer how to choose among one or more alternative sequences of steps. The values of selected program data determine which of the alternatives listed in the decision step is actually executed.

One possible use of a decision step would be in the simple payroll problem discussed in Chapter 1. In the program shown in Fig. 1.21, a tax of $25 is deducted regardless of the employee's salary. It would be more desirable to base the tax amount on the employee's gross salary using this *decision step:*

If gross salary exceeds $100, deduct a tax of $25; otherwise, deduct no tax.

The refinement of this step should show that there are two alternative courses of action: either deduct a tax or do not deduct a tax. To determine what to do, a payroll clerk might ask the question "Is gross salary greater than $100?" The clerk would perform one action (deduct tax) if the answer is "yes" and the other action (deduct no tax) if the answer is "no."

The decision step is restated below in *pseudocode*, a mixture of English and FORTRAN.

IF gross salary is greater than $100.00 THEN
    Deduct a tax of $25.00
ELSE
    Deduct no tax
ENDIF

This decision step specifies that either the action "Deduct a tax of $25.00" or the action "Deduct no tax" will take place, but not both. We will often use pseudocode to represent algorithms, because it allows us to state algorithms concisely and in a form that can easily be translated into FORTRAN.

Conditions and Relational Operators

The first line of the decision step above contains the *condition* "gross salary is greater than $100.00." A condition is a *logical expression*, that is, an expression that evaluates to either true or false. The value of the condition determines which action will take place. If the condition value is true, the task following the word THEN is executed; if the condition value is false, the task following the word ELSE is executed instead.

An alternative representation of this decision step, called a *flow diagram*, is shown in Fig. 2.3. The diamond-shaped box in the flow diagram represents a condition; the rectangles represent processes. The flow diagram shows that the condition enclosed in the diamond symbol is evaluated. If the condition value is true, the arrow on the right is followed; if the condition value is false, the arrow on the left is followed.

Figure 2.3. *Flow Diagram of a Decision Step*

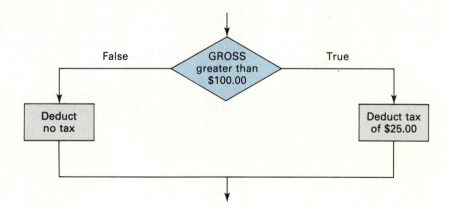

We can rewrite the condition "gross salary is greater than $100.00" in FORTRAN as

    GROSS .GT. 100.00

where the symbol .GT. means greater than. Most conditions that we use will have one of the forms

   variable relational operator variable as in GROSS .GT. CUTOFF
   or *variable relational operator constant* as in GROSS .GT. 100.00

where the *relational operators* are the symbols .LT. (less than), .LE. (less than or equal to), .GT. (greater than), .GE. (greater than or equal to), .EQ. (equal to), and .NE. (not equal to).

EXAMPLE 2.1
The relational operators and some sample conditions are shown in Table 2.1. Each condition is evaluated assuming the variable values below. ■

X	POWER	MAXPOW	Y	ITEM	MIN	MOMDAD	NUM	SENTNL
−5	1024	1024	7	1.5	−999.0	'M'	999	999

Table 2.1. *FORTRAN Relational Operators and Sample Conditions*

OPERATOR	CONDITION	MEANING	VALUE
.LE.	X .LE. 0	X less than or equal to 0	true
.LT.	POWER .LT. MAXPOW	POWER less than MAXPOW	false
.GE.	X .GE. Y	X greater than or equal to Y	false
.GT.	ITEM .GT. MIN	ITEM greater than MIN	true
.EQ.	MOMDAD .EQ. 'M'	MOMDAD equal to 'M'	true
.NE.	NUM .NE. SENTNL	NUM not equal to SENTNL	false

IF Statement Examples

The IF statement in Fig. 2.4 (see page 79) has two alternatives, but only one will be executed for a given value of GROSS. An IF statement can also have a single alternative that is executed only when the condition is true, as shown next.

EXAMPLE 2.2
The following IF statement has one alternative that is executed only when X is not equal to zero. It causes PRODCT to be multiplied by X; the new value is saved in PRODCT and printed. If X is equal to zero, these steps are not performed. ■

```
C Multiply PRODCT by a nonzero X only
      IF (X .NE. 0) THEN
          PRODCT = PRODCT * X
          PRINT *, 'New product is ', PRODCT
      ENDIF
```

EXAMPLE 2.3
The following IF statement has two alternatives. It will print either 'Hi Mom' or 'Hi Dad' depending on the character stored in character variable MOMDAD.

```
      IF (MOMDAD .EQ. 'M') THEN
          PRINT *, 'Hi Mom'
      ELSE
          PRINT *, 'Hi Dad'
      ENDIF
```

The IF statement below has one alternative; the message 'Hi Mom' will be printed only when MOMDAD has the value 'M'. Regardless of whether or not 'Hi Mom' is printed, the message 'Hi Dad' will always be printed because it follows the IF statement. ∎

```
IF (MOMDAD .EQ. 'M') THEN
    PRINT *, 'Hi Mom'
ENDIF
PRINT *, 'Hi Dad'
```

Syntax of IF Statements

The syntax of FORTRAN IF statements is described in the next displays. Remember that an IF statement must always end with the word ENDIF, and the words ELSE (if present) and ENDIF must always be on lines by themselves. Later, we will see that IF statements with several (more than two) alternatives are also possible in FORTRAN.

IF Statement (Two Alternatives)

SYNTAX: IF (*condition*) THEN
         $Task_T$
      ELSE
         $Task_F$
      ENDIF

EXAMPLE: IF (X .GE. 0) THEN
        PRINT *, X, ' is positive'
      ELSE
        PRINT *, X, ' is negative'
        X = −X
      ENDIF

INTERPRETATION: If the *condition* evaluates to true, then $Task_T$ (the true alternative) is executed and $Task_F$ (the false alternative) is skipped; otherwise, $Task_T$ is skipped and $Task_F$ is executed. $Task_T$ or $Task_F$ can be one or more FORTRAN statements.

IF Statement (One Alternative)

SYNTAX: IF (*condition*) THEN
        $Task_T$
      ENDIF

EXAMPLE: IF (X .GT. 0) THEN
        POSSUM = POSSUM + X
        COUNT = COUNT + 1
      ENDIF

INTERPRETATION: If the *condition* evaluates to true, then *Task*$_T$ (the true alterna-tive) is executed; otherwise, it is skipped. *Task*$_T$ can be one or more FORTRAN statements.

Program Style

Structuring the IF Statement

In all our IF statement examples, the true and false alternatives are indented. If the word ELSE appears, it must be entered on a separate line and aligned under the word IF. Finally, the word ENDIF must appear on a separate line at the end of the IF statement and aligned with IF and ELSE.

Indenting *Task*$_T$ and *Task*$_F$ makes the IF statement easier to read and its meaning more apparent. This is done solely to improve program readability; the indentation used makes no difference to the compiler.

SELF-CHECK EXERCISES FOR SECTION 2.5

1. Assuming X is 15.0 and Y is 25.0, what are the values of the following conditions?

   X .NE. Y   X .LT. X   X .GE. (Y − X)   X .EQ. (Y + X − Y)

2. What do the following statements display?

   a. IF (X .LT. X) THEN
          PRINT *, 'Always'
        ELSE
          PRINT *, 'Never'
        ENDIF

   b. VAR1 = 15.0
        VAR2 = 25.12
        IF (VAR2 .LE. 2.0 * VAR1) THEN
          PRINT *, 'O.K.'
        ELSE
          PRINT *, 'NOT O.K.'
        ENDIF

3. Write FORTRAN statements to carry out the steps below.

   a. If ITEM is nonzero, then multiply PRODCT by ITEM and save the result in PRODCT; otherwise, skip the multiplication. In either case, print the value of PRODCT.

   b. Store the absolute difference of X and Y in Z, where the absolute differ-ence is X − Y or Y − X, whichever is positive.

   c. If X is zero, then add 1 to ZROCNT; if X is negative, add X to MINSUM; if X is positive, add X to PLUSUM.

2.6  Solving Problems with Decision Steps

This section contains three problems that use decision steps in their solutions.

Case Study: Modified Payroll Problem

Problem

Modify the simple payroll program to deduct a $25.00 tax only if an employee earns more than $100.00; deduct no tax otherwise.

Design Overview

We will analyze this problem using the tools developed so far in this chapter. First, we list the data requirements and the algorithm.

Data Requirements

Problem Parameters

maximum salary without a tax deduction (TXBRAK = 100.00)
amount of tax deducted (TAX = 25.00)

Problem Inputs

hours worked (REAL HOURS)
hourly rate (REAL RATE)

Problem Outputs

gross pay (REAL GROSS)
net pay (REAL NET)

Unlike a problem input, whose value may vary, a problem parameter has a constant value for each run of the program. Each constant value is associated with a symbolic name (TXBRAK and TAX). The program style display following this case study describes the reason for this association.

Initial Algorithm

1. Enter hours worked and hourly rate.
2. Compute gross salary.
3. Compute net salary.
4. Print gross salary and net salary.

Case Study: Modified Payroll Problem, continued

Algorithm Refinement

Algorithm step 3 is the only one needing refinement; its refinement follows. The program is shown in Fig. 2.4.

Figure 2.4. *Program for Modified Payroll Problem*

```
PROGRAM MYPAY4
C Compute and print gross pay and net pay given an hourly
C rate and number of hours worked. Deduct a tax of $25 if
C gross salary exceeds $100; otherwise, deduct no tax.

C Declarations
      REAL TXBRAK, TAX
      PARAMETER (TXBRAK = 100.00)
      PARAMETER (TAX = 25.00)
      REAL HOURS, RATE, GROSS, NET

C Enter HOURS and RATE
      PRINT *, 'Enter hours worked:'
      READ *, HOURS
      PRINT *, 'Enter hourly rate:'
      READ *, RATE

C Compute gross salary
      GROSS = HOURS * RATE

C Compute net salary
      IF (GROSS .GT. TXBRAK) THEN
         NET = GROSS - TAX
      ELSE
         NET = GROSS
      ENDIF

C Print GROSS and NET
      PRINT *, 'Gross salary is $', GROSS
      PRINT *, 'Net salary is $', NET
      STOP
      END

Enter hours worked:
40
Enter hourly rate:
5.00
Gross salary is $    200.00000
Net salary is $    175.00000
```

Case Study: Modified Payroll Problem, continued

Step 3 Refinement

3.1 IF GROSS is greater than TXBRAK THEN
　　　3.2 Deduct TAX
　　ELSE
　　　3.3 Deduct no tax
　　ENDIF

Coding

Figure 2.4 shows the program. In Fig. 2.4, the IF statement

```
IF (GROSS .GT. TXBRAK) THEN
    NET = GROSS - TAX
ELSE
    NET = GROSS
ENDIF
```

implements the decision step (step 3) shown earlier.

Testing

To test this program, run it with at least three sets of data. One data set should yield a gross salary greater than $100.00, one should yield a gross salary less than $100.00, and one should yield a gross salary that is exactly $100.00.

Program Style

Use of Parameters

In Fig. 2.4, the constant values 25.00 and 100.00 are associated with the parameters TAX and TXBRAK, respectively. These parameters are referenced in the IF statement. We could just as easily have inserted the constant values directly in the IF statement and written

```
IF (GROSS .GT. 100.00) THEN
    NET = GROSS - 25.00
ELSE
    NET = GROSS
ENDIF
```

There are two advantages to using parameters. First, the original IF statement is easier to understand since it uses the names TAX and TXBRAK, which are descriptive, rather than numbers, which have no intrinsic meaning. Second, a program written with parameters is much easier to modify than one that is not. If we wish to use different constant values in Fig. 2.4, we need to change only the parameter declaration statement. If the constant values were inserted directly in the IF statement as shown above, then we would have to change the IF statement and any other statements that use the constant values.

Case Study: Finding the Smallest of Three Numbers

Problem

Read three integer values and find and print the smallest one.

Design Overview

From our prior experience with conditions and decision steps, we know how to compare two items at a time to see which one is smaller using the relational operator .LT.. The problem inputs and outputs are listed next, followed by the algorithm.

Data Requirements

Problem Input

three numbers (INTEGER NUM1, NUM2, NUM3)

Problem Output

the smallest number (INTEGER MINNUM)

Initial Algorithm

1. Read three numbers into NUM1, NUM2, and NUM3.
2. Save the smallest of NUM1, NUM2, and NUM3 in MINNUM.
3. Print the smallest number.

Algorithm Refinements

Step 2 can be performed by first comparing NUM1 and NUM2 and saving the smaller number in MINNUM; this result can then be compared to NUM3. The refinement of step 2 follows.

Step 2 Refinement

2.1 Save the smaller of NUM1 and NUM2 in MINNUM.
2.2 Save the smaller of NUM3 and MINNUM in MINNUM.

Steps 2.1 and 2.2 require further refinement as shown next.

Case Study: Finding the Smallest of Three Numbers, continued

Step 2.1 Refinement

2.1.1 IF NUM1 is less than NUM2 THEN
        2.1.2 Store NUM1 in MINNUM
    ELSE
        2.1.3 Store NUM2 in MINNUM
    ENDIF

Step 2.2 Refinement

2.2.1 IF NUM3 is less than MINNUM THEN
        2.2.2 Store NUM3 in MINNUM
    ENDIF

Coding

Figure 2.5 shows the program. In Fig. 2.5, the IF statement with two alternatives saves either NUM1 or NUM2 in MINNUM. The IF statement with one alternative stores NUM3 in MINNUM if NUM3 is less than the value already in MINNUM.

Figure 2.5. *Finding the Smallest Number*

```
      PROGRAM SMALL3
C Finds and prints the smallest number.

C Declarations
      INTEGER NUM1, NUM2, NUM3, MINNUM

C Read three numbers
      PRINT *, 'Enter three integers separated by blanks:'
      READ *, NUM1, NUM2, NUM3

C Store the smaller of NUM1 and NUM2 in MINNUM
      IF (NUM1 .LT. NUM2) THEN
         MINNUM = NUM1
      ELSE
         MINNUM = NUM2
      ENDIF

C Store the smaller of NUM3 and MINNUM in MINNUM
      IF (NUM3 .LT. MINNUM) THEN
         MINNUM = NUM3
      ENDIF

C Print result
      PRINT *, MINNUM, ' is the smallest number.'
      STOP
      END
```

Case Study: Finding the Smallest of Three Numbers, continued

```
Enter three integers separated by blanks:
2 3 1
         1 is the smallest number.
```

Testing

To test this program, make sure it works when the smallest number is in any of the three positions. Section 2.7 describes the four cases that should be tested. You should also see what happens when two or more of the numbers are the same and when one or more of the numbers is negative.

Case Study: Testing Column Safety

Problem

Acme Construction needs a program that computes the stress on a rectangular column and displays a message indicating whether the column is safe or unsafe. Assume that the column is safe if the stress is less than or equal to 2000 pounds per square inch (p.s.i.).

Design Overview

The stress on a short column is calculated by dividing the force (or weight) on the column by the cross-sectional area (width × depth) of the rectangular column. If force, depth, and width are provided as data, the program can calculate the stress and compare it to the maximum allowed stress. The data requirements and algorithm follow.

Data Requirements

Problem Parameter

the maximum stress allowed (REAL MXSTRS = 2000.0)

Problem Inputs

the force applied in pounds (REAL FORCE)
the width of the column in inches (REAL WIDTH)
the depth of the column in inches (REAL DEPTH)

Case Study: Testing Column Safety, continued

Problem Outputs

the computed stress (REAL STRESS)
a message indicating whether the column is safe or unsafe

Initial Algorithm

1. Enter the force on the column and its width and depth.
2. Compute the stress on the column.
3. Display the stress value.
4. Display a message indicating whether the column is safe or unsafe.

Algorithm Refinements

Steps 2 and 4 need refinement. For step 2, we can use the equations

$area = depth \times width$
$stress = force \,/\, area$

to compute the stress. We need an additional program variable to store the cross-sectional area.

Additional Program Variable

the cross-sectional area of the column (REAL AREA)

Step 2 Refinement

2.1 AREA = DEPTH * WIDTH
2.2 STRESS = FORCE / AREA

We can implement step 4 using the following decision step.

Step 4 Refinement

4.1 IF STRESS is less than or equal to the maximum allowed THEN
     4.2 Print that the column is safe
  ELSE
     4.3 Print that the column is unsafe
  ENDIF

Coding

The program appears in Fig. 2.6.

Case Study: Testing Column Safety, continued

Figure 2.6. *Computing Column Stress and Safety*

```
      PROGRAM COLUMN
C Determines whether a short column is safe or unsafe.
C The user enters the depth and width of a column along with
C the force on it. The area and stress are computed.

C Declarations
      REAL MXSTRS
      PARAMETER (MXSTRS = 2000.0)
      REAL DEPTH, WIDTH, FORCE, STRESS

C Enter data
      PRINT *, 'Enter force on the column (in pounds)'
      READ *, FORCE
      PRINT *, 'Enter column width (in inches)'
      READ *, WIDTH
      PRINT *, 'Enter column depth (in inches)'
      READ *, DEPTH

C Compute area and stress
      AREA = WIDTH * DEPTH
      STRESS = FORCE / AREA

C Display stress
      PRINT *, 'The stress on the column is ', STRESS, ' psi'

C Determine whether column is safe or unsafe
      IF (STRESS .LE. MXSTRS) THEN
         PRINT *, 'The column is within safety limits.'
      ELSE
         PRINT *, 'Warning the column is UNSAFE!!!!!'
      ENDIF

C Exit the program
      STOP
      END


Enter force on the column (in pounds)
20000.0
Enter column width (in inches)
8.0
Enter column depth (in inches)
12.0
The stress on the column is  208.3333 psi
The column is within safety limits.
```

Case Study: Testing Column Safety, continued

Testing

To test the program, try values of stress that are less than, equal to, and greater than MXSTRS (2000 p.s.i.). One easy way to get a stress value equal to MXSTRS is to use a force of 20000 pounds and a cross-sectional area of 10.

SELF-CHECK EXERCISES FOR SECTION 2.6

1. What value is assigned to X for each of the following segments given that Y is 15.0? What if Y is 10.0?

   a. ```
   X = 25.0
   IF (Y .NE. (X - 10.00)) THEN
      X = X - 10.0
   ELSE
      X = X / 2.0
   ENDIF
   ```

   b. ```
   IF (Y .LT. 15.0) THEN
      X = 5.0 * Y
   ELSE
      X = 2.0 * Y
   ENDIF
   ```

2. Modify the algorithm and program in Fig. 2.5 to find the largest of three numbers.

3. Modify the algorithm and program in Fig. 2.5 to find the smallest of four numbers.

2.7 ▬▬▬ Tracing an Algorithm or Program

A critical step in the design of an algorithm or program is to verify that the algorithm is correct before extensive time is spent translating it to FORTRAN, typing in the FORTRAN program, and testing and debugging the program. It makes no sense to proceed with these steps if the algorithm is not correct in the first place. Often, a few extra minutes spent verifying the correctness of an algorithm will save hours of testing later.

One important technique for checking the correctness of an algorithm or program is a *hand trace* or *desk check*. This consists of a careful, step-by-step simulation on paper of how the algorithm or program would be executed by the computer. The results of the simulation should show the effect of each step as it is executed on data that are relatively easy to manipulate by hand.

As an example, the refined algorithm for the smallest of three numbers problem appears next.

Refined Algorithm

1.   Read three numbers into NUM1, NUM2, and NUM3.
2.1.1 IF NUM1 is less than NUM2 THEN
      2.1.2 Store NUM1 in MINNUM
    ELSE
      2.1.3 Store NUM2 in MINNUM
    ENDIF
2.2.1 IF NUM3 is less than MINNUM THEN
      2.2.2 Store NUM3 in MINNUM
    ENDIF
3.   Print the smallest number.

Table 2.2 shows a trace of the algorithm for the data values 12, 10, and 5. Each step is listed at the left in order of its execution. If an algorithm step changes the value of a variable, then the new value is shown; the effect of each step is described at the far right. For example, the table shows that step 1 (Read three numbers) stores the numbers 12, 10, and 5 in the variables NUM1, NUM2, and NUM3, respectively.

Table 2.2. *Trace of Smallest Number Algorithm*

STEP	NUM1	NUM2	NUM3	MINNUM	EFFECT
	?	?	?	?	
1.	12	10	5		Reads the data.
2.1.1					12 < 10 is false –
2.1.3				10	Store 10 in MINNUM.
2.2.1					5 < 10 is true –
2.2.2				5	Store 5 in MINNUM.
3.					Display 5.

The trace in Table 2.2 shows that the algorithm is correct when NUM2 is smaller than NUM1 (step 2.1.1 is false), and NUM3 is the smallest of all three numbers (step 2.2.1 is true). To completely verify that the algorithm is correct, you should select data that test all possible combinations. Since steps 2.1.1 and 2.2.1 each have two possible outcomes (true or false), you should try at least 2 × 2, or 4, different sets of data.

You should also check that an algorithm works correctly for unusual data. For example, what would happen if all three numbers or a pair of numbers were the same? Would the algorithm still provide the correct result? To complete the desk check, it would be necessary to show that the algorithm does indeed handle special situations properly.

After you verify that the algorithm is correct, you should convert it to a FORTRAN program. It is still a good idea to trace the final program before you type it into the computer. As an example, Table 2.3 traces the program in Fig. 2.5 for the same data values (12, 10, and 5).

Table 2.3. *Trace of Program in Fig. 2.5*

PROGRAM STATEMENT	NUM1	NUM2	NUM3	MINNUM	EFFECT
	?	?	?	?	
PRINT *, 'Enter three...'					Prints a prompt.
READ *, NUM1, NUM2, NUM3	12	10	5		Reads the data.
IF (NUM1 .LT. NUM2) THEN					Is 12 < 10? Value is false.
MINNUM = NUM2				10	10 is smallest so far.
IF (NUM3 .LT. MINNUM)...					Is 5 < 10? Value is true.
MINNUM = NUM3				5	5 is smallest.
PRINT *, MINNUM...					Prints 5 is the smallest number.

In performing each trace, you must be very careful to execute the program exactly as it would be executed by the computer. It is easy to carry out the operations that you expect to be performed without explicitly testing each condition and tracing each program step. A trace that is performed in this way is of little value.

SELF-CHECK EXERCISES FOR SECTION 2.7

1. Provide sample data and traces for the remaining three cases of the smallest number problem. Also, test the case where all three numbers are the same. Trace the algorithm and program.
2. Trace the program in Fig. 2.4 when HOURS is 30.0 and RATE is 5.00. Perform the trace when HOURS is 20.0 and RATE is 3.00.

2.8 ▬▬ Problem-Solving Strategies

Often what appears to be a new problem will turn out to be a variation of one that you have already solved. Consequently, an important skill in problem solving is the ability to recognize that a problem is similar to one solved earlier. As you progress through the course, you will start to build up a *library* of programs. Whenever possible, you should try to adapt or reuse parts of a program that have been shown to work correctly.

Extending a Problem Solution

An experienced programmer usually writes programs that can be easily changed or modified to fit other situations. One of the reasons for this is the fact that programmers (and program users) often wish to make slight improvements to a program after having used it. If the original program is designed carefully from the beginning, we can accommodate changing specifications with a minimum of effort. Often, we can modify the code corresponding to one or two algorithm steps rather than rewrite the entire program. This technique is illustrated next.

Case Study: Computing Overtime Pay

Problem

We wish to modify the payroll program so that employees who work more than 40 hours a week are paid double for all overtime hours.

Design Overview

This problem is an extension of the Modified Payroll Problem solved earlier (see Fig. 2.4). Overtime pay must be added for those employees who are eligible. We can solve this problem by adding a new step (step 2A) after step 2 in the original algorithm. The data requirements are listed below, followed by the new algorithm.

Data Requirements

Problem Parameters

maximum salary for no tax deduction (TXBRAK = 100.00)
amount of tax deducted (TAX = 25.0)
maximum hours without overtime pay (MXHOUR = 40.0)

Problem Inputs

hours worked (REAL HOURS)
hourly rate (REAL RATE)

Problem Outputs

gross pay (REAL GROSS)
net pay (REAL NET)

Case Study: Computing Overtime Pay, continued

Initial Algorithm

1. Enter hours worked and hourly rate.
2. Compute gross salary.
2A. Add any overtime pay to gross salary.
3. Compute net salary.
4. Print gross salary and net salary.

Algorithm Refinement

The refinement for the new step follows.

Step 2A Refinement

2A.1 IF hours worked exceeds maximum without overtime THEN
      Add overtime pay to GROSS
  ENDIF

Coding

As shown below, the IF statement that implements step 2A should follow the statement in Fig. 2.4 used to compute gross salary.

```
C Compute gross salary
      GROSS = HOURS * RATE

C Add overtime pay to GROSS
      IF (HOURS .GT. MXHOUR) THEN
          GROSS = GROSS + ((HOURS - MXHOUR) * RATE)
      ENDIF
```

The assignment statement above involves three arithmetic operators: +, −, and *. In Chapter 1 we saw that the parentheses cause the operators above to be evaluated in the following order: − first, * next, and + last. Consequently, the overtime hours (HOURS − MXHOUR) will be multiplied by RATE and added to the value of GROSS computed in algorithm step 2; the result will be the new value of GROSS.

Testing

To test the overtime computation, rerun the program with values of HOURS less than MXHOUR, equal to MXHOUR, and greater than MXHOUR. Make sure the value assigned to GROSS includes overtime pay only in the third case.

Solution by Analogy

Sometimes a new problem is simply an old one presented in a new guise. You should try to determine whether you have solved a similar problem before and, if so, adapt the earlier solution. This requires a careful reading of the problem statement to detect similar requirements that may be worded differently.

Case Study: Computing the Price of Concrete

Problem

You work for a building supply company that charges $44.75 a cubic yard for concrete. For quantities over 30 cubic yards, a 5% discount is given. Your boss needs a program to calculate the price of any amount of concrete.

Design Overview

This problem is quite similar to the overtime payroll problem. You can determine the price of the concrete by first multiplying the amount purchased by the unit cost, then subtracting the discount when applicable. (In the overtime pay problem, we followed a similar algorithm by first computing gross pay, then adding in overtime pay when earned.)

Data Requirements

Problem Parameters

the cost per cubic yard (REAL COST = 44.75)
the minimum amount for a discount (REAL DISAMT = 30.0)
the discount rate of 5% (REAL DISRAT = 0.05)

Problem Input

the amount sold (REAL AMOUNT)

Problem Output

the price of the concrete (REAL PRICE)
the discount when applicable (REAL DISCNT)

Initial Algorithm

1. Enter amount sold.
2. Compute the initial price.
3. Get the final price by deducting any discount.
4. Display the final price.

Case Study: Computing the Price of Concrete, continued

Algorithm Refinements

The refinements of steps 2 and 3 follow.

Step 2 Refinement

2.1 PRICE = AMOUNT * COST

Step 3 Refinement

3.1 IF the amount sold is greater than 30 cubic yards THEN
      3.2 Subtract the discount from PRICE.
      3.3 Display the discount
   ENDIF

Step 3.2 Refinement

3.2.1 DISCNT = DISRAT * PRICE
3.2.2 PRICE = PRICE − DISCNT

Coding

The complete program is shown in Fig. 2.7. Because FORTRAN possesses no % operator, decimal fractions are required. Thus, the discount rate of 5% is written as the decimal fraction 0.05. One PARAMETER statement defines all three program parameters.

Figure 2.7. *Computing the Price of Concrete*

```
      PROGRAM CONCRT
C Calculates the price of any amount of concrete.

C Declarations
      REAL COST, DISAMT, DISRAT
      PARAMETER (COST = 44.75, DISAMT = 30.0, DISRAT = 0.05)
      REAL AMOUNT, PRICE, DISCNT

C Enter amount sold.
      PRINT *, 'Enter concrete amount (in cubic yards)'
      READ *, AMOUNT

C Compute the initial price.
      PRICE = AMOUNT * COST

C Deduct any discount.
      IF (AMOUNT .GT. DISAMT) THEN
         DISCNT = DISRAT * PRICE
         PRICE = PRICE - DISCNT
         PRINT *, 'The discount is $', DISCNT
      ENDIF
```

Case Study: Computing the Price of Concrete, continued

```
C Display the final price.
      PRINT *, 'The final price is $', PRICE
      STOP
      END

Enter concrete amount (in cubic yards)
40.0
The discount is $          89.500000
The final price is $       1700.500000
```

Testing

To test the price computation, run the program with values of AMOUNT that are less than DISAMT, equal to DISAMT, and greater than DISAMT.

**SELF-CHECK
EXERCISES FOR
SECTION 2.8**

1. Provide the complete program for the Overtime Pay Problem.
2. Rewrite the algorithm for the Overtime Pay Problem so that the computation of gross salary is performed in one step rather than in two (i.e., combine steps 2 and 2A). Use an IF statement with two alternatives.

2.9 ▬▬▬ The General IF Statement

Earlier we introduced IF statements with one and two alternatives. We will first review these statements and then provide a more general form of the IF statement.

EXAMPLE 2.4

The IF statement in Fig. 2.8 orders the values in X and Y so that the smaller number will be in X and the larger number will be in Y. If the two numbers are already in the proper order, the true task will not be executed.

Figure 2.8. *IF Statement to Order X and Y*

```
IF (X .GT. Y) THEN
   TEMP = X
   X = Y
   Y = TEMP
ENDIF
```

The variables X, Y, and TEMP should all be the same type. Although the values of X and Y are being switched, an additional variable, TEMP, is needed for storage of a copy of one of these values. The need for TEMP is illustrated in Table 2.4, assuming X and Y have original values of 12.5 and 5.0, respectively. ∎

Table 2.4. *Switching a Pair of Values*

STATEMENT	X	Y	TEMP	EFFECT
	12.5	5.0	?	
IF (X .GT. Y) THEN				12.5 > 5.0 is true:
TEMP = X			12.5	stores old X in TEMP;
X = Y	5.0			stores old Y in X;
Y = TEMP		12.5		stores old X in Y.

The Logical IF Statement

If a single alternative decision has just one statement in its true task, it can be implemented using a simpler FORTRAN statement called the logical IF statement. A logical IF statement and an equivalent IF structure are shown below. The logical IF is described in the display that follows.

Logical IF	IF Structure

IF (X .GT. LARGE) LARGE = X	IF (X .GT. LARGE) THEN
	  LARGE = X
	ENDIF

Logical IF Statement

SYNTAX: IF (*condition*) *dependent statement*

EXAMPLE: IF (X .EQ. 0.0) PRINT *, 'ZERO'

INTERPRETATION: The *condition* is evaluated. If it is true, the *dependent statement* is executed; otherwise, the *dependent statement* is not executed.

NOTES: Only one FORTRAN statement may follow the *condition*. The *dependent statement* may be any single executable statement such as assignment, STOP, READ, or PRINT. It may not be another logical IF statement or a control structure.

Some more examples of IF statements with two alternative tasks, a true task and a false task, are discussed next.

EXAMPLE 2.5

The IF statement below may be used to process a positive transaction amount (AMOUNT) that represents a check (TYPE is 'C') or a deposit. In either case, an appropriate message is printed and the account balance (BALANC) is updated. ∎

```
      IF (TYPE .EQ. 'C') THEN
C     Deduct check amount
      PRINT *, 'Check for $ ', AMOUNT
      BALANC = BALANC - AMOUNT
      ELSE
C     Add deposit amount
      PRINT *, 'Deposit of $ ', AMOUNT
      BALANC = BALANC + AMOUNT
      ENDIF
```

EXAMPLE 2.6   The IF statement below finds and prints the average value of a list of items given their sum. If the value of NUMITM is less than or equal to zero, the true task is executed and an error message is printed; otherwise, the average is computed and printed.

```
      IF (NUMITM .LE. 0) THEN
         PRINT *, 'Invalid number of items - average undefined'
      ELSE
         AVERGE = SUM / NUMITM
         PRINT *, 'Average is ', AVERGE
      ENDIF
```

When NUMITM is zero or negative, the division is not performed and a message is printed instead. If the division were attempted when NUMITM is zero, an execution error would result and the error diagnostic "division by zero" would be printed by FORTRAN. Rather than have an execution error occur, it is much better to have your program test for this possible error and print its own diagnostic.   ∎

Nested IF Structures

Until now, we used IF statements to implement decisions involving two alternatives. In this section, we will see how IF statements can be nested to implement decisions involving several alternatives. A *nested* IF structure occurs when the true or false task of an IF statement contains another IF statement.

EXAMPLE 2.7   The FORTRAN code fragment below illustrates a nested IF structure with three alternatives. The false task of the *outer* IF statement is itself an IF statement. This nested IF structure causes one of three variables (NUMPOS, NUMNEG, or NUMZER) to be increased by one depending on whether X is greater than zero, less than zero, or equal to zero, respectively. Both of the ENDIF lines at the end of this structure are required. As before, we have used indentation to make the nested IF structure more readable. The indentation is ignored by the compiler.

```
C Increment NUMPOS, NUMNEG, or NUMZER depending on X
      IF (X .GT. 0) THEN
         NUMPOS = NUMPOS + 1
```

```
        ELSE
            IF (X .LT. 0) THEN
                NUMNEG = NUMNEG + 1
            ELSE
                NUMZER = NUMZER + 1
            ENDIF
        ENDIF
```

The execution of this IF structure proceeds as follows: the first condition (X .GT. 0) is tested; if it is true, NUMPOS is incremented and the rest of the IF statement is skipped. If the first condition is false, the second condition (X .LT. 0) is tested; if it is true, NUMNEG is incremented; otherwise, NUMZER is incremented. It is important to realize that the second condition is tested only when the first condition is false. A trace of this statement is shown in Table 2.5, assuming X is –7. ∎

Table 2.5. *Trace of IF Statement in Example 2.7 for X = −7*

STATEMENT	EFFECT
IF (X .GT. 0) THEN	–7 > 0 is false;
IF (X .LT. 0) THEN	–7 < 0 is true;
NUMNEG = NUMNEG + 1	adds 1 to NUMNEG.

Flow Diagram of a Nested IF Structure

As an aid to understanding nested IF structures, it is sometimes helpful to draw a flow diagram of the decision-making process. A flow diagram of the decision step from Example 2.7 is shown in Fig. 2.9. Each condition is shown

Figure 2.9. *Flow Diagram of a Nested IF Structure*

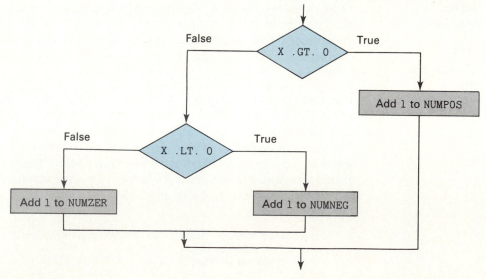

in a diamond shaped box, and the true and false tasks are enclosed in rectangular boxes. There are two paths leading from each condition. The path labeled True indicates the true task for that condition; the path labeled False indicates the false task for that condition.

Multiple Alternative Decisions

Nested IF structures can become quite complex. If there are more than three alternatives and indentation is not done consistently, it may be difficult to determine to which IF line a given ELSE line belongs. In most cases, a single general IF statement can be used instead of a nest of IF structures.

EXAMPLE 2.8

The nested IF structure of Example 2.7 is implemented below using a general IF statement.

```
C Increment NUMPOS, NUMNEG, or NUMZER depending on X
      IF (X .GT. 0) THEN
         NUMPOS = NUMPOS + 1
      ELSE IF (X .LT. 0) THEN
         NUMNEG = NUMNEG + 1
      ELSE
         NUMZER = NUMZER + 1
      ENDIF
```

In this form, the first condition appears on the IF header line, and the second condition appears on the first ELSE IF line. Since this is a single control structure, only one ENDIF line is needed. If the first condition is true, then NUMPOS is incremented. If the first condition is false but the second condition is true, then NUMNEG is incremented. If both conditions are false, then NUMZER is incremented. The general IF statement, or Block IF, is described in the next display; a flow diagram appears in Fig. 2.10. ■

General IF Statement (Block IF)

SYNTAX:
```
IF condition₁ THEN
    task₁
ELSE IF condition₂ THEN
    task₂
        .
        .
        .
ELSE IF conditionₙ THEN
    taskₙ
ELSE
    taskₑ
ENDIF
```

EXAMPLE:
```
IF (N .LT. 0) THEN
    PRINT *, 'N is negative'
ELSE IF (N .EQ. 0) THEN
    PRINT *, 'N is zero'
```

```
      ELSE
         PRINT *, 'N is positive'
      ENDIF
```

INTERPRETATION: The conditions in a general IF statement are evaluated in sequence until a true condition is reached. If a condition is true, the task following it is executed and the rest of the general IF statement is skipped. If a condition is false, the task following it is skipped and the next condition is tested. If all conditions are false, then $task_e$ (between the lines ELSE and ENDIF) is executed. Exactly one of the tasks $task_1$, $task_2$, ..., $task_e$ is executed.

NOTE: If there is no $task_e$, then ELSE may be omitted. In this case, no task within the general IF statement is executed when all conditions are false.

Figure 2.10. *Flow Diagram of General IF Statement*

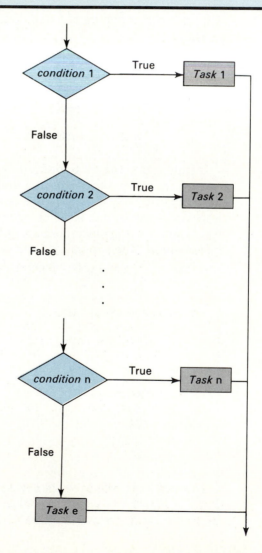

Program Style

> *Writing the General IF Statement*
>
> In Example 2.8, the keywords IF, ENDIF, and all the words ELSE are aligned, and each *dependent task* is indented under the condition that controls its execution. This is done to make the general IF statement more readable; indentation is ignored by the FORTRAN compiler.

Order of Conditions

Very often, the conditions in a multiple-alternative decision are not *mutually exclusive*. This means that it may be possible for more than one condition to be true for given data values. If this is the case, the order of the conditions becomes very important, because only the statement following the first true condition will be executed.

EXAMPLE 2.9

The table below describes the assignment of grades based on exam scores.

Exam Score	Grade Assigned
90 and above	A
80–89	B
70–79	C
60–69	D
below 60	F

The multiple-alternative decision below prints the letter grade assigned according to this table. The last three conditions are true for an exam score of 85; however, a grade of B is assigned because the first true condition is SCORE .GE. 80.

```
C Correct grade assignment
      IF (SCORE .GE. 90) THEN
          PRINT *, 'A'
      ELSE IF (SCORE .GE. 80) THEN
          PRINT *, 'B'
      ELSE IF (SCORE .GE. 70) THEN
          PRINT *, 'C'
      ELSE IF (SCORE .GE. 60) THEN
          PRINT *, 'D'
      ELSE
          PRINT *, 'F'
      ENDIF
```

It would be wrong to write the decision as shown next. All passing exam scores (60 or above) would be incorrectly categorized as a grade of D because the first condition would be true and the rest would be skipped.   ■

```
C Incorrect grade assignment
      IF (SCORE .GE. 60) THEN
          PRINT *, 'D'
      ELSE IF (SCORE .GE. 70) THEN
          PRINT *, 'C'
      ELSE IF (SCORE .GE. 80) THEN
          PRINT *, 'B'
      ELSE IF (SCORE .GE. 90) THEN
          PRINT *, 'A'
      ELSE
          PRINT *, 'F'
      ENDIF
```

EXAMPLE 2.10   A general IF statement may be used to implement a *decision table* that describes several alternatives. Table 2.6 provides information needed to compute income tax due for people whose salaries fall within one of five tax brackets. Each line of Table 2.6 indicates a salary range and a base tax amount and tax percentage for that bracket. Given a salary amount, the tax is calculated by adding the *base tax* for that bracket to the product of the *percentage of excess* and the amount of salary over the minimum salary for that bracket:

tax due = (salary − minimum salary) × percentage + base tax

Table 2.6. *Tax Table for Example 2.10*

RANGE	SALARY	BASE TAX	PERCENTAGE OF EXCESS
1	0.00– 1499.99	0.00	15%
2	1500.00– 2999.99	225.00	16%
3	3000.00– 4999.99	465.00	18%
4	5000.00– 7999.99	825.00	20%
5	8000.00–14999.99	1425.00	25%

As an example, the second line of the table specifies that the tax due on a salary of $2000.00 is $225.00 plus 16% of the excess salary over $1500.00 (i.e., 16% of $500.00). Therefore, the total tax due is $305.00, as shown next.

tax due = (2000.00 − 1500.00) × 0.16 + 225.00
= 500.00 × 0.16 + 225.00 = 80.00 + 225.00 = 305.00

The general IF statement in Fig. 2.11 implements the tax table. If the value of SALARY is within the table range (0.00 to 14999.99), exactly one of the statements assigning a value to TAX will be executed.

Figure 2.11. *General IF Statement for Table 2.6*

```
IF (SALARY .LT. 0.0) THEN
   PRINT *, 'Error! Negative salary $', SALARY
ELSE IF (SALARY .LT. 1500.00) THEN
   TAX = 0.15 * SALARY
ELSE IF (SALARY .LT. 3000.000) THEN
   TAX = (SALARY - 1500.00) * 0.16 + 225.00
ELSE IF (SALARY .LT. 5000.00) THEN
   TAX = (SALARY - 3000.00) * 0.18 + 465.00
ELSE IF (SALARY .LT. 8000.00) THEN
   TAX = (SALARY - 5000.00) * 0.20 + 825.00
ELSE IF (SALARY .LT. 15000.00) THEN
   TAX = (SALARY - 8000.00) * 0.25 + 1425.00
ELSE
   PRINT *, 'Error! Too large salary $', SALARY
ENDIF
```

A trace of the IF statement for SALARY = 2000.00 is shown in Table 2.7. The value assigned to TAX is 305.00, as desired.   ∎

Table 2.7. *Trace of General IF Statement in Fig. 2.11 for SALARY = 2000.00*

STATEMENT	SALARY	TAX	EFFECT
	2000.00	?	
IF (SALARY .LT. 0.0)			2000.00 < 0.0 is false.
ELSE IF (SALARY .LT. 1500.00)			2000.00 < 1500.00 is false.
ELSE IF (SALARY .LT. 3000.00)			2000.00 < 3000.00 is true.
TAX = (SALARY - 1500.00)			Evaluates to 500.00.
* 0.16			Evaluates to 80.00.
+ 225.00		305.00	Evaluates to 305.00.

Using a Multiple-Alternative Decision

The next problem uses a multiple-alternative decision.

Program Style

Validating the Value of Variables

It is important to validate the value of a variable before performing computations with invalid or meaningless data. Instead of computing an incorrect tax amount, the general IF statement in Fig. 2.11 prints an error message if the value of SALARY is outside the range covered by the table (0.0 to 14999.99). The first condition is used to detect negative salaries and an error message is printed if SALARY is less than zero. All conditions will evaluate to false if SALARY is greater than 14999.99, and the alternative following ELSE would cause an error message to be printed.

Case Study: Computing Compass Bearings

Problem

While spending the summer as a surveyor's assistant, you decide to write a program that transforms compass headings in degrees (0 to 360 degrees) to compass bearings. The program enters a compass heading such as 110 degrees and displays the corresponding bearing (south 70 degrees east).

Design Overview

The compass bearing indicates a direction of travel corresponding to a compass heading. In this example, if you have a compass heading of 110 degrees, then you should first face due south and then turn 70 degrees toward the east (see Fig. 2.12). Each compass bearing consists of three items: the direction you face (north or south), an angle between 0 and 90 degrees, and the direction you turn before walking (east or west). Table 2.8 indicates how to transform compass headings to compass bearings. From the second line of this table, we see that a heading of 110 degrees corresponds to a bearing of south (180.0 − 110.0) east, or south 70 degrees east.

Figure 2.12. *Compass Headings*

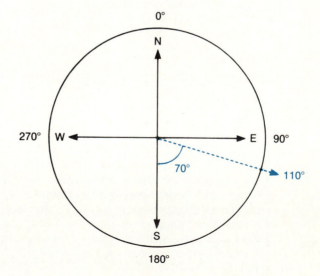

Case Study: Computing Compass Bearings, continued

Table 2.8. *Computing Compass Bearings*

HEADING IN DEGREES	BEARING COMPUTATION
0– 89.999 . . .	north (heading) east
90–179.999 . . .	south (180.0 − heading) east
180–269.999 . . .	south (heading − 180.0) west
270–360	north (360.0 − heading) west

Data Requirements

Problem Input

the compass heading in degrees (REAL HEAD)

Problem Outputs

the direction to face (CHARACTER *5 FACE)
the compass bearing in degrees (REAL BEAR)
the direction to turn (CHARACTER *4 TURN)

Initial Algorithm

1. Enter the compass heading.
2. Compute the compass bearing.
3. Display the compass bearing.

Algorithm Refinements

To refine step 2, we must specify Table 2.8 as a multiple-alternative decision step.

Step 2 Refinement

2.1 IF heading is less than zero THEN
    2.2 Bearing is undefined.
  ELSE IF heading is less than 90.0 THEN
    2.3 Use north (HEAD) east as the bearing.
  ELSE IF heading is less than 180.0 THEN
    2.4 Use south (180.0 − HEAD) east as the bearing.
  ELSE IF heading is less than 270.0 THEN
    2.5 Use south (HEAD − 180.0) west as the bearing.

Case Study: Computing Compass Bearings, continued

Figure 2.13. *Computing Compass Bearings*

```
        PROGRAM COMPAS
C Transforms a compass heading to a compass bearing

C Type declarations
        REAL HEAD, BEAR
        CHARACTER *5 FACE
        CHARACTER *4 TURN

C Enter compass heading
        PRINT *, 'Enter a compass heading (0 - 360 degrees)'
        READ *, HEAD

C Compute compass bearing
        IF (HEAD .LT. 0.0) THEN
            FACE = '?????'
        ELSE IF (HEAD .LT. 90.0) THEN
            FACE = 'north'
            BEAR = HEAD
            TURN = 'east'
        ELSE IF (HEAD .LT. 180.0) THEN
            FACE =  'south'
            BEAR = 180.0 - HEAD
            TURN = 'east'
        ELSE IF (HEAD .LT. 270.0) THEN
            FACE = 'south'
            BEAR = HEAD - 180.0
            TURN = 'west'
        ELSE IF (HEAD .LE. 360.0) THEN
            FACE = 'north'
            BEAR = 360.0 - HEAD
            TURN = 'west'
        ELSE
            FACE = '?????'
        ENDIF

C Display compass bearing
        IF (FACE .EQ. '?????') THEN
            PRINT *, 'Error - heading must be between 0 and 360'
        ELSE
            PRINT *, 'The bearing is ', FACE, BEAR,
     +            ' degrees ', TURN
        ENDIF

        STOP
        END

Enter a compass heading (0 - 360 degrees)
110.0
The bearing is south   70.00000 degrees east
```

Case Study: Computing Compass Bearings, continued

```
    ELSE IF heading is less than 360.0 THEN
        2.6 Use north (360.0 - HEAD) west as the bearing.
    ELSE IF heading is greater than 360.0 THEN
        2.7 Bearing is undefined.
    ENDIF
```

Coding

The program appears in Fig. 2.13. In the general IF statement, the assignment statement

```
    FACE = '?????'
```

executes when the value of HEAD is out of range (less than zero or greater than 360), indicating that the bearing is undefined. Three assignment statements implement each of the algorithm steps 2.3 through 2.6, assigning values to FACE, BEAR, and TURN. The IF statement at the end of the program displays either an error message (FACE is '?????') or the values assigned to FACE, BEAR, and TURN.

Testing

To test this program, try compass headings in each of the four quadrants. Also, try compass headings at the quadrant boundaries: 0, 90, 180, 270, and 360 degrees. Finally, see what happens when the heading value is out of range.

SELF-CHECK EXERCISES FOR SECTION 2.9

1. Write an IF statement that assigns the larger of X and Y to LARGER and the smaller to SMALLR. Your statement should print 'X larger' or 'Y larger' depending on the situation.
2. Explain what is wrong with the nested IF structure below.

```
IF (GPA .GE. 3.0) THEN
    PRINT *, 'Dean''s list'
ELSE
    IF (GPA .LT. 2.0) THEN
        PRINT *, 'On probation'
    ELSE IF (GPA .LT. 1.0) THEN
        PRINT *, 'Flunked out'
    ENDIF
ENDIF
```

3. Trace the execution of the general IF statement in Fig. 2.11 for SALARY = 13500.00.

4. What would be the effect of reversing the order of the first two conditions in the IF statement of Fig. 2.11?
5. Rewrite the IF statement for Example 2.9 using only the relational operator .LT. in all conditions.
6. Implement the decision table below using a general IF statement. Assume that the grade point average is within the range 0.0 through 4.0.

Grade Point Average	Transcript Message
0.0–0.99	Failed semester—registration suspended
1.0–1.99	On probation for next semester
2.0–2.99	(no message)
3.0–3.49	Dean's list for semester
3.5–4.0	Highest honors for semester

2.10 ▮▮ Common Programming Errors

When writing IF statements, remember that the words ELSE and ENDIF must always appear on a line by themselves. To improve program readability, we recommend that you indent the true and false tasks.

Be careful to write the conditions in a multiple-alternative decision in the correct order. If the conditions are not mutually exclusive (i.e., more than one condition may be true), the most restrictive condition should come first.

Chapter Review

In the first part of this chapter, we outlined the steps for solving problems on the computer:

1. Understand the problem.
2. Identify the input and output data for the problem as well as other relevant data and make a list of the data requirements.
3. Formulate a precise statement of the problem.
4. Develop a list of steps for solving the problem (an algorithm).
5. Refine the algorithm.
6. Desk check or hand trace the algorithm.
7. Implement the algorithm in FORTRAN.

Several guidelines for using program comments were discussed. Well-placed, carefully worded comments and a refined algorithm can provide all the documentation necessary for a program.

In the remainder of the chapter, we discussed the representation of the various steps in an algorithm and illustrated the stepwise refinement of algorithms. We used pseudocode to represent the decision steps of an algorithm.

We showed how to implement decisions with one or two alternatives using the FORTRAN IF statement. We also saw how to use nested IF statements and the general IF structure to implement decisions with several alternatives.

Desk checks or traces are used to verify that an algorithm or program is correct. Careful tracing can help you discover errors in logic. You will save considerable time and effort if you find these logic errors before entering the program in the computer. Remember to carefully "execute" each step just as the computer would; the trace is meaningless if you assume that a step does what it is supposed to do without checking it.

New FORTRAN Statements

The new FORTRAN statements introduced in this chapter are described in Table 2.9.

Table 2.9. *Summary of New FORTRAN Statements*

STATEMENT	EFFECT
Comment	
```C This is a comment``` ```* So is this!```	Comments document the use of variables and statements in a program. They are ignored by the compiler.
IF Statement (One Alternative)	

```IF (X .NE. 0.0) THEN```
```   PRODCT = PRODCT * X```
```ENDIF```
	Multiplies PRODCT by X only if X is nonzero.

IF Statement (Two Alternatives)	

```IF (X .GE. 0.0) THEN```
```   PRINT *, X, ' is positive'```
```ELSE```
```   PRINT *, X, ' is negative'```
```ENDIF```
	IF X is greater than or equal to 0.0, the message ' is positive' is printed; otherwise, the message ' is negative' is printed.

Logical IF Statement	
```IF (NUMRET .GT. 0) PRINT *, NUMRET```	Prints the value of NUMRET only when NUMRET is greater than zero.

Table 2.9. *Continued*

STATEMENT	EFFECT
Multiple Alternative Decision	

```
IF (SCORE .GE. 90) THEN
    PRINT *, 'A'
    COUNTA = COUNTA + 1
ELSE IF (SCORE .GE. 80) THEN
    PRINT *, 'B'
    COUNTB = COUNTB + 1
ELSE
    PRINT *, 'C'
    COUNTC = COUNTC + 1
ENDIF
```

If SCORE is greater than or equal to 90, increment COUNTA; otherwise, if SCORE is greater than or equal to 80, increment COUNTB; otherwise, increment COUNTC. Also, display score category (A, B, or C).

Quick-Check Exercises

1. Does a compiler translate comments?
2. Each statement in a program should have a comment. True or false?
3. What are two ways to denote comments?
4. An IF statement implements a(n) _____ step.
5. What is pseudocode?
6. What values can a conditional expression have?
7. The relational operator .NE. means _____ .
8. A(n) _____ is used to verify that an algorithm is correct.
9. What value is assigned to FEE by the following IF statement when SPEED is 75?

```
IF (SPEED .GT. 35) THEN
    FEE = 20.00
ELSE IF (SPEED .GT. 50) THEN
    FEE = 40.00
ELSE IF (SPEED .GT. 75) THEN
    FEE = 60.00
ENDIF
```

10. Answer question 9 for the IF statement below. Which IF statement is correct?

```
IF (SPEED .GT. 75) THEN
    FEE = 60.0
ELSE IF (SPEED .GT. 50) THEN
    FEE = 40.00
ELSE IF (SPEED .GT. 35) THEN
    FEE = 20.00
ENDIF
```

11. What output line(s) are displayed by the following statements when X is 5.53? When X is 9.95?

```
IF (X .GT. 7.5) THEN
    X = 90.0
    PRINT *, 'X is ', X
ELSE
    X = 25.0
ENDIF
PRINT *, 'X is ', X
```

12. Explain the difference between the statements on the left and the statements on the right. For each of them, what is the final value of X if the initial value of X is 1?

```
IF (X .GE. 0) THEN              IF (X .GE. 0) THEN
    X = X + 1                       X = X + 1
ELSE IF (X .GE. 1) THEN         ENDIF
    X = X + 2                    IF (X .GE. 1) THEN
ENDIF                               X = X + 2
                                ENDIF
```

Answers to Quick-Check Exercises

1. no
2. false
3. * or C in column 1
4. decision
5. a mixture of English and FORTRAN used to describe algorithm steps
6. true or false
7. not equal
8. hand trace
9. 20.00
10. 40.00; the statement in question 10
11. X is 25.0; X is 90.00 is printed twice.
12. A multiple-alternative decision is on the left; a sequence of IF statements is on the right. X becomes 2 on the left; X becomes 4 on the right.

Review Questions

1. Briefly describe the steps to derive an algorithm for a given problem.
2. A decision in FORTRAN is actually an evaluation of a(n) _____ expression.
3. List the six relational operators discussed in this chapter.
4. What should be done by the programmer after the algorithm is written but before the program is entered (typed) into the computer?
5. Trace the following program fragment and indicate what will be done if a data value of 27.34 is entered.

```
PRINT *, 'Enter a temperature: '
READ *, TEMP
IF (TEMP .GT. 32.0) THEN
    PRINT *, 'NOT FREEZING'
ELSE
    PRINT *, 'ICE FORMING'
ENDIF
```

6. Write the appropriate IF statement to compute GROSS given that the hourly rate is stored in the variable RATE and the total hours worked is stored in the variable HOURS. Pay time and a half for more than forty hours worked.

7. Implement the following flow diagram using a nested IF structure.

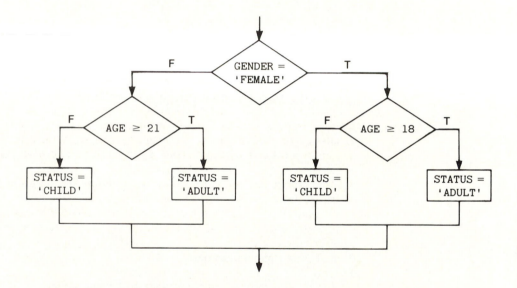

8. Use a general IF statement to display whether a student is in elementary school (0 ≤ GRADE ≤ 5), middle school (6 ≤ GRADE ≤ 8), high school (9 ≤ GRADE ≤ 12), or college (GRADE > 12).

Programming Projects

1. a. Write a program to print the "message" XXOXOX in block letters. Each block letter should be printed using six columns and six rows. Print the block letters down the page.

   b. Modify your program so that any six-letter message consisting of X's and 0's will be printed in block-letter form. The message to be printed should be entered and displayed one character at a time. *Hint:* Use a decision.

2. Write a program to simulate a state police radar gun. The program should read an automobile speed and print the message "speeding" if the speed exceeds 55 mph.

3. A program is needed that will read a character value and a number. Depending on what is read, certain information will be printed. The character should be either an S or a T. If an S is read and the number is 100.50, the program will print

   ```
   Send money!   I need $100.50
   ```

   If a T is read instead of S, the program will print

   ```
   The temperature last night was 100.50 degrees
   ```

4. Write a program that reads in three numbers and finds and prints the smallest and the largest number.

5. Write a program that will determine the additional state tax owed by an employee. The state charges a 4% tax on net income. Net income is determined by subtracting a $500 allowance for each dependent from gross income. Your program will read gross income, number of dependents, and tax amount already deducted. It will then compute the actual tax owed and print the difference between tax owed and tax deducted, followed by the message 'SEND CHECK' or 'REFUND' depending on whether the difference is positive or negative.

6. A monthly magazine wants a program that will print out renewal notices to its subscribers and cancellation notices when appropriate. Your program should first read in the current month number (1 though 12) and year. For each subscription processed, read in four data items: the account number, the month and year the subscription started, and the number of years paid for the subscription.

   Read in each set of subscription information and print a renewal notice if the current month is either the month prior to expiration or the month of expiration. A cancellation notice should be printed if the current month comes after the expiration month.

   Sample input might be:

10 90	for a current month of October 1990
1364 4 89 3	for account 1364 whose three-year subscription began in April 1989

7. Write a program that will read in the number of credit hours (HOURS) completed by a student at a university. Based on the number of credit hours completed, classify the student as a freshman, sophomore, junior, or senior. Each student should be classified according to the following rules:

Classification	Credit Hours
Freshman	HOURS $<$ 32
Sophomore	32 $\leq$ HOURS $<$ 64
Junior	64 $\leq$ HOURS $<$ 96
Senior	96 $\leq$ HOURS

   After reading in a student's number of credit hours completed, print the appropriate classification for that student.

8. The New Telephone Company has the following rate structure for long-distance calls:

   ■ Any call started after 6 p.m. (1800 hours) gets a 50% discount.
   ■ Any call started after 8 a.m. (0800 hours) is charged full price.
   ■ All calls are subject to a 4% federal tax.
   ■ The regular rate for a call is $0.40 per minute.
   ■ Any call longer than 60 minutes receives a 15% discount on its cost (after any other discount is taken but before tax is added).

   Write a program that reads the start time for a call based on a 24-hour clock and the length of a call. The gross cost (before any discounts or tax) should be printed, followed by the net cost (after discounts are deducted and tax is added).

9. Modify the program in Fig. 2.6 to read in the maximum allowable stress as a data value. Also, compute and display the safety factor when the column is judged to be safe. The safety factor is defined as the ratio of the maximum stress to the computed stress and should always be greater than 1.

10. Concrete weighs about 150 pounds per cubic foot. Have a user enter a pipe thickness (in inches), outside diameter (in inches), and the length of the pipe (in feet). Then calculate the weight of the pipe. *Hint:* To find the volume of concrete in the pipe, subtract the volume of a cylinder of the inside diameter from the volume of a cylinder with the outside diameter. An example run would be

    ```
    Please enter the pipe thickness in inches
    3
    Enter the outside diameter in inches
    36
    Enter the pipe length in feet
    10
    The weight of the pipe is    3239.768    pounds
    ```

3. Repetition and Loops

THE CONTROL structures of a programming language enable the programmer to control the sequence and the frequency of execution of program segments. In the last chapter, we introduced the IF statement for implementing decision steps. In this chapter, you will see how to specify the repetition of a group of program statements (called a *loop*) using the standard FORTRAN DO loop and the nonstandard WHILE loop. We will discuss how and when to use each of these looping structures.

Although the WHILE loop is not part of FORTRAN 77, it is provided as an extension to many FORTRAN compilers. Normally, we avoid using features that are nonstandard; however, the WHILE loop is such an important control structure that we make an exception in its case. Also, it will be included in FORTRAN 8X.

We will also discuss what happens when we nest control structures or place one control structure inside another. Several case studies will also be presented.

3.1 ■■■■■ Repetition in Programs

Just as the ability to instruct the computer to make decisions is an important programming tool, so is the ability to specify that a group of operations is to be repeated. For example, we might like to carry out the gross pay and net pay computations shown in Fig. 2.4 once for each employee in a company. This could be expressed in pseudocode as follows:

    DO for each employee
        Read hours worked and hourly rate
        Compute gross salary
        Compute net salary
        Print gross pay and net pay
    CONTINUE

This pseudocode indicates that a group of operations is to be repeatedly performed. The operations to be repeated are listed between the lines that begin with DO and CONTINUE.

This text describes two control statements for specifying repetition. The first one, the DO loop, is introduced next. The second, the WHILE loop, is introduced in Section 3.5.

The DO Loop   The DO loop can be used to specify certain forms of repetition quite easily, as shown in the next examples.

EXAMPLE 3.1   The following two statements have the same effect.

```
PRINT *, 'Hi Mom'                DO 10 LINE = 1, 5
PRINT *, 'Hi Mom'                    PRINT *, 'Hi Mom'
PRINT *, 'Hi Mom'             10 CONTINUE
PRINT *, 'Hi Mom'
PRINT *, 'Hi Mom'
```

If LINE is declared as an integer variable, the DO loop causes the message 'Hi Mom' to be printed five times. More lines can be printed by simply changing the integer 5 to some larger value.

The *loop header*

```
DO 10 LINE = 1, 5
```

specifies that the statement(s) that follow should be repeated five times, once each for values of LINE equal to 1, 2, 3, 4, and 5. It may help you understand the FORTRAN syntax if you read the header above as "DO through label 10 for values of LINE from 1 to 5." The *loop terminator*

```
10 CONTINUE
```

follows the last statement that is to be repeated.

The integer 10 appearing in both the loop header and the loop terminator is a *label*. It does not matter what integer is used as a label; however, the same label must be used in both the header and the terminator statements of a loop. The label must appear in the *label field* (columns 1 through 5) of the terminator statement. Any integer from 1 through 99999 may be used as a label, and it does not matter where the label is placed in the label field. We will not use labels in pseudocode descriptions of DO loops.   ∎

The DO loop is used to implement loops where the exact number of loop repetitions required is known at the start of the loop and may be specified as a variable or constant value. Such a loop is called a *counting loop*. In Example 3.1, the number of repetitions was specified by the integer 5. The DO loop specifies that the variable LINE should take on each of the values in the range 1 to 5 during successive loop repetitions. This means that the value of LINE is 1 during the first loop repetition, 2 during the second loop repetition, and 5 during the last loop repetition.

The variable LINE is called the *loop-control variable*, because its value controls the loop repetition. The loop-control variable in this case is initialized to 1 when the DO loop is first reached; after each execution of the loop body, the loop-control variable is incremented by 1 and tested to see whether loop repetition should continue.

The loop-control variable may also be referenced in the loop body, but its value cannot be changed. The next example shows a DO loop whose loop-control variable is referenced in the loop body.

EXAMPLE 3.2   The program in Fig. 3.1 uses a DO loop to print a list of integer values and their squares. During each repetition of the loop, the statements

```
SQUARE = I * I
PRINT *, I, SQUARE
```

cause the value of the loop-control variable I (an integer from 1 to 4) and its square (an integer from 1 through 16) to be printed. A trace of this program is shown in Table 3.1.   ■

Figure 3.1. *Program to Print a List of Integers and Their Squares*

```
      PROGRAM INTSQU
C Prints a list of integer values and their squares.
      INTEGER I, SQUARE, MAXI
      PARAMETER (MAXI = 4)
      PRINT *, '      I          I * I'
      DO 20 I = 1, MAXI
         SQUARE = I * I
         PRINT *, I, SQUARE
 20   CONTINUE
      STOP
      END


      I          I * I
      1            1
      2            4
      3            9
      4           16
```

Table 3.1. *Trace of Program in Fig. 3.1*

STATEMENT	I	SQUARE	EFFECT
	?	?	
DO 20 I = 1, MAXI	1		Initializes I to 1;
			1 <= 4 is true —
SQUARE = I * I		1	assigns 1 * 1 to SQUARE;
PRINT *, I, SQUARE			prints 1 and 1.
Increment and test I	2		2 <= 4 is true —
SQUARE = I * I		4	assigns 2 * 2 to SQUARE;
PRINT *, I, SQUARE			prints 2 and 4.
Increment and test I	3		3 <= 4 is true —
SQUARE = I * I		9	assigns 3 * 3 to SQUARE;
PRINT *, I, SQUARE			prints 3 and 9.
Increment and test I	4		4 <= 4 is true —
SQUARE = I * I		16	assigns 4 * 4 to SQUARE;
PRINT *, I, SQUARE			prints 4 and 16.
Increment and test I	5		5 <= 4 is false —
			exits loop.

The trace in Table 3.1 shows that the loop-control variable I is initialized to 1 when the DO loop is reached. The DO loop causes the PRINT statement to be repeated. Before each repetition, I is incremented by one and tested to see whether its value is still less than or equal to MAXI (4). If the test result is true, then the loop body is executed again, and the next value of I and SQUARE are printed. I is equal to 4 during the last loop repetition.

Counting Loops (Special Form of DO Loop)

SYNTAX: DO *label counter* = 1, *repetitions*
                      statement$_1$
                      statement$_2$
                      ⋮   *loop body*
                      statement$_n$
             label CONTINUE

EXAMPLE: DO 10 I = 1, 5
                    PRINT *, I
          10 CONTINUE

INTERPRETATION: The number of times each *statement*$_i$ in the *loop body* is executed is determined by the value of *repetitions*. The value of the loop-control variable *counter* is set to 1 before the first execution of the *loop body*; *counter* is incremented by 1 after each execution of the *loop body*. The variable *counter* must be type INTEGER; *repetitions* may be a type INTEGER variable, an INTEGER constant, or an expression with an INTEGER value. The value of *label* must be an integer from 1 to 99999 and must appear in columns 1 through 5 of the loop terminator (the CONTINUE statement).

NOTE: If the value of *repetitions* is less than 1, the *loop body* will not be executed. The value of *counter* cannot be changed within the *loop body*.

Accumulating a Sum

We can use a counting loop to accumulate the sum of a collection of data values, as shown in the next problem.

Case Study: Sum of Integers

Problem

Write a program that finds the sum of all integers from 1 to N.

Case Study: Sum of Integers, continued

Design Overview

In order to solve this problem, it will be necessary to find some way to form the sum of the first N integers. The data requirements and algorithm follow.

Data Requirements

Problem Input

the last integer in the sum (INTEGER N)

Problem Output

the sum of integers from 1 to N (INTEGER SUM)

Initial Algorithm

1. Read the last integer (N).
2. Find the sum (SUM) of all the integers from 1 to N inclusive.
3. Print the sum.

Algorithm Refinements

Step 2 is the only step needing refinement. One possible refinement is shown next.

Step 2 Refinement

2.0 Store 0 in SUM
2.1 Add 1 to SUM
2.2 Add 2 to SUM
2.3 Add 3 to SUM

$\vdots$

2.N Add N to SUM

For a large value of N, it would be rather time-consuming to write this list of N steps. We would also have to know the value of N before writing this list; consequently, the program would not be general since it would work for only one value of N.

However, steps 2.1 through 2.N are all quite similar and can, in fact, be represented in the general form

2.*i* Add *i* to SUM

Case Study: Sum of Integers, continued

To accomplish the same task as steps 2.1 through 2.N, the general step must be executed for all values of *i* from 1 to N, inclusive. This suggests the use of a counting loop with I as the loop-control variable.

Step 2 Refinement

2.0 Store 0 in SUM
2.1 DO for each integer I from 1 to N
        Add I to SUM
    CONTINUE

The variable I will take on the successive values 1, 2, 3, ..., N. Each time the loop is repeated, the current value of I will be added to SUM. The description of I follows.

Additional Program Variable

loop-control variable—represents each integer from 1 through N to be included in the sum (INTEGER I)

Coding

The complete program is shown in Fig. 3.2. The statements

```
      SUM = 0
      DO 10 I = 1, N
         SUM = SUM + I
10 CONTINUE
```

are used to perform step 2. To ensure that the final sum is correct, the value of SUM must be *initialized* to zero before the first addition operation.

Figure 3.2. *Program for Sum of Integers from 1 to N*

```
      PROGRAM SUMINT
C Finds and prints the sum of all integers from 1 to N.

C Declarations
      INTEGER N, SUM, I

C Read the last integer (N)
      PRINT *, 'Enter the last integer in the sum'
      READ *, N

C Find the sum (SUM) of all the integers from 1 to N inclusive
      SUM = 0
      DO 10 I = 1, N
         SUM = SUM + I
   10 CONTINUE
```

Case Study: Sum of Integers, continued

```
C Print the sum
        PRINT *, 'The sum is ', SUM
        STOP
        END

Enter the last integer in the sum
6
The sum is              21
```

The DO loop causes the assignment statement

        SUM = SUM + I

to be repeated N times. Each time, the current value of I is added to the sum being accumulated and the result is saved back in SUM. This is illustrated in Fig. 3.3 for the first two loop repetitions.

Figure 3.3. *Effect of First Two Loop Repetitions*

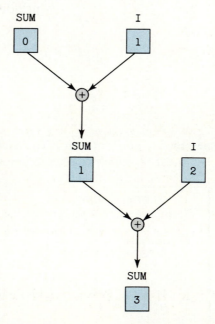

Testing

A trace of the program for a data value of 3 is shown in Table 3.2. The trace verifies that the program performs as desired, because the final value stored

Case Study: Sum of Integers, continued

Table 3.2. *Trace of Program in Fig. 3.2*

STATEMENT	N	I	SUM	EFFECT
	?	?	?	
PRINT *, 'Enter the...'				Prints a prompt.
READ *, N	3			Reads 3 into N.
SUM = 0			0	Initializes SUM.
DO 10 I = 1, N		1		Initializes I to 1;
				1 <= 1 is true —
SUM = SUM + I			1	adds 1 to SUM.
Increment and test I		2		2 <= 3 is true —
SUM = SUM + I			3	adds 2 to SUM.
Increment and test I		3		3 <= 3 is true —
SUM = SUM + I			6	adds 3 to SUM.
Increment and test I		4		4 <= 3 is false —
				exits loop.
PRINT *, 'The sum...'				Prints the sum, 6.

in SUM is 6 (1+2+3). The loop exit occurs when the value of the loop-control variable I becomes greater than N. As shown in the table, the statement

    SUM = SUM + I

is executed exactly three times.

You should run this program for several different values of N. Use the formula

$$SUM = \frac{N(N + 1)}{2}$$

to check your results.

Case Study: Physics of Falling Bodies

Problem

Your skydiving club wants a program that will compute and display the distance a skydiver falls from a plane at one-second intervals from *time* = 1 second until *time* = 10 seconds.

Case Study: Physics of Falling Bodies, continued

Design Overview

From physics, we know that the distance an object falls from a plane (ignoring air resistance) is given by the equation

$$distance = \tfrac{1}{2}\, acceleration \times time^2$$

where the acceleration due to gravity is approximately 9.81 meters/sec². We can use this equation in a loop to compute distance for each value of *time* from 1 second through 10 seconds. We can make the program more general by reading in the maximum time in seconds.

Data Requirements

Problem Parameter

the acceleration due to gravity in meters/sec² (REAL GACCEL = 9.80665)

Problem Input

the maximum time in seconds (INTEGER MXTIME)

Problem Output

the distance fallen at the end of each second (REAL DISTNC)

Initial Algorithm

1. Enter the maximum time (in seconds) for the fall.
2. Compute and display the distance fallen at the end of each second in the time interval from 1 second to the maximum.

Algorithm Refinements

To refine step 2, we must introduce a new program variable, TIME, that will be used to control loop repetition.

Additional Program Variable

the elapsed time since the parachutist left the plane (INTEGER TIME)

Step 2 Refinement

```
2.1 DO for values of TIME between 1 and MXTIME
        2.2 Compute distance fallen.
        2.3 Display distance fallen.
    CONTINUE
```

Case Study: Physics of Falling Bodies, continued

Coding

The program appears in Fig. 3.4. The assignment statement

```
DISTNC = 0.5 * GACCEL * TIME ** 2
```

implements the equation, shown earlier, that describes the relationship among distance, acceleration, and elapsed time.

Figure 3.4. *Computing a Skydiver's Flight*

```
      PROGRAM SKYDIV
C Computes and displays the distance fallen by a skydiver in one-
C second intervals. The maximum time is entered as data.

C Declarations
      REAL GACCEL
      PARAMETER (GACCEL = 9.80665)
      INTEGER TIME, MXTIME, DISTNC

C Enter maximum time of fall
      PRINT *, 'Enter maximum freefall time (in seconds)'
      READ *, MXTIME

C Compute and display distance fallen after each second
      DO 10 TIME = 1, MXTIME
         DISTNC = 0.5 * GACCEL * TIME ** 2
         PRINT *, 'Time (secs) = ', TIME,
     +        '   Distance (meters) = ', DISTNC
   10 CONTINUE

C Exit program
      STOP
      END
Enter maximum freefall time (in seconds)
10
Time (secs) =           1   Distance (meters) =          4.903325
Time (secs) =           2   Distance (meters) =         19.613300
Time (secs) =           3   Distance (meters) =         44.129920
Time (secs) =           4   Distance (meters) =         78.453200
Time (secs) =           5   Distance (meters) =        122.583100
Time (secs) =           6   Distance (meters) =        176.519700
Time (secs) =           7   Distance (meters) =        240.262900
Time (secs) =           8   Distance (meters) =        313.812800
Time (secs) =           9   Distance (meters) =        397.169300
Time (secs) =          10   Distance (meters) =        490.332500
```

Case Study: Physics of Falling Bodies, continued

Testing

You should run this program for several increasing values of MXTIME. As MXTIME increases, the table size should grow, but the beginning lines of each succeeding table should be the same as for the previous table. You should check certain values of DISTNC that are relatively easy to calculate. For example, line 1 of each table (TIME is 1) should contain a value of GACCEL / 2 (DISTNC is 4.903325); line 2 of each table (TIME is 2) should contain a value of 2 * GACCEL (DISTNC is 19.6133); and line 10 of each table (TIME is 10) should contain a value of 50 * GACCEL (DISTNC is 490.3325).

SELF-CHECK EXERCISES FOR SECTION 3.1

1. Explain what the DO loop header below means in English. How many times is the loop executed?

```
DO 15 I5 = 1, 5
```

2. Trace the execution of the DO loop below. What is printed?

```
      N = 5
      DO 10 COUNT = 1, N
         PRINT *, '*****'
   10 CONTINUE
```

3. Trace the execution of the DO loop below. What is printed?

```
      PROD = 1
      DO 20 I = 1, 5
         PROD = PROD * I
         PRINT *, I, PROD
   20 CONTINUE
```

4. There is generally more than one way to solve a problem. It so happens that the formula

$$SUM = \frac{N(N + 1)}{2}$$

may be used to compute the sum of the integers from 1 to N inclusive. Write a program that compares the results of both methods and prints an appropriate message indicating whether the results are the same.

5. Write a program that finds the product of the integers from 1 to N inclusive.

3.2 ▬▬▬ Generalizing a Solution

After finishing a program, someone will often ask a "what if?" question. The person asking the question usually wants to know if the program would still work if some of the restrictions implied by the problem statement were removed. If the answer is "no," then you may have to modify the program to make it work. You will be much better off if you try to anticipate these questions in advance and make your programs as general as possible right from the start. Sometimes this can easily be accomplished by making a problem parameter or constant a problem input.

One question comes to mind for the sum of N integers problem: What if we wanted to find the sum of any list of numbers, not just the first N integers; would the program still work? Clearly, the answer to this question is "no." However, it would not be too difficult to modify the program to solve this more general problem. In fact, we will extend our solution to compute the average value as well as the sum.

▬▬▬ Case Study: Average of a Set of Measurements

Problem

The control engineers at ACME Hydraulics need a program that will compute the average value for a set of measurements taken during the day. They would like to use the same program to calculate the average temperature, pressure, and so on.

Design Overview

Besides the measurement values, the program must read the units of measurement (e.g., degrees, p.s.i.) and the total number of measurement values (NUMMES). Each measurement value can be temporarily stored in the same memory cell (ITEM) and added to an accumulating sum (SUM). The average can be obtained using the equation

    AVERGE = SUM / NUMMES

Data Requirements

Problem Inputs

units of measurement (CHARACTER *15 UNITS)
number of measurements to be averaged (INTEGER NUMMES)
each observed value (REAL ITEM)

Case Study: Average of a Set of Measurements, continued

Problem Outputs

sum of the observed values (SUM)
average of the data items (AVERGE)

Initial Algorithm

1. Read the units of measurement.
2. Read the number of observed values.
3. Read each measurement and add it to the sum.
4. Compute the average value.
5. Print the average value.

Algorithm Refinements

Step 3 is similar to step 2 of the algorithm in the preceding sum-of-integers case study; its refinement follows.

Step 3 Refinement

3.1 Initialize SUM to zero.
3.2 DO for each data item
    3.3 Read the next data item into ITEM.
    3.4 Add ITEM to SUM.
CONTINUE

In the refinement above, the variable ITEM is used to store each number to be summed, and each new value that is read into ITEM replaces the previous value. After each number is read into ITEM, it will be added to SUM. This process will be repeated until all the data items have been read in and added to SUM.

In step 2, the number of data items to be summed is read into NUMMES. This value determines the number of loop repetitions that are required. We need a loop-control variable to count the data items as they are processed and ensure that all data are summed.

Additional Program Variables

loop-control variable—the number of data items added so far (INTEGER COUNT)

The refinement of step 4 (Compute the average value) is shown below.

Step 4 Refinement

4.1 Divide SUM by the number of items.

Case Study: Average of a Set of Measurements, continued

Coding

Figure 3.5 shows the program. The DO loop in Fig. 3.5 begins with the header

```
DO 10 COUNT = 1, NUMMES
```

where the value of NUMMES determines how many times the loop is repeated. If this value is not correctly defined prior to loop execution, the loop will not work properly. By using a READ statement to enter this value, we have made the program as general as possible. However, invalid data values can cause serious problems, as described in the program style display on page 128.

Figure 3.5. *Computing the Average of a Set of Measurements*

```
      PROGRAM MEASUR
C Finds and prints the average value of a set of measurements.
C The units of measurement, the number of values, and the values are
C provided as data.

C Declarations
      INTEGER NUMMES, COUNT
      REAL ITEM, SUM, AVERGE
      CHARACTER *15 UNITS

C Read the units of measurement and number of measurements.
      PRINT *, 'Enter units (enclosed in apostrophes)'
      READ *, UNITS
      PRINT *, 'Enter number of observed values'
      READ *, NUMMES

C Read each measurement and add it to the sum.
      SUM = 0
      DO 10 COUNT = 1, NUMMES
         PRINT *, 'Enter next value (in ', UNITS, ')'
         READ *, ITEM
         SUM = SUM + ITEM
   10 CONTINUE

C Compute the average value.
      AVERGE = SUM / NUMMES

C Print the average value.
      PRINT *, ' '
      PRINT *, 'The average value is ', AVERGE, ' ', UNITS
      STOP
      END
Enter units (enclosed in apostrophes)
'degrees Celsius'
```

Case Study: Average of a Set of Measurements, continued

```
Enter number of observed values
3
Enter next value in (degrees Celsius)
45.0
Enter next value in (degrees Celsius)
54.6
Enter next value in (degrees Celsius)
100.4

The average value is 66.66667 degrees Celsius
```

Testing

You should test this program with a varying number of data values. Make sure that the average computed is correct for negative measurement values as well as for positive ones. You will find that the program does not work properly when NUMMES is zero or negative. The next program style display discusses the reason for this and a way to correct the problem.

Program Style

Defensive Programming

In Fig. 3.5, the assignment statement

```
    AVERGE = SUM / NUMMES
```

cannot be executed if the divisor is zero. Instead, the computer will print an error message such as "attempted division by zero" and program execution will be stopped.

You are correct if you are thinking that no reasonable person would enter a data value of zero for NUMMES, but program users often do not know what is reasonable and what is not. Also, it is possible for anyone to make a typing error. Therefore, experienced programmers often practice "defensive programming" to ensure that a program operates properly even for invalid data.

In Fig. 3.5, it would be safer to compute AVERGE using the IF statement

```
    IF (NUMMES .LE. 0) THEN
        PRINT *, 'Invalid number of items: ', NUMMES
    ELSE
        AVERGE = SUM / NUMMES
    ENDIF
```

This statement causes an error message to be displayed when NUMMES is invalid; the program computes the value of AVERGE only when NUMMES is valid. In either case, program execution will continue. This is preferable to having the computer stop the program because of an error.

1. Write a general program to find the product of a list of data items. Ignore any data values of 0.

3.3 Repeating a Program Body

When we began the discussion of repetition in programs, we mentioned that we would like to be able to execute the payroll program (see Fig. 2.4) for several employees in a single run. We will see how to do this next.

Case Study: Computing the Payroll for Several Employees

Problem

Modify the payroll program to compute gross pay and net pay for a group of employees. Also, compute and display the total payroll amount.

Design Overview

The number of employees must be provided as input data followed by the hourly rate and the hours worked for each employee. The same variables (HOURS, RATE, GROSS, NET) will be used to hold the data and computational results for each employee. The computations will be performed in the same way as before. The total payroll will be the sum of all employees' net pay.

Problem Parameters

maximum salary for no tax deduction (TXBRAK = 100.00)
amount of tax deducted (TAX = 25.00)

Problem Inputs

number of employees (INTEGER NUMEMP)
hours worked by each employee (REAL HOURS)
hourly rate for each employee (REAL RATE)

Problem Outputs

gross pay for each employee (REAL GROSS)
net pay for each employee (REAL NET)
total payroll amount (REAL PAYROL)

Case Study: Computing the Payroll for Several Employees, continued

Initial Algorithm

1. Enter the number of employees (NUMEMP).
2. For each employee, read the payroll data, compute and display gross pay and net pay, add net pay to the total payroll amount.
3. Display the total payroll amount.

Algorithm Refinements

An additional variable (shown below) is needed to count the number of employees processed and to control the DO loop in step 2.

Additional Program Variable

loop-control variable—counts the employees that are processed
                    (INTEGER CNTEMP)

Step 2 Refinement

2.1 PAYROL = 0.0
2.2 DO for each employee
      2.3 Enter employee data.
      2.4 Compute gross pay.
      2.5 Compute net pay.
      2.6 Display gross pay and net pay.
      2.7 Add net pay to PAYROL.
   CONTINUE

Coding

Figure 3.6 shows the payroll program. The DO loop header

```
DO 10 CNTEMP = 1, NUMEMP
```

implements step 2.2.

Figure 3.6. *Payroll Program*

```
     PROGRAM PAYER
C Computes and prints each employee's gross pay and net pay given hourly
C rate and number of hours worked. Deducts a tax of $25 if
C gross pay exceeds $100; otherwise, deducts no tax.
C Also computes total payroll
```

Case Study: Computing the Payroll for Several Employees, continued

```
C Declarations
      REAL TXBRAK, TAX
      PARAMETER (TXBRAK = 100.00)
      PARAMETER (TAX = 25.00)
      REAL HOURS, RATE, GROSS, NET, PAYROL
      INTEGER NUMEMP, CNTEMP


C Enter total number of employees
      PRINT *, 'Enter number of employees:'
      READ *, NUMEMP


C Compute and print gross pay and net pay for NUMEMP employees
C and total payroll amount
      PAYROL = 0.0
      DO 10 CNTEMP = 1, NUMEMP
C        Enter HOURS and RATE
         PRINT *, 'Enter hours worked:'
         READ *, HOURS
         PRINT *, 'Enter hourly rate:'
         READ *, RATE


C        Compute gross pay
         GROSS = HOURS * RATE


C        Compute net pay
         IF (GROSS .GT. TXBRAK) THEN
            NET = GROSS - TAX
         ELSE
            NET = GROSS
         ENDIF


C        Print GROSS and NET
         PRINT *, 'Gross pay is $', GROSS
         PRINT *, 'Net pay is $', NET
         PRINT *


C        Add NET to PAYROL
         PAYROL = PAYROL + NET
 10   CONTINUE


C Display total payroll
      PRINT *, 'Total Payroll is $', PAYROL
      STOP
      END
```

Case Study: Computing the Payroll for Several Employees, continued

```
Enter number of employees:
2
Enter hours worked:
25
Enter hourly rate:
3.50
Gross pay is $  87.50000
Net pay is $  87.50000

Enter hours worked:
40
Enter hourly rate:
4.80
Gross pay is $  192.0000
Net pay is $  167.0000

Total payroll is $  254.50
```

Testing

Run the payroll program for ten employees where some of the employees pay a tax amount and some do not. Make sure that the program runs properly for the simple case of just one employee.

SELF-CHECK EXERCISES FOR SECTION 3.3

1. Trace the execution of the DO loop below for the data 5, 3, –5, 7, 0, –9. What value is read into N? What values are read into NEXT? What is printed?

```
      READ *, N
      SUM = 0
      DO 30 I = 1, N
         READ *, NEXT
         IF (NEXT .GE. 0) THEN
            SUM = SUM + NEXT
         ELSE
            SUM = SUM - NEXT
         ENDIF
   30 CONTINUE
      PRINT *, SUM
```

2. Write a DO loop that reads N items and accumulates the sum of all positive data items in one variable and the sum of all negative data items in another variable. Print both sums when done. Assume that N is the first data value to be read.

3.4 ▬▬▬ The General DO Loop

So far, we have used the DO loop to implement counting loops, or loops that are executed once for each integer value between 1 and a specified final value. In a counting loop, the loop-control variable is a special variable whose value is increased by 1 each time the loop is repeated.

The DO Loop Step Parameter

It is actually possible to specify any positive or negative change to the value of a DO loop-control variable in the loop header. Thus, the value of the DO loop-control variable may increase or decrease after each loop repetition, as illustrated in the next examples.

EXAMPLE 3.3

The DO loop in Fig. 3.7 computes the sum of all odd integers in the range from 1 to N. The DO loop header

```
DO 10 ODD = 1, N, 2
```

Figure 3.7. *Computing the Sum of Odd Integers*

```
      PROGRAM SUMODD
C Demonstration of general DO

C Declarations
      INTEGER N, ODD, SUM

C Read last integer
      PRINT *, 'Enter an integer'
      READ *, N

C Add the odd integers between 1 and N
      SUM = 0
      DO 10 ODD = 1, N, 2
         SUM = SUM + ODD
   10 CONTINUE

C Print the sum
      PRINT *, 'The value of ODD is ', ODD
      PRINT *, 'The sum of odd integers from 1 to ', N, ' is', SUM

      STOP
      END

Enter an integer
5
The value of ODD is             7
The sum of odd integers from 1 to             5 is             9
```

has a third parameter, 2 (the *step parameter*), which causes the value of the loop-control variable ODD to increase by 2 instead of 1. In the sample run shown, N is 5 so the values of ODD that are summed are 1, 3, and 5. Note that loop exit occurs when the value of ODD *passes* (becomes larger than) N, so the value of ODD printed after loop exit is 7. If the value entered for N is 6 instead of 5, the same values of ODD and SUM would be printed (i.e., 7 and 9). ■

EXAMPLE 3.4

The program in Fig. 3.8 "counts down" from a specified starting value (an input variable) to "blast-off." Since INTERV is -1, the value of the loop-control variable, TIME, decreases by one each time the loop is repeated. ■

Figure 3.8. *Counting Down to Blast-off*

```
      PROGRAM BLAST
C Counting down to blast-off

C Declarations
      INTEGER INTERV
      PARAMETER (INTERV = -1)
      INTEGER TIME, START

      PRINT *, 'Enter starting time (an integer) in seconds:'
      READ *, START

C Begin count down
      PRINT *, 'Begin count down'
      DO 10 TIME = START, 1, INTERV
         PRINT *, 'T -', TIME
   10 CONTINUE
      PRINT *, 'Blast-off!'

      STOP
      END


Enter starting time (an integer) in seconds:
5
Begin count down
T -           5
T -           4
T -           3
T -           2
T -           1
Blast-off!
```

DO Loop Syntax

Although we have used only integer constants or variables as DO loop parameters, we can also use expressions. For example, the DO loop header

```
      DO 100 I = J + 3, 2 * JMAX
```

is valid. In this header, the initial parameter is the value of the expression J + 3, and the limit parameter is the value of the expression 2 * JMAX. These expression values are computed once, when the loop header is first reached, and are used to fix the minimum and maximum values of loop-control variable I during loop repetition. Even if the value of JMAX is later changed during loop execution, the number of loop repetitions will not be affected.

Although FORTRAN permits type REAL expressions as DO loop parameters, we strongly discourage this practice. This is because DO loops with type REAL parameters will not always execute the same number of times on different computers. The reason for this is discussed in Section 4.2 under ''Numerical Inaccuracies.''

DO Loop Structure (General Form)

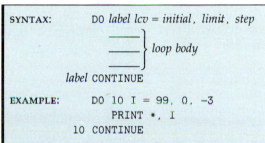

SYNTAX: DO *label lcv = initial, limit, step*

             } *loop body*

     label CONTINUE

EXAMPLE: DO 10 I = 99, 0, −3
             PRINT *, I
     10 CONTINUE

INTERPRETATION: The loop parameters *initial*, *limit*, and *step* are expressions that represent the initial value, limit value, and step value for the loop-control variable, *lcv*. The *lcv* is set to the value of *initial* when the loop header is first reached. Before each repetition of the *loop body* (including the first), the value of *lcv* is tested to see whether it has ''passed'' the value of *limit*. If so, control passes to the first statement following the loop terminator (loop exit); otherwise, the *loop body* is executed. After the *loop body* is executed, the value of *lcv* is incremented by *step* and retested as explained next.

If *step* is positive, repetition will continue as long as *lcv* is less than or equal to *limit*; the loop will be exited when *lcv* becomes greater than *limit*. If *step* is negative, repetition will continue as long as *lcv* is greater than or equal to *limit*; the loop will be exited when *lcv* becomes less than *limit*. Upon exit, *lcv* retains the last value assigned to it, i.e., the value that caused the exit.

NOTES: The loop parameters may be arbitrary arithmetic expressions. Each expression is evaluated only once—when the loop is first entered. It is permissible for the values of variables in these expressions (but not the *lcv*) to be changed in the loop body; however, this will not affect the values of *initial*, *limit*, or *step*, nor will it change the number of loop repetitions.

A *step* value of zero is not allowed. If *step* is omitted, it is assumed to be one. The same statement *label* must be used in the DO loop header and terminator lines.

Since the loop parameters may be arbitrary arithmetic expressions, they may contain constants, variables, arithmetic operators, and parentheses. The *step* value determines the magnitude and direction of change in the loop-control variable after each loop repetition. It is possible for the loop body not to be executed at all.

- If *step* is negative (*step* < 0), the loop will not be executed if *initial* is less than *limit* (e.g., DO 10 I = 4, 10, –1).
- If *step* is positive (*step* > 0), the loop will not be executed if *initial* is greater than *limit* (e.g., DO 15 I = 10, 4, 1).

If the loop is not executed, the value of the loop-control variable is set equal to the value of *initial,* and the first statement following the loop terminator is executed.

EXAMPLE 3.5

The program in Fig. 3.9 prints a table for converting Celsius temperatures to Fahrenheit temperatures. Because of the values of CBEGIN and CLIMIT, the table runs from 20 degrees Celsius to –20 degrees Celsius. Since CSTEP is –5, the DO loop header

```
DO 10 CELSUS = CBEGIN, CLIMIT, CSTEP
```

causes the value of CELSUS to decrease by 5 after each loop repetition. Loop exit occurs when CELSUS becomes less than CLIMIT, i.e., when CELSUS is –25. ∎

Program Style

Printing a Table

The statement

```
PRINT *, '       Celsius     Fahrenheit'
```

before the loop prints an output line consisting of two words separated by a group of blanks. This is the first output line printed and will serve as a heading for the table of numbers that is printed by the loop.

Inside the loop, the statement

```
PRINT *, CELSUS, '      ', FARHEN
```

prints a pair of numbers each time it is executed. The actual position of these numbers will differ depending on the compiler used. If your compiler aligns these numbers in columns, you can insert or remove spaces as needed in the first PRINT statement to align each heading (Celsius or Fahrenheit) over its respective column of numbers.

Unfortunately, some compilers will not align these numbers in columns. In Chapter 4, we will learn another method of printing a table that will produce the same output for all compilers.

Figure 3.9. *Printing a Table for Temperature Conversions*

```
      PROGRAM TEMPER
C Conversion of Celsius to Fahrenheit temperature

C Declarations
      INTEGER CBEGIN, CLIMIT, CSTEP
      PARAMETER (CBEGIN = 20, CLIMIT = -20, CSTEP = -5)
      INTEGER CELSUS
      REAL FAHREN

C Print the table heading
      PRINT *, '      Celsius     Fahrenheit'

C Print table
      DO 10 CELSUS = CBEGIN, CLIMIT, CSTEP
         FAHREN = 1.8 * CELSUS + 32.0
         PRINT *, CELSUS, '        ', FAHREN
   10 CONTINUE

      STOP
      END

      Celsius     Fahrenheit
        20         68.00000
        15         59.00000
        10         50.00000
         5         41.00000
         0         32.00000
        -5         23.00000
       -10         14.00000
       -15         5.000000
       -20         -4.000000
```

Using a DO Loop to Evaluate a Series[M]

There are a number of mathematical quantities that can be represented using a series approximation where a series is represented by a summation of an infinite number of terms. For example, the base of the natural logarithms, $e = 2.71828 \ldots$, may be determined by evaluating the expression

$$1 + 1/1! + 1/2! + 1/3! + \ldots + 1/n!$$

where $n!$ represents the factorial of n (i.e., $n! = 1 \times 2 \times 3 \times \ldots \times n$). The number of terms in the series is dependent on n. As the value of n increases, $1/n!$ becomes smaller and the series *converges* to a value. The more terms included in the sum, the more accurate is the value computed.

[M] The superscript "M" will be used throughout this text to indicate material requiring mathematics beyond algebra.

This expression may also be represented as

$$\sum_{i=0}^{n} 1/i!$$

using *summation notation*. This notation is shorthand for the series

$$1/0! + 1/1! + 1/2! + \dots + 1/n!$$

where the first term is obtained by substituting 0 for *i*, the second term is obtained by substituting 1 for *i*, and so on. Since 0! is defined to be 1, the first term is 1, as in the original series above. As shown next, DO loops are a convenient tool for evaluating series such as these.

EXAMPLE 3.6

The program in Fig. 3.10 computes and prints the value of *e*.

Figure 3.10. *Finding the Value of* e *Using a DO Loop*

```
      PROGRAM FINDE
C Computing the value of e using a DO loop

C Declarations
      REAL E, TERM
      INTEGER N, NEXT

      PRINT *, 'Enter the number of terms to be summed'
      READ *, N

C Compute the next value of TERM and add it to the approximation for e
      TERM = 1.0
      E = 1.0
      DO 10 NEXT = 1, N
          TERM = TERM / NEXT
          E = E + TERM
   10 CONTINUE

C Print the result
      PRINT *, 'The value of e is ', E
      STOP
      END

Enter the number of terms to be summed
10
The value of e is    2.718282
```

The input variable N determines how many terms will be summed, where 1/N! is the last term added to the sum. The larger the value of N, the more accurate is the final sum.

Inside the DO loop, the statement

        TERM = TERM / NEXT

computes the value of the next term by dividing the previous term by NEXT (an integer from 1 to N). Since the initial value of TERM is 1.0, this repeated division causes TERM to be assigned the value of 1/NEXT! as desired. The statement

        E = E + TERM

adds the new value of TERM to the sum being accumulated in E. The values of NEXT, TERM, and E are traced in Table 3.3 for three loop iterations.   ■

Table 3.3. *Trace of Program in Fig. 3.10*

STATEMENT	NEXT	TERM	E	EFFECT
TERM = 1.0		1.0		
E = 1.0			1.0	
DO 10 NEXT = 1, N	1			Initializes NEXT;
TERM = TERM / NEXT		1.0/1		TERM is 1.0.
E = E + TERM			2.0	
DO 10 NEXT = 1, N	2			Increments NEXT;
TERM = TERM / NEXT		1.0/2		TERM is 1/2! or 0.5.
E = E + TERM			2.5	
DO 10 NEXT = 1, N	3			Increments NEXT;
TERM = TERM / NEXT		0.5/3		TERM is 1/3!
E = E + TERM			2.6666...	or 0.1666....

SELF-CHECK EXERCISES FOR SECTION 3.4

1. Trace the execution of the loop in Fig. 3.7. Show values of ODD and SUM for each loop iteration.

2. Given the parameter values in Fig. 3.9 and repeated below

        PARAMETER (CBEGIN = 20, CLIMIT = -20, CSTEP = -5)

   indicate what values of CELSUS would appear in the table printed if the DO loop header was rewritten as shown below:

   a. DO 10 CELSUS = CLIMIT, CBEGIN, CSTEP
   b. DO 10 CELSUS = CLIMIT, CBEGIN, -CSTEP
   c. DO 10 CELSUS = CLIMIT, CSTEP, CBEGIN
   d. DO 10 CELSUS = CSTEP, CBEGIN, CLIMIT

3. The value of e^x is represented by the series

   $$1 + x + x^2/2! + x^3/3! + x^4/4! + \ldots$$

   Write a program to compute and print the value of this series. *Hint: x* and the number of terms to be summed should be input variables.

3.5   The WHILE Loop

Whenever a DO loop is used, the exact number of loop repetitions that will be performed is determined when the loop header is first reached. Even if we were to change the loop-parameter values in the loop body, this would have no effect on the number of loop repetitions.

In many programming situations, the exact number of loop repetitions cannot be determined before loop execution begins. It may depend on some aspect of the data that is not known beforehand, but it usually can be stated by a condition. For example, we may wish to continue writing checks as long as our bank balance is positive, as indicated by the pseudocode description below:

```
DO WHILE the balance is still positive
     Read in the next transaction.
     Update and print the balance.
ENDDO
```

The actual number of loop repetitions performed depends on the type of each transaction (deposit or withdrawal) and the amount. In this text, we will use the WHILE loop to implement such a *conditional loop*.

EXAMPLE 3.7   The program in Fig. 3.11 traces the progress of a hungry worm approaching an apple. Each time it moves, the worm reduces the distance between itself and the apple by its own length until the worm is close enough to reach the apple. A WHILE loop is the correct looping structure to use because we have no idea beforehand how many moves will be required.

The variable DISTNC is the loop-control variable in Fig. 3.11. The statement

```
READ *, DISTNC
```

reads in the initial value of DISTNC before the loop is reached. The *loop header*

```
DO WHILE (DISTNC .GT. WRMLEN)
```

tests the value of DISTNC before each loop repetition. If the current value of DISTNC is greater than the worm's length (WRMLEN), the loop is repeated; otherwise, the loop is exited and the first statement after ENDDO is executed. Within the loop, the statement

```
DISTNC = DISTNC - WRMLEN
```

reduces the value of DISTNC each time the loop is repeated.   ∎

Figure 3.11. *Printing Distances between a Worm and an Apple*

```
      PROGRAM WORM
C Prints the distances between a worm and an apple
C until the worm is close enough to reach the apple.

C Declarations
      REAL DISTNC, WRMLEN

C Enter initial distance and worm length.
      PRINT *, 'Enter initial distance between the worm'
      PRINT *, 'and the apple (in inches)'
      READ *, DISTNC
      PRINT *, 'Enter the worm length (in inches)'
      READ *, WRMLEN

C Reduce the distance until worm is close enough to reach it.
      DO WHILE (DISTNC .GT. WRMLEN)
         PRINT *, 'The distance is ', DISTNC
         DISTNC = DISTNC - WRMLEN
      ENDDO

C Display result.
      PRINT *, 'The distance is ', DISTNC
      PRINT *, 'The worm will reach the apple on its next move.'
      STOP
      END

Enter initial distance between the worm
and the apple (in inches)
12.5
Enter the worm length (in inches)
3.5
The distance is        12.500000
The distance is         9.000000
The distance is         5.500000
The distance is         2.000000
The worm will reach the apple on its next move.
```

These three steps

- initializing the loop-control variable before the loop is reached
- testing the loop-control variable before each loop repetition
- updating the loop-control variable in the loop body

must be performed in every program that uses a WHILE loop. If the first step is omitted, the initial test of the loop-control variable will be meaningless. If the last step is omitted, the loop-control variable value cannot change and the loop will execute "forever."

WHILE Loop Syntax

Because the WHILE loop is nonstandard, your computer may use a different syntax from the one shown in Fig. 3.11, or it may not recognize any form of the WHILE loop. We show two forms of the WHILE loop in the syntax display that follows. The form shown on the left is used on Digital Equipment Corporation VAX computers and will appear in the new FORTRAN standard. The form shown on the right is used on some FORTRAN 77 compilers written for Control Data Corporation computers. We show how to implement the WHILE loop in standard FORTRAN later in this section.

WHILE Loop

```
SYNTAX:    DO WHILE (condition)          WHILE (condition) DO
              loop body                     loop body
           ENDDO                         ENDWHILE

EXAMPLE:   DO WHILE (N .NE. 0)           WHILE (N .NE. 0) DO
              PRINT *, 'Enter N?'           PRINT *, 'Enter N?'
              READ *, N                     READ *, N
           ENDDO                         ENDWHILE
```

INTERPRETATION: The *condition* is tested; if it is true, the *loop body* is executed and the *condition* is retested. The *loop body* is repeated as long as the *condition* is true. When the *condition* is tested and found to be false, loop exit occurs and the next program statement after ENDDO (or ENDWHILE) is executed.

NOTES: If the *condition* evaluates to false the first time it is tested, the *loop body* will not be executed. Since the WHILE loop is nonstandard, it may not be implemented on your computer or may be implemented differently.

More WHILE Loop Examples

Several examples of programs with WHILE loops follow.

EXAMPLE 3.8

The WHILE loop below could be used in Fig. 3.5 to ensure that a valid value was read into NUMMES. The loop body is repeated as long as the value of NUMMES is less than or equal to zero. The loop body will not be executed at all if the first value read is positive.

```
PRINT *, 'Enter number of observed values'
READ *, NUMMES
DO WHILE (NUMMES .LE. 0)
   PRINT *, 'Number not positive — try again:'
   READ *, NUMMES
ENDDO
```

The interaction that would result for the data –3, 0, 7 is shown next.

```
Enter number of observed values
-3
Number not positive - try again:
0
Number not positive - try again:
7
```

In this example, the READ statement appears twice, before the WHILE loop and at the end of the loop body. The first READ (called a *priming read*) reads the first data value (–3); the second READ statement would read any additional values of NUMMES (0 and 7). The priming read initializes the loop-control variable and is needed whenever the initial value of the loop-control variable is an input data item.   ∎

EXAMPLE 3.9   The program in Fig. 3.12 prints each power, POWER, of an input integer N that is less than 1000 (MAXPOW). The WHILE loop is exited when the value of NEXPOW becomes greater than or equal to 1000. The assignment statement

    NEXPOW = 1

initializes NEXPOW to the zero power. The *loop-repetition condition*

    (NEXPOW .LT. MAXPOW)

ensures that loop exit will occur at the proper time.
Within the loop body, the statement

    NEXPOW = NEXPOW * N

computes the next power of N by multiplying the previous power by N. If the new value is less than MAXPOW, the loop is repeated causing the current value of NEXPOW to be printed and the next one to be computed.
In the sample run shown in Fig. 3.12, the last value printed is 512; however, the last value assigned to NEXPOW in the loop body is 1024. Since 1024 is greater than 1000, the loop repetition test fails the next time it is evaluated, and the loop is exited.   ∎

It is important to realize that loop exit does not occur at the exact instant that NEXPOW is assigned the value 1024. If there were more statements following the assignment statement in the loop body, they would be executed. Loop exit does not occur until the loop repetition test is reevaluated at the top of the loop.

Figure 3.12. *Program POWERS*

```
      PROGRAM POWERS
C Prints all powers of N less than 1000.

C Declarations
      INTEGER MAXPOW
      PARAMETER (MAXPOW = 1000)
      INTEGER N, NEXPOW

C Read an integer N
      PRINT *, 'This program prints all powers < 1000 of an integer'
      PRINT *, 'Enter an integer:'
      READ *, N
      PRINT *, 'Powers of ', N

C Print each power of N less than MAXPOW
      NEXPOW = 1
      DO WHILE (NEXPOW .LT. MAXPOW)
         PRINT *, NEXPOW
         NEXPOW = NEXPOW * N
      ENDDO

      STOP
      END

This program prints all powers < 1000 of an integer
Enter an integer:
2
Powers of         2
          1
          2
          4
          8
         16
         32
         64
        128
        256
        512
```

EXAMPLE 3.10ᴹ   The distance traveled by a body dropped from a tower in *t* seconds is represented by the formula

$$distance = 1/2 \times gt^2$$

where *g* is the gravitational constant. The program in Fig. 3.13 prints a table showing the height of an object at fixed time intervals after it has been dropped from a tower while the object is still above the ground.

Figure 3.13. *Table of Heights for an Object Dropped from a Tower*

```
      PROGRAM DROPIT
C Shows the height of an object until it hits the ground

C Declarations
      REAL G
      PARAMETER (G = 9.80665)
      REAL HEIGHT, TIME, INTERV, TOWER

C Enter tower height and time interval between data points
      PRINT *, 'Enter the tower height in meters:'
      READ *, TOWER
      PRINT *, 'Enter the time in seconds between height displays:'
      READ *, INTERV

C Initialize TIME AND HEIGHT
      TIME = 0.0
      HEIGHT = TOWER

C Print the object height until it hits the ground
      PRINT *
      PRINT *, '    Time          Height'
      DO WHILE (HEIGHT .GT. 0.0)
         PRINT *, TIME, HEIGHT
         TIME = TIME + INTERV
         HEIGHT = TOWER - 0.5 * G * TIME ** 2
      ENDDO

      PRINT *
      PRINT *, 'SPLAT!!!'
      STOP
      END

Enter the tower height in meters:
100
Enter the time in seconds between height displays:
1.0

    Time          Height
0.000000       100.0000
1.000000       95.09667
2.000000       80.38670
3.000000       55.87008
4.000000       21.54680

SPLAT!!!
```

The number of lines in the table shown in Fig. 3.13 depends on the time interval between displays (INTERV) and the tower height (TOWER). During each loop repetition, the current time (starting at 0.0) and the current object height, HEIGHT, are printed. Next, the elapsed time is increased by INTERV, and the object height is recomputed. HEIGHT is the loop-control variable, and the loop is repeated as long as the object height is positive. The message following the table is printed when the object hits the ground.

Compare this program with the one in Fig. 3.4 that uses a DO loop to control loop repetition. Why would a DO loop be inappropriate here?   ■

Figure 3.14. *Doubling Your Money*

```
      PROGRAM BANKER
C Finds and prints the time required to double your money

C Declarations
      REAL DEPOS, BALANC, RATE, INTRST, DOUBLE
      INTEGER YEAR

      PRINT *, 'Enter the deposit amount in dollars:'
      READ *, DEPOS
      PRINT *, 'Enter the interest rate as a decimal fraction:'
      READ *, RATE

C Initialize YEAR, BALANC, and DOUBLE
      YEAR = 0
      BALANC = DEPOS
      DOUBLE = 2.0 * DEPOS

C Recompute BALANC until the initial deposit amount is doubled
      DO WHILE (BALANC .LT. DOUBLE)
         YEAR = YEAR + 1
         INTRST = BALANC * RATE
         BALANC = BALANC + INTRST
      ENDDO

      PRINT *, 'Deposit amount is doubled after ', YEAR, ' years'
      PRINT *, 'New balance is ', BALANC

      STOP
      END


Enter the deposit amount in dollars:
100.00
Enter the interest rate as a decimal fraction:
0.075
Deposit amount is  doubled after          10 years
New balance is      206.1032
```

EXAMPLE 3.11   The program in Fig. 3.14 determines the number of years required to double your money if you purchase a certificate of deposit that returns a fixed interest rate (RATE) each year. Before the loop is reached, the statements

```
YEAR = 0
BALANC = DEPOS
DOUBLE = 2.0 * DEPOS
```

initialize YEAR to zero, BALANC to the deposit amount, and DOUBLE to twice the deposit amount. The loop-repetition condition

```
(BALANC .LT. DOUBLE)
```

causes the loop to be repeated until the current balance is twice the deposit amount. Within the loop, the statements

```
INTRST = BALANC * RATE
BALANC = BALANC + INTRST
```

recompute the balance at the end of each year by adding the interest earned (INTRST) during the year to the current balance. Note that BALANC, not YEAR, is the loop-control variable. (Why?)   ■

Comparison of WHILE and DO Loops

As shown in the next example, a WHILE loop can also be used to implement a counting loop.

EXAMPLE 3.12   The WHILE loop below could be used to find the sum of the first N integers. The loop body is the pair of statements between the lines beginning with DO WHILE and ENDDO. The loop body is repeated as long as (WHILE) the value of NXTINT is less than or equal to N. In the loop body, each value of NXTINT (starting with 1) is added to SUM and NXTINT is incremented by 1. Loop execution stops when NXTINT is equal to N + 1. The equivalent DO loop is provided for comparison.   ■

WHILE Loop	DO Loop
```SUM = 0```	```SUM = 0```
```NXTINT = 1```	```DO 10 NXTINT = 1, N```
```DO WHILE (NXTINT .LE. N)```	``` SUM = SUM + NXTINT```
``` SUM = SUM + NXTINT```	```10 CONTINUE```
``` NXTINT = NXTINT + 1```	
```ENDDO```	

The most obvious difference between the loops above is that the WHILE loop is longer. This illustrates that the WHILE loop should not be used to implement a counting loop. The DO loop is easier to write and should be used when the number of loop repetitions needed can be determined before loop entry.

The main reason for the extra length of the WHILE loop involves the manner in which the loop-control variable NXTINT is manipulated:

- NXTINT is set to an initial value of 1 (NXTINT = 1).
- NXTINT is tested before each loop repetition (NXTINT .LE. N).
- NXTINT is updated during each loop repetition (NXTINT = NXTINT + 1).

Although these three steps are implicit in the DO loop, they must be specified explicitly when the WHILE loop is used. If the loop-control variable is not initialized properly before the WHILE statement is reached, the loop-repetition test will be meaningless. If the loop-control variable is not updated, the loop-repetition test will always be true and the loop will not be exited (*infinite loop*).

Implementing the WHILE Loop in Standard FORTRAN

Although the WHILE loop is a convenient control structure, it is not part of standard FORTRAN 77. Consequently, your particular version of FORTRAN may not support it. So, a program written for one computer using the WHILE loop may have to be rewritten to run on another computer with a FORTRAN 77 compiler that does not support the WHILE loop. In this section, we will describe how to implement the WHILE loop in standard FORTRAN.

EXAMPLE 3.13

The WHILE loop from Fig. 3.12 is rewritten below and its implementation in standard FORTRAN is shown on the right. The comments preceding and following the control structure identify it as a WHILE loop.

```
        Nonstandard FORTRAN                 Standard FORTRAN

                                      C     WHILE loop
  DO WHILE (NEXPOW .LT. MAXPOW)          9 IF (NEXPOW .LT. MAXPOW) THEN
     PRINT *, NEXPOW                           PRINT *, NEXPOW
     NEXPOW = NEXPOW * N                        NEXPOW = NEXPOW * N
  ENDDO                                         GOTO 9
                                             ENDIF
                                      C     End of WHILE loop
```

If the condition

```
(NEXPOW .LT. MAXPOW)
```

is true, the true task of the IF structure is executed. The statement

```
GOTO 9
```

transfers control back to the IF structure header (label 9) after each execution of the true task. Consequently, the true task is repeated while the above condition is true. When the condition is false, the true task is skipped and execution continues with the first statement after the ENDIF. This is analogous to exiting a WHILE loop.   ■

The GOTO statement and the standard FORTRAN implementation of the WHILE loop are described next.

GOTO Statement

> SYNTAX: GOTO *label*
>
> EXAMPLE: GOTO 9
>
> INTERPRETATION: An immediate transfer of control to the statement specified by *label* occurs. The *label* must appear in columns 1 through 5 of exactly one FORTRAN statement.

WHILE Loop (Standard FORTRAN)

> SYNTAX: *label* IF (*condition*) THEN
>   *loop body*
>   GOTO *label*
>   ENDIF
>
> EXAMPLE: 9 IF (N .LE. 0) THEN
>   PRINT *, 'Enter N:'
>   READ *, N
>   GOTO 9
>   ENDIF
>
> INTERPRETATION: The *condition* is tested and if it is true, the *loop body* is executed, the GOTO statement transfers control back to the IF statement header, and the *condition* is retested. This sequence is repeated as long as the *condition* is true. When the *condition* is tested and found to be false, loop exit occurs and the next program statement (following ENDIF) is executed.
>
> NOTE: If the *condition* evaluates to false the first time it is tested, the *loop body* will not be executed.

Using a Sentinel Value

Very often, we do not know exactly how many data items there will be when a program begins execution. In a batch or interactive program, this may be because there are too many data items to count them beforehand (e.g., a stack of exam scores for a very large class). In an interactive program, the number of data items provided may depend on how the computation proceeds.

There are two ways to handle this situation. Before each data item is read, the program user could be asked whether or not there are any more data. The user would enter 'Y' (for Yes) or 'N' (for No), and the program would either read the next item ('Y') or terminate data entry ('N').

EXAMPLE 3.14

In the loop below, the CHARACTER *1 variable MORE is used as a loop-control variable. It must be initialized to 'Y' before the start of the loop. A new string value ('Y' or 'N') is read into MORE at the end of each loop repetition. The data being summed are read into NUM and added to SUM.

```
SUM = 0
MORE = 'Y'
DO WHILE (MORE .EQ. 'Y')
        PRINT *, 'Enter next data item:'
        READ *, NUM
        SUM = SUM + NUM
        PRINT *, 'Any more data? Enter ''Y'' (Yes) or ''N'' (No):'
        READ *, MORE
ENDDO
```

The sample dialogue below would be used to enter the data 3, 5, and –7. The problem with this approach is that the program user must enter a string ('Y') before each actual data item that is entered. ∎

```
Enter next data item:
3
Any more data? Enter 'Y' (Yes) or 'N' (No):
'Y'
Enter next data item:
5
Any more data? Enter 'Y' (Yes) or 'N' (No):
'Y'
Enter next data item:
–7
Any more data? Enter 'Y' (Yes) or 'N' (No):
'N'
```

A second approach would be to instruct the user to enter a unique data value when done. The program would test each data item and terminate after this *sentinel value* is read. This approach is more convenient since the program user enters only the required data. ∎

EXAMPLE 3.15   The program in Fig. 3.15 finds the product of a collection of data values. It stops reading data after a value of zero is entered. ∎

The program in Fig. 3.15 illustrates the proper use of a sentinel value. In order to determine whether or not data entry is complete, each data item must be compared to the value stored in SNTNEL (0.0). For this test to make sense in the beginning, the first number must be read before the WHILE loop is reached. The last step in the WHILE loop must read the next number so that it can be tested to determine whether or not the loop body should be repeated. This general pattern is illustrated after Fig. 3.15.

Figure 3.15. *Program to Multiply Nonzero Data*

```
      PROGRAM NOZERO
C Finds the product of all nonzero data items — stops at first 0.0

C Declarations
      REAL SNTNEL
      PARAMETER (SNTNEL = 0.0)
      REAL ITEM, PRODCT
      PRODCT = 1.0


C Multiply PRODCT by each nonzero data item
      PRINT *, 'Enter first number or 0 to stop:'
      READ *, ITEM
      DO WHILE (ITEM .NE. SNTNEL)              9 IF (...) THEN
         PRODCT = PRODCT * ITEM
         PRINT *, 'Next number or 0:'
         READ *, ITEM
      ENDDO                                      GOTO 9
C                                                ENDIF
C Print result
      PRINT *, 'The product is ', PRODCT
      STOP
      END

Enter first number or 0 to stop:
10
Next number or 0:
12
Next number or 0:
22
Next number or 0:
0
The product is    2640.000
```

> Read first data item
> DO WHILE current data item is not the sentinel value
>   Process current data item
>   Read the next data item
> ENDDO

Remember, proper use of a sentinel value requires that the READ statement appear twice: before the WHILE header (the priming read) and at the end of the loop body (the loop-control variable update).

Program Style

> *Writing WHILE Loops in Programs*
>
> We will continue to use the WHILE loop in programs because it is available in several FORTRAN compilers. However, since the WHILE loop is nonstandard, we will also show the standard FORTRAN implementation of each WHILE loop in the right margin. In Fig. 3.15, the line
>
> ```
>     DO WHILE (ITEM .NE. SNTNEL)                        9 IF (...) THEN
> ```
>
> means that the standard FORTRAN IF structure header has label 9 and the IF condition is the same as the nonstandard WHILE condition shown on the left.

1. What values would be printed if the order of the statements in the loop body of Fig. 3.12 were reversed?
2. Modify the program in Fig. 3.12 to print both the power and its value. For the example shown, the table printed should begin

   ```
   POWER   VALUE
      0       1
      1       2
      2       4
      3       8
   ```

3. What does the following segment do? Rewrite it using a DO loop.

   ```
   VAL = 100
   DO WHILE (VAL .GE. -100)
      VAL = VAL - 5
      PRINT *, VAL
   ENDDO
   ```

4. Write a program that prints the cumulative product of all numbers entered as long as that product is less than a specified maximum. Your procedure should ignore zero data values.
5. Modify the program that computes the value of *e* (see Fig. 3.10) to use a WHILE loop. The new program should continue to add terms until the value of $1/n!$ becomes less than 0.0005. Print the final value of *e*.

3.6 ▬▬ Nested Control Structures

Each section in this chapter describes a FORTRAN control structure. In many programming situations, it will be necessary to nest one control structure inside another. We saw an example of a nested IF structure in Section 2.9; another example follows.

EXAMPLE 3.16   A nested IF structure is shown at the top of Fig. 3.16. As we discussed earlier, we can often avoid nesting decision structures by using a general IF statement instead. The two program fragments in Fig. 3.16 are equivalent.   ■

Figure 3.16. *Nested* IF *Structure (top) and General* IF *Statement (bottom)*

```
IF (GPA .GE. 3.0) THEN
    PRINT *, 'Dean''s list'
ELSE
    IF (GPA .LT. 1.0) THEN
        PRINT *, 'Flunked out'
    ELSE IF (GPA .LT. 2.0) THEN
        PRINT *, 'On probation'
    ENDIF
ENDIF
```

```
IF (GPA .GE. 3.0) THEN
    PRINT *, 'Dean''s list'
ELSE IF (GPA .LT. 1.0) THEN
    PRINT *, 'Flunked out'
ELSE IF (GPA .LT. 2.0) THEN
    PRINT *, 'On probation'
ENDIF
```

EXAMPLE 3.17   The program in Fig. 3.17 contains a logical IF statement nested within a WHILE loop. It finds the product (PRODUC) of all data items that are nonzero. Each data value is read into DATITM and tested; the nonzero values are included in the product being accumulated in PRODUC. The loop is exited after the sentinel value (SNTNEL) is read into DATITM.   ■

Nested DO Loops   The last category of nested structures that we will consider is nested DO loops. Nested DO loops are the most difficult of all nested structures to deal with. For each iteration of the outer loop in a nest, the control structure that is the inner loop is entered and repeated until done.

EXAMPLE 3.18   If we assume that there are always K iterations in the inner loop and the outer loop is repeated M times, then each statement in the inner loop is repeated M × K times. This is shown after Fig. 3.17 for a pair of nested DO loops.

Figure 3.17. *Finding the Product of Nonzero Data Items*

```
        PROGRAM NONZER
C Finds product of nonzero data

C Declarations
        REAL SNTNEL
        PARAMETER (SNTNEL = -1000.0)
        REAL PRODUC, DATITM

C Initialize product and read first data value
        PRODUC = 1.0
        PRINT *, 'Enter next data item:'
        READ *, DATITM

C Multiply only nonzero data values
        DO WHILE (DATITM .NE. SNTNEL)                 9 IF (...) THEN
          IF (DATITM .NE. 0.0) PRODUC = PRODUC * DATITM
          PRINT *, 'Enter next data item:'
          READ *, DATITM
        ENDDO                                           GOTO 9
C                                                       ENDIF
C Print the result
        PRINT *, 'The product of nonzero data is ', PRODUC
        STOP
        END


Enter next data item:
3.0
Enter next data item:
0.0
Enter next data item:
-1.0
Enter next data item:
-1000.0
The product of nonzero data is    -3.000000
```

```
        PRINT *, 'LOOP              I              J'
        DO 10 I = 1, M
          PRINT *, 'OUTER ', I        ← repeated M times
          DO 20 J = 1, K
            PRINT *, 'INNER ', I, J ← repeated M × K times
20        CONTINUE
10      CONTINUE
```

Note that the inner loop and the outer loop must have different loop control variables and labels. Also, the inner-loop terminator must always come before the outer-loop terminator (i.e., 20 CONTINUE must precede 10 CONTINUE). If M is 3 and K is 2, the output is shown next. ∎

```
LOOP          I          J
OUTER         1
INNER         1          1
INNER         1          2
OUTER         2
INNER         2          1
INNER         2          2
OUTER         3
INNER         3          1
INNER         3          2
```

SELF-CHECK EXERCISE FOR SECTION 3.6

1. What is displayed by the following program segments assuming N is 5?

a.
```
      DO 10 I = 1, N
          DO 20 J = 1, I
              PRINT *, I, J
   20     CONTINUE
          PRINT *
   10 CONTINUE
```

b.
```
      DO 10 I = 1, N
          DO 20 J = N, I, -1
              PRINT *, I, J
   20     CONTINUE
          PRINT *
   10 CONTINUE
```

c.
```
      DO 10 I = 1, N
          PRINT *, 'I = ', I
          DO 20 J = I, 0, -1
              PRINT *, I + J
   20     CONTINUE
   10 CONTINUE
```

3.7 ▬▬▬ Problem Solving Illustrated

In this section, we will examine two programming problems that illustrate most of the concepts discussed in this chapter. Each problem contains a general IF statement and a WHILE loop.

The *top-down design* process will be demonstrated in solving these problems. The program will be implemented in a stepwise manner, starting with a list of major algorithm steps and continuing to add detail through refinement until the program can be written.

Case Study: Balancing a Checkbook

Problem

You have just received a new home computer and would like to write a program to help balance your checkbook. The program will read your initial checkbook balance and each transaction (check or deposit). It will print the new balance after each transaction and a warning message if the check amount exceeds the balance and is returned for insufficient funds. A penalty of $20 will be assessed for each check that is returned. At the end of the session, the starting and final balances should be printed along with a count of the number of checks and deposits processed and the number of checks returned.

Design Overview

After the starting balance is read, each transaction will be read and processed separately. We can use a simple code ('C' or 'D') to distinguish between checks and deposits. The transaction amount will be a real number. The starting balance must be available at the end, so we will save it in variable STBAL and use a different variable (CURBAL) to keep track of the current balance.

Data Requirements

Problem Parameter

penalty for returned check (PENLTY = 20.00)

Problem Inputs

starting checkbook balance (REAL STBAL)
transaction data
   type of transaction (CHARACTER *1 TYPE)
   amount of transaction (REAL AMOUNT)

Problem Outputs

current balance after each transaction (REAL CURBAL)
number of checks (INTEGER NUMCHK)
number of deposits (INTEGER NUMDEP)
number of returned checks (INTEGER NUMRET)

Initial Algorithm

1. Display the instructions and read the starting balance.
2. For each transaction: read the transaction, update and print the current balance, and increment the count of checks, deposits, or returned checks.

Case Study: Balancing a Checkbook, continued

3. Print the starting and final balances, and the number of checks, deposits, and returned checks.

Algorithm Refinements

Step 2 of the algorithm needs further refinement. All program outputs should be initialized before any transactions are processed. The three output variables beginning with NUM (NUMCHK, NUMDEP, and NUMRET) are used as *counters* and should be initialized to 0 (e.g., there are 0 checks to begin with). The initial value of CURBAL should be the same as STBAL. The refinement of step 2 is listed below.

Step 2 Refinement

2.1 Set counters to 0 and current balance to starting balance.
2.2 Read the first transaction type.
2.3 DO WHILE there are more transactions
    2.4 Read the transaction amount.
    2.5 Update current balance and increment the appropriate counter.
    2.6 Read the next transaction type.
  ENDDO

Step 2.5 is a multiple-alternative decision structure as shown below.

Refinement of Step 2.5

2.5.1 IF transaction is a deposit THEN
    Increment NUMDEP
    Add AMOUNT to CURBAL and print new balance
  ELSE IF transaction is not a check THEN
    Print an "illegal transaction" message
  ELSE IF current balance $\geq$ check amount THEN
    Increment NUMCHK
    Subtract AMOUNT from CURBAL and print new balance
  ELSE
    Increment NUMRET
    Deduct PENLTY from CURBAL and print new balance
    Print an "Insufficient funds" message
  ENDIF

Coding

Figure 3.18 shows the program. The third executable statement

```
PRINT *, 'Enter ''C'' (Check), ''D'' (Deposit), or ''Q'' (Quit)'
```

Case Study: Balancing a Checkbook, continued

Figure 3.18. *The Checkbook-Balancing Program*

```
      PROGRAM CHECKS
C Processes each transaction. Reads each transaction, updates and
C prints the current balance, and increments the count of checks,
C deposits, or returned checks.

C Declarations
      REAL PENLTY
      CHARACTER *1 SENVAL
      PARAMETER (SENVAL = 'Q', PENLTY = 20.00)
      REAL STBAL, CURBAL, AMOUNT
      INTEGER NUMCHK, NUMDEP, NUMRET
      CHARACTER *1 TYPE

C Print instructions
      PRINT *, 'Balance your checking account!'
      PRINT *
      PRINT *, 'Enter ''C'' (Check), ''D'' (Deposit), or ''Q'' (Quit)'
      PRINT *, 'after prompt ''C'', ''D'', or ''Q'':'
      PRINT *
      PRINT *, 'Enter a positive number after prompt AMOUNT'
      PRINT *

C Read starting balance
      PRINT *, 'Begin by entering a starting balance:'
      READ *, STBAL

C Initialize counters to zero and CURBAL to STBAL
      NUMCHK = 0
      NUMDEP = 0
      NUMRET = 0
      CURBAL = STBAL

C Read the first transaction TYPE
      PRINT *
      PRINT *, '''C'', ''D'', or ''Q'':'
      READ *, TYPE
C Process each transaction until done
      DO WHILE (TYPE .NE. SENVAL)                    9 IF (...) THEN
C         Read the transaction amount
          PRINT *, 'AMOUNT:'
          READ *, AMOUNT

C         Process the transaction
          IF (TYPE .EQ. 'D') THEN
              CURBAL = CURBAL + AMOUNT
              NUMDEP = NUMDEP + 1
```

Case Study: Balancing a Checkbook, continued

```
               PRINT *, 'Depositing $', AMOUNT, ' Balance of $', CURBAL
            ELSE IF (TYPE .NE. 'C') THEN
               PRINT *, 'Invalid transaction type ', TYPE,
     +                   ' - transaction ignored.'
            ELSE IF (CURBAL .GE. AMOUNT) THEN
               CURBAL = CURBAL - AMOUNT
               NUMCHK = NUMCHK + 1
               PRINT *, 'Check for $', AMOUNT, '      Balance of $', CURBAL
            ELSE
               CURBAL = CURBAL - PENLTY
               NUMRET = NUMRET + 1
               PRINT *, 'Check returned for insufficient funds.'
               PRINT *, 'Service charge of $', PENLTY, ' deducted.'
               PRINT *, 'Check for $', AMOUNT, '      Balance of $', CURBAL
            ENDIF

C        Read the next transaction TYPE
         PRINT *
         PRINT *, '''C'', ''D'', or ''Q'':'
         READ *, TYPE
      ENDDO                                            GOTO 9
C                                                      ENDIF
C Print summary
      PRINT *
      PRINT *, 'Starting balance was $', STBAL
      PRINT *, 'Final    balance is  $', CURBAL
      PRINT *, 'Number of checks paid: ', NUMCHK
      PRINT *, 'Number of deposits made: ', NUMDEP
      PRINT *, 'Number of checks returned: ', NUMRET

      STOP
      END
```

uses two consecutive apostrophes to denote a single apostrophe in a string. This point is discussed further in Section 4.6.

Testing

Figure 3.19 shows a sample run of the checkbook-balancing program. When you test this program, make sure you provide invalid as well as valid transaction types. Also make sure that invalid transaction types are not counted as either checks or deposits and that the amount associated with an invalid transaction type is ignored.

Case Study: Balancing a Checkbook, continued

Figure 3.19. *Sample Run of Check-book-Balancing Program*

```
Balance your checking account!

Enter 'C' (Check), 'D' (Deposit), or 'Q' (Quit)
after prompt 'C', 'D', or 'Q':

Enter a positive number after prompt AMOUNT

Begin by entering a starting balance:
1000.00

'C', 'D', or 'Q':
'D'
AMOUNT:
100.00
Depositing $    100.0000     Balance of $    1100.000

'C', 'D', or 'Q':
'C'
AMOUNT:
200.00
Check for $     200.0000     Balance of $   900.0000

'C', 'D', or 'Q':
'C'
AMOUNT:
1200.00
Check returned for insufficient funds.
Service charge of $   20.00000    deducted.
Check for $    1200.000     Balance of $   880.0000

'C', 'D', or 'Q':
'X'
AMOUNT
500.00
Invalid transaction type X — transaction ignored.

'C', 'D', or 'Q':
'Q'

Starting balance was $   1000.000
Final    balance  is $   880.0000
Number of checks paid:           1
Number of deposits made:          1
Number of checks returned:         1
```

Program Style

Case Study: Computing Radiation Levels

Problem

In a certain building at a top secret research lab, some Yttrium-90 has leaked into the computer programmers' coffee room. It would currently expose personnel to 150 millirems of radiation a day. The half-life of the substance is about three days, which means that the radiation level is only half of what it was three days previously. The programmers want to know how long it will be before the radiation is down to a safe level of 0.466 millirem a day so they can get back to their "hot" coffee. They would like a chart that displays the radiation level for every three days with a message UNSAFE or SAFE after every line. The chart should stop just before the radiation level is one-tenth of the safe level, because the more cautious programmers will require a safety factor of 10.

Design Overview

The chart can be printed by a WHILE loop whose loop-control variable is the current radiation level. Since the radiation level is cut in half every three days, we can use the formulas

> *day = day + 3*
> *radiation level = radiation level / 2.0*

inside the loop. The data requirements and algorithm follow.

Data Requirements

Program Parameters

the safe radiation level in millirems (REAL SAFRAD = 0.466)
the safety factor (REAL SAFFAC = 10.0)

Case Study: Computing Radiation Levels, continued

Problem Outputs

the day number (INTEGER DAY)
the radiation level in millirems (INTEGER RADLEV)

Initial Algorithm

1. Initialize DAY to zero and read the initial radiation level into RADLEV.
2. Compute and display the day number and the radiation level every three days that the radiation level exceeds the safe level divided by the safety factor. Also, indicate whether each level is safe or unsafe.

Algorithm Refinements

We will use a WHILE loop to implement step 2. For reasons of efficiency that will be discussed after the program, we will introduce a new variable to hold the stopping level of radiation, which is the safe level divided by the safety factor.

Additional Program Variable

the stopping level of radiation (REAL RADMIN)

Step 2 Refinements

2.1 Compute RADMIN.
2.2 DO WHILE RADLEV exceeds RADMIN
      2.3 Display the value of DAY, RADLEV, and the string
          'UNSAFE' or 'SAFE'.
      2.4 Add 3 to the value of DAY.
      2.5 Compute RADLEV for the next period.
   ENDDO

The refinement of step 2.3 is the decision step below.

Step 2.3 Refinement

2.3.1 IF RADLEV exceeds SAFRAD THEN
      Display DAY, RADLEV, and 'UNSAFE'.
   ELSE
      Display DAY, RADLEV, and 'SAFE'.
   ENDIF

Coding

The program appears in Fig. 3.20.

Case Study: Computing Radiation Levels, continued

Figure 3.20. *Computing Radiation Levels*

```
      PROGRAM NUKE
C Calculates safe zone of a coffee room

C Type declarations
      REAL SAFRAD, SAFFAC
      PARAMETER (SAFRAD = 0.466, SAFFAC = 10.0)
      INTEGER DAY
      REAL RADLEV, RADMIN

C Initialize DAY and RADLEV
      DAY = 0
      PRINT *, 'Enter the radiation level (in millirems)'
      READ *, RADLEV

C Display table
      RADMIN = SAFRAD / SAFFAC
      PRINT *,'         Day  Radiation      Status'
      PRINT *,'              (millirems)'
      DO WHILE (RADLEV .GT. RADMIN)
         IF (RADLEV .GT. SAFRAD) THEN
            PRINT *, DAY, RADLEV, '         UNSAFE'
         ELSE
            PRINT *, DAY, RADLEV, '         SAFE'
         ENDIF
         DAY = DAY + 3
         RADLEV = RADLEV / 2.0
      ENDDO

C Exit program
      STOP
      END

Enter the radiation level (in millirems)
150.0

        Day  Radiation      Status
             (millirems)
          0   150.0000       UNSAFE
          3   75.00000       UNSAFE
          6   37.50000       UNSAFE
          9   18.75000       UNSAFE
         12   9.375000       UNSAFE
         15   4.687500       UNSAFE
         18   2.343750       UNSAFE
         21   1.171875       UNSAFE
         24   0.5859375      UNSAFE
         27   0.2929688      SAFE
         30   0.1464844      SAFE
         33   7.3242188E-02    SAFE
```

Case Study: Computing Radiation Levels, continued

Testing

The only data item for this program is the initial radiation level of 150 millirems, so one run should suffice. Check that each radiation value is one-half the previous value and that the number of days always increases by 3. Also, check that the first safe value is less than 0.466 millirem. If you divide the last radiation value displayed by 2.0, you must get a value that is less than or equal to 0.0466 (0.466 / 10.0 is 0.0466).

Program Style

Removing Redundant Computations from Loops

In Fig. 3.20, we introduce an additional program variable, RADMIN, and use the assignment statement below to define RADMIN prior to loop entry.

```
RADMIN = SAFRAD / SAFFAC
DO WHILE (RADLEV .GT. RADMIN)
```

Instead, we could combine these two statements, as follows.

```
DO WHILE (RADLEV .GT. (SAFRAD / SAFFAC))
```

The loop header above is less efficient because it recomputes the quotient SAFRAD / SAFFAC each time the loop is repeated. Because both variables involved in the computation are parameters and thus the value of the quotient cannot change, it makes no sense to recompute it. You should look for redundant computations like this and remove them from a loop. Some FORTRAN compilers will *optimize* a program by removing redundant computations for you.

SELF-CHECK EXERCISES FOR SECTION 3.7

1. Replace the general IF statement in Fig. 3.18 with a nested IF structure that implements the decision table below.

Transaction Type	Action
'D'	Add AMOUNT to balance and increment NUMCHK.
'C'	Subtract AMOUNT from balance.
	Increment NUMCHK.
	Print a message if balance becomes negative.
Anything else	Print an illegal transaction message.

2. Discuss how to modify the check-balancing program to send a record of each transaction to an output file as well as to the display screen.
3. How would you get the program in Fig. 3.20 to stop the table display *after* the radiation level becomes less than or equal to the safe level of radiation divided by the safety factor, instead of before?

3.8 ▬▬▬▬ Debugging and Testing Programs

In Section 1.11, we described the general categories of error messages that you are likely to see: syntax errors and run-time errors. It is also possible for a program to execute without generating any error messages, but still produce incorrect results. Sometimes the cause of a run-time error or the origin of incorrect results is apparent and the error can easily be fixed. However, very often the error is not obvious and may require considerable effort to locate.

The best approach to debugging is to prevent errors from occurring in the first place (called *antibugging*). If you carefully desk check the refined algorithm using one or more data samples, you may be able to determine that a logic error exists (and correct it) before you implement the incorrect algorithm as a buggy program.

The first step in debugging is to determine what part of the program is generating incorrect results. If the final answer does not match your hand-computed result, this may be due to an earlier partial result that was also incorrect. Check all prior displayed values to determine where the first error occurred. If no partial results are displayed, then add extra *diagnostic* PRINT *statements* to display partial results. If one partial result is correct, but the next one is incorrect, the statements that lie between these two diagnostic PRINT statements must contain the source of the error. Once you have located the buggy section of the program, you should zero in on the computations performed in that section.

As an example of this process, refer to the program in Fig. 3.5, which computes the average value (AVERGE) of a set of measurements whose sum is accumulated in SUM. If the value of AVERGE displayed in Fig. 3.5 is incorrect, you will want to insert a diagnostic PRINT statement that displays the value of SUM. If SUM is correct, the assignment statement used to compute AVERGE from SUM must be wrong. However, if SUM is also incorrect, focus on the DO loop used to compute SUM. To trace the execution of the DO loop, insert the diagnostic PRINT statement shown below as the last statement in the loop body.

```
      DO 10 COUNT = 1, NUMMES
         PRINT *, 'Enter next value (in ', UNITS, ')'
         READ *, ITEM
         SUM = SUM + ITEM
         PRINT *, '****** COUNT = ', COUNT, ' ITEM = ', ITEM,
     +              ' SUM = ', SUM
      10 CONTINUE
```

Each time the loop executes, this diagnostic PRINT statement displays the current values of COUNT and ITEM and each partial sum that is accumulated. The PRINT statement displays a string of asterisks at the beginning of its output line. This makes it easier to identify diagnostic output in the debugging runs and to locate the diagnostic PRINT statements in the source program.

Once it appears that you have located the error, you will want to take out the extra diagnostic statements. As a temporary measure, it is sometimes advisable to turn these diagnostic statements into comments by placing a c (or an *) in column 1. If errors crop up again in later testing, it is easier to remove the c (or *) than to retype the diagnostic statements.

Using Debugger Programs

Many computer systems have *debugger programs* to help you debug a program. A debugger program lets you execute your program one statement at a time so you can see the effect of each statement. You can also instruct the debugger program to display the values of selected variables after each statement executes, so you can trace those variables. If you don't want your program to pause after every statement, you can set *breakpoints* at certain key statements. Then you can instruct the debugger to execute all statements from the current statement to the next breakpoint.

Testing a Program

After all errors have been corrected and the program appears to execute as expected, the program should be tested thoroughly to make sure that it works. In Section 2.7, we discussed tracing an algorithm and suggested that enough sets of test data be provided to ensure that all possible paths are traced. The same is true for the completed program. Make enough test runs to verify that the program works properly for representative samples of all possible data combinations. Always investigate how your program reacts to zero and negative numbers entered as data.

3.9 ▬▬▬ Common Programming Errors

Students sometimes confuse decision steps with conditional loops because the header statement for both structures contains a condition. Make sure that you use an IF statement to implement a decision step and a WHILE loop for a conditional loop.

The first words in the header statement of a control structure (IF, DO, or DO WHILE) indicates the type of the control structure. The corresponding structure terminator (ENDIF, CONTINUE, or ENDDO) should be used to mark the end of the control structure.

The syntax of the DO loop header is repeated below.

DO *label lcv = initial, limit, step*

Remember to use an integer of five digits or less as a label between the keyword DO and the variable *lcv*. This same integer must be placed in the label field (columns 1 through 5) of the loop terminator (CONTINUE) statement.

A comma is required as a separator between the *initial* and the *limit* parameters. If this comma is omitted, FORTRAN will attempt to translate the DO loop header as an assignment statement. For example, DO 10 I = 1 5 assigns the value 15 to the variable DO10I. The reason for this is that FORTRAN ignores spaces after column 7 (except in strings), so the characters to the left and to the right of the equal sign are treated as a variable (DO10I) and an integer (15), respectively.

Another common mistake is placing the last digit of the label for a CONTINUE statement in column 6 instead of column 5. Since the last digit appears in the continuation column (column 6), FORTRAN will not include it as part of the label. This may cause a missing-label syntax error.

Finally, be careful not to mistype the letter O as the digit 0 (or vice versa). For example, ending the reserved word DO with a zero will lead to syntax errors. Similarly, mistyping a "zero" in a label as an "oh" may cause a missing-label syntax error.

Missing terminator statements can be detected easily by the FORTRAN compiler, which will print a diagnostic message indicating that the terminator is missing. When control structures are nested, the terminator for the innermost structure must come first. If the terminator statements are in the wrong order, the structures will *overlap* and the compiler will not be able to translate these structures (see Fig. 3.21). The compiler will print a diagnostic message indicating that the structures overlap or are terminated improperly.

Figure 3.21. *Overlapping Structures*

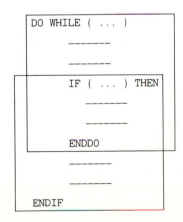

Be very careful when using tests for inequality to control the repetition of a WHILE loop. The loop below is intended to process all transactions for a bank account while the balance is positive.

```
DO WHILE (BALANC .NE. 0.0)
    .
    .
    .
ENDDO
```

If the bank balance goes from a positive to a negative amount without being exactly 0.0, the loop will not terminate. The loop below would be safer.

```
DO WHILE (BALANC .GT. 0.0)
    .
    .
    .
ENDDO
```

You should verify that the repetition condition for a WHILE loop will eventually become false; otherwise, an *infinite loop* (nonterminating loop) may result. If a sentinel value is used to control loop repetition, make sure that the program user is told what value to enter to stop loop repetition.

Chapter Review

This chapter described how to repeat steps in a program. You learned how to implement counting loops using DO statements. A counting loop with the header

> DO *label counter* = 1, N

performs N iterations. You also learned how to use the general DO statement. A DO loop with the header

> DO *label lcv = initial, limit, step*

executes for values of *lcv* equal to *initial, initial + step, initial + 2 ∗ step*, and so on, until the value of *lcv* passes *limit*.

A conditional looping structure, the WHILE loop, is used to implement loops whose repetition is controlled by a condition. The WHILE loop is useful when the exact number of repetitions required is not known before the loop begins. Separate FORTRAN statements are needed for initializing, updating, and testing the value of the loop-control variable associated with a WHILE loop.

One common technique for controlling the repetition of a WHILE loop involves using a special sentinel value to indicate that all required data have been processed. In this case, the loop-control variable is a problem input. Its initial value (the first data value) is read prior to loop entry; its value is updated at the end of the loop when the next data value is read. Loop repetition terminates after the sentinel value is read into the loop-control variable.

New FORTRAN Statements

The new FORTRAN statements introduced in this chapter are described in Table 3.4.

Table 3.4. *Summary of New FORTRAN Statements*

STATEMENT	EFFECT
Counting Loop	
```DO 10 NUM = 1, 25 PRINT *, NUM, NUM ** 2 10 CONTINUE```	Prints 25 lines, each containing an integer from 1 to 25 and its square.
General DO Loop	
```DO 30 VOLTS = 20, −20, −10 CURENT = VOLTS / RESIST PRINT *, VOLTS, CURENT 30 CONTINUE```	For values of VOLTS equal to 20, 10, 0, −10, −20, computes the value of CURENT and displays VOLTS and CURENT.
Nonstandard WHILE Loop	
```SUM = 0.0 PRINT *, 'Enter first number' READ *, NEXT DO WHILE (NEXT .NE. SENVAL) SUM = SUM + NEXT PRINT *, 'Next number' READ *, NEXT ENDDO```	Accumulates the sum (SUM) of a group of numbers entered as data. The sum is complete when the sentinel value (SENVAL) is read into NEXT.
WHILE Loop in Standard FORTRAN	
```SUM = 0.0 PRINT *, 'Enter first number' READ *, NEXT 9 IF (NEXT .NE. SENVAL) THEN SUM = SUM + NEXT PRINT *, 'Next number' READ *, NEXT GOTO 9 ENDIF```	See WHILE loop, above.

Quick-Check Exercises

1. A _____ loop is used to implement a counting loop.
2. A _____ loop is called a conditional loop.
3. A sentinel value is used to terminate the execution of a _____ loop.
4. If we change the *limit* parameter of a DO loop during loop execution, we can change the number of iterations performed. True or false?
5. The *lcv* for a DO loop can decrease in value. True or false?
6. The priming step for a sentinel-controlled loop is what kind of statement? Where must this statement appear in the program?
7. The sentinel value is the last value added to a sum being accumulated in a sentinel-controlled loop. True or false?
8. For the loop headers below, how many times will each loop execute? What will be the value of I after loop exit?
   a. DO 10 I = 1, 15
   b. DO 20 I = -10, 5, 10
   c. DO WHILE (I .LE. 10)
9. What does the following program segment display? What can you say about X after loop exit?

   ```
   PRODUC = 1
   READ *, X
   DO WHILE (X .GT. 0)
       PRODUC = PRODUC * X
       READ *, X
   ENDDO
   PRINT *, PRODUC
   ```

10. How many times does the PRINT statement below execute? What are the output lines?

    ```
        DO 10 I = 1, 3
           DO 20 J = I, 2
              PRINT *, I, J
    20     CONTINUE
    10 CONTINUE
    ```

11. How many times does the PRINT statement below execute? What are the output lines?

    ```
        DO 10 I = 1, 2
           DO 20 J = I, 3
              PRINT *, I, J
    20     CONTINUE
    10 CONTINUE
    ```

Answers to Quick-Check Exercises

1. DO
2. WHILE

3. WHILE
4. false
5. true
6. A READ statement. It appears twice, just before the loop and at the end of the loop body.
7. False. The sentinel should not be processed with the normal data.
8. a. fifteen; 16
   b. five; 15
   c. unknown; I is greater than 10
9. It displays the product of an initial sequence of positive data values. X is less than or equal to zero after loop exit.
10. three times
    ```
    1   1
    1   2
    2   2
    ```
11. five times
    ```
    1   1
    1   2
    1   3
    2   2
    2   3
    ```

Review Questions

1. Explain the difference between the two control structures below.

```
IF (X .GT. 0.0) THEN
    X = X - 2.0
    PRINT *, X
ENDIF

DO WHILE (X .GT. 0.0)
    X = X - 2.0
    PRINT *, X
ENDDO
```

2. For question 1, indicate what would be printed by each control structure for the following values of X: 8.0, 7.0, 0.0, -7.0, -8.0.
3. Which control structure (IF, DO, or WHILE) would you use for the following situations?
   a. Print a message indicating whether or not a person is old enough to vote.
   b. Compute the gross pay for five employees.
   c. Select one of five tax rates to use for a particular employee based on gross pay.
   d. Count the number of zeros in a data collection of unknown size.
   e. Find the product of all odd integers from 1 through 99.
   f. Determine the letter grade corresponding to a particular exam score.

g. Keep dividing a data value in half until it is smaller than 0.5 and print all quotients.

4. Provide sample control structures for each situation in question 3. Don't bother to declare or initialize variables.

5. Explain the difference between a WHILE loop and a DO loop.

6. Define a sentinel value.

7. For a sentinel value to be used properly when reading in data, where should the READ statements appear?

8. Write a WHILE loop to sum a collection of payroll amounts entered at the keyboard until a sentinel value of –1.0 is entered.

9. Hand trace the program below given the following data:

4.0	2.0	8.0	4.0
9.0	3.0	3.0	1.0
0.0	0.0	0.0	0.0

```
PROGRAM ENTER4
REAL SENVAL, SLOPE, Y2, Y1, X2, X1
PARAMETER (SENVAL = 0.0)
PRINT *, 'Enter four real numbers:'
READ *, Y2, Y1, X2, X1
SLOPE = (Y2 - Y1) / (X2 - X1)
DO WHILE (SLOPE .NE. SENVAL)
    PRINT *, 'Slope is ', SLOPE
    PRINT *
    PRINT *, 'Enter four real numbers:'
    READ *, Y2, Y1, X2, X1
    SLOPE = (Y2 - Y1) / (X2 - X1)
ENDDO
STOP
END
```

10. What is printed by the following program fragment for the data values 3, 5, 1, 2, 0, –1, –2, 0?

```
READ *, X
DO WHILE (X .GE. 0)
    IF (X .GE. 3) THEN
        PRINT *, 'GOOD'
    ELSE IF (X .GE. 2) THEN
        PRINT *, 'FAIR'
    ELSE
        PRINT *, 'POOR'
    ENDIF
    READ *, X
ENDDO
```

11. Explain the effect of deleting the second READ statement in question 10.

Programming Projects

1. Write a program that will find the product of a collection of data values. Your program should terminate when a zero value is read.

2. Write a program to read in an integer N and compute

$$\text{SLOW} = \sum_{i=1}^{N} i = 1 + 2 + 3 + \ldots + N$$

(the sum of all integers from 1 to N). Then compute

$$\text{FAST} = (N \times (N + 1)) / 2$$

and compare FAST and SLOW. Your program should print both FAST and SLOW and indicate whether or not they are equal. (You will need a loop to compute SLOW.) Which computation method is preferable?

3. Write a program to read a list of integer data items and find and print the index of the first occurrence and the last occurrence of the number 12. Your program should print index values of 0 if the number 12 is not found. The index is the sequence number of the data item 12. For example, if the eighth data item is the only 12, then the index value 8 should be printed for the first and last occurrences.

4. Write a program to read in a collection of exam scores ranging in value from 1 to 100. Your program should count and print the number of outstanding scores (90–100), the number of satisfactory scores (60–89), and the number of unsatisfactory scores (1–59). Test your program on the following data:

63	75	72	72	78	67	80	63	75
90	89	43	59	99	82	12	100	

In addition, print each exam score and its category.

5. Write a program to process weekly employee time cards for all employees of an organization. Each employee will have three data items: an identification number, the hourly wage rate, and the number of hours worked during a given week. Each employee is to be paid time-and-a-half for all hours worked over 40. A tax amount of 3.625 percent of gross salary will be deducted. The program output should show the employee's number and net pay.

6. Suppose you own a beer distributorship that sells Piels (ID number 1), Coors (ID number 2), Bud (ID number 3), and Iron City (ID number 4) by the case. Write a program to (a) read in the case inventory for each brand for the start of the week; (b) process all weekly sales and purchase records for each brand; and (c) print out the final inventory. Each transaction will consist of two data items. The first item will be the brand identification number (an integer). The second will be the amount purchased (a positive integer value) or the amount sold (a negative integer value). The weekly inventory for each brand (for the start of the week) will

also consist of two items: the identification and initial inventory for that brand. For now, you may assume that you always have foresight to prevent depletion of your inventory for any brand. (*Hint:* Your data entry should begin with eight values representing the case inventory. These should be followed by the transaction values.)

7. Write a program to find the largest, smallest, and average values in a collection of N numbers, where the value of N will be the first data item read.

8. a. Write a program to process a collection of savings account transactions (deposits or withdrawals). Your program should begin by reading in the previous account balance and then read and process each transaction. Enter a positive value for a deposit and a negative value for a withdrawal. For each transaction, print the message 'Withdrawal' or 'Deposit' and the new balance. Print an error message if a withdrawal would result in a negative balance and do not change the balance.

   b. Compute and print the number of deposits, the number of withdrawals, the number of invalid withdrawals, and the total dollar amount for each type of transaction.

9. a. Write a program that computes and prints the fractional powers of two (1/2, 1/4, 1/8, etc.). The program should also print the decimal value of each fraction as shown below:

Power	Fraction	Decimal Value
1	1/2	0.5
2	1/4	0.25
3	1/8	0.125

   Print all values through power equal to 10.

   b. Add an extra output column that shows the sum of all decimal values so far. The first three sums are 0.5, 0.75, 0.875.

10. a. The trustees of a small college are considering voting a pay raise for the twelve faculty. They want to grant a 5.5% pay raise; however, before doing so, they want to know how much this will cost. Write a program that will print the pay raise for each faculty member and the total amount of the raises. Also, print the total faculty payroll before and after the raise. Test your program for these salaries:

$22500	$24029.50	$26000	$23250
$25500	$22800	$30000.50	$28900
$23780	$27300	$24120.25	$24100

   b. Redo the program assuming that faculty members earning less than $24000 receive a 4% raise, faculty earning more than $26500 receive a 7% raise, and all others receive a 5.5% raise. For each faculty member, print the raise percentage as well as the amount.

11. The assessor in your town has estimated the market value of all fourteen properties and would like a program that determines the tax owed on each property and the total tax to be collected. The tax rate is 125 mils per dollar of assessed value. (A mil is 0.1 cent.) The assessed value of each property is 28% of its estimated market value. The market values are:

    $150000 $148000 $145500 $167000 $137600 $147100 $165000
    $153350 $128000 $158000 $152250 $148000 $156500 $143700

12. Patients required to take many kinds of medication often have difficulty in remembering when to take their medicine. Given the following set of medications, write a program that prints an hourly table indicating what medication to take at any given hour. Use a counter variable CLOCK to go through a 24-hour day. Print the table based upon the following prescriptions:

Medication	Frequency
Iron pill	0800, 1200, 1800
Antibiotic	Every 4 hours starting at 0400
Vitamin	0800, 2100
Calcium	1100, 2000

13. The square root of a number N can be approximated by repeated calculation using the formula

    $NG = .5(LG + N / LG)$

    where NG stands for next guess and LG stands for last guess. Write a program that calculates the square root of a number using this method.

    The initial guess will be the starting value of LG. The program will compute a value for NG using the formula above. The difference between NG and LG is checked to see whether these two guesses are almost identical. If so, NG is the square root; otherwise, the new guess (NG) becomes the last guess (LG) and the process is repeated (another value is computed for NG, the difference is checked, etc.).

    For this program, the loop should be repeated until the difference is less than 0.005 (DELTA). Use an initial guess of 1.0 and test the program for the numbers 4, 120.5, 88, 36.01, 10000.

M14. The function $sin^2 X$ can be determined by the following series equation:

$$sin^2 X = X^2 - \frac{2^3 X^4}{4!} + \frac{2^5 X^6}{6!} + \ldots = \sum_{n=1}^{\infty} \frac{(-1)^{n+1} 2^{2n-1} X^{2n}}{(2n)!}$$

Write a program that will read in a value for X and calculate the value of $sin^2 X$ using the formula above. Continue the calculation until n reaches 100. Note that the first term is X^2 and each subsequent term is the previous term multiplied by

$$\frac{-(2X)^2}{2n(2n - 1)}$$

M15. The value for π can be determined by the series equation:

$$\pi = 4 * (1 - 1/3 + 1/5 - 1/7 + 1/9 - 1/11 + 1/13 - ...)$$

Write a program to calculate the value of π using the formula above until the term 1/99 is reached.

16. Write a program to create a table showing the underwater pressure (in pounds per square inch) from 1 foot to 30 feet. Water weighs 62.4 pounds per cubic foot, which means that a column 1 foot high and 1 inch square will weigh 0.433 pound. Have it look something like the following:

Underwater	Pressure Table
Depth	Pressure
(ft.)	(p.s.i.)
1	0.4333333
2	0.8666667
3	1.300000
.	.
.	.
.	.
29	12.56667
30	13.00000

17. Bunyan Lumber Co. needs to create a table of the engineering properties of its lumber. The dimensions of the wood are given as base and height in inches. Engineers need to know the following information about lumber:

- cross-sectional area (*base* ∗ *height*)
- moment of inertia [(*base* × *height*³)/12]
- section modulus [(*base* × *height*²)/6]

The owner, Paul, makes lumber with base sizes 2, 4, 6, 8, 10, and 12 inches. The height sizes are also 2, 4, 6, 8, and 10 inches. Produce a table to show these values. Use a nested DO loop to create it. In the chart, do not duplicate a 2-by-6 with a 6-by-2 board. Have it look like the following:

Bunyan Lumber Company
882 Blue Ox Drive
Engineering Properties of Our Lumber

Base (in.)	Height (in.)	Area (sq. in.)	Moment of Inertia (in. 4)	Section Modulus (in. 3)
2	2	4.000000	1.333333	1.333333
2	4	8.000000	10.66667	5.333333
2	6	12.00000	36.00000	12.00000
2	8	16.00000	85.33334	21.33333
2	10	20.00000	166.6667	33.33333
2	12	24.00000	288.0000	48.00000

Base (in.)	Height (in.)	Area (sq. in.)	Moment of Inertia (in. 4)	Section Modulus (in. 3)
4	4	16.00000	21.33333	10.66667
4	6	24.00000	72.00000	24.00000
4	8	32.00000	170.6667	42.66667
4	10	40.00000	333.3333	66.66666
4	12	48.00000	576.0000	96.00000
6	6	36.00000	108.0000	36.00000
6	8	48.00000	256.0000	64.00000
6	10	60.00000	500.0000	100.0000
6	12	72.00000	864.0000	144.0000
8	8	64.00000	341.3333	85.33334
8	10	80.00000	666.6667	133.3333
8	12	96.00000	1152.000	192.0000
10	10	100.0000	833.3333	166.6667
10	12	120.0000	1440.000	240.0000
12	12	144.0000	1728.000	288.0000

4. Simple Data Types

So FAR, we have used four data types: INTEGER, REAL, CHARACTER, and LOGICAL (conditions in IF and WHILE structures). In this chapter, we take a closer look at these data types and introduce new operators and operations that can be performed on them. We describe the library functions of FORTRAN and demonstrate how they are used to simplify computations.

In addition, we review input/output operations and learn how to use FORMAT statements to gain more control over the appearance of program output.

4.1 ▬ Declaring a Data Type

In Chapter 1, we introduced the general form of the type declaration statement as

> *type variable-list*

where *type* may be any of the keywords REAL, INTEGER, LOGICAL, or CHARACTER *∗n*. A type declaration statement specifies the data type of each variable in its *variable-list*. Only a value of the correct type may be stored in a variable, as described in Table 4.1.

Table 4.1. *Data Types and Values*

VARIABLE TYPE	VALID VALUES
INTEGER	15, −34567, 0
REAL	3.0, −15.567, 1.234E−5, 3.98E6
CHARACTER	'ABCDE', 'Joe''s hat', 'Alice', '1234'
LOGICAL	.TRUE., .FALSE.

The last two values listed for type REAL are real numbers in FORTRAN scientific notation. A number in FORTRAN scientific notation has the form

> $mantissa \mathrm{E}^{exponent}$

where the *mantissa* may be an integer or real number and the *exponent* must be an integer. Both the *mantissa* and the *exponent* may be signed numbers. If the sign is missing, it is assumed to be +.

FORTRAN scientific notation is like normal scientific notation except that it is written on a single line. Consequently, the value of a number written in FORTRAN scientific notation is

> $mantissa \times 10^{exponent}$

Those of you familiar with normal scientific notation will recognize that 1.234E–5 is the FORTRAN form of 1.234×10^{-5}, or 0.00001234. This value is obtained by shifting the decimal point five positions to the left. Similarly, the value of 3.98E6 is 3,980,000. This value is obtained by shifting the decimal point six positions to the right. Normally, only very large numbers (i.e., greater than 1000) or very small fractions (less than 0.0001) are written in scientific notation.

CHARACTER Data Type

Type CHARACTER variables can store string values consisting of combinations of letters, digits, and special characters. For example, the declaration

```
CHARACTER *9 OBJECT
```

identifies OBJECT as a variable that may contain a string of exactly nine characters. The assignment statement

```
OBJECT = 'ABCD12345'
```

stores the nine characters ABCD12345 in variable OBJECT.

Suppose we want to store the nine characters Joe's hat, where the fourth character is an apostrophe and the sixth character is a blank. We can use the assignment below to accomplish this.

```
OBJECT = 'Joe''s hat'
```

Since FORTRAN uses an apostrophe to mark the beginning and the end of a string, we must use something else (i.e., two consecutive apostrophes) to tell FORTRAN that we want to store an apostrophe inside a string.

In the character variable OBJECT (CHARACTER *9) below, the blank character is represented by the symbol □.

```
OBJECT
```

```
Joe's□hat
```

LOGICAL Data Type

Only two values, .TRUE. and .FALSE., may be stored in a type LOGICAL variable. The periods are required when writing a LOGICAL value.

We shall discuss each of these data types in more detail in the rest of this chapter.

Implicit Types

When a variable whose type has not been declared appears in a program, FORTRAN allocates a memory cell for the variable and makes an assumption about its type. The *implicit typing rules* used by FORTRAN are described below.

Rules for Implicit Data Typing

- A variable beginning with any of the letters I through N is considered to be type INTEGER.
- All other variables are considered to be type REAL.

If you forget a type declaration or misspell a variable name, FORTRAN will not detect this as an error, but will use the rules above to determine the type of this variable. However, if you attempt to store a string or a LOGICAL value in an implicitly typed variable, an error will be detected. This is because all implicitly typed variables are either type REAL or type INTEGER.

We strongly recommend that you do not attempt to take advantage of the implicit typing capability of FORTRAN; instead, you should declare the type of each variable used in a program. Besides reducing the chance of error, the type declarations are an excellent source of internal program documentation. The type declarations clearly indicate what variables will be manipulated by the program.

4.2 ▬▬▬ Numeric Data Types—INTEGER and REAL

The data types INTEGER and REAL are used to represent numeric information. Thus far, we have used INTEGER variables as loop counters and to represent data, such as exam scores, that were whole numbers. In most other instances, we have used type REAL numeric data.

You may be wondering why it is necessary to have two numeric types. Can the data type REAL be used for all numbers? The answer is yes, but on many computers, operations involving integers are faster, and less storage space is needed to store integers. Also, operations with integers are always precise, whereas there may be some loss of accuracy when dealing with real numbers.

These differences result from the way real numbers and integers are represented internally in memory. All data are represented in memory as *binary strings*, strings of 0's and 1's. However, the binary string stored for the integer 13 is not the same as the binary string stored for the real number 13.0. The actual internal representation used is computer dependent, but generally follows the sample integer and real formats shown in Fig. 4.1.

Figure 4.1. *Integer and Real Formats*

Integer format

binary number

Real format

mantissa	exponent

In Fig. 4.1, each integer is represented as a standard binary number. If you are familiar with the binary number system, you know that the integer 13 is represented as the binary number 1101. There will be a string of leading 0's preceeding this number when it is stored in a memory cell.

Real format is analogous to scientific notation. The storage area occupied by a real number is divided into two sections: the mantissa and the exponent. The mantissa is a binary fraction between 0.5 and 1.0 (−0.5 and −1.0 for a negative number). The exponent is a power of 2, and the mantissa and exponent are chosen so that the formula below is correct.

$$real\text{-}number = mantissa \times 2^{exponent}$$

Besides the capability of storing fractions, the range of numbers that may be represented in real format is considerably larger than for integer format. For example, on Control Data Corporation Cyber series computers, real numbers range in value from 10^{-294} (a very small fraction) to 10^{+322}, whereas the range of positive integers extends from 1 to approximately 10^{15}.

Type of an Arithmetic Expression

All the arithmetic operators can have either INTEGER or REAL operands. If both operands are the same type, then the result of an arithmetic operation has the same type as its operands. This means that the result of 3.0 * 4.0 is the real number 12.0; the result of 3 * 4 is the integer 12. If one operand is type REAL and the other is type INTEGER, the type INTEGER operand is converted to type REAL, and the result will be type REAL (e.g., the expressions 7.0/2 and 7/2.0 are evaluated as 7.0 / 2.0).

In FORTRAN, the result of a division operation must be type INTEGER when both operands are type INTEGER. This means that the value of 7 / 2 cannot be the same as the value of 7 / 2.0. The value of the latter expression is 3.5; the value of the former expression is the integral part of this result (i.e., the integer 3). In general, when two integers are divided, the result is the integral part of their quotient; the fractional part is lost.

Figure 4.2. *Evaluation Tree for 3 * 6 / 4*

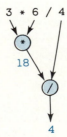

EXAMPLE 4.1   In Fig. 4.2, the expression

        3 * 6 / 4

involving three integer operands is shown to evaluate to the integer 4. In Fig. 4.3, the expression

        3.0 * 6 / 4

is shown to evaluate to the real number 4.5. The reason for the discrepancy is the fact that the left operand of the division operator in Fig. 4.3 is a real number (18.0) due to the prior multiplication. Consequently, the result of the division is also a real number.   ■

Figure 4.3. *Evaluation Tree for 3.0 * 6 / 4*

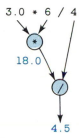

We can conclude from Example 4.1 that expressions involving the division operator and mixed-type operands often lead to unexpected results. For this reason, you should avoid using mixed-type expressions, especially when division is involved.

Mixed-Type Assignment Statements   When an assignment statement is executed, the expression is first evaluated and then the result is assigned to the variable listed to the left of the assignment operator (=). Only an integer can be stored in a type INTEGER variable, and only a real number can be stored in a type REAL variable. Consequently, if the expression and the value being assigned are the same type, the expression value will be stored directly. If they are not the same type, a type conversion occurs and the value stored may not be what is intended.

EXAMPLE 4.2   The expression in the assignment statements

        X = 3.0 * 6 / 4
        I = 3.0 * 6 / 4

evaluates to the real number 4.5, as shown in Fig. 4.3. If X is type REAL, the real number 4.5 is stored in X, as expected. If I is type INTEGER, only the integral part of the expression value (the integer 4) is stored in I, as shown below.

The expression in the assignment statements

```
X = 3 * 6 / 4
I = 3 * 6 / 4
```

evaluates to the integer 4, as shown in Fig. 4.2. If I is type INTEGER, the integer 4 is stored. If X is type REAL, the integer 4 is converted to its equivalent real value (4.0) before being stored in X.   ■

A common error is to assume that the type of X (the variable being assigned) causes the expression to be evaluated as if its operands were that type too. Remember, the expression is evaluated before the assignment is made, and the type of the variable being assigned has no effect whatsoever on the expression value.

Numerical Inaccuracies

One of the problems in processing real numbers is that there is sometimes an error in representing real data. Just as there are certain numbers that cannot be represented exactly in the decimal number system (e.g., the fraction 1/3 is 0.333333...), so there are numbers that cannot be represented exactly in REAL format on a computer. In fact, many decimal fractions cannot be represented exactly in the internal binary format used for real numbers. The *representational error* will depend on the number of bits used in the mantissa: the more bits, the smaller the error.

The number 0.1 is an example of a real number that has a representational error. Although this error is quite small, its effect can become magnified through repeated computations. The result of adding 0.1 ten times is not exactly 1.0, so the loop below may fail to terminate on some computers:

```
TRIAL = 0.0
DO WHILE (TRIAL .NE. 1.0)
    . . . . . . . . . . . . . . .
    TRIAL = TRIAL + 0.1
ENDDO
```

If the loop repetition test is changed to (TRIAL .LT. 1.0), the loop will terminate; however, it may execute ten times on one computer and eleven times on another. For this reason, it is best to use type INTEGER variables whenever possible in loop-repetition tests. The variable TRIAL takes on the same values in the loop below as in the one above; however, the type INTEGER variable NUMTRY is used for loop control. Consequently, this loop always executes exactly ten times.

```
      TRIAL = 0.0
      DO 10 NUMTRY = 1, 10
         . . . . . . . . . . . . . . . .
         TRIAL = TRIAL + 0.1
   10 CONTINUE
```

Other problems occur when manipulating very large and very small real numbers. When a large number and a small number are added, the larger number may "cancel out" the smaller number (a *cancellation error*). If X is much larger than Y, X + Y and X may have the same value (e.g., 1000.0 + 0.000001234 is equal to 1000.0 on some computers).

If two very small numbers are multiplied, the result may be too small to be represented accurately and will become zero. This is called *arithmetic underflow*. Similarly, if two very large numbers are multiplied, the result may be too large to be represented. This is called *arithmetic overflow* and is handled in different ways by different computers. Arithmetic underflow and overflow also can occur when very large and very small integer values are processed.

SELF-CHECK EXERCISES FOR SECTION 4.2

1. Given the declarations

```
   REAL PI, X, Y
   INTEGER MAXI, A, B, I
   PARAMETER (PI = 3.14159, MAXI = 1000)
```

find the value of each of the statements below that are valid. Also indicate which statements are invalid and why. Assume that A is 3, B is 4, and Y is −1.0.

a. I = A * B
b. I = (990 − MAXI) / A
c. I = A * Y
d. X = PI * Y
e. I = A / B
f. X = A / B
g. X = A * (A / B)
h. I = B / 0
i. I = A * (990 − MAXI)

j. I = (MAXI − 990) / A
k. X = A / Y
l. I = PI * A
m. X = PI / Y
n. I = B / A
o. I = (MAXI − 990) * A
p. I = A * 0
q. I = A * (MAXI − 990)

2. What values are assigned by the legal statements in exercise 1, assuming A is 5, B is 2, and Y is 2.0?

3. Assume that you have the following variable declarations:

```
INTEGER COLOR, LIME, STRAW, YELLOW, RED, ORANGE
REAL BLACK, WHITE, GREEN, BLUE, PURPLE, CRAYON
```

Evaluate each of the statements below given the values: COLOR is 2, BLACK is 2.5, CRAYON is –1.3, STRAW is 1, RED is 3, PURPLE is 0.3E1.

a. WHITE = COLOR * 2.5 / PURPLE
b. GREEN = COLOR / PURPLE
c. ORANGE = COLOR / RED
d. BLUE = (COLOR + STRAW) / (CRAYON + 0.3)
e. LIME = RED / COLOR
f. PURPLE = STRAW / RED * COLOR

4. Let A, B, C, and X be the names of four type REAL variables and I, J, and K the names of three type INTEGER variables. Each of the statements below contains a violation of the rules for forming arithmetic expressions. Rewrite each statement so that it is consistent with the rules.

a. X = 4.0 A * C
b. A = AC
c. I = 2 * –J
d. K = 3(I + J)
e. X = 5A / BC
f. I = 5J3

4.3 ▬▬ Functions in Arithmetic Expressions

Functions are features of FORTRAN that are helpful in specifying numerical computations. Each function performs a different mathematical operation (square root, cosine, etc.) and computes a single value. Functions are referenced directly in an expression: the value computed by the function is substituted for the function reference when the expression is evaluated.

EXAMPLE 4.3   SQRT is the name of a function that computes the square root of a positive value. In the assignment statement

```
Y = 5.7 + SQRT(20.25)
```

the value computed by the function reference SQRT(20.25) is 4.5; this value replaces the function reference in the expression and is added to 5.7. The result of the addition, 10.2 (5.7 + 4.5), is stored in the real variable Y.   ■

FORTRAN provides a number of *library* or *intrinsic* functions, such as SQRT, that may be used by the programmer. The names and descriptions of some commonly used functions are given in Table 4.2; the function name is always followed by one or more *arguments* enclosed in parentheses, as shown in Example 4.3 (argument is 20.25). Any legal arithmetic expression of the proper type may be used as an argument for these functions. A complete list of FORTRAN library functions appears in Appendix A.

Table 4.2. *Table of FORTRAN Library Functions*

FUNCTION REFERENCE	OPERATION	ARGUMENT TYPE	RESULT TYPE
INT(*arg*)	Converts *arg* to an integer by dropping the fractional part	REAL	INTEGER
NINT(*arg*)	Rounds *arg* to nearest integer	REAL	INTEGER
REAL(*arg*)	Converts *arg* to a real value	INTEGER	REAL
ABS(*arg*)	Finds absolute value of *arg*	REAL	REAL
IABS(*arg*)	Finds absolute value of *arg*	INTEGER	INTEGER
SQRT(*arg*)	Computes square root of *arg* (*arg* $\geq$ 0.0)	REAL	REAL
EXP(*arg*)	Computes e^{arg}	REAL	REAL
ALOG(*arg*)	Computes natural logarithm, ln(*arg*) (*arg* $>$ 0.0)	REAL	REAL
ALOG10(*arg*)	Computes logarithm, log(*arg*) (*arg* $>$ 0.0)	REAL	REAL
SIN(*arg*)	Computes sine of angle *arg* in radians	REAL	REAL
COS(*arg*)	Computes cosine of angle *arg* in radians	REAL	REAL
TAN(*arg*)	Computes tangent of angle *arg* in radians	REAL	REAL
MOD(*a1*, *a2*)	Computes remainder of *a1/a2*	INTEGER	INTEGER
MAX0(*a1*,...,*an*)	Selects largest value from list *a1*,...,*an*	INTEGER	INTEGER
AMAX1(*a1*,...,*an*)	Selects largest value from list *a1*,...,*an*	REAL	REAL
MIN0(*a1*,...,*an*)	Selects smallest value from list *a1*,...,*an*	INTEGER	INTEGER
AMIN1(*a1*,...,*an*)	Selects smallest value from list *a1*,...,*an*	REAL	REAL

The names used in this table are fairly descriptive of the operation performed by the function. Also, the type of result returned by each function is determined using the implicit type convention. A function whose name begins with the letters I through N returns a type INTEGER result; otherwise, the function returns a type REAL result. This is the reason for having two similar functions named ABS (type REAL result) and IABS (type INTEGER result) and for function names such as ALOG and AMAX1 instead of LOG and MAX1.

The type of argument(s) required by each function is also listed in Table 4.2. Using a type REAL argument where a type INTEGER argument is specified may cause a syntax error or incorrect results.

The first three functions listed in Table 4.2 convert a value of one numeric type to the other numeric type. The function INT converts a type REAL value to an integer value by *truncating* it, or removing the fractional part.

EXAMPLE 4.4   The functions INT and NINT are used to convert a REAL value to an integer, as shown below. The fractional part is always removed by function INT, whereas NINT rounds a real value to the nearest integer.   ■

```
INT(5.3) is 5       NINT(5.3) is 5
INT(5.8) is 5       NINT(5.8) is 6
INT(-5.3) is -5     NINT(-5.3) is -5
INT(-5.8) is -5     NINT(-5.8) is -6
```

EXAMPLE 4.5   The function REAL converts an integer value to a real number. If TOTAL and NUMITM are both type INTEGER and AVE is type REAL, the assignment statement

```
AVE = REAL(TOTAL) / REAL(NUMITM)
```

stores the value of TOTAL divided by NUMITM in AVE, including any fractional remainder. For example, if TOTAL is 7 and NUMITM is 2, the value of AVE becomes 3.5. What would be stored in AVE by the assignment statement below?   ■

```
AVE = TOTAL / NUMITM
```

EXAMPLE 4.6   The program in Fig. 4.4 illustrates the use of three functions. The function references are inserted in the output list of the PRINT statement

```
PRINT *, I, SQRT(REAL(I)), EXP(REAL(I))
```

The program prints a table of square roots and exponential values for integers from 1 through 10. Because SQRT and EXP require type REAL arguments, the function REAL is used to convert each integer to a real number before the SQRT or EXP function is called. The output list item SQRT(REAL(I)) is called a *nested function reference*; the innermost function reference (i.e. REAL(I)) is evaluated first.   ■

The last few functions in Table 4.2 have multiple arguments. The function MOD must always have two arguments, while the number of arguments for the functions MAX0 (pronounced "max zero"), AMAX1, MIN0, and AMIN1 may vary.

Figure 4.4. *Printing a Table of Square Roots and Exponential Values*

```
      PROGRAM ROOTS
C Prints square roots and exponential function values
      INTEGER I

      PRINT *, '        I  Square Root     Exponential'
      DO 10 I = 1, 10
         PRINT *, I, SQRT(REAL(I)), EXP(REAL(I))
   10 CONTINUE

      STOP
      END

      I  Square Root     Exponential
      1    1.000000         2.718282
      2    1.414214         7.389056
      3    1.732051        20.08554
      4    2.000000        54.59815
      5    2.236068       148.4132
      6    2.449490       403.4288
      7    2.645751      1096.633
      8    2.828427      2980.958
      9    3.000000      8103.084
     10    3.162278     22026.46
```

EXAMPLE 4.7

If I is 5 and J is –7, the function reference

    MAX0(3, 6, I + J, I - J)

returns the largest value in its argument list, which is the value of I - J, or 12. The function reference

    MIN0(3, 6, I + J, I - J)

returns the smallest value in its argument list, which is the value of I + J, or –2. ∎

EXAMPLE 4.8

The MOD function determines the integer remainder of an integer division. The value of the expression

    MOD(N, 3)

is the integer remainder of N divided by 3. The only possible values for this expression are the integers 0 (no remainder), 1, or 2. The value of MOD(17, 3) is 2, as shown below.

$$
\begin{array}{r}
5 \longleftarrow \text{quotient} \\
3\overline{)17} \\
\underline{15} \\
2 \longleftarrow \text{remainder}
\end{array}
$$

The function reference MOD(3, 17) is not the same as the one above. The value returned by this function reference is 3, which is the integer remainder of 3 divided by 17.

The MOD function is often used to determine whether one integer is an exact divisor of another. If the condition

```
(MOD(N, M) .EQ. 0)
```

is true, then M must be an exact divisor of N since the remainder of N divided by M is zero.   ∎

EXAMPLE 4.9   Einstein's theory of relativity demonstrates that mass increases with speed, that is,

$$m = m_o/(1 - (v/c)^2)^{1/2}$$

where m_o is the mass of an object at rest, v is the velocity with respect to the observer, and c is the speed of light. We implement this equation in FORTRAN as

```
M = MO / SQRT(1.0 - (V/C) ** 2)
```

where the SQRT function raises its argument to the power 1/2 (its square root).

We can also use the assignment statement

```
M = MO / (1.0 - (V/C) ** 2) ** (1.0/2.0)
```

to compute the mass, M. However, it is more efficient and more accurate to call the SQRT function. Note that the exponent 1/2 must be written in FORTRAN as (1.0/2.0), not (1/2). FORTRAN evaluates (1/2) using integer division, so (1/2) is zero in FORTRAN.

EXAMPLE 4.10   The quadratic formula

$$\frac{-B \pm \sqrt{B^2 - 4AC}}{2A}$$

may be used to compute the roots of a quadratic equation in x:

$$Ax^2 + Bx + C = 0, \quad A \text{ not equal to } 0$$

The value of the *discriminant*, $B^2 - 4AC$, of the quadratic formula determines whether the equation has real or complex roots. If the discriminant is negative, the roots are complex; otherwise, they are real. The program in Fig. 4.5 prints the root value(s) or, if the roots are complex, an appropriate message.

The program in Fig. 4.5 uses the assignment statement

```
DISC = B ** 2 - 4.0 * A * C
```

to compute the value of the discriminant. (Note that it is correct to use the

Figure 4.5. *Finding the Roots of a Quadratic Equation*

```
      PROGRAM QUADEQ
C Program to compute the roots of a quadratic equation
      REAL A, B, C, ROOT1, ROOT2, DISC

      PRINT *, 'Enter the three coefficients A, B, C'
      PRINT *, 'Leave spaces between the three values:'
      READ *, A, B, C

C Find and print the roots or print a message
      DISC = B ** 2 - 4.0 * A * C
      IF (A .EQ. 0) THEN
          ROOT1 = -C / B
          PRINT *, 'Equation is not quadratic'
          PRINT *, 'The single real root is: ', ROOT1
      ELSE IF (DISC .GT. 0) THEN
          ROOT1 = (-B + SQRT(DISC)) / (2.0 * A)
          ROOT2 = (-B - SQRT(DISC)) / (2.0 * A)
          PRINT *, 'The two real roots are: ', ROOT1, ROOT2
      ELSE IF (DISC .EQ. 0) THEN
          ROOT1 = -B / (2.0 * A)
          PRINT *, 'There is only one real root'
          PRINT *, 'The root is: ', ROOT1
      ELSE
          PRINT *, ' There are two complex roots'
      ENDIF

      STOP
      END

Enter the three coefficients A, B, C
Leave spaces between the three values:
1 -1 -2
The two real roots are:    2.000000      -1.000000
```

integer 2 as an exponent with the real variable B.) The assignment statements

```
ROOT1 = (-B + SQRT(DISC)) / (2.0 * A)
ROOT2 = (-B - SQRT(DISC)) / (2.0 * A)
```

store the root values in ROOT1 and ROOT2 when they are real. ∎

The assignment statements above illustrate the correct way to write a complicated formula in FORTRAN. Rather than recompute the value of the discriminant each time it is needed, the value is computed once and saved in DISC. Then the variable DISC is referenced whenever the discriminant value is needed. Besides being more efficient, this reduces the chances of error because the resultant formulas for ROOT1 and ROOT2 are much simpler. It would also be reasonable to introduce another variable to store the value of `2.0 * A`, which appears in two assignment statements. However, this is not done because this expression is so simple.

Parentheses are used to set off the numerator and the denominator in the expressions for ROOT1 and ROOT2. Without parentheses, the division would be performed too early and the root values would not be correct.

EXAMPLE 4.11[M]   Prince Valiant is trying to rescue Rapunzel by shooting an arrow with a rope attached through her tower window, which is 100 feet off the ground. We will assume that the arrow travels at a constant velocity. The laws of physics tell us that the time (t) of flight of the arrow is given by the formula

$$t = \frac{d}{v(\cos\theta)}$$

where d is the distance the prince is standing from the tower, v is the velocity of the arrow, and θ is its angle of elevation.

To help him perfect his aim, Prince Valiant needs a computer program that will compute the height of the arrow when it reaches the tower. To rescue Rapunzel, the arrow's height (h) must be between 100 and 110 feet, as given by the formula

$$h = v \cdot t \cdot \sin\theta - \frac{g \cdot t^2}{2}$$

where g is the gravitational constant and t is the value computed by the first formula.

The required program is shown in Fig. 4.6. The assignment statement

```
RADIAN = THETA * (PI / 180.0)
```

is used to convert the angle THETA from degrees to radians as required for input to the FORTRAN SIN and COS functions.   ∎

SELF-CHECK EXERCISES FOR SECTION 4.3

1. Write a program that computes and prints

   $$e^a \times \ln(b)$$

   for several different values of a and b using functions EXP and ALOG. What does this program compute?
2. Using the NINT function, write FORTRAN statements to round any real value X to the nearest two decimal places. *Hint:* You will have to multiply by 100 before rounding.
3. Modify the program in Fig. 4.5 to find and print complex roots as well. *Hint:* Save the real part and the imaginary part of the complex roots in separate variables.

Figure 4.6. *Prince Valiant Takes Aim at Rapunzel*

```
      PROGRAM RESCUE
C Prince Valiant Takes Aim at Rapunzel

C Declarations
      REAL PI, G, BOTTOM, TOP
      PARAMETER (PI = 3.14159, G = 32.17, BOTTOM = 100.0, TOP = 110.0)
      REAL HEIGHT, TIME, VEL, THETA, DIST, RADIAN

C Read and print input data
      PRINT *, 'Distance from tower in feet:'
      READ *, DIST
      PRINT *, 'Velocity of arrow in feet per second:'
      READ *, VEL
      PRINT *, 'Angle of elevation in degrees:'
      READ *, THETA

C The FORTRAN trig functions require input angles in radians.
C Convert THETA from degrees to radians
      RADIAN = THETA * (PI / 180.0)
C Compute travel time of arrow
      TIME = DIST / (VEL * COS(RADIAN))
C Compute arrow height
      HEIGHT = VEL * TIME * SIN(RADIAN) - G / 2.0 * TIME ** 2

C Print message to correct Prince's aim
      IF (HEIGHT .LT. 0.0) THEN
         PRINT *, 'Arrow did not reach the tower'
      ELSE IF (HEIGHT .LT. BOTTOM) THEN
         PRINT *, 'Arrow was too low, height was ', HEIGHT
      ELSE IF (HEIGHT .LT. TOP) THEN
         PRINT *, 'Good shot, Prince!'
      ELSE
         PRINT *, 'Arrow was too high, height was ', HEIGHT
      ENDIF

      STOP
      END

Distance from tower in feet:
100.0
Velocity of arrow in feet per second:
500.0
Angle of elevation in degrees:
47.0
Good shot, Prince!
```

4.4 ▆▆▆▆ LOGICAL Data Type

We introduced the LOGICAL data type in Chapter 1. We used LOGICAL expressions (expressions that evaluate to true or false) to control WHILE loop repetition and to select an alternative in an IF structure.

LOGICAL Variables and Values

The simplest LOGICAL expression is a LOGICAL variable or value. A LOGICAL variable can be set to either of the LOGICAL values, .TRUE. or .FALSE.. The statements

```
LOGICAL DEBUG
PARAMETER (DEBUG = .TRUE.)
LOGICAL FLAG, SWITCH
```

declare SWITCH and FLAG to be LOGICAL variables, i.e., variables that may be assigned only the values .TRUE. and .FALSE.. DEBUG is a LOGICAL parameter with the value .TRUE..

The expression parts of the assignment statements

```
SWITCH = .FALSE.
FLAG = SWITCH
```

are a LOGICAL value (.FALSE.) and a LOGICAL variable (SWITCH). The result of executing these statements is pictured below.

```
    SWITCH           FLAG
  ┌─────────┐     ┌─────────┐
  │ .FALSE. │     │ .FALSE. │
  └─────────┘     └─────────┘
```

Most of the time, we will use relational operators to form LOGICAL expressions that are used as conditions in IF statements and as loop-repetition tests. Some examples of LOGICAL expressions used in earlier programs are

```
GROSS .GT. TXBRAK
ITEM .NE. SENVAL
TYPE .EQ. 'D'
```

LOGICAL Operators

In this section, we will discuss five LOGICAL operators: .AND., .OR., .NOT., .EQV., .NEQV.. These operators are used with operands that are LOGICAL expressions to form other LOGICAL expressions. Some examples are

```
(SALARY .LT. MINSAL) .OR. (NUMDEP .GT. 5)
(TEMP .GT. 90) .AND. (HUMID .GT. 0.90)
ATHLET .AND. (.NOT. FLUNK)
```

The first LOGICAL expression can be used to determine whether an employee pays no income tax. It evaluates to true if either condition in parentheses is true. The second LOGICAL expression can be used to describe an unbearable summer day: temperature over 90° Fahrenheit and humidity over 90%. The expression evaluates to true only when both conditions are true. The third LOGICAL expression manipulates two LOGICAL variables (ATHLET and FLUNK). Any individual for whom this expression is true is eligible for intercollegiate sports. As we will see, this condition is true if ATHLET has the value .TRUE. and FLUNK has the value .FALSE..

The LOGICAL operators can be used with LOGICAL expressions only. The .AND., .OR., and .NOT. operators are described in Tables 4.3, 4.4, and 4.5.

Table 4.3. *.AND. Operator*

OPERAND1	OPERAND2	OPERAND1 .AND. OPERAND2
.TRUE.	.TRUE.	.TRUE.
.TRUE.	.FALSE.	.FALSE.
.FALSE.	.TRUE.	.FALSE.
.FALSE.	.FALSE.	.FALSE.

Table 4.4. *.OR. Operator*

OPERAND1	OPERAND2	OPERAND1 .OR. OPERAND2
.TRUE.	.TRUE.	.TRUE.
.TRUE.	.FALSE.	.TRUE.
.FALSE.	.TRUE.	.TRUE.
.FALSE.	.FALSE.	.FALSE.

Table 4.5. *.NOT. Operator*

OPERAND1	.NOT. OPERAND1
.TRUE.	.FALSE.
.FALSE.	.TRUE.

Table 4.3 shows that the .AND. operator yields a true result only when both its operands are true; Table 4.4 shows that the .OR. operator yields a false result only when both its operands are false. The .NOT. operator has a single operand; Table 4.5 shows that the .NOT. operator yields the *logical complement*, or negation, of its operand.

EXAMPLE 4.12   The nested `IF` structure

```
IF (AGE .GT. 25) THEN
    IF (STATUS .EQ. 'SINGLE') THEN
        IF (SEX .EQ. 'FEMALE') THEN
            PRINT *, NAME
        ENDIF
    ENDIF
ENDIF
```

can be used to print the names of all single females over 25 years of age. The `.AND.` operator is used below to implement this decision structure without nesting.

```
IF ((AGE .GT. 25) .AND. (STATUS .EQ. 'SINGLE') .AND.
+    (SEX .EQ. 'FEMALE')) THEN
    PRINT *, NAME
ENDIF
```

The symbol + in column six of the second line indicates that the first line is continued. ∎

The operators `.EQV.` (*equivalent*) and `.NEQV.` (*not equivalent*) are used instead of the relational operators `.EQ.` and `.NE.` to compare two `LOGICAL` expressions. They are described in Tables 4.6 and 4.7.

Table 4.6. *.EQV. Operator*

OPERAND1	OPERAND2	OPERAND1 .EQV. OPERAND2
.TRUE.	.TRUE.	.TRUE.
.TRUE.	.FALSE.	.FALSE.
.FALSE.	.TRUE.	.FALSE.
.FALSE.	.FALSE.	.TRUE.

Table 4.7. *.NEQV. Operator*

OPERAND1	OPERAND2	OPERAND1 .NEQV. OPERAND2
.TRUE.	.TRUE.	.FALSE.
.TRUE.	.FALSE.	.TRUE.
.FALSE.	.TRUE.	.TRUE.
.FALSE.	.FALSE.	.FALSE.

EXAMPLE 4.13   If `SWITCH` and `FLAG` are type `LOGICAL`, the expression

```
SWITCH .EQV. FLAG
```

is correct and true if SWITCH and FLAG have the same LOGICAL value (both .TRUE. or both .FALSE.). The expression

    SWITCH .EQ. FLAG

causes a syntax error because the relational operator .EQ. cannot have type LOGICAL operands.   ■

Operator Precedence

The precedence of an operator determines its order of evaluation. Table 4.8 shows the precedence of all operators discussed so far, including the relational operators.

Table 4.8. *Operator Precedence*

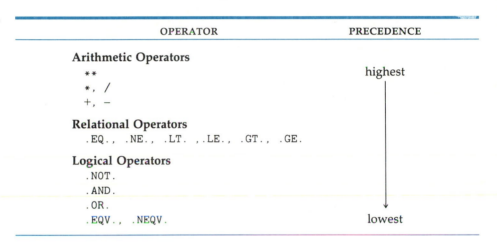

OPERATOR	PRECEDENCE
Arithmetic Operators	
**	highest
*, /	
+, −	
Relational Operators	
.EQ., .NE., .LT. ,.LE., .GT., .GE.	
Logical Operators	
.NOT.	
.AND.	
.OR.	
.EQV., .NEQV.	lowest

Table 4.8 shows that the arithmetic operators have the highest precedence. Next are the relational operators and, last, the LOGICAL operators. When in doubt, you should use parentheses to specify the order of expression evaluation.

EXAMPLE 4.14

The expression

    X .LT. Y + Z

involving the real variables X, Y, and Z is interpreted correctly as

    X .LT. (Y + Z)

since + has higher precedence than .LT..
    The expression

    X .LT. W * Y .OR. Z .LT. W * Y

is interpreted as

```
(X .LT. (W * Y)) .OR. (Z .LT. (W * Y))
```

since `* > .LT. > .OR.` (read ">" as "has higher precedence than"). The use of parentheses helps to clarify the meaning of the expression. ∎

EXAMPLE 4.15 The expressions in Table 4.9 are all valid if X, Y, and Z are type REAL, and FLAG is type LOGICAL. The value of each expression is shown on the right, assuming that X is 3.0, Y is 4.0, Z is 2.0, and FLAG is .FALSE..

Table 4.9. *Expressions with X = 3.0, Y = 4.0, Z = 2.0, FLAG = .FALSE.*

EXPRESSION	VALUE
1. (X .GT. Z) .AND. (Y .GT. Z)	.TRUE.
2. (X + Y / Z) .LE. 3.5	.FALSE.
3. (Z .GT. X) .OR. (Z .GT. Y)	.FALSE.
4. .NOT. FLAG	.TRUE.
5. (X .EQ. 1.0) .OR. (X .EQ. 3.0)	.TRUE.
6. (0.0 .LT. X) .AND. (X .LT. 3.5)	.TRUE.
7. (X .LE. Y) .AND. (Y .LE. Z)	.FALSE.
8. .NOT. FLAG .OR. ((Y + Z) .GE. (X − Z))	.TRUE.
9. .NOT. (FLAG .OR. ((Y + Z) .GE. (X − Z)))	.FALSE.

Expression 1 gives the FORTRAN form of the relationship "X and Y are greater than Z." It is often tempting to write this as

```
X .AND. Y .GT. Z
```

However, this is an illegal LOGICAL expression because the real variable X cannot be an operand of the LOGICAL operator .AND..

Figure 4.7. *Evaluation Tree for .NOT. FLAG .OR. ((Y + Z) .GE. (X − Z))*

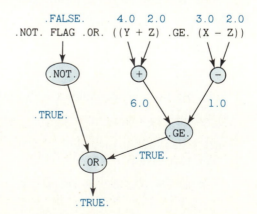

In expression 2, the arithmetic expression $(X + Y / Z)$ evaluates to 5.0 (not 3.5), so the LOGICAL expression is false.

Expression 5 shows the correct way to express the relationship "X is equal to 1.0 or to 3.0."

Expression 6 is the FORTRAN form of the relationship $0.0 < X < 3.5$, i.e., "X is in the range 0.0 to 3.5." Similarly, expression 7 shows the FORTRAN form of the relationship $X \le Y \le Z$, i.e., "Y is in the range X to Z, inclusive."

Finally, expression 8 is evaluated in Fig. 4.7; the values given at the beginning of Example 4.15 are shown above the expression.   ∎

LOGICAL Assignment

We can write assignment statements that assign the value of a LOGICAL expression to a LOGICAL variable.

EXAMPLE 4.16

The statement

```
SAME = X .EQ. Y
```

assigns the value .TRUE. to the LOGICAL variable SAME when the REAL variables X and Y are equal; otherwise, the value .FALSE. is assigned. The assignment above is more efficient than the IF structure

```
IF (X .EQ. Y) THEN
    SAME = .TRUE.
ELSE
    SAME = .FALSE.
ENDIF
```

which has the same effect.   ∎

Complementing a Condition

The logical operator .NOT. is used to form the complement, or opposite, of a condition. If a logical expression is true, then its complement must be false and vice versa.

EXAMPLE 4.17

Two forms of the complement of the condition

```
(ITEM .EQ. SENVAL)
```

are

```
(ITEM .NE. SENVAL)          (.NOT. (ITEM .EQ. SENVAL))
```

The form on the left is obtained by flipping the relational operator (from .EQ. to .NE.); the complement on the right is obtained by applying the .NOT. operator to the original condition.   ∎

It is generally easier to flip the relational operator when you are dealing with simple conditions like the one shown in Example 4.17. The relational operator .LE. should be changed to .GT., .LT. to .GE., etc. To complement more complicated conditions, it is easier to place the .NOT. operator in front of the entire condition.

EXAMPLE 4.18   The condition

        (AGE .GT. 25) .AND. (STATUS .EQ. 'Single')

is true for a single person over 25. The complement of this condition is written below.   ∎

        .NOT. ((AGE .GT. 25) .AND. (STATUS .EQ. 'Single'))

DeMorgan's Theorem

DeMorgan's theorem can also be used to form the complement of a LOGICAL expression. DeMorgan's theorem is stated below.

- The complement of *expr1* .AND. *expr2* is written as *comp1* .OR. *comp2*, where *comp1* is the complement of *expr1* and *comp2* is the complement of *expr2*.
- The complement of *expr1* .OR. *expr2* is written as *comp1* .AND. *comp2*, where *comp1* is the complement of *expr1* and *comp2* is the complement of *expr2*.

EXAMPLE 4.19   Using DeMorgan's theorem, the complement of

        (AGE .GT. 25) .AND. (STATUS .EQ. 'Single' .OR. STATUS .EQ. 'Divorced')

may be written as

        (AGE .LE. 25) .OR. (STATUS .NE. 'Single' .AND. STATUS .NE. 'Divorced')

The original condition is true for anyone who is over 25 and either single or divorced. The complement would be true for anyone who is 25 or younger or anyone who is currently married.   ∎

Using LOGICAL Variables as Program Flags

LOGICAL variables are often used as *program flags* to signal whether a special event occurs in a program. The fact that such an event occurs is important to the future execution of the program. A LOGICAL variable used as a program flag is initialized to one of its two possible values (.TRUE. or .FALSE.) and is reset to the other if and when the event being monitored occurs.

EXAMPLE 4.20   Program GUESS (see Fig. 4.8) prompts the user to guess a number in its "secret interval." The WHILE loop continues to read integer values into N until an integer between NMIN and NMAX is entered.

The LOGICAL variable BETWEN is the loop-control variable for the WHILE loop. BETWEN is a program flag whose value signals whether a data value between

Figure 4.8. *Using a Program Flag*

```
      PROGRAM GUESS
C Displays the first data value in the interval defined by
C parameters NMIN and NMAX

C Declarations
      INTEGER NMIN, NMAX
      PARAMETER (NMIN = 1, NMAX = 10)
      INTEGER N
      LOGICAL BETWEN

C Initially assume an integer between NMIN and NAMX is not
C entered
      BETWEN = .FALSE.

C Keep reading until an integer between NMIN and NMAX is entered
      DO WHILE (.NOT. BETWEN)            9    IF (.NOT. BETWEN) THEN
         PRINT *, 'Guess an integer in my secret interval?'
         READ *, N
         BETWEN = (N .GE. NMIN) .AND. (N .LE. NMAX)
      ENDDO                                  GOTO 9
C                                            ENDIF
C Display result
      PRINT *, N, ' is the first guess in the interval ', NMIN,
     +             ' to ', NMAX

C Exit program
      STOP
      END

Guess an integer in my secret interval?
15
Guess an integer in my secret interval?
3
         3 is the first guess in the interval      1 to       10
```

NMIN and NMAX has been read. BETWEN is initialized to .FALSE. before the loop is reached. Inside the loop, the LOGICAL assignment statement

        BETWEN = (N .GE. NMIN) .AND. (N .LE. NMAX)

resets BETWEN to .TRUE. when an integer between NMIN and NMAX is entered. The loop is repeated as long as BETWEN is still .FALSE.. ∎

SELF-CHECK EXERCISES FOR SECTION 4.4

1. Draw the evaluation tree for expression 9 in Table 4.9.
2. Write the following LOGICAL assignment statements:
   a. Assign a value of .TRUE. to BETWEN if the value of N lies between –K and +K, inclusive; otherwise, assign a value of .FALSE..

b. Assign a value of .TRUE. to UPCASE if CH is a letter; otherwise, assign a value of .FALSE..
c. Assign a value of .TRUE. to DIVISR if M is a divisor of N; otherwise, assign a value of .FALSE..

4.5 CHARACTER Data Type

There are many features provided in FORTRAN for the manipulation of CHARACTER data. These features are the subject of Chapter 9. In this section, we discuss storing and comparing CHARACTER data.

Length of a CHARACTER Data Item

The *length* of a CHARACTER variable is specified when the variable is declared. The length of a string can be determined by counting the number of characters between the apostrophes delimiting the string. Some examples are provided in Table 4.10.

Table 4.10. *Length of CHARACTER Variables and Strings*

VARIABLE OR STRING	LENGTH
CHARACTER LETTER	1
CHARACTER *3 INITLS	3
CHARACTER *10 ALPA	10
'ABCDEFGHIJ'	10
'Joe''s hat'	9

The first entry in Table 4.10 shows that the length of a CHARACTER variable is assumed to be 1 unless it is declared to be otherwise. The last entry shows that two consecutive apostrophes inside a string represent the single symbol '.

CHARACTER Declaration

The length specifier (e.g., *10) for a CHARACTER declaration does not have to follow the reserved word CHARACTER. Instead, it can come after each variable listed in the CHARACTER declaration. For example, the statement

```
CHARACTER NAME *10, ZIPCOD *5
```

declares two character variables of different lengths, NAME (length 10) and ZIPCOD (length 5).

**CHARACTER
Declaration**

> SYNTAX: CHARACTER *len variable list*
>   CHARACTER *variable1* *len1, *variable2* *len2, . . .
>
> EXAMPLE: CHARACTER *10 NAME1, NAME2
>   CHARACTER STATE *10, CITY *10, ZIP *5
>
> INTERPRETATION: The first form allocates memory space for each of the character variables specified in the *variable list*. Each variable has the capacity for storing *len* characters, where *len* is an integer constant. The second form allocates memory space for one or more character variables. The length of each character variable is specified separately by the integer constant appearing after each variable name.

**CHARACTER
Assignment**

Assignment statements or READ statements can be used to store strings in CHARACTER variables according to the rules below.

Rules for Storing Strings in CHARACTER Variables

- If the CHARACTER variable and string length are the same, then all characters in the string will be stored in the character variable.
- If the CHARACTER variable is longer than the string, then *blank padding* will be added at the right of the string to equalize the lengths.
- If the CHARACTER variable is shorter than the string, the string will be truncated, that is, the extra string characters will be removed from the right end of the string.

EXAMPLE 4.21

If ALPHA is type CHARACTER *10, the assignment

```
ALPHA = 'ABCDEFGHIJ'
```

yields the result

    ALPHA

```
ABCDEFGHIJ
```

If INITLS is type CHARACTER *3, the effect of the assignments

```
ALPHA = 'Joe''s hat'
INITLS = 'ABCDEFGHIJ'
```

is

    ALPHA   INITLS

```
Joe's□hat□         ABC
```

The symbol □ stored in ALPHA represents a blank character. ∎

EXAMPLE 4.22

It is also possible to assign the value of one CHARACTER variable to another. The assignment statements

```
ALPHA = INITLS
LETTER = INITLS
```

store the value of CHARACTER variable INITLS (string 'ABC') in ALPHA and LETTER (type CHARACTER), as shown below. The string 'ABC' is padded with seven blanks when it is stored in ALPHA. ∎

ALPHA   LETTER

| ABC□□□□□□□ | | A |

Reading String Data

When READ * is used to read string data into a CHARACTER variable, the string to be read must be enclosed in apostrophes. The same rules for padding and truncation apply when the string value being read is not the same length as the CHARACTER variable receiving it.

EXAMPLE 4.23

The statements below read a string and a numeric value into the variables NAME (type CHARACTER *10) and RATE (type REAL).

```
PRINT *, 'Enter the employee name and rate:'
READ *, NAME, RATE
```

The data line

```
'JOHNNY JONES'  3.50
```

would result in the variable values below. ∎

NAME   RATE

| JOHNNY□JON | | 3.50 |

Comparing CHARACTER Data

In earlier program fragments, we used the relational operator .EQ. to test for matching strings. For example, the conditions

```
MOMDAD .EQ. 'M'
STATUS .EQ. 'SINGLE'
```

were used to test whether a CHARACTER variable contains a particular string value. Order comparisons can also be performed on CHARACTER variables and strings using other relational operators (e.g., .LT., .GE.).

To understand the result of an order comparison, we must know something about the way characters are represented internally. Each character has its own unique numeric code that is stored as a binary number. A string stored in a CHARACTER variable is represented as the binary number formed by joining the individual numeric codes. This means that the internal representation for 'ABC' is the binary number formed by joining the codes for the letters A, B, and C.

To compare two strings of equal length, the computer simply compares the binary numbers representing each string. If the strings are not the same length, the shorter string is first padded with blanks until it contains as many characters as the longer string. The binary numbers representing each of these equal-length strings are then compared.

It should be obvious that the result of comparing two strings depends on the numeric codes for the characters in these strings. Unfortunately, the code values assigned are not the same for every computer, so the internal representation for a string may vary from computer to computer. However, FORTRAN requires the following *collating sequence* or relative ordering of certain characters regardless of their actual numeric codes.

FORTRAN Collating Sequence

- The blank character precedes (is less than) all the digit characters and all the letters.
- The letters follow the normal alphabetic sequence (i.e., the letter A precedes the letter B, the letter B precedes the letter C, etc.).
- The digit characters follow the normal numeric sequence (i.e., digit 0 precedes digit 1, digit 1 precedes 2, etc.).
- The digits and letters cannot be intermixed in the collating sequence.

The FORTRAN collating sequence ensures that two strings consisting of letters only will follow their normal dictionary sequence. This results in the string ordering 'ACE' < 'BAT' < 'CAT', since A precedes B and B precedes C. Similarly, the string 'BAT' is less than the string 'BIGGER' because A is less than I.

To compare the strings 'BAT' and 'BATTY', FORTRAN compares the binary numbers representing the two equal length strings 'BAT□□' and 'BATTY'. The string 'BAT' is less than the string 'BATTY' because the blank character precedes the letter T in the collating sequence.

EXAMPLE 4.24 The IF structure below prints the "smallest" of the strings stored in NAME1, NAME2, NAME3 (type CHARACTER *10). ∎

```
IF ((NAME1 .LE. NAME2) .AND. (NAME1 .LE. NAME3)) THEN
   PRINT *, NAME1, ' is smallest'
ELSE IF ((NAME2 .LE. NAME1) .AND. (NAME2 .LE. NAME3)) THEN
   PRINT *, NAME2, ' is smallest'
ELSE IF ((NAME3 .LE. NAME1) .AND. (NAME3 .LE. NAME2)) THEN
   PRINT *, NAME3, ' is smallest'
ENDIF
```

The ASCII Code   There are several different sets of binary codes for characters. The most prevalent code is the American Standard Code for Information Interchange, or ASCII (pronounced "askey"). In ASCII, 8 binary digits (*bits*) are used to encode 127 different characters.

EXAMPLE 4.25   The ASCII binary codes for the letters A, B, and C are shown below.

```
A        01000001
B        01000010
C        01000011
```

Therefore, the string 'ABC' is represented by the binary number

```
01000001 01000010 01000011
    A        B        C
```

in ASCII.   ■

Even though there are 127 characters in the ASCII character set, standard FORTRAN requires only 49 characters. They are the digits 0 through 9, the uppercase letters A through Z, and the thirteen *special characters* (=+−*/(),.$': and blank).

Table 4.11 shows the ASCII code for twelve characters. The numbers listed under the columns labelled "Code" are the decimal values corresponding to the actual eight-bit strings (e.g., decimal 65 corresponds to 01000001, the code for A). Some features of Table 4.11 are listed next; Appendix B shows the complete ASCII code.

- The blank character has a code value of 32.
- The digit characters 0 through 9 have the code values 48 through 57.
- The uppercase letters have smaller code values than the lowercase letters (not part of standard FORTRAN).
- The difference between the code values for each lowercase letter and its corresponding uppercase letter is always 32.

Table 4.11. *Some ASCII Codes (in decimal)*

CHARACTER	CODE	CHARACTER	CODE	CHARACTER	CODE
blank	32	+	43	−	45
0	48	A	65	a	97
1	49	B	66	b	98
9	57	Z	90	z	122

Numeric Strings

Numeric strings are strings that consist of digit characters only, for example, '123' or '345'. Arithmetic operations cannot be performed on numeric strings (e.g., '123' + '345' is illegal). They can only be manipulated in the same way as other strings.

The FORTRAN collating sequence ensures that two equal-length numeric strings will follow their normal numeric sequence (e.g., '123' is less than '345'). However, unexpected results may occur when numeric strings of different lengths are compared. For example, to compare the strings '12345' and '345', FORTRAN compares the binary numbers representing the equal-length strings '12345' and '345□□'. The string '12345' is less than '345' because the digit 1 precedes the digit 3 in the collating sequence. To avoid this kind of error, use leading or trailing zeros in numeric strings as required. The string '12345' is greater than the string '00345' but less than the string '34500'.

SELF-CHECK EXERCISES FOR SECTION 4.5

1. Show what string is stored in memory for each assignment or READ statement below. Represent a blank character by using the symbol □.

   a. CHARACTER *8 CITY
      CITY = 'NEW YORK'
   b. CHARACTER *5 TRIP
      TRIP = 'HONEYMOON'
   c. CHARACTER *6 FIRST, LAST
      READ *, FIRST, LAST
      data: 'Bill'   'Smith'

   d. CHARACTER *12 LASTNA
      LASTNA = 'JACKSON'
   e. CHARACTER *9 TEAM
      TEAM = 'ORIOLES'
   f. CHARACTER *9 TEAM
      TEAM = 'RED STOCKINGS'

2. Write an appropriate sequence of type declarations and READ statements for entering the data shown below. The first line of data contains a student ID number, name, class, and major. The next group of lines will be read into the same three variables. The data items in each line are the course ID, number of credits, and grade.

   ```
   700007    'J.A. OSHEA'    'SENIOR'    'MARKETING'
   'SOC101'    3    'A'
   'CIS120'    4    'B'
   'MAT201'    3    'C'
   ```

3. What is the value of each of the conditions shown below?

   a. 'SMITH' .LE. 'SMYTHE'
   b. '120'   .GE. '34'
   c. '34'   .EQ. '34 '
   d. 'JONES' .LT. 'JONES '
   e. 'FREE' .LT. 'BUSY'
   f. '120' .GE. '034'
   g. '34 ' .EQ. '340'
   h. 'JO'   .LT. 'JOSEPH'
   i. '*/+' .NE. ' */+'
   j. '*/+' .NE. '*/+ '

4.6 ▬▬▬ Introduction to FORMAT Statements

In our programming so far, we were able to exercise very little control over the appearance of an output line. It was fairly difficult to align table values under table headings. The compiler determined how many decimal places to use in printing a real value and the number of spaces to leave between consecutive values on the same output line. In this section, we will learn how to specify the exact form of our program output through the use of *formatted* PRINT statements. We will also see how to use a FORMAT statement to simplify reading a character string.

FORMAT Statements

In our programs so far, we have used PRINT * to display output values. The * following the word PRINT indicates *list-directed* output. This means that the data type of each output list item determines the form of the value printed.

In a *formatted* PRINT statement, a statement label replaces the symbol * following the word PRINT. The label references a FORMAT statement, as shown next.

EXAMPLE 4.26

The formatted PRINT and FORMAT statements

```
    PRINT 15,  NAME,    GROSS,    DEPEND
 15 FORMAT (1X, A10, 3X, F7.2, 2X, I2)
```

are used to specify how the values of NAME, GROSS, and DEPEND should be printed. The FORMAT statement with label 15 is referenced by the formatted PRINT. The FORMAT statement consists of a list of *edit descriptors* enclosed in parentheses. Some of the edit descriptors describe how a value is to be printed (A10, F7.2, I2); others specify how many spaces are to be left between values (3X, 2X). Each edit descriptor is explained in Table 4.12. ∎

Table 4.12. *Edit Descriptors in FORMAT Statement 15*

DESCRIPTOR	EFFECT
1X	Inserts a blank in the output line
A10	Prints a string value right-justified in ten columns
3X	Leaves three spaces (between the first and second values)
F7.2	Prints a real value right-justified in seven columns with two decimal places
2X	Leaves two spaces (between the second and third values)
I2	Prints an integer value right-justified in two columns

FORMAT statement 15 is a template that specifies the exact appearance (as described in Table 4.12) of any output line that is printed using it. In the form sketched below, the A's indicate where the string value will be printed, the F's indicate where the real value will be printed, and the I's indicate where the integer will be printed. The symbol □ indicates which columns will be left blank.

```
□AAAAAAAAAA□□FFFF.FF□□II
```

The position of the decimal point in the real value is also shown in the sketch. Recall that the edit descriptor F7.2 specifies that there are two decimal places in the real value and a total of seven print columns, including the decimal point itself. Counting characters from the left, we can determine that the decimal point must appear in column 19.

In this example, the formatted PRINT statement has three output list items: NAME, GROSS, DEPEND. Each of these is paired with an edit descriptor that begins with the letter A, F, or I. The first output list item is paired with the first such descriptor (NAME with A10), the second output list item with the second such descriptor (GROSS with F7.2), and the third output list item with the third such descriptor (DEPEND with I2). To illustrate this pairing, each output list item appears directly above its corresponding edit descriptor.

Once this pairing is determined, the output values are printed according to the template shown earlier. Given the variable values

NAME	GROSS	DEPEND
JOHNNY□JONES	346.976	3

the line that would be printed is shown next under its template.

```
□AAAAAAAAAA□□FFFF.FF□□II
JOHNNY JON    346.98    3
```

Note that the value of NAME is truncated to 10 characters, the value of GROSS is rounded to two decimal places, and the numeric values are each printed right-justified (with a leading blank) in their *output fields*.

It is essential that each edit descriptor and its associated output list item be the same type. The type of data item required for each edit descriptor and the general form of the edit descriptors are described in Table 4.13. In this table, n, w, and d represent integer constants (parameters may not be used).

As shown in Table 4.13, the edit descriptor A by itself instructs the compiler to use as many output columns as there are characters in the string value being printed. If the output list item is a CHARACTER variable, its declared length determines the number of columns used.

The FORMAT statement is a nonexecutable statement and may be placed

Table 4.13. *General Form of Edit Descriptors*

DESCRIPTOR	EFFECT
Aw	Exactly w characters are printed. If there are more than w characters in the associated string value, the extra characters on the right are not printed. If there are fewer than w characters, the string value is padded with blanks on the left (right-justified).
A	The number of characters printed exactly matches the length of the output list item.
Fw.d	A real number is printed right-justified in w columns. The fractional part is rounded to d decimal places.
Iw	An integer is printed right-justified in w columns.
nX	There are n blanks or spaces "printed."

anywhere in a program. Generally, it follows the first PRINT statement that references it. There may be more than one formatted PRINT statement that references a particular FORMAT statement. Each FORMAT statement must have a unique label. The FORMAT statement is described in the next display.

FORMAT Statement

SYNTAX: *label* FORMAT (*edit descriptors*)

EXAMPLE: 15 FORMAT (1X, A, 2X, I6)

INTERPRETATION: The *edit descriptors* provide a template describing the form of an output line. This template applies to any line printed by each formatted PRINT statement that references the FORMAT statement *label*. The first edit descriptor beginning with A, F, or I is paired with the first output list item in the formatted PRINT, the second edit descriptor beginning with A, F, or I is paired with the second output list item, and so on.

Review of Edit Descriptors

In this section, we will provide more examples of the use of some FORTRAN edit descriptors.

EXAMPLE 4.27

Table 4.14 shows some integer values printed using different edit descriptors. Each edit descriptor must begin with the letter I. The symbol □ represents a blank space. ■

As shown in Table 4.14, an integer value is always printed right-justified in its field. There should be enough columns specified to print the integer value and its sign. If there are not enough columns specified, the value displayed is compiler-dependent; however, many compilers display a string of asterisks.

Table 4.14. *Printing Integer Values Using Edit Descriptors*

VALUE	DESCRIPTOR	PRINTED OUTPUT
234	I4	□234
234	I5	□□234
234	I6	□□□234
234	I2	compiler-dependent
−234	I4	−234
−234	I5	□−234
−234	I6	□□−234
−234	I3	compiler-dependent

EXAMPLE 4.28 Table 4.15 shows some real values printed using different edit descriptors. Each edit descriptor must begin with the letter F. ■

Table 4.15. *Printing Real Values Using Edit Descriptors*

VALUE	DESCRIPTOR	PRINTED OUTPUT
3.14159	F5.2	□3.14
3.14159	F5.1	□□3.1
3.14159	F6.3	□3.142
3.14159	F4.0	□□3.
3.14159	F3.2	compiler-dependent
−5.678	F4.1	−5.7
−5.678	F6.2	□−5.68
−5.678	F4.0	□−6.
−5.678	F9.5	□−5.67800
−5.678	F7.5	compiler-dependent

As shown in this table, a real value is always rounded before it is printed. It is all right to specify zero decimal places. In this case, the real value is rounded to the nearest whole number. Make sure that you leave enough columns for all the digits required, the decimal point, and the sign of the number. If there are not enough columns specified, the value displayed is compiler-dependent; however, many compilers display a string of asterisks.

EXAMPLE 4.29 Table 4.16 shows some string values printed using different edit descriptors. Each edit descriptor must begin with the letter A. ■

As shown in Table 4.16, a string value is always printed right-justified in its output field. If there are not enough columns specified to print the complete string, then only the part of the string that fits in the output field will be printed.

Table 4.16. *Printing String Values Using Edit Descriptors*

VALUE	DESCRIPTOR	PRINTED OUTPUT
'*'	A	*
'*'	A1	*
'*'	A2	□*
'*'	A3	□□*
'ACES'	A	ACES
'ACES'	A1	A
'ACES'	A2	AC
'ACES'	A3	ACE
'ACES'	A4	ACES
'ACES'	A5	□ACES

Table 4.16 assumes that the string values `'*'` and `'ACES'` are inserted directly in an output list. The situation is a bit different when we store a string in a CHARACTER variable first and then display the CHARACTER variable. For example, if CARD is type CHARACTER *10, the assignment

```
CARD = 'ACES'
```

stores the string ACES followed by six blanks in variable CARD. Consequently, if we print CARD using format specification A or A10, FORTRAN displays the string ACES followed by six blanks (the value of CARD). If we print CARD using format specification A15, FORTRAN displays the value of CARD right-justified, so we see five blanks before the string ACES and six blanks after the string.

Line-Control Characters

The first edit descriptor in FORMAT statement 15 is 1X. This edit descriptor causes the template to begin with a blank and is required on some terminals (and all line printers) that use the first character in a formatted output line to determine spacing between lines. On such terminals, the first blank would not be printed but instead would cause the current output line to be printed on the line following the previous line (single-line spacing).

The line-control character can also be specified using a string value as the edit descriptor. The FORMAT statement

```
15 FORMAT (' ', A10, 3X, F7.2, 2X, I2)
```

is equivalent to the earlier one. Table 4.17 shows the line-control characters in FORTRAN.

If you forget to specify the line-control character when one is expected, FORTRAN will use the first output character for line control instead of printing it. This can lead to some very undesirable results.

If your terminal does not process the line-control character, you may prefer

Table 4.17. *Line-Control Characters*

DESCRIPTOR	EFFECT
' ' or 1X	Prints the current line on the line following the previous line (single-line spacing)
'0'	Leaves one blank line between the current line and the previous line (double-line spacing)
'1'	Prints the current line at the top of the next page
'+'	Prints the current line over the previous line

to omit it. If the line-control character 1X or ' ' is not processed, an initial blank is displayed, which can easily be ignored. However, if the line-control character '1' is not processed, a 1 will appear in the first output column.

More Formatted PRINT Statements

We can use formatted PRINT statements to simplify the process of setting up output tables.

EXAMPLE 4.30

The formatted PRINT statement

```
      PRINT 25, 'EMPLOYEE', 'RATE', 'DEPENDENTS'
   25 FORMAT ('1', A15, 5X, A10, 5X, A15)
```

prints a table heading line at the top of the next output page. It should precede a loop that prints the table values. The template described by FORMAT statement 25 and the table heading are shown next.

```
1AAAAAAAAAAAAAAA□□□□□AAAAAAAAAA□□□□□AAAAAAAAAAAAAAA
       EMPLOYEE             RATE           DEPENDENTS
```

Within the loop body, the formatted PRINT statement

```
      PRINT 35, NAME, RATE, DEPEND
   35 FORMAT (' ', A15, 5X, F10.2, 5X, I15)
```

could be used to print an output value under each column heading. Because the output field widths specified in FORMAT statements 25 and 35 are the same (15, 10, 15), each output value would right-align with its respective column heading. The template for FORMAT statement 35 is shown next under the template for FORMAT statement 25.

```
1AAAAAAAAAAAAAAA□□□□□AAAAAAAAAA□□□□□AAAAAAAAAAAAAAA
□AAAAAAAAAAAAAAA□□□□□FFFFFFF.FF□□□□□IIIIIIIIIIIIIII
```

The table heading and two sample output lines are shown next.

```
          EMPLOYEE             RATE           DEPENDENTS
      SMITH, JOHN              55.95                  10
      WILEY, WILLIAMS        123.00                   3
```

The strings stored in variable NAME (type CHARACTER * 15) appear to be left-aligned rather than right-aligned. The reason is that a string that is too short is padded with blanks when it is stored in NAME. All characters stored, including the blank padding, are displayed when the value of NAME is printed. ∎

Formatted WRITE Statements

We can use FORMAT statements with WRITE statements to control the appearance of each line of an output file. To specify formatted output with a WRITE statement, replace the symbol * with a FORMAT statement label. The WRITE statement below writes a new line to the output file associated with unit number 1; FORMAT statement 36 describes the layout of that line. We did not specify a line-control character because the new line is being sent to a disk file, not to the printer. The new line has the same form as the lines shown in Example 4.30.

```
    WRITE (1, 36) NAME, RATE, DEPEND
36 FORMAT (A15, 5X, F10.2, 5X, I15)
```

Format Specifications in PRINT Statements

Generally when debugging programs, we need to insert statements that print key variable values. A shorter version of formatted PRINT statements can be used for this purpose.

FORTRAN permits us to insert a *format specification string* directly in a PRINT statement. In the statement below, the string '(1X, A, I2)' appears after the word PRINT (instead of a statement label) and eliminates the need for a separate FORMAT statement. Don't forget the comma after this string.

```
    PRINT '(1X, A, I2)', 'Value of COUNT is ', COUNT
```

This form is particularly convenient when the format specification is relatively short as it would be in PRINT statements used for debugging.

Assuming COUNT has the integer value 15, the formatted PRINT statement above would display the output line

```
    Value of COUNT is 15
```

The edit descriptor A causes the string value to be printed in an output field that matches the string length, that is, the *default* width of the output field is the same as the string length.

In the format specification string '(1X, A, I2)', shown above, the symbols 1X denote a blank line-control character. You can also use a string to denote the line-control character, as shown next.

```
    PRINT '(''0'', A, I2)', 'Value of COUNT is ', COUNT
```

In this case, the line-control character is the symbol 0 so FORTRAN would insert a blank line before displaying the output list. You must place two consecutive apostrophes on each side of the line-control character (''0'') inside a format specification string used with a PRINT statement.

Format Specifications in READ Statements

We discuss formatted READ statements in Chapter 8. For the time being, we will use formatted READ statements to enter character data only. The formatted READ statement

```
PRINT *, 'Enter your first name?'
READ '(A)', NAME
```

reads character data into character variable NAME. The format specifier A tells FORTRAN that character data will be read, so do not enclose the character data in apostrophes (e.g., enter Bill Jones instead of 'Bill Jones'). Also, you must not insert a line-control character in a format specification string that is part of a READ statement.

EXAMPLE 4.31

The program in Fig. 4.9 uses Manning's equation, shown below, to calculate the flow of water through a pipe.

$$Q = \frac{1.49}{N} AR^{2/3} S^{1/2}$$

where Q is the flow of water (cubic feet per sec), N is the roughness coefficient (unitless), A is the area (square feet), R is the hydraulic radius (feet), and S is the slope (feet/foot). For readability, the program uses the variables FLOW, RUFNES (for roughness coefficient), AREA, RADIUS, and SLOPE.

In Fig. 4.9, all formats are inserted directly as strings in READ and PRINT statements. The list-directed READ statement

```
READ *, RUFNES, AREA, RADIUS, SLOPE
```

enters all four REAL data values. In the sample run, the program user enters each data value under its units.

Figure 4.9. *Computing Flow Using Manning's Equation*

```
      PROGRAM MANNING
C Computes the flow of water through a pipe
C in cubic feet per second (cfs)

C Declarations
      CHARACTER STREET *30
      REAL FLOW, RUFNES, AREA, RADIUS, SLOPE

C Enter data
```

```
          PRINT *, 'Enter street name'
          READ '(A)', STREET
          PRINT *, 'Enter the roughness,        area, ',
         +          'hydraulic radius, and slope'
          PRINT *, '           (unitless), (sq. ft.), ',
         +          ' (feet) (feet/foot)'
          READ *, RUFNES, AREA, RADIUS, SLOPE

C Perform calculations
          FLOW = (1.49/RUFNES) * AREA * (RADIUS ** (2.0/3.0)) *
         +          SQRT(SLOPE)

C Echo the input values and display results
          PRINT '( ''0'', A)', 'City of Byran Civil Engineering Report'
          PRINT '(1X, A, A)', 'Hydraulic data for ', STREET
          PRINT *
          PRINT '(1X, A, F6.4)', 'The roughness coefficient is ',
         +      RUFNES
          PRINT '(1X, A, F6.2, A)', 'The area of the culvert is ',
         +      AREA, ' square feet'
          PRINT '(1X, A, F5.2, A)', 'The hydraulic radius is ',
         +      RADIUS, ' feet'
          PRINT '(1X, A, F7.5, A)', 'The slope is ', SLOPE,
         +      ' feet/foot'
          PRINT *
          PRINT '(1X, A, F8.1, A)', 'The calculated flow is ', FLOW,
         +      ' cfs'

          STOP
          END

Enter street name
Aggie Drive
Enter the roughness,        area, hydraulic radius, and slope
          (unitless), (sq. ft.),            (feet), (feet/foot)
          .0130          28.27            1.5        .0015

City of Byran Civil Engineering Report
Hydraulic data for Aggie Drive

The roughness coefficient is  .0130
The area of the culvert is  28.27 square feet
The hydraulic radius is  1.50 feet
The slope is  .00150 feet/foot

The calculated flow is     164.4 cfs
```

**SELF-CHECK
EXERCISES FOR
SECTION 4.6**

1. Which of the following format specifications are correct? Which contain syntax errors? Correct the syntax errors that you find.

    a. (A, 3X, I4, F12.2)

b. (A, 4I, 2X, F12.1)
c. (A, F16.35X)
d. (A, 2A, F3.3, X6)
e. (A, I4, 4X, F4.2)

2. Let K contain the value 1234 and ALPHA contain the value 555.4567. What would be printed by each of the statements below?

a. PRINT '(1X, I4, F12.4)', K, ALPHA
b. PRINT '(1X, I4, 4X, F8.4)', K, ALPHA
c. PRINT '(1X, A, I4)', 'K = ', K
d. PRINT '(1X, A, F8.2)', 'ALPHA = ', ALPHA
e. PRINT '(1X, A, I5, 10X, A, F10.3)', 'K = ', K, 'ALPHA = ', ALPHA

3. Consider these variable values:

SSNO1	SSNO2	SSNO3	LAST	FIRST	HOURS	RATE	PAY
219	40	9677	DOG	HOT	40.00	4.50	180.00

Write a segment of a FORTRAN program (including declarations) to produce the following output:

Line 1 SOCIAL SECURITY NUMBER 219-40-9677
Line 2
Line 3 DOG, HOT
Line 4
Line 5 HOURS RATE PAY
Line 6 40.00 4.50 180.00

4.7 Problem Solving Illustrated

The next two case studies illustrate some of the concepts discussed in this chapter. The first case study processes character data and uses formatted output to display the result; the second case study performs a sequence of computations and uses formatted output to display a table.

Case Study: Registered Voters List

Problem

Three clerks, Abraham, Martin, and John, were appointed to supervise the town elections and verify that each person attempting to vote is legally registered. Abraham will check voters whose last names begin with A–I, Martin

Case Study: Registered Voters List, continued

will check voters whose last names begin with J–R, and John will check voters whose last names begin with S–Z.

Design Overview

We need a program that will read in each voter's name and print out the clerk assigned. The program should also print the number of voters assigned to each clerk so that we can check whether their workloads are comparable. A sample run follows.

```
Enter each voter name in the form:
last name, first name
When done, enter * as the voter name.

Enter voter:
Johnson, William
Clerk assigned: Martin

Enter voter:
Washington, George
Clerk assigned: John

Enter voter:
Adams, John
Clerk assigned: Abraham

Enter voter:
*

 CLERK    NUMBER OF VOTERS
Abraham          1
Martin           1
John             1
```

Data Requirements

Problem Parameters

the three clerks (CLERK1 = 'Abraham', CLERK2 = 'Martin',
                   CLERK3 = 'John')
the first letter of each group (GROUP1 = 'A', GROUP2 = 'J', GROUP3 = 'S')
the sentinel name (SENVAL = '*')

Problem Input

the name of each voter (CHARACTER *20 VOTER)

Case Study: Registered Voters List, continued

Problem Output

the count of voters assigned to each clerk (INTEGER N1, N2, N3)

Initial Algorithm

1. Read each voter name, assign a clerk, and keep track of the count of voters assigned to each clerk.
2. Print the count of voters assigned to each clerk.

Algorithm Refinements

Step 1 is the only step that needs refinement, as shown next.

Step 1 Refinement

1.1 Initialize the counts of voters to zero
1.2 Read the first voter name
1.3 DO WHILE there are more voters
     1.4 Find and print the clerk's name and increment his counter
     1.5 Read the next voter name
  ENDDO

Step 1.4 is a decision structure that determines which clerk should be assigned to a voter. Its refinement follows.

Step 1.4 Refinement

1.4.1 IF voter name begins with A–I THEN
     Print CLERK1 and increment N1
  ELSE IF voter name begins with J–R THEN
     Print CLERK2 and increment N2
  ELSE IF voter name begins with S–Z THEN
     Print CLERK3 and increment N3
  ELSE
     Print a message that voter's name is invalid
  ENDIF

Coding

The final program is shown in Fig. 4.10. (A sample run was provided earlier as part of the problem discussion.)

We introduced three parameters in Fig. 4.10 besides SENVAL. These parameters are GROUP1, GROUP2, and GROUP3, and they are used to specify the first letter

Case Study: Registered Voters List, continued

Figure 4.10. *Program to Assign Voting Clerks*

```
      PROGRAM VOTING
C Assigns voters to clerks and counts voters assigned to each clerk
C Voters with names A - I are assigned to Abraham.
C Voters with names J - R are assigned to Martin.
C Voters with names S - Z are assigned to John.

C Declarations
      CHARACTER *10 CLERK1, CLERK2, CLERK3
      PARAMETER (CLERK1 = 'Abraham', CLERK2 = 'Martin', CLERK3 = 'John')
      CHARACTER SENVAL, GROUP1, GROUP2, GROUP3
      PARAMETER (SENVAL = '*', GROUP1 = 'A', GROUP2 = 'J', GROUP3 = 'S')
      CHARACTER *20 VOTER
      CHARACTER *10 CLERK
      INTEGER N1, N2, N3

C Read each voter name, assign a clerk, and keep track of counts.
C Initialize counts
      N1 = 0
      N2 = 0
      N3 = 0

C Read the first voter's name.
      PRINT *, 'Enter each voter name in the form:'
      PRINT *, ' last name, first name '
      PRINT *, 'When done, enter * as the voter name.'
      PRINT *
      PRINT *, 'Enter voter:'
      READ '(A)', VOTER

C Find and print the clerk assigned.
      DO WHILE (VOTER .NE. SENVAL)              9 IF (...) THEN
         IF (VOTER .GE. GROUP1 .AND. VOTER .LT. GROUP2) THEN
            PRINT *, 'Clerk assigned: ', CLERK1
            N1 = N1 + 1
         ELSE IF (VOTER .GE. GROUP2 .AND. VOTER .LT. GROUP3) THEN
            PRINT *, 'Clerk assigned: ', CLERK2
            N2 = N2 + 1
         ELSE IF (VOTER .GE. GROUP3 .AND. VOTER .LE. 'ZZZZZZZZZZ') THEN
            PRINT *, 'Clerk assigned: ', CLERK3
            N3 = N3 + 1
         ELSE
            PRINT *, 'Voter name is invalid. No clerk assigned.'
         ENDIF

C        Read the next voter's name
         PRINT *
```

Case Study: Registered Voters List, continued

```
         PRINT *, 'Enter voter:'
         READ '(A)', VOTER
      ENDDO                                       GOTO 9
C                                                 ENDIF
C Print counts of voters
      PRINT *
      PRINT 10, 'CLERK', 'NUMBER OF VOTERS'
   10 FORMAT (1X, A7, 10X, A)
      PRINT 20, CLERK1, N1
      PRINT 20, CLERK2, N2
      PRINT 20, CLERK3, N3
   20 FORMAT (1X, A7, 10X, I9)

C Exit Program
      STOP
      END
```

of each group of voters. The use of these parameters enables us to change the makeup of each group easily in case the group sizes are very uneven and we need to rerun the program.

Testing

When testing this program, be sure to enter some names that begin with the letters at each group boundary (A, J, and S). Make sure that these names are assigned to the correct clerk.

Case Study: Computing Maximum Tensile Loads

Problem

Joe Bob's steel company produces steel reinforcing bars (rebars). The size of a rebar is designated by a number. That number divided by 8 gives the diameter of the bar in inches (e.g., a number 5 rebar is $\frac{5}{8}$ of an inch in diameter). The company needs to produce a chart showing the maximum tensile load of the bars when they are made from certain grades of steel. Joe Bob makes number 2 to number 11 rebars. Each chart should have the form shown next.

Case Study: Computing Maximum Tensile Loads, continued

```
                    Joe Bob's Steel Company
                        Rebar load chart
           For bars with a steel strength of 8000.00 psi

        Bar                 Cross-sectional            Max. Load
      Number                 Area (sq. in.)              (lbs.)
      -------               ----------------           ----------
         2                        0.05                    393.
         3                        0.11                    884.
         4                        0.20                   1571.
         5                        0.31                   2454.
         6                        0.44                   3534.
         7                        0.60                   4811.
         8                        0.79                   6283.
         9                        0.99                   7952.
        10                        1.23                   9817.
        11                        1.48                  11879.
```

Design Overview

The maximum tensile load on a bar is the amount of force the bar can hold in tension. It is calculated by multiplying the cross-sectional area of the bar by the tensile strength of the steel:

load = area × steel strength

For a given tensile strength, we can display each line of the preceding table by first determining the cross-sectional area corresponding to that number rebar. We can then use the formula above to compute the maximum load.

Data Requirements

Problem Input

tensile strength of the steel (REAL STRNTH)

Problem Outputs

the rebar number (INTEGER BARNUM)
the cross-sectional area (REAL AREA)
the maximum tensile load (REAL LOAD)

Initial Algorithm

1. Read the steel strength
2. Display the table heading
3. DO for each rebar from number 2 to 11

Case Study: Computing Maximum Tensile Loads, continued

      4. Compute cross-sectional area
      5. `LOAD = AREA * STRNTH`
      6. Display rebar number, area, and load
  `CONTINUE`

Algorithm Refinements

Step 4 needs further refinement. We can use the steps below to compute the cross-sectional area for a particular rebar number.

Additional Program Variable

the radius of the cross-section (`REAL RADIUS`)

Step 4 Refinement

4.1 *radius = rebar number/16.0*
4.2 *area = $\pi \times radius^2$*

Coding

Figure 4.11 shows the program.

Figure 4.11. *Computing Table of Loads for Rebars*

```
      PROGRAM REBAR
C Prints a table of maximum tensile load on rebars

C  Declarations
      REAL PI
      PARAMETER (PI = 3.14159)
      REAL STRNTH, AREA, LOAD, RADIUS
      INTEGER BARNUM

C  Read steel strength
      PRINT *, 'Enter steel tensile strength (in psi)'
      READ *, STRNTH

C  Display table heading
      PRINT *, '          Joe Bob''s Steel Company'
      PRINT *, '            Rebar load chart'
      PRINT *, 'For bars with a steel strength of ', STRNTH, ' psi'
      PRINT *
      PRINT *, 'Bar            Cross-sectional           Max. Load'
      PRINT *, 'Number         Area (sq. in.)             (lbs.)'
      PRINT *, '--------       ----------------         -----------'
```

Case Study: Computing Maximum Tensile Loads, continued

```
C  Perform calculations and print table.
      DO 10 BARNUM = 2, 11
         RADIUS = REAL(BARNUM) / 16.0
         AREA = PI * RADIUS ** 2
         LOAD = AREA * STRNTH
         PRINT 5, BARNUM, AREA, LOAD
    5    FORMAT (1X, I6, 13X, F6.2, 14X, F8.0)
   10 CONTINUE

C  Exit program
      STOP
      END
```

Testing

A sample run would begin with the prompt

```
Enter steel tensile strength (in psi)
```

If a positive data value is entered, the program should display a meaningful table of values (see sample table on page 222).

SELF-CHECK EXERCISES FOR SECTION 4.7

1. Compute the weight per linear foot of each rebar. Steel has a weight of 490 lb./cu. ft.
2. After the first `READ` statement in Fig. 4.11, add a `WHILE` loop that executes until a positive value is read.

4.8 Common Programming Errors

Errors in type declarations are generally caused by spelling mistakes or failure to declare a variable used in a program. In either case, the compiler will not detect an error but instead will allocate another memory cell for the new variable using the implicit type convention. If type `LOGICAL` or `CHARACTER` data are stored in the implicitly declared variable, an error message will be printed. If type `REAL` or `INTEGER` data are stored in the implicitly declared variable, no error message will be printed; however, the program results may be incorrect.

The type of each data value entered during program execution must correspond to the variable in which it is stored. If the data type required is not obvious, the program should print a prompting message with appropriate instructions for the program user. The apostrophes enclosing a character string must be entered as must the periods enclosing a type LOGICAL value.

Be careful to use the correct type of operator with each operand. The arithmetic operators can be used only with type INTEGER or REAL operands. If a type REAL expression is assigned to a type INTEGER variable, the fractional part of the result will be lost. The fractional remainder is lost when two integers are divided.

For the time being, only the relational operators should be used with type CHARACTER data. The LOGICAL expression

    (3 .NE. '3')

is invalid because it compares an integer to a character value.

The LOGICAL .AND. and .OR. operators can be used only with LOGICAL expressions. In the expression

    (FLAG .AND. (X .LE. Y))

the variable FLAG must be type LOGICAL. Remember to enclose a LOGICAL expression used with IF or WHILE in parentheses.

A good deal of care is required when working with complicated expressions. It is easy to omit parentheses or operators inadvertently, especially the * operator. If an operator or a single parenthesis is omitted, a syntax error will be detected. If a pair of parentheses is omitted, then the expression, although syntactically correct, may compute the wrong value.

Sometimes it is beneficial to break a complicated expression into subexpressions that are separately assigned to *temporary variables* and then to manipulate these temporary variables. For example, it is easier to write correctly the three assignment statements

    TEMP1 = SQRT(X + Y)
    TEMP2 = 1.0 + TEMP1
    Z = TEMP1 / TEMP2

than the single assignment statement

    Z = SQRT(X + Y) / (1.0 + SQRT(X + Y))

which has the same effect. Using three assignment statements is also more efficient because the square-root operation is performed only once; it is performed twice in the single assignment statement.

Be careful to use the right type and number of arguments in a function call. A type REAL argument cannot be used with the functions MOD, REAL, IABS, MAXO, and MINO. A negative value cannot be passed as the argument of SQRT, ALOG, or ALOG10.

Chapter Review

The FORTRAN language provides a capability for manipulating a number of different *types* of data. We have introduced four of these types (INTEGER, REAL, LOGICAL, and CHARACTER) in this chapter.

All information is stored in the computer as a binary string. The format of this string is determined by the type of data being represented. In order for the FORTRAN compiler to generate the correct machine language instructions for a program, it must know the types of all data being manipulated. Thus, the types of all constants and variable names used in a program must be clearly indicated to the compiler.

The types of variable names can be specified either by using type declaration statements or by allowing the compiler to assign a type to each name according to the implicit typing convention (not recommended). Under this convention, all variable names beginning with the letters I through N are automatically typed INTEGER; names beginning with A through H or O through Z are automatically typed REAL. Examples of the four type declarations introduced in this chapter are shown in Table 4.18.

Table 4.18. *Examples of Type Declarations*

DECLARATION	EFFECT
CHARACTER *20 NAME CHARACTER NAME *20	Declares a variable for storing a character string of length 20
CHARACTER LETTER	Declares a variable for storing a character string of length 1
REAL X, ALPHA	Declares two variables for storing real data items
INTEGER I, COUNT	Declares two variables for storing integer data items
LOGICAL FLAG	Declares a variable for storing a logical data item (having a value of either .TRUE. or .FALSE.)

Constants are typed according to the way in which they are written. Real constants are numbers that contain a decimal point; integer constants do not contain a decimal point. Character-string constants consist of a string of legal FORTRAN characters enclosed in apostrophes. The only two logical constants are .TRUE. and .FALSE..

In this chapter, we have also provided rules for forming and evaluating arithmetic expressions. This capability is most useful in numerically oriented problems. Knowledge of these rules will enable you to apply FORTRAN correctly to perform calculations. One useful guideline, which should always be kept in mind when transforming an equation or formula to FORTRAN, is "when in doubt of the meaning, insert parentheses."

Integer arithmetic was also discussed. Of the basic arithmetic operators, +,

$-$, $*$, $/$, and $**$, only the slash (division) produces different results when used with integers instead of reals. This is due to the fact that the internal fixed-point format used for storage of integers does not permit the representation of a fractional remainder.

Library functions were also introduced. Their use will enable you to perform numerical calculations more efficiently, since calling a function to compute a result is much faster and easier than trying to perform the calculation using the basic arithmetic operations.

Finally, we discussed formatted output and the use of the format specification to control the appearance of a printed line. Edit descriptors beginning with A, F, and I are used for printing character, real, and integer data, respectively.

The x descriptor is used for horizontal spacing in a line. On some computer systems, each output list should begin with one of the characters blank, 0, 1, or +; this character is used for vertical spacing, or line control.

New FORTRAN Statements

The new FORTRAN statements introduced in this chapter are described in Table 4.19.

Table 4.19. *Summary of New FORTRAN Statements*

STATEMENT	EFFECT
Arithmetic Assignment	
`I = J / K + MOD(L + 5, N)`	Adds the result of J / K to the integer remainder of (L + 5) divided by N. L and N must be type INTEGER.
CHARACTER Assignment	
`FLOWER = 'ROSE'`	Assigns the string 'ROSE' to the type CHARACTER variable FLOWER.
LOGICAL Assignment	
`EVEN = .NOT. ODD`	Assigns the LOGICAL complement of ODD to EVEN. ODD and EVEN must be type LOGICAL.
Formatted PRINT	
`    PRINT 25, MONTH, DAY` `25 FORMAT ('1', A, 1X, I2)`	Displays a character value (MONTH), a blank, and a two-digit integer value (DAY) on a new page.
Formatted WRITE	
`    WRITE (2, 26) MONTH, DAY` `26 FORMAT (A, I2)`	Writes the values of MONTH (a string) and DAY (a two-digit integer) to unit 2.
Formatted READ	
`    READ '(A)', DATE`	Enters a string of characters into DATE.

Quick-Check Exercises

1. When does the operator / mean real division and when does it mean integer division?
2. Evaluate the following when X is 22.0 and Y is 3.0.

   ```
   X + Y / SQRT(X + Y)
   ```

3. Complete the formula below for integers N and M:

   ```
   N = (N / M) * ___ + MOD(___, ___)
   ```

4. Write a FORTRAN expression to compute the real average of N values stored in SUM where N and SUM are type INTEGER.
5. Assign LOGICAL variable SWITCH the value .TRUE. if N is a multiple of 3.
6. Evaluate the LOGICAL expressions

   ```
   .FALSE. .AND. (3.14593 / (1.1234 * 2.0456) .LE. 1.3690)
   .TRUE. .AND. (MOD(30, 10) .EQ. 0)
   ```

   For each expression, is the outer pair of parentheses required? What about the inner pair? Explain your answers.
7. List the following characters in sequence according to their ASCII codes: a, B, blank, 0. What is the absolute difference between the codes for a and B?
8. Arrange the three strings that follow in sequence according to their internal codes:
   ' 10', '3', and '010'.
9. Assume X is 5.9456, Y is 6.1234, and Z is 'Donald Duck'. Show the output displayed by the statements

   ```
       PRINT 15, '+', X, Y, Z
   15 FORMAT (1X, A, F5.2, F8.5, 1X, A6)
       PRINT '(''0'', A, F4.1, A12, F6.3)', '+', X, Z, Y
   ```

Answers to Quick-Check Exercises

1. The operator / means real division if one or both of its operands is type REAL; it means integer division only when both of its operands are type INTEGER.
2. 22.0 + (3.0 / SQRT(25.0)) is 22.0 + (3.0 / 5.0) is 22.6.
3. N = (N / M) * M + MOD(N, M)
4. REAL(SUM) / REAL(N)
5. SWITCH = MOD(N, 3) .EQ. 0
6. .FALSE. .AND. *any expression* is always .FALSE.
   .TRUE. .AND. (0 .EQ. 0) is .TRUE.
   The outer pair is not needed because the logical operator .AND. has lower precedence and would be evaluated last. The inner pair is needed in the first expression because otherwise the division would be done first. The inner pair is needed in the second expression because it encloses the function arguments.

7. blank, 0, B, a. The difference between a and A is 32, so the difference between a and B is 31.
8. ' 10', '010', '3' (blank < 0 < 3)
9. + 5.95 6.12340 Donald

    + 5.9 Donald Duck   6.123

Review Questions

1. What are the advantages of data type INTEGER over data type REAL?
2. What is the result of the expression (3 + 5.0 / 2) + 8 − 15 / 4?
3. Given the following declarations, indicate the data type and value of each expression below when X is 7.0, Y is 2.0, A is 2, B is 7.

    REAL X, Y
    INTEGER A, B

	Type	Value
X * Y		
A * B		
B / Y		
B / A		
X / Y		
MOD(A, B)		
MOD(X, Y)		

4. Indicate the answer to the operations presented below.

MOD(11, 2)		ABS(−37.5 + 20)	
INT(−3.5)		SQRT(12 + 13)	
MAX0(−27,50,4)		INT(−25.7)	
MIN0(−27,50,4)		NINT(−18.7)	

5. Write an assignment statement that rounds a real variable NUM1 to two digits after the decimal point leaving the result in NUM1.
6. List and explain three computational errors that may occur in type REAL expressions.
7. Write an IF structure that will write out TRUE or FALSE according to the following conditions: either FLAG is .TRUE. or COLOR is 'RED', or both MONEY is 'PLENTY' and TIMEUP is .FALSE..
8. Write a statement that assigns a value of .TRUE. to the LOGICAL variable OVRTIM only if a worker's HOURS are greater than 40.
9. Write statements that print the values of NAME, HOURS, RATE, and PAY in the table form below. Show one PRINT and FORMAT pair for the heading and one for the table values. Leave five spaces between the values shown in the table.

NAME	HOURS	RATE	PAY
AAAAAAAAAA	XXX.X	XXX.XX	XXXXX.XX

Programming Projects

1. A company has ten employees, many of whom work overtime (more than 40 hours) each week. The company wants a payroll program that reads the weekly time records (containing employee name, hourly rate (*rate*), and hours worked (*hours*) for each employee) and computes the gross salary and net pay as follows:

$$gross = \begin{cases} hours \times rate \text{ (if } hours <= 40) \\ 1.5 \times rate \times (hours - 40) + 40 \times rate \text{ (if } hours > 40) \end{cases}$$

$$net = \begin{cases} gross \text{ (if } gross <= \$65) \\ gross - (15 + 0.45 \times gross) \text{ (if } gross > \$65) \end{cases}$$

The program should print a five-column table listing each employee's name, hourly rate, hours worked, gross salary, and net pay. The total amount of the payroll should be printed at the end, and can be computed by summing the gross salaries for all employees. Test your program on the following data:

Name	Rate	Hours
IVORY HUNTER	3.50	35
TRACK STAR	4.50	40
SMOKEY BEAR	3.25	80
OSCAR GROUCH	6.80	10
THREE BEARS	1.50	16
POKEY PUPPY	2.65	25
FAT EDDIE	2.00	40
PUMPKIN PIE	2.65	35
SARA LEE	5.00	40
HUMAN ERASER	6.25	52

2. Write a program to read in a collection of integers and determine whether each is a prime number. Test your program with the four integers 7, 17, 35, 96. All numbers should be processed in one run.

3. Let N be a positive integer consisting of up to ten digits, $d_{10}d_9...d_1$. Write a program to list in one column each of the digits in the number N. The rightmost digit, d_1, should be listed at the top of the column. *Hint:* If N is 3704, what is the value of digit as computed according to the following formula?

```
DIGIT = MOD(N, 10)
```

Test your program for values of N equal to 6, 3704, and 170498.

4. An integer N is divisible by 9 if the sum of its digits is divisible by 9. Use the algorithm developed for project 3 and write a program to determine whether or not the following numbers are divisible by 9.

```
N =   154368
N =   621594
N =   123456
```

5. Write a program that reads in a collection of words enclosed in apostrophes. The program should print the total number of words read, the number of words that are in the first half of the alphabet (first letter is A-M), the number of words that begin with the letter T, and the number of occurrences of the word 'THE'.

6. Each month a bank customer deposits $50 in a savings account. The account earns 6.5 percent interest, calculated on a quarterly basis (one-fourth of 6.5 percent each quarter). Write a program to compute the total investment, the total amount in the account, and the interest accrued, for each of 120 months of a 10-year period. You may assume that the rate is applied to all funds in the account at the end of a quarter regardless of when the deposits were made.

   Print all values accurate to two decimal places. The table printed by your program should begin as follows:

MONTH	INVESTMENT	NEW AMOUNT	INTEREST	TOTAL SAVINGS
1	50.00	50.00	0.00	50.00
2	100.00	100.00	0.00	100.00
3	150.00	150.00	2.44	152.44
4	200.00	202.44	0.00	202.44
5	250.00	252.44	0.00	252.44
6	300.00	302.44	4.91	307.35
7	350.00	357.35	0.00	357.35

7. The interest paid on a savings account is compounded daily. This means that if you start with STBAL dollars in the bank, at the end of the first day you will have a balance of

$$\text{STBAL} \times (1 + rate/365)$$

dollars, where *rate* is the annual interest rate (0.10 if the annual rate is 10 percent). At the end of the second day, you will have

$$\text{STBAL} \times (1 + rate/365) \times (1 + rate/365)$$

dollars, and at the end of N days you will have

$$\text{STBAL} \times (1 + rate/365)^N$$

dollars. Write a program that processes a set of data records, each of which contains values for STBAL, *rate*, and N and computes the final account balance.

8. Compute the monthly payment and the total payment for a bank loan, given:

   a. the amount of the loan
   b. the duration of the loan in months
   c. the interest rate for the loan

   Your program should read in one record at a time (each containing a loan value, a months value, and a rate value), perform the required computation, and print the values of the loan, months, rate, the monthly payment, and the total payment.

Test your program with at least the following data (and more if you want).

Loan	Months	Rate
16000	300	12.50
24000	360	13.50
30000	300	15.50
42000	360	14.50
22000	300	15.50
300000	240	15.25

Notes:
The formula for computing monthly payment is

$$monthly = \left[\frac{rate}{1200} \times \left(1 + \frac{rate}{1200}\right)^{months} \times loan \right] \Big/ \left[\left(1 + \frac{rate}{1200}\right)^{months} - 1 \right]$$

The formula for computing the total payment is

$$total = monthly \times months$$

Also, you may find it helpful to introduce the following additional variables to simplify the computation of the monthly payment. You can print the values of *ratem* and *expm* to see whether your program's computations are accurate.

$ratem = rate/1200$
$expm = (1 + ratem)$

Hint: You will need a loop to multiply *expm* by itself *months* times.

9. The rate of decay of a radioactive isotope is given in terms of its half-life, H, the time lapse required for the isotope to decay to one-half of its original mass. The isotope strontium 90 (Sr^{90}) has a half-life of 28 years. Compute and print in table form the amount of this isotope remaining after each year for 50 years, given the initial presence of 50.0 grams. The amount of Sr^{90} remaining can be computed by using the following formula:

   $$r = amount * C^{(y/H)}$$

   where *amount* is 50.0 grams as the initial amount, C is expressed as $e^{-0.693}$ ($e = 2.71828$), y is the number of years elapsed, and H is the half-life of the isotope in years.

10. An employee time card is represented as one long line of data items. Write a program that processes a collection of these lines. Assume that the data items follow the sequence below.

Positions	Data
1–10	Employee's last name enclosed in apostrophes
12–20	Employee's first name enclosed in apostrophes
22–24	Contains 'C' for city office or 'S' for suburban office
26–28	Contains 'U' (union) or 'N' (non-union)
30–35	Employee's identification number in apostrophes
37–38	Number of regular hours (a whole number)

40–45	Hourly rate (dollars and cents)
47–48	Number of dependents
50–54	Number of overtime hours (a real number)

a. Compute gross pay using the formula:

gross = regular hours × rate + overtime hours × 1.5 × rate

b. Compute net pay by subtracting the following deductions:

federal tax = .14(gross − 13 × dependents)
social security = 0.052 × gross
city tax = .04(gross) (if employee works in the city)
union dues = 6.75(gross) (for union member)

11. A concrete channel is being designed to bring water to Mono Lake. It will have vertical walls and a width of 15 feet. It will be 10 feet deep, have a slope of .0015 feet/foot, and a roughness coefficient of .014. How deep will the water be when 5,000 cubic feet per second is flowing through it?
    To solve this problem, we can use Manning's equation

$$Q = \frac{1.49}{N} AR^{2/3}S^{1/2}$$

where Q is the flow of water (cubic feet per sec), N is the roughness coefficient (unitless), A is the area (square feet), S is the slope (feet/foot), and R is the hydraulic radius (feet).

The hydraulic radius is the cross-sectional area divided by the wetted perimeter. For square channels, like the one in this example,

*Hydraulic radius = depth * width/(2.0 * depth + width)*

To solve this problem, we will guess a depth and then calculate the corresponding flow. If the flow is too little, we guess a depth a little higher; if the flow is too high, we guess a depth a little lower. This is repeated until we are within .1 percent of the flow desired.

For the initial guess, try half the channel depth. Example run:

trial depth	trial flow	target flow	difference
5.217247	643.0518	1000.000	−356.9482
5.406021	682.4061	1000.000	−317.5939
5.570860	716.9747	1000.000	−283.0253
5.715399	747.4297	1000.000	−252.5703
.	.	.	.
.	.	.	.
6.888953	998.6530	1000.000	−1.346985
6.889561	998.7847	1000.000	−1.215332
6.890110	998.9034	1000.000	−1.096558
6.890604	999.0106	1000.000	−0.9893799

The depth will be   6.890604   feet.

5. Subprograms

$\mathbf{I}$N THE last chapter, you learned how to use library functions to simplify computations. In this chapter, we will illustrate how to write your own functions to implement computational steps in an algorithm. You will learn how to define functions and how to reference these functions in expressions.

A function is an independent program module, or *subprogram*, that returns a single result. We will introduce another type of subprogram, a subroutine, which can return more than one result. The use of functions and subroutines will enable you to implement each major program step as an independent program module. You can implement and test each subprogram individually. Then you can combine these subprograms as "building blocks" to form a complete program. You can also reuse a subprogram when the operation it performs is required again in the same program or another program.

5.1 ▬▬▬ User-Defined Functions

Library functions are convenient in that they permit us to perform a particular computation as often as we wish simply by referencing a function name in an expression. Each time we perform this computation, different argument(s) can be passed to the function. We can also define our own functions to perform other computations that are not part of the FORTRAN function library.

EXAMPLE 5.1   The function FACTRL in Fig. 5.1 computes the factorial of an integer argument. The integer whose factorial will be computed is represented by the *dummy argument* N in the function description; its value is passed into the function when it is called.   ∎

The factorial function in Fig. 5.1 looks a lot like a program. The differences are the following:

- A function begins with a special header statement of the form

    ftype FUNCTION *fname* (*dummy argument list*)

- The last statement executed in a function is RETURN instead of STOP. Although more than one RETURN statement is permitted, it is generally best to have only a single RETURN.
- A function does not print its result; instead, the result is assigned to the function name by a statement such as

    FACTRL = PRODUC

The last value assigned to the function name is "returned" as the function result.

Figure 5.1. *Function to Compute Factorial*

```
      INTEGER FUNCTION FACTRL (N)
C Computes the factorial of N
C Pre : N is greater than or equal to zero.
C Post: Function result is N!

C Argument Declarations
      INTEGER N

C Local Declarations
      INTEGER I, PRODUC

C Accumulate partial products in PRODUC
      PRODUC = 1
      DO 10 I = N, 2, -1
      PRODUC = PRODUC * I
   10 CONTINUE

C Define function result
      FACTRL = PRODUC

C Exit function
      RETURN
      END
```

The variables PRODUC and I are called *local variables* because they are declared in the function and, therefore, can be manipulated only within the function body. Except for special COMMON data (to be discussed in Chapter 7), a function can reference only its own local variables and dummy arguments. Function definitions are described next.

Function Definition

SYNTAX: *ftype* FUNCTION *fname* (*dummy argument list*)
          function interface
          dummy argument declarations
          local declarations
          function body

EXAMPLE:
```
      INTEGER FUNCTION SQUARE (N)
C Computes the square of N
C Pre : N is defined
C Post: Function result is N ** 2

C Argument declarations
      Integer N
```

```
      C Define result and return
            SQUARE = N * N
            RETURN
            END
```

INTERPRETATION: The FUNCTION header statement specifies the function name, *fname*, and the type of the result returned, *ftype*. The *dummy argument list* provides a list of symbolic names that are used as function dummy arguments. The type of each *dummy argument* must be declared. Also, the type of any local variable manipulated by the function should be declared in the *local declarations*. The next program style display describes the *function interface*.

The *function body* describes the data manipulation performed on the function arguments and local variables. The function name, *fname*, must be defined in the *function body*. The last value stored in *fname* is returned as the function value when a RETURN statement is executed or the END statement is reached. The END statement is used to mark the end of the function definition.

NOTE: If the function does not have any arguments, an empty pair of parentheses ( ) must appear in the FUNCTION header statement following *fname*.

Program Style

Function Interface

The first few lines of function FACTRL in Fig. 5.1 contain all the information that anyone needs to know in order to use this function. The initial comment describes what the function does.
The comment line

```
      C Pre : N is greater than or equal to zero.
```

describes the condition that should be true before the function is called; this condition is known as the *precondition*. The condition

```
      C Post: Function result is N!
```

describes the condition that must be true after the function execution is completed; this condition is called the *postcondition*. Next, the lines

```
      C Argument Declarations
            INTEGER N
```

identify and declare the function arguments.

We recommend that you begin all function declarations in this way. These comments and dummy argument declarations provide valuable documentation to other programmers who might want to reuse your functions in a new program. If you list explicit preconditions and postconditions, other programmers can determine what your function does without having to read the code.

Figure 5.2. *Main Program with Function FACTRL*

```
      PROGRAM FUNCAL
C Illustrates a function call

C Declarations
      INTEGER NUM, FACT
      INTEGER FACTRL

      PRINT *, 'Enter an integer between 0 and 10'
      READ *, NUM
      IF (NUM .GE. 0) THEN
         FACT = FACTRL(NUM)
         PRINT *, 'The factorial of ', NUM, ' is ', FACT
      ELSE
         PRINT *, 'The factorial of a negative number is undefined.'
      ENDIF
C Exit program
      STOP
      END


C _____

      INTEGER FUNCTION FACTRL (N)
C Computes the factorial of N
C Pre : N is greater than or equal to zero.
C Post: Function result is N!

C Argument Declarations
      INTEGER N

C Local Declarations
      INTEGER I, PRODUC

C Accumulate partial products in PRODUC
      PRODUC = 1
      DO 10 I = N, 2, -1
      PRODUC = PRODUC * I
   10 CONTINUE

C Define function result
      FACTRL = PRODUC

C Exit function
      RETURN
      END


Enter an integer between 0 and 10
6
The factorial of          6 is          720
```

Using a Function   Function FACTRL in Fig. 5.1 is an independent program module, or *subprogram.* A subprogram cannot be executed by itself; it must be called into execution by another subprogram or a *main program.*

EXAMPLE 5.2   Fig. 5.2 shows a main program that reads in an integer value, calls function FACTRL to compute its factorial, and prints the result returned by FACTRL.

The top part of Fig. 5.2 (through the first END) is the main program; the bottom part is the function FACTRL. The main program begins with a declaration statement that declares the type of the input variable NUM whose factorial is to be computed. The type of the result returned by function FACTRL (type INTEGER) is also declared so that the compiler knows what type of value to expect.

If a non-negative integer is read into NUM, the statement

        FACT = FACTRL(NUM)

in the main program is executed. The expression references function FACTRL, so function FACTRL is called into execution and the assignment statement above waits for the function result. The value of NUM is passed into FACTRL as its *actual argument* (i.e., the actual value to be used in the factorial computation), and the function body is executed. The result of the function execution is returned to the main program, assigned to variable FACT, and printed. Program execution terminates when STOP is reached.

A trace of the execution of the function call and return is shown in Fig. 5.3 when NUM (the actual argument) is 6. The top arrow shows that 6 is passed into the function as the value of N (the dummy argument). After the function is executed, the value 720 is returned to the main program and stored in FACT.

∎

EXAMPLE 5.3   A formula from probability theory can be used to compute the number of different ways in which r items can be selected from a collection of n items without regard to order. This formula is written as

$$C(n, r) = \frac{n!}{r!(n-r)!}$$

This formula represents the number of different combinations of n items taken r at a time. For example, if we have a class of five students and we want to know the number of different pairs of students that can be selected, we perform the computation

$$C(5, 2) = \frac{5!}{2!(5-2)!} = \frac{5!}{2!3!} = \frac{120}{2 \times 6} = 10$$

The answer is 10 different pairs of students.

Figure 5.3. *Effect of Execution of FACTRL When NUM is 6*

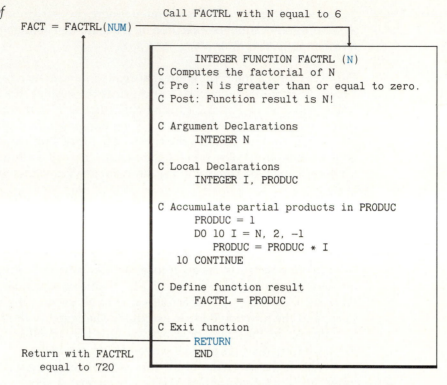

```
                                    Call FACTRL with N equal to 6
FACT = FACTRL(NUM)
                        INTEGER FUNCTION FACTRL (N)
                     C Computes the factorial of N
                     C Pre : N is greater than or equal to zero.
                     C Post: Function result is N!

                     C Argument Declarations
                           INTEGER N

                     C Local Declarations
                           INTEGER I, PRODUC

                     C Accumulate partial products in PRODUC
                           PRODUC = 1
                           DO 10 I = N, 2, -1
                               PRODUC = PRODUC * I
                        10 CONTINUE

                     C Define function result
                           FACTRL = PRODUC

                     C Exit function
                           RETURN
 Return with FACTRL        END
    equal to 720
```

The program in Fig. 5.4 uses function FACTRL to perform this computation. First N and R are read. If R is not greater than N, the statement

$$C = FACTRL(N) / (FACTRL(R) * FACTRL(N-R))$$

calls function FACTRL with three different actual arguments (N, R, N–R). The results of these calls are manipulated, as described above, and the number of different combinations of N items taken R at a time is saved in variable C. ■

In the main program of Fig. 5.4, a different actual argument is passed in each call to function FACTRL; consequently, a different result is computed each time. The effect of each call to function FACTRL is summarized in Table 5.1.

Table 5.1. *Effect of Each Call to FACTRL*

CALL	ACTUAL ARGUMENT	ARGUMENT VALUE	FUNCTION RESULT
1	N	5	120
2	R	2	2
3	N–R	3	6

Figure 5.4. *Finding Combinations of N Items Taken R at a Time*

```
      PROGRAM COMBIN
C Computes the number of combinations of N items taken R at a time

      INTEGER N, R, C
      INTEGER FACTRL

      PRINT *, 'Enter number of items in the collection:'
      READ *, N
      PRINT *, 'Enter number of items to be selected:'
      READ *, R
      IF (R .LE. N) THEN
         C = FACTRL(N) / (FACTRL(R) * FACTRL(N-R))
         PRINT *, 'The number of combinations is ', C
      ELSE
         PRINT *, 'Items to be selected cannot exceed total items'
      ENDIF

C Exit program
      STOP
      END

C -------------------------------------------------------------------

      INTEGER FUNCTION FACTRL (N)
C Computes the factorial of N
C Pre : N is greater than or equal to zero.
C Post: Function result is N!

C Argument declarations
      INTEGER N

C Local Declarations
      INTEGER I, PRODUC

C Accumulate partial products in PRODUC
      PRODUC = 1
      DO 10 I = N, 2, -1
      PRODUC = PRODUC * I
   10 CONTINUE

C Define function result
      FACTRL = PRODUC

C Exit function
      RETURN
      END

Enter number of items in the collection:
5
Enter number of items to be selected:
2
The number of combinations is          10
```

Table 5.1 illustrates one of the most important reasons for using functions. A function may be called several times in a program, each time with a different actual argument. Each call to the function causes the program statements associated with the function definition to be executed. Without using functions, these program statements would have to be listed several times in the main program. It is certainly easier to insert a function reference in a program instead of inserting the entire function body.

Name Independence

Figure 5.5 shows the data storage area for the main program and function FACTRL just after the data values for N and R are read into the main program and before the function is called. There is a memory cell in the main program allocated for variable N (value 5) and a memory cell for dummy argument N (initially undefined) in the function data area. Even though they have the same names, dummy argument N and variable N in the main program are unrelated. Consequently, when the value 5 is read into main program variable N, the value of dummy argument N is unaffected. Each call to function FACTRL redefines the value of dummy argument N, and this value may be different from that of main program variable N (value is 5). This is perfectly natural when you consider that their values are stored in different memory cells.

Figure 5.5. *Data Areas for Main Program and Function FACTRL*

By the same reasoning, local variables I and PRODUC in FACTRL are unrelated to any other use of these names in either the main program or any other function. A similar statement may be made regarding the use of label 10 in function FACTRL: this use of label 10 is unrelated to any other use of label 10 in the main program. Although label 10 may be associated with only one statement in FACTRL, this label may also appear in the main program or another subprogram.

Finally, variables C and R are declared in the main program and may be manipulated only in the main program. It would be illegal for the function to attempt to reference either C or R.

A Reminder About Declarations

Remember to declare the type of each user-defined function in the program unit that references it. This type should match the type specified in the FUNC-TION header statement and is determined by the type of the result returned by the function.

Also, remember to declare the type of each dummy argument listed in a FUNCTION header and the types of any local variables. As mentioned in the last section, it does not matter whether a name was used elsewhere in the program; its type must still be declared in the function definition. Its use in the function is independent of any other use of that name elsewhere.

Argument Type Correspondence

It is very important that the type of each actual argument used in a call to function FACTRL be the same as the type (INTEGER) of the dummy argument (N). If this is not the case, an error diagnostic such as "illegal argument type" may be printed. If your compiler does not detect this error, the function will be called and may return an incorrect result.

Functions with Multiple Arguments

We can also define functions with multiple arguments.

Figure 5.6. *Function ENTER*

```
      INTEGER FUNCTION ENTER (NMIN, NMAX)
C Returns the first data value read between NMIN and NMAX
C Pre : NMIN is less than or equal to NMAX.
C Post: Function result lies between NMIN and NMAX.

C Argument Declarations
      INTEGER NMIN, NMAX

C Local Declarations
      INTEGER N
      LOGICAL BETWEN

C Initially assume an integer between NMIN and NMAX is not entered
      BETWEN = .FALSE.

C Keep reading until an integer between NMIN and NMAX is entered
      DO WHILE (.NOT. BETWEN)              9 IF (.NOT. BETWEN) THEN
         PRINT *, 'Enter an integer between ',
     +            NMIN, ' and ', NMAX
         READ *, N
         BETWEN = (N .GE. NMIN) .AND. (N .LE. NMAX)
      ENDDO                                  GOTO 9
C                                            ENDIF
C Define result
      ENTER = N

C Exit function
      RETURN
      END
```

EXAMPLE 5.4   Function ENTER (see Fig. 5.6) returns the first data value read that lies between its arguments, NMIN and NMAX. The body of function ENTER is based on the body of program GUESS, shown in Fig. 4.8. The WHILE loop continues to execute until a valid data value is read into local variable N, thereby causing the program flag BETWEN to be set to .TRUE.. After loop exit, the statement

        ENTER = N

defines the function result as the last value read into N.
    The statement

        NUM = ENTER(1, 10)

calls function ENTER to read a data value between 1 and 10, which is stored in NUM. NUM should be declared as a type INTEGER variable in the program that contains this statement.

EXAMPLE 5.5   Function ROUND in Fig. 5.7 is used to round its first argument to the number of decimal places indicated by its second argument. This means that the function reference

        ROUND(2.51863, 3)

returns the real number 2.519.
    If PLACES is greater than or equal to zero, the rounding operation is performed. Table 5.2 traces the execution of the function reference

        ROUND(2.51863, 3)

The function result is 2519 / 1000.0 or 2.519, as desired.   ∎

Table 5.2. *Trace of ROUND (2.51863, 3)*

STATEMENT	X	PLACES	POWER	TEMPX	EFFECT
	2.51863	3	?	?	
IF (PLACES .GE. 0)					True—does True task
POWER = 10.0 ** PLACES			1000.0		
TEMPX = X * POWER				2518.63	
ROUND = NINT(TEMPX)					Assigns 2519
/ REAL(POWER)					/ 1000.0 to ROUND

Function ROUND illustrates that a user-defined function can call a FORTRAN library function. Both NINT and REAL are called by ROUND. It is also possible for one user-defined function to call another, but a function cannot call itself.

Figure 5.7. *Function ROUND*

```
      REAL FUNCTION ROUND (X, PLACES)

C Rounds the value of X
C Pre : X is defined and PLACES is greater than or equal to zero.
C Post: Function result is X rounded to PLACES decimal points.

C Argument Declarations
      REAL X
      INTEGER PLACES

C Local Declarations
      REAL TEMPX, POWER

      IF (PLACES .GE. 0) THEN
         POWER = 10.0 ** PLACES
         TEMPX = X * POWER
         ROUND = NINT(TEMPX) / POWER
      ELSE
         PRINT *, 'Negative argument for PLACES — no rounding done'
         ROUND = X
      ENDIF

C Exit function
      RETURN
      END
```

When using multiple-argument functions, you must be careful to use the correct number of actual arguments in the function reference. Also, the order of actual arguments used in the function reference must correspond to the order of dummy arguments listed in the function definition.

Finally, the type of each actual argument must be the same as the type of its corresponding dummy argument. The function reference

```
      ROUND(3, 2.51863)
```

is illegal. The first actual argument, 3, cannot correspond to the first dummy argument, X, because dummy argument X (the number to be rounded) is supposed to be type REAL. The rules for argument list correspondence are listed next.

Argument List Correspondence

- The number of actual arguments used in each call to a function must be the same as the number of dummy arguments listed in the function definition.
- Each actual argument must be the same type as its corresponding dummy argument. The first actual argument corresponds to the first dummy argu-

ment, the second actual argument corresponds to the second dummy argument, and so on.

Program Style

Validating Function Arguments

The IF structure in Fig. 5.7 validates the value of the second dummy argument, PLACES. The function cannot be executed in a meaningful way if PLACES is negative. Rather than compute an answer that makes no sense, the function prints an error message and returns its first argument as the result. In this way, the function user is warned that the computation did not take place; however, the program is able to continue execution since a reasonable value is returned as the function result.

Program Style

Side Effects of Functions

Function dummy arguments are used to store values passed into a function. Although FORTRAN allows you to change the value of a dummy argument inside a function, this is a bad programming practice and should not be done. Changing the value of a dummy argument may modify the value of the corresponding actual argument in the calling program. This undesirable change is called a function *side effect*. In section 5.3, we will introduce subroutines, and we will see that it is all right, and even desirable, for a subroutine to modify its dummy arguments.

Testing Functions

A function is an independent program module, and as such it should be tested separately from the program that uses it. To test a function, you should write a short *driver* program that defines the function argument, calls the function, and then prints the value returned. For example, the main program in Fig. 5.8 could act as a driver program to test function FACTRL.

You should execute the driver program with function FACTRL appended to the end of it until you are satisfied that function FACTRL works correctly. As illustrated, you should test the function operation with several actual arguments, including zero.

Figure 5.8. *Driver Program to Test Function FACTRL*

```
      PROGRAM DRIVER
C Driver program to test FACTRL
      INTEGER SENVAL
      PARAMETER (SENVAL = 99)
      INTEGER N, FACT
      INTEGER FACTRL
```

```
      PRINT *, 'Enter a nonnegative integer or 99 to stop:'
      READ *, N
      DO  WHILE (N .NE. SENVAL)                    9 IF (...) THEN
         FACT = FACTRL(N)
         PRINT *, 'The result is ', FACT
         PRINT *, 'Enter another integer:'
         READ *, N
      ENDDO                                          GOTO 9
C                                                     ENDIF
C Exit program
      STOP
      END


C ---------------------------------------------------------------
      INTEGER FUNCTION FACTRL (N)
C Computes the factorial of N
C Pre : N is greater than or equal to zero.
C Post: Function result is N!

C Argument Declarations
      INTEGER N

C Local Declarations
      INTEGER I, PRODUC

C Accumulate partial products in PRODUC
      PRODUC = 1
      DO 10 I = N, 2, -1
      PRODUC = PRODUC * I
  10    CONTINUE

C Define function result
      FACTRL = PRODUC

C Exit function
      RETURN
      END


Enter a nonnegative integer or 99 to stop:
6
The result is          720
Enter another integer:
3
The result is            6
Enter another integer:
0
The result is            1
Enter another integer:
99
```

Single-Statement Functions

Occasionally, a function definition can be written in a single line. FORTRAN provides the *single-statement function* to implement such functions.

EXAMPLE 5.6

The single-statement function RAISE defined below can be used to raise a number (represented by X) to the power N.

```
REAL X, Z
INTEGER N
REAL RAISE
RAISE(X, N) = X ** N
```

Although it has the appearance of an executable statement, a single-statement function definition is actually a declaration. Therefore, it should come directly after all other declarations and before the executable statements of a program. The type of the single-statement function and its arguments should also be declared before the function, as shown above. The dummy argument names (X and N for RAISE) may be reused for other purposes in the program. ∎

A single-statement function is called just like any other function. The assignment statement

```
Z = RAISE(1.5, 10)
```

calls function RAISE to raise the value of 1.5 to the power 10; the result is stored in Z. The single-statement function is described next.

Definition of the Single-Statement Function

> SYNTAX: *fname* (*dummy argument list*) = *expression*
>
> EXAMPLE: SQUARE(X) = X * X
>
> INTERPRETATION: *fname* is defined as a single-statement function whose value is determined by evaluating *expression*. The *expression* may reference variables, constants, and other functions as well as the *dummy arguments*. When the function *fname* is called, each actual argument value is substituted for its corresponding *dummy argument* in the *expression*, and the *expression* is evaluated.
>
> NOTE: *fname* and *expression* must be the same data type, or one may be type REAL and the other type INTEGER. In the latter case, the compiler will convert the *expression* value to match the type of *fname*.

EXAMPLE 5.7

A common operation is finding the square root of a sum of squares, for example,

$$\sqrt{X^2 + Y^2}$$

The single-statement functions HYPOT and SQUARE defined below can be used for this purpose.

```
      REAL X, Y, C
      REAL HYPOT, SQUARE
      SQUARE(X) = X * X
      HYPOT(X, Y) = SQRT(SQUARE(X) + SQUARE(Y))
```

The statement

```
      C = HYPOT(X, 2.0)
```

uses HYPOT to assign the square root of $x^2 + 4.0$ to C. ■

LOGICAL Functions

Functions can return LOGICAL results. A LOGICAL function is often used to make a condition more readable.

EXAMPLE 5.8

Function POSTIV in Fig. 5.9 returns .TRUE. when its REAL argument, NUM, is positive (greater than zero). The function returns .FALSE. when its argument is zero or negative.

Figure 5.9. *Function POSTIV*

```
      LOGICAL FUNCTION POSTIV (NUM)
C Indicates whether NUM is positive
C Pre : None
C Post: Returns .TRUE. if NUM is greater than 0;
C       otherwise, returns .FALSE.

C Argument Declarations
      REAL NUM

      POSTIV = NUM .GE. 0.0

C Exit function
      RETURN
      END
```

Function POSTIV is used in the IF structure below, which prints the square root of X. ■

```
      IF (X .EQ. 0.0) THEN
         PRINT *, 'Square root is 0.0'
      ELSE IF (POSTIV(X)) THEN
         PRINT *, 'Square root is ', SQRT(X)
      ELSE
         PRINT *, 'Square root is imaginary'
      ENDIF
```

**SELF-CHECK
EXERCISES FOR
SECTION 5.1**

1. Assuming the main program declarations

```
INTEGER MAXINT
PARAMETER (MAXINT = 32767)
REAL X, Y, Z, MASSAG
INTEGER M, N
```

and function MASSAG, declared as follows,

```
REAL FUNCTION MASSAG (A, B, X)
REAL A, B
INTEGER X
```

which of the following references to function MASSAG are incorrect in the main program and why?

a. MASSAG(A, B, X)   e. MASSAG(X, Y, M)
b. MASSAG(MASSAG, Y, M)   f. MASSAG(X, Y)
c. MASSAG(Y, Z, N)   g. MASSAG(Z, X, MAXINT)
d. MASSAG(3.5, 4.5, 6)   h. MASSAG(3.5, 4.5, 6.7)

2. Write a function that returns the larger of two type REAL values. Show how to use this function to find the largest of three values.
3. Write a function POWER(N, K) that computes N^K by repeated multiplication (i.e., don't use the operator **). Assume that N and K are type INTEGER and that K is positive. The function should be type INTEGER.
4. Write a function that calls POWER from exercise 3 to compute N^K for any integer K (positive, negative, or zero). The function should be type REAL.
5. Write a single-statement function ROUND(X, N) to round a real number (represented by X) to N decimal digits (N is a nonnegative integer).
6. a. Write a single-statement function CONVRT(C) that converts temperatures given in degrees Celsius (C) to temperatures in degrees Fahrenheit (F), where

   ```
   F = 1.8 * C + 32.0
   ```

   b. Using the function CONVRT defined in part a., write a FORTRAN program segment (a DO loop) to generate a table for Celsius to Fahrenheit conversion for degrees C = 0,1,2, . . . 99,100.
7. The coordinates of two points on the x-y plane are represented by (X1, Y1) and (X2, Y2), respectively. Write a FORTRAN statement that uses the single statement functions HYPOT and SQUARE to find the distance between these points.

$$distance = \sqrt{(X2 - X1)^2 + (Y2 - Y1)^2}$$

5.2 ▬▬▬ Top-Down Design Using Functions

This section illustrates how functions facilitate the top-down design process. We can implement a complicated computation step as a separate function and then reference this function in the main program. Removing the computation from the main program simplifies the main program body and makes it easier to read and understand. Since each function is a self-contained program module that performs a particular task, the individual functions are also relatively easy to read and understand.

▬▬▬ Case Study: Finding Prime Numbers

Problem

The prime numbers have been studied by mathematicians for many years. A prime number is an integer that has no divisors other than 1 and itself. Examples of prime numbers are the integers 2, 3, 5, 7, and 11. Write a program that finds the smallest divisor of a number or determines that the number is a prime number.

Design Overview

To determine whether an integer N is a prime number, our program will test all integers smaller than N until it finds an integer that is a divisor. The data requirements and algorithm follow.

Data Requirements

Problem Parameter

the largest number that can be tested (NMAX = 1000)

Problem Input

the number to be tested (INTEGER N)

Problem Output

the smallest divisor greater than 1 (INTEGER MINDIV)

Initial Algorithm

1. Read in the number to be tested for a prime number.
2. Find the smallest divisor or determine that the number is prime.
3. Print the smallest divisor or a message that the number is prime.

Case Study: Finding Prime Numbers, continued

Algorithm Refinements

Since N must be an integer greater than 1, we will use function ENTER (see Fig. 5.6) to read a value into N. We will write a new function, FINDIV, to implement step 2. FINDIV will return the smallest divisor of N that is greater than 1. If N is prime, FINDIV will return N. The value returned by FINDIV will be stored in MINDIV and tested in step 3. The refinement for step 3 follows.

Step 3 Refinement

```
3.1 IF the smallest divisor is N THEN
        Print a message that N is prime
    ELSE
        Print the smallest divisor of N
    ENDIF
```

Coding the Main Program

We can now write the main program (see Fig. 5.10). The statements

```
N = ENTER(2, NMAX)
MINDIV = FINDIV(N)
```

call functions ENTER and FINDIV to perform steps 1 and 2 of the algorithm. The IF statement implements step 3. Next, we turn our attention to function FINDIV.

Coding Function FINDIV

Function FINDIV finds the smallest divisor of N that is greater than 1. It does this by testing each integer that is a possible divisor of N, starting with 2. If 2 does not divide N, then no other even integer divides N; consequently, only 2 and the odd integers need to be tested. The local variables and algorithm for FINDIV follow.

Local Variables for FINDIV

logical flag that indicates whether a divisor is found (DIVFND is .TRUE.) or not found (DIVFND is .FALSE.) (LOGICAL DIVFND)
each trial divisor starting with 2 (INTEGER TRIAL)

Algorithm for FINDIV

```
1. Initialize TRIAL to 2
2. IF 2 is a divisor of N THEN
        Set DIVFND to .TRUE.
```

Case Study: Finding Prime Numbers, continued

Figure 5.10. *Program to Identify a Prime or Find Smallest Divisor*

```
      PROGRAM PRIME
C Finds and prints the smallest divisor (other than 1) of the integer N
C Prints that N is a prime number if no divisor is found

C Declarations
      INTEGER NMAX
      PARAMETER (NMAX = 1000)
      INTEGER N, MINDIV
      INTEGER FINDIV, ENTER

C Read in the number to be tested for a prime number
      PRINT *, 'Enter a number that you think is a prime number.'
      N = ENTER(2, NMAX)

C Find the smallest divisor, MINDIV, that divides N
      MINDIV = FINDIV(N)

C Print the smallest divisor or a message that N is prime
      IF (MINDIV .EQ. N) THEN
          PRINT *, N, ' is a prime number'
      ELSE
          PRINT *, MINDIV, ' is the smallest divisor of ', N
      ENDIF

C Exit program
      STOP
      END
```

```
      ELSE
          Set DIVFND to .FALSE. and reset TRIAL to 3
      ENDIF
```
3. Test each odd integer (TRIAL) as a possible divisor of N until a divisor is found or TRIAL is greater than $\sqrt{N}$
4. IF a divisor was not found THEN
          Return N
      ELSE
          Return TRIAL
      ENDIF

First, TRIAL is initialized to 2 (step 1) and DIVFND is defined (step 2). If N is even, DIVFND is set to .TRUE., causing step 3 to be skipped. If N is odd, DIVFND is set to .FALSE., TRIAL is set to the smallest odd integer (3), and the loop in step 3 is executed. Step 3 is used to test each odd integer less than or equal to $\sqrt{N}$

Case Study: Finding Prime Numbers, continued

Figure 5.11. *Function FINDIV*

```
      INTEGER FUNCTION FINDIV (N)
C Finds smallest divisor of N between 2 and N
C Pre : N is greater than 1.
C Post: Returns the smallest divisor; returns N
C       if N is prime.

C Argument Declarations
      INTEGER N

C Local Declarations
      INTEGER TRIAL
      LOGICAL DIVFND

C Test whether N is even
      TRIAL = 2
      IF (MOD(N, TRIAL) .EQ. 0) THEN
C         N is even
          DIVFND = .TRUE.
      ELSE
C         N is odd
          DIVFND = .FALSE.
          TRIAL = 3
      ENDIF

C Test each odd integer as a divisor of N until a divisor is found
      DO WHILE (.NOT. DIVFND .AND. (TRIAL .LE. SQRT(REAL(N))))    9 IF ...
          IF (MOD(N, TRIAL) .EQ. 0) THEN
              DIVFND = .TRUE.
          ELSE
C             Reset trial to next odd integer
              TRIAL = TRIAL + 2
          ENDIF
      ENDDO                                                       GOTO 9
C                                                                 ENDIF
C Define result
C Return TRIAL or N if no divisor is found
      IF (.NOT. DIVFND) THEN
          FINDIV = N
      ELSE
          FINDIV = TRIAL
      ENDIF

C Exit function
      RETURN
      END
```

Case Study: Finding Prime Numbers, continued

as a possible divisor. The loop will be exited when a divisor is found or TRIAL is greater than $\sqrt{N}$. The refinement of step 3 follows.

Step 3 Refinement

3.1 DO WHILE a divisor is not found and TRIAL is less than or equal to $\sqrt{N}$
      IF TRIAL is a divisor of N THEN
            Set DIVFND to .TRUE.
      ELSE
            Reset TRIAL to the next odd integer
      ENDIF
   ENDDO

As shown above, it is only necessary to test integers less than or equal to $\sqrt{N}$ as possible divisors. In FINDIV (see Fig. 5.11), the condition

```
(MOD(N, TRIAL) .EQ. 0)
```

is used to test whether TRIAL divides N, as explained in Example 4.8. If a divisor is found, DIVFND is reset to .TRUE. and the WHILE loop is exited. If no divisor is found, the loop is exited when TRIAL becomes greater than $\sqrt{N}$.

Function FINDIV should be inserted after the main program in source file PRIME.FOR. We should also include function ENTER (see Fig. 5.6) in the source file. Once the source file is completed, we can compile and run the program.

Testing

The complete program should be tested for both small and large integers that are prime numbers. You should be able to find a table of primes to help you select sample cases. Make sure you test odd numbers that are nonprimes and even numbers. Also, test function ENTER using data values that are not in range.

Several sample runs of the prime number program are shown in Fig. 5.12. The test values used for N were selected to exercise all parts of the program and to verify that the program works for numbers that are prime as well as numbers that are not prime. The operation of the program at the boundaries (2 and 1000) was also checked, as well as the operation of the program for invalid data values (0 and 1001). A very large prime number (997) was used as a test case as well as odd and even numbers that were not prime. Although many valid data values were not tested, the sample selected is representative and provides a fair indication that the program is correct.

You should use a similar strategy when selecting test data to exercise your programs. Avoid choosing sample test data that are similar. Also, select test data that are at or near any boundary values.

Case Study: Finding Prime Numbers, continued

Figure 5.12. *Four Sample Runs of the Program PRIME*

```
Enter a number that you think is a prime number.
Enter an integer between 2 and 1000?
1000
          2 is the smallest divisor of          1000

Enter a number that you think is a prime number.
Enter an integer between 2 and 1000?
997
          997 is a prime number

Enter a number that you think is a prime number.
Enter an integer between 2 and 1000?
35
          5 is the smallest divisor of            35

Enter a number that you think is a prime number.
Enter an integer between 2 and 1000?
0
Enter an integer between 2 and 1000?
1001
Enter an integer between 2 and 1000?
2
          2 is a prime number
```

Program Style

Top-Down Design Using Functions

The program in Fig. 5.10 uses functions to facilitate the top-down design process. The main program is very short and includes two function calls. Each function is a self-contained module that performs a single task. The functions are also relatively short and one function has already been written. The variables DIVFND and TRIAL, which were not part of the original data requirements, are declared as local variables in function FINDIV.

   Since the main program and each function are short, it is relatively easy to read and understand each of these modules. Since each function performs only a single task, it should be easy to test and debug the functions. Once the functions are debugged, the entire program can be put together and tested as a unit. As illustrated here, you should make use of functions whenever practical, particularly if a function that has been previously written and tested is available.

SELF-CHECK EXERCISE FOR SECTION 5.2

1. Modify FINDIV to print all divisors of N where N is an integer greater than 1. If N is prime, the only divisors printed should be 1 and N.

5.3 ▬▬▬ Defining a Subroutine

A *subroutine* is a FORTRAN subprogram that can be used to return any number of results, or zero results. The subroutine in the next example simply displays a table heading and does not return any results back to the calling program.

EXAMPLE 5.9

Subroutine TABHED in Fig. 5.13 displays the table heading for the rebar strength program shown in Fig. 4.11. When called, the subroutine displays each of the messages in the PRINT statements.

Figure 5.13. *A Subroutine with Zero Results*

```
      SUBROUTINE TABHED (STRNTH)
C Displays the heading for the rebar table

C Argument Declarations
      REAL STRNTH

      PRINT *, '          Joe Bob''s Steel Company'
      PRINT *, '             Rebar load chart'
      PRINT *, 'For bars with a steel strength of ', STRNTH, ' psi'
      PRINT *
      PRINT *, 'Bar          Cross-sectional          Max. Load'
      PRINT *, 'Number       Area (sq. in.)            (lbs.)'
      PRINT *, '--------     ------------------      ------------'

C Exit subroutine
      RETURN
      END
```

The definition of subroutine TABHED is very similar to the declaration of a function. It begins with the word SUBROUTINE. There is one argument, STRNTH, whose value is displayed. The statement

    RETURN

returns control back to the calling program; the statement

    END

marks the end of the subroutine definition.   ■

We stated earlier that a subroutine can return any number of results, or even zero results as does TABHED. A result is returned when a dummy argument is given a value. The arguments of a subroutine can be used both to pass data into the subroutine and to return results back to the calling program.

EXAMPLE 5.10 Subroutine BREAK in Fig. 5.14 returns the whole and fractional parts of its first argument. This argument value is passed into dummy argument X and is used to determine the values assigned to dummy arguments WHOLE and FRAC. The statements

```
WHOLE = INT(X)
FRAC = X - REAL(WHOLE)
```

reference the type conversion functions INT and REAL (see Table 4.2). These statements assign values to the *output arguments* WHOLE and FRAC. Since the value passed into X is not modified by the subroutine execution, X is called an *input argument*. ∎

Because all values are returned through the output arguments, there is no value assigned to the subroutine name in Fig. 5.14. It is, in fact, illegal to reference the subroutine name within the subroutine body. It is also unnecessary and illegal to declare the type of a subroutine in the calling program.

Figure 5.14. *Subroutine BREAK*

```
      SUBROUTINE BREAK (X, WHOLE, FRAC)

C Breaks a real number into its whole and fractional parts

C Input Argument
C   X - The value to be split (REAL)
C Output Arguments
C   WHOLE - The whole part of X (INTEGER)
C   FRAC - The fractional part of X (REAL)

C Argument Declarations
      REAL X, FRAC
      INTEGER WHOLE

C Define results
      WHOLE = INT(X)
      FRAC = X - REAL(WHOLE)

C Exit subroutine
      RETURN
      END
```

Subroutine Definition

SYNTAX: SUBROUTINE *sname* (*dummy argument list*)
          interface section
          local declaration section

```
            ----  }
            ----  }     subroutine body
            ----  }

        RETURN
        END
EXAMPLE: SUBROUTINE STUB
        PRINT *, 'STUB entered'
        RETURN
        END
```

INTERPRETATION: The SUBROUTINE statement specifies the subroutine name, *sname*; the *dummy argument list* is a list of symbolic names. The dummy arguments are used either to receive data (as *input arguments*) from the calling program or to return results to the calling program (*output arguments*). Occasionally a dummy argument will be used for both purposes. We will refer to such arguments as *input/output arguments*. The *interface section* contains descriptions and declarations for all the *dummy arguments*.

Other symbolic names not appearing in the dummy argument list but required for writing the subroutine should be declared in the separate *local declaration section*.

The *subroutine body* describes the data manipulation performed by the subroutine. The RETURN statement transfers control back to the calling statement. The END statement terminates the subroutine definition.

Program Style

Documentation of Subroutines

Subroutine BREAK illustrates some conventions for writing subroutines that will be used throughout the text. Each subroutine begins with an interface section that describes both the purpose of the subroutine and its arguments. The interface section (in black type in Fig. 5.14) consists of comments describing the subroutine and its arguments followed by the dummy argument declarations. This is all the documentation that a potential user of the subroutine needs to determine whether the subroutine can be used for a specific purpose and, if so, how to call it. There is no need to look beyond the interface section.

SELF-CHECK EXERCISES FOR SECTION 5.3

1. What does the following subroutine do? If its argument is 3 when the subroutine is called, what value is returned through its argument?

```
SUBROUTINE CUBE (N)
INTEGER N
N = N * N * N
RETURN
END
```

2. Write a subroutine that returns both the square and the square root of the absolute value of its first argument. The subroutine should also return a LOGICAL flag indicating whether its argument is positive (flag value is .TRUE.) or negative (flag value is .FALSE.). *Hint:* There should be one input argument and three output arguments.

5.4 ▬▬ Calling a Subroutine

A function is called by simply referencing it in an expression; however, a special FORTRAN statement, the CALL statement, is used to call a subroutine. Assuming X (type REAL), I1 (type INTEGER), and R1 (type REAL) are declared in a program, the statement

```
CALL BREAK (X, I1, R1)
```

can be used to call subroutine BREAK. The argument correspondence would be

Actual Argument		Dummy Argument
X	⟷	X
I1	⟷	WHOLE
R1	⟷	FRAC

Within the body of the subroutine, each reference to a dummy argument causes its corresponding actual argument to be manipulated. This situation is depicted in Fig. 5.15 assuming the variable X in the main program has the value 7.234 and main-program variables I1 and R1 are initially undefined.

Figure 5.15. *Argument Correspondence for CALL BREAK(X, I1, R1)*

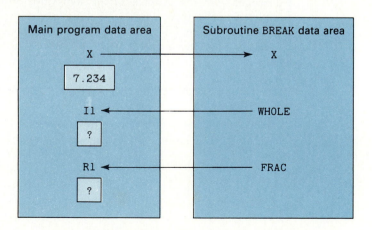

The statement

```
WHOLE = INT(X)
```

causes the integral part (7) of X to be stored in I1; the statement

```
FRAC = X - REAL(WHOLE)
```

causes the fractional part (0.234) of X to be stored in R1. The effect of the subroutine call is illustrated in Fig. 5.16.

Figure 5.16. *Effect of CALL BREAK (X, I1, R1)*

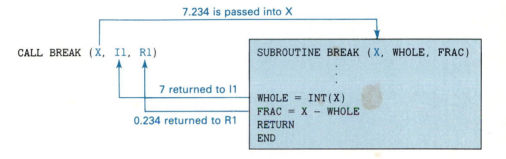

Each dummy argument for subroutine BREAK is used either for input (X) or for output (WHOLE, FRAC). An argument whose initial value is passed into the subroutine and then modified is called an *input/output* argument.

EXAMPLE 5.11   Subroutine ORDER in Fig. 5.17 places its arguments in numerical order. After execution of ORDER, the smaller value is in S and the larger value is in L. It may be necessary to switch the original values passed into S and L to accomplish this.

The argument correspondence specified by the statement

```
CALL ORDER (NUM1, NUM2)
```

is shown next.

Actual Argument		Dummy Argument
NUM1	⟷	S
NUM2	⟷	L

If the value of NUM1 is 8.0 and the value of NUM2 is 6.0 before the call, the value of NUM1 would be 6.0 and the value of NUM2 would be 8.0 after the execution of subroutine ORDER. The effect of the subroutine call is illustrated in Fig. 5.18.

This execution of the subroutine is traced in Table 5.3. The actual argument represented by each dummy argument is shown in parentheses in the table

Figure 5.17. *Subroutine ORDER*

```
        SUBROUTINE ORDER (S, L)

C Arranges its arguments in numerical order

C Input/Output Argument
C   S - Smaller number after execution of ORDER
C   L - Larger number after execution of ORDER

C Argument Declarations
        REAL S, L

C Local Declarations
        REAL TEMP

C Compare S and L and switch if necessary
        IF (S .GT. L) THEN
            TEMP = S
            S = L
            L = TEMP
        ENDIF

C Exit subroutine
        RETURN
        END
```

heading. The statement

```
    S = L
```

stores the value (6.0) passed into dummy argument L in the actual argument (NUM1) that corresponds to dummy argument S. The statement

```
    L = TEMP
```

stores the value (8.0) that was passed into dummy argument S and saved in local variable TEMP in the actual argument (NUM2) that corresponds to dummy argument L. The subroutine execution switches the values stored in the actual arguments NUM1 and NUM2 as desired.   ∎

Table 5.3. *Trace of CALL ORDER (NUM1, NUM2) for NUM1 = 8.0, NUM2 = 6.0*

STATEMENT	S(NUM1)	L(NUM2)	TEMP	EFFECT
	8.0	6.0	?	
IF (S .GT. L) THEN				8.0 > 6.0 is true
TEMP = S			8.0	Saves 8.0 in TEMP
S = L	6.0			Saves 6.0 in NUM1
L = TEMP		8.0		Saves 8.0 in NUM2

Figure 5.18. *Effect of CALL ORDER (NUM1, NUM2)*

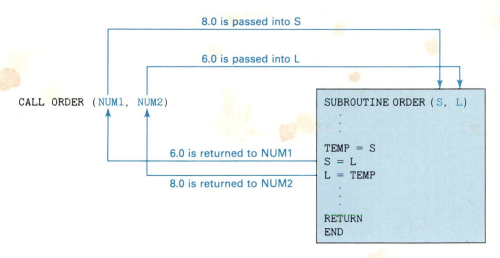

Subroutine Call

SYNTAX: CALL *sname* (*actual argument list*)

EXAMPLE: CALL ORDER (A, B)

INTERPRETATION: Subroutine calls begin with the word CALL, followed by the name of the subroutine to be referenced, *sname*, and the *actual argument list*. The actual arguments may be variable names, expressions, or constants. Expressions and constants may be used only to pass data into the subroutine and must correspond to dummy input arguments. The parentheses should be omitted if there are no subroutine arguments.

Summary of Rules for Using Subroutines

- A CALL statement must be used to call each subroutine.
- There should be the same number of actual arguments as there are dummy arguments in the subroutine definition.
- Each actual argument must have the same type as its corresponding dummy argument.

Your FORTRAN compiler may not check to see whether each actual argument list appearing in a subroutine call satisfies these rules. Consequently, violating one of these rules may lead to errors that are difficult to track down.

SELF-CHECK EXERCISES FOR SECTION 5.4

1. Show the output displayed by the following program in the form of a table of values for X, Y, and Z.

```
PROGRAM SHOW
INTEGER X, Y, Z
X = 5
```

```
      Y = 3
      PRINT *, '   X   Y   Z'
      CALL SUM (X, Y, Z)
      PRINT 5, X, Y, Z
    5 FORMAT (1X, I4, I4, I4)
      CALL SUM (Y, X, Z)
      PRINT 5, X, Y, Z
      CALL SUM (Z, Y, X)
      PRINT 5, X, Y, Z
      CALL SUM (Z, Z, X)
      PRINT 5, X, Y, Z
      CALL SUM (Y, Y, Y)
      PRINT 5, X, Y, Z
      STOP
      END

      SUBROUTINE SUM (A, B, C)
      INTEGER A, B, C
      C = A + B
      RETURN
      END
```

2. Rewrite SUM as a function and replace the CALL statements in the main program with assignment statements.
3. Write a program fragment that reads in a data value and calls the subroutine from exercise 2 at the end of Section 5.3 to find its square and square root. Your fragment should print the values returned and a message indicating that the square root is imaginary if the flag value returned is .FALSE..

5.5 ▭ Structure Chart

With the introduction of the subroutine, we now have the capability to write subprogram modules that return any number of values. We will use functions for modules that return a single value and subroutines for all other modules.

We can use this capability to implement programs in a top-down or stepwise manner in a way analogous to how we refine algorithms. We will write the initial algorithm as a list of steps (or subproblems) and decide whether to implement each algorithm step in-line (as part of the main program) or as a separate subprogram. If we decide to use a separate subprogram, we will implement the algorithm step as a function if it returns a single value; otherwise, we will implement it as a subroutine. The main program will be written as a sequence of calls to its subprogram modules.

We will use a *structure chart* to illustrate the flow of control and data between the main program and its subprograms. We will illustrate this design technique by reexamining the case study in Section 4.7 concerned with displaying a table of maximum tensile loads for different-size steel reinforcing bars (rebars). (We suggest that you review the problem statement and desired problem outputs outlined in Section 4.7.)

Case Study: Computing Maximum Tensile Loads with Subprograms

(See Section 4.7 for problem statement and design overview. The data requirements and initial algorithm for this problem are repeated below.)

Data Requirements

Problem Input

tensile strength of the steel (REAL STRNTH)

Problem Outputs

the rebar number (INTEGER BARNUM)
the cross-sectional area (REAL AREA)
the maximum tensile load (REAL LOAD)

Initial Algorithm

1. Read the steel strength
2. Display the table heading
3. DO for each rebar from number 2 through 11
    4. Compute cross-sectional area
    5. LOAD = AREA * STRNTH
    6. Display rebar number, area, and load
  CONTINUE

Structure Chart and Refinements

We will implement steps 2 and 4 using subprograms and write the rest of the algorithm as part of the main program. We will implement step 2 as a subroutine (TABHED). We will implement step 4 as a function (DOAREA) because it computes a single result (the cross-sectional area). We will write the remaining steps in-line since they are relatively straightforward and involve one or two lines of code. The structure chart is shown in Fig. 5.19.

Case Study: Computing Maximum Tensile Loads with Subprograms, continued

Figure 5.19. *Structure Chart for Tensile Load Problem*

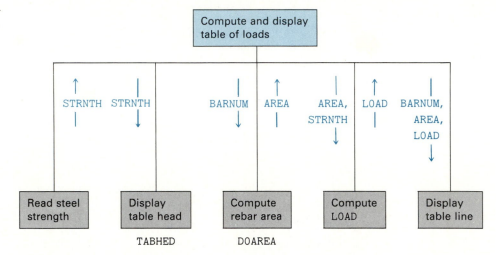

The structure chart shows each of the major subproblems in the algorithm. The name of a subprogram (TABHED or DOAREA) appears under its subproblem description.

The labeled arrows in the structure chart show the data flow between subproblems. For example, the value of STRNTH is an output of the subproblem "Read steel strength." The rebar number, BARNUM, is an input to function DOAREA (solves subproblem "Compute rebar area"), and the value of AREA is the function output. The values of BARNUM, AREA, and LOAD are inputs to the subproblem "Display table line." This may be surprising at first, because these three variables are outputs of the original problem; however, they are still considered inputs to the subproblem that displays them.

Coding the Main Program

With the structure chart in mind, we can write the main program, called REBAR2 and shown in Fig. 5.20. Program REBAR2 is much more concise and readable than program REBAR shown in Fig. 4.11. The statement

```
CALL TABHED (STRNTH)
```

calls subroutine TABHED to display the table heading. Within the DO loop, the statement

```
AREA = DOAREA(BARNUM)
```

calls function DOAREA, passing DOAREA the current value of BARNUM. The function result is returned to the main program and stored in variable AREA.

Case Study: Computing Maximum Tensile Loads with Subprograms, continued

Figure 5.20. *Main Program for Computing Tensile Loads Using Subprograms*

```
      PROGRAM REBAR2
C Prints a table of maximum tensile load on rebars
C using subprograms

C Declarations
      REAL STRNTH, AREA, LOAD, DOAREA
      INTEGER BARNUM

C Read steel strength
      PRINT *, 'Enter steel tensile strength (in psi)'
      READ *, STRNTH

C Write table headings
      CALL TABHED (STRNTH)

C Perform calculations and print table
      DO 10 BARNUM = 2, 11
         AREA = DOAREA(BARNUM)
         LOAD = AREA * STRNTH
         PRINT 5, BARNUM, AREA, LOAD
   5     FORMAT (1X, I6, 13X, F6.2, 14X, F8.0)
  10  CONTINUE

C Exit program
      STOP
      END
```

Coding the Subprograms

Subroutine TABHED appears in Fig. 5.13. Function DOAREA computes the cross-sectional area for a bar whose rebar number is given by the function argument. Function DOAREA uses the formulas

$$radius = rebar\ number/16.0$$
$$area = \pi \times radius^2$$

Figure 5.21 shows function DOAREA. Note that parameter PI and variable RADIUS are declared locally in function DOAREA and not in the main program. This is because PI and RADIUS are used only in the cross-sectional area computation and are not needed in the main program. Function DOAREA and subroutine TABHED should be inserted in the source program file that contains program REBAR2.

Case Study: Computing Maximum Tensile Loads with Subprograms, continued

Figure 5.21. *Function DOAREA*

```
      REAL FUNCTION DOAREA (BARNUM)
C Calculates the area of a circular rebar with number BARNUM
C Pre : BARNUM is greater than zero.
C Post: Returns the cross-sectional area

C Argument Declarations
      INTEGER BARNUM

C Local Declarations
      REAL PI
      PARAMETER (PI = 3.14159)
      REAL RADIUS

C Compute RADIUS
      RADIUS = BARNUM / 16.0

C Return cross-sectional area
      DOAREA = PI * RADIUS ** 2

C Exit function
      RETURN
      END
```

5.6 ▬▬ Multiple Calls to a Subroutine

Often we need to *sort* a collection of data values or rearrange the values so they are in numerical order (alphabetical order for character data). We can use subroutine ORDER (see Fig. 5.17) to place two numbers in numerical order. We can call this subroutine repeatedly to place several numbers in order, as shown in the next case study.

▬▬ Case Study: Simple Sorting Problem

Problem

Write a program that reads any three numbers into the variables NUM1, NUM2, and NUM3 and rearranges the data so that the smallest number is stored in NUM1, the next smallest number in NUM2, and the largest number in NUM3.

Case Study: Simple Sorting Problem, continued

Design Overview

This is a special case of a sorting problem. Since there are only three items to be sorted, we will solve this special case now; the general sorting problem is a bit more complicated and will be considered later.

Data Requirements

Problem Inputs

three numbers (REAL NUM1, NUM2, NUM3)

Problem Outputs

the three numbers stored in increasing order in NUM1, NUM2, NUM3

Initial Algorithm

1. Read the three numbers into NUM1, NUM2, and NUM3.
2. Place the smallest number in NUM1, the next smallest in NUM2, and the largest number in NUM3.
3. Print NUM1, NUM2, and NUM3.

Algorithm Refinements

We can think of the three variables NUM1, NUM2, NUM3 as representing a list of consecutive storage cells. To perform step 2, we can compare pairs of numbers, always moving the smaller number in the pair closer to the front of the list (NUM1) and the larger number closer to the end of the list (NUM3). It should take three comparisons to sort the numbers in the list; one possible sequence of comparisons is shown next.

Step 2 Refinement

2.1 Compare NUM1 and NUM2 and store the smaller number in NUM1 and the larger number in NUM2.
2.2 Compare NUM1 and NUM3 and store the smaller number in NUM1 and the larger number in NUM3.
2.3 Compare NUM2 and NUM3 and store the smaller number in NUM2 and the larger number in NUM3.

Table 5.4 traces this refinement for the input sequence: 8.0, 10.0, 6.0. The final order is correct.

Case Study: Simple Sorting Problem, continued

Table 5.4. *Trace of Step 2 Refinement for Input Data 8, 10, 6*

ALGORITHM STEP	NUM1	NUM2	NUM3	EFFECT
	8.0	10.0	6.0	
2.1	8.0	10.0	6.0	NUM1, NUM2 are in order.
2.2	6.0	10.0	8.0	Switches NUM1 and NUM3.
2.3	6.0	8.0	10.0	Switches NUM2 and NUM3.

Figure 5.23 shows the structure chart for this algorithm. The data-flow information for subproblem "Order NUM1 and NUM2" shows that subroutine ORDER uses NUM1 and NUM2 for input and output in performing this step.

Coding

The final program is shown in Fig. 5.22. The three statements

```
CALL ORDER (NUM1, NUM2)
CALL ORDER (NUM1, NUM3)
CALL ORDER (NUM2, NUM3)
```

that call subroutine ORDER each have a different argument list. Consequently, a different pair of variables will be manipulated each time the ORDER executes.

Figure 5.22. *Program to Order Three Numbers*

```
      PROGRAM SORT3
C Test subroutine ORDER and order three numbers

C Declarations
      REAL NUM1, NUM2, NUM3

C Enter test data
      PRINT *, 'Enter three numbers:'
      READ *, NUM1, NUM2, NUM3

C Order the three numbers
      CALL ORDER (NUM1, NUM2)
      CALL ORDER (NUM1, NUM3)
      CALL ORDER (NUM2, NUM3)

C Print results
      PRINT *, 'The numbers in ascending order are: ', NUM1, NUM2, NUM3

C Exit program
      STOP
      END
```

Case Study: Simple Sorting Problem, continued

```
C--------------------------------------------------------------------

      SUBROUTINE ORDER (S, L)

C Arranges its arguments in numerical order.

C Input/Output Arguments
C   S - Smaller number after execution of ORDER
C   L - Larger number after execution of ORDER

C Argument Declarations
      REAL S, L

C Local Declarations
      REAL TEMP

C Compare S and L and switch if necessary
      IF (S .GT. L) THEN
          TEMP = S
          S = L
          L = TEMP
      ENDIF

C Exit subroutine
      RETURN
      END

Enter three numbers:
7.5   5.5   9.6
The numbers in ascending order are: 5.5000000    7.5000000    9.6000000
```

Figure 5.23. *Structure Chart for Sorting Problem*

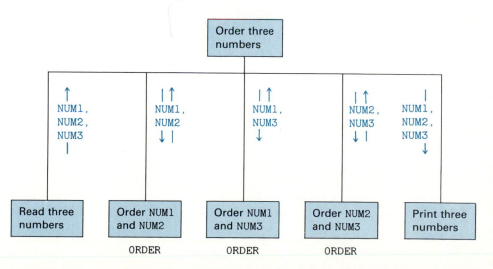

1. Draw a diagram like Fig. 5.15 showing the main program data area and subroutine data area before and after the first execution of subroutine ORDER in the program of Fig. 5.22. Use the data shown in the sample run.
2. What would be the effect of the call statements below?

```
CALL ORDER (NUM3, NUM2)
CALL ORDER (NUM2, NUM1)
CALL ORDER (NUM3, NUM2)
```

5.7 ▭ Debugging and Testing a Program System

As the number of modules and statements in a program grows, the possibility of error also increases. If each module or subprogram is kept to a manageable size, then the likelihood of error will increase much more slowly. Short subprograms are also easier to read and understand, particularly if they are carefully documented, as illustrated in the text.

Whenever possible, test each subprogram separately before including it in the program system. This can be done by writing a short driver program. The driver program should define all subprogram inputs, call the subroutine, and display the subprogram outputs.

EXAMPLE 5.12

The main program in Fig. 5.24 is a driver program that tests subroutine BREAK (see Fig. 5.14). The driver program reads each test value for the input argument X, calls BREAK, and displays the subroutine outputs that are stored in main program variables N and Y.

Figure 5.24. *Driver Program for Subroutine BREAK*

```
      PROGRAM DRIVER
C Driver program to test BREAK

C Declarations
      REAL X, Y
      INTEGER N

      PRINT *, 'Enter a value to be split — enter 0.0 when done:'
      READ *, X
      DO WHILE (X .NE. 0.0)                           9 IF (...) THEN
         CALL BREAK (X, N, Y)
         PRINT *, 'N = ', N, ' Y = ', Y
```

```
          PRINT *, 'Enter a value to be split — enter 0.0 when done:'
          READ *, X
       ENDDO                                       GOTO 9
C                                                  ENDIF
C Exit program
       STOP
       END

C—————————————————————————————————————————————————————————————————————

       SUBROUTINE BREAK (X, WHOLE, FRAC)

C Breaks a real number into its whole and fractional parts

C Input Argument
C   X — The value to be split (REAL)
C Output Arguments
C   WHOLE — The whole part of X (INTEGER)
C   FRAC — The fractional part of X (REAL)

C Argument Declarations
       REAL X, FRAC
       INTEGER WHOLE

C Define results
       WHOLE = INT(X)
       FRAC = X — REAL(WHOLE)

C Exit subroutine
       RETURN
       END

Enter a value to be split — enter 0.0 when done:
2.5
N =            2   Y =   0.5000000
Enter a value to be split — enter 0.0 when done:
—3.7
N =           —3   Y =  —0.7000000
Enter a value to be split — enter 0.0 when done:
25.
N =           25   Y =   0.0000000
Enter a value to be split — enter 0.0 when done:
1.25678E3
N =         1256   Y =   0.7800000
Enter a value to be split — enter 0.0 when done:
0.0
```

To properly test subroutine BREAK, the program user should enter positive numbers, negative numbers, whole numbers, and numbers in scientific notation. When satisfied that BREAK performs correctly on a variety of input data, the user enters 0.0 to stop the test.   ■

Pretesting a subprogram helps us to remove any obvious bugs and gives us some confidence that the subprogram is correct. If most subprograms are pretested in this way, it will be easier to debug the entire program system. The process of separately testing each subprogram is called *bottom-up testing*.

Another technique that helps us test the main program or a subprogram that has several subordinate subprograms is the use of a stub. A *stub* is a dummy subprogram consisting of a PRINT statement that simply prints a message indicating that the subroutine was called. A stub may be used in place of a subprogram that has not yet been written. When the main program calls the stub, a message will be printed. Execution of the stub does not cause any meaningful results to be computed; however, it does enable us to check the flow of control through the program system and to test those subprograms that are ready.

As an example, let's suppose we have completed program REBAR2 (see Fig. 5.20) and subroutine TABHED, and we would like to test them before writing function DOAREA. If we substitute the stub in Fig. 5.25 for function DOAREA in the source file, we can compile the source file and determine whether the main program and subroutine TABHED perform as expected. Because a function must always return a single result, the stub for DOAREA returns a value of 1.0 each time it is called. This means that program REBAR2 will not display the correct value for LOAD, but we can still observe its overall operation. Once the actual function DOAREA is written and tested, we can substitute it for the stub in the source file and complete the debugging and testing process. The use of stubs as described here is called *top-down testing*.

Figure 5.25. *Stub for Function DOAREA*

```
      REALFUNCTION DOAREA (BARNUM)
C Stub for function DOAREA

C Argument Declaration
      INTEGER BARNUM
      PRINT *, 'Entering function DOAREA'

C Define result and exit
      DOAREA = 1.0
      RETURN
      END
```

A list of suggestions for debugging complete program systems follows.

Debugging Tips for Program Systems

1. Carefully document each subprogram argument with comments. Also describe the subprogram operation with comments.
2. Separately test each subprogram on a variety of input data using a short driver program before inserting the subprogram in the system.
3. When debugging the system, leave a trace of execution by printing each subprogram name as it is entered.
4. To test the flow of control and completed segments of an incomplete program system, use stubs for all subprograms that are not yet written.
5. During debugging, print the values of all input arguments upon entry to a subprogram. Make sure that these values make sense.
6. During debugging, print the values of all output arguments upon returning from a subprogram.

5.8 ▭▭▭ Common Programming Errors

When writing functions, make sure that the function name is always defined (given a value) before the function RETURN is executed. If you fail to do this, a syntax error such as "return function value not set" may occur. Within a function body, the function's name should appear only on the left side of an assignment statement and not at all in an expression. You should also declare the data type of a function in every program module that uses it.

The local variables declared inside a subprogram cannot be referenced outside the subprogram body. If you attempt to do this, the compiler will allocate another memory cell (contents undefined) and use that cell instead. The same thing will happen if you attempt to reference inside the subprogram body a variable or parameter that is declared in the main program. Only subprogram arguments and local variables and parameters may be referenced inside the subprogram.

To call a subroutine, use a CALL statement; to call a function, reference its name in an expression. Make sure that the number of actual arguments in a subprogram call is the same as the number of dummy arguments for that subprogram, and that each argument appears in its correct position. The type of each actual argument must be the same as its corresponding dummy argument or an "argument type mismatch" syntax error may occur.

Finally, make sure that you spell each subprogram name consistently and that you include in the source program file the main program together with all subprograms called. If a subprogram is missing or if its name is misspelled, an "undefined external reference" error will occur when you attempt to link and run your program.

Chapter Review

This chapter introduced the concept of modular programming using subprograms. A subprogram can be called repeatedly in a program to perform a particular operation. By changing the actual arguments listed in the subprogram call, we can get it to perform this operation on different data. A subprogram written for one program system can also be reused in another. This capability allows us to create our own libraries of subprograms and to use them as building blocks or modules to facilitate the design of larger program systems.

Table 5.5 shows the two types of subprograms discussed in this chapter: functions and subroutines. You can write your own functions, which are used in the same way as library functions. A user-defined function must always return a single result. The function result is the last value assigned to the function name during its execution. A function is called when an expression is evaluated that contains the function name followed by its actual arguments. Each actual argument is substituted for a dummy argument listed in the function header statement; the correspondence between actual arguments and dummy arguments is determined by position in the argument list (i.e., first actual argument corresponds to first dummy argument, and so on).

Subroutines are subprograms that can return any number of results, or zero results. A subroutine returns a value by modifying one or more of its arguments. The correspondence between a subroutine's actual arguments and dummy arguments is also determined by position. A subroutine is called when a CALL statement is executed.

Finally, we showed how to use a structure chart to summarize the control flow and data flow between the main program and its subprograms. We recommend that you use structure charts for this purpose in your own programming. A structure chart provides valuable documentation for the program system. A structure chart also helps you determine what variables must be declared in the main program and what arguments are needed for each subprogram call.

Table 5.5. *Summary of New FORTRAN Statements*

STATEMENT	EFFECT
Function Definition	

`LOGICAL FUNCTION POSTIV (N)`
`INTEGER N`
`POSTIV = (N .GT. 0)`
`RETURN`
`END`
	Function `POSTIV` returns the value `.TRUE.` if the value of `N` is greater than zero; otherwise, the function result is `.FALSE.`.

Single-Statement Function	

`REAL X, Y`
`REAL SUMSQ`
`SUMSQ(X, Y) = X ** 2 + Y ** 2`
	Function `SUMSQ` (type `REAL`) returns the sum of the squares of its two arguments.

Subroutine Definition	

`SUBROUTINE SWITCH (X, Y)`
`REAL X, Y`
`REAL TEMP`
`TEMP = X`
`X = Y`
`Y = TEMP`
`RETURN`
`END`
	Switches the values stored in the actual arguments corresponding to dummy arguments X and Y. The actual arguments must be two type `REAL` variables.

Subroutine Call	
`CALL SWITCH (A, B)`	Calls subroutine `SWITCH` to exchange the data stored in variables A and B.

Quick-Check Exercises

1. The _____ arguments appear in the subprogram call, and the _____ arguments appear in the subprogram definition.
2. The correspondence between dummy arguments and actual arguments is by _____.
3. Functions return _____ result(s); subroutines may return _____ result(s).
4. A(n) _____ returns results by assigning a value to the _____ name; a(n) _____ returns results by assigning a value to a(n) _____.
5. Which arguments can be expressions, actual or dummy?
6. Which kind of subprogram requires a special statement to call it? Which kind of subprogram should have its type declared in the calling program?

7. For the subroutine that begins

```
SUBROUTINE CONFUS (X, Y, N)
INTEGER X
REAL Y, N
```

indicate the argument correspondence for the call statement

```
CALL CONFUS (N, Y, X)
```

8. What are the requirements for the CALL statement in exercise 7 to be valid?
9. Which of the following subprogram headers are valid and which are invalid? Explain your answers.
   a. REAL FUNCTION (X, N)
   b. SUBROUTINE CHOP (X, N, RESULT)
   c. INTEGER FUNCTION ROUND (SQRT(I))
   d. SUBROUTINE FIXIT (W, 4.0)
   e. FUNCTION ROUND (X, N)
10. Functions may not return character or logical results. True or false?
11. Character type variables may not be used as dummy arguments in subroutines. True or false?
12. Which of the following is not always an advantage of subprograms: more readable programs, separation of tasks, reduction in lines of code, easier debugging, reusability of modules? Explain your answer.
13. What is the value of main program variable X after the following program executes?

```
PROGRAM MAIN
REAL X
CALL SILLY (X)
STOP
END

SUBROUTINE SILLY (Y)
REAL Y
REAL X
X = 25.0
Y = 2.0 * X
RETURN
END
```

Answers to Quick-Check Exercises

1. actual, dummy
2. position
3. one, any number including zero
4. function, function, subroutine, argument
5. actual

6. subroutine, function
7. actual N to dummy X, actual Y to dummy Y, actual X to dummy N
8. In the calling program, N must be type INTEGER, and X and Y must be type REAL.
9. a. illegal—function name is missing
   b. legal
   c. illegal—dummy argument is an expression
   d. illegal—dummy argument is a constant
   e. legal—implicit type REAL is assumed for function
10. false
11. false
12. reduction in lines of code. If a subprogram is called only once, there may be more lines of code due to the subprogram documentation.
13. Main program variable X corresponds to dummy argument Y and has the value 50.0.

Review Questions

1. Write a function that converts an amount in dollars and cents to pennies. Assume the function has two arguments: the first is the number of dollars and the second is the number of pennies. For example, the function reference CHANGE(3, 75) returns 375 as its result.
2. Write a subroutine that has one input parameter called Score and displays the corresponding letter grade using a straight scale (90–100 is an A, 80–89 is a B, and so on).
3. Redo question 2 using a function that returns the letter grade instead of displaying it.
4. Explain the allocation of memory cells when a subprogram is called.
5. Explain the use of a stub.
6. Explain the use of a driver program.
7. Explain the use of a structure chart.
8. Which of the three items mentioned in questions 5, 6, and 7 is used during algorithm development?
9. Argue against the following statements: It is silly to use subprograms because a program together with its subprograms has many more lines than a program written without subprograms. Also, the use of subprograms leads to more errors because of mistakes in using argument lists.

Programming Projects

1. Two positive integers I and J are considered to be *relatively prime* if there exists no integer greater than 1 that divides them both. Write a logical function RELPRM that has two parameters, I and J, and returns a value of true if and only if I and J are relatively prime. Otherwise, RELPRM should return a value of false.

2. The *greatest common divisor*, GCD, of two positive integers I and J is an integer N with the property that N divides both I and J (with 0 remainder) and is the largest integer dividing them both. An algorithm for determining N was devised by the famous mathematician Euclid:
   1. Let I be the smaller integer and J the larger.
   2. Let R be the remainder of I divided by J.
   3. DO WHILE R is nonzero
      4. Let I be J
      5. Let J be R
      6. Let R be the remainder of I divided by J
   ENDDO
   7. Print the value of J as the greatest common divisor.

   Write a program to read in four positive integers N1, N2, N3, and N4 and find the GCD of all four numbers. *Hint:* The GCD of the four integers is the largest N that divides all four of them. Implement the above algorithm as an integer function and call it as many times as needed to solve the problem.
   Note that GCD (N1, N2, N3, N4) = GCD (GCD(N1, N2), GCD(N3, N4)). Print N1, N2, N3, and N4 and the resulting GCD.

3. Given the lengths a, b, c of the sides of a triangle, write a function to compute the area, A, of the triangle. The formula for computing A is given by

   $$A = \sqrt{s(s - a)(s - b)(s - c)}$$

   where s is the semiperimeter of the triangle:

   $$s = \frac{a + b + c}{2}$$

   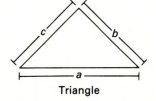

   Triangle

   Write a program to read in values for a, b, and c and call your function to compute A. Your program should print A, a, b, and c.

4. Write a program that will help you determine the maximum number of traffic lights that can be purchased for $50,000. Assume that the purchase cost of each light is $5000 and the installation cost is $1000. Each light uses 420 kilowatt-hours of electricity a year, and kilowatts are charged at $0.047 per kilowatt-hour. Enter a guess as to how many lights can be purchased and keep rerunning the program until the best answer is printed.

5. Read a series of integer numbers and determine the following information about each:
   a. Is it a multiple of 7, 11, or 13?
   b. Is the sum of the digits odd or even?
   c. What is the square root value (if positive)?
   d. Is it a prime number?

   You should have at least four functions and label all output. Some sample input data might be: 104 3773 13 121 77 30751.

6. Whatsamata U. offers a service to its faculty in computing grades at the end of each semester. A program will process three weighted test scores and calculate a student's average and letter grade (based on 90–100 is an A, 80–89 is a B, etc.).

   Write a program to provide this valuable service. The data will consist of the three test weights followed by three test scores and a student ID number (four digits) for each student. You should calculate the weighted average for each student and the corresponding grade. This information should be printed along with the initial three test scores. The weighted average for each student is equal to

   $$weight1 \times grade1 + weight2 \times grade2 + weight3 \times grade3$$

   For summary statistics, print the "highest average," "lowest average," "average of the averages," and "total number of students processed."

   Sample data might be

   ```
   .35    .25    .40
   100    76     88    1014
    96    91     99    2222
    45    15     65    3051
    35    88     86    4067
   ```

7. To design a square timber column in a structure, three formulas must be satisfied:

   a. Buckling load

   $$maximum\ load = (0.30 \times E \times Area)/(length/width)^2$$

   b. Compressive stress:

   $$maximum\ load = area/maximum\ compressive\ strength$$

   c. Slenderness limits:

   $$length/width \le 50$$

   where E is the modulus of elasticity (1,700,000 psi), A is the area (square inches), and *maximum compressive strength* = 445 psi (Douglas fir).

   Write a program that uses these three formulas to give an initial design to a structural engineer. Assume the columns to be used are square and are available in intervals of 2 inches (i.e., 2 by 2, 4 by 4, . . .).

   Have the output look like the following.

   ```
   Please enter the expected load in pounds
   9000
   Please enter the length of the column in inches
   120
   Testing a beam with width of    2.000000      inches
   The current width has failed the tests.
   Testing a beam with width of    4.000000      inches
   The current width has failed the tests.
   Testing a beam with width of    6.000000      inches
   ```

```
For a load of      9000.000      pounds
and a length of     120.0000      inches
recommend a square beam with sides of    6.000000    inches
```

8. It was a dark and stormy night. Our secret agent, Mr. Rogers, is behind enemy lines at a fuel depot. He walks over to a huge upright cylindrical fuel tank. It is 20 feet tall and 8 feet in diameter. He opens the 2-inch-diameter circular nozzle. He instinctively knows that the volume of fuel leaving the tank is

$$volume\ lost = velocity \times (area\ of\ the\ nozzle) \times time$$

and that

$$velocity = 8.02 * \sqrt{(height\ of\ fluid\ in\ the\ tank)}$$

How long will it take for the tank to empty?

Hint: Although this is really a calculus problem, we can simulate it with a computer and get a close answer. We can calculate the volume lost over a brief period of time, like a minute, and assume the loss of fluid is constant. We can then subtract the volume from the tank to arrive at the new height of fluid in the tank at the end of that minute. We can then calculate the loss for the next minute. This can be done over and over until the tank is dry. Print a table showing the elapsed time, the volume lost, and the height of the fluid. At the very end, convert the total elapsed seconds to minutes. The fluid height can be negative on the last line. Have the table look like the following:

Time (secs)	Volume Lost (cubic feet)	Fluid Height (feet)
60.	46.95	19.07
120.	45.84	18.15
180.	44.73	17.26
.	.	.
.	.	.
.	.	.
2340.	3.93	0.06
2400.	2.62	0.01
2460.	1.05	−0.01

```
Total time to drain is 41.00000   minutes
```

9. The electric company charges according to the following rate schedule:

8 cents a kilowatt-hour (kwh) for the first 300 kwh
6 cents a kwh for the next 300 kwh (up to 600 kwh)
5 cents a kwh for the next 400 kwh (up to 100 kwh)
3 cents a kwh for all electricity used over 1000 kwh

Write a function to compute the total charge for each customer. Write a program to call this function using the following data:

Customer Number	Kilowatt-hours Used
123	725
205	115
464	600
596	327
601	915
613	1011
722	47

The calling program should print a three-column table listing the customer number, hours used, and the charge for each customer. It should also compute and print the number of customers, total hours used, and total charges.

10. Each week, the employees of a local manufacturing company turn in time cards containing the following information:
   a. an identification number (a five-digit integer)
   b. hourly pay rate (a real number)
   c. time worked Monday, Tuesday, Wednesday, Thursday, and Friday (each a four-digit integer of the form HHMM, where HH is hours and MM is minutes)

For example, last week's time cards contained the following data:

		Time Worked (Hours, Minutes)				
Employee Number	Hourly Rate	Monday	Tuesday	Wednesday	Thursday	Friday
16025	4.00	0800	0730	0800	0800	0420
19122	4.50	0615	0800	0800	0800	0800
21061	4.25	0805	0800	0735	0515	0735
45387	3.50	1015	1030	0800	0945	0800
50177	6.15	0800	0415	0800	0545	0600
61111	5.00	0930	0800	0800	1025	0905
88128	4.50	0800	0900	0800	0800	0700

Write a program system that will read the above data and compute for each employee the total hours worked (in hours and minutes), the total hours worked (to the nearest quarter-hour), and the gross salary. Your system should print the data shown above with the total hours (both figures) and gross pay for each employee. You should assume that overtime is paid at 1½ times the normal hourly rate and that it is computed on a weekly basis (only on the total hours in excess of 40), rather than on a daily basis. Your program system should contain the following subprograms:
   a. a function for computing the sum (in hours and minutes) of two four-digit integers of the form HHMM (*Example:* 0745 + 0335 = 1120)
   b. a function for converting hours and minutes (represented as a four-digit integer) into hours rounded to the nearest quarter hour (*Example:* 1120 = 11.25)
   c. a function for computing gross salary given total hours and hourly rate
   d. a function for rounding gross salary accurate to two decimal places

Test your program using the time cards shown above.

6. Arrays

$\mathbf{I}$N ALL previous programs in this text, each variable was associated with a single memory cell. Such variables are called *simple variables*. In this chapter, we study a FORTRAN data structure. A *data structure* is a grouping of related data items in memory. The items in a data structure can be processed individually, although some operations may be performed on the structure as a whole.

An *array* is a data structure used for storage of a collection of data items that are all the same type (e.g., all the exam scores for a class). By using an array, we will be able to associate a single variable name (e.g., SCORES) with a group of related data items (exam scores). The individual data items in an array are stored in adjacent cells of main memory (one item per memory cell). Since each item is saved in a separate memory cell, we can process the individual items more than once and in any order we wish.

In earlier programs we reused the same memory cell to store each exam score. Each time a new item was read into the cell, its previous content was lost. Consequently, we could no longer access the third score after the fourth score was read. By using an array to store each score in a separate memory cell, this will no longer be a problem.

6.1 ▬▬▬ Declaring and Referencing Arrays

An array is a collection of two or more adjacent memory cells, called *array elements,* that are associated with a particular symbolic name. To set up an array in memory, we must declare both the name of the array and the number of cells associated with it.

The declaration

```
REAL X(8)
```

instructs the compiler to associate eight memory cells with the name X; these memory cells will be adjacent to each other in memory. Each element of array X may contain a single real value, so a total of eight real values may be stored and referenced using the array name X.

In order to process the data stored in an array, we must be able to reference each individual element. To reference a particular element, we need to specify the array name and identify the element desired (e.g., the third element of array X). The *subscripted variable* X(1) (read as X sub 1) may be used to reference the first element of the array X, X(2) the second element, and X(3) the third element. The integer enclosed in parentheses is the *array subscript.*

EXAMPLE 6.1   If x is the array declared as

    REAL X(8)

then we may refer to the elements of the array x as shown in Fig. 6.1.   ∎

Figure 6.1. *The Eight Elements of the Array X*

Array X

X(1)	X(2)	X(3)	X(4)	X(5)	X(6)	X(7)	X(8)
16.0	12.0	6.0	8.0	2.5	12.0	14.0	−54.5

First element   Second element   Third element   Eighth element

EXAMPLE 6.2   Let x be the array shown in Fig. 6.1. A sequence of statements that manipulate this array is shown in Table 6.1.

Table 6.1. *Statements that Manipulate Array X*

STATEMENT	EXPLANATION
PRINT *, X(1)	Displays the value of X(1) or 16.0.
X(4) = 25.0	Stores the value 25.0 in X(4).
SUM = X(1) + X(2)	Stores the sum of X(1) and X(2) or 28.0 in the variable SUM.
SUM = SUM + X(3)	Adds X(3) to SUM. The new SUM is 34.0.
X(4) = X(4) + 1.0	Adds 1.0 to X(4). The new X(4) is 26.0.
X(3) = X(1) + X(2)	Stores the sum of X(1) and X(2) in X(3). The new X(3) is 28.0.

The contents of array x after execution of these statements are shown below. Only X(3) and X(4) are changed.   ∎

Array X

X(1)	X(2)	X(3)	X(4)	X(5)	X(6)	X(7)	X(8)
16.0	12.0	28.0	26.0	2.5	12.0	14.0	−54.5

First element   Second element   Third element   Eighth element

EXAMPLE 6.3   Two arrays are declared below:

    CHARACTER *20 NAMES(50)
    INTEGER SCORES(50)

The arrays NAMES and SCORES have fifty elements. Each element of array NAMES can be used to store a string of up to twenty characters; each element of array

SCORES can be used to store an integer value. If these declarations are used in the exam score problem, the first student's name can be stored in NAMES(1), and the first student's score can be stored in SCORES(1). Because the data stored in NAMES(I) and SCORES(I) relate to the Ith student ($1 \leq I \leq 50$), the two arrays are called *parallel arrays*. Samples of these arrays are shown next.

NAMES(1)	SMITH, BILLY	SCORES(1)	75
NAMES(2)	JONES, JOHNNY	SCORES(2)	85
NAMES(3)	STRUTHERS, SALLY	SCORES(3)	88
	. .		. . .
NAMES(50)	SYKES, DAN	SCORES(50)	92

EXAMPLE 6.4

The type declaration

```
LOGICAL ANSWER(10)
```

declares an array ANSWER with ten elements; each element can store a LOGICAL value. This array could be used to store the ten answers for a true-false quiz (e.g., ANSWER(1) is .TRUE., ANSWER(2) is .FALSE.). A sample array is shown next.

ANSWER(1)	.TRUE.
ANSWER(2)	.FALSE.
ANSWER(3)	.FALSE.
	. .
ANSWER(10)	.TRUE.

EXAMPLE 6.5

More than one array may be declared in a single type declaration. The statements

```
REAL CACTUS(5), NEEDLE, PINS(6)
INTEGER FACTOR(12), N, INDEX
```

declare CACTUS and PINS to be arrays with five and six type REAL elements, respectively. FACTOR is an array with twelve type INTEGER elements. In addition, individual memory cells will be allocated for storage of the simple variables NEEDLE, N, and INDEX.

It is often desirable to use a parameter to specify the number of array elements to allocate. This makes it easy to change the size of an array.

EXAMPLE 6.6   The statements

```
INTEGER MAX
PARAMETER (MAX = 20)
CHARACTER *10 FIRNAM(MAX), LASNAM(MAX)
```

allocate storage for two arrays of character strings. Each array can hold twenty strings consisting of ten characters each. Changing the value of MAX will change the array sizes but not the length of the strings.   ∎

EXAMPLE 6.7   It is also possible to allocate storage for an array whose smallest subscript value is different from 1. The array VOLTS

```
INTEGER LOW, HIGH
PARAMETER (LOW = -2, HIGH = 2)
REAL VOLTS(LOW : HIGH)
```

has elements VOLTS(-2), VOLTS(-1), VOLTS(0), VOLTS(1), VOLTS(2). A sample array is shown next.   ∎

Volts(-2)	15.5
Volts(-1)	12.0
Volts(0)	16.1
Volts(1)	14.2
Volts(2)	15.0

All the points illustrated so far are summarized in the next display.

Array Declaration

> SYNTAX: *element-type aname(size)*
> *element-type aname(minval : maxval)*
>
> EXAMPLE: REAL A(5), B(-2 : 2)
>
> INTERPRETATION: The first form of the array declaration above allocates storage space for array *aname* consisting of *size* memory cells. Each memory cell can store one data item whose data type is specified by *element-type* (i.e., REAL, INTEGER, CHARACTER, or LOGICAL). The individual array elements are referenced by the subscripted variables *aname*(1), *aname*(2), ... , *aname*(size). An INTEGER constant or parameter must be used to specify *size*.

In the second form of the array declaration, storage space is allocated for an array with subscripts *minval*, *minval* + 1, ..., *maxval* − 1, *maxval*. This form may be used to declare an array whose smallest subscript is different from 1. Both *minval* and *maxval* must be INTEGER constants or parameters, and *minval* must be less than or equal to *maxval*.

SELF-CHECK EXERCISES FOR SECTION 6.1

1. What is the difference between X3 and X(3)?
2. For the declaration

   ```
   CHARACTER *1 GRADES(5)
   ```

   how many memory cells are allocated for data storage? What type of data can be stored there?
3. Allocate one array for storing the square roots of the integers from 1 through 10 and a second array for storing the cubes of the integers from −5 through 5.
4. Allocate an array for storing the twenty-one readings of a pressure gauge that are recorded at one-second intervals (from $t − 10$ seconds through $t + 10$ seconds) during a satellite launch.

6.2 ▬▬▬ Array Subscripts

A subscript is used to differentiate between the individual array elements and to allow us to specify which array element is to be manipulated. Any INTEGER expression may be used as an array subscript. However, the value of this subscript expression must lie between 1 and the declared size of the array (or between *minval* and *maxval* if *minval* is not 1); otherwise, an "out-of-range subscript" run-time error may occur.

It is essential to understand the distinction between an array subscript value and an array element value. The original array X from Fig. 6.1 is redrawn below. The subscripted variable X(I) references a particular element of this array. If I has the value 1, the subscript value is 1, so X(1) is referenced. The value of X(I) in this case is 16.0. If I has the value 3, the subscript value is 3 and the value of X(I) is 6.0. If I has the value 9, the subscript value is 9 and the value of X(I) is undefined because the subscript value is out of the allowable range.

Array X

X(1)	X(2)	X(3)	X(4)	X(5)	X(6)	X(7)	X(8)
16.0	12.0	6.0	8.0	2.5	12.0	14.0	−54.5

EXAMPLE 6.8

Table 6.2 lists some sample statements involving the array X above. I is assumed to be an INTEGER variable with value 6. Make sure you understand each statement.

Table 6.2. *Some Sample Statements for Array X When I is 6*

STATEMENT	EFFECT
PRINT *, 5, X(5)	Displays 5 and 2.5 (value of X(5))
PRINT *, I, X(I)	Displays 6 and 12.0 (value of X(6))
PRINT *, X(I) + 1	Displays 13.0 (value of X(6) plus 1)
PRINT *, X(I) + I	Displays 18.0 (value of X(6) plus 6)
PRINT *, X(I+1)	Displays 14.0 (value of X(7))
PRINT *, X(I+I)	Illegal attempt to display X(12)
PRINT *, X(2*I)	Illegal attempt to display X(12)
PRINT *, X(2*I-4)	Displays -54.5 (value of X(8))
PRINT *, X(INT(X(5)))	Displays 12.0 (value of X(2))
X(I-1) = X(I)	Assigns 12.0 (value of X(6)) to X(5)
X(I) = X(I+1)	Assigns 14.0 (value of X(7)) to X(6)
X(I) - 1 = X(I)	Illegal assignment statement

There are two illegal attempts to display element X(12), which is not in the array. These attempts may result in a *"subscript out of range"* run-time error.

The last PRINT statement uses INT(X(5)) as a subscript expression. Since this evaluates to 2, the value of X(2) (and not X(5)) is printed. If the value of INT(X(5)) is outside the range 1 through 8, it would be an illegal subscript expression. ∎

Array Subscripts

SYNTAX: *aname(subscript)*

EXAMPLE: B(I+1)

INTERPRETATION: The *subscript* may be any INTEGER expression. Each time a subscripted variable is encountered in a program, the subscript is evaluated and its value determines which element of array *aname* is referenced.

NOTE: If the value of *subscript* is not within the declared range, an "out-of-range subscript" error may occur.

SELF-CHECK EXERCISES FOR SECTION 6.2

1. Show the contents of array X after executing the statements in Table 6.2.
2. For the new array derived in exercise 1, describe what happens when the statements in Table 6.2 are executed for I = 3.

6.3 ▬▬▬ Using DO Loops to Process Arrays

Very often, we wish to process the elements of an array in sequence, starting with the first. An example would be entering data into the array or printing its contents. In FORTRAN, this can be accomplished easily using a DO loop with a loop-control variable (e.g., I) that is also used as the array subscript (e.g., X(I)). Increasing the value of the loop-control variable by 1 causes the next array element to be processed.

EXAMPLE 6.9

The array CUBE declared below will be used to store the cubes of the first ten integers (e.g., CUBE(1) is 1, CUBE(10) is 1000).

```
INTEGER CUBE(10), I
```

The DO loop

```
DO 10 I = 1, 10
   CUBE(I) = I ** 3
10 CONTINUE
```

initializes this array, as shown below.   ■

Array CUBE

(1)	(2)	(3)	(4)	(5)	(6)	(7)	(8)	(9)	(10)
1	8	27	64	125	216	343	512	729	1000

Statistical Computations Using Arrays

One common use of arrays is for storage of a collection of related data values. Once the values are stored, some simple statistical computations may be performed. The array X is used for this purpose in the program discussed next.

The program in Fig. 6.2 uses three DO loops to process the array X. The parameter MAXITM determines the size of the array. The variable I is used as the loop-control variable and array subscript in each loop.

The first DO loop,

```
DO 10 I = 1, MAXITM
   READ *, X(I)
10 CONTINUE
```

reads one data value into each element of array X (the first item is stored in X(1), the second item in X(2), etc.) The READ statement is repeated for each value of I from 1 to 8; each repetition causes a new data value to be read and stored in X(I). The subscript I determines which array element receives the

Figure 6.2. *Printing a Table of Differences*

```
      PROGRAM AVESTD
C Computes the average value and standard deviation of an array of
C data and prints the difference between each value and the average

      INTEGER MAXITM
      PARAMETER (MAXITM = 8)
      INTEGER I
      REAL X(MAXITM), AVERAG, STDEV, SUM, SUMSQR

C Enter the data
      PRINT *, 'Enter ', MAXITM, ' numbers, one per line:'
      DO 10 I = 1, MAXITM
         READ *, X(I)
  10  CONTINUE

C Compute the sum and sum of the squares of all elements
      SUM = 0.0
      SUMSQR = 0.0
      DO 20 I = 1, MAXITM
         SUM = SUM + X(I)
         SUMSQR = SUMSQR + X(I) ** 2
  20  CONTINUE

C Compute and print the average and standard deviation
      AVERAG = SUM / REAL(MAXITM)
      STDEV = SQRT(SUMSQR / REAL(MAXITM) - AVERAG ** 2)
      PRINT *
      PRINT 15, 'The average value is ', AVERAG
      PRINT 15, 'The standard deviation is ', STDEV
  15  FORMAT (1X, A, F8.1)

C Display the difference between each item and the average
      PRINT *
      PRINT *, 'Table of differences between X(I) and average'
      PRINT 25, 'I', 'X(I)', 'Difference'
  25  FORMAT (1X, A4, 3X, A8, 3X, A14)
      DO 30 I = 1, MAXITM
         PRINT 35, I, X(I), X(I)-AVERAGE
  35     FORMAT (1X, I4, 3X, F8.1, 3X, F14.1)
  30  CONTINUE

C Exit program
      STOP
      END

Enter           8 numbers, one per line:
16
12
6
8
```

```
2.5
12
14
-54.5

The average value is       2.0
The standard deviation is      21.8

Table of differences between X(I) and average
   I       X(I)        Difference
   1       16.0            14.0
   2       12.0            10.0
   3        6.0             4.0
   4        8.0             6.0
   5        2.5             0.5
   6       12.0            10.0
   7       14.0            12.0
   8      -54.5           -56.5
```

next data value. The data shown in the sample run cause the array to be initialized as in Fig. 6.1.

The second DO loop (with label 20) is used to accumulate (in SUM) the sum of all values stored in the array. It also accumulates (in SUMSQR) the sum of the squares of all element values. The formulas implemented by this loop are

$$SUM = X(1) + X(2) + ... + X(7) + X(8) = \sum_{I=1}^{MAXITM} X(I)$$

$$SUMSQR = X(1)^2 + X(2)^2 + ... + X(7)^2 + X(8)^2 = \sum_{I=1}^{MAXITM} X(I)^2$$

This loop will be discussed in more detail later.

The last DO loop

```
     DO 30 I = 1, MAXITM
        PRINT 35, I, X(I), X(I)-AVERAG
 35     FORMAT (1X, I4, 3X, F8.1, 3X, F14.1)
 30 CONTINUE
```

prints a table. Each line of the table displays an array subscript, an array element, and the difference between that element and the average value, X(I) − AVERAG. Note how the edit descriptors in FORMAT statements 25 and 35 cause each column of values in the output table to be right-aligned with its respective column heading.

Now that we have seen the entire program, we will take a closer look at the DO loop with label 20, which is repeated below.

```
C Compute the sum and the sum of the squares of all elements
       SUM = 0.0
       SUMSQR = 0.0
       DO 20 I = 1, MAXITM
          SUM = SUM + X(I)
          SUMSQR = SUMSQR + X(I) ** 2
    20 CONTINUE
```

This loop accumulates the sum of all eight elements of array x in the variable SUM. Each time the DO loop is repeated, the next element of array x is added to SUM. Then this array element value is squared, and its square is added to the sum being accumulated in SUMSQR. The execution of this program fragment is traced in Table 6.3 for the first three repetitions of the loop.

Table 6.3. *Partial Trace of DO Loop with Label 20*

STATEMENT	I	X(I)	SUM	SUMSQR	EFFECT
SUM = 0.0			0.0		Initializes SUM.
SUMSQR = 0.0				0.0	Initializes SUMSQR.
DO 20 I = 1, MAXITM	1	16.0			$1 \leq 8$ is true;
SUM = SUM + X(I)			16.0		Adds X(1) to SUM$_2$
SUMSQR = SUMSQR + ...				256.0	Adds 256.0 to SUMSQR.
increment and test I	2	12.0			$2 \leq 8$ is true;
SUM = SUM + X(I)			28.0		adds X(2) to SUM,
SUMSQR = SUMSQR + ...				400.0	adds 144.0 to SUMSQR.
increment and test I	3	6.0			$3 \leq 8$ is true;
SUM = SUM + X(I)			34.0		adds X(3) to SUM,
SUMSQR = SUMSQR + ...				436.0	adds 36.0 to SUMSQR.

The standard deviation of a set of data is a measure of the spread of the data values around the average value. A small standard deviation means that the data values are all relatively close to the average value. For MAXITM data items, the standard deviation is given by the formula

$$standard\ deviation = \sqrt{\frac{\sum_{I=1}^{MAXITM} X(I)^2}{MAXITM} - AVERAG^2}$$

In Fig. 6.2, this formula is implemented by the statement

```
STDEV = SQRT(SUMSQR / REAL(MAXITM) - AVERAG ** 2)
```

Program Style

Using DO Loop-Control Variables as Array Subscripts

In Fig. 6.2, the DO loop-control variable I determines which array element is manipulated during each loop repetition. The use of the loop-control variable as an array subscript is common, because it allows the programmer to specify easily the sequence in which the elements of an array are to be manipulated. Each time the loop-control variable is increased, the next array element is automatically selected. Note that the same loop-control variable is used in all three loops. This is not necessary but is permitted since the loop control variable is always initialized at loop entry. Thus, I is reset to 1 when each loop is entered.

SELF-CHECK EXERCISE FOR SECTION 6.3

1. Write DO loops to fill the arrays described in exercise 1 at the end of Section 6.1 with data. Each array element should be assigned the value specified for it.

6.4 ▬▬ Input and Output of Arrays

In Fig. 6.2, a DO loop was used to read in the eight elements of array X. This program fragment is repeated next.

```
      PRINT *, 'Enter ', MAXITM, ' numbers, one per line:'
      DO 10 I = 1, MAXITM
         READ *, X(I)
   10 CONTINUE
```

Each data item was entered by the program user on a separate line. Two other methods that may be used to read in an array of values will be discussed next.

Reading an Array of Data

The program fragment

```
      PRINT *, 'Enter ', MAXITM, ' numbers:'
      READ *, X
```

could also be used to read MAXITM values and store them in consecutive elements of the array X (i.e., the first data item in X(1), the second data item in X(2), etc.). The program user could enter one value on each of eight lines as before, all eight values on one line, or any other combination.

In the READ statement above, no subscripts are used to identify specific elements in array X. Whenever an array name appears without subscripts, the entire array is being referenced.

There are two advantages to using the program fragment above. First, it is simpler than using a DO loop. Second, it allows the program user to enter several data items on one line. The only disadvantage is that the number of data items needed is determined by the declared size of the array, and the program user must always enter exactly that number of data items.

EXAMPLE 6.10

The program fragment below could be used to read data into the arrays NAMES and SCORES assuming that MAXSTU students took the exam, where MAXSTU is the declared size of both arrays.

```
PRINT *, 'Enter the name of each student'
READ *, NAMES
PRINT *, 'Enter each score in the same order as the names'
READ *, SCORES
```

The program user must enter all the student names first and then all the exam scores as directed by the prompting messages. There are two problems with this approach. First, the program user must be careful that the ith score in the list of scores belongs to the ith student in the list of names. Second, even if fewer than MAXSTU students sit for the exam, MAXSTU names and MAXSTU scores must still be entered. We will discuss alternative techniques that do not have these problems next. ∎

Reading Data into Part of an Array

In many applications, we will not know beforehand exactly how many data items will need to be saved in an array. In fact, the number of data items will often change from one run of a program to another. For example, a grading program must be able to handle different-size classes. For this reason, we need to declare an array that is large enough to hold the largest expected set of data; we then instruct the program to read in the actual number of data items processed in a given run.

EXAMPLE 6.11

The program fragment in Fig. 6.3 reads the number of students taking an exam into the variable NUMSTU; the program then reads the students' names and scores into the parallel arrays NAMES and SCORES (size MAXSTU).

Figure 6.3. *DO Loop to Read Data into Part of an Array*

```
      PRINT *, 'Enter number of students'
      READ *, NUMSTU

C Enter the exam data
      DO 10 I = 1, NUMSTU
         PRINT *, 'Enter next name and score pair'
         READ *, NAMES(I), SCORES(I)
  10  CONTINUE
```

The prompting message

```
Enter next name and score pair
```

is printed each time the loop is repeated and a new name and score are read into the next pair of array cells. If NUMSTU is less than MAXSTU, only part of the arrays NAMES and SCORES will be defined, as shown by the darker color in Fig. 6.4.

Figure 6.4. *A Partially Defined Array*

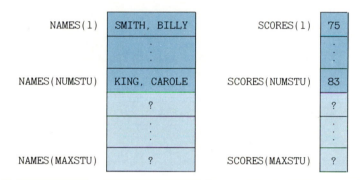

Since the data for NAMES(I) and SCORES(I) are entered together, it is less likely that student names and scores will not match. The variable NUMSTU should be used as the upper limit in any later DO loop that processes the arrays to ensure that only elements with subscripts 1 through NUMSTU are manipulated. ∎

Program Style

> *Verifying Array Bounds*
>
> The variable NUMSTU serves a very important role in the processing of arrays NAMES and SCORES, because it denotes the portion of these arrays that is filled with meaningful data. If the value of NUMSTU does not lie within the range 1 to MAXSTU, inclusive, a "subscript out of range" diagnostic may occur during program execution. For this reason, it is a good idea to use a function, such as ENTER (see Fig. 5.6), that not only reads a value into NUMSTU but verifies that this value is within the allowable range.

Implied DO Loop

The need to read data into part of an array is so common that a special form of the DO loop, called the *implied DO loop*, is available for this purpose. An implied DO loop is inserted directly in the input list of a READ statement or the output list of a PRINT statement. The part of the output list that makes up the implied DO loop is enclosed in parentheses. The DO loop variable and control parameters appear at the end of the implied DO loop.

EXAMPLE 6.12 The input list below contains an implied DO loop:

```
READ *, (NAMES(I), I = 1, 10)
```

The control portion (I = 1, 10) appears at the end of the implied DO loop and specifies that the data-entry operation is to be repeated for each integer value of I from 1 to 10. The input list specified by the implied DO loop is equivalent to NAMES(1), NAMES(2), ... , NAMES(10). ∎

EXAMPLE 6.13 An implied DO loop can be used to replace the explicit DO loop shown in Fig. 6.3. If the implied DO loop below is used, the prompt

```
Enter each name and score pair until done
```

is displayed one time. The program user must enter exactly NUMSTU name and score pairs after the prompt appears.

```
        PRINT *, 'Enter number of students'
        NUMSTU = ENTER(1, MAXSTU)

C Enter the exam data
        PRINT *, 'Enter each name and score pair until done'
        READ *, (NAMES(I), SCORES(I), I = 1, NUMSTU)
```

In this example, the input list specified by the implied DO loop is equivalent to NAMES(1), SCORES(1), NAMES(2), SCORES(2), ... , NAMES(NUMSTU), SCORES(NUMSTU). ∎

The implied DO loop is the most flexible technique for reading data into an array. Unlike the explicit DO loop shown earlier, it is possible to enter more than one name and score pair on a data line. The implied DO loop is also shorter and simpler to write than the explicit DO loop, because there is no CONTINUE statement or label required. In most cases, you will find this the best technique to use for data entry.

End-of-File Specifier

In the examples so far, we assumed that we knew beforehand the number of data items being read. Often, this is not the case. In Section 3.5, we showed how to use a sentinel value as an extra data item entered at the terminal to signal that all actual data were read. Although we could insert a sentinel value at the end of a data file, it is much easier to use an end-of-file specifier in a READ statement that enters data from a file.

EXAMPLE 6.14 The DO loop in Fig. 6.5 reads the student exam data from a data file. Each time it executes, the statement

```
READ (2, *, END = 99) NAMES(I), SCORES(I)
```

enters a new student name and score from the data file associated with unit 2 and stores the data in the next pair of array elements. A sample data file is shown in Fig. 6.6. ▪

Figure 6.5. *Loop to Read a Data File*

```
        DO 20 I = 1, MAXSTU
            READ (2, *, END = 99) NAMES(I), SCORES(I)
20      CONTINUE
        PRINT *, 'WARNING — ARRAY FILLED BEFORE END OF FILE REACHED'

C File read operation completed
C Adjust counter
    99 NUMSTU = I - 1
```

Figure 6.6. *Sample Data File*

```
'SMITH, BILLY'    75
'JONES, GORDY'    92
'KING, CAROLE'    83
```

We would expect DO loop 20 to execute MAXSTU times, where MAXSTU is the declared size of the arrays. However, what happens if the data file contains fewer than MAXSTU pairs of data? In this case, we would like to exit the DO loop after the last pair of data items is stored. The file specifier END = 99 causes this to happen.

The end of the data file in Fig. 6.6 is reached after the last data pair is read into array elements NAMES(3) and SCORES(3). When the READ statement executes again, the file specifier END = 99 causes a transfer of control to the statement with label 99. Without this specifier, an "attempt to read beyond the end of file" run-time error would occur.

If the data file contains more than MAXSTU data pairs, the arrays will be filled with data before the end of the data file is reached. In this case, normal loop exit occurs after the last element in each array receives its data (I is MAXSTU + 1). The PRINT statement displays a message warning that there may be more data left on the file. Normal loop exit also occurs if the data file contains exactly MAXSTU data pairs. In this case, the program user may ignore the warning message.

After loop exit, the assignment statement with label 99

```
99 NUMSTU = I - 1
```

stores in NUMSTU the number of data pairs read. The value stored, $I - 1$, represents the value of I during the last successful READ operation.

End-of-File Specifier

> SYNTAX: READ (*unum*, *, END = *label*) *input list*
>
> EXAMPLE: READ (1, *, END = 99) X(I), Y(I), Z(I)
>
> INTERPRETATION: The READ statement attempts to satisfy its *input list* by reading data from the next line of the file associated with unit number *unum*. If the file does not contain sufficient data, control transfers to the statement denoted by *label*.

End-of-File Specifier with Implied DO

We can also use an implied DO loop with a READ statement that has an end-of-file specifier. For example, the statement

```
READ (2, *, END = 99) (NAMES(I), SCORES(I), I = 1, MAXSTU)
```

reads data pairs into arrays NAMES and SCORES, transferring control to label 99 when there is no more data on the file associated with unit 2. If both arrays become filled with data, the statement following the READ statement executes next. It is not necessary to list each data pair on a separate line of the data file.

Review of Array-Input Methods

The properties of the four array-input methods discussed so far are summarized in Table 6.4, assuming that N represents the number of data pairs available. N must be less than or equal to the array size.

Array Output

The techniques for array input may also be used for array output. However, since we generally prefer to have array data displayed in a table, the explicit DO loop is most commonly used. The other methods display as many values as will fit across an output line.

EXAMPLE 6.15

Given the arrays NAMES and SCORES described earlier, the statement

```
PRINT *, NAMES, SCORES
```

causes a list of student names to be printed, followed by a list of student scores. Remember that whenever arrays are referred to by name only (no subscripts) the entire array is indicated. The number of values printed on a line depends on the field width used for each value and the line length. There are exactly $2 \times$ MAXSTU values printed, where MAXSTU is the declared size of each array. Since all names are printed first and then all scores, it is difficult to determine which score goes with which name. This is equivalent to the out-

Table 6.4. *Three Array-Input Methods*

EXAMPLE	DATA FORMAT	COMMENTS
`READ *, NAMES, SCORES`	`'BILL'  'JILL' ... 'JOE'` `95  67 ... 85`	Entire array must be filled (first NAMES, then SCORES). Many data items may be on each line.

`      DO 10 I = 1, N`
`          READ *, NAMES(I),`
`     +      SCORES(I)`
`10 CONTINUE`
	`'BILL'  95`
	`'JILL'  67`
	`'SUE'  88`
		Part of array may be filled. Only one data pair may be on a line.

`      READ *, (NAMES(I),` `     +  SCORES(I), I = 1, N)`	`'BILL'  95  'JILL'  67` `'SUE'  88`	Part of array may be filled. Many data items may be on each line.

`      DO 20 I = 1, MAXSTU`
`          READ (2, *, END = 99)`
`     +        NAMES(I), SCORES(I)`
`20 CONTINUE`
	`'BILL'  95`
	`'JILL'  67`
	`'SUE'  88`
		Part of array may be filled. Only one data pair may be on a line.

put list NAMES(1), NAMES(2), ... , NAMES(MAXSTU), SCORES(1), SCORES(2), ... , SCORES(MAXSTU). ∎

EXAMPLE 6.16   The DO loop

```
      DO 10 I = 1, NUMSTU
          PRINT *, NAMES(I), SCORES(I)
10 CONTINUE
```

prints one name and score pair on each output line. The number of pairs printed, NUMSTU, may be between 1 and MAXSTU. This gives the most legible output and is the form commonly used for tables. ∎

EXAMPLE 6.17   The PRINT statement with implied DO loop

```
      PRINT *, (NAMES(I), SCORES(I), I = 1, NUMSTU)
```

prints a name followed by a score. As many name and score pairs as will fit are displayed on each line. The number of pairs printed, NUMSTU, may be between 1 and MAXSTU. This is equivalent to the output list NAMES(1), SCORES(1), NAMES(2), SCORES(2), ... , NAMES(NUMSTU), SCORES(NUMSTU).

The three array output methods are summarized in Table 6.5, assuming that N represents the number of data pairs stored in the arrays. N must be less than or equal to the array size. ∎

Table 6.5. *Three Array-Output Methods*

EXAMPLE	OUTPUT	COMMENTS
PRINT *, NAMES, SCORES	BILL JILL SUE ,..., JOE 95 67 88, ..., 85	Both arrays are printed (NAMES and then SCORES). As many values as will fit appear on each line.

DO 10 I = 1, N
     PRINT *, NAMES(I),
  +   SCORES(I)
10 CONTINUE
	BILL 95
	JILL 67
	SUE 88
		Part of array may be printed. Only one pair of values appears on a line.

PRINT *, (NAMES(I), + SCORES(I), I = 1, N)	BILL 95 JILL 67 SUE 88	Part of array may be printed. As many values as will fit appear on each line.

The implied DO loop is described in the next display.

Implied DO Loop

> **SYNTAX:**   READ *, (*input list*, *lcv* = *initial*, *final*, *step*)
>   PRINT *, (*output list*, *lcv* = *initial*, *final*, *step*)
>
> **EXAMPLE:** READ *, (X(I), I = 1, N)
>
> **INTERPRETATION:** The READ (or PRINT) statement is executed. The *input list* (or *output list*) is repeated once for each integer value of *lcv* from *initial* to *final* in increments of *step*. Thus, the statement
>
>   PRINT *, (A(I), B(I), I = 1, 3)

has the same effect as the statement

```
    PRINT *, A(1), B(1), A(2), B(2), A(3), B(3)
```

The rules for specifying the implied DO loop parameters are the same as for the explicit DO (see Section 3.4).

Using Implied DO Loop in a Formatted Print

One problem with using the implied DO loop to print data in parallel arrays is that more than one set of data may be printed on each line, so the data will not be printed in a table. FORMAT statements can be used to solve this problem. If a FORMAT statement is written to describe the appearance of one set of data, then that FORMAT statement can be reused when more than one set of data is printed. Each time a FORMAT statement is reused, a new line of output is automatically started.

EXAMPLE 6.18

The formatted PRINT statement

```
      PRINT 5, (I, NAMES(I), SCORES(I), I = 1, NUMSTU)
    5 FORMAT (1X, I3, 2X, A, 5X, I3)
```

causes a student number (1 through NUMSTU) and a name and score pair to be displayed on each output line. FORMAT statement 5 describes how three output list items should be printed. If NUMSTU is greater than 1, there will be more items in the output list than there are edit descriptors in the FORMAT statement, so the format specification must be reused. Each time the specification is reused, a new output line is started. The student names and scores will be printed in a table similar to that produced by an explicit DO loop. ■

SELF-CHECK EXERCISES FOR SECTION 6.4

1. Using the arrays in exercise 3 at the end of Section 6.1, write a DO loop to print the square roots and cubes of the integers from 1 through 5. Each output line should show an integer value followed by its square root and cube.
2. Rewrite DO loop 30 in Fig. 6.2 as an implied DO loop. Use a formatted PRINT to ensure that the output remains in table form.

6.5 ▬▬▬ Array Arguments

Until now, all subprogram arguments were simple variables. In this section, we will study how to use arrays as subprogram arguments.

EXAMPLE 6.19   Function GETMAX in Fig. 6.7 returns the largest value that is stored in the array represented by dummy argument LIST. Within the DO loop, the current array element value, LIST(I), is compared to the largest value found so far, CURLRG. If the current element value is larger, it is stored in CURLRG. CURLRG is initialized to the first array element; its final value is returned as the function result.

Figure 6.7. *Function GETMAX*

```
      INTEGER FUNCTION GETMAX (LIST, N)

C Returns the largest of the first N values in array LIST
C Pre : First N elements of array LIST are defined and N > 0.
C Post: Function result is LIST(i) (1 <= i <= N) where
C        LIST(i) is the largest of the first N elements.

C Argument Declarations
      INTEGER N, LIST(N)

C Local Declarations
      INTEGER I, CURLRG

C     Assume the first element is the largest so far
      CURLRG = LIST(1)

C Compare each element to the largest so far; save the larger value
      DO 10 I = 2, N
         IF (LIST(I) .GT. CURLRG) THEN
            CURLRG = LIST(I)
         ENDIF
   10 CONTINUE

C Define result and exit function
      GETMAX = CURLRG
      RETURN
      END
```

The declaration statement

```
      INTEGER N, LIST(N)
```

indicates to the compiler that dummy argument LIST represents an array with N elements. Dummy argument N is used as the end value in the DO loop and determines how many array elements are processed. N may be passed any value from 1 to the declared size of the array.   ∎

If X is an INTEGER array with five elements, the statement

```
      XLARGE = GETMAX(X, 5)
```

calls function GETMAX to search array X and find its largest element; this value is returned and stored in variable XLARGE. If Y is an INTEGER array with ten elements, the statement

        YLARGE = GETMAX(Y, 10)

causes the largest value in array Y to be stored in YLARGE. The statement

        YLARGE = GETMAX(Y, 5)

causes the largest value in the first half (subscripts 1 through 5) of array Y to be stored in YLARGE.

Argument Correspondence for Arrays

The argument correspondence for GETMAX(X, 5) is shown in Fig. 6.8 for a particular array X. There is no need to copy array X in the function data area; instead, the location in memory of the first array element is stored in the function data area. This enables the function to access array X. Consequently, each reference to dummy array element LIST(I) causes X(I) to be manipulated. The value returned by the function reference GETMAX(X, 5) is 37; the value returned by the function reference GETMAX(X, 3) is 15. In the latter case, only the first three elements of array X are examined.

Figure 6.8. *Argument Correspondence for GETMAX(X, 5)*

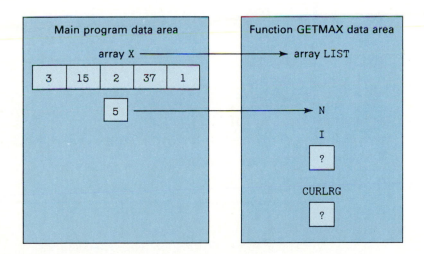

Returning an Array of Values

A subroutine can return several values using different output arguments. It can also return an array of values using one output argument, as shown in the next example.

EXAMPLE 6.20

Subroutine ADDER in Fig. 6.9 adds two arrays. The sum of arrays A and B is defined as the array C such that C(I) is equal to A(I) + B(I) for each subscript I. The last argument, N, specifies how many array elements are summed. The declaration

```
REAL A(*), B(*), C(*)
```

indicates that dummy arguments A, B, and C are type REAL arrays. The * specifies that each array size is the same as the declared size of its corresponding actual array. This allows us to use the subroutine with any size arrays. Arrays A, B, and C are called *assumed-size dummy arrays*. ∎

Figure 6.9. *Subroutine ADDER*

```
      SUBROUTINE ADDER (A, B, C, N)

C Stores element—by—element sum of arrays A and B in array C

C Input Arguments
C   A, B — Arrays being summed
C   N — Number of elements summed
C Output Argument
C   C — Sum of arrays A and B

C Argument Declarations
      REAL A(*), B(*), C(*)
      INTEGER N

C Local Declarations
      INTEGER I

C Add elements of arrays A and B with the same subscript
      DO 10 I = 1, N
         C(I) = A(I) + B(I)
   10 CONTINUE

C Exit subroutine
      RETURN
      END
```

The argument correspondence specified by

```
CALL ADDER (X, Y, Z, 5)
```

is shown in Fig. 6.10. The values stored in arrays X and Y in the main program are added together and saved in array Z. Dummy argument N (not shown) corresponds to the constant 5.

Figure 6.10. *Argument Correspondence for ADDER (X, Y, Z, 5)*

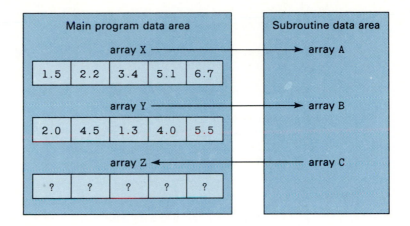

After execution of the subroutine, $Z(1)$ will contain the sum of $X(1)$ and $Y(1)$, or 3.5; $Z(2)$ will contain the sum of $X(2)$ and $Y(2)$, or 6.7; and so on; arrays X and Y will be unchanged. The new contents of array Z are shown next.   ∎

array Z after subroutine execution

3.5	6.7	4.7	9.1	12.2

EXAMPLE 6.21

Subroutine ENTSTU in Fig. 6.11 reads data into a pair of parallel arrays. The first dummy argument (MAXSIZ) is an input argument that specifies the declared size of the arrays. The remaining arguments are input/output arguments used to store the array data (NAMES, SCORES) and the number of array elements (NUMSTU) that are currently filled with data. ENTSTU can be called more than once; each time it is called, additional data are entered and positioned after the data entered during the previous call.

NUMSTU is used to select the next pair of array elements that receive data. The value of NUMSTU passed into the subroutine is the subscript of the last pair of elements that currently contain data and should be zero the first time ENTSTU is called. NUMSTU is increased by 1 before each data pair is stored. The value of NUMSTU returned to the calling program specifies the number of element pairs that contain data after the new data are entered.

Each name and score pair is temporarily saved in NXTNAM and NXTSCR before being stored in the arrays. The subroutine return occurs after the sentinel name is read or the arrays become filled (NUMSTU is MAXSIZ). The sentinel name ('*') and score (0) are not saved in the arrays.

Dummy arrays NAMES and SCORES are considered input/output arguments,

Figure 6.11. *Subroutine ENTSTU*

```
      SUBROUTINE ENTSTU (MAXSIZ, NAMES, SCORES, NUMSTU)

C Returns data in the parallel arrays NAMES and SCORES
C and updates NUMSTU

C Input Argument
C   MAXSIZ - The array size
C Input/Output Arguments
C   NAMES - Array of student names
C   SCORES - Array of exam scores
C   NUMSTU - Number of array elements currently filled with data

C Argument Declarations
      INTEGER MAXSIZ, NUMSTU, SCORES(MAXSIZ)
      CHARACTER *20 NAMES(MAXSIZ)
C Local Declarations
      INTEGER NXTSCR
      CHARACTER *20 NXTNAM

C Print instructions
      PRINT *, 'Enter a name (in quotes) and a score'
      PRINT *, 'Enter the sentinel pair ''*'' 0 when done'

C Read each name and score pair and store it in the arrays
      READ *, NXTNAM, NXTSCR
      DO WHILE ((NXTNAM .NE. '*') .AND.
     +        (NUMSTU .LT. MAXSIZ))
         NUMSTU = NUMSTU + 1
         SCORES(NUMSTU) = NXTSCR
         NAMES(NUMSTU) = NXTNAM
         PRINT *, 'Enter next name and score'
         READ *, NXTNAM, NXTSCR
      ENDDO                                     GOTO 9
C                                               ENDIF
C Exit subroutine
      RETURN
      END
```

because they may be partially defined before each call to ENTSTU. Any new data entered during each call are returned to the calling program along with the original data.

The main program data area is shown in Fig. 6.12 before and after the statement

```
CALL ENTSTU (MAXSIZ, NAMES, SCORES, NUMSTU)
```

Figure 6.12. *Effect of Call to ENTSTU*

Before the call to ENTSTU

NUMSTU	NAMES(1)	JANE DOE	SCORES(1)	87
2	NAMES(2)	JOHN DOE	SCORES(2)	77

After the call to ENTSTU

NUMSTU	NAMES(1)	JANE DOE	SCORES(1)	87
4	NAMES(2)	JOHN DOE	SCORES(2)	77
	NAMES(3)	BILLY JOEL	SCORES(3)	75
	NAMES(4)	CHRIS BRINK	SCORES(4)	93

is executed, assuming MAXSIZ is 100 and NUMSTU is 2 before the call. Only the array elements with defined values are shown. The new data are

```
'BILLY JOEL' 75
'CHRIS BRINK' 93
'*' 0
```

The value returned for NUMSTU is 4.   ■

Using Individual Array Elements as Arguments

We can also use individual array elements as actual, but not dummy, arguments. An array element used as an actual argument must correspond to a dummy argument that is a simple variable of the same type as the array element. For example, the statement

```
CALL ORDER (X(1), X(2))
```

calls subroutine ORDER (see Fig. 5.17) to place the first two elements of actual array X in ascending order. The call statement establishes a correspondence between array element X(1) and the first dummy argument, and between array element X(2) and the second dummy argument. Since both dummy arguments of subroutine ORDER are type REAL, the calling program must declare X as a type REAL array with at least two elements. Remember, it is illegal for an array element to be listed as a dummy argument in either a function or a subroutine definition.

Case Study: Finding the Area of a Polygon[M]

Problem

Your math professor needs a program for computing the area of a polygon. The (X, Y) coordinates of each point of the polygon are stored on a data file in which each line contains the X and Y coordinates of a single point.

Design Overview

Assume the points of a polygon with n sides are numbered in sequence, as shown in Fig. 6.13, where point (X_1, Y_1) lies between points (X_n, Y_n) and (X_2, Y_2), and point (X_2, Y_2) lies between points (X_1, Y_1) and (X_3, Y_3). We can store the points of the polygon in a pair of parallel arrays, x and y, of size NMAX and then find the area of the polygon. According to your math professor, you can use the formula

$$area = \tfrac{1}{2}|X_1Y_2 + X_2Y_3 + \ldots + X_{n-1}Y_n + X_nY_1$$
$$- Y_1X_2 - Y_2X_3 - \ldots - Y_{n-1}X_n - Y_nX_1|$$

to find the area.

Figure 6.13. *Sample Polygon with Five Sides*

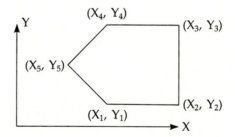

Data Requirements

Problem Parameters

the maximum number of sides in a polygon (NMAX =20)

Problem Inputs

the array of X coordinates (REAL X(NMAX))
the array of Y coordinates (REAL Y(NMAX))

Problem Output

the area of the polygon (REAL AREA)

Case Study: Finding the Area of a Polygon[M], continued

Additional Program Variable

the actual number of sides in the polygon (INTEGER N)

Initial Algorithm

1. Read the coordinates into arrays X and Y and define the number of sides in the polygon.
2. Display the coordinates.
3. Compute the area of the polygon.
4. Display the area.

Structure Chart and Algorithm Refinements

Figure 6.14 shows the structure chart. We will implement steps 1 and 2 using subroutines ENTCOR and SHOCOR, respectively; we will implement step 3 using function SUMSID. Arrays X and Y and variable N are returned as outputs from ENTCOR and are passed as inputs to SHOCOR and SUMSID.

Figure 6.14. *Structure Chart for Finding the Area of a Polygon*

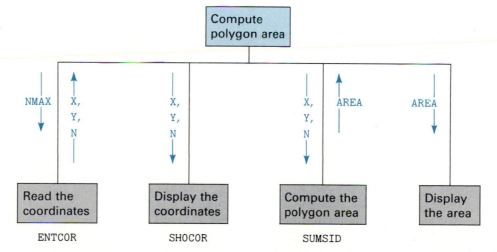

Coding the Main Program

Figure 6.15 shows the main program. The program begins by calling ENTCOR and SHOCOR to enter and display the coordinates. Next, the statement

```
AREA = SUMSID(X, Y, N)
```

Case Study: Finding the Area of a Polygon^M, continued

calls function SUMSID, passing arrays X and Y as arguments along with N. The function result is stored in AREA and displayed by the PRINT statement in the main program.

Figure 6.15. *Main Program for Computation of Polygon Area*

```
      PROGRAM POLGON
C Computes the area of a polygon whose coordinates are read from
C a data file

C Declarations
      INTEGER NMAX
      PARAMETER (NMAX = 20)
      REAL X(NMAX), Y(NMAX), AREA
      INTEGER N

C Read the array coordinates into arrays X and Y
      CALL ENTCOR (NMAX, X, Y, N)

C Display the coordinates
      CALL SHOCOR (X, Y, N)

C Compute area of polygon
      AREA = SUMSID (X, Y, N)

C Display area
      PRINT, 'Area is ', AREA
    5 FORMAT ('0', A, F10.2)

C Exit program
      STOP
      END
```

Coding the Subprograms

Subroutines ENTCOR and SHOCOR are relatively straightforward and are shown in Fig. 6.16. ENTCOR uses a READ statement with an end-of-file specifier to read the coordinates, and SHOCOR uses an implied DO loop to display them. The declaration

```
      REAL X(NMAX), Y(NMAX)
```

identifies dummy arguments X and Y as type REAL arrays with NMAX elements. The variable I is used as a loop-control variable and array subscript in each subroutine. It is declared as a local variable in each subprogram.

Case Study: Finding the Area of a Polygon[M], *continued*

Figure 6.16. *Sub-routines ENTCOR and SHOCOR*

```fortran
      SUBROUTINE ENTCOR (NMAX, X, Y, N)
C Reads up to NMAX coordinates into arrays X and Y

C Input Arguments
C   NMAX — the maximum number of coordinates

C Output Arguments
C   X, Y — the coordinate points
C   N — the number of points read

C Argument Declarations
      INTEGER NMAX, N
      REAL X(NMAX), Y(NMAX)

C Local Declarations
      INTEGER I

C Prepare data file for input
      OPEN (UNIT = 1, FILE = 'POLY.DAT', STATUS = 'OLD')

C Read the coordinate pairs
      DO 10 I = 1, NMAX
          READ (1, *, END = 99) X(I), Y(I)
   10 CONTINUE
      PRINT *, 'WARNING — ARRAY FILLED BEFORE END OF FILE'

C Exit loop and adjust number of points read
   99 N = I - 1

C Exit subroutine
      RETURN
      END

C-------------------------------------------------------------------

      SUBROUTINE SHOCOR (X, Y, N)
C Displays the first N values in parallel arrays X and Y

C Input Arguments
C   X, Y — the coordinate points
C   N — the number of points

C Argument Declarations
      INTEGER N
      REAL X(*), Y(*)

C Local Declarations
      INTEGER I
```

Case Study: Finding the Area of a Polygon^M, continued

```
C Display the table heading
      PRINT 25, 'X', 'Y'
   25 FORMAT (1X, A10, 2X, A10)

C Display N pairs of points
      PRINT 35, (X(I), Y(I), I = 1, N)
   35 FORMAT (1X, F10.2, 2X, F10.2)

C Exit subroutine
      RETURN
      END
```

SUMSID must implement the formula for the area of a polygon given earlier. The number of product terms in this formula increases with N. We can use summation notation to write this formula for any N.

$$area = \tfrac{1}{2} \left| \left(\sum_{i=1}^{N-1} X_i Y_{i+1} \right) + X_N Y_1 - \left(\sum_{i=1}^{N-1} Y_i X_{i+1} \right) - Y_N X_1 \right|$$

Rearranging terms, we get

$$area = \tfrac{1}{2} \left| \sum_{i=1}^{N-1} (X_i Y_{i+1} - Y_i X_{i+1}) + X_N Y_1 - Y_N X_1 \right|$$

We can use a single DO loop to compute the sum. The algorithm for SUMSID follows. Figure 6.17 shows function SUMSID.

Local Variables

the array subscript and loop-control variable (INTEGER I)
the sum of the XY products (REAL SUM)

Figure 6.17. *Function SUMSID*

```
      REAL FUNCTION SUMSID (X, Y, N)
C Computes the area of a polygon of N sides whose coordinates
C are stored in arrays X and Y
C Pre : Arrays X and Y contain N polygon coordinates and N lies
C        between 3 and NMAX.
C Post: Returns the polygon area

C Argument Declarations
      INTEGER N
      REAL X(*), Y(*)
```

Case Study: Finding the Area of a Polygon^M, continued

```
C Local Declarations
      INTEGER I
      REAL SUM

C Compute SUM
      SUM = 0.0
      DO 20 I = 1, N - 1
         SUM = SUM + X(I) * Y(I + 1) - Y(I) * X(I + 1)
   20 CONTINUE
      SUM = SUM + X(N) * Y(1) - Y(N) * X(1)

C Define result
      SUMSID = ABS(SUM) / 2.0

C Exit function
      RETURN
      END
```

Algorithm for SUMSID

1. Set SUM to zero
2. DO I = 1, N-1
      $$SUM = SUM + X_iY_{i+1} - Y_iX_{i+1}$$
   CONTINUE
3. $SUM = SUM + X_NY_1 - Y_NX_1$
4. SUMSID = ABS(SUM) / 2.0

Testing

Figure 6.18 shows a sample run of the area-computation program for a square centered around the origin of the coordinate system. To test it, use simple polygons such as triangles and rectangles whose areas can be verified using well-known formulas. Make sure the program works for coordinates that are negative as well as positive.

Figure 6.18. *Sample Run of Area-Computation Program*

```
              X          Y
          -2.00      -2.00
           2.00      -2.00
           2.00       2.00
          -2.00       2.00

Area is       16.00
```

Program Style

Checking for Subscript-Range Errors

In function SUMSID, DO loop 20 adds together a collection of products of elements in arrays X and Y. The array subscripts used within the DO loop are I and I + 1. It is important to verify that these subscripts are in range during all loop iterations. We can do this by checking their values when I is 1 and I is $N - 1$. When I is 1, the two subscript values are 1 and 2. When I is $N - 1$, the two subscript values are $N - 1$ and N. Since the subscript values are in range for the first and last loop iterations, we can be fairly certain that they will be in range for all loop iterations.

SELF-CHECK EXERCISES FOR SECTION 6.5

1. Write a subroutine that negates the values stored in an array. The first argument should be the array, and the second should be the number of elements being negated.

2. Assume a main program contains declarations for three arrays, C, D, and E, each with six elements. Explain the effect of each valid CALL statement to subroutine ADDER (see Fig. 6.9). Explain why each invalid CALL statement is invalid.

   a. CALL ADDER (A, B, C, 6)
   b. CALL ADDER (C(6), D(6), E(6), 6)
   c. CALL ADDER (C, D, E, 6)
   d. CALL ADDER (C, D, E, 7)
   e. CALL ADDER (C, D, E, 5)
   f. CALL ADDER (C, D, 6, E)
   g. CALL ADDER (E, D, C, 6)
   h. CALL ADDER (C, C, C, 6)
   i. CALL ADDER (C, D, E, C(1))
   j. CALL ADDER (C, D, E, INT(C(1)))
   k. CALL ADDER (C, D, E, INT(AMIN1(ABS(C(1)), 6.0)))

6.6 ▬▬▬ The DATA Statement

The DATA statement provides a convenient method for initializing the values of simple variables and arrays.

EXAMPLE 6.22

The DATA statement

```
DATA A, B, C /2.5, 6.5, 9.0/
```

initializes the three variables listed as shown below.

The DATA statement

    DATA A /2.5/, B /6.5/, C /9.0/

would have the same effect.

EXAMPLE 6.23   The statements

```
INTEGER CNTSIZ
PARAMETER (CNTSIZ = 20)
INTEGER COUNTR(CNTSIZ)
DATA COUNTR /CNTSIZ * 0/
```

initialize an array of counters (COUNTR) to all zeros. Since array COUNTR appears without a subscript in the DATA statement, the entire array is initialized. The notation CNTSIZ * 0 means that the value 0 is to be repeated twenty (value of CNTSIZ) times.   ■

EXAMPLE 6.24   If LETTER is an array declared as

    CHARACTER *1 LETTER(26)

the DATA statement

```
DATA LETTER /'A','B','C','D','E','F','G','H','I','J','K','L','M',
+            'N','O','P','Q','R','S','T','U','V','W','X','Y','Z'/
```

initializes LETTER(1) to 'A', LETTER(2) to 'B', and so on.   ■

When only part of an array is to be initialized, an implied DO loop may be used in the DATA statement.

EXAMPLE 6.25   If I is type INTEGER, the DATA statement

    DATA (LETTER(I), I = 1, 5) /'A','B','C','D','E'/

initializes only the first five elements of array LETTER. The implied DO loop specifies that the string constants listed should be placed in elements LET-TER(1) through LETTER(5), inclusive.   ■

The DATA Statement

SYNTAX: DATA *variable list* / *constant list* /   DATA *variable$_1$/constant$_1$/*, *variable$_2$/constant$_2$/*, . . .
EXAMPLE: DATA N, X /0, 0.0/   DATA N/0/, X/0.0/

INTERPRETATION: The *variable list* may contain combinations of the following:

- variable names
- array element names (array names with subscripts)
- array names (for initializing entire arrays)
- implied loops (for initializing portions of arrays)

The *constant list* provides the corresponding initial values for the items in the *variable list*. There may be numeric, character, or logical constants or named constants previously declared in a PARAMETER statement.

The type of each constant and its corresponding variable should be the same. The correspondence is established in left-to-right order. There should be the same number of constants as there are memory cells being initialized. The notation $n * c$ can be used to specify n repetitions of the constant c. (n must be a positive integer constant or parameter, and c must be a constant.)

DATA statements must be placed after the type and parameter declarations.

NOTES: Any subscripts must be integer constants or parameters or expressions involving integer constants and parameters. Any loop parameters should be integer constants or parameters or expressions involving integer constants and parameters.

The DATA statement must appear at the beginning of a program following the type and PARAMETER declarations. The DATA statement is a nonexecutable statement and is processed when the program is loaded into computer memory. Since the DATA statement is not an executable statement, it has no effect whatsoever once program execution begins. Consequently, a DATA statement cannot be reused in a program to reset an array after the array has already been processed.

Care must be taken when using DATA statements to initialize local variables or arrays declared in a subprogram. The local variable will be initialized correctly the first time the subprogram is called. However, there is no guarantee that this initialization will occur in subsequent calls. If you wish the local variable to be reinitialized each time the subprogram is called, then an assignment statement must be used.

Plotting a Function

The next example illustrates how an array may be used to store successive lines in a function plot. See Chapter 10 for additional discussion of function plots and graphs.

EXAMPLE 6.26

The program in Fig. 6.19 plots the value of the function $T^2 - 4T + 5$ for values of T between 0 and 10. It accomplishes this by storing an asterisk in the element of CHARACTER array PLOT corresponding to the function value, while all other elements contain the blank character. The first element of array PLOT has

Figure 6.19. *Plot of Function $T^2 - 4T + 5$*

```
      PROGRAM PLOTIT
C Plots the function T ** 2 - 4 * T + 5 for T between 0 and 10

C Declarations
      INTEGER MAXVAL
      PARAMETER (MAXVAL = 65)
      CHARACTER *1 PLOT(0 : MAXVAL)
      DATA PLOT /' ', MAXVAL * ' '/
      INTEGER F, T, I, FUNVAL
      F(T) = T ** 2 - 4 * T + 5

C Display heading lines
      PRINT 5, (I, I = 0, MAXVAL, 5)
    5 FORMAT (1X, 14I5)
      PRINT 15, ('     !', I = 0, MAXVAL, 5)
   15 FORMAT (1X, 14A)

C Compute and print function value for each T between 0 and 10
      DO 10 T = 0, 10
         FUNVAL = F(T)
         PLOT(FUNVAL) = '*'
         PRINT 25, 'T=', T, PLOT
   25    FORMAT (1X, A2, I2, 66A1)
         PLOT(FUNVAL) = ' '
   10 CONTINUE

C Exit program
      STOP
      END

      0   5  10  15  20  25  30  35  40  45  50  55  60  65
      !   !   !   !   !   !   !   !   !   !   !   !   !   !
T= 0     *
T= 1   *
T= 2 *
T= 3   *
T= 4      *
T= 5         *
T= 6            *
T= 7                 *
T= 8                      *
T= 9                            *
T=10                                  *
```

a subscript of zero; the array is initialized to all blanks using the DATA statement

```
DATA PLOT /' ', MAXVAL * ' '/
```

Because MAXVAL is 65, 66 blanks are stored.

Within the DO loop, the assignment statement

```
FUNVAL = F(T)
```

calls the single-statement function F and saves the value returned in FUNVAL. The assignment

```
PLOT(FUNVAL) = '*'
```

places an asterisk in the element that corresponds to the function value. The formatted PRINT

```
      PRINT 25, 'T=', T, PLOT
25 FORMAT (1X, A2, I2, 66A1)
```

displays a line that begins with the value of T followed by array PLOT. The edit descriptor 66A1 is equivalent to the edit descriptor A1 repeated 66 times. Consequently, the array elements will be printed one after the other in adjacent columns across the output line. Since all but one of the elements contain blanks, a single asterisk will be displayed; the position of the asterisk depends on the value of FUNVAL. After each line is printed, the assignment statement

```
PLOT(FUNVAL) = ' '
```

resets the nonblank element back to a blank.

There are three formatted PRINT statements in Fig. 6.19. The first one prints the heading line consisting of the integers 0, 5, 10, and so on, spaced five columns apart. The second one prints a line directly beneath the first consisting of fourteen occurrences of the symbol '!' spaced five columns apart. As mentioned above, the last formatted PRINT statement prints the current value of T and the corresponding function value (denoted by the symbol *). The first output line shows that F(0) is 5. ∎

General Function Plot[M]

The function in Fig. 6.19 was relatively easy to plot because its values range from 1 (T = 0) to 65 (T = 10), and there is an array element corresponding to each integer value within this range. This approach can be generalized to plot any function. You will first need to change the definition of the single-statement function F. If the new function values do not lie within the range 0 to 65, you will have to scale them so that they do fall in this range.

As an example, consider a function with values between −30 and 250. A value of −30 should cause an asterisk to be placed in PLOT(0), and a value of 250 should cause an asterisk to be placed in PLOT(65). For such a function, the assignment statement

```
SCALED = 65 * (FUNVAL + 30) / 280
```

can be used to compute a scaled function value (SCALED) based on the actual function value (FUNVAL). In the expression above, the argument of function NINT is derived from the formula

65 × (FUNVAL − *minval*) / (*maxval* − *minval*)

where *minval* (−30) and *maxval* (250) are the smallest and largest function values to be plotted, respectively.

The assignment statements

```
PLOT(SCALED) = '*'
PLOT(SCALED) = ' '
```

can be used to insert and remove the asterisk in array PLOT. They should be used instead of

```
PLOT(FUNVAL) = '*'
PLOT(FUNVAL) = ' '
```

shown in Fig. 6.19.

Program Style

> *Checking Boundary Values*
>
> The discussion above states that the value of SCALED ranges from 0 to 65 as the function value goes from −30 to 250. It is always a good idea to check the accuracy of these assumptions. This can be done by checking the boundaries of the range, as shown in Table 6.6. Since the value of SCALED is correct at the boundaries, it should be correct throughout the range.

Table 6.6. *Computation of SCALED at Boundary Values*

FUNVAL	COMPUTATION OF SCALED	SCALED
−30	65 * (−30 + 30) / 280	
	65 * 0 / 280	0
250	65 * (250 + 30) / 280	
	65 * 280 / 280	65

SELF-CHECK EXERCISES FOR SECTION 6.6

1. Declare an array PRIME for storing the first ten prime numbers and write a DATA statement to initialize the array PRIME to those numbers.
2. Modify the program in Fig. 6.19 to plot the function $T^3 − 10 * T$ for values of T between −5 and 5. Determine the smallest and largest function values and write an assignment statement that scales these values into the range 0 to 70. Make sure that you change the heading for the function plot as well.

6.7   Array Processing Illustrated

We have written programs that accumulate the sum of all input data items in a single variable. Often, we have different categories of data items, and we might want to accumulate a separate total for each category rather than lump all items together. The problem that follows uses an array to accomplish this.

The next problem also illustrates two common ways of selecting array elements for processing. Sometimes we need to manipulate all elements of an array in some uniform manner (e.g., initialize them all to zero). In situations like this, it makes sense to process the array elements in sequence (*sequential access*), starting with the first and ending with the last.

At other times, the order in which the array elements are accessed is completely dependent on the order of the problem data. This is called *random access*, since the order is not predictable beforehand.

Case Study: Budget Problem

Problem

Your consulting firm separates its monthly expenses into ten categories (computer supplies, salaries, equipment, rent, etc.) You need a program that keeps track of the monthly expenditures in each category. The program should read each expense amount, add it to the appropriate category total, and print the total expenditure by category. The input data consist of the category number and amount of each purchase made during the past month.

Design Overview

There are ten separate totals to be accumulated; each total can be associated with a different element of a ten-element array. The program must read each expenditure, determine to which category it belongs, and then add the expense amount to the appropriate array element. When done with all expenditures, the program can print a table showing each category and its accumulated total. As in all programs that accumulate a sum, each total must be initialized to zero. The program inputs, outputs, and algorithm follow.

Data Requirements

Problem Parameters

the number of budget categories (NUMCAT = 10)

Problem Inputs

each expense category and amount

Case Study: Budget Problem, continued

Problem Outputs

the array of budget totals (REAL BUDGET(NUMCAT))

Initial Algorithm

1. Initialize all budget totals to zero.
2. For each expenditure, read the category and expense amount and add the amount to the appropriate total.
3. Print the accumulated total for each category.

Structure Chart and Refinements

The structure chart in Fig. 6.20 shows the relationship among the three steps. The array BUDGET is an output of step 1 (performed in the main program), an input/output argument for step 2 (subroutine POST), and an input argument for step 3 (subroutine REPORT).

Figure 6.20. *Structure Chart for Budget Problem*

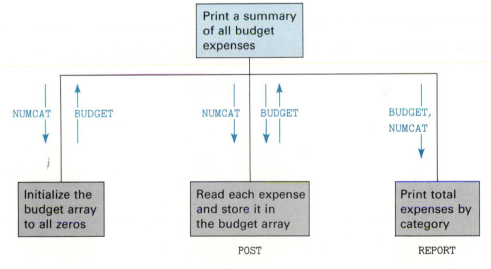

Coding the Main Program

Figure 6.21 shows the main program. The statement

```
DATA BUDGET /NUMCAT * 0.0/
```

initializes all elements of array BUDGET to zero. Only parameter NUMCAT and array BUDGET are declared in the main program.

Case Study: Budget Problem, continued

```
      PROGRAM DOBUDG
C Prints a summary of all expenses by budget category

C Declarations
      INTEGER NUMCAT
      PARAMETER (NUMCAT = 10)
      REAL BUDGET(NUMCAT)

C Initialize array BUDGET to all zeros
      DATA BUDGET /NUMCAT * 0.0/

C Read each expense amount and add it to the appropriate category
      CALL POST (BUDGET, NUMCAT)

C Print each category and its budget total
      CALL REPORT (BUDGET, NUMCAT)

C Exit program
      STOP
      END
```

```
      SUBROUTINE REPORT (BUDGET, NUMCAT)
C Prints each category and its expense total

C Input Arguments
C    BUDGET - array of expenses
C    NUMCAT - number of expense categories

C Argument Declarations
      INTEGER NUMCAT
      REAL BUDGET(NUMCAT)

C Local Declarations
      INTEGER NEXCAT

C Display heading
      PRINT 15, 'Category', 'Expenses'
   15 FORMAT ('0', A10, 5X, A15)

C Display each category number and budget total
      PRINT 25, (NEXCAT, BUDGET(NEXCAT), NEXCAT = 1, NUMCAT)
   25 FORMAT (1X, I10, 5X, F15.2)

C Exit subroutine
      RETURN
      END
```

Case Study: Budget Problem, continued

Coding the Subprograms

Subroutine REPORT (Fig. 6.22) uses a formatted PRINT statement with an implied DO loop in its output list to display each budget category and expense amount on a separate line.

Subroutine POST (Fig. 6.23) must read each expense amount and add it to the appropriate budget category. A sentinel value for each category will be used to indicate the end of data. The data requirements and algorithm for POST follow Fig. 6.23.

Figure 6.23. *Subroutine POST*

```
      SUBROUTINE POST (BUDGET, NUMCAT)
C Prints each category and its expense total

C Input Arguments
C   NUMCAT - number of expense categories

C Input/Output Arguments
C   BUDGET - array of expenses

C Argument Declarations
      INTEGER NUMCAT
      REAL BUDGET(NUMCAT)

C Local Declarations
      INTEGER SENVAL
      PARAMETER (SENVAL = 0)
      INTEGER ENTER
      INTEGER NEXCAT, CATGRY
      REAL EXPENS

C Read each budget category, expense amount, and save it
      PRINT *, 'Enter the budget category or 0 to stop:'
      CATGRY = ENTER(SENVAL, NUMCAT)
      DO WHILE (CATGRY .NE. SENVAL)            9 IF (...) THEN
         PRINT *, 'Enter the expenditure'
         READ *, EXPENS
         BUDGET(CATGRY) = BUDGET(CATGRY) + EXPENS
         PRINT *, 'Enter the budget category or 0 to stop:'
         CATGRY = ENTER(SENVAL, NUMCAT)
      ENDDO                                      GOTO 9
C                                                ENDIF
C Exit subroutine
      RETURN
      END
```

Case Study: Budget Problem, continued

Local Parameter

the sentinel category (SENVAL = 0)

Local Variables

the category of the current expenditure (INTEGER CATGRY)
the amount of the current expenditure (REAL EXPENS)

Algorithm for POST

1. Read in the budget category for each expenditure.
2. DO WHILE there are more expenditures

Figure 6.24. *Sample Run of Budget Program*

```
Enter the budget category or 0 to stop:
Enter an integer between          0 and          10
4
Enter the expenditure
10.00
Enter the budget category or 0 to stop:
Enter an integer between          0 and          10
10
Enter the expenditure
15.00
Enter the budget category or 0 to stop:
Enter an integer between          0 and          10
4
Enter the expenditure
35.00
Enter the budget category or 0 to stop:
Enter an integer between          0 and          10
11
Enter an integer between          0 and          10
0

    Category          Expenses
        1              0.00
        2              0.00
        3              0.00
        4             45.00
        5              0.00
        6              0.00
        7              0.00
        8              0.00
        9              0.00
       10             15.00
```

Case Study: Budget Problem, continued

> 3. Read in the expense amount.
> 4. Add the amount to the appropriate budget total.
> 5. Read in the category of the next expenditure.
>
> ENDDO

Subroutine POST calls function ENTER (see Fig. 5.6) to perform steps 1 and 5, so ENTER (type INTEGER) must be declared in POST. If the value returned to CATGRY by ENTER is a valid budget category, the statement

```
BUDGET(CATGRY) = BUDGET(CATGRY) + EXPENS
```

adds the expense amount (EXPENSE) to the element of array BUDGET selected by the subscript CATGRY.

Testing

Make sure you insert the main program, subroutines POST and REPORT, and function ENTER in the source file before attempting to compile and run the budget program. Figure 6.24 shows a sample run of the budget program. As shown in this run, the budget categories can be entered in arbitrary (random) order. You should verify that all budget categories without purchases remain zero. Also, verify that an out-of-range category value does not cause a run-time error.

Program Style

> *Allowing for Array Expansion*
>
> The constant NUMCAT is used throughout the Budget program to represent the number (10) of budget categories. This enables us to easily extend the program to handle more budget categories by changing the value of a single constant. This is consistent with our prior use of program parameters to write general programs.

Program Style

> *Avoiding Out-of-Range Errors*
>
> Several measures are taken in Fig. 6.24 to prevent the occurrence of a "subscript out of range" execution error. Function ENTER ensures that only valid category values are assigned to the variable CATGRY. The WHILE loop is exited when CATGRY is 0 so there will be no attempt to increment the nonexistent array element BUDGET(0).

6.8 ▭ Common Programming Errors

It is very important that you declare each array used in a program and its size. You must also consistently spell the array name correctly. If you forget to declare an array or its size, the compiler will assume that you are referencing a function, since both array and function names can be followed by a left parenthesis. For example, the statement

```
GRADES(I) = 0
```

is valid if GRADES is declared as an array; it is invalid and will be detected as an illegal function reference during program execution if array GRADES is not declared.

Another common error in using arrays is a subscript-range error. This occurs when the subscript value is outside the range specified in the array declaration. For the array VOLTS

```
REAL VOLTS(-5 : 5)
```

a subscript-range error occurs when VOLTS is used with a subscript that has a value less than –5 or greater than 5. If the value of I is 15, a reference to the subscripted variable VOLTS(I) may cause an error message such as

```
SUBSCRIPT RANGE ERROR AT LINE NO. 28 FOR ARRAY VOLTS, I = 15
```

Subscript-range errors are not syntax errors; consequently, they will not be detected until program execution begins. They are most often caused by an incorrect subscript expression or by a loop parameter error or nonterminating loop. Before considerable time is spent in debugging, all suspect subscript calculations should be carefully checked for out-of-range errors. This can be done most easily by inserting diagnostic output statements in your program, to print subscript values that might be out of range.

If a subscript range error occurs inside a DO loop, you should verify that the subscript is in range for both the initial and the final values of the loop-control variable. If these values are in range, it is likely that all other subscript references in the loop are in range as well.

If a subscript-range error occurs in a WHILE loop, verify that the loop-control variable is being updated as required. If it is not, the loop may be repeated more often than expected, causing the subscript-range error. This could happen if the control-variable update step was placed after the ENDDO statement or was inadvertently omitted.

As with all FORTRAN data types, make sure that there are no type inconsistencies. The type of each subscript expression must be type INTEGER; the type of data stored in an array element must correspond to the type specified in the array declaration.

Table 6.7. *Summary of New FORTRAN Statements*

STATEMENT	EFFECT
Array Declaration	
`INTEGER CUBE(10), Y(0 : 5)`	Allocates storage for ten INTEGER items in array CUBE (CUBE(1), . . . , CUBE(10)) and six INTEGER items in array Y (Y(0), . . . , Y(5)).
Array References	

`DO 10 I = 1, 10`
`   CUBE(I) = I ** 3`
`10 CONTINUE`
	Saves I^3 in the Ith element of array CUBE.

`IF (CUBE(5) .GT. 100) THEN`	Compares CUBE(5) to 100.
`PRINT *, CUBE(1), CUBE(2)`	Displays the first two cubes.
Array Initialization	
`DATA Y /6 * 0/`	Initializes each element of Y to 0.
`DATA (CUBE(I), I = 1, 4)` `+        /1, 8, 27, 64/`	Initializes the first four cubes.
Array Read and Print	
`READ *, Y` `PRINT *, Y`	Reads and prints the entire array. More than one value may appear on a line.

`DO 10 I = 2, 5`
`   PRINT *, 'Enter value ', I`
`   READ *, Y(I)`
`   PRINT *, Y(I)`
`10 CONTINUE`
	Reads and prints the values stored in Y(2) through Y(5), one value per line.

`PRINT *, 'Enter Y(2) through Y(5)'`
`READ *, (Y(I), I = 2, 5)`
`PRINT *, (Y(I), I = 2, 5)`
	Reads and prints the values in Y(2) through Y(5). More than one value may appear on a line.

`PRINT '(1X, I4, 2X, I4)', CUBES`	Displays all elements of array CUBES, two values per line.
Read with End-of-File Specifier	

`DO 20 I = 1, 10`
`   READ (1, *, END = 99) Y(I)`
`20 CONTINUE`
	Reads up to ten values into array Y from the data file on unit 1. Continues at label 99 if there are fewer than ten data values.

When using DATA statements, the size of the constant list must be the same as the size of the variable list. Any DATA statements should be placed right after the type declarations. Remember that a DATA statement is not an executable statement; consequently, if it is placed in a subprogram, the variables listed in the DATA statement will have the initial values specified only during the first execution of the subprogram. During subsequent executions, the DATA statement will have no effect whatsoever.

Chapter Review

In this chapter, we introduced a special data structure called an array, which is a convenient facility for naming and referencing a collection of like items. We discussed how to declare an array and how to reference an individual array element by placing a subscript in parentheses, following the array name.

The DO loop enables us to easily reference the elements of an array in sequence. We used DO loops to initialize arrays, read and print arrays, and control the manipulation of individual array elements.

New FORTRAN Statements

The new FORTRAN statements introduced in this chapter are described in Table 6.7.

Quick-Check Exercises

1. What is a data structure?
2. Of the data types REAL, INTEGER, CHARACTER, and LOGICAL, which cannot be used to subscript an array?
3. Can values of different types be stored in an array?
4. If an array is declared to have ten elements, must the program use all ten?
5. When can the assignment operator be used with an array as its operand? Answer the same question for the relational operators such as .EQ., .LE., .GT..
6. The two methods of array access are _____ and _____ .
7. The _____ loop allows us to access the elements of an array in _____ order.
8. What is the difference between the following two declarations?

```
CHARACTER *18 NAME
```

and

```
CHARACTER NAME(18)
```

9. Let `SCORES(12)` be an array of twelve integers. Describe how each of the following two FORTRAN loops will work. Discuss any differences between the loops.

```
    READ (2, *, END = 99) (SCORES(I), I = 1, 12)
99 ...

    DO 10 I = 1, 12
        READ (2, *, END = 99) SCORES(I)
10 CONTINUE
99 ...
```

Answers to Quick-Check Exercises

1. A data structure is a grouping of related values in main memory.
2. REAL, CHARACTER, and LOGICAL
3. no
4. no
5. not allowed under any circumstances
6. random and sequential
7. DO, sequential
8. The first declares a simple variable to be used to store a string of eighteen characters; the second declares an eighteen-element array in which each element is a character string of length 1.
9. Both loops behave the same. They read up to twelve integer values from the file associated with unit 2. Reading will terminate as soon as twelve values are read or the end of the file is reached, whichever comes first.

   The second loop reads each data item from a separate line. The second loop does impose this requirement.

Review Questions

1. Identify the error in the following segment of FORTRAN statements:

```
    INTEGER X(1 : 8), I
    DO 10 I = 1, 9
        X(I) = I
10 CONTINUE
```

   When will the error be detected?
2. Declare an array of real values called SALES that can be referenced by using any day of the week as a subscript where 0 represents Sunday.
3. Identify the error in the following segment:

```
CHARACTER *10 NAMES(100)
INTEGER I
I = 1
NAMES(I) = 8.384
```

4. The statement with label 5 in the following segment is a valid FORTRAN statement. True or false?

```
    INTEGER COUNTS(10), I
    REAL X(5)
    PRINT *, Enter a small integer'
    I = 1
    READ *, COUNTS(I)
  5 X(COUNTS(I)) = 8.384
```

5. What are the two common ways of selecting array elements for processing?
6. Write a FORTRAN program segment to print out the index of the smallest and the largest numbers in an array X of 20 integers. Array X has a range of values of 0 to 100. Assume array X already has values assigned to each element.
7. Declare arrays X and Y, each of which may store up to 100 REAL numbers. Let N represent the number of items currently stored in array X. Write a DO loop that copies the values in array X to array Y in reverse order (e.g., Y(1) gets X(N), Y(N) gets X(1)).

Programming Projects

1. Write a program to read N data items into two arrays X and Y of size 20. Store the product of corresponding elements of X and Y in a third array Z, also of size 20. Print a three-column table displaying the arrays X, Y, and Z. Then compute and print the square root of the sum of the items in Z. Make up your own data, with N less than 20.

2. Let A be an array containing twenty integers. Write a program that first reads up to twenty data items into A and then finds and prints the subscript of the largest item in A and that item.

3. The Department of Traffic Accidents each year receives accident-count reports from a number of cities and towns across the country. To summarize these reports, the department provides a frequency-distribution printout that gives the number of cities reporting accident counts in the following ranges: 0–99, 100–199, 200–299, 300–399, 400–499, and 500 or above. The department needs a computer program to read the number of accidents for each reporting city or town and to add one to the count for the appropriate accident range. After all the data have been processed, the resulting frequency counts are to be printed.

4. Assume for the moment that your computer has the very limited capability of being able to read and print only single decimal digits and to add together two integers consisting of one decimal digit each. Write a program to read in two integers of up to ten digits each, add these numbers together, and print the result. Test your program on the following numbers.

```
X = 1487625
Y =   12783
```

```
X = 60705202
Y = 30760832

X = 1234567890
Y = 9876543210
```

Hints: Store the numbers X and Y in two integer arrays X and Y of size 10, one decimal digit per element. If the number is less than ten digits in length, enter enough leading zeros (to the left of the number) to make the number ten digits long.

Array X

(1) (2) (3) (4) (5) (6) (7) (8) (9) (10)

0	0	0	1	4	8	7	6	2	5

Array Y

(1) (2) (3) (4) (5) (6) (7) (8) (9) (10)

0	0	0	0	0	1	2	7	8	3

You will need a loop to add together the digits in corresponding array elements, starting with the element with subscript 10. Don't forget to handle the carry if there is one! Use a LOGICAL variable CARRY to indicate whether or not the sum of the last pair of digits is greater than 9.

5. Consider the situation in which the pricing of official Baltimore Oriole banners is based upon the quantity purchased as illustrated in the following table.

Number Purchased	Price Per Hundred
0– 100	$ 32.50
101– 300	$ 32.00
301– 500	$ 31.50
501– 800	$ 31.00
801–1200	$ 30.00
1201–1600	$ 29.00
1601–2000	$ 28.00
2001–2500	$ 26.00
2501–3000	$ 24.00
3001–4000	$ 21.00
4001–5000	$ 18.00
5001–7500	$ 15.00
7501–9999	$ 12.00
more than 10,000	$ 5.00

Write a program which, given a count, COUNT, of banners to be purchased will determine the price for this number of banners. Use a pair of parallel arrays NUMPUR and PURPRO in which to store an appropriate value for each category of

purchase quantity and the corresponding price per hundred respectively. Use a
DATA statement to initialize both arrays.

6. Write a program for the following problem. You are given a collection of scores for
the last exam in your computer course. You are to compute the average of these
scores and then assign grades to each student according to the following rule: If a
student's score is within 10 points (above or below) of the average, assign the
student a grade of SATISFACTORY. If the score is more than 10 points higher than
the average, assign the student a grade of OUTSTANDING. If the score is more than
10 points below the average, assign the student a grade of UNSATISFACTORY. Test
your program on the following data:

RICHARD LUGAR	55
FRANK RIZZO	71
DONALD SCHAEFFER	84
KEVIN WHITE	93
JAMES RIEHLE	74
ABE BEAME	70
TOM BRADLEY	84
WALTER WASHINGTON	78
RICHARD DALEY	64
RICHARD HATCHER	82

Hint: The output from your program should consist of a labeled three-column list
containing the name, exam score, and grade of each student.

7. Write a program to read N data items into each of two arrays X and Y of size 20.
Compare each of the elements of X to the corresponding element of Y. In the
corresponding element of a third array Z, store

+ 1	if X is larger than Y
0	if X is equal to Y
− 1	if X is less than Y

Then print a three-column table displaying the contents of the arrays X, Y, and Z,
followed by a count of the number of elements of X that exceed Y and a count of
the number of elements of X that are less than Y. Make up your own test data with
N less than 20.

8. It can be shown that a number is prime if there is no smaller prime number that
divides it. Consequently, to determine whether N is prime, it is sufficient to check
only the prime numbers less than or equal to N as possible divisors (see Section

5.2). Use this information to write a program that stores the first 100 prime numbers in an array. Have your program print the array after it is done.

9. Modify the area-computation program in Fig. 6.15 to find the area of a piece of land that is shaped like a polygon. The X and Y coordinates (in feet) at the edges of the property are available in a data file. Compute and display the acreage where 1 acre = 43,560 square feet. Use the following sample data file.

```
12.342   34.476
19.564   43.556
34.451   55.026
46.735   77.323
50.034   70.432
43.958   65.361
30.985   59.207
22.894   38.976
15.347   36.890
```

10. Generate a table indicating the rainfall for the city of Bedrock that can be used to compare the average rainfall for the city with the previous year's rainfall. Print some summary statistics that will indicate: (1) annual rainfall for each year and (2) average monthly rainfall for each year. The input data will consist of twelve pairs of numbers. The first number in each pair will be the average rainfall for a month, and the second number will be what fell the previous year. The first data pair will represent January, the second will be February, and so forth. Assuming the data begin

```
3.2   4   (for January)
2.2 1.6 (for February)
```

the output should resemble the following:

```
                   Table of monthly rainfall

               January   February   March ...
This year        3.2        2.2
Last year        4.0        1.6

Total rainfall this year: 35.7
Total rainfall last year: 42.8

Average monthly rainfall for this year: 3.6
Average monthly rainfall for last year: 4.0
```

11. The results of a survey of the households in your township have been made available. Each record contains data for one household, including a four-digit integer identification number, the annual income for the household, and the number of members of the household. Write a program to read the survey results into three arrays and perform the following analyses:
   a. Count the number of households included in the survey and print a three-column table displaying the data read in. (You may assume that no more than twenty-five households were surveyed.)

b. Calculate the average household income and list the identification number and income of each household that exceeds the average.

c. Determine the percentage of households having incomes below the poverty level. The poverty level income may be computed using the formula

$$P = \$6500.00 + \$750.00 * (m - 2)$$

where m is the number of members of each household. This formula shows that the poverty level depends on the number of family members, m, and the poverty level increases as m gets larger.

Test your program on the following data.

Identification Number	Annual Income	Household Members
1041	$12,180	4
1062	13,240	3
1327	19,800	2
1483	22,458	8
1900	17,000	2
2112	18,125	7
2345	15,623	2
3210	3,200	6
3600	6,500	5
3601	11,970	2
4725	8,900	3
6217	10,000	2
9280	6,200	1

12. Write a program that, given the taxable income for a single taxpayer, will compute the income tax for that person. Use Schedule X shown in Fig. 6.25. Assume that "line 47," referenced in this schedule, contains the taxable income. *Example:* If the individual's taxable income is $8192, your program should use the tax amount and percent shown in column 3 of line 7 (arrow). The tax in this case is $1590 + 0.25(8192.00 − 8000) = $1638. For each individual processed, print taxable earnings and the total tax. *Hint:* Set up three arrays, one for the base tax (column 3), one for the tax percent (column 3), and the third for the excess base (column 4). Your program must then compute the correct index to these arrays, given the taxable income.

13. Write a program that reads one character at a time into an array of individual characters. Your program should remove all the blanks in this array and "compact" all nonblank characters in the array so that all the blanks are at the end. You should have to scan the array only once from left to right. Print the array contents so that it appears as a single word both before and after the compaction.

14. Write an interactive program that plays the game of HANGMAN. Read the word to be guessed into successive elements of an array (WORD) of individual characters. The player must guess the letters belonging to WORD. The program should terminate when either all letters have been guessed correctly (player wins) or a specified

Figure 6.25. *Schedule X (from IRS Form 1040)*

Tax Rate Schedules

SCHEDULE X—Single Taxpayers Not Qualifying for Rates in Schedule Y or Z

Use this schedule if you checked the box on Form 1040, line 1—

If the amount on Form 1040, line 47, is:		Enter on Form 1040, line 16a:	
Not over $509...14% of the amount on line 47.			
Over—	But not over—		of the amount over—
$500	$1,000	$70+15%	$500
$1,000	$1,500	$145+16%	$1,000
$1,500	$2,000	$225+17%	$1,500
$2,000	$4,000	$310+19%	$2,000
$4,000	$6,000	$690+21%	$4,000
$6,000	$8,000	$1,110+24%	$6,000
$8,000	$10,000	$1,590+25%	$8,000
$10,000	$12,000	$2,090+27%	$10,000
$12,000	$14,000	$2,630+29%	$12,000
$14,000	$16,000	$3,210+31%	$14,000
$16,000	$18,000	$3,830+34%	$16,000
$18,000	$20,000	$4,510+36%	$18,000
$20,000	$22,000	$5,230+38%	$20,000
$22,000	$26,000	$5,990+40%	$22,000
$26,000	$32,000	$7,590+45%	$26,000
$32,000	$38,000	$10,290+50%	$32,000
$38,000	$44,000	$13,290+55%	$38,000
$44,000	$50,000	$16,590+60%	$44,000
$50,000	$60,000	$20,190+62%	$50,000
$60,000	$70,000	$26,390+64%	$60,000
$70,000	$80,000	$32,790+66%	$70,000
$80,000	$90,000	$39,390+68%	$80,000
$90,000	$100,000	$46,190+69%	$90,000
$100,000		$53,090+70%	$100,000

number of incorrect guesses have been made (computer wins). *Hint:* Use another array, GUESSD, to keep track of the solution so far. Initialize GUESSD to a string of symbols '*'. Each time a letter in WORD is guessed, replace the corresponding '*' in GUESSD with that letter.

7. More Arrays and Subprograms

THIS CHAPTER covers additional features of arrays and subprograms. It introduces multidimensional arrays, that is, arrays with two or more dimensions. We will use two-dimensional arrays to represent tables of data, matrices, and other two-dimensional objects.

We will discuss two common operations performed on arrays, searching and sorting, and describe one technique for searching an array and one technique for sorting an array. We will write subprograms for implementing these operations and show how to reuse these subprograms in other applications.

The chapter contains two case studies that involve multiple subprograms. We focus on the reusability of subprograms and introduce COMMON blocks for data communication between subprograms. We also describe the SAVE statement and show how to use it to write a random-number function. Finally, we show how to use a random-number function in the simulation of an experiment.

7.1   Multidimensional Arrays

In this section, we will see how to store tables of data and how to represent multidimensional objects using arrays. A two-dimensional object we are all familiar with is a tic-tac-toe board. The array declaration

```
CHARACTER *1 TICTAC(3, 3)
```

allocates storage for a two-dimensional array (TICTAC) with three rows and three columns.

This array has nine elements, each of which must be referenced by specifying a row subscript (1, 2, or 3) and a column subscript (1, 2, or 3). Each array element contains a character value. The array element TICTAC(2,3) pointed to in Fig. 7.1 is in row 2, column 3 of the array; it contains the character 0. The diagonal line consisting of array elements TICTAC(1,1), TICTAC(2,2), and TICTAC(3,3) represents a win for player X, because each cell contains the character X.

Figure 7.1. *A Tic-tac-toe Board Stored as Array TICTAC*

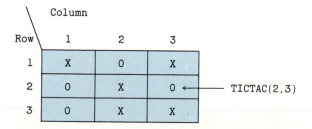

Array Declaration (for Multidimensional Arrays)

SYNTAX: *element-type aname(size$_1$, size$_2$, ... , size$_n$)*
element-type aname(minval$_1$: maxval$_1$, minval$_2$: maxval$_2$, ... , minval$_n$: maxval$_n$)

EXAMPLE: REAL TABLE(10, 0 : 6)

INTERPRETATION: The first form above allocates storage space for an array *aname* consisting of *size$_1$* $\times$ *size$_2$* $\times$ ... $\times$ *size$_n$* memory cells. Each memory cell can store one data item whose data type is specified by *element-type* (i.e., REAL, INTEGER, CHARACTER, LOGICAL). The individual array elements are referenced by the subscripted variables *aname*(1, 1, ... , 1) through *aname*(size$_1$, size$_2$, ... , size$_n$). An INTEGER constant or parameter must be used to specify *size$_i$*.

In the second form of the array declaration, the minimum value for the subscript associated with dimension *i* is *minval$_i$* and the maximum value is *maxval$_i$*. Both *minval$_i$* and *maxval$_i$* must be INTEGER constants or parameters, and *minval$_i$* must be less than or equal to *maxval$_i$*.

NOTE: A multidimensional array can have a maximum of seven dimensions.

EXAMPLE 7.1

The array TABLE

```
REAL TABLE(7, 5, 6)
```

consists of three dimensions: the first subscript may take on values from 1 to 7; the second, from 1 to 5; and the third from 1 to 6. A total of 7 $\times$ 5 $\times$ 6, or 210, real numbers may be stored in the array TABLE. All three subscripts must be specified in each reference to array TABLE (e.g., TABLE(2,3,4)). ∎

Manipulation of Two-Dimensional Arrays

A row and a column subscript must be specified to reference an element of a two-dimensional array. If I is type INTEGER, the statement

```
PRINT *, (TICTAC(1,I), I = 1, 3)
```

displays the first row of array TICTAC (TICTAC(1,1), TICTAC(1,2), and TICTAC(1,3)) on the next output line. The indexed DO loop

```
    DO 10 I = 1, 3
    PRINT *, TICTAC(I,2)
 10 CONTINUE
```

displays the second column of TICTAC (TICTAC(1,2), TICTAC(2,2), and TICTAC(3,2)) in a vertical line.

Nested loops are used to access all elements of a multidimensional array in a predetermined order. In the next examples, the outer loop determines the row being accessed, and the inner loop is used to select each element in that row.

EXAMPLE 7.2

The program fragment in Fig. 7.2 displays the current status of a tic-tac-toe board. A sample output of this fragment is also shown in Fig. 7.2.

Figure 7.2. *Printing a Tic-tac-toe Board*

```
C Display the status of a tic-tac-toe board (array TICTAC)
      PRINT *, '————'
      DO 10 ROW = 1, 3
C       Print all columns of current row
        PRINT 15, ('!', TICTAC(ROW,COLUMN), COLUMN = 1, 3), '!'
  15    FORMAT (1X, 7A1)
        PRINT *, '————'
  10  CONTINUE


 ————
!X!0! !

!0!X!0!
 ————
!X! !X!
```

In Fig. 7.2, the formatted PRINT statement

```
      PRINT 15, ('!', TICTAC(ROW,COLUMN), COLUMN = 1, 3), '!'
```

is used to display each row of the tic-tac-toe board. The implied DO loop causes the three columns across a row to be printed. Since the first '!' is included in the output-list controlled by the implied DO, it is printed before each array element. A final '!' is printed at the end of each row. ∎

EXAMPLE 7.3

The program fragment below assigns a value of .TRUE. to FILLED if a tic-tac-toe board is all filled up; it assigns a value of .FALSE. if there is at least one empty cell (contains a blank). ∎

```
C Assign a value of .TRUE. to FILLED if TICTAC is filled
C Assign a value of .FALSE. to FILLED if TICTAC is not filled

C Assume the board is filled
      FILLED = .TRUE.

C Reset FILLED to .FALSE. if an empty cell is found
      DO 10 ROW = 1, 3
         DO 20 COLUMN = 1, 3
            IF (TICTAC(ROW,COLUMN) .EQ. ' ') THEN
               FILLED = .FALSE.
            ENDIF
  20     CONTINUE
  10  CONTINUE
```

Row-Major vs. Column-Major Order

The programs shown for examples 7.2 and 7.3 process the array TICTAC one row at a time. This is because the row subscript is the loop-control variable for the outer loop of each pair of nested loops. An array that is processed one row at a time is processed in *row-major* order.

If we make the column subscript the loop-control variable for the outer loop, the arrays will be processed one column at a time. This is called *column-major* order.

EXAMPLE 7.4

The program fragment below enters array data, one column at a time. Since there are five rows in the array, five data values should be entered after each prompt. Since there are three columns, the prompt will be displayed three times.

```
      INTEGER TABLE(5, 3), ROW, COLUMN

C Enter one column of data at a time
      DO 10 COLUMN = 1, 3
         PRINT *, 'Enter the data for column ', COLUMN
         READ *, (TABLE(ROW, COLUMN), ROW = 1, 5)
   10    CONTINUE
```

Column-major order is not as natural for people as row-major order. We generally process array data one row at a time. However, FORTRAN uses column-major order to store arrays in memory. Consequently, the statements below will also cause fifteen data values to be stored in the same array elements as the nested DO loop above. ∎

```
      PRINT *, 'Enter the 15 array values starting with column one'
      READ *, TABLE
```

When you use a two-dimensional array name without subscripts in a READ, PRINT, or DATA statement, the entire array will be processed in column-major order. If you do not want to process the entire array or if you prefer row-major order, then you must use subscripts.

DATA Statements with Multidimensional Arrays

The DATA statement can also be used to initialize multidimensional arrays. The statement

```
      DATA TABLE /15 * 0.0/
```

initializes array TABLE declared above to all zeros. The DATA statement

```
      DATA ((TABLE(I, J), J = 1, 3), I = 1, 5)
     +     /1, 2, 3,  4, 5, 6,  7, 8, 9,  10, 11, 12,  13, 14, 15/
```

stores 1, 2, 3 in the first row of TABLE; 4, 5, 6 in the second row of TABLE, and so on. The implied-DO list in the DATA statement references the array elements in row-major order.

Arrays with Several Dimensions

So far, we have concentrated on arrays with two dimensions. In standard FORTRAN, you can declare arrays with up to seven dimensions, although it is difficult to visualize arrays with more than three dimensions.

The array ENROLL declared below

```
INTEGER ENROLL(MAXCRS, 5, 4)
```

course   *campus*   *year*

and pictured in Fig. 7.3 is a three-dimensional array that may be used to store the enrollment data for an undergraduate college. We will assume that the college offers 100 (MAXCRS) courses at five different campuses. ENROLL(1, 3, 4) represents the number of seniors taking course 1 at campus 3. The range of values for the subscript denoting year is 1 (for first year) through 4 (for senior).

Figure 7.3. *Three-Dimensional Array ENROLL*

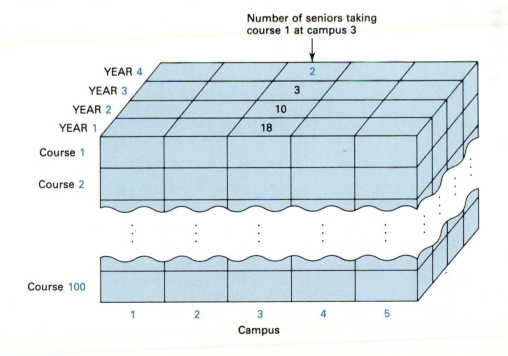

There are a total of 2000 (100 × 5 × 4) elements in array ENROLL. This points out a potential pitfall when you are dealing with multidimensional arrays. Memory space can be used up rapidly if several multidimensional arrays are declared in the same program. You should be aware of the amount of memory space required by each large array in a program.

There are many different ways to process the data in Fig. 7.3. We could determine the total number of students taking courses at a particular campus, the total number of students taking a particular course, the number of juniors in course 2 at all campuses, and so on. The type of information desired determines the order in which we must reference the array elements.

EXAMPLE 7.5   The program fragment below finds and prints the total number of students in each course.

```
C Find and print number of students in each course
      DO 10 COURSE = 1, MAXCRS
         CRSSUM = 0
         DO 20 CAMPUS = 1, 5
            DO 30 RANK = 1, 4
               CRSSUM = CRSSUM + ENROLL(COURSE, CAMPUS, RANK)
   30       CONTINUE
   20    CONTINUE
         PRINT *, 'Number of students in course', COURSE, ' is', CRSSUM
   10 CONTINUE
```

Since we are printing the number of students in each course, the loop-control variable for the outermost DO loop is the subscript that denotes the course.

The program fragment below prints the number of students at each campus. This time the loop-control variable for the outermost DO loop is the subscript that denotes the campus.   ■

```
C Find and print number of students at each campus
      DO 10 CAMPUS = 1, 5
         CMPSUM = 0
         DO 20 COURSE = 1, MAXCRS
            DO 30 RANK = 1, 4
               CMPSUM = CMPSUM + ENROLL(COURSE, CAMPUS, RANK)
   30       CONTINUE
   20    CONTINUE
         PRINT *, 'Number of students in campus', CAMPUS, ' is',
     CMPSUM
   10 CONTINUE
```

SELF-CHECK EXERCISE FOR SECTION 7.1

1. Redefine MAXCRS as 5 and write and test program segments that perform the following operations:
   a. Enter the enrollment data.
   b. Find the number of juniors in all classes at all campuses. Students will be counted once for each course in which they are enrolled.

c. Find the number of sophomores on all campuses who are enrolled in course 2.
d. Compute and print the number of students at campus 3 enrolled in each course and the total number of students at campus 3 in all courses. Students will be counted once for each course in which they are enrolled.
e. Compute and print the number of upperclass students in all courses at each campus, as well as the total number of upperclass students enrolled. (Upperclass students are juniors and seniors.) Again, students will be counted once for each course in which they are enrolled.

7.2 ▬▬ Multidimensional Array Arguments

Multidimensional arrays may be used as subroutine arguments. In Chapter 11, we will discuss some matrix operations involving two-dimensional arrays. A short example is provided next.

EXAMPLE 7.6 Subroutine ADDER can be easily modified to form the sum of two matrixes. If matrixes A and B have the same number of rows (M) and columns (N), they can be added together to form a new M × N matrix. If their sum is stored in matrix C, then each element C(i,j) must equal A(i,j) + B(i,j). Subroutine ADDMAT in Fig. 7.4 performs this operation.

The declaration

```
REAL A(M,N), B(M,N), C(M,N)
```

indicates that A, B, and C are matrixes. The number of rows is determined by dummy argument M, and the number of columns is determined by dummy argument N. ■

When a multidimensional array is used as an argument, the size of the last dimension may be left unspecified. The argument declaration

```
REAL A(M,*), B(M,*), C(M,*)
```

indicates that A, B, and C are assumed-size dummy arrays with M rows. The number of columns in each array is determined by the actual argument declaration.

The next case study illustrates the processing of a two-dimensional array as a rectangular grid of integer values. In this problem, we need to reference the individual elements of the grid in sequence and also access the eight neighbors of each element.

Figure 7.4. *Subroutine ADDMAT*

```
      SUBROUTINE ADDMAT (A, B, C, M, N)

C Stores element-by-element sum of matrixes A and B in matrix C

C Input Arguments
C   A, B - Matrixes being summed
C   M - Number of rows in the matrixes
C   N - Number of columns in the matrixes
C Output Argument
C   C - Sum of matrixes A and B

C Argument declarations
      INTEGER M, N
      REAL A(M,N), B(M,N), C(M,N)

C Local declarations
      INTEGER ROW, COL

C Add corresponding elements of matrixes A and B
      DO 10 ROW = 1, M
         DO 20 COL = 1, N
            C(ROW,COL) = A(ROW,COL) + B(ROW,COL)
  20     CONTINUE
  10  CONTINUE

C Exit subroutine
      RETURN
      END
```

Case Study: Image Enhancement

Problem

A secret military satellite has taken a digital image of a foreign military base. The information from the satellite is in an array of integers with each element having a value from 0 through 9. Each number in the array is called a pixel (picture element). However, because the transmission was jammed, random noise has entered into the image. This noise can be detected when the value of a pixel is very different from its neighbors. For example, in the image section

```
24456
34187
48899
```

the pixel with the value of 1 can be assumed to be noise since its value is so different from its neighbors. If a pixel has a value that is different from its

Case Study: Image Enhancement, continued

eight neighbors (the numbers in color in the above image section) by 3 or more, it can be assumed to be noise. We will ignore the pixels on the edge of the picture. A noisy value should be replaced with the rounded average of all those neighbors. In the example, the 1 should be replaced with a 6:

$$value = (4 + 4 + 4 + 5 + 8 + 8 + 8 + 9)/8 = 6$$

Another problem with digital images is that detail is often blurred by the many numbers. Because humans discern shapes better with fewer symbols, in our image we will lump all the numbers 0 to 3 into one category and set them to 0. The numbers 4, 5, and 6 should be set to 1. Finally 7, 8, and 9 should be set to 4. This will increase the contrast and allow our photo interpreters to see the message in the image. Figure 7.5 shows an image before and after this enhancement.

Design Overview

Our task is to write a program to remove the noise and increase the contrast in a digital image.

We will read the digital image from a data file into a two-dimensional array IMAGE that is twenty-four rows by seventy-eight columns. Next, we will check for noise, as described earlier, and then reduce the number of different symbols in the image to render it more readable. Finally, we will display the resulting image.

Data Requirements

Problem Parameters

the number of rows in the array (MAXROW = 24)
the number of columns in the array (MAXCOL = 78)

Problem Input

the original digital image (INTEGER IMAGE(MAXROW, MAXCOL))

Problem Output

the enhanced digital image (array IMAGE)

Initial Algorithm

1. Read the digital image into array IMAGE.
2. Check each element (except the edges) for noise and redefine any noisy elements.

Case Study: Image Enhancement, continued

Figure 7.5. *Digital Image Before (top) and After (bottom) Enhancement*

```
211111122221211111221212222112121112112221111111333111111111122112121111211111
121100013233221110033130322013222123222210200021233200001012232002020000032011
128808870021322117778999219888779979799997898911128899958770113232177787888220
101464447221211284554549166655404541656565449202465464565912222136645644458333
114564545822300946406802455545544465166154071236651655449312022264165655821
236140414582228460454258224464604146545455545800065646154471233213555646649032
126452565159186664546458326504445450566446464700254545654580092122652454569222
135514466464965645651548321222014445569321193331156614646470132131565455447323
126554745646651565146649032221125650568233333330156665465481226220464245549101
105504814646566652146569202021104664649233333311165516515470112365456454812333
104646700465454511165467323231104450659349333333134666645659119225656154471123
125404721255664020264149101822105544418222333332326651455149212126456565681122
116464800012221401454581331080240446573323333300065466554471233325616614691213
236645912211111112154048232810004545559211333339091454155155701356465544722232
216565702211111110165658121123815404553333333333332664464644703145052540610022
226654710213333311144067203823126565533333333333331606514145711165446464712310
224555711113333311146459222121114406467222333332111255066454471545604447212213
124464200113333312146540122832814445662326333332213126664565645665566671019012
623200102111111112020000210202220110003233333333333333333330033330232212311312
122002011111111110101101228008080808281613333310013232311000232322322101119210
222331121333132322201000113421101010121220333330002202121101101132232110011112
```

```
00000000000000000000000000000000000000000000000000000000000000000000000000000000
00000000000000000000000000000000000000000000000000000000000000000000000000000000
00440444000000000444444400444444444444444444000044444144400000000044444444000
00011114000000041111114011111111111141111111114000011111111140000000111111114000
00111111400000041111011400111111111111111111114000111111111400000001111111114000
00111011114000041111110140011111111111111111114000111111111400000001111111114000
00111011111404111111101400110111111111111111114000111111111400000001101111114000
00110111111141111111111400000000111111400000000001111111114000000011111111114000
00111141111111111011114000000001111111400000000001111111114000000011101111114000
00111140111111111001114000000001111114000000000001111111114000001111111114000
00111140011111110001114000000001111114010000000001111111114000001111111114000
00111140001111100001114000000001111114000000000001111111114000001111111114000
00111400000000010011140000000011111140000000000011111111114000011111111114000
00111400000000000111140000000011111140000000000011111111114000111111111400000
00111140000000000011114000000001111100000000000001111111114000111101111100000
00111140000000000001114000000001111100000000000010110111140001111111114000000
00111140000000000001114000000001111114000000000000110111114011111111114000000
00111100000000001111000000000111110000000000000001111111111111111114000000
10000000000000000000000000000000000000000000000000000000000000000000000000000000
00000000000000000000000000000000000000000000000000000000000000000000000000000000
00000000000000000000000000000000000000000000000000000000000000000000000000000000
```

3. Reduce the number of distinct symbols in IMAGE.
4. Display the reduced image.

Structure Chart and Refinements

As shown in the structure chart (Fig. 7.6), we will use separate subroutines to perform each algorithm step. The data passed between the main program and its subprograms consist of the array IMAGE and the two parameters representing its dimensions (MAXROW and MAXCOL).

Case Study: Image Enhancement, continued

Figure 7.6. *Structure Chart for Image Enhancement*

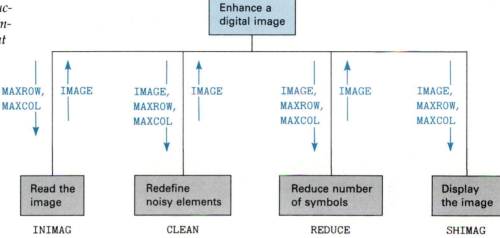

Coding the Main Program

The main program declares the three subroutine parameters and then calls the subroutines. Figure 7.7 shows the main program.

Subroutine INIMAG

Subroutine INIMAG (Fig. 7.8) reads the digital image from file DIGITAL.DAT using a READ statement with an implied DO loop in its input list. Each line of the data file is read into a row of array IMAGE. The FORMAT statement referenced in the READ statement

```
15 FORMAT (78I1)
```

specifies that each line of the data file contains seventy-eight single-digit integer values.

Figure 7.7. *Main Program for Image Enhancement*

```
      PROGRAM ENHANC
C Enhances digital images in two steps:
C   1. Reduces noise fluctuations. If a pixel is different from all its
C      neighbors by 3 or more, it is set to their average value.
C   2. Reduces the number of symbols by setting each pixel to
C      one of three standard values.
C Declarations
      INTEGER MAXROW, MAXCOL
      PARAMETER (MAXROW = 24, MAXCOL = 78)
      INTEGER IMAGE (MAXROW, MAXCOL)
```

Case Study: Image Enhancement, continued

```
C Read the digital image
      CALL INIMAG (IMAGE, MAXROW, MAXCOL)

C Replace each noisy pixel
      CALL CLEAN (IMAGE, MAXROW, MAXCOL)

C Reduce the number of symbols
      CALL REDUCE (IMAGE, MAXROW, MAXCOL)

C Display the reduced image
      CALL SHIMAG (IMAGE, MAXROW, MAXCOL)

C Exit program
      STOP
      END
```

Figure 7.8. *Subroutine INIMAG*

```
      SUBROUTINE INIMAG (IMAGE, MAXROW, MAXCOL)
C Reads the image

C Input Arguments
C    MAXROW - number of rows in IMAGE
C    MAXCOL - number of columns in IMAGE
C Output Arguments
C    IMAGE - the array of pixels

C Argument Declarations
      INTEGER MAXROW, MAXCOL
      INTEGER IMAGE(MAXROW, MAXCOL)

C Local Declarations
      INTEGER I,J

C Read each row of data until done
      OPEN (UNIT = 2, FILE = 'DIGITAL.DAT', STATUS = 'OLD')
      DO 10 I = 1, MAXROW
         READ (2, 15) (IMAGE(I, J), J = 1, MAXCOL)
   15    FORMAT (7I1)
   10 CONTINUE

C Exit subroutine
      RETURN
      END
```

Case Study: Image Enhancement, continued

Subroutine CLEAN

Subroutine CLEAN must check each element to see whether its value is noisy. If so, we should replace it with the average value of its neighbors. We do not check elements on the edge of the image (rows 1 and 24 and columns 1 and 78).

> ***Local Parameter***
>
> the noise level (NOSLEV = 3)
>
> ***Local Variables***
>
> the row subscript (INTEGER I)
> the column subscript (INTEGER J)
> a flag indicating whether an element contains noise (LOGICAL NOISY)
> the value of the current element of IMAGE (INTEGER CELL)

Algorithm for CLEAN

1. DO for each row I not on the edge
2.   DO for each column J not on the edge
3.   Set NOISY to .TRUE. if IMAGE(I,J) is noisy.
4.   IF (NOISY) THEN
5.   Replace IMAGE(I,J) with the average
            of its neighbors
         ENDIF
      CONTINUE
   CONTINUE

In step 3, we must compare the value in IMAGE(I,J) with the values stored in its eight neighbors. To facilitate the comparison, we can store the value of IMAGE(I,J) in local variable CELL. The neighbors are the eight elements with row subscripts I−1, I, or I+1 and column subscripts J−1, J, or J+1. The eight neighbors of IMAGE(I,J) are listed in the LOGICAL assignment statement shown in the subroutine (see Fig. 7.9). The first subexpression in the LOGICAL assignment

    (IABS(CELL − IMAGE(I−1,J−1)) .GE. NOSLEV)

compares the value of CELL with its neighbor in row I−1, column J−1. If the absolute difference of these values is greater than or equal to the noise threshold, the subexpression is .TRUE.. NOISY is set to .TRUE. only if all eight subexpressions are .TRUE..

Case Study: Image Enhancement, continued

Figure 7.9. *Subroutine CLEAN*

```
      SUBROUTINE CLEAN (IMAGE, MAXROW, MAXCOL)
C Finds noisy pixels and substitutes their neighbors' average value
C Input Arguments
C    MAXROW - number of rows in IMAGE
C    MAXCOL - number of columns in IMAGE
C Input/Output Arguments
C    IMAGE - the array of pixels

C Argument Declarations
      INTEGER MAXROW, MAXCOL
      INTEGER IMAGE(MAXROW, MAXCOL)

C Local Declarations
      INTEGER NOSLEV
      PARAMETER (NOSLEV) = 3)
      INTEGER CELL
      INTEGER I, J
      LOGICAL NOISY

C Check for noise and replace noisy pixels
      DO 10 I = 2, MAXROW-1
         DO 20 J = 2, MAXCOL-1
            CELL = IMAGE(I,J)
            NOISY = (IABS(CELL - IMAGE(I-1,J-1)) .GE. NOSLEV) .AND.
     +              (IABS(CELL - IMAGE(I-1,J  )) .GE. NOSLEV) .AND.
     +              (IABS(CELL - IMAGE(I-1,J+1)) .GE. NOSLEV) .AND.
     +              (IABS(CELL - IMAGE(I  ,J-1)) .GE. NOSLEV) .AND.
     +              (IABS(CELL - IMAGE(I  ,J+1)) .GE. NOSLEV) .AND.
     +              (IABS(CELL - IMAGE(I+1,J-1)) .GE. NOSLEV) .AND.
     +              (IABS(CELL - IMAGE(I+1,J  )) .GE. NOSLEV) .AND.
     +              (IABS(CELL - IMAGE(I+1,J+1)) .GE. NOSLEV)
C           Redefine IMAGE(I,J) if noisy
            IF (NOISY) THEN
               IMAGE(I,J) = NINT(REAL(IMAGE(I-1,J-1) + IMAGE(I-1,J)
     +                      + IMAGE(I-1,J+1) + IMAGE(I,J-1)
     +                      + IMAGE(I,J+1) + IMAGE(I+1,J-1)
     +                      + IMAGE(I+1,J)
     +                      + IMAGE(I+1,J+1)) / 8.0)
            ENDIF
20       CONTINUE
10    CONTINUE

C Exit subroutine
      RETURN
      END
```

Case Study: Image Enhancement, continued

The IF statement replaces a noisy value with the average value of its eight neighbors. Function REAL converts the sum of these eight values to a real number, and function NINT returns the nearest integer value after the sum is divided by eight.

Subroutine REDUCE

Subroutine REDUCE (Fig. 7.10) simply replaces each value in IMAGE with one of three standard symbols. SYMBL1 replaces values 0–3, SYMBL2 replaces values 4–6, and SYMBL3 replaces values 7–9. A pair of nested DO loops is used to access the array elements in sequence. The IF statement selects the appropriate standard symbol.

Figure 7.10. *Subroutine REDUCE*

```
      SUBROUTINE REDUCE (IMAGE, MAXROW, MAXCOL)
C Replaces each of the symbols in IMAGE with a standard symbol
C Input Arguments
C    MAXROW - number of rows in IMAGE
C    MAXCOL - number of columns in IMAGE
C Input/Output Arguments
C    IMAGE - the array of pixels

C Argument Declarations
      INTEGER MAXROW, MAXCOL
      INTEGER IMAGE(MAXROW, MAXCOL)

C Local Declarations
      INTEGER SYMBL1, SYMBL2, SYMBL3
      PARAMETER (SYMBL1 = 0, SYMBL2 = 1, SYMBL3 = 4)
      INTEGER I, J

C Perform the replacement
      DO 10 I = 1, MAXROW
         DO 20 J = 1, MAXCOL
            IF (IMAGE(I,J) .LE. 3) THEN
               IMAGE(I,J) = SYMBL1
            ELSE IF (IMAGE(I,J) .LE. 6) THEN
               IMAGE(I,J) = SYMBL2
            ELSE
               IMAGE(I,J) = SYMBL3
            ENDIF
 20      CONTINUE
 10   CONTINUE

C Exit subroutine
      RETURN
      END
```

Case Study: Image Enhancement, continued

Subroutine SHIMAG

Subroutine SHIMAG (Fig. 7.11) displays the enhanced image. The FORMAT statement

```
15 FORMAT (1X, 78I1)
```

causes the value of each array element to be displayed as a single-digit integer.

Figure 7.11. *Subroutine SHIMAG*

```
      SUBROUTINE SHIMAG (IMAGE, MAXROW, MAXCOL)
C Displays the enhanced image

C Input Arguments
C   IMAGE - the array of pixels
C   MAXROW - number of rows in IMAGE
C   MAXCOL - number of columns in IMAGE

C Argument Declarations
      INTEGER MAXROW, MAXCOL
      INTEGER IMAGE(MAXROW, MAXCOL)

C Local Declarations
      INTEGER I, J

C Display each row of the image
      DO 10 I = 1, MAXROW
         PRINT 15, (IMAGE(I,J), J = 1, MAXCOL)
   15    FORMAT (1X, 78I1)
   10 CONTINUE

C Exit subroutine
      RETURN
      END
```

Testing

You can construct your own test file by drawing a "stick figure" and then "encoding" it as a set of digits that all reduce to the same value. Pick "random" values outside this range for all other points in your image. Write each row of values to data file DIGITAL.DAT and see what happens. You will probably want to redefine MAXROW and MAXCOL to smaller values for test purposes. Programming project 9 at the end of this chapter discusses how to construct a noisy image.

7.3 ▬▬▬ Searching an Array

A common problem is searching an array to determine the location of a desired value. For example, we might wish to search an array of student names to locate a particular student name (called the *target*). This can be accomplished by examining each array element in a loop and testing to see whether it matches the target name. The search loop should be exited when the target name is found. A search algorithm follows.

Algorithm

1. Assume the target has not been found.
2. Start with the first array element.
3. DO WHILE the target is not found and there are more elements
   4. IF the current element matches the target THEN
      5. Set a flag to indicate that the target is found.
      ELSE
      6. Advance to the next array element.
      ENDIF
   ENDDO
7. IF the target was found THEN
   8. Return the target index as the search result.
   ELSE
   9. Return 0 as the search result.
   ENDIF

A function that implements this algorithm is shown in Fig. 7.12. This function returns the index of the target if it is present in the array; otherwise, it returns zero. The local variable I (initial value 1) selects the array element that is compared to the target value.

The LOGICAL flag FOUND is used for loop control in Fig. 7.12. The value of FOUND indicates whether the target has been found. It is initially set to .FALSE. (target is not found prior to search) and is reset to .TRUE. only if the target is found. After FOUND becomes .TRUE., the search loop is exited and the IF statement following the loop defines the value returned.

If array NAMES is defined in the calling program, the assignment statement

```
INDEX = SEARCH(NAMES, 'JANE DOE', 20)
```

calls function SEARCH to search the first twenty elements of array NAMES for the target name 'JANE DOE'. The subscript of the first occurrence of 'JANE DOE' is saved in INDEX. If 'JANE DOE' is not found, then INDEX is set to zero.

Figure 7.12. *Function SEARCH*

```
          INTEGER FUNCTION SEARCH (NAMES, TARGET, N)

C Searches for TARGET item in first N elements of array NAMES
C Returns TARGET index or 0 if not found
C Pre : TARGET and first N elements of array NAMES are
C       defined and N > 0.
C Post: Function result is subscript of first occurrence
C        of TARGET or 0 if no element is TARGET.

C Argument Declarations
       INTEGER N
       CHARACTER *20 NAMES(*), TARGET

C Local Declarations
       INTEGER I
       LOGICAL FOUND

C Assume TARGET is not yet found
       FOUND = .FALSE.

C Compare each element to TARGET starting with the first element
       I = 1
       DO WHILE (.NOT. FOUND .AND. I .LE. N)       9 IF (...) THEN
          IF (NAMES(I) .EQ. TARGET) THEN
             FOUND = .TRUE.
          ELSE
             I = I + 1
          ENDIF
       ENDDO                                         GOTO 9
C                                                    ENDIF
C Set result to TARGET index or 0
       IF (FOUND) THEN
          SEARCH = I
       ELSE
          SEARCH = 0
       ENDIF

C Exit function
       RETURN
       END
```

1. What value is returned by function SEARCH if the first, third, and fifth array elements all contain the target? Modify SEARCH so that the index of the last occurrence of the target is always returned.

7.4 ▬▬▬ Sorting an Array

In Section 5.3 we discussed a simple sort operation involving three numbers. We performed the sort by examining pairs of numbers and exchanging them if they were out of order. There are many times when we would like to sort the elements in an array. For example, we might prefer to have a grade report printed out in alphabetical order or in order by score.

In this section, a fairly simple (but not very efficient) algorithm called the *bubble sort* will be discussed. The bubble sort compares adjacent array elements and exchanges their values if they are out of order. In this way, the smaller values "bubble" to the top of the array (toward the first element), while the larger values sink to the bottom of the array. The data requirements and algorithm for a bubble sort subroutine follow.

> ***Subroutine Inputs***
>
> the array being sorted
> the number of array elements
>
> ***Subroutine Output***
>
> the sorted array

Algorithm for Bubble Sort Subroutine

1. DO WHILE the array is not sorted
   2. Examine every pair of adjacent array elements and exchange any values that are out of order.
   ENDDO

As an example, we will trace through one execution of step 2 above, that is, one *pass* through an array being sorted. By scanning the diagrams in Fig. 7.13 from left to right, we see the effect of each comparison. The pair of array

Figure 7.13. *One Pass of Bubble Sort of Array M*

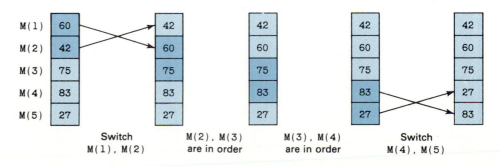

elements being compared is shown in a darker color in each diagram. The first pair of values (M(1) is 60, M(2) is 42) is out of order, so the values are exchanged. The next pair of values (M(2) is now 60, M(3) is 75) is compared in the second array shown in Fig. 7.13; this pair is in order, and so is the next pair (M(3) is 75, M(4) is 83). The last pair (M(4) is 83, M(5) is 27) is out of order, so the values are exchanged, as shown in the last diagram.

The last array shown in Fig. 7.13 is closer to being sorted than is the original. The only value that is out of order is the number 27 in M(4). Unfortunately, it will be necessary to complete three more passes through the entire array before this value bubbles to the top of the array. In each of these passes, only one pair of values will be out of order, so only one exchange will be made. The contents of array M after the completion of each pass are shown in Fig. 7.14.

Figure 7.14. *Array M after Completion of Each Pass*

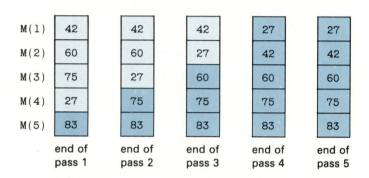

We can tell by looking at the contents of the array at the end of pass 4 that the array is now sorted; however, the computer can recognize this only by making one additional pass without doing any exchanges. If no exchanges are made, then all pairs must be in order. This is the reason for the extra pass shown in Fig. 7.14 and for the LOGICAL flag SORTED described below.

Local Variables for Bubble Sort

flag to indicate whether any exchanges were made in a pass (LOGICAL SORTED)
loop-control variable and subscript (INTEGER FIRST)
number of the current pass starting with 1 (INTEGER PASS)

Refinement of Step 2 of Bubble Sort

2.1 Initialize SORTED to .TRUE.
2.2 DO for each pair of adjacent array elements
      2.3 IF the values in a pair are out of order THEN

2.4 Exchange the values
2.5 Set SORTED to .FALSE.
            ENDIF
        CONTINUE

Step 2 will be implemented using a DO loop. The DO loop-control variable, FIRST, will also be the subscript of the first element in each pair; consequently, FIRST+1 will be the subscript of the second element in each pair. During each pass, the initial value of FIRST is 1. The final value of FIRST must be less than the number of array elements so that FIRST+1 will be in range.

For an array of n elements, the final value of FIRST can be $n-$PASS, where PASS is the number of the current pass, starting with 1 for the first pass. The reason for this is that at the end of pass 1 the last array element must be in its correct place, at the end of pass 2 the last two array elements must be in their correct places, at the end of pass 3 the last three array elements must be in their correct places, and so on. There is no need to examine array elements that are already in place. The section of the array that is already sorted is shown in a darker color in Fig. 7.14.

Subroutine BUBBLE in Fig. 7.15 performs a bubble sort on the array represented by LIST. If the pair of elements represented by LIST(FIRST) and LIST(FIRST+1) is out of order, their values are exchanged and SORTED is set to .FALSE.. When BUBBLE is done, the array elements will be in order.

Subroutine BUBBLE begins by setting SORTED to .FALSE.. Although this step is not listed in the algorithm shown earlier, it is done to ensure that the WHILE loop will be executed at least one time.

Figure 7.15. *Bubble Sort Subroutine*

```
      SUBROUTINE BUBBLE (LIST, N)
C Sorts the data in array LIST

C Input Argument
C   N - Number of array elements to be sorted
C Input/Output Argument
C   LIST - Array being sorted

C Argument Declarations
      INTEGER LIST(*), N

C Local Declarations
      INTEGER FIRST, PASS, TEMP
      LOGICAL SORTED

C Start with pass 1
      PASS = 1
```

```
C Exchange out of order pairs while array is not sorted
      SORTED = .FALSE.
      DO WHILE (.NOT. SORTED)                        9  IF (...) THEN
         SORTED = .TRUE.
         DO 10 FIRST = 1, N-PASS
            IF (LIST (FIRST) .GT. LIST(FIRST+1)) THEN
C              Exchange pair
               TEMP = LIST(FIRST)
               LIST(FIRST) = LIST(FIRST+1)
               LIST(FIRST+1) = TEMP
               SORTED = .FALSE.
            ENDIF
  10     CONTINUE
         PASS = PASS + 1
      ENDDO                                           GOTO 9
C                                                     ENDIF
C Exit subroutine
      RETURN
      END
```

**SELF-CHECK
EXERCISE FOR
SECTION 7.4**

1. Modify BUBBLE to place the array values in descending order (largest value first).

7.5   Using Subprograms in a Large-Scale Problem

In this section, we use many of the subprograms developed in the last two chapters to solve a rather large programming problem. The problem solution demonstrates the advantage of using subprograms to split a large problem into manageable modules. Since many of these subprograms are general and were not written specifically for this problem, they can be reused in other programs.

Case Study: Grading Problem

Problem

The instructors at your college would like a grading program to help them assign grades for an examination. They would like to use this program to display data for either all students or a particular student, to calculate exam statistics, to assign letter grades, and even to chart the distribution of grades.

Case Study: Grading Problem, continued

Since each instructor will have a different use for the program, the program should be *menu driven*. The program user can request a display of the menu below after completing each task (or before the first task); the number entered by the program user determines which task will be performed next.

```
Select one of the operations below by number.

 0.  Display the menu
 1.  Enter exam data
 2.  Find the score of a particular student
 3.  Change a score and grade
 4.  Sort the student data by name
 5.  Sort the student data by score
 6.  Find the low score
 7.  Find the high score
 8.  Find the mean and standard deviation
 9.  Find the median
10.  Assign a letter grade
11.  Plot a histogram of grades
12.  Display the student exam data
13.  Exit the program
```

Design Overview

We will write a separate subprogram to accomplish each of the tasks listed above. In fact, we already have subprogram solutions to several of these tasks. The input data for the new grading program consist of the name and score of each student. Also, each menu selection will be read as data. The outputs consist of the letter grades assigned and the exam statistics. The student names, scores, and grades will be stored in a set of parallel arrays. The problem data requirements and algorithm follow.

Data Requirements

Problem Parameters

the maximum array sizes (MAXSIZ = 100)
the number of the exit option (EXITCH = 13)

Problem Inputs

the number of students taking the exam (INTEGER NUMSTU)
the name of each student (CHARACTER *20 NAMES(MAXSIZ))
the score of each student (INTEGER SCORES(MAXSIZ))
the operation to be performed (INTEGER CHOICE)

Case Study: Grading Problem, continued

Problem Outputs

the lowest score (INTEGER MINSCR)
the highest score (INTEGER MAXSCR)
the average score (REAL AVERAG)
the standard deviation (REAL STDEV)
the median score (INTEGER MEDIAN)
the assigned letter grades (CHARACTER *1 GRADES(MAXSIZ))

Initial Algorithm

1. DO WHILE the user is not done
      2. Read and validate the user's choice.
      3. Perform the option selected.
ENDDO

Structure Chart and Algorithm Refinements

The structure chart corresponding to this algorithm is shown in Fig. 7.16. Subroutine OPRATE will contain the code required to perform each option selected by the program user. It is in color in the structure chart to indicate that it has subordinate subprograms, which will be shown later.

Figure 7.16. *Structure Chart for New Grading Program*

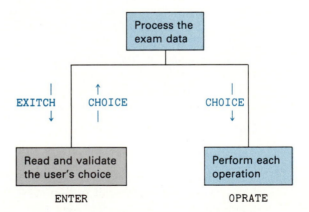

Only variable CHOICE and parameter EXITCH are shown as arguments in Fig. 7.16. None of the other problem inputs or outputs listed earlier appears, because these variables are manipulated by subroutine OPRATE and its subordinate subprograms. For this reason, only CHOICE and EXITCH should be declared

Case Study: Grading Problem, continued

in the main program; the other problem inputs and outputs will be declared in subroutine OPRATE.

Coding the Main Program

The main program (Fig. 7.17) begins by setting CHOICE to 0 to ensure that the main loop is entered and executed at least once. Function ENTER (see Fig. 5.6) is used to read the user's choice into CHOICE. The first-time user should select option 0 to see the menu. After CHOICE is read, subroutine OPRATE is called.

Figure 7.17. *Main Program for New Grading Program*

```
      PROGRAM GRADER
C Grades student exams
C Performs a set of operations on student exam data

C Declarations
      INTEGER CHOICE, EXITCH, ENTER
      PARAMETER (EXITCH = 13)

C Read and process each option until user is done
      CHOICE = 0
      DO WHILE (CHOICE .NE. EXITCH)                    9 IF (...) THEN
        PRINT *
        PRINT *, 'Enter your choice — enter 0 to see the menu'
        CHOICE = ENTER(0, EXITCH)
        CALL OPRATE (CHOICE, EXITCH)
      ENDDO                                               GOTO 9
C                                                         ENDIF
C Exit program
      STOP
      END
```

Subroutine OPRATE

Each time it is called, OPRATE must perform the operation selected by its first input argument, CHOICE. Consequently, the algorithm for OPRATE consists of a multiple-alternative decision structure.

Certain preconditions must be satisfied before some of the operations can be performed. For example, the student exam data must be read before any of the other operations can be performed (i.e., NUMSTU must be non-zero). The exam data must be sorted by score before the median score can be determined. Also, the letter grades must be assigned before a histogram can be

Case Study: Grading Problem, continued

drawn. The program flags listed below will be used to signal whether the last two preconditions are satisfied.

Local Variables for OPRATE

program flag to indicate whether data is sorted by score (LOGICAL SORTED)
program flag to indicate whether grades are assigned (LOGICAL GRADED)
the mean or average score (REAL MEAN)
the standard deviation of the scores (REAL STDEV)
the median score (REAL MEDIAN)

Algorithm for OPRATE

1. IF CHOICE is 0 THEN
    2. Print the menu.
ELSE IF CHOICE is not 1 and NUMSTU is 0 THEN
    3. Print a message to read in student data first.
ELSE IF CHOICE is 1 THEN
    4. Read the student data and set flags to .FALSE..
ELSE IF CHOICE is 2 THEN
    5. Read a student's name and display the score.
ELSE IF CHOICE is 3 THEN
    6. Read a student's name and change that score and grade.
ELSE IF CHOICE is 4 THEN
    7. Sort the student data by name and set SORTED to .FALSE..
ELSE IF CHOICE is 5 THEN
    8. Sort the student data by score and set SORTED to .TRUE..
ELSE IF CHOICE is 6 THEN
    9. Find the low score.
ELSE IF CHOICE is 7 THEN
    10. Find the high score.
ELSE IF CHOICE is 8 THEN
    11. Find the mean score and standard deviation.
ELSE IF CHOICE is 9 and scores are sorted THEN
    12. Find the median score.
ELSE IF CHOICE is 9 THEN
    13. Print a message that scores must be sorted first.
ELSE IF CHOICE is 10 THEN
    14. Assign letter grades and set GRADED to .TRUE..
ELSE IF CHOICE is 11 and grades are assigned THEN
    15. Plot the histogram of grades.

Case Study: Grading Problem, continued

```
ELSE IF CHOICE is 11 THEN
```
   16. Print a message that letter grades must be assigned.
```
ELSE IF CHOICE is 12 THEN
```
   17. Display all student data.
```
ELSE IF CHOICE is EXITCH THEN
```
   18. Exit from the grading program.
```
ELSE
```
   19. Print a message that CHOICE is invalid.
```
ENDIF
```

Steps 2, 3, 13, 16, 18, and 19 consist of simple PRINT statements. Of the rest, only steps 14 and 15 require subprograms that are unfamiliar to us. The structure chart for subroutine OPRATE is shown in Fig. 7.18.

Because of space limitations, subroutine PRMENU is omitted from the structure chart. All the subprograms shown in Fig. 7.18 are subroutines with the exception of GETMIN, which should be implemented as a function because it returns a single result. The functions GETMAX (returns the high score—see Fig. 6.7) and GETMED (returns the median value) are not shown in the structure chart; however, they have the same input arguments as GETMIN. Subroutine AVESTD, which returns both the average value and the standard deviation, also is not shown. Subroutine OPRATE is shown in Fig. 7.19.

The statement

```
SAVE NAMES, SCORES, GRADED, SORTED, NUMSTU
```

is used in Fig. 7.19 to instruct the compiler to retain the values of the local variables that are listed after SAVE between successive calls to OPRATE. The SAVE statement is described in detail in Section 7.6.

The statement

```
DATA NUMSTU /0/
```

initializes the value of NUMSTU to 0 when the subroutine is first loaded into memory. Consequently, NUMSTU will be zero the very first time that ENTSTU is called to enter student data. The DATA statement has no effect during subsequent calls to OPRATE, so NUMSTU will not be reset to zero.

The top-down approach has been utilized in designing the grading program. We have progressed fairly far in writing the program and have an overall design that is clear, readable, and well documented. However, we still have not explored the details of many subprograms that actually perform the grading operations. Most of these will be left as exercises. Functions GETMED and PLOT are discussed next.

Case Study: Grading Problem, continued

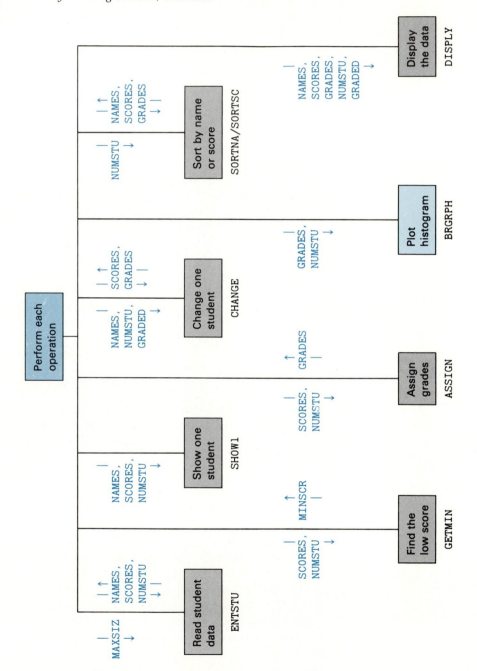

Figure 7.18. *Structure Chart for OPRATE*

Case Study: Grading Problem, continued

Figure 7.19. *Subroutine OPRATE*

```
      SUBROUTINE OPRATE (CHOICE, EXITCH)
C Performs the option selected by CHOICE
C Input Arguments
C   CHOICE - The number of the option selected (0 to EXITCH)
C   EXITCH - The number of the exit option

C Argument Declarations
      INTEGER CHOICE, EXITCH

C Local Declarations
      INTEGER MAXSIZ
      PARAMETER (MAXSIZ = 100)
      INTEGER SCORES(MAXSIZ), NUMSTU
      INTEGER MINSCR, MAXSCR
      CHARACTER *20 NAMES(MAXSIZ)
      CHARACTER *1 GRADES(MAXSIZ)
      REAL MEAN, STDEV, MEDIAN
      LOGICAL SORTED, GRADED

      INTEGER GETMIN, GETMAX
      REAL GETMED

C Save all local data between calls
      SAVE NAMES, SCORES, GRADES, GRADED, SORTED, NUMSTU
      DATA NUMSTU /0/

C Perform option selected
      IF (CHOICE .EQ. 0) THEN
          CALL PRMENU
      ELSE IF ((CHOICE .NE. 1) .AND. (NUMSTU .EQ. 0)) THEN
          PRINT *, 'Read student data first'
      ELSE IF (CHOICE .EQ. 1) THEN
          CALL ENTSTU (MAXSIZ, NAMES, SCORES, NUMSTU)
          GRADED = .FALSE.
          SORTED = .FALSE.
      ELSE IF (CHOICE .EQ. 2) THEN
          CALL SHOW1 (NAMES, SCORES, NUMSTU)
      ELSE IF (CHOICE .EQ. 3) THEN
          CALL CHANGE (GRADED, NUMSTU, NAMES, SCORES, GRADES)
      ELSE IF (CHOICE .EQ. 4) THEN
          CALL SORTNA (NUMSTU, NAMES, SCORES, GRADES)
          SORTED = .FALSE.
      ELSE IF (CHOICE .EQ. 5) THEN
          CALL SORTSC (NUMSTU, NAMES, SCORES, GRADES)
          SORTED = .TRUE.
      ELSE IF (CHOICE .EQ. 6) THEN
          MINSCR = GETMIN(SCORES, NUMSTU)
          PRINT *, 'The lowest score is ', MINSCR
```

Case Study: Grading Problem, continued

```
      ELSE IF (CHOICE .EQ. 7) THEN
         MAXSCR = GETMAX(SCORES, NUMSTU)
         PRINT *, 'The highest score is ', MAXSCR
      ELSE IF (CHOICE .EQ. 8) THEN
         CALL AVESTD (SCORES, NUMSTU, MEAN, STDEV)
         PRINT *, 'The mean score is ', MEAN
         PRINT *, 'with a standard deviation of ', STDEV
      ELSE IF ((CHOICE .EQ. 9) .AND. SORTED) THEN
         MEDIAN = GETMED(SCORES, NUMSTU)
         PRINT *, 'The median score is ', MEDIAN
      ELSE IF (CHOICE .EQ. 9) THEN
         PRINT *, 'Scores must first be sorted'
      ELSE IF (CHOICE .EQ. 10) THEN
         CALL ASSIGN (SCORES, NUMSTU, GRADES)
         GRADED = .TRUE.
      ELSE IF (CHOICE .EQ. 11 .AND. GRADED) THEN
         CALL BRGRPH (GRADES, NUMSTU)
      ELSE IF (CHOICE .EQ. 11) THEN
         PRINT *, 'Assign grades first'
      ELSE IF (CHOICE .EQ. 12) THEN
         CALL DISPLY (NAMES, SCORES, GRADES, NUMSTU, GRADED)
      ELSE IF (CHOICE .EQ. EXITCH) THEN
         PRINT *, 'Exiting from the grading program'
      ELSE
         PRINT *, 'Choice must be between 0 and ', EXITCH
      ENDIF

C Exit subroutine
      RETURN
      END
```

Finding the Median Value

Function GETMED in Fig. 7.20 returns the median score. The median item in a list is defined as the item that occupies the middle position when the list is sorted. Function GETMED is called only when the scores are in order. This makes it easier to determine the median score, as explained next.

If the items are in order and there are an odd number of items, then the median is the middle item. If the items are in order but there are an even number of items, then the median is the average of the two middle items.

Both cases are illustrated in Fig. 7.21. The value of NUMSTU is 7 for the diagram on the left and 8 for the diagram on the right. In the diagram on the left, the median, 78, is shaded in grey. In the diagram on the right, the median, 83, is the average of the two items in grey.

Figure 7.20. *Function GETMED*

```
      REAL FUNCTION GETMED (SCORES, NUMSTU)
C Returns the median value in the sorted array SCORES
C Pre : The first NUMSTU elements of array SCORES are in
C        ascending order and NUMSTU > 0.
C Post: The function result is the median of
C        the first NUMSTU values in score.

C Argument Declarations
      INTEGER SCORES(*), NUMSTU

C Define median value
      IF (MOD(NUMSTU, 2) .EQ. 1) THEN
C        Median is the middle item of an odd item count
         GETMED = REAL(SCORES(NUMSTU/2 + 1))
      ELSE
C        Median is the average of two middle items of an even item count
         GETMED = REAL(SCORES(NUMSTU/2) + SCORES(NUMSTU/2 + 1)) / 2.0
      ENDIF

C Exit function
      RETURN
      END
```

Figure 7.21. *The Median of a Sorted Array*

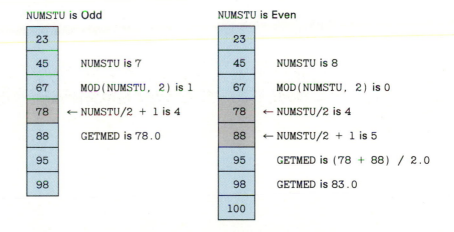

Plotting a Histogram

Choice 11 of the grading program requests a histogram of the grade distribution. A numerical value is represented in a histogram, or bar graph, by a bar whose length is proportional to the size of the value.

Before the grade distribution can be plotted, it is necessary to first determine the number of scores in each letter grade category (the number of A's, B's, etc.). Two local arrays, CATGRY and COUNTS, will be used to store the five letter grades and a counter for each grade category. The local data requirements and algorithm for subroutine BRGRPH follow.

Local Parameters

the number of grade categories (NUMCAT = 5)
the character plotted (STAR = '*')

Local Variables

the array of grade categories (CHARACTER *1 CATGRY(NUMCAT))
the array of category counters (INTEGER COUNTS(NUMCAT))
subscript for array of assigned grades (INTEGER NXTGRD)
subscript for array of grade categories (INTEGER NXTCAT)
loop-control variable (INTEGER NSTAR)

Algorithm for BRGRPH

1. Count the number of assigned grades in each of the five letter grade categories.
2. Plot the array of counters as a bar graph.

Subroutine CNTGRD will be called by subroutine BRGRPH to determine the number of grades in each of the five grade categories. The structure chart segment in Fig. 7.22 shows the data flow between BRGRPH and CNTGRD. The subroutines are shown in Fig. 7.23, and a sample histogram appears in Fig. 7.24.

Figure 7.22. *Structure Chart for BRGRPH and CNTGRD*

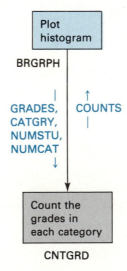

Figure 7.23. *Subroutines BRGRPH and CNTGRD*

```
      SUBROUTINE BRGRPH (GRADES, NUMSTU)
C Plots the distribution of GRADES as a bar graph (histogram)

C Input Arguments
C    GRADES - The array of grades
C    NUMSTU - The number of elements in GRADES

C Argument Declarations
      CHARACTER *1 GRADES(*)
      INTEGER NUMSTU

C Local Declarations
      CHARACTER *1 STAR
      PARAMETER (STAR = '*')
      INTEGER NUMCAT
      PARAMETER (NUMCAT = 5)
      INTEGER NXTCAT, NSTAR
      INTEGER NUMGRD, NXTGRD
      INTEGER COUNTS(NUMCAT)
      CHARACTER *1 CATGRY(NUMCAT)
      DATA CATGRY /'A', 'B', 'C', 'D', 'F'/

C Print the title
      PRINT 5, 'HISTOGRAM OF GRADE DISTRIBUTION'
    5 FORMAT ('1', A)
      PRINT *

C Count the number of occurrences of each grade
      CALL CNTGRD (GRADES, CATGRY, NUMSTU, NUMCAT, COUNTS)

C Plot a bar for the count associated with each grade category
      DO 10 NXTCAT = 1, NUMCAT
         PRINT 15, CATGRY(NXTCAT), ' I',
     +               (STAR, NSTAR = 1, COUNTS(NXTCAT))
   15    FORMAT (1X, A, A, 50A1)
   10 CONTINUE

C Print a legend at the bottom
      PRINT *, '   I----I----I----I----I----I----I----I----I----I----I'
      PRINT *, '   0    5   10   15   20   25   30   35   40   45   50'

C Exit subroutine
      RETURN
      END

C----------------------------------------------------------------------
```

```
      SUBROUTINE CNTGRD (GRADES, CATGRY, NUMSTU, NUMCAT, COUNTS)
C Count the number of grades in each category

C INPUT ARGUMENTS
C    GRADES - The array of grades
C    CATGRY - The array of categories
C    NUMSTU - The number of GRADES
C    NUMCAT - The number of categories

C OUTPUT ARGUMENTS
C    COUNTS - The array of counters

C Argument Declarations
      CHARACTER *1 GRADES(*), CATGRY(*)
      INTEGER COUNTS(*), NUMSTU, NUMCAT

C Local Declarations
      INTEGER NXTCAT, NXTGRD

C Initialize all counters to zero
      DO 10 NXTCAT = 1, NUMCAT
          COUNTS(NXTCAT) = 0
   10 CONTINUE

C Categorize each grade
      DO 20 NXTGRD = 1, NUMSTU
C         Compare the current grade to each grade category
C         and increment the counter for the matched category
          IF (GRADES(NXTGRD) .EQ. CATGRY(1)) THEN
              COUNTS(1) = COUNTS(1) + 1
          ELSE IF (GRADES(NXTGRD) .EQ. CATGRY(2)) THEN
              COUNTS(2) = COUNTS(2) + 1
          ELSE IF (GRADES(NXTGRD) .EQ. CATGRY(3)) THEN
              COUNTS(3) = COUNTS(3) + 1
          ELSE IF (GRADES(NXTGRD) .EQ. CATGRY(4)) THEN
              COUNTS(4) = COUNTS(4) + 1
          ELSE IF (GRADES(NXTGRD) .EQ. CATGRY(5)) THEN
              COUNTS(5) = COUNTS(5) + 1
          ELSE
              PRINT *, 'Invalid grade ', GRADES(NXTGRD)
          ENDIF
   20 CONTINUE

C Exit subroutine
      RETURN
      END
```

Figure 7.24. *Sample Histogram Printed by BRGRPH*

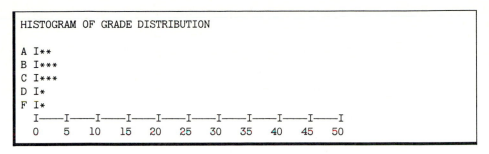

```
HISTOGRAM OF GRADE DISTRIBUTION

A I**
B I***
C I***
D I*
F I*
  I———I———I———I———I———I———I———I———I———I———I
  0    5   10   15   20   25   30   35   40   45   50
```

Subroutine BRGRPH begins by calling subroutine CNTGRD

        CALL CNTGRD (GRADES, CATGRY, NUMSTU, NUMCAT, COUNTS)

to define the array of counters (COUNTS). The IF structure in subroutine CNTGRD attempts to match each element of array GRADES to one of the five grade categories and increments the counter for the matched category.

In subroutine BRGRPH, the formatted PRINT statement

```
         PRINT 15, CATGRY(NXTCAT), ' I',
     +             (STAR, NSTAR = 1, COUNTS(NXTCAT))
     15  FORMAT (1X, A, A, 50A1)
```

is executed once for each of the letter grade categories. It displays a letter grade label for a bar, the symbol ' I', and then the bar itself as a string of adjacent STAR characters. The implied DO loop (second line) uses the value of COUNTS(NXTCAT) to determine how many asterisks are printed in each bar.

Testing the Grading Program

Before you can test the grading program completely, you must supply the missing subprograms. You can perform a partial test by using a dummy subprogram or stub in place of each subprogram that is not yet completed (see Section 5.7). This will allow you to compile the grading program. Make sure you do not select an option that calls a missing subroutine.

You should complete subroutine DISPLY before you begin the testing process. This will allow you to view the letter grade assignments and verify that all data items were stored properly.

SELF-CHECK EXERCISES FOR SECTION 7.5

1. Write a DO loop containing a LOGICAL IF statement that can be used to replace the IF structure in subroutine CNTGRD of Fig. 7.23.
2. Write the remaining subroutines and functions that are called by subroutine OPRATE.

7.6 ▬▬▬▬ The SAVE Statement and Simulation

The SAVE statement was used in subroutine OPRATE (see Fig. 7.19) to save the values of several local variables declared in that subroutine. Otherwise, the local variables could become undefined when we exit from OPRATE and could be lost.

This has not been a problem before because each subprogram either was called just once or if called multiple times, there was no need to retain local variable values between calls. Also in earlier programs, any data that needed to be saved between subprogram calls were stored in main program variables instead of in local variables. The SAVE statement is summarized in the next display.

SAVE Statement

SYNTAX: SAVE
          SAVE *list*

EXAMPLE: SAVE A, B, C

INTERPRETATION: The *list* contains the names of local variables or arrays whose values are to be saved following the execution of a subprogram RETURN. Otherwise, the values of these local variables may be lost. If the SAVE statement appears without a *list,* all local variable values will be saved. The SAVE statement is nonexecutable and must appear in the declaration section of a subprogram, before any executable statements. A SAVE statement in the main program has no effect.

NOTE: The SAVE statement must appear with the declarations and before any executable statements. The *list* must not contain the names of subprograms or dummy arguments. Items defined by a DATA statement and not redefined do not have to be included in the SAVE statement.

Random-Number Generation

The SAVE statement can be used within a function that generates random numbers. Although a computer cannot generate a truly random number, it can generate what is called a *pseudorandom number*. Pseudorandom numbers are not really random, but they are close. Random numbers are used in many computer applications, for example, simulation of ship arrivals at a port or traffic flow through a city.

EXAMPLE 7.7

Function RANDOM (see Fig. 7.25) generates pseudorandom numbers. Its argument, SEED, is the initial *seed* of the random-number generator and should be a large prime number. The idea behind random-number generation is to multiply the seed value by a very large number and then perform a division operation, thereby returning a "random" result.

Figure 7.25. *Function RANDOM*

```
      REAL FUNCTION RANDOM (SEED)
C Generates a random number using SEED as the initial seed for the
C random-number generator
C Pre : SEED is defined and OLDSED contains the previous
C       seed value.
C Post: Returns a value between 0.0 and 1.0 and OLDSED contains
C       the next seed value.

C Argument Declarations
      INTEGER SEED

C Local Declarations
      INTEGER C1, C2
      PARAMETER (C1 = 19423, C2 = 811)
      INTEGER OLDSED
      SAVE OLDSED
      DATA OLDSED /0/

C Set OLDSED to SEED if this is the first call
      IF (OLDSED .EQ. 0) THEN
          OLDSED = SEED
      ENDIF

C Generate a new value of OLDSED
      OLDSED = MOD(C1 * OLDSED, C2)

C Define the result
      RANDOM = REAL(OLDSED) / REAL(C2)

C Exit function
      RETURN
      END
```

The local variable OLDSED represents the current seed value. The DATA statement initializes OLDSED to 0 when the function is loaded into memory. OLDSED is set to SEED the first time function RANDOM executes. Thereafter, the statement

```
      OLDSED = MOD(C1 * OLDSED, C2)
```

computes a new value for OLDSED by first multiplying it by a very large prime number (parameter C1) and then finding the remainder after division by another prime number (parameter C2). The statement

```
      RANDOM =  REAL(OLDSED) / REAL(C2)
```

divides OLDSED by C2 to get a pseudorandom number between 0.0 and 1.0. The SAVE statement is used to ensure that OLDSED retains its value during successive calls to function RANDOM.

EXAMPLE 7.8   The DO loop below calls function RANDOM ten times in succession and displays the values returned for an initial seed of 20029.

```
DO 20 I = 1, 10
   X = RANDOM(20029)
   PRINT *, X
20 CONTINUE
```

As another example of the use of function RANDOM, the statement

```
N = 1 + INT(10 * RANDOM(20029))
```

assigns a random integer between 1 and 10 to N. In general, the expression

```
A + INT(B * RANDOM(SEED))
```

yields a random integer in the range A to A + B − 1.   ∎

In Example 7.8, we used a large prime number, 20029, as the initial seed value. The theory behind random-number generation is beyond the scope of this text; refer to other texts for more information.[1]

Simulation Using Random Numbers

Interestingly enough, we can estimate the value of π using random numbers. We can divide the first quadrant of a graph into two regions by drawing the arc of a circle with radius 1 (see Fig. 7.26). The area of region 1 is $\pi r^2/4$ or simply $\pi/4$ when r is 1. The area of the entire quadrant (region 1 and region 2) is 1. Therefore, the ratio of region 1 to the entire quadrant area is $\pi/4$.

Figure 7.26. *Regions of a Unit Circle*

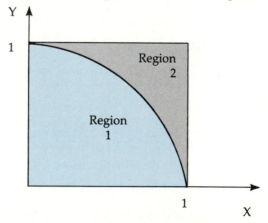

If we "throw darts" into the quadrant, the number of darts landing in region 1 should be proportional to the area of region 1. We can simulate throwing a dart by generating a pair of random numbers that represent the X, Y coordinates of the point where the dart lands. If we divide the number of

[1] See, for example, Donald Knuth, *The Art of Computer Programming, Seminumerical Algorithms,* vol. 1 (Reading, Mass.: Addison-Wesley, 1981).

darts landing in region 1 by the total number of darts thrown, we should get an estimate of $\pi/4$.

How do we know whether a dart lands in region 1? If the distance of the dart from the origin is less than 1, the dart must lie within region 1. The distance formula is

$$distance = \sqrt{X^2 + Y^2}$$

If we throw a large number of darts (say, 1000 or more), we should come pretty close to an accurate estimate of $\pi/4$. Multiplying this value by 4 gives us an estimate of π. Figure 7.27 shows a sample run of a program that estimates the value of π using function RANDOM.

Figure 7.27. *Estimating Pi*

```
      PROGRAM PIEST
C Estimates the value of pi using random numbers

C Declarations
      INTEGER SEED
      PARAMETER (SEED = 20029)
      INTEGER DART, TRIES, HITS
      REAL X, Y, PI, RANDOM

C Enter number of darts to throw
      PRINT *, 'How many tries?'
      READ *, TRIES

C Throw each dart and count the number of hits inside the circle
      HITS = 0
      DO 10 DART = 1, TRIES
         X = RANDOM(SEED)
         Y = RANDOM(SEED)
         IF (SQRT(X ** 2 + Y ** 2) .LT. 1.0) THEN
            HITS = HITS + 1
         ENDIF
   10 CONTINUE

C Estimate pi
      PI = (REAL(HITS) / REAL(TRIES)) * 4.0
      PRINT '(1X, A, F10.7)', 'Pi is ', PI

C Exit program
      STOP
      END


How many tries?
1000
Pi is  3.1640000
```

7.7 ▰▰▰▰ COMMON Blocks

The only data communication between main programs and subprograms discussed so far is through argument lists. FORTRAN also provides the capability of data communication through a storage area called a *COMMON block*. We could use the declarations

```
INTEGER MAXSIZ
PARAMETER (MAXSIZ = 100)
COMMON SCORES(MAXSIZ)
INTEGER SCORES
```

in OPRATE (see Fig. 7.19) to allocate a COMMON block for storage of an integer array (SCORES) with MAXSIZ elements. The statement beginning with COMMON is called a COMMON statement, and it lists the names of variables in the COMMON block. The type of each variable in the COMMON block must be declared either before or after the COMMON statement. If the variable is an array, its size may be declared in the COMMON statement or in the type declaration.

Placing the array SCORES in the COMMON block enables other subprograms called by OPRATE to reference the data in SCORES without the need to pass SCORES as an argument. The interface section for function GETMED (see Fig. 7.20) is rewritten in Fig. 7.28 to include the COMMON statement above. The array SCORES must be deleted from the dummy argument list for GETMED. The assignment statement

```
MEDIAN = GETMED(NUMSTU)
```

can be used in subroutine OPRATE to call GETMED.

Figure 7.28. *Interface Section for Subroutine GETMED*

```
      REAL FUNCTION GETMED (NUMSTU)
C Returns the median value in the sorted array SCORES

C Pre : The first NUMSTU elements of array SCORES are in
C        ascending order and NUMSTU > 0.
C Post: The function result is the median of
C        the first NUMSTU values in score.

C Argument Declarations
      INTEGER NUMSTU

C Common Declarations
      INTEGER MAXSIZ
      PARAMETER (MAXSIZ = 100)
      COMMON SCORES(MAXSIZ)
      INTEGER SCORES
```

The advantage of using COMMON statements is that they enable us to shorten the argument lists used in subprogram definitions and calls by deleting items in COMMON storage. The disadvantage is that it becomes less clear exactly what external data are being referenced by a subprogram when some external data are passed as arguments and some are not. This problem is exacerbated when a team of programmers is working together on a large project.

A COMMON statement may also be used in a main program to enable easy reference to data that are manipulated by many of its subprograms. When the COMMON statement appears in the main program, the data in the COMMON block are called *global data*. Each subprogram that references the global data must contain a COMMON statement similar to the one in the main program.

There are some restrictions on the use of COMMON storage. They are listed next.

Restrictions on the Use of COMMON Storage

- A parameter cannot be stored in a COMMON block.
- A variable listed in a COMMON statement in a subprogram cannot also be a dummy argument for that subprogram.
- Character data cannot be combined with data of other types in a COMMON block.
- Items in a COMMON block cannot appear in a SAVE or DATA statement.

These restrictions prevent us from placing MAXSIZ (a parameter) and NUMSTU (initialized by a DATA statement) in the COMMON block declared for subroutine OPRATE. It also is not possible to place the array NAMES (type CHARACTER * 20) and the array SCORES together in a COMMON block.

The data in the COMMON block declared above are automatically saved between calls to subroutine OPRATE. Therefore, it is unnecessary (and illegal) to include SCORES in the variable list associated with the SAVE statement in OPRATE. The SAVE statement from Fig. 7.19,

```
SAVE NAMES, SCORES, GRADES, GRADED, SORTED, NUMSTU
```

should be rewritten as

```
SAVE NAMES, GRADES, GRADED, SORTED, NUMSTU
```

Name Independence of COMMON Data

The COMMON block declared in the previous section contains an array of 100 type INTEGER values. A different array name may be used to reference these INTEGER data in another subprogram. In fact, there is no requirement that the structure of the data be the same in all subprograms that reference the same COMMON block.

EXAMPLE 7.9

The declarations

```
COMMON FIRST, MIDDLE(98), LAST
INTEGER FIRST, MIDDLE, LAST
```

could be used in another subprogram to reference the 100 type INTEGER values in the COMMON block shown earlier. In this case, the COMMON data would have the correspondence shown in Fig. 7.29. In the subprogram containing the above COMMON statement, the variable FIRST references the first cell of the COMMON block, and the variable LAST references the last cell of the COMMON block. In subroutine OPRATE, the names of these cells are SCORES(1) and SCORES(100), respectively. ∎

Figure 7.29. *Correspondence of COMMON Data*

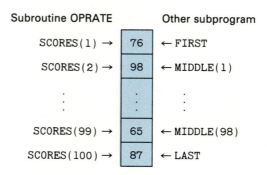

Even though this flexibility exists, we strongly recommend that you be consistent in naming items in a COMMON block and simply duplicate the COMMON statement in each subprogram that contains it. Remember to declare the structure of each item in the COMMON block as well as its data type.

Named COMMON Blocks

In some cases, there may be variables that are shared by a group of subprograms in a program system but not by all the subprograms. Rather than include these variables in the general common storage area, one or more additional *named COMMON blocks* may be declared. The COMMON block described earlier is called the *blank COMMON block* because it has no name.

EXAMPLE 7.10

Several of the subprograms in Fig. 7.19 reference data stored in the character arrays NAMES and GRADES. These variables are not included in the blank COMMON block because there are many subprograms that do not reference them. Also, it is not possible to combine character data with noncharacter data in a COMMON block.

The declaration

```
COMMON /STUDAT/ NAMES(MAXSIZ), GRADES(MAXSIZ)
```

identifies NAMES and GRADES as belonging to the named COMMON block STUDAT. This named COMMON statement must appear in OPRATE and any subprogram that references these data without the use of argument lists. The type and structure of variables in named COMMON blocks must also be declared. The declarations for subroutine OPRATE shown in Fig. 7.30 include the blank COMMON block and the COMMON block named STUDAT. The new SAVE statement is explained in the next subsection, "The SAVE Statement and Named COMMON Blocks."

∎

Figure 7.30. *Declarations for Subroutine OPRATE*

```
      SUBROUTINE OPRATE (CHOICE, EXITCH)
C Performs the option selected by CHOICE

C Input Arguments
C    CHOICE - The number of the option selected (0 through EXITCH)
C    EXITCH - The number of the exit option

C Common Data
C    SCORES - Array of scores in blank COMMON
C    NAMES - Array of names in COMMON block STUDAT
C    GRADES - Array of grades in COMMON block STUDAT

C Argument Declarations
      INTEGER CHOICE, EXITCH

C Common Declarations
      INTEGER MAXSIZ
      PARAMETER (MAXSIZ = 100)
      COMMON SCORES(MAXSIZ)
      INTEGER SCORES
      COMMON /STUDAT/ NAMES(MAXSIZ), GRADES(MAXSIZ)
      CHARACTER *20 NAMES
      CHARACTER *1 GRADES

C Local Declarations
      INTEGER NUMSTU
      INTEGER MINSCR, MAXSCR
      REAL MEAN, STDEV, MEDIAN
      LOGICAL SORTED, GRADED
      INTEGER GETMIN, GETMAX
      REAL GETMED

C Save all local data between calls
      SAVE GRADED, SORTED, NUMSTU, /STUDAT/
      DATA NUMSTU /0/
```

EXAMPLE 7.11　The interface section for subroutine SORTNA ("sort by name") is shown in Fig. 7.31. The blank COMMON block and named COMMON block are both declared in SORTNA. The argument list for SORTNA contains only the dummy argument NUMSTU. The statement

```
        CALL SORTNA (NUMSTU)
```

must be used in OPRATE to call subroutine SORTNA.　∎

Figure 7.31. *Interface Section for SORTNA*

```
        SUBROUTINE SORTNA (NUMSTU)
C Sorts the data in arrays NAMES, SCORES, and GRADES. When done,
C the data will be in alphabetical order by student name.

C Input Argument
C    NUMSTU - The number of students in the arrays

C Common Data
C    SCORES - Array of scores in blank COMMON
C    NAMES - Array of names in COMMON block STUDAT
C    GRADES - Array of grades in COMMON block STUDAT

C Argument Declarations
        INTEGER NUMSTU

C Common Declarations
        INTEGER MAXSIZ
        PARAMETER (MAXSIZ = 100)
        COMMON SCORES(MAXSIZ)
        INTEGER SCORES
        COMMON /STUDAT/ NAMES(MAXSIZ), GRADES(MAXSIZ)
        CHARACTER *20 NAMES
        CHARACTER *1 GRADES
```

The COMMON statement for declaring blank and named COMMON is described in the next display.

COMMON Declaration

SYNTAX:　　COMMON *list*
　　　　　　 COMMON */name/ list*

EXAMPLE:　COMMON A, B(10)
　　　　　　 COMMON /HAT/ C, D

INTERPRETATION: The defined COMMON block is treated as one large array of consecutive memory cells containing data in the order indicated by the variables and arrays appearing in *list*. The statement

　　　　COMMON */name/ list*

defines a COMMON block called *name*. The declaration

>   COMMON *list*

defines a COMMON block with a blank name (the blank COMMON block). The COMMON declarations must precede the executable statements.
NOTE: Character data may not be placed in a COMMON block containing data of any other type (REAL, INTEGER, or LOGICAL).

Program Style

Type Declarations for COMMON Data

Each COMMON statement used in a module should be preceded or followed by one or more type declarations defining the type of each of the items listed in the COMMON statement. If arrays are included in a COMMON block, it is a good practice to define the array sizes in the COMMON statement and not in the type declarations. This can help to provide a clearer indication of the organization and structure of the COMMON block. All COMMON declarations should precede any executable statements. We recommend placing COMMON declarations at the very beginning of a main program and immediately following the argument descriptions in a subprogram.

The SAVE Statement and Named COMMON Blocks

Unlike data in the blank COMMON block, data in a named COMMON block can become undefined when a subprogram RETURN is executed. The contents of a named COMMON block are automatically saved upon return from a subprogram only if that block is declared in the main program or the subprogram that has called the current one. In all other cases, the COMMON block name must be listed in a SAVE statement to ensure that its contents are saved.

Since COMMON block STUDAT is declared in OPRATE, its contents are automatically saved upon return from any subprogram called by OPRATE. However, the SAVE statement

```
SAVE GRADED, SORTED, NUMSTU, /STUDAT/
```

is needed in OPRATE to ensure that the data in STUDAT are also saved upon return to the main program. The COMMON block name preceded and followed by a slash must be used in the SAVE list; the names of individual variables stored in blank COMMON or a named COMMON block cannot appear in a SAVE statement.

Warnings

COMMON blocks appear to be a panacea to beginning programmers because they lead to shorter argument lists and, in some cases, to the elimination of argument lists altogether. Unfortunately, improper use of COMMON blocks can cause program errors that are difficult to detect.

Passing data through argument lists has the advantage that the variables being used to pass and receive data are clearly listed in the subprogram call. This provides a valuable piece of program documentation. Conversely, there is no indication of which variables in a COMMON block are likely to be modified by a subprogram. For this reason, extensive use of COMMON blocks can lead to programs that are difficult to read, understand, and maintain.

Another problem is that as COMMON blocks grow, it becomes easier to make an error in the COMMON statement and to omit a variable name or to transpose two names. Since the correspondence between COMMON data items is based on relative position in the COMMON declaration, the wrong correspondence will be established. This error often is not detected by the compiler and is extremely difficult to find. The best way to avoid such an error is to use your system editor to duplicate the COMMON statement wherever it is needed.

Another potential problem is choosing a name for a local variable that happens to be a name listed in a COMMON statement. References to this "local variable" in the subprogram can cause the corresponding data item in COMMON to be modified as a *side effect* of the subprogram execution. This type of error is also difficult to detect and correct; it becomes more likely as the number of variables in the COMMON block increases.

The use of named COMMON blocks enables you to shorten individual COMMON statements, because only data items that are manipulated together are declared in the same named block. Also, only those named COMMON blocks that are needed by a particular subprogram are declared in that subprogram. For these reasons, it is preferable to use several named COMMON blocks instead of a single blank COMMON block.

Program Style

What to Put in COMMON Storage

The discussion in this section has focused on potential problems associated with the use of COMMON blocks. This does not mean that they should be avoided altogether, but they should be used with discretion. We recommend that you place only data that are referenced by almost all the subprograms in a program system in the blank COMMON block. You should assume that these data can be manipulated by every subprogram and would be included in almost every argument list anyway.

You can place data that are referenced by a smaller group of subprograms in a named COMMON block. Only subprograms containing the declaration of this named COMMON block will be able to manipulate these data directly. Individual variables in a named COMMON block may be passed as arguments to other subprograms that do not declare the named COMMON block.

Finally, it is reasonable to have more than one named COMMON block declared in a program. One group of subprograms may reference certain data, and another group may reference a different collection of data. By setting up several named COMMON blocks, you can restrict access to the named COMMON block(s) needed in each subprogram.

SELF-CHECK EXERCISES FOR SECTION 7.7

1. What values are printed as a result of the execution of the following program and subroutine?

```
PROGRAM TSTCOM
COMMON A, B
REAL A, B
REAL C
CALL JUMBLE (C)
PRINT *, A, B, C
STOP
END
```

```
SUBROUTINE JUMBLE (X)
REAL X
COMMON A, B
REAL A, B
A = 1.0
B = 2.0
X = 4.0
RETURN
END
```

2. What values are printed as a result of the execution of the following program and subroutines?

```
PROGRAM TEST2
COMMON /WHAT/ NEXT(5)
INTEGER NEXT
INTEGER I
CALL DEFINE(NEXT, 5)
CALL EXCH(1, 4)
I = 2
CALL EXCH(I, I+1)
PRINT *, NEXT
STOP
END
```

```
SUBROUTINE DEFINE (ARRAY, SIZE)
INTEGER SIZE, ARRAY(*)
INTEGER I
DO 40 I = 1, SIZE
    ARRAY(I) = 2 * I - 1
40 CONTINUE
RETURN
END

SUBROUTINE EXCH (S1, S2)
INTEGER S1, S2
COMMON /WHAT/ NEXT(5)
INTEGER NEXT
INTEGER TEMP
TEMP = NEXT(S1)
NEXT(S1) = NEXT(S2)
NEXT(S2) = TEMP
RETURN
END
```

What is the relationship between the variable I in the main program and the variable I in subroutine DEFINE? Why is it unnecessary to declare the COMMON block WHAT in subroutine DEFINE?

7.8 ▬▬▬ Common Programming Errors

When you use multidimensional arrays, make sure the subscript for each dimension is always in range. If any subscript value is out of range, a run-time error will occur.

If you declare a multidimensional array as a subprogram dummy argument, you must specify the correct sizes for all dimensions except the last one. The symbol * may be used to represent the size of the last dimension only.

If you use nested DO loops to process the elements of a multidimensional array, make sure the loop-control variables used as array subscripts are in the correct order. The order of the loop-control variables determines the sequence in which the array elements are processed.

Algorithms for searching and sorting arrays can sometimes cause subscript-range errors. Make sure each array reference is in range at the boundary values of the loop-control variable.

Argument list errors are the major source of difficulty in using subroutines. The actual argument list must have the same number of arguments as the dummy argument list. Also, the data type and structure (variable or array) of each actual argument must match the data type and structure of its corresponding dummy argument.

Passing some data through COMMON blocks may help to reduce the length of the argument list; however, COMMON blocks can cause problems of their own. Changing the value of a "local" variable that also happens to be declared in a COMMON block can cause a side-effect error. These errors are extremely difficult to detect, since there may be no documentation in a subroutine indicating what COMMON block data should be manipulated by the subroutine. When all data are communicated through argument lists, this documentation is automatically provided by the argument list itself. Make sure that you do not attempt to list either a dummy argument or a parameter in a COMMON block.

Chapter Review

In this chapter, we showed how to use multidimensional arrays to represent tables of information and game boards. A nested loop structure is needed to manipulate the elements of a multidimensional array in a systematic way. The correspondence between the loop-control variables and the array subscripts determines the order in which the array elements are processed.

We introduced one technique for searching an array and one technique for sorting an array. We provided several examples of subprograms with array arguments.

We also wrote a function that generates random numbers and showed how to use this function in a simulation program.

New FORTRAN Statements

The new FORTRAN statements introduced in this chapter are described in Table 7.1.

Table 7.1. *Summary of New FORTRAN Statements*

STATEMENT	EFFECT
Multidimensional Array Declaration `REAL SALES(52, 7)`	Allocates storage for 52 × 7, or 364, REAL numbers. The first subscript may represent the week (1 to 52) and the second subscript the day (1 to 7).
Array References `PRINT *, SALES(3, 5)`	Displays the sales amount for week 3 and day 5.

`DO 10 WEEK = 1, 52`
`  DO 20 DAY = 1, 7`
`    SALES(WEEK, DAY) = 0.0`
`20    CONTINUE`
`10 CONTINUE`
	Initializes each element of SALES to zero.

Array Initialization `DATA SALES /364 * 0.0/`	Initializes each element of SALES to zero.

Blank COMMON Declaration
`COMMON X(100), N`
`REAL X`
`INTEGER N`
	Declares a blank COMMON block consisting of an array X with 100 type REAL elements and an INTEGER variable N.

Named COMMON Declaration
`COMMON / INBLOK/ Y(100), Z(5)`
`REAL Y, Z`
	Declares a COMMON block named INBLOK consisting of an array Y with 100 REAL elements and an array Z with five REAL elements.

SAVE Statement `SAVE COUNT, FLAT, /INBLOK/`	Specifies that the values of local variables COUNT and FLAG and COMMON block INBLOK are to be saved between subprogram calls.

Quick-Check Exercises

1. How many subscripts can a FORTRAN array have?
2. What is the difference between row-major and column-major order? Which does FORTRAN use for array storage?
3. How many elements does array MULTI(5, -5:5, 10) have? List the first six elements in the array storage area and the last element.
4. What control structure is used to process all the elements in a multidimensional array?
5. If array LIST is an array with six REAL elements, what does the following program fragment do?

```
      DO 10 I = 1, 5
         LIST(I + 1) = LIST(1)
   10 CONTINUE
```

6. Answer exercise 5 for the program fragment

```
      DO 20 I = 2, 6
         LIST(I - 1) = LIST(I)
   20 CONTINUE
```

7. Subroutine SWITCH has two type REAL arguments, and SWITCH exchanges the values of its arguments. Write a statement that calls SWITCH to exchange the first and last elements in array LIST.
8. Are type and structure correspondence for the items in two COMMON block lists as important as for argument lists? Is this correspondence required for COMMON block lists?
9. List one advantage and two disadvantages of using COMMON blocks.
10. Are all local variable values automatically saved between calls of a subprogram with a SAVE statement? Explain your answer.

Answers to Quick-Check Exercises

1. seven
2. Row-major order means the elements are processed one row at a time; column-major order means they are processed one column at a time. FORTRAN uses column-major order.
3. 5 × 11 × 10, or 550, elements. The first six elements are MULTI(1, -5, 1), MULTI(2, -5, 1), MULTI(3, -5, 1), MULTI(4, -5, 1), MULTI(5, -5, 1), MULTI (1, -4, 1). The last element is MULTI(5, 5, 10).
4. nested DO loops
5. It copies the value of LIST(1) into all elements of array LIST.
6. It shifts all array elements up by one position (i.e., LIST(2) moves up to LIST(1), LIST(3) moves up to LIST(2), and so on.)
7. CALL SWITCH (LIST(1), LIST(6))
8. Yes, they are just as important to prevent misalignment of COMMON list elements. Type and structure correspondence of individual items are not required.

9. An advantage is shorter argument lists. One disadvantage is lack of documentation regarding the COMMON list elements that are being manipulated in a subprogram. Another disadvantage is the possibility of inadvertent side effects caused by misalignment of COMMON list items.
10. Only the local variables listed in the SAVE statement are saved. If there is no list of variables, all local variables are saved.

Review Questions

1. Declare an array that can be used to store each title of the top ten hits for each week of the year. Each title can be up to twenty characters.
2. Declare an array HOURS to store the hours that each of five employees works each day of the week, each week of the year. Write a nest of DO loops that initializes this array to all zeros. Also, provide a DATA statement that does the same task.
3. Write a program segment to display the sum of the REAL values in each row of array TABLE(5, 3). How many row sums will be displayed? How many elements are included in each sum?
4. Answer question 3 for the column sums.
5. Trace the operation of a bubble sort on the array

        20 30 25 80 40 60

   Show the array after each pass is completed.
6. Write a DO loop that shifts all elements of the array LIST(6) down one position (i.e., move LIST(1) down to LIST(2), LIST(2) down to LIST(3), and so on).
7. What is the reason for using both named COMMON and blank COMMON blocks?
8. The subroutine PSUM computes the sum of element I through J of an array. PSUM has six arguments:

   - the name of the array of items to be summed (real, input)
   - the size of the array (integer, input)
   - the index of the first array element included in the sum (integer, input)
   - the index of the last array element included in the sum (integer, input)
   - a flag used to indicate whether an illegal array index occurred (an array index is illegal if it is out of bounds or if the index of the first element to be summed exceeds the index of the last element to be summed) (logical, output)
   - the sum of the selected elements (sum is zero if an index is illegal) (real, output)

   Write a CALL statement for each of the circumstances described below. Assume A is a real array of MAXSIZ elements and FIRST and LAST are integer variables. Use the actual output arguments VALID (logical) and SUM (real) for each reference to PSUM.
   a. Compute the sum of all of the elements of A.
   b. Compute the sum of the FIRST through LAST elements of A.
   c. Compute the sum of the FIRST + 4 through LAST elements of A.

d. Compute the sum of the second through seventh elements of A.

e. Compute the sum of the FIRST through 2 * LAST elements of A.

9. Assume that A, MAXSIZ, FIRST, and LAST contain the values shown.

A(1)	A(2)	A(3)	A(4)	A(5)	A(6)	A(7)	A(8)	A(9)	A(10)
4.2	1.1	0.0	3.0	7.1	2.2	0.0	8.1	3.7	6.8

MAXSIZ	FIRST	LAST
10	3	6

What are the values of SUM and VALID after execution of each of the CALL statements you wrote for question 8?

10. Write the COMMON declaration and type declarations needed to define a COMMON block named EMPBLK, which contains the following items in the order listed:
   - an integer array NUMDEP of size 50
   - a real array SALARY of size 100
   - an integer variable N
   - an integer variable COUNT
   - a real variable X
   - a real variable Y

   Could you include a CHARACTER *30 array NAME in this COMMON block?

11. Write the subroutine PSUM described in question 8.

Programming Projects

1. Use a two-dimensional array of individual characters to store a collection of five words where each word is up to twenty characters in length. Enter each word one character at a time. For each word read, your program should do the following:
   a. Print the actual length of the word.
   b. Count the number of occurrences of four-letter words.

2. The results from the mayor's race have been reported by each precinct as follows:

Precinct	Candidate A	Candidate B	Candidate C	Candidate D
1	192	48	206	37
2	147	90	312	21
3	186	12	121	38
4	114	21	408	39
5	267	13	382	29

Write a program to do the following:

a. Print the table with appropriate headings for the rows and columns.

b. Compute and print the total number of votes received by each candidate and the percentage of the total votes cast.

c. If any one candidate received over 50 percent of the votes, the program should print a message declaring that candidate the winner.

d. If no candidate received 50 percent of the votes, the program should print a message declaring a run-off between the two candidates receiving the highest number of votes; the two candidates should be identified by their letter names.

e. Run the program once with the above data and once with candidate C receiving only 108 votes in precinct 4.

3. Write a subroutine, MERGE, that will merge together the contents of two sorted (ascending order) real arrays A and B, storing the result (still in ascending order) in the real array C.

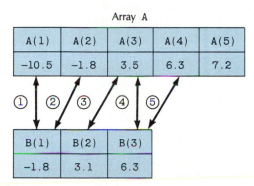

Array A

A(1)	A(2)	A(3)	A(4)	A(5)
-10.5	-1.8	3.5	6.3	7.2

B(1)	B(2)	B(3)
-1.8	3.1	6.3

Array B

Array C

C(1)	C(2)	C(3)	C(4)	C(5)	C(6)
-10.5	-1.8	3.1	3.5	6.3	7.2

Hint: When one of the input arrays has been exhausted, do not forget to copy the remaining data in the other array into the array C. Test your subroutine using a representative set of unsorted data in the arrays A and B. Sort both arrays before calling your MERGE subroutine. Use either COMMON blocks or subprogram arguments for data communication among the various modules that you write.

4. The binary search algorithm below may be used to search an array when the elements are in order.

Algorithm for Binary Search

1. Let BOTTOM be the subscript of the first array element.
2. Let TOP be N.

3. Let FOUND be false.
4. DO WHILE BOTTOM is less than TOP and FOUND is false
     5. Let MIDDLE be the subscript of the element halfway between BOTTOM and TOP.
     6. IF the element at MIDDLE is the KEY THEN
        Set FOUND to true and INDEX to MIDDLE.
       ELSE IF the element at MIDDLE is larger than KEY THEN
        Let TOP be MIDDLE-1.
       ELSE
        Let BOTTOM be MIDDLE+1.
       ENDIF
  ENDDO

Write and test subroutine BNSRCH. Which of the subroutines SEARCH and BNSRCH do you think is faster when N is a large number?

5. The selection sort is another technique for sorting an array. In the selection sort, the first pass through the array finds the largest value in the array and the subscript of the largest value. The largest value is then switched with the value in the last position of the array. This puts the largest value in the last position, where it belongs, much like the bubble sort. The process is then repeated (the second pass) but the last position is not included in the search for the largest value. After the second pass, the second-largest value is now known and can be switched with the value currently in the second position from the end of the array. This process continues until each item is in its correct location and requires N-1 passes to sort an array of N elements (why?). Write and test a subroutine that implements this method to sort an array.

ᴹ 6. Write a program fragment that will determine the dot product of two square (N × N) arrays. The dot product, array C, of some elements of arrays A and B is defined as

```
C(1,1) = A(1,1) * B(1,1) + A(1,2) * B(2,1) + A(1,3) * B(3,1)
C(2,3) = A(2,1) * B(1,3) + A(2,2) * B(2,3) + A(2,3) * B(3,3)
C(i,j) = A(i,1) * B(1,j) + A(i,2) * B(2,j) + A(i,3) * B(3,j)
```

The dot product of arrays A and B is shown below.

$$
N = 3
$$

$$
A = \begin{vmatrix} 4 & 5 & 1 \\ 0 & 2 & 5 \\ 1 & 6 & 1 \end{vmatrix} \quad B = \begin{vmatrix} 2 & 1 & 10 \\ 5 & 20 & 0 \\ 4 & 0 & 5 \end{vmatrix}
$$

$$
C = \begin{vmatrix} 37 & 104 & 45 \\ 30 & 40 & 25 \\ 36 & 121 & 15 \end{vmatrix}
$$

7. Write a program to test the uniform nature of function RANDOM in Fig. 7.25. Use this function to generate 500 integer values between 1 and 10, save the occurrence counts in an array, and then draw a bar graph of the occurrence counts. We would expect to see approximately the same number of occurrences of each integer.

8. Write a program that simulates the movement of radioactive particles in a two-dimensional shield around a reactor. A particle in the shield can move in one of four directions. The direction for the next second of travel is determined by generation of a random number between 1 and 4 (forward, backward, left, right). A change in direction is interpreted as a collision with another particle, which results in a dissipation of energy. Each particle can have only a limited number of collisions before it dies. For each particle that enters the shield, determine whether that particle exits the shield before it dies. A particle exits the shield if its net forward travel time is N seconds before K collisions occur (i.e., it takes N more forward steps than backward steps). Determine the percentage of particles that exit the shield where N, K, and the number of particles are data items.

9. For the case study in Section 7.2, we wrote a program that removed noise from a picture. We can generate a noisy image from a nonnoisy one by adding random noise. Write a program that randomly selects the coordinates of several points (say 10 percent of the total) in a two-dimensional image and then randomly selects an integer value for that pixel. Next, for each pixel that is not on the edge of the image, select one of three values (−1, 0, 1) at random and add it to the pixel value. Make sure you change any negative pixel values back to zero. After perturbing your image in this way, run it through the image enhancement program to see what you get.

10. Mahogany Airlines stores its reservation information in a file RESERV. For each flight, there are up to 100 lines of information, one for each row in the plane. Each line consists of up to ten values, one for each seat in a row. For any seat, a value of 0 indicates the seat is empty; a value of 1 indicates that the seat is full.

    Write a FORTRAN program to read the reservation information on file RESERV into a two-dimensional integer array SEATS and find and print all pairs of adjacent empty seats. You may ignore the aisles in the plane and assume that seats on either side of an aisle are adjacent; thus, the location of the aisle(s) is irrelevant to the problem. If more than two adjacent seats are empty, all adjacent empty pairs should still be printed (for example, if four adjacent seats are empty, three pairs should be printed).

    Use PARAMETER statements wherever possible, in case larger planes are ever built (of course, they already exist).

    Your output should appear as follows.

```
              MAHOGANY AIRLINES
        ADJACENT PAIRS OF SEATS ANALYSIS

             Available Seat Pairs

        Row Number      Seat Number
        _____      _____

           xxx             xx-xx
           xxx             xx-xx
            .               .
            .               .
            .               .
```

11. Statistical analysis of data makes heavy use of arrays. One such analysis, called cross-tabulation, is used to help decide whether a relationship exists between two or more variables. For example, the following data might represent opinions from a survey taken concerning an amendment to the U.S. Constitution making it illegal to destroy or damage the U.S. flag in any way.

	Sex		*Row*
Opinion	*Male*	*Female*	*Total*
In Favor	63	27	90
Opposed	19	42	61
No Opinion	6	39	45
Column Total	88	108	196

Write a FORTRAN program that will read in the pairs of male/female response totals (one pair per line)

```
63   27
19   42
 6   39
```

and print out the above cross-tabulation matrix including the row totals and the column totals.

The program should also print out the percentage in each category. For example, we would want to know that the 39 females with no opinion represent 36 percent of the total females interviewed and 87 percent of those with no opinion. Make the percentage tabulation and, for that matter, all output as attractive as possible.

12. The game of Life, invented by John H. Conway, is supposed to model the genetic laws for birth, survival, and death (see *Scientific American*, October 1970, p. 120). We will play it on a board consisting of twenty-five squares in the horizontal and vertical directions. Each square can be empty or contain an X indicating the presence of an organism. Each square (except the border squares) has eight neighbors. The small square shown in the segment of the board drawn below connects the neighbors of the organism in row three, column three.

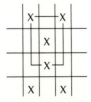

Generation 1

The next generation of organisms is determined according to the following criteria:

a. Birth: An organism will be born in each empty location that has exactly three neighbors.

b. Death: An organism with four or more organisms as neighbors will die from overcrowding. An organism with fewer than two neighbors will die from loneliness.

c. Survival: An organism with two or three neighbors will survive to the next generation. Generations 2 and 3 for the sample follow:

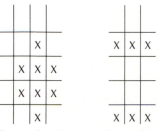

Generation 2   Generation 3

Read in an initial configuration of organisms. Print the original game array, calculate the next generation of organisms in a new array, copy the new array into the original game array, and repeat the cycle for as many generations as you wish. *Hint:* Assume that the borders of the game array are infertile regions where organisms can neither survive nor be born; you will not have to process the border squares.

13. A mail order house with the physical facilities for stocking up to twenty items decides that it wants to maintain inventory control records on a small computer. For each stock item, the following data are to be stored on the computer:
   1. the stock number (a five-digit integer)
   2. a count of the number of items on hand
   3. the total year-to-date sales count
   4. the price
   5. the date (month and day) of the last order for restocking an item (a four-digit integer of the form MMDD)
   6. the number of items ordered

   Both items 5 and 6 will be zero if there is no outstanding order for an item.

   Design and implement a program system to keep track of the data listed in 1 through 6. You will need six arrays, each of size 20. Your system should contain subprograms to perform the following tasks:
   a. Change the price of an item (given the item stock number and the new price).
   b. Add a new item to the inventory list (given the item number, the price, and the initial stock on hand).
   c. Enter information about the date and size of a restock order.
   d. Reset items 5 and 6 to zero and update the amount on hand when a restock order is received.
   e. Increase the total sales and decrease the count on hand each time a purchase order is received (if the order cannot be filled, print a message to that effect and reset the counts).
   f. Search for the array element that contains a given stock number.

The following information should be initially stored in memory (using data initialization (DATA) statements). This information should be printed at the start of execution of your program system.

Stock Numbers	On-Hand Count	Price
02421	12	100.00
00801	24	32.49
63921	50	4.99
47447	100	6.99
47448	48	2.25
19012	42	18.18
86932	3	67.20

Write a menu-driven program that can be used to keep the inventory up-to-date. Your program should handle options a through f by reading in the required data and calling the appropriate subprogram. Each subprogram should print an appropriate informative message for each transaction, indicating whether the transaction was processed and giving other pertinent information about changes in the stored data that were affected by the processing of the transaction.

14. Write a program that reads the five cards representing a poker hand into a two-dimensional array (first dimension—suit, second dimension—rank). Evaluate the poker hand by using functions to determine whether the hand is a flush (all one suit), a straight (five consecutive cards), a straight flush (five consecutive cards of one suit), four of a kind, a full house (three of one kind, two of another), three of a kind, two pair, or one pair.

8. Formats and Files

N SECTION 4.6, we introduced FORMAT statements and described how to use them with PRINT statements. In this chapter, we will provide additional features of formatted output and describe formatted input.

In Section 1.9, we explained how to store data on secondary storage devices such as disks. The use of secondary storage enables us to save *files of data* that may contain much more information than can normally be saved in main memory. A file saved on disk also has the advantage that it is *permanent* and will remain in secondary memory (disk) even after our program has stopped running.

In this chapter, we will review how to instruct a FORTRAN program to read its data from a file and/or to save its output results in a file. We will see that all FORTRAN files can be accessed in sequential order, starting with the first file *record*. Also, we will learn how to create and process files (called *direct access files*) whose records can be accessed in arbitrary or random order.

8.1 ▭ Review of Formatted Output

This section provides a brief review of formatted output statements. It also introduces two new edit descriptors, T and /.

The T Descriptor   We discussed the alignment of output columns in Section 4.6. The X descriptor was used to position output data under column headings. This can be done more easily using the T descriptor, which is analogous to setting a tab position on a typewriter.

EXAMPLE 8.1   The statements below print a line of column headings at the top of a page followed by a line of output data.

```
      PRINT 35
 35 FORMAT ('1', 'NAME', T15, 'SALARY', T25, 'DEPENDENTS')
      PRINT 45, NAME, GROSS, DEPEND
 45 FORMAT (1X, A10, T15, F6.2, T25, I5)
```

```
NAME        SALARY      DEPENDENTS
CALDWELL    347.82          3
```

The edit descriptors T15 and T25 cause an advance to positions 15 and 25 of the output line. You must be careful when specifying tab positions. For example, in FORMAT 35, if T20 was specified instead of T25, SALARDEPENDENTS would be printed as the second column heading.   ■

The Slash Descriptor

We can use a single FORMAT statement to describe the appearance of more than one line of output. The slash, /, may be used in a format specification to separate the description of one output line from the next. When a slash is encountered, the current line is terminated, and a new line is started.

A string of consecutive slashes has the effect of causing blank lines to appear on a page. The number of blank lines will be one less than the number of consecutive slashes if the slashes are in the middle of the format specification. The number of blank lines will be equal to the number of slashes if the slashes appear at the very beginning or very end of the format specification. Commas are not required to separate consecutive slashes nor to separate slashes from other format descriptors. A large number of consecutive slashes may be indicated using the descriptor form $n(/)$, where n is a positive integer constant indicating the number of slashes to be used.

EXAMPLE 8.2

The statements

```
        PRINT 18, X, Y
    18 FORMAT (1X, F8.2, 5(/), 1X, F8.2)
```

cause four blank lines to appear between the values of X and Y. The first slash in FORMAT 18 terminates the output line containing the value of X; the next four slashes terminate blank output lines.

The format specification begins with the edit descriptor 1X, which represents a blank space. This blank would be used for carriage control.   ∎

EXAMPLE 8.3

The Raisem Higher Home Loan Association maintains lists of home loan mortgage interest payments. A sample page of these lists is shown next.

```
RAISEM HIGHER HOME LOAN ASSOCIATION          07-04-91

HOME LOAN MORTGAGE INTEREST PAYMENT TABLES

AMOUNT = $30000.00       LOAN DURATION (MONTHS) = 300

RATE (PERCENT)     MONTHLY PAYMENT       TOTAL PAYMENT
    10.50              XXX.XX               XXXXXX.XX
    10.75              XXX.XX               XXXXXX.XX
      .                   .                     .
      .                   .                     .
      .                   .                     .
    13.50              349.69               104908.04
      .                   .                     .
      .                   .                     .
      .                   .                     .
    16.00              XXX.XX               XXXXXX.XX
```

The person who wrote the program to print this table used six variables:

1. the date the loan was made (CHARACTER *8 DATE)
2. the amount of the loan (REAL AMOUNT)
3. the period of time (in months) for loan repayment (INTEGER MONTHS)
4. the interest rate (percent) applied to the loan (REAL RATE)
5. the monthly payment required from borrower (REAL MPAYMT)
6. total amount to be paid over entire loan period (REAL TPAYMT)

The program contains three PRINT statements:

```
a.    PRINT 26, DATE, AMOUNT, MONTHS
     26 FORMAT ('1', 'RAISEM HIGHER HOME LOAN ASSOCIATION', 9X, A8/
        A '0', 'HOME LOAN MORTGAGE INTEREST PAYMENT TABLES'/
        B '0', 'AMOUNT = $', F8.2, 6X, 'LOAN DURATION (MONTHS) = ', I3)
b.    PRINT 27
     27 FORMAT ('0', 'RATE (PERCENT)', 4X, 'MONTHLY PAYMENT', 4X,
        + 'TOTAL PAYMENT')
c.    PRINT 28, RATE, MPAYMT, TPAYMT
     28 FORMAT (1X, 5X, F5.2, 13X, F6.2, 10X, F9.2)
```

Together these three statements produce the sample page of output just shown. Statement a prints the three lines of page-heading information that appear at the top of the page. The values of the variables DATE, AMOUNT, and MONTHS are included as part of the heading. Statement b prints the column heading labels, and statement c is used inside a loop in the program to print the numbers appearing in each output line, the values of RATE, MPAYMT, TPAYMT.

You should convince yourself that FORMATS 26, 27, and 28 do indeed produce the output shown in Example 8.3. To help you, Table 8.1 provides a detailed description of the formation of the three output lines defined in FORMAT 26.   ∎

8.2 ▬▬▬ Input Formats

Partitioning a Data Line into Fields

The function of an input format is analogous to that of an output format. Output formats provide a line-by-line description of the external appearance of data that are to be printed. Input formats, on the other hand, are normally used to describe the line-by-line appearance of input data.

The format specification in a formatted READ statement partitions the data line (sometimes called a *record*) into fields. It may cause some columns to be skipped and enables strings to be typed without enclosing quotes.

As was the case with list-directed input, each execution of a READ statement causes at least one new data line to be read. The data items in these lines are placed into the memory cells designated by the input list.

Table 8.1.
FORMAT Statement 26

EDIT DESCRIPTOR	CORRESPONDING OUTPUT LIST ITEM	MEANING
Line 1 of FORMAT 26		
'1', 'RAISEM . . . ASSOCIATION'	None	The string 'RAISEM . . . ASSOCIATION' is to be entered into the line being formed. (The 1 is not printed; it is used for carriage control.)
9X	None	A field of 9 blanks is to be entered into the line being formed.
A8	DATE	A field of width 8 (8 print positions) is to be used to print the character string stored in DATE.
/	None	Indicates the end of the output line being formed.
Continuation Line A		
'0', 'HOME . . . TABLES'	None	The string 'HOME . . . TABLES' is to be entered into the line being formed. (The 0 is not printed; it is used for carriage control.)
/	None	Indicates the end of an output line.
Continuation Line B		
'0', 'AMOUNT = $'	None	The string 'AMOUNT = $' is to be entered into the line being formed. (The 0 is not printed; it is used for carriage control.)
F8.2	AMOUNT	A field of width 8 is to be used to print the real number stored in AMOUNT (two digits will appear to the right of the decimal point).
6X	None	Skip 6 spaces.
'LOAN . . . MONTHS) = '	None	The string 'LOAN . . . MONTHS) = ' is to be entered into the line being formed.
I3	MONTHS	A field of width 3 is to be used to print the integer stored in MONTHS.

EXAMPLE 8.4   If the data 07–04–91 are typed in columns 1–8 of a data line, then the statements

```
      READ 62, MONTH, DAY, YEAR
   62 FORMAT (I2, 1X, I2, 1X, I2)
```

will have the effect shown below.

MONTH	DAY	YEAR
7	4	91

FORMAT 62 partitions the data line into five fields, as shown below. Three of these fields contain integer data that are stored in memory, and two fields (columns 3 and 6) are skipped. The column numbers are shown under the data. ∎

```
07 – 04 – 91
1 2  3 4 5  6  7 8 9 10 . . .
```

EXAMPLE 8.5   The list-directed READ statement

```
READ *, FIRST, LAST, IDEMPL, HOURS, RATE, OTHRS
```

```
'JOHN' 'CAGE' 37458   35.0 6.75   0.0
1 2 3 4 5 6 7 8 9 1011121314151617181920212223242526272829303132333435
```

will cause the data line that follows it to be read and its contents to be stored in memory, as shown below where FIRST and LAST are type CHARACTER *4.

FIRST	LAST	IDEMPL	HOURS	RATE	OTHRS
JOHN	CAGE	37458	35.0	6.75	0.0

Character data   Integer data   Real data

Given a similar line without apostrophes, the statements

```
      READ 25, FIRST, LAST, EMPLNO, HOURS, RATE, OTHRS
   25 FORMAT (1X, A4, 3X, A4, 2X, I5, 1X, F5.1, 1X, F4.2, 1X, F4.1)
```

will have the same effect. FORMAT 25 partitions the data line into the fields shown below.

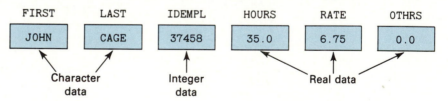

```
 |JOHN|   |CAGE|   |37458| 35.0| |6.75| |0.0 |
1 |2 3 4 5| 6 7 8| 9 101112|1314|1516171819|20|2122232425|26|27282930|31|32333435|
```

To see why the second set of statements has the same effect as the first statement, it is necessary to understand the meaning of the edit descriptors listed in FORMAT 25. They are described in Table 8.2. ∎

Table 8.2. *Meaning of Edit Descriptors in FORMAT 25*

EDIT DESCRIPTOR	CORRESPONDING INPUT LIST ITEM	MEANING
1X	None	Skip the first column in the line.
A4	FIRST	The next four columns in the line (2–5, in this case) are to be treated as a field containing a string (JOHN), which is to be stored in the variable FIRST.
3X	None	Skip the next three columns in the line (columns 6, 7, and 8).
A4	LAST	The next four columns in the line (9–12) are to be treated as a field containing a string (CAGE), which is to be stored in the variable LAST.
2X	None	Skip the next two columns in the line (columns 13, 14).
I5	EMPLNO	The next five columns (15–19) are to be treated as containing a 5-digit integer (37458) to be stored in variable EMPLNO.
1X	None	Skip the next column in the line (column 20).
F5.1	HOURS	The next five columns (21–25) are to be treated as containing a real number (35.0) with one digit (0) to the right of the decimal point. This number is to be stored in variable HOURS.
1X	None	Skip the next column in the line (column 26).
F4.2	RATE	The next four columns (27–30) are to be treated as containing a real number (6.75) with two digits (75) to the right of the decimal point. This number is to be stored in variable RATE.
1X	None	Skip the next column in the line (column 31).
F4.1	OTHRS	The next four columns (32–35) are to be treated as containing a real number (0.0), with one digit to the right of the decimal point. This number is to be stored in the variable OTHRS.

The rules that must be followed when using formatted input are summarized next.

Rules for Formatted Input

1. The FORMAT statement determines which data columns are to be skipped and which are to be read. It also describes the type and width (number of columns) of the information contained in each field and the number of decimal places in each type real data item.
2. As is the case with output formats, all edit descriptors in an input format except the slash should be separated from one another with commas.
3. The data descriptors (A, F, or I) must be compatible with the corresponding variable type (character, real, or integer). Also, the type of data in the data field must be compatible with the data descriptor (i.e., digits and a sign for I; digits, a sign, and a decimal point for F).
4. The field width (w) information for each data descriptor, where w is an integer constant, immediately follows the type indication.
   - Aw: The A indicates that a string of characters is to be read into a memory cell; the w indicates the total width (or number of characters) contained in the string. If the w is omitted, the field width is the same as the length of the corresponding input variable. Any legal FORTRAN character may appear in the string. If the length, w, of the data string is less than the length, n, of the variable, then the string will be stored with blank padding on the right. If the length, w, of the data string is greater than the length, n, of the variable, then only the rightmost n characters of the string will be stored.
   - Iw: I indicates that a type integer value is to be read. The w indicates the width (the number of decimal digits) contained in the integer.
   - $Fw.d$: F indicates that a type real value is to be read. The w indicates the total width (including the sign and the decimal point); the d indicates the number of decimal places in the real number that are assumed to be to the right of the decimal point if no explicit decimal point appears.
5. The edit descriptor nX indicates that a field of n columns is to be skipped. These columns need not contain blanks; they will be skipped regardless of what they contain.
6. It is not necessary that the data occupying a character, integer, or real data field fill the entire field. However, the following guidelines should be followed:
   a. Integer values should appear in the rightmost portion of the field;
   b. Real values may appear anywhere in the field as long as the decimal point is included. If the decimal point is not typed, the number should appear in the rightmost portion of the field, and the decimal point will

be assumed to be placed as indicated by the *d* parameter of the format descriptor. If the decimal point is typed, then it overrides the *d* parameter in the F*w.d* edit descriptor.

7. A single FORMAT statement may be used to describe the layout of more than one line. The edit descriptor slash, /, can be used to mark the end of the description of one line and the start of the description of a new line.

Rule 6 is concerned with the position of real and integer values in a data field. These values generally should be right-justified, since some systems may read any blanks in an integer or real data field as zeros. An I or F field with all blanks will be read as the number 0. Real values may be typed with or without a decimal point.

EXAMPLE 8.6   Given the READ statement

```
      READ 672, X, Y, Z
672 FORMAT (F4.1, F4.2, F4.2)
```

and the data line

the real variables X, Y, and Z will be defined as

X	Y	Z
-2.5	6.3	.623

In the first field, the decimal point is assumed to be between the 2 and the 5, according to the format descriptor F4.1. In the last two fields, the decimal point overrides the format descriptor. ∎

EXAMPLE 8.7   The FORMAT statement

```
562 FORMAT (A8 / F10.4 / I6, I4)
```

describes the appearance of three lines. The first line is described as containing one field that is to be treated as a character string of width 8. The second line is described as having a field of width 10 containing a real number. If the decimal point is not typed in this number, it will be assumed to be between the digits in columns 6 and 7. The third line is described as containing two integer fields, the first of width 6 and the second of width 4. ∎

The general form of the edit descriptors used in input formats is summarized in Table 8.3.

Table 8.3. *Edit Descriptors for Formatted Input*

EDIT DESCRIPTOR	MEANING
nX	A field of n columns is to be skipped.
Iw	A field of width w (w columns) is to be treated as an integer.
Aw	A field of width w is to be treated as a character string. The w may be omitted.
F$w.d$	A field of width w is to be treated as a real number with d digits to the right of the decimal point. If a decimal point is present, it overrides the d specification.

It is often desirable to echo print data being read. In such cases, it is tempting to try to use the same FORMAT statement for both the READ and the PRINT statements. You should avoid this temptation because there is no guarantee that the first character read will be suitable for use as a carriage-control character for printing.

The E Format Descriptor*

Another method for reading (or displaying) real numbers is to use the E format descriptor (rather than F). A number to be read under E format must be typed in exponential notation, using the letter E. The E descriptor E$w.d$ contains a total width specification, w, and a count of the number of decimal digits to the right of the decimal point, d. However, the width specification must include not only the sign and the decimal point (if present), but also the letter E and the sign and the value of the integer exponent. Thus, in the E format descriptor, w should normally be larger than $d + 5$.

For example, the number

$$-6.245\text{E}-6$$

could be read using a format descriptor of E9.3. Here again, if the decimal point appears in the data line, it overrides the d parameter of the E descriptor.

The E format descriptor may also be used for printing real data. It is often convenient to use the E descriptor when the magnitude of a real number is not known, or it is so large that the use of the F format descriptor is impractical. Real data printed using the E format descriptor will usually appear in the form

$$\pm 0.\text{X}_1\text{X}_2 \ldots \text{X}_d\text{E}\pm exp$$

where the X_i are the d most significant digits of the number (after rounding) and exp is the base 10 exponent. When the E descriptor is used for output, w must include the zero (if present), the two signs, the decimal point, the E, and

---

* This section may be omitted.

the width of the exponent, as well as the d digits to the right of the decimal point. Therefore, w should always be greater than $d + 7$ when E$w.d$ is used in output (the exponent should not exceed two digits in width).

EXAMPLE 8.8

The READ statement

```
        READ 37, INDEX, A, B, C
     37 FORMAT (I5, E10.3, E10.3, E10.3)
```

will cause the information in the data line

36	6.107E+02	3.993E+4	−92.6E−3
1 2 3 4 5	6 7 8 9 10 11 12 13 14 15	16 17 18 19 20 21 22 23 24 25	26 27 28 29 30 31 32 33 34 35

to be placed in the named variables as shown below. ∎

INDEX	A	B	C
36	610.7	39930.0	−.0926

SELF-CHECK EXERCISES FOR SECTION 8.2

1. You are given a data line with the following format:

Columns	Contents	Sample Data
1–11	Social security number	552–63–0179
12–31	Last name	BROWN
32–44	First name	JERRY
45	Middle initial	L
46–48	Blanks	
49–50	Age	38
51–54	Blanks	
55–59	Total years of education	23
60–63	Blanks	
64–66	Occupation code	12
67–80	Blanks	

Assign variable names to the data in each of the nonblank fields. Give these names appropriate types and write a READ statement and appropriate FORMAT for reading such a line. Draw a picture of the line and show how the sample data would be arranged in each field (left-adjusted, right-adjusted, and so on).

2. Design a data line layout for an account records program. For each account, the following information must appear on a single line:

Information	Form
Account number	a 6-digit integer
Name of firm	character string (maximum width of 25)

Information	*Form*
Previous account balance	a real number between −9999.99 and 9999.99
Charges for current month	a real number between 0.0 and 999.99
Credits for current month	a real number between 0.0 and 999.99
Total amount due	a real number between −999.99 and 999.99

You should ensure that there is at least one space between each of the six data items listed. Write the appropriate variable declarations, READ statement, and FORMAT statement for reading in the line that you designed.

3. Suppose you decided that you did not want to have to type the decimal points in the four real values in exercise 2 and that you didn't want to bother typing zero entries (if any) for these four values. Will your FORTRAN statements for exercise 2 still work? Why? If not, change them.

4. You are given the following declarations and READ statement:

```
REAL ALPHA, BETA
INTEGER GAMMA, EPS
CHARACTER *4 DELTA
READ 30, ALPHA, GAMMA, DELTA, BETA, EPS
```

Write FORMAT 30 so that the information in the three data lines shown on the left will be read in as indicated on the right.

```
16.3
1 2 3 4 5 6 7 8 9 1011

   12  DAWN
1 2 3 4 5 6 7 8 9 1011

   −32.1 49
1 2 3 4 5 6 7 8 9 1011
```

ALPHA	GAMMA	DELTA	BETA	EPS
16.3	12	DAWN	−32.1	49

5. How would you type the data shown in exercise 4 if FORMAT 30 appeared as shown below?

```
30 FORMAT (F3.1, I2, A4, F4.1, 3X, I3)
```

8.3 ▭ Using Formats with Arrays

When using formats with arrays, the compiler requires an edit descriptor for each array element read or printed. If the FORMAT statement does not have enough edit descriptors, it will be reused as explained below.

EXAMPLE 8.9

Given the declaration

    INTEGER K(4)

and the PRINT statement

    PRINT 10, K

FORMAT 10 should have four edit descriptors beginning with the letter I. They can be provided individually, as in

    10 FORMAT (1X, I3, 2X, I3, 2X, I3, 2X, I3, 2X)

or by specifying the *repetition* of one or more edit descriptors, as in

    10 FORMAT (1X, 4(I3, 2X))

In FORMAT 10 above, the notation 4(I3, 2X) indicates that the *descriptor group* (I3, 2X) is to be repeated four times. ∎

EXAMPLE 8.10

Let W be a real array consisting of 200 elements. We wish to print the elements of W in 10 columns across a line. We can do this using the following PRINT and FORMAT statements:

    PRINT 62, W
    62 FORMAT (20(1X, 10F12.3/))

The descriptors that are repeated (1X, 10F12.3/) describe a single line consisting of ten real numbers, each of width 12, with three digits to the right of the decimal point. The slash (/) is used to mark the end of the line. Without the slash, some compilers assume that all 200 real elements of W are to be printed in F12.3 format on the same line. It is not likely that a printer exists that can accommodate such a long line—2,400 characters. The repeat count 20 will cause the line description (1X, 10F12.3/) to be repeated twenty times during the printing of the array W. Each time, a blank will be used for carriage control resulting in single-line spacing. ∎

In all our previous examples, the number of *data descriptors* (beginning with I, F, or A) appearing in a format specification matched the number of items to be read or printed. If there are not enough data descriptors in a format specification to satisfy the input or output list, then the format specification will be automatically reused. Thus, input or output continues until all items specified in the list have been processed, regardless of the number of data descriptors in the format. This feature can be extremely useful when the exact number of array elements to be processed depends on a value that is determined during program execution.

EXAMPLE 8.11

Again, let W be a real array of 200 elements and let N be an integer variable used to indicate the number of data items to be stored in W. If the value of N is typed on one line (in I3 format) and the N values to be read into W are typed on successive data lines (8 items per line in F10.3 format), then the statements

```
    READ 40, N
40  FORMAT (I3)
    READ 50, (W(I), I = 1, N)
50  FORMAT (8F10.3)
```

can be used to read in N, and the items to be stored in array W. FORMAT 50 will work regardless of the size of N (as long as N is in range). Each time the format specification is exhausted during the execution of the READ 50 statement, a new line will be read and the format specification will be reused automatically. The format still describes the layout of a single line, but it will be repeated as often as necessary, until all N elements of W have been filled with data.

The statements

```
    PRINT 60
60  FORMAT ('1', 'THE DATA IN W ARE:')
    PRINT 70, (W(I), I = 1, N)
70  FORMAT (1X, 12F10.3)
```

print a short heading at the top of a page and then print the data in the array W, 12 items per line. FORMAT 70 describes a single line of output, but the format specification will be reused as often as necessary until all N elements in W have been printed. Each time the format is reused, a new line is started, and a blank is used for carriage control.   ∎

The input or output list in a READ or PRINT statement completely determines the number of data items to be processed regardless of the number of data descriptors in the associated FORMAT statement. During processing, each item in the input or output list is matched with the corresponding data descriptor. If there are more data descriptors than items in the input or output list, any extra data descriptors are ignored (although leftover space descriptors, including strings, are processed up to the next data descriptor).

If there are more items than data descriptors, all or part of the format specification will be reused. If the format specification contains no internal parentheses, the entire format specification will be reused. If the format specification contains internal parentheses, format control reverts to the left parenthesis that matches the next-to-last right parenthesis. The re-scan of the format specification will begin with the repetition count, if any, preceding this left parenthesis.

Reading Character Arrays

A formatted READ can be very useful in reading textual data. To store a paragraph or page of text in memory, we would normally type the information on consecutive data lines. Each eighty-column line could then be entered into a separate element of an array, as shown below.

```
      INTEGER MAXLIN, NUMLIN, CURLIN
      PARAMETER (MAXLIN = 1000)
      CHARACTER *80 TEXT(MAXLIN)
      READ *, NUMLIN
      DO 10 CURLIN = 1, NUMLIN
         READ 17, TEXT(CURLIN)
17       FORMAT (A80)
10 CONTINUE
```

The array TEXT declared above has 1000 elements where each element can be used to store a string of eighty characters. FORMAT 17 specifies that each line contains a single character data field of length 80. The input variable NUMLIN determines how many lines will be read (NUMLIN must be between 1 and MAXLIN).

Often, we wish to examine individual characters of a string. For example, we might want to know how many times the letter E or the word THE occurs in a string. One way to do this would be to read each character of a data line into a separate element of a character array using a formatted READ, as shown in the following example. We will study other techniques for manipulating character strings in the next chapter.

EXAMPLE 8.12

The following statements can be used to read the contents of an eighty-character line into an eighty-element array.

```
      CHARACTER *1 BUFFER(80)
      READ 27, BUFFER
27 FORMAT (80A1)
```

FORMAT 27 specifies that the data line contains eighty individual character fields of width one. Consequently, each column will be stored separately in an element of the array BUFFER. We can then process any character on the data line by specifying its corresponding array subscript (e.g., BUFFER(1) represents the first column).

The statement

```
      READ '(80A)', BUFFER
```

would have the same effect as the READ 27 statement. Each line contains eighty fields; the width of each field must be the same as the length of an element of BUFFER (length 1). ∎

1. How would array W be printed if FORMAT 62 in Example 8.10 were rewritten as

   ```
   62 FORMAT (1X, 10F12.3)
   ```

2. What would happen if FORMATS 17 and 27 were interchanged in the two code segments shown in the subsection "Reading Character Arrays"?

3. Describe the information read by the following statements for the line images shown. For b and c, remember that multiple format descriptors are required when an array name (without a subscript) appears in the input list. (You may assume that the variables involved in each operation have been declared consistent with the type of the data.)

   a.
   ```
       READ 527, COLOR, ID, COST
   527 FORMAT (3X, A4, 5X, I5, 3X, F6.2)

          BLUE      37288    672.25
      1 2 3 4 5 6 7 8 9 10111213141516171819202122232425 26
   ```

   b.
   ```
      READ 65, NAME, FLIGHT, AIRLIN, DATE
   65 FORMAT (A3, 3X, I3, A6, I2, 1X, I2, 1X, I2)
   ```

   Assume DATE is an integer array of size 3.

   ```
      DEBBIE698UNITED06/13/90
      1 2 3 4 5 6 7 8 9 1011121314151617181920212223
   ```

   c.
   ```
        READ 2231, NAME, AB, RUNS, HITS, RBI, AVE
   2231 FORMAT (A4, A4, I3, I3, I3, I3, F5.3)
   ```

   Assume NAME is a string array of size 2.

   ```
      ELIEKOFF6241262140420.312
      1 2 3 4 5 6 7 8 9 101112131415161718192021222324 25
   ```

4. a. Let WCF be an integer array of size 12 containing values ranging from −130°F to +50°F, and TEMP be an integer variable whose values range from −50° to +50°. Write the PRINT and FORMAT statement to output the contents of TEMP and WCF in one row:

   ```
   TEMP WCF(1) WCF(2) . . . WCF(12)
   ```

   The value of TEMP should be separated from WCF(1) by at least five blanks, and the contents of the elements of WCF should be separated from one another by at least two blanks.

   b. Suppose you want to put your PRINT statement from part a into a loop in which TEMP ranges from −50 to +50 in increments of 5, and the contents of WCF are recomputed for each of these twenty-one values of TEMP. Would any changes be required in either your PRINT or your FORMAT statement? What would be the result of the execution of such a loop containing your PRINT statement?

c. Write one PRINT and one FORMAT statement to display the following heading:

```
WIND CHILL FACTOR TABLE (DEGREES F)
TEMPERATURE              WIND VELOCITY (MILES PER HOUR)
READING (DEG F)           5    10    15    20  . . . 50
```

5. Write the PRINT and FORMAT statements needed to produce the output described below. Start each new line described by your format with the descriptor 1X. This will indicate a blank for line control for these lines.
   a. Let X be a real array of twenty elements, each containing positive real numbers ranging in value from 0 to 99999.99. Print the contents of X, accurate to two decimal places, four elements per line.
   b. Do the same as for part a, but print the contents of the variable N (containing an integer ranging in value from 1 to 20) on one line and then print the contents of the first N elements of the array X, four per line.
   c. Let QUEUE be a 1000-element array of real numbers whose range of values is not easily determined but is known to be very large. Print the contents of QUEUE six elements per line, accurate to six decimal places.
   d. Let ROOM and TEMP be 120-element arrays. ROOM contains the numbers of the rooms in a nine-story building (these range from 101 through 961). TEMP contains the temperatures of these rooms on a given day, accurate to one decimal place. Print two parallel columns of output, one containing all room numbers and the other containing the temperature of each room.

8.4 Sequential Files

In most of the program examples in the text, the program user receives prompts and types in all data requested at the keyboard while the program is running. Some of the programs also read data from a previously prepared data file. In this section, we will focus on the use of input data files and output files.

In many computer applications, it is important to be able to share data among programs, enabling data generated by one program to be processed by another. Also, it is often desirable to read data from more than one input data file or to combine these data to form a new output file. For example, a bank that has a file of accounts and a file of daily transactions might want to update the file of accounts based on today's transactions. This new file of accounts could become an input file to be processed later with tomorrow's transactions.

Because files are physically located in secondary storage, they can be extremely large. Normally, only one component of a file, called a *record,* will be stored in main memory and processed at a given time.

There are two kinds of files in FORTRAN: sequential files and direct access files. A *sequential file* has the property that its records must always be processed serially, starting with the first. At any point, the next record to be processed is the record following the last one processed. On the other hand, it is possible to reference any record in a *direct access file* at any time; hence, we say that the access order is *random.* To facilitate random access to a direct access file, all records must be of uniform length. There is no requirement of this type for a sequential file.

A FORTRAN program is actually stored in secondary storage as a file; each program line is a record in this source file. Similarly, each line printed by a program is a record in the program output file. Both are sequential files because they are processed in serial order (e.g., the first five program lines must be read before the sixth line). In the remainder of this chapter, we shall study both file types, starting with sequential files.

Creating a Sequential File

In order to create a file for later use, we must read or generate data under program control and write those data onto a file. In the next example, we illustrate a number of new FORTRAN statements needed to accomplish this task.

EXAMPLE 8.13

The program in Fig. 8.1 creates a file of the odd numbers from 1 to 999. Each odd number becomes an individual record of the newly created file named ODDNUM, as shown below.

file ODDNUM

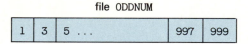

The OPEN statement is used to *connect* a file so that it can be read or written. The OPEN statement in Fig. 8.1 specifies a number of properties of the file, including its unit number (UNIT = 3), its name (FILE = 'ODDNUM'), that it is written using formatted output (FORM = 'FORMATTED'), that it is a sequential file (ACCESS = 'SEQUENTIAL'), and that the file is newly created (STATUS = 'NEW') by this program.

The file properties listed above are all quite straightforward given our knowledge so far. Files are either sequential (ACCESS = 'SEQUENTIAL') or direct access (ACCESS = 'DIRECT'). A file may be processed using list-directed or formatted input/output (FORM = 'FORMATTED'); otherwise, the file is considered unformatted (FORM = 'UNFORMATTED').

Figure 8.1. *Creating a File of Odd Numbers*

```
      PROGRAM DOODD
C Create a sequential file of odd numbers

C Declarations
      INTEGER ODDMAX
      PARAMETER (ODDMAX = 999)
      INTEGER NEXODD

C Open file ODDNUM for output
      OPEN (UNIT = 3, FILE = 'ODDNUM', FORM = 'FORMATTED',
     +      ACCESS = 'SEQUENTIAL', STATUS = 'NEW')

C Write each odd number to file ODDNUM
      DO 10 NEXODD = 1, ODDMAX, 2
          WRITE (UNIT = 3, FMT = 19) NEXODD
   19     FORMAT (I3)
   10 CONTINUE

C Terminate and close file
      ENDFILE (UNIT = 3)
      CLOSE (UNIT = 3)

C Exit program
      STOP
      END
```

The file specifier STATUS = 'NEW' is used when a new file is being created; the file specifier STATUS = 'OLD' is used when a previously created file is being read. If we do not wish to retain a file that is being created, we use the file specifier STATUS = 'SCRATCH'.

The file name is used to locate and identify each file that is in secondary storage. On some systems, the file name must follow a prescribed form. Files with a STATUS parameter of 'SCRATCH' should not be given names, since they are not retained after the execution of the program.

The unit number is an integer value associated with the file. There are usually restrictions unique to each computer system as to what integers may be specified as unit numbers. On most systems, the integers 5 and 6 are reserved for the primary input and output devices being used by the computer system (job-control stream and line printer for a batch program; the terminal for an interactive program). The unit number must appear in all subsequent program statements that manipulate the file.

In Fig. 8.1, the statement

```
WRITE (UNIT = 3, FMT = 19) NEXODD
```

is used to write the output list (NEXODD) to the file designated by unit number 3 using FORMAT statement 19. You can also use the shorter version

```
WRITE (3, 19) NEXODD
```

Note that a carriage-control character is not specified in FORMAT 19; carriage control is needed only when writing to a unit that represents the line printer. The statement

```
ENDFILE (UNIT = 3)
```

is used to mark the end of a file by appending a special end-of-file record to the newly created file. This should be done whenever a new sequential file is created or written. The statement

```
CLOSE (UNIT = 3)
```

disconnects the file associated with unit number 3 from the program. Every file that is opened should be closed before the program terminates. ∎

The OPEN, ENDFILE, and CLOSE statements are described in the displays that follow.

OPEN Statement

SYNTAX: OPEN (*speclist*)

INTERPRETATION: The OPEN statement connects a file to the program. *Speclist* is a list of file specifiers separated by commas. The file specifiers describe the properties of the file being connected.

Required specifiers
UNIT = *unum*: *unum* is the unit number (a nonnegative integer expression).

Optional specifiers
FILE = *name*: *name* is a string giving the file name (not required for 'SCRATCH' files).

ACCESS = *acc*: The value of *acc* must be 'SEQUENTIAL' or 'DIRECT'. If omitted, 'SEQUENTIAL' is assumed

FORM = *frm*: The value of *frm* must be 'FORMATTED' or 'UNFORMATTED'. If omitted, 'FORMATTED' is assumed for sequential files; 'UNFORMATTED' for direct access.

STATUS = *stat*: The value of *stat* must be 'NEW', 'OLD', 'SCRATCH', or 'UNKNOWN'. If omitted, 'UNKNOWN' is assumed.

Other specifiers
RECL = *len*: *len* is an integer expression indicating the length of each record in a direct access file (used only when ACCESS = 'DIRECT').

NOTES: The values allowed for *unum* and *name* may depend on your computer system. If STATUS = 'SCRATCH', then omit the specifier FILE = *name*.

ENDFILE
Statement

> SYNTAX: ENDFILE (UNIT = *unum*)
>
> INTERPRETATION: The ENDFILE statement writes a special end-of-file record onto the file specified by *unum*. No data may be written following the end-of-file record.

CLOSE
Statement

> SYNTAX: CLOSE (UNIT = *unum*)
>
> INTERPRETATION: The CLOSE statement disconnects the file specified by *unum* from the program. Unit number *unum* can be reconnected to another file.

The internal binary forms of data are stored directly in an unformatted file. In a formatted file, each data item is represented as a string of characters. Consequently, formatted files are easier to move from one computer to another. On the other hand, the particular computer system used to create an unformatted file determines the form of each record of that file. Although they are less portable, unformatted files can generally be processed more quickly.

On some systems, file properties may be specified using special control statements as well as the OPEN statement. You should find out what special statements, if any, are required on your system. Many systems write an end-of-file record automatically when the file is closed or the program terminates.

Reading an
Existing File

We mentioned that one motivation for files was to enable the output generated by one program to be used as data by another program. This process is illustrated next.

EXAMPLE 8.14

The program in Fig. 8.2 reads the file 'ODDNUM' created by the execution of the program in Fig. 8.1 and echo prints each file record. Note that the OPEN statement is the same as before except that the value of STATUS is now 'OLD'. The ENDFILE statement is no longer needed since the file is being read, not written. The unit number for file 'ODDNUM' is still specified as 3, although another unit number could be used instead.   ∎

Within the WHILE loop, each record of file 'ODDNUM' is read (using FORMAT 25) into the variable NEXNUM. A list-directed output statement prints each value of NEXNUM. Since the loop-repetition condition is always true, the loop could execute "forever." However, we want the loop to terminate when all file records have been read, or the end of the file is reached. The optional *control specifier* END = 35 causes a transfer to label 35 when the end-of-file record is read. Since the repeat condition is always true, this is the only method provided for loop exit.

Figure 8.2. *Echo Printing the File ODDNUM*

```
      PROGRAM ODDFIL
C Read the file ODDNUM

C Declarations
      INTEGER NEXNUM

C Open file ODDNUM for input
      OPEN (UNIT = 3, FILE = 'ODDNUM', FORM = 'FORMATTED',
     +     ACCESS = 'SEQUENTIAL', STATUS = 'OLD')

C Read and print each record
      PRINT *, 'List of file data'
      DO  WHILE (.TRUE.)                               9 CONTINUE
          READ (UNIT = 3, FMT = 25, END = 35) NEXNUM
  25      FORMAT (I3)
          PRINT *, NEXNUM
      ENDDO                                            GOTO 9

C End of file reached
   35 CONTINUE
      CLOSE (UNIT = 3)
      PRINT *, 'File read completed'

C Exit program
      STOP
      END
```

The general READ and WRITE statements are described next.

General READ/WRITE Statements

SYNTAX: READ (UNIT = *unum, control list*) *input list*
        WRITE (UNIT = *unum, control list*) *output list*

INTERPRETATION: The READ or WRITE operation is performed on the file associated with unit *unum*. The variables receiving data (for READ) are provided in *input list*; the variables and values to be written (for WRITE) are provided in *output list*.

Control list

FMT = *flab:*   Specifies the label of the FORMAT statement to be used with a formatted file (omitted if the file is unformatted). FMT = * specifies list-directed input/output.

END = *endlab:* Specifies the label to transfer to when the end-of-file record is read. This specifier may not appear in a WRITE statement or with a direct access file.

REC = *recnum:* Specifies the record number (a positive integer) of a direct access file (omitted if the file is sequential).

NOTE: There are additional control specifiers; however, they are beyond the scope of this discussion. The symbols UNIT = and FMT = may be omitted from a READ or WRITE statement. In that case, FORTRAN assumes that the first item in the control list is the unit number and the second item is the format label (or *) for formatted files.

Figure 8.3. *Main Program for Creating the Inventory File INVEN*

```
      PROGRAM BOOKST
C Writes the book store inventory to a file

C Declarations
      INTEGER SENVAL
      PARAMETER (SENVAL = 0)
      INTEGER STOCK, QUANT, TOTAL
      REAL PRICE
      CHARACTER *20 AUTHOR, TITLE
      CHARACTER *8 DATE

C Open file INVEN for output
      OPEN (UNIT = 1, FILE = 'INVEN', FORM = 'UNFORMATTED',
     +      ACCESS = 'SEQUENTIAL', STATUS = 'NEW')

C Get date and initialize TOTAL
      PRINT *, 'Enter the date in the form ''MM/DD/YY'' :
      READ *, DATE
      PRINT *, 'Enter each book record as of ', DATE
      TOTAL = 0

C Read each book record, write it to file INVEN,
C and accumulate the total number of books in TOTAL
      CALL GETREC (STOCK, AUTHOR, TITLE, PRICE, QUANT)
      DO WHILE (STOCK .NE. SENVAL)                    9 IF ( . . .) THEN
         WRITE (UNIT = 1) STOCK, AUTHOR, TITLE, PRICE, QUANT
         TOTAL = TOTAL + QUANT
         CALL GETREC (STOCK, AUTHOR, TITLE, PRICE, QUANT)
      ENDDO                                              GOTO 9
C                                                        ENDIF
C Print final TOTAL and terminate and close file INVEN
      PRINT *
      PRINT *, 'Total number of books in stock = ', TOTAL
      PRINT *, 'File INVEN created'
      ENDFILE (UNIT = 1)
      CLOSE (UNIT = 1)

C Exit program
      STOP
      END
```

Creating a File from Keyboard Data

The program in Fig. 8.1 generated data to be stored in a sequential file. It is also possible to read or enter data from the keyboard and to save these data in a file for later use. This process is illustrated in the next example.

EXAMPLE 8.15

The inventory for a bookstore is read from a keyboard by the program in Fig. 8.3. Each input record consists of the stock number, author's name, title, cost, and quantity on hand. GETREC is called to read each data record. The statement

```
WRITE (UNIT = 1) STOCK, AUTHOR, TITLE, PRICE, QUANT
```

writes this record to the file (INVEN) associated with unit number 1; there is no format specified since the file is unformatted.

The WHILE loop in Fig. 8.3 terminates when the sentinel record (stock number is 0) is read. The total number of books is counted and displayed after loop exit. A sample of the output for this program is shown in Fig. 8.4. (See exercise 2 at the end of this section for a description of subroutine GETREC.)■

Figure 8.4. *Sample Run of File Creation Program*

```
Enter the date in the form 'MM/DD/YY' :
'12/25/90'
Enter each book record as of 12/25/90

Stock Number (enter 0 when done):
1
Author in quotes:
'Ty Cobb'
Title in quotes:
'No Place Like Home'
Price:
5.95
Quantity:
18

Stock Number (enter 0 when done):
15
Author in quotes:
'Pete Rose'
Title in quotes:
'My Greatest Hits'
Price:
9.95
Quantity:
500

Stock Number (enter 0 when done):
0

Total Number of Books in stock =      518
File INVEN created
```

EXAMPLE 8.16   The program in Fig. 8.5 could be used to update file INVEN by adding additional data records to the end of this file. The first WHILE loop advances to the current end of the file. It does this by reading each record until the end-of-file record is read. After loop exit, the statement

```
        BACKSPACE (UNIT = 1)
```

repositions the file to the start of the last record read (the current end-of-file record). The additional data records are then written onto the file INVEN, erasing the original end-of-file record. A new end-of-file record is written following the last data record added to the file.   ∎

Figure 8.5. *Adding More Records to File INVEN*

```
        PROGRAM FEXTEN
C Extends existing inventory file

C Declarations
        INTEGER STOCK, QUANT, TOTAL
        REAL PRICE
        CHARACTER *20 AUTHOR, TITLE

C Open file INVEN for extension
        OPEN (UNIT = 1, FILE = 'INVEN', FORM = 'UNFORMATTED',
     +        ACCESS = 'SEQUENTIAL', STATUS = 'OLD')

C Find current end of file
        DO WHILE (.TRUE.)                             9 CONTINUE
            READ (UNIT = 1, END = 25) STOCK, AUTHOR,
                TITLE, PRICE, QUANT
            PRINT *, STOCK, AUTHOR, TITLE, PRICE, QUANT
        ENDDO                                         GOTO 9

C Add new data starting at the end of the current file
   25 CONTINUE
        BACKSPACE (UNIT = 1)
        CALL GETREC (STOCK, AUTHOR, TITLE, PRICE, QUANT)
        DO WHILE (STOCK .NE. 0)                       19 IF (...) THEN
            WRITE (UNIT = 1) STOCK, AUTHOR,
     +          TITLE, PRICE, QUANT
            CALL GETREC (STOCK, AUTHOR, TITLE, PRICE, QUANT)
        ENDDO                                         GOTO 19
C                                                     ENDIF
C Terminate and close file
        PRINT *, 'Extension of INVEN complete'
        ENDFILE (UNIT = 1)
        CLOSE (UNIT = 1)

C Exit program
        STOP
        END
```

Another command

```
REWIND (UNIT = unum)
```

may be used to reposition a sequential file to its first record. This enables the data in a sequential file to be processed more than once during the execution of a program.

BACKSPACE Statement

> SYNTAX: BACKSPACE (UNIT = *unum*)
>
> INTERPRETATION: The file position pointer for the file connected to unit number *unum* is repositioned before the record last processed. If the file position pointer is past the end-of-file record, it is repositioned just before the end-of-file record.

REWIND Statement

> SYNTAX: REWIND (UNIT = *unum*)
>
> INTERPRETATION: The file position pointer for the file connected to unit number *unum* is positioned just before the first file record.

SELF-CHECK EXERCISES FOR SECTION 8.4

1. Write the OPEN statement needed to connect an existing, sequential, unformatted file named 'TEXT' to unit number 3.
2. Write subroutine GETREC, to consist of the prompt and the READ statements needed to enter one book record.

8.5 Problem Solving Illustrated

We present two case studies in this section. The first case study shows how to *merge*, or combine, the data in two existing files into a third file. One of the two existing files is considered the *master file;* the other is considered the *update file,* which contains new information. The merged file contains the data in both of the previous files and is considered the *new master file.* The second case study contains several subroutines and illustrates the use of formatted and unformatted files.

Case Study: Merging Files

Problem

The Junk Mail Company has recently received a new mailing list (file UPDATE) that it wishes to merge with its master file (file OLDMST). Each of the files is in

Case Study: Merging Files, continued

alphabetical order by name. The company wants to produce a new master file (NEWMST) that is also in alphabetical order. Each client name and address on either mailing list is represented by four character strings, as shown below:

```
'CLAUS, SANTA'
'1 STAR LANE'
'NORTH POLE'
'ALASKA, 99999'
```

A sentinel name and address are at the end of each of the files UPDATE and OLDMST. The sentinel is the same for both files; one copy should be written at the end of the NEWMST file. The sentinel entry consists of four character strings containing all z's. We shall assume that there are no names that appear on both files OLDMST and UPDATE.

Design Overview

In addition to the two input files (OLDMST and UPDATE), we will need an output file (NEWMST) that will contain the merged data from OLDMST and UPDATE. NEWMST will then serve as the new master file of mailing labels.

Figure 8.6 illustrates the result of merging two small sample files. For simplicity, only the name portion of each record is shown. The original mailing list and the update list each contain four records (including the sentinel); the new mailing list contains seven records. The records on all three files are in alphabetical order by name.

Data Requirements

Input Files

the original mailing list in alphabetical order by name (OLDMST)
the additions to be made to OLDMST, also in alphabetical order by name (UPDATE)

Output Files

the final mailing list, formed by merging OLDMST and UPDATE (NEWMST)

Initial Algorithm

1. Read first records from OLDMST and UPDATE.
2. Compare names of current records. Copy the record with the alphabetically first name into NEWMST. Read the next record from the file containing the record that was just copied. Continue to merge until the end of both files is reached.

Case Study: Merging Files, continued

Figure 8.6. *Sample File Merge*

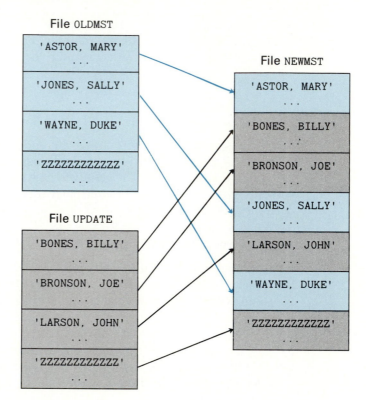

Algorithm Refinements

The program must read one name and address entry at a time from each input file. These two entries are compared, and the one that comes first alphabetically is copied to the output file (NEWMST). Another entry is then read from the file containing the entry just copied, and the comparison process is repeated.

When the end of one of the input files (OLDMST or UPDATE) is reached, the program should copy the remaining information from the other input file to NEWMST and then write the sentinel record.

To simplify the implementation of the algorithm, we will use two string arrays, OLDATA and UPDATA, to hold the current records from OLDMST and UPDATE, respectively. Each array provides storage for four strings of length 20.

The additional data requirements and the refinement of algorithm step 2 follow Fig. 8.7.

Case Study: Merging Files, continued

Figure 8.7. *Merging Two Sequential Files*

```
      PROGRAM MERGE
C Merges OLDMST and UPDATE to NEWMST
C Records in all 3 files are in alphabetical order by name
C Uses OLDATA and UPDATA to store file data

C Declarations
      CHARACTER *20 OLDATA(4), UPDATA(4)

C Open three sequential files
      OPEN (UNIT = 1, FILE = 'OLDMST', FORM = 'UNFORMATTED',
     +      ACCESS = 'SEQUENTIAL', STATUS = 'OLD')
      OPEN (UNIT = 2, FILE = 'UPDATE', FORM = 'UNFORMATTED',
     +      ACCESS = 'SEQUENTIAL', STATUS = 'OLD')
      OPEN (UNIT = 3, FILE = 'NEWMST', FORM = 'UNFORMATTED',
     +      ACCESS = 'SEQUENTIAL', STATUS = 'NEW')

C Read first data entries from each input file
      READ (UNIT = 1, END = 94) OLDATA
      READ (UNIT = 2, END = 95) UPDATA

C Merge alphabetically smaller data to NEWMST and
C get next record from input file with smaller
C data.  Continue until end of either file is read
      DO WHILE (.TRUE.)                                29 CONTINUE
C        Copy record with smaller name
         IF (OLDATA(1) .LT. UPDATA(1)) THEN
            WRITE (UNIT = 3) OLDATA
            READ (UNIT = 1, END = 40) OLDATA
         ELSE
            WRITE (UNIT = 3) UPDATA
            READ (UNIT = 2, END = 40) UPDATA
         ENDIF
      ENDDO                                            GOTO 29

C Close files and exit program
   40 CONTINUE
      PRINT *, 'Merge completed'
      ENDFILE (UNIT = 3)
      CLOSE (UNIT = 1)
      CLOSE (UNIT = 2)
      CLOSE (UNIT = 3)
      STOP

C Error section
C Print error message if either input file is empty
   94 CONTINUE
      PRINT *, 'File OLDMST is empty'
      STOP
```

Case Study: Merging Files, continued

```
95 CONTINUE
   PRINT *, 'File UPDATE is empty'
   STOP
   END
```

Input Variables

string array to hold current record from OLDMST (CHARACTER *20 OLDATA(4))

string array to hold current record from UPDATE (CHARACTER *20 UPDATA(4))

Step 2 Refinement

2.1 DO WHILE (.TRUE.)
    IF OLDATA(1) is less than UPDATA(1) THEN
        2.2 Copy OLDATA to NEWMST. Read next record from OLDMST to OLDATA. Exit loop when the end-of-file record is read.
    ELSE
        2.3 Copy UPDATA to NEWMST. Read next record from UPDATE to UPDATA. Exit loop when the end-of-file record is read.
    ENDIF
  ENDDO

Coding

It is important to verify that all the remaining data on one file will be copied into NEWMST when the end-of-file record on the other file has been read. Just before reaching the end-of-file record on UPDATE (or OLDMST), the sentinel record will be read into UPDATA (or OLDATA). Since the sentinel name (all Z's) alphabetically follows any other client name, the remaining client data on the unfinished file will be copied to NEWMST, as desired. During the last repetition of the loop, both OLDATA and UPDATA will contain the sentinel record, which is copied to NEWMST just before loop exit.

In the program shown in Fig. 8.7, a transfer to label 94 or 95 occurs if either UPDATE or OLDMST is empty (a file consisting of an end-of-file record only). In this case, there is no need to perform the merge operation since the other file contains the required alphabetical list.

Testing

To test the merge program, provide files that contain only the sentinel record as well as files with one or more actual records. Make sure the merge program

Case Study: Merging Files, continued

works properly regardless of which of the two input files has all of its data processed first. Also, make sure there is exactly one sentinel record on the merged file.

Case Study: Land Boundary Survey

Problem

The surveying firm of Harris, Neilson, and Gallop has completed a land boundary survey. The result consists of the X and Y coordinates of points defining the edges of a piece of property. These coordinates are stored in a data file named SURVIN.DAT, one pair per line. The firm needs to know the distance between adjacent points and the total length of the boundary. For error correction purposes, the firm would also like to know the percentage of the total length of each line and the cumulative percentage, starting with the first line. The output results will be written to an output file and also displayed in tabular form, as shown in Fig. 8.8.

Figure 8.8. *Land Survey Table*

```
        Harris, Neilson, and Gallop, Surveyors

The number of points read was  6
Total boundary length is     1365.685 feet

Line         Start Point      Line Length    % of     Cumulative
Number     X           Y      (in feet)    Boundary       %
  1      100.000     100.000    141.421     10.355      10.355
  2      200.000     200.000    141.421     10.355      20.711
  3      300.000     300.000    141.421     10.355      31.066
  4      400.000     400.000    400.000     29.289      60.355
  5        .000      400.000    400.000     29.289      89.645
  6        .000        .000     141.421     10.355     100.000
```

Design Overview

The program first reads the survey data into a pair of arrays, X and Y. The distance between adjacent points, (X_i, Y_i), and (X_j, Y_j), is given by the formula

$$distance = \sqrt{(X_i - X_j)^2 + (Y_i - Y_j)^2}$$

Case Study: Land Boundary Survey, continued

The total length of the land boundary is the sum of the individual lengths. After computing the total length, we can determine the percentage of each individual length, add it to the cumulative percentage, and write the required output file and table.

The problem data requirements and algorithm follow. Note that the first element in array CUMPCT has a subscript of 0. The reason for this will be discussed later.

Data Requirements

Input File

the coordinate file (SURVIN.DAT)

Output File

the line lengths and percentages (SURVOUT.DAT)

Problem Parameters

the size of the arrays (MAX = 100)

Problem Inputs

the X coordinates of edge points (REAL X(MAX))
the Y coordinates of edge points (REAL Y(MAX))

Problem Outputs

the coordinates of edge points (arrays X and Y)
the distance between adjacent points (REAL LENGTH(MAX))
the percentage of total boundary length (REAL PERCNT(MAX))
the cumulative percentage so far (REAL CUMPCT(0 : MAX))
the number of points on the boundary (INTEGER N)
the total boundary length (REAL PERIM)

Initial Algorithm

1. Read all coordinate points and count the number of points read.
2. Calculate the length of each line and the total boundary length.
3. Compute percentages of individual line lengths and cumulative percentages.
4. Write the output file and table.

Case Study: Land Boundary Survey, continued

Algorithm Refinements

We will use subroutines to perform each step of the algorithm. Figure 8.9 shows the structure chart.

Figure 8.9. *Structure Chart for Surveying Problem*

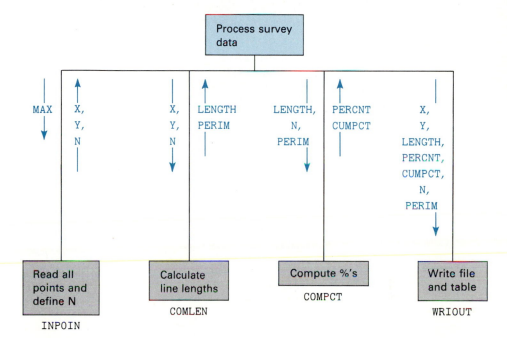

Coding the Main Program

Figure 8.10 shows the main program. The main program contains declarations for all arrays and simple variables listed in the data requirements section and calls to the four subroutines.

Subroutine INPOIN

Subroutine INPOIN (see Fig. 8.11) begins by connecting the data file SURVIN.DAT to unit number 1. It uses a READ statement with an end-of-file specifier to read coordinates into arrays X and Y. The value of N is defined after loop exit.

Subroutine COMLEN

Subroutine COMLEN (see Fig. 8.12) computes the length of each line on the boundary. The first line connects point 1 and point 2, the second line connects

Case Study: Land Boundary Survey, continued

Figure 8.10. *Main Survey Program*

```
      PROGRAM SURVEY
C This program reads the X, Y coordinates of a collection
C of edge points around the boundary of a plot of land and
C computes the distances between adjacent points. The
C coordinates of the individual lines, their lengths, the
C percentages of total length, and the cumulative percentages
C are written to an output file and displayed in a table.

C Declarations
      INTEGER MAX, N
      PARAMETER (MAX = 100)
      REAL X(MAX), Y(MAX), LENGTH(MAX)
      REAL PERCNT(MAX), CUMPCT(MAX), PERIM

C Read all coordinate points
      CALL INPOIN (MAX, X, Y, N)

C Calculate the length of each line and the total boundary
      CALL COMLEN (X, Y, N, LENGTH, PERIM)

C Compute individual line percentages
      CALL COMPCT (LENGTH, N, PERIM, PERCNT, CUMPCT)

C Write output file and table
      CALL WRIOUT (X, Y, LENGTH, PERCNT, CUMPCT, N, PERIM)

C Exit program
      STOP
      END
```

point 2 and point 3, and so on. The last line connects point N and point 1. The algorithm follows.

Algorithm for COMLEN

1. Set PERIM to zero.
2. DO I = 1, N − 1
   3. Set LENGTH(I) to the length of the line from point I to point I + 1.
   4. Add the new line length to PERIM.
   CONTINUE
5. Set LENGTH(N) to the length of the line from point N to point 1.
6. Add the new line length to PERIM.

Case Study: Land Boundary Survey, continued

Figure 8.11. *Subroutine INPOIN*

```
      SUBROUTINE INPOIN (MAX, X, Y, N)
C Enters survey data from file SURVIN.DAT and defines N

C Input Arguments
C   MAX - The maximum number of points

C Output Arguments
C   X - the X coordinate of each point
C   Y - the Y coordinate of each point
C   N - the number of points read (0 <= N <= MAX)

C Argument Declarations
      INTEGER MAX, N
      REAL X(MAX), Y(MAX)

C Local Declarations
      INTEGER I

C Open data file
      OPEN (UNIT = 1, FILE = 'SURVIN.DAT', FORM = 'FORMATTED',
     +      ACCESS = 'SEQUENTIAL', STATUS = 'OLD')

C Read coordinate points
      DO 10 I = 1, MAX
         READ (UNIT = 1, FMT = *, END = 99) X(I), Y(I)
   10 CONTINUE
      PRINT *, 'WARNING - ARRAY FILLED BEFORE END OF FILE'

C File read operation completed, adjust N
   99 N = I - 1

C Close file and exit subroutine
      CLOSE (UNIT = 1)
      RETURN
      END
```

Figure 8.12 shows subroutine COMLEN along with function DISTNC. Function DISTNC calculates the distance of the line whose end points are passed as the function arguments.

Subroutine COMPCT

Subroutine COMPCT performs the percentage calculations for each line, defining arrays PERCNT and CUMPCT. Figure 8.13 shows subroutine COMPCT. In the DO

Case Study: Land Boundary Survey, continued

Figure 8.12. *Subroutine COMLEN and Function DISTNC*

```
      SUBROUTINE COMLEN (X, Y, N, LENGTH, PERIM)
C Calculates the length of each line and the total boundary

C Input Arguments
C    X - the X coordinate of each point
C    Y - the Y coordinate of each point
C    N - the number of points read

C Output Arguments
C    LENGTH - the length of each line
C    PERIM - the total boundary length

C Argument Declarations
      INTEGER N
      REAL X(*), Y(*), LENGTH(*), PERIM

C Local Declarations
      INTEGER I
      REAL DISTNC

C Define each individual line length and add it to the total
      PERIM = 0.0
      DO 10 I = 1, N - 1
          LENGTH(I) = DISTNC(X(I), Y(I), X(I + 1), Y(I + 1))
          PERIM = PERIM + LENGTH(I)
   10 CONTINUE
      LENGTH(N) = DISTNC(X(N), Y(N), X(1), Y(1))
      PERIM = PERIM + LENGTH(N)

C Exit subroutine
      RETURN
      END


C ----------------------------------------------------------------

      REAL FUNCTION DISTNC (XSTART, YSTART, XEND, YEND)
C Computes the distance of the line between points
C START and END.
C Pre : The X, Y coordinates of points START and END
C       are defined.
C Post: The function result is the length of the line
C       between these coordinates.

C Argument Declarations
      REAL XSTART, YSTART, XEND, YEND
```

Case Study: Land Boundary Survey, continued

```
C Define function result
      DISTNC = SQRT((XEND - XSTART) ** 2 +
     +                 (YEND - YSTART) ** 2)

C Exit function
      RETURN
      END
```

Figure 8.13. *Subroutine COMPCT*

```
      SUBROUTINE COMPCT (LENGTH, N, PERIM, PERCNT, CUMPCT)
C Calculates the % length of each line and the cumulative %

C Input Arguments
C    LENGTH - the length of each line
C    N - the number of points read
C    PERIM - the total boundary length

C Output Arguments
C    PERCNT - the percentage length of each line
C    CUMPCT - the cumulative percentage so far

C Dummy Argument Declarations
      INTEGER N
      REAL PERIM, LENGTH(*), PERCNT(*)
      REAL CUMPCT(0 : *)

C Local Declarations
      INTEGER I

C Compute the percentage of each line and the
C cumulative percentage so far
      CUMPCT(0) = 0.0
      DO 10 I = 1, N
         PERCNT(I) = (LENGTH(I) / PERIM) * 100.00
         CUMPCT(I) = CUMPCT(I - 1) + PERCNT(I)
   10 CONTINUE

C Exit subroutine
      RETURN
      END
```

Case Study: Land Boundary Survey, continued

loop, the statements

```
PERCNT(I) = (LENGTH(I) / PERIM) * 100.00
CUMPCT(I) = CUMPCT(I - 1) + PERCNT(I)
```

define the percentage of the current line, PERCNT(I), and the cumulative percentage so far, CUMPCT(I). The latter is obtained by adding PERCNT(I) to the previous cumulative percentage, CUMPCT(I - 1). When I is 1, the value of PERCNT(1) is added to CUMPCT(0) (value is zero). This is the reason for the extra element in array CUMPCT. The declaration

```
REAL CUMPCT(0 : *)
```

identifies CUMPCT as an assumed-size dummy array with a smallest subscript of zero.

Subroutine WRIOUT

Subroutine WRIOUT writes the output file, SURVOUT.DAT, as an unformatted file. This file contains one record for each boundary line. The record for each line consists of the coordinates of its endpoints, its length, the percentage of the total length, and the cumulative percentage so far.

After file SURVOUT.DAT is completed, we can verify its correctness by reading each record and echo printing it on the screen in the body of the display table. Because of screen width limitations, we will display only the starting point of each line. (The ending point of line i is the same as the starting point of line i + 1.)

Figure 8.14 shows subroutine WRIOUT. DO loop 10 creates the output file, and

Figure 8.14. *Subroutine WRIOUT*

```
      SUBROUTINE WRIOUT (X, Y, LENGTH, PERCNT, CUMPCT, N, PERIM)
C Writes the output file, SURVOUT.DAT, and
C echo prints it in a display table.

C Input Arguments
C    X - the X coordinate of each point
C    Y - the Y coordinate of each point
C    LENGTH - the length of the ith line
C    PERCNT - the percentage length of each line
C    CUMPCT - the cumulative percentage so far
C    N - the number of points read
C    PERIM - the total boundary length

C Argument Declarations
      INTEGER N
      REAL X(*), Y(*), LENGTH(*), PERCNT(*), PERIM
      REAL CUMPCT(0 : *)
```

Case Study: Land Boundary Survey, continued

```
C Local Declarations
      INTEGER I
      REAL XSTART, YSTART, XEND, YEND,
     +     TEMLEN, TEMPER, TEMCUM

C Open output file and write records 1 through N - 1
      OPEN (UNIT = 2, FILE = 'SURVOUT.DAT',
     +      FORM = 'UNFORMATTED', ACCESS = 'SEQUENTIAL',
     +      STATUS = 'NEW')

      DO 10 I = 1, N - 1
         WRITE (UNIT = 2) X(I), Y(I), X(I + 1), Y(I + 1),
     +                 LENGTH(I), PERCNT(I), CUMPCT(I)
   10 CONTINUE

C Write record N and end of file
      WRITE (UNIT = 2) X(N), Y(N), X(1), Y(1),
     +                 LENGTH(N), PERCNT(N), CUMPCT(N)
      ENDFILE (UNIT = 2)

C Write table heading
      WRITE (6, *) '           Harris, Neilson, and ',
     +             'Gallop, Surveyors'
      WRITE (6, 11) N
   11 FORMAT ('0', 'The number of points read was ', I3)
      WRITE (6, 12) PERIM
   12 FORMAT ('Total boundary length is ', F12.3, ' feet')
      WRITE (6, *)
      WRITE (6, *) 'Line        Start Point ',
     +             '   Line Length      % of      Cumulative'
      WRITE (6, *) 'Number      X         Y',
     +             '        (in feet)    Boundary        %'

C Read and echo print all records of file SURVOUT.DAT
      REWIND (UNIT = 2)
      DO 20 I = 1, N
         READ (UNIT = 2)  XSTART, YSTART, XEND, YEND,
     +                 TEMLEN, TEMPER, TEMCUM
         WRITE (UNIT = 6, FMT = 13) I, XSTART, YSTART,
     +                 TEMLEN, TEMPER, TEMCUM
   13 FORMAT (1X, I3, 5F12.3)
   20 CONTINUE

C Close file and exit subroutine
      CLOSE (UNIT = 2)
      RETURN
      END
```

Case Study: Land Boundary Survey, continued

DO loop 20 displays the output table. Just before DO loop 20 begins, the statement

```
REWIND (UNIT = 2)
```

rewinds file SURVOUT.DAT so its records can be read and echo printed in the body of the table. DO loop 20 reads the file data into local variables instead of back into the arrays.

Testing

A sample run of the survey program will produce a table similar to the one shown in the statement of the problem. Make sure that all values printed are positive and that the final cumulative percentage is 100. To verify the correctness of the table, try some adjacent points with the same X coordinates but different Y coordinates (or same Y but different X). In this case, the line length should be the absolute value of the difference between the Y coordinates. Also, see what happens to the display table when point 1 is placed at the end of the data file instead of the beginning. The table lines should all move up one position, and the last line displayed should be the same as the old first line.

SELF-CHECK EXERCISES FOR SECTION 8.5

1. Modify the program in Fig. 8.7 to handle the situation in which the UPDATE file may contain some of the same names as the OLDMST file. In this case, only one address should appear on the NEWMST file; the address in file UPDATE should be used since it is more recent. Also, print a count of the number of file entries in each of the three files.
2. Discuss the changes necessary in program MERGE if the sentinel records were deleted from all files.

8.6 ▬▬▬ Direct Access Files

A direct access file is analogous to an array that is stored in secondary memory rather than main memory. Like an array, the records of a direct access file may be accessed in arbitrary or random order.

Each record of a direct access file is assigned a unique record number, starting with 1. Since each record is a fixed size, FORTRAN can determine where on disk a particular record is stored and access it. For example, if all records are twenty characters in length, record 1 occupies the first twenty characters allocated to the file, record 2 occupies the next twenty characters, and so on.

The *record length* must be declared by a file specifier in the OPEN statement (i.e., RECL = *len,* where *len* is an integer). The length of a formatted record is equal to the number of characters specified by the associated FORMAT statement. For an unformatted record, the length depends on the computer system.

The OPEN statement

```
OPEN (UNIT = 2, FILE = 'DIRINV', FORM = 'FORMATTED',
+     ACCESS = 'DIRECT', RECL = 54, STATUS = 'NEW')
```

declares file DIRINV as a new direct access file with formatted records consisting of fifty-four characters each.

EXAMPLE 8.17 Before writing data to a direct access file, it is a good idea to initialize each record of the file to a string of blank characters. This enables us to determine at a later time whether a particular record exists. Subroutine INTLIZ in Fig. 8.15 may be called to initialize a direct access file. The DO loop-control variable

Figure 8.15. *Subroutine INTLIZ*

```
      SUBROUTINE INTLIZ (UNUM)
C Writes blank records to the direct access file on unit number UNUM.

C Input Argument
      UNUM - the unit number of the file being initialized

C Dummy argument declaration
      INTEGER UNUM

C Local declarations
      INTEGER MAXSTK
      PARAMETER (MAXSTK = 1000)
      INTEGER RECNUM

C Write all blank records.
      DO 10 RECNUM = 1, MAXSTK

C Write next blank record
         WRITE (UNIT = UNUM, FMT = 11, REC = RECNUM)
   11    FORMAT (A54)
   10 CONTINUE

C Exit subroutine.
      RETURN
      END
```

RECNUM is used to access each file record in sequence. The WRITE statement

```
      WRITE (UNIT = UNUM, FMT = 11, REC = RECNUM)
   11 FORMAT (A54)
```

initializes the record selected by RECNUM to all blank characters. The unit number, UNUM, is an input argument.   ■

A direct access file may be created from a sequential file or by reading in data from the terminal. The program in Fig. 8.3 may be modified to create a direct access file instead of a sequential file.

EXAMPLE 8.18   The program in Fig. 8.16 can be used to write the book store inventory as a direct access file instead of a sequential file. It uses subroutine GETREC (not shown) to enter each book record and subroutine INTLIZ to initialize the direct access file. Each stock number (STOCK) entered by GETREC is used as a record number, provided it is between 1 and MAXSTK (1000). Only the records specified by the program user will be changed. The program output will be similar to that shown in Fig. 8.4. If the call to INTLIZ is omitted, this program could be used to modify or insert new records in an existing file (STATUS = 'OLD').

Note that the WRITE statement in Fig. 8.16 uses FORMAT 21 to control the layout of the record being written. Adding up the number of "print positions" described by this format gives us a record length of exactly fifty-four characters. This is the same as the record length specified in the OPEN statement for file DIRINV.

We could also use the sequential file INVEN that was created earlier as an input file and create a new direct access file from it. To accomplish this, we would need to open both files using the statements

```
      OPEN (UNIT = 1, FILE = 'INVEN', FORM = 'UNFORMATTED',
     +      ACCESS = 'SEQUENTIAL', STATUS = 'OLD')
      OPEN (UNIT = 2, FILE = 'DIRINV', FORM = 'FORMATTED',
     +      ACCESS = 'DIRECT', RECL = 54, STATUS = 'NEW')
```

The loop in Fig. 8.16 would be rewritten as shown below.

```
C Read each book record from file INVEN, write it to file DIRINV,
C and accumulate the total number of books in TOTAL.
      DO WHILE (.TRUE.)                            19 CONTINUE
         READ (UNIT = 1, END = 99)
     +      STOCK, AUTHOR, TITLE, PRICE, QUANT
         WRITE (UNIT = 2, FMT = 21, REC = STOCK)
     +      STOCK, AUTHOR, TITLE, PRICE, QUANT
   21    FORMAT (I4, A20, A20, F6.2, I4)
         TOTAL = TOTAL + QUANT
      ENDDO                                        GOTO 19
C
   99 CONTINUE
```

Figure 8.16. *Creating the Inventory File DIRINV*

```
        PROGRAM CREATE
C Write the book store inventory to a direct access file.
C The file data are read from the keyboard.

C Declarations
      INTEGER SENVAL, MAXSTK
      PARAMETER (SENVAL = 0, MAXSTK = 1000)
      INTEGER STOCK, QUANT, TOTAL
      REAL PRICE
      CHARACTER *20 AUTHOR, TITLE
      CHARACTER *8 DATE

C Open file INVEN for output.
      OPEN (UNIT = 2, FILE = 'DIRINV', FORM = 'FORMATTED',
     +      ACCESS = 'DIRECT', RECL = 54, STATUS = 'NEW')

C Get date, initialize TOTAL, and initialize file DIRINV to blanks.
      PRINT *, 'Enter the date in the form ''MM/DD/YY'' :'
      READ *, DATE
      PRINT *, 'Enter each book record as of ', DATE
      PRINT *, 'Stock (record) numbers must be between 1 and ', MAXSTK
      TOTAL = 0
      CALL INTLIZ (2)

C Read each book record, write it to file DIRINV,
C and accumulate the total number of books in TOTAL.
      CALL GETREC (STOCK, AUTHOR, TITLE, PRICE, QUANT)
      DO WHILE ((STOCK .GT. SENVAL) .AND. (STOCK .LE. MAXSTK))  9 IF ...
         WRITE (UNIT = 2, FMT = 21, REC = STOCK)
     +      STOCK, AUTHOR, TITLE, PRICE, QUANT
   21    FORMAT (I4, A20, A20, F6.2, I4)
         TOTAL = TOTAL + QUANT
         CALL GETREC (STOCK, AUTHOR, TITLE, PRICE, QUANT)
      ENDDO                                                        GOTO 9
C                                                                  ENDIF
C Print final TOTAL and terminate and close file DIRINV.
      IF (STOCK .GT. MAXSTK) PRINT *, 'Record number out-of-range'
      PRINT *
      PRINT *, 'Total number of books in stock = ', TOTAL
      PRINT *, 'File DIRINV created'
      CLOSE (UNIT = 2)

C Exit program
      STOP
      END
```

Records are read from file INVEN and written to file DIRINV in the order in which they are read. Each record of file DIRINV would be formatted, even though the corresponding record in INVEN was unformatted. The control specifier REC = STOCK uses the stock number of each record read to determine where it will be stored in DIRINV.

8.7 Updating a Direct Access File

A direct access file has the property that any record may be read or written without disturbing the rest of the file. For this reason, direct access files are used when a relatively small number of randomly selected records of a file are likely to be modified during a file update. Sequential files are used when most, or all, of the records are likely to be changed during a file update and the records are modified in serial order.

Case Study: Direct Access File Update

Problem

A program is needed to update a bookstore inventory file. The input data for the program consist of the record number (RECNUM) and amount sold (ORDER) for each book that is purchased. These data are not arranged in any special order.

Design Overview

Considering the random nature of the input data, a direct access file (DIRINV) should be used. We will assume that all inventory records contain the same information about a book as the records shown in example 8.18 (stock number, title, author, price, quantity). This information must be read from each inventory record that is to be modified; the inventory amount (QUANT) should then be updated and the new inventory record written to the file.

Data Requirements

Program Parameter

maximum record number for file DIRINV (MAXSTK = 1000)

Input/Output Files

direct access inventory file (DIRINV)

Case Study: Direct Access File Update, continued

Problem Inputs

the stock number of book ordered (INTEGER RECNUM)
the quantity purchased (INTEGER ORDER)
the current inventory file record is read from INVEN and saved in the variables listed below:

(INTEGER STOCK)
(CHARACTER *20 AUTHOR)
(CHARACTER *20 TITLE)
(REAL PRICE)
(INTEGER QUANT)

Problem Outputs

each updated inventory file record is written to file DIRINV

Initial Algorithm

1. For each order, read the record number (RECNUM) and order amount (ORDER) from the keyboard and update the corresponding record of the inventory file (DIRINV).

Step 1 Refinement

1.1 Read the order stock number
1.2 DO WHILE the order stock number is in range
    1.3 Read the order amount
    1.4 Read the inventory record from DIRINV
    1.5 IF the order is valid THEN
            Update the inventory record and write it to DIRINV
        ELSE
            Print an error message
        ENDIF
    1.6 Read the order stock number
ENDDO

Algorithm Refinements

Step 1.5 updates the inventory record selected by the order stock number (RECNUM), provided the order is valid. The order is considered valid if the stock number of the inventory record (STOCK) matches the order stock number and the inventory quantity is sufficient to fill the order. Otherwise, an appropriate error message is printed.

Case Study: Direct Access File Update, continued

Figure 8.17. *Updating the Inventory File DIRINV*

```
        PROGRAM UPDATE
C Updates a direct access inventory file
C Reads the record number and quantity ordered
C from the keyboard. Updates the inventory amount for each record
C selected.

C Declarations
        INTEGER SENVAL, MAXSTK
        PARAMETER (SENVAL = 0, MAXSTK = 1000)
        INTEGER STOCK, QUANT, TOTAL, ORDER, RECNUM
        REAL PRICE
        CHARACTER *20 AUTHOR, TITLE

C Open file INVEN for update
        OPEN (UNIT = 2, FILE = 'DIRINV', FORM = 'FORMATTED',
     +       ACCESS = 'DIRECT', RECL = 54, STATUS = 'OLD')

C Read the record number and quantity of each book sold
C Update the inventory record if order is valid
        PRINT *, 'Enter record number of book sold (or 0 to stop):'
        READ *, RECNUM
        DO WHILE ((RECNUM .GT. SENVAL) .AND. (RECNUM .LE. MAXSTK)) 9 IF ...
           PRINT *, 'Enter quantity sold:'
           READ *, ORDER
C          Get record RECNUM
           READ (UNIT = 2, FMT = 21, REC = RECNUM)
     +        STOCK, AUTHOR, TITLE, PRICE, QUANT

C          If order is valid, update the inventory quantity
           IF ((STOCK .EQ. RECNUM) .AND. (QUANT .GE. ORDER)) THEN
              QUANT = QUANT - ORDER
              PRINT *, 'New inventory amount = ', QUANT
              WRITE (UNIT = 2, FMT = 21, REC = RECNUM)
     +           STOCK, AUTHOR, TITLE, PRICE, QUANT
   21         FORMAT (I4, A20, A20, F6.2, I4)
           ELSE IF (STOCK .EQ. 0) THEN
              PRINT *, 'Error - record does not exist'
           ELSE IF (STOCK .NE. RECNUM) THEN
              PRINT *, 'Error - record and stock number don''t match'
           ELSE
              PRINT *, 'Inventory insufficient to fill order'
           ENDIF

           PRINT *, 'Enter record number of book sold (or 0 to stop):'
           READ *, RECNUM
        ENDDO                                                    GOTO 9
```

Case Study: Direct Access File Update, continued

```
C                                                              ENDIF
        IF (RECNUM .GT. MAXSTK) PRINT *, 'Record number out-of-range'
        CLOSE (UNIT = 2)

C Exit program
        STOP
        END
```

Coding

Figure 8.17 shows program UPDATE. The program user enters the stock number, RECNUM, and quantity of each book sold. The corresponding record is retrieved from file DIRINV. The error message Error - record does not exist is displayed when the inventory record has a stock number of 0. This should happen when a blank record is read from file DIRINV. (This is the reason DIRINV was initialized to all blanks.) The error message Error - record and stock number don't match is displayed if the stock number field of the record read is different from its record number; however, this should never happen.

Testing

Figure 8.18 shows a sample run of the update program for a direct access file. This run assumes that there are two inventory records (record 1, quantity 18

Figure 8.18. *Sample Run of Update Program*

```
Enter record number of book sold (or 0 to stop):
5
Enter quantity sold:
300
New inventory amount =       200

Enter record number of book sold (or 0 to stop):
3
Error - record does not exist

Enter record number of book sold (or 0 to stop):
1
Enter quantity sold:
30
Inventory insufficient to fill order

Enter record number of book sold (or 0 to stop):
0
```

Case Study: Direct Access File Update, continued

and record 5, quantity 500). As shown in this sample, make sure your test data cause all the normal warning messages to be displayed. The error message

```
Error — record and stock number don't match
```

should not be displayed unless your computer system accesses the file incorrectly. After completing the file update, run a program with a DO loop that reads and echos each of the records in file DIRINV in sequence (see exercise 1 below). You should examine the output of this program to make sure that the file update was performed correctly.

---

1. Write a DO loop that echo prints the records in file DIRINV in sequence. Use the loop-control variable as the record number in the READ statement.
2. Modify the program in Fig. 8.17 so that it deletes a record in file DIRINV if the ORDER for that record exceeds the quantity, QUANT. *Hint:* To delete a record, replace it with a blank record.

8.8 ◼️◼️ Common Programming Errors

Format Errors

A number of very common errors can be made in working with formatted input and output. Some of the errors are described in the list below. Errors 3, 5, and 6 are not unique to formatted input and output and can just as easily be made in working with list-directed input and output.

1. Type mismatches in the correspondence between variable names and edit descriptors will result in execution-time errors. A diagnostic message may be printed, and many FORTRAN compilers will immediately terminate execution of your program. Failure to provide a sufficient number of descriptors to accommodate an input or output list may result in type mismatches.
2. If an integer is not right-justified in its field, the blanks on the right may be interpreted as trailing zeros during input. This may change the value of the input data. Similarly, embedded blanks in an integer field may be read as zeros. These comments also apply to real numbers that are typed without a decimal point.
3. If apostrophes in character strings are not carefully paired, the format specification will not be interpreted correctly, and a compile-time syntax error will occur.

4. Attempting to print a number in a field that is too small may result in an execution-time error on some systems. However, many compilers will print only part of the number along with one or more asterisks; no explicit diagnostic will be printed.

5. Not providing sufficient data to satisfy the input variable list will result in an execution-time error. The diagnostic message will indicate that there were insufficient input data or the end of the input file was reached.

6. Failure to provide a line-control character (1, +, 0, or blank) in an output format for the line printer will produce unpredictable program output. This failure may be noted by a warning diagnostic but usually will go undetected during compilation.

File Errors

When working with files, you should use the OPEN statement to connect each file before it is processed. Check with your instructor to determine the local restrictions on file names and unit numbers. If the file is formatted, you must be careful to use the same format to read it as was used to create it.

Make sure that an END = *lab* control specifier is used in each READ statement associated with a sequential file. This is generally the only way to determine when all the file records have been processed; otherwise, an "attempt to read beyond end of file" error may occur. When writing a sequential file, make sure that you always append an end-of-file record before disconnecting the file. When performing a READ/WRITE operation with a direct access file, the record number of the file being accessed must always be specified via a REC = *recnum* control specifier. You should also verify that the integer expression for *recnum* is within range for the file being processed. Otherwise, a file access error will occur.

Chapter Review

A detailed description of the meaning of the more frequently used FORTRAN format descriptors was given. The descriptors X, I, F, E, A, T, and / were described. The use of formatted READ statements was also discussed. This is most helpful when reading character data or data that have been previously written to a data file.

Formatted output permits direct control over the use of every print position of every line printed on a page. When such detailed control is necessary for the generation of precisely spaced output, formats must be used, and the programmer must provide all details of spacing, data types, and data widths.

No list-directed output facility allows the degree of horizontal and vertical space control that can be achieved with formats.

We also provided an introduction to file processing in FORTRAN. We introduced both sequential files and direct access files. The essential difference between them is that the records of sequential files are always processed in a fixed, serial order, whereas the records of a direct access file may be processed in random order.

Table 8.4. *New FORTRAN Statements*

STATEMENT	EFFECT
OPEN Statement	

`OPEN (UNIT = 1, FILE = 'ERZA',`
`+      STATUS = 'OLD',`
`+      FORM = 'UNFORMATTED',`
`+      ACCESS = 'SEQUENTIAL' )`
	Connects an existing sequential file named ERZA to the program. The file is associated with unit number 1.

REWIND Statement	
`REWIND (UNIT = 1)`	Resets the file position pointer for the file associated with unit number 1 to precede the first record.
BACKSPACE Statement	
`BACKSPACE (UNIT = 1)`	Moves the file position pointer to precede the record just processed.
ENDFILE Statement	
`ENDFILE (UNIT = 1)`	Appends an end-of-file record to the file associated with unit number 1.
CLOSE Statement	
`CLOSE (UNIT = 1)`	Disconnects the file associated with unit number 1.
General READ	
`READ (UNIT = 1, FMT = 10,` `+      END = 11) N, A`	Reads two data values from the file with unit number 1 using FORMAT 10. If the end-of-file record is read, a transfer to label 11 occurs.
General WRITE	
`WRITE (UNIT = 2,` `+       REC = I) N, A`	Writes the value of N and A as the Ith record on the file with unit number 2.

We described the OPEN, CLOSE, REWIND, BACKSPACE, and ENDFILE statements and the file parameters that must be specified in the OPEN statement. We also discussed the general READ/WRITE in FORTRAN and the control specifiers that are needed for file input/output operations. The new statements for this chapter are described in Table 8.4.

Quick-Check Exercises

1. A group of data items accessed by a single READ or WRITE statement is called a _____.
2. The records of a _____ _____ file may be accessed _____, but the records of a _____ file must be accessed in order, beginning with the first record.
3. An _____ _____ is used to connect a file to a program that references it.
4. The _____ descriptor may be used when a single format specification describes the appearance of several output lines.
5. The ENDFILE statement is used to write an _____ to a _____ file.
6. Which format descriptor is used for entering (or displaying) the following?
   a. an integer
   b. a real number
   c. a character string
7. How is the X format descriptor used?
8. Why is it not always possible to reuse an input format specification as an output format specification?
9. Write an OPEN statement for a preexisting, unformatted direct access file named YRFILE, with records of length 100.

Answers to Quick-Check Exercises

1. record
2. direct access; randomly; sequential
3. OPEN statement
4. slash
5. end-of-file record; sequential
6. a. I   b. F or E   c. A
7. to enter blank characters into a line of output; to skip over columns of an input line
8. An input format does not specify a carriage-control character, which is required for each output line printed by the line printer.
9.   OPEN (UNIT = 3, FILE = 'YRFILE', FORM = 'UNFORMATTED',
      +   ACCESS = 'DIRECT', RECL = 100, STATUS = 'OLD')

Review Questions

1. Write a READ and a FORMAT statement to enter the input line described below into the variables listed.

Columns	Contents	Variable	Type
1–14	Name	NAME	CHARACTER *15
15–19	Weekly salary (2 decimal places)	WKSAL	REAL
20–21	Age	AGE	INTEGER
22–27	Favorite author	AUTHOR	CHARACTER *10
28	Number of children	NCHILD	INTEGER

2. Assume that the READ statement written for question 1 has been used to enter the input line below, which begins with 2 blanks:

```
BOB SOLOMON 1476384ARTHUR8
```

Show the output displayed by the statements

```
    PRINT 15, NAME, AGE, WKSAL
 15 FORMAT ('1', A, 'IS ', I2, ' YEARS OLD' / ' HE EARNS ',
   +  F6.2, ' DOLLARS PER WEEK')
    PRINT 19, ' HIS FAVORITE AUTHOR IS ', AUTHOR,
   +  ' AND HE HAS', NCHILD, ' CHILDREN'
 19 FORMAT (A, A6, A, I1, A)
```

3. What is wrong with each of the following statements?

```
a.  OPEN (FILE = 'AFILE', FORM = 'FORMATTED', ACCESS = 'DIRECT',
   +      RECL = 100, STATUS = 'OLD')
b.  PRINT '(3X, 2Z10, 3A10, 5X, A4)', A,B,C,D,E,F
c.  FORMAT (' ', 2I4, 5X, A10)
```

4. Write a READ statement to read the Nth record of a direct access file into the variable INREC. Assume that the direct access file is unformatted, contains MAXNUM records, and is associated with unit 2. Be sure to verify that N is in range.

5. Show the output generated by the program segment below.

```
    INTEGER I
    CHARACTER *10 NAMES(12)
    DATA NAMES / 'PATRICIA', 'CHARLES', 'MARY', 'MEG', 'MARIE',
   +   'CHUCK', 'RICHARD', 'SHEILA', 'IRENE', 'HOWARD', 'EDWARD',
   +   'HELEN' /

    PRINT 10, NAMES
 10 FORMAT ((1X, 4(A10, 5X)))
```

Programming Projects

1. Write a program to read in the addresses of all the students in the class and print each address on an envelope. You may assume that a "skip to the top of the next page" operation implies that the next envelope is put in position for the first line of an address.

   Each address will be printed on three lines. The information to be printed on the first line is in columns 1–20 of each input line. The second line of information is in columns 21–40, and the third line is contained in columns 41–80. For example,

```
MR. JOHN JONES      325 CEDAR ST.      PHILADELPHIA      PA. 19122
1                   21                 41                61
```

2. Especially during the colder months of the year, weather forecasters frequently inform us not only of the Fahrenheit-degree temperature (TEMP) reading at a given hour, but also of the wind-chill factor (WCF) at that time. This factor is used to indicate the relative degree of coldness that we are likely to experience if we are outside. Its calculation is based on the thermometer reading (TEMP) and the velocity (V) of the wind at the time. Write a program to compute the wind-chill factor for temperatures ranging from −50° to +50° in increments of 5° and for wind velocities of from 5 to 60 miles per hour, also in increments of 5°. Your output should appear similar to the following table.

```
WIND-CHILL FACTOR TABLE (DEGREES F)
TEMPERATURE                 WIND VELOCITY (MILES PER HOUR)
READING (DEG F)        5 10 15 20 25 30 35 . . .
      -50
      -45
      -40
       .                         .
       .                         .
       .                         .
        0
        5
       .
       .
       .
       20          . . .                 -16
       .
       .
       .
       50
```

The formula for computing the wind-chill factor is

$$WCF = 91.4 - (.486 + .305\sqrt{V} - .020v) \times (91.4 - temp)$$

Your answers should be rounded to the nearest whole degree. The WCF of −16 has been given as a test value. It is the WCF when TEMP is 20 degrees and V is 25.

3. *Base 2 addition, using the multiple-alternative decision structure.* Write a program to read two 15-digit binary numbers (strings of 0's and 1's) into the arrays I and J (both of size 15), using the 15I1 format. Then compute the decimal (base 10) representation of these numbers and print both the binary and decimal representations.

Next, compute the column-by-column sum of these two numbers, moving *right to left*. Use the variable CARRY to indicate whether a previous addition contained a CARRY. A value of 0 for CARRY should indicate that the previous addition had no carry; a value of 1 should be used when a carry occurs. (Initially, CARRY is 0.) Store the column-by-column sum in the array SUMIJ of size 16. The value of each element SUMIJ(L+1) and the next value of CARRY is determined by adding the values of elements I(L), J(L), and CARRY, as shown next.

For all L from 15 to 1:

If only one of I(L), J(L), or CARRY is 1, then

SUMIJ(L+1) is 1, and CARRY must be set to 0.

If all three of I(L), J(L), and CARRY are 1, then

SUMIJ(L+1) is 1 and CARRY must be set to 1.

If any two of I(L), J(L), or CARRY are 1, then

SUMIJ(L+1) is 0 and CARRY must be set to 1.

Otherwise, SUMIJ(L+1) is 0 and CARRY must be set to 0.

This will define the values of SUMIJ(16) through SUMIJ(2), from I(15), J(15) through I(1) and J(1), respectively. SUMIJ(1) can be defined directly from CARRY, once the other "additions" are done. Compute the decimal representation of the SUM and print the binary and decimal representations.

Test your program on the following strings:

```
I = 00000 00010 11011
J = 00000 01010 11110
I = 00000 00010 00110
J = 00000 00001 11101
I = 10001 00010 00100
J = 11100 11101 11001
```

Your output, for example, for the second set of data might appear as follows:

```
    I =   00000 00010 00110
    J =   00000 00001 11101
SUMIJ = 000000 00100 00011
```

Use functions and subroutines as needed and draw a structure chart.

4. *Determining the collating sequence on your computer.* On a single data line, type the following character string (starting in column 1):

```
+JB4PUD(OFY3RH2MCAT)=7Z N.W8KLG56$9QIV*/X-E,0'1S
1          10        20        30          40
```

There should be a total of forty-eight characters in your line. Write a program that will read these characters into an array CHARS one character per array element and sort them. Print the string before the sort and after. The result will tell you the

Figure 8.19. *Questionnaire for Programming Project 5*

POLITICS AS USUAL—A PREFERENCE POLL

1. Name: — — — — — — — — — — — —,   — — — — — — — —,   —
       1 2 3 4 5 6 7 8 9 10 11 12   14 15 16 17 18 19 20 21   23
              Last   First   M.I.

2. Academic year:

        — —
        25 26

(Fr, So, Jr, Sr; use 0 for other)

3. Age:

      — —
     28 29

For items 4 through 10, answer yes (Y) or no (N).

4. Have you ever voted in a presidential election?
    —
    31

5. Do you think that most politicians are basically honest?
    —
    32

6. Do you think that most politicians are responsive to the needs of their constituents?
    —
    33

7. Do you think that the federal government has taken steps sufficient to prevent another Watergate?
    —
    34

8. Have you ever taken a political science course?
    —
    35

9. Are you very interested in national politics?
    —
    36

10. Have you ever paid any Federal income taxes?
    —
    37

exact collating sequence for these characters on the computer you are using. *Hint:* Use the subroutine SORT shown in Section 7.4 or an equivalent subroutine of your own to perform the sort. Remember to change the declarations in this subroutine: you will be using it to sort character strings and not real numbers. Use the edit descriptor A1. *Warning to instructors:* For desired results, these hints may require modification on some computers.

5. Complete the questionnaire shown in Fig. 8.19 by filling in the blanks as instructed. Each blank shown has a number below it. These numbers indicate the columns of the data line in which your responses will be typed for processing by the computer. Write a program that will read in the responses to the questionnaire for all students in your class and tabulate the results as follows:

   a. Compute and print the total number of responses and a breakdown according to class and according to age: under 18, 18–22, over 22.
   b. Compute and print the number of yes and no answers to each of questions 4–10.

   Label all output appropriately and use formats for all input and output.
   Hint: Read the answers to questions 4 through 10 into an array (ANSWER) of size 7, using 7A1 format. To compare the responses to the letter Y, use a statement such as

   ```
   IF (ANSWER(I) .EQ. 'Y') THEN
   ```

6. Write a program to print a table (with headings) for values of n, n^2, n^3, $\sqrt{n}$, and $\sqrt[3]{n}$, where n is an integer that ranges from 1 to 100 in steps of 1. Use formats.

M7. Write a program that, given the size of an angle in degrees, computes the size in radians and then computes the sine, cosine, and tangent of the angle. The program should print a neatly arranged, appropriately labeled five-column table for degrees, radians, sine, cosine, and tangent of angles from $-90°$ to $+90°$ in steps of $1°$. Note that the SIN, COS, and TAN functions all require real arguments in radians and that tan 90° and tan $-90°$ are not mathematically defined. You should note undefined computations in a meaningful way in your table. Keep your answers accurate to five decimal places. Use the following formula for degrees-to-radians conversion:

$$number\ of\ radians = 0.01745 * number\ of\ degrees$$

8. We can consider a single sheet of printer paper as a piece of graph paper containing a grid of 50×100—50 rows and 100 columns (with space left over). We can use this grid to plot a function f on x, y-axes, in much the same way as we would plot f on a piece of graph paper. To do this, we set up two 100-element real arrays, Y and XLIST, and a CHARACTER *1 array LINE of size 100. LINE will be used to define 50 lines of 100 print positions each. Initially, LINE is to contain all blanks. Y will be used to store 100 values of f (one for each of 100 values of x along the x-axis). XLIST will be used to define the index of each x in the 100-item list used to compute $f(x)$. Thus, initially, XLIST$(i) = i$ for all values of i between 1 and 100.

These indices will be used to indicate which of the 100 horizontal grids corresponds to each value of x for which $f(x)$ was computed.

Now proceed as shown in the following algorithm.

Algorithm

1. Let XMIN be the smallest value of X and XMAX the largest value of X
2. Define a subinterval length, SUBINT, equal to (XMAX − XMIN) / 99.0
3. Initialize X to XMIN
4. DO for each value of LV from 1 to 100
     5. Compute f(X) and store it in Y(LV)
     6. Increment X by SUBINT
  CONTINUE

This will compute a value of f for each of the 100 values of X used. Each x index and the corresponding value $f(x)$ will be stored in corresponding elements of XLIST and Y, respectively.

Next we sort, in descending order, the array Y, exchanging the contents of the elements in XLIST in parallel with the exchanges in Y.

Then we determine 50 y-axis values (one for each line of output) as follows: Compute YINT as

$$YINT = \frac{Y(1) - Y(100)}{49.0}$$

where Y(1) now contains the largest value of f, and Y(100) contains the smallest value. We must print each of the 50 lines of the grid. The first line corresponds to the value Y(1), the second Y(1) − YINT, the third to Y(1) − 2 * YINT, . . . , and the 50th to Y(1) − 49 * YINT, or Y(100). (For example, if Y(1) = 1000.0 and Y(100) = 100.0, then the lines would correspond to

1000.00, 981.63, 963.26, . . . , 136.74, 118.37, 100.00.

Note that 900./49. = 18.37.)
We do this as follows.

Algorithm

1. Initialize array `LINE` to all blanks
2. Initialize `LINVAL` to `Y(1)`
3. `DO WHILE LINVAL` is greater than or equal to `Y(100)`
  4. For each K such that `Y(K)` is closer to `LINVAL` than to `LINVAL` − `YINT`, place a '$' in `LINE(XLIST(K))`
  5. Display `LINE`
  6. Replace each '$' in `LINE` with ' '
  7. Reset `LINVAL` to `LINVAL` − `YINT`

`ENDDO`

The implementation of step 4 is simplified since the data in array Y has been sorted. We illustrate by example, using the *y*-axis values computed earlier. Suppose the first few elements in Y and XLIST are defined as follows.

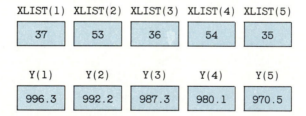

The first time through loop 3, `LINVAL` will be equal to 1000. Since both 996.3 and 992.2 are closer in value to 1000 than to 981.63, a $ will be entered into `LINE(37)` and `LINE(53)`. The next time through loop 2, `LINVAL` will be 981.63. Since 987.3 and 980.1 are closer to 981.63 than to 963.26, a $ will be placed in `LINE(36)` and `LINE(54)`. Therefore, the test for the condition

$$\text{ABS}(Y(K) - \text{LINVAL}) < \text{ABS}(Y(K) - (\text{LINVAL} - \text{YINT}))$$

must be made only for consecutive elements in Y, starting where the previous test failed and continuing until the test fails again.

Write a program to implement the above algorithms. Use subroutines whenever practicable. Test your program on the function

$$f(x) = (x - 1)^4/(x - 6),$$

where x ranges from -1 to $+6$ ($[-1,6]$). Provide a structure chart to describe the components of your system.

9. Let FILEA and FILEB be two files containing the name and identification number of the students in two different programming classes. Assume that these files are arranged in ascending order by student number and that no student is in both classes. Write a program to read the information on FILEA and FILEB and merge them onto a third file (FILEC) retaining the ascending order.

10. Write a program that reads a name and a list of three exam scores for each student in a class and copies this information onto a sequential file called GRADES. Test your program on the following data:

```
IVORY    47 82 93
CLARK    86 42 77
MENACE   99 88 92
BUMSTEAD 88 74 81
```

Provide a subroutine that reads and echo prints the file GRADES. Then write a program that adds a fourth exam score to each component of the file GRADES. Assume that each student's name and fourth exam score are provided as input data.

11. Write a program to read the sequential file created in Example 8.15, sort the file in ascending order according to stock number and write the results on a new file. You may assume that the entire sequential file will fit in memory at once.

12. Create a sequential file SALMEN containing the salaries of ten men, and a second sequential file SALWOM containing the salaries of ten women. For each employee on these files, there is an employee number (four digits), an employee name (a string), and an employee salary. Each file is arranged in ascending order by employee number. Write a program that will read each of these files and merge the contents onto a third file, SALARY, retaining the ascending order of employee numbers. For each employee written to the file SALARY, write an M (for male) or an F (for female) following the employee number.

13. Write a program to read and print the file SALARY and compute the average salary for all employees.

14. Assume you have a file of records each containing a person's last name, first name, birth date, and sex. Create a new file containing only first names and sex. Also, print out the complete name of every person whose last name begins with the letter A, C, F, or P through Z and was born in a month that begins with the letter J.

15. Write a program that prints every record of a direct access file whose record number ends with a zero.

16. Write a menu-driven program that will update a direct access book store inventory file. The menu options should include:

a. creating an initial blank file
b. inserting records in a file
c. updating selected records
d. displaying selected records
e. displaying all nonblank records

If option b or c is chosen, the new record data should be entered at the terminal. The program user should be able to verify that the record is correct before it is written to the file.

9. String Manipulation

So FAR, we have seen limited use of character data. Character variables have appeared in the list portion of data initialization and READ and PRINT statements, and they have been used for storing character strings that were later displayed to identify program output. Strings have also been used in PRINT statements to annotate program output and for format specification.

Many computer applications are concerned with the manipulation of textual data rather than numerical data. Computer-based *word processing systems* enable a user to compose letters, term papers, newspaper articles, and even books at a computer terminal instead of using a typewriter. The advantage of using such a system is that words and sentences can be modified, whole paragraphs can be moved, and then a fresh copy can be printed without mistakes or erasures.

Additional applications include the use of computerized typesetters in the publishing industry; text editors are used to update telephone directories and annual reports on a regular basis; computers are used in the analysis of great works of literature.

In the sections that follow, we will introduce some fundamental operations that can be performed on character data. We will describe how to reference a character substring and how to concatenate (or join) two strings. We will learn how to search for a substring in a larger string and how to delete a substring or replace it with another.

9.1 Character String Declaration

We have already used the CHARACTER statement to declare character strings and string arrays. For example, the declaration

```
CHARACTER *10 A(20), FLOWER
```

allocates storage space for twenty-one character strings consisting of ten characters each. (Twenty of these strings are elements of the array A.)

The notion of the length of a character string is important to the discussion of character-type data. We will introduce this concept by defining what is meant by the length of a character string constant or variable. The definition of the length of other character entities will be given as they are introduced in later sections.

Length of Character String Constants and Variables

1. The length of a character string constant is equal to the number of characters in the constant (excluding the apostrophes used to delimit the con-

stant) except that a pair of adjacent apostrophes within the constant is counted as a single character.
2. The length of a character variable is defined to be the length given to the variable when it is declared.

Note that the length of any character entity is a positive number and may not change. Zero-length character strings are not permitted in FORTRAN.

As indicated above, the length of a character variable remains unchanged, although character data of different lengths may be assigned to the variable. Any character string that is shorter than the declared length of a variable will be padded on the right with blanks when assigned to that variable; any string that is too long cannot be stored in its entirety and is truncated.

FORTRAN provides a library function LEN that can be used to determine the length of its character string argument. We will describe this function and provide examples of its use in Section 9.5.

9.2 ▭ Substrings

We frequently need to reference substrings of a longer character string. For example, we might want to examine the day, '25', in the string 'JUNE 25, 1990' or remove the substring 'Machinery' from the string 'Association for Computing Machinery'. In this section, we will see how to use special features of FORTRAN to segment a character string into substrings or to extract part of a longer string.

To specify a substring of a character variable or character array element, we write the substring name in the form shown next.

Substring References

> SYNTAX: *cname* (*exp$_1$* : *exp$_2$*)
>
> EXAMPLE: FLOWER(4 : 8)
>
> INTERPRETATION: *Cname* is a character variable or character array element, and *exp$_1$*, *exp$_2$* are substring expressions. The values of *exp$_1$* and *exp$_2$* should be type integer. *exp$_1$* and *exp$_2$* are used to specify which substring of *cname* should be referenced. The value of *exp$_1$* indicates the position in *cname* of the first character of the substring; the value of *exp$_2$* indicates the position in *cname* of the last character of the substring.
>
> NOTE: The reference *cname*(*exp$_1$* : *exp$_2$*) is called the *substring name*. The integer values of *exp$_1$* and *exp$_2$* must satisfy the following constraints:
>
> $$1 \le exp_1 \le exp_2 \le length\ of\ cname$$

If *exp₁* is omitted, it is considered to be 1; if *exp₂* is omitted, it is considered to be the same as the length of *cname*. The substring length is defined as $exp_2 - exp_1 + 1$.

EXAMPLE 9.1

The names of three substrings of the character variable PRES are shown below.

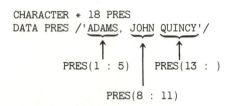

EXAMPLE 9.2

The program segment

```
CHARACTER *11 SOSSEC
CHARACTER *3 SSN1
CHARACTER *2 SSN2
CHARACTER *4 SSN3
PRINT *, 'Enter a social security number in apostrophes'
READ *, SOSSEC
SSN1 = SOSSEC(1 : 3)
SSN2 = SOSSEC(5 : 6)
SSN3 = SOSSEC(8 : 11)
```

reads a character string representing a social security number. If the string '042–30–0786' is read, this program segment breaks the social security number into substrings, as shown below:

SOSSEC	SSN1	SSN2	SSN3
042–30–0786	042	30	0786

The assignment statements in this program are *character assignment statements*; they each assign a character string to a character variable. We will discuss character assignments in more detail later in this chapter.

EXAMPLE 9.3

The program in Fig. 9.1 prints each word of the sentence SENTNC on a separate line. It assumes that a single blank occurs between words.

The statement

```
CHARACTER *(LENGTH) SENTNC
```

declares a character variable whose length is determined by the parameter LENGTH. Any expression involving integer constants and parameters may be used to specify the length of a character variable. The expression must be enclosed in parentheses.

Figure 9.1. *Program to Print Words in a Sentence*

```
      PROGRAM WORDS
C Print each word in a sentence

C Declarations
      INTEGER LENGTH
      CHARACTER *1 BLANK
      PARAMETER (LENGTH = 80, BLANK = ' ')
      CHARACTER *(LENGTH) SENTNC
      INTEGER FIRST, NEXT

C Enter data string
      PRINT *, 'Enter a string:'
      READ '(A)', SENTNC

C Print each word (the characters between the blanks)
      FIRST = 1
      DO 10 NEXT = 1, LENGTH
         IF (SENTNC(NEXT : NEXT) .EQ. BLANK) THEN
            PRINT *, SENTNC(FIRST : NEXT)
            FIRST = NEXT + 1
         ENDIF
   10 CONTINUE

C Print the last word if it is not yet printed
         IF (SENTNC(LENGTH : LENGTH) .NE. BLANK) THEN
            PRINT *, SENTNC(FIRST : LENGTH)
         ENDIF

C Exit program
      STOP
      END

Enter a string:
THE QUICK BROWN FOX JUMPED
THE
QUICK
BROWN
FOX
JUMPED
```

The program variable FIRST always points to the start of the current word and is initialized to 1. During each execution of the loop, the condition

```
(SENTNC(NEXT : NEXT) .EQ. BLANK)
```

tests to see whether the next character is a blank. If it is, the statements

```
PRINT *, SENTNC(FIRST : NEXT)
FIRST = NEXT + 1
```

cause all characters in the current word (from FIRST through the blank) to be printed, and FIRST to be reset to point to the first character following the blank.

The statement

```
PRINT *, SENTNC(FIRST : LENGTH)
```

following the loop is used to print the last word. This is necessary only when the last character (SENTNC(LENGTH : LENGTH)) is not a blank. ■

The formatted READ statement

```
READ '(A)', SENTNC
```

is used to enter the data line as one long string (length 80) into SENTNC. The data string should not be enclosed in quotes.

1. Given the character variables SSN1 and PRES (defined in examples 9.1 and 9.2), list the characters that would be printed by the statements

```
PRINT *, SSN1(1 : 3)
PRINT *, PRES(6 : )
PRINT *, PRES( : 6)
PRINT *, PRES( : )
```

2. Indicate how you could modify the program in Fig. 9.1 to convert a sentence to "pig latin," in which the first letter of each word is moved to the end of the word, followed by the letters AY. The string 'THE QUICK BROWN FOX JUMPED' would become 'HETAY UICKQAY ROWNBAY OXFAY UMPEDJAY'.
Hint: It is necessary to change only the two PRINT statements.

3. Modify Example 9.3 so that the restriction of a single blank between words is removed. Your program will have to skip over a group of consecutive blanks.

9.3 ▰▰▰ Character Expressions

Until now, character expressions have consisted of individual character variables, substrings, or character string constants. In FORTRAN, we can join strings using the *concatenation operator* // (two consecutive slashes). The concatenation operator comes between the arithmetic operators and the relational operators in the precedence table shown in Section 4.4 (Table 4.8).

The Concatenation Operator

> SYNTAX: $S_1 \; // \; S_2$
>
> INTERPRETATION: The character string S_1 is concatenated with the character string S_2. This means the string S_2 is joined to the right end of the string S_1. The length of the resulting string is equal to the sum of the lengths of S_1 and S_2.

EXAMPLE 9.4

1. The expression

    ```
    'ABC' // 'DE'
    ```

    concatenates the strings `'ABC'` and `'DE'` together to form one string of length 5, `'ABCDE'`.

2. Given a string MESSAG with eleven or more characters, the expression

    ```
    MESSAG (1 : 5) // '*****' // MESSAG (11 : )
    ```

    creates a new string that differs from MESSAG only in character positions 6 through 10 (replaced with asterisks).

3. Given the string

    ```
    'ADAMS, JOHN QUINCY'
    ```

    stored in the character variable PRES (length 18), the expression

    ```
    PRES(8 : 12) // PRES(13 : 13) // '. ' // PRES( : 5)
    ```

    forms the string

    ```
    'JOHN Q. ADAMS'
    ```

    of length 13 (5 + 1 + 2 + 5). ∎

Use of Character Expressions

Character expressions may be used in FORTRAN in character assignment statements, as operands of relational operators in logical expressions, in PRINT statements, and as arguments in subprogram calls. In this section, we will describe the rules for the first two of these uses of character expressions; character string arguments will be discussed later in this chapter.

The character assignment statement is described next.

Character Assignment Statement

> SYNTAX: *cname = expression*
>
> INTERPRETATION: *Cname* may be a character variable, an array element, or a substring name. A character *expression* consists of a sequence of character string constants, character variables, character array elements, substrings, or character-valued functions connected by the concatenation operator //.

> NOTES: If the length of *cname* exceeds the length of *expression*, *expression* will be padded on the right with blanks before being stored.
>
> If the length of *cname* is less than the length of *expression*, the extra characters at the right of *expression* will be discarded.
>
> If *cname* is a substring name, only the specified substring is defined by the assignment; all other characters in the string are unchanged, for example, NAME(2 : 4) = *expression* changes only characters 2 through 4 of NAME.
>
> None of the character positions being defined in *cname* may be part of *expression*. For example, NAME(1 : 2) = NAME(1 : 1) // 'A' is illegal since NAME(1 : 1) is being defined (NAME(2 : 2) = NAME(1 : 1) would be legal).

EXAMPLE 9.5

Consider the following sample program segment.

```
CHARACTER BIGGER *17, SMALLR *8, SAME *12
BIGGER = 'EXTRASENSORY'
SMALLR = BIGGER
SAME = BIGGER
```

The CHARACTER declaration allocates storage for three strings of different lengths. The result of executing the assignment statements is shown next.

The assignment statement

```
BIGGER(6 : ) = SAME
```

would change BIGGER as shown below.

BIGGER

| EXTRAEXTRASENSORY |

This result could also be obtained using the assignment statement

```
BIGGER = SMALLR(1 : 5) // SAME
```                           ■

EXAMPLE 9.6

Consider the sample program segment

```
CHARACTER *8 NAME, HERS, HIS
CHARACTER *4 FIRST, FIRSTA, FIRSTB, INITLS
CHARACTER *9 LSTFST
NAME = 'JOHN DOE'
FIRST = 'JIM'
FIRSTA = NAME(1 : 2)
FIRSTB = NAME
HIS = FIRST // NAME(6 : )
LSTFST = NAME(6 : ) // ', ' // NAME( : 4)
```

```
INITLS = NAME(1 : 1) // '.' // NAME(6 : 6) // '.'
HERS = NAME
HERS(3 : 3) = 'A'
```

The execution of the assignment statements in this segment will result in the following string assignments. ■

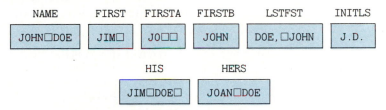

SELF-CHECK
EXERCISES FOR
SECTION 9.3

1. Given the string PRES

   'ADAMS, JOHN QUINCY'

   write the strings formed by the following expressions:

   ```
   PRES(8 : 11) // ' ' // PRES( : 5)
   PRES(1 : 5) // PRES(7 : 8) // '.' // PRES(13 : 13) // '.'
   ```

2. Let HIPPO, QUOTE, QUOTE1, QUOTE2, and BIGGER be declared and initialized as

   ```
   CHARACTER *12 HIPPO, BIGGER
   CHARACTER *30 QUOTE1
   CHARACTER *24 QUOTE2, QUOTE
   DATA HIPPO, BIGGER / 'HIPPOPOTAMUS', 'SMALL' /
   DATA QUOTE1 / 'STRUCTURED PROGRAMS ARE BETTER' /
   ```

   Carry out each of the following assignment statements in sequence. Indicate if any are illegal.

   ```
   a. QUOTE( : 24) = QUOTE1(21 : 24) // QUOTE1( : 20)
   b. QUOTE2 = QUOTE(21 : 24) // QUOTE( : 20)
   c. QUOTE(1 : 24) = QUOTE2
   d. HIPPO(4 : ) = 'S'
   e. BIGGER = 'LARGE'
   f. BIGGER(1 : 6) = BIGGER(7 : 12)
   g. BIGGER(6 : 7) = 'ST'
   ```

9.4 ▬▬▬ String Comparisons

The comparison of character strings was discussed in Chapter 4. We learned that the order relationship between two strings is based on the FORTRAN collating sequence, as described below.

Collating Sequence

1. The blank character precedes (is less than) all of the digits (0, 1, 2, . . . , 9) and all of the letters (A, B, C, . . . , Z).
2. The letters are ordered lexigraphically (in dictionary sequence), that is, A precedes B, B precedes C, . . . , Y precedes Z.
3. The digits follow their normal numeric sequence, that is, the character 0 precedes 1, 1 precedes 2, . . . , 8 precedes 9.

It is important to note what is not specified by the collating sequence. In particular,

- The relationship between the special characters (punctuation symbols, arithmetic operators, etc.) and A–Z, 0–9, and blank depend on the character code used.
- The relationship between the letters A–Z and the characters 0–9 depend on the character code used.

As mentioned in Chapter 4, the collating sequence ensures that order comparisons between strings of letters will follow their dictionary sequence; however, little else is guaranteed.

EXAMPLE 9.7 The relationships between the pairs of character strings shown below are not specified.

'ALLEN, R.' and 'ALLEN, RICHARD'	Depends on relative order of period and I.
'X123' and 'XYZ'	Depends on relative order of 1 and Y.
'./*' and '.*//*='	Depends on relative order of / and *.
'***' and '*'	Depends on relative order of * and blank. ∎

All relationships not specified are compiler-dependent and are based on the internal code used by the compiler. Three common codes are shown in Appendix B. It is important that you learn the collating sequence defined for the compiler that you are using. The special functions described next may be of some help.

CHAR and ICHAR FORTRAN has a library function, ICHAR, which can be used to determine the relative position of a character in the collating sequence. For example, the statement

```
PRINT *, ICHAR(' '), ICHAR('A'), ICHAR('O')
```

prints the relative positions in the collating sequence of the three characters shown (blank, letter A, and zero).

The function CHAR is the *inverse* of the function ICHAR; CHAR can be used to determine the character in a specified position of the collating sequence. The statement

```
PRINT *, CHAR(0)
```

will print the first character of the collating sequence (position 0).

The functions CHAR and ICHAR are described next.

**Function
ICHAR**

SYNTAX: ICHAR(*character*)

EXAMPLE: ICHAR('A')

INTERPRETATION: The integer function ICHAR determines the relative position of *character* in the FORTRAN collating sequence.

**Function
CHAR**

SYNTAX: CHAR(*pos*)

EXAMPLE: CHAR(27)

INTERPRETATION: The character function CHAR determines the character at relative position *pos* in the collating sequence. The value of *pos* must be between 0 and $n-1$, where n is the number of characters in the collating sequence.

EXAMPLE 9.8

The program in Fig. 9.2 prints the position in the collating sequence of each character in the FORTRAN character set. The character set is stored in the character variable CHRSET. The PRINT statement prints a character, CHRSET (POS : POS), followed by its position in the collating sequence, ICHAR (CHRSET (POS : POS)). Try this program on your computer.   ∎

Figure 9.2. *Position of FORTRAN Characters in the Collating Sequence*

```
      PROGRAM COLLAT
C Prints the relative positions in the collating sequence
C of all characters in the FORTRAN character set

C Declarations
      INTEGER SETSIZ
      PARAMETER (SETSIZ = 49)
      INTEGER POS
      CHARACTER *(SETSIZ) CHRSET
```

```
C FORTRAN character set
      DATA CHRSET
     + /' ABCDEFGHIJKLMNOPQRSTUVWXYZ0123456789+-*/()=$,.''':'/

C Print each character and its relative position
      PRINT *, 'Collating sequence positions for FORTRAN characters'
      PRINT *
      PRINT *, 'Character      Position'
      DO 10 POS = 1, SETSIZ
         PRINT '(5X, A, 11X, 13)',
     +      CHRSET(POS : POS), ICHAR(CHRSET(POS : POS))
   10 CONTINUE

C Exit program
      STOP
      END
```

EXAMPLE 9.9   The program in Fig. 9.3 counts and prints the number of occurrences of each character in an input string (TEXT). The array CHRCNT (subscripts 0 through 255) is used to keep track of the number of occurrences of each character. This array is initialized to all zeros. Since ICHAR(NEXCHR) is the position of character NEXCHR in the collating sequence, the statement

    CHRCNT(ICHAR(NEXCHR)) = CHRCNT(ICHAR(NEXCHR)) + 1

increments the array element corresponding to character NEXCHR. The statement

    PRINT '(4X, A, 17X, I2)', CHAR(POS), CHRCNT(POS)

in DO loop 30 prints each character followed by its number of occurrences.

Figure 9.3. *Counting Character Occurrences in a String*

```
      PROGRAM OCCURS
C Finds the number of occurrences of each character in text

C Declarations
      INTEGER COLLEN, TXTLEN
      PARAMETER (COLLEN = 255, TXTLEN = 80)
      INTEGER CHRCNT(0 : COLLEN), POS, NEXT
      CHARACTER *(TXTLEN) TEXT
      CHARACTER *1 NEXCHR

C Initialize array of counters and enter data string
      DATA CHRCNT /0, COLLEN * 0/
      PRINT *, 'Enter a string:'
      READ '(A)', TEXT

C Increase count of each character in text
      DO 20 NEXT = 1, TXTLEN
         NEXCHR = TEXT(NEXT : NEXT)
         CHRCNT(ICHAR(NEXCHR)) = CHRCNT(ICHAR(NEXCHR)) + 1
   20 CONTINUE
```

```
C Print results
      PRINT *, 'Character        Occurrence'
      DO 30 POS = 0, COLLEN
         IF (CHRCNT(POS) .NE. 0) THEN
            PRINT '(4X, A, 17X, I2)', CHAR(POS), CHRCNT(POS)
         ENDIF
   30 CONTINUE

C Exit program
      STOP
      END
```

The program shown in Fig. 9.3 works regardless of the collating sequence used on a particular computer. The decision step inside loop 30 ensures that counts are printed only for those characters that actually appear in the text string. A sample run is shown in Fig. 9.4.   ∎

Figure 9.4. *Sample Output for Program in Fig. 9.3*

```
Enter a string:
THE QUICK BROWN FOX JUMPED OVER THE LAZY DOG.

Character          Occurrence
                        8
    .                   1
    A                   1
    B                   1
    C                   1
    D                   2
    E                   4
    F                   1
    G                   1
    H                   2
    I                   1
    J                   1
    K                   1
    L                   1
    M                   1
    N                   1
    O                   4
    P                   1
    Q                   1
    R                   2
    T                   2
    U                   2
    V                   1
    W                   1
    X                   1
    Y                   1
    Z                   1
```

9.5 ▬▬▬ String Length and Search Functions

The FORTRAN library function LEN determines the length (number of characters) in its character string argument, as described next.

String Length Function LEN

> SYNTAX: LEN(*string*)
>
> INTERPRETATION: *String* may be any character expression (including character string constants and variables). The value returned is an integer denoting the length of *string*.
>
> NOTES: If *string* is a character string constant, its length is determined by counting the characters inside the enclosing apostrophes [e.g., LEN ('ABC') is 3; LEN('A''S') is also 3 (why?)].
>
> If *string* is a character variable (or array element), its length is defined by the variable (or array) declaration statement.
>
> If *string* is a substring of the form S(exp_1 : exp_2), its length is equal to $exp_2 - exp_1 + 1$.
>
> If *string* is a character expression involving the concatenation operator, //, its length is equal to the sum of the individual string lengths of the operands of //.

EXAMPLE 9.10

1. LEN ('ABCDE') returns a value of 5.
2. LEN ('MY' // 'NAME') returns a value of 6.
3. If WORD is declared as a character variable of length 10, LEN(WORD) always returns a value of 10. Thus, the sequence of statements

```
WORD = 'ABCDE'
I = LEN(WORD)
PRINT *, I
```

prints the value 10, the length of the string 'ABCDE   ' that is stored in WORD. ∎

The Function GETLEN

As indicated above, the length of a character variable is independent of the data stored in it. There are times when we would like to know exactly how many characters are stored in a string, excluding any blank padding.

EXAMPLE 9.11

Often we want to disregard any padding characters when determining the length of a string. Standard FORTRAN does not provide a library function for this purpose, so we must write our own. The user-defined function GETLEN in

Fig. 9.5 determines the "actual" length of an input string, excluding any blank padding. It does this by starting with the last character and skipping over blanks until the first nonblank character is reached. If the last character in string S is not a blank, the value of GETLEN(S) is the same as LEN(S). If all characters are blank, GETLEN returns a value of zero. (The statement

```
CHARACTER *(*) STRING
```

in Fig. 9.5 is explained in the next section.)   ■

Figure 9.5. *Function GETLEN*

```
      INTEGER FUNCTION GETLEN (STRING)
C Determines length of string excluding any blank padding
C Pre : STRING is defined.
C Post: The function result is the actual string length
C       and includes only the characters preceding the padding.

      CHARACTER *(*) STRING

C Local Declarations
      CHARACTER *1 BLANK
      PARAMETER (BLANK = ' ')
      INTEGER NEXT

C Start with the last character and find the first nonblank
      DO 10 NEXT = LEN(STRING), 1, -1
         IF (STRING(NEXT : NEXT) .NE. BLANK) THEN
            GETLEN = NEXT
            RETURN
         ENDIF
   10 CONTINUE

C All characters are blanks
      GETLEN = 0

C Exit function
      RETURN
      END
```

The GETLEN function is very useful when concatenating strings. If SHORTS is a character variable, there may be a number of extraneous blanks before the letter M in the character string formed by the expression

```
SHORTS // ' MORE STUFF'
```

There is only one blank before the letter M in the character string formed by

```
SHORTS(1 : GETLEN(SHORTS)) // ' MORE STUFF'
```

Length of Character Arguments

Character arguments in a subprogram call can be character expressions (including character string constants or character variables). Character arguments used in a subprogram call must, of course, correspond to type character dummy arguments.

The type declaration of a character dummy argument specifies its length. The declared length of a character dummy argument may not exceed the length of its associated actual argument. If the length, L, of a dummy argument is less than the actual argument length, then only the leftmost L characters of the actual argument will be associated with the dummy argument.

In most cases, we wish the length of a character dummy argument to be the same as its corresponding actual argument. However, the dummy argument lengths cannot be predetermined since the subprogram arguments (and their lengths) change from one call to the next. Consequently, FORTRAN allows the programmer to use the symbols (*) to declare the length of a character dummy argument. The statement

```
CHARACTER *(*) STRING
```

in Fig. 9.5 indicates that the dummy argument STRING will assume the length of its corresponding actual argument. The actual argument length may vary from one call to the next and may be determined by the function LEN, as illustrated in the DO loop header in Fig. 9.5.

Searching for a Substring

In this section, we will introduce a library function that is helpful in examining and manipulating a string stored in memory. The string search function, INDEX, can be used to search a string (the *subject string*) for a desired substring (the *target string*). For example, if SENTNC is the subject string shown below

SENTNC

```
WHAT NEXT
```

we could use this function to determine whether a target string 'AT' is a substring in SENTNC; the INDEX function should tell us that 'AT' appears at position 3 (counting from the left). If we tried to locate a target string 'IT', the INDEX function would return a value of zero since 'IT' is not a substring of SENTNC. The function INDEX is described next.

String Search Function INDEX

SYNTAX: INDEX (*subject, target*)

EXAMPLE: INDEX (SENTNC, '.')

INTERPRETATION: The function INDEX returns an integer value indicating the starting position in the character string *subject* of a substring matching the string *target*.

NOTES: If there is more than one occurrence of *target*, the starting position of the first occurrence is returned.

If *target* does not occur in *subject*, the value 0 is returned.

EXAMPLE 9.12

The program in Fig. 9.6 replaces all occurrences of the string `'AIN''T'` in SENTNC with the string `'IS NOT'`. The statement

```
COPY = SENTNC( : POSIT-1) //
+          'IS NOT' // SENTNC(POSIT+LEN('AIN''T') : )
```

replaces the substring (`'AIN''T'`) in positions POSIT through POSIT+4 of SENTNC with the string `'IS NOT'`. A more general version of a string replacement program is described later in this chapter.   ∎

Figure 9.6. *Program and Output for Example 9.12*

```
      PROGRAM AINT
C Replaces AIN'T with IS NOT

C Declarations
      CHARACTER *80 SENTNC, COPY
      INTEGER POSIT

C Enter data string
      PRINT *, 'Old sentence:'
      READ '(A)', SENTNC

C Find each occurrence of AIN'T in SENTNC
      POSIT = INDEX(SENTNC, 'AIN''T')
      DO WHILE (POSIT .NE. 0)                    19 IF (...) THEN
         COPY = SENTNC( : POSIT-1) //
     +      'IS NOT' // SENTNC(POSIT+LEN('AIN''T') : )
         SENTNC = COPY
         POSIT = INDEX(SENTNC, 'AIN''T')
      ENDDO                                          GOTO 19
C                                                    ENDIF
C Print results
      PRINT *, 'New sentence:'
      PRINT *, SENTNC

C Exit program
      STOP
      END


Old sentence:
HE AIN'T MY FRIEND.
New sentence:
HE IS NOT MY FRIEND.
```

1. Rewrite function GETLEN so that it has only one RETURN statement. *Hint:* Use a WHILE loop.
2. Evaluate the following:

   a. INDEX ('HAND ME THE CUP AND SAUCER', 'AND')
   b. INDEX ('HAND ME THE CUP AND SAUCER', 'and')
   c. INDEX ('HAND ME THE CUP AND SAUCER', ' AND ')
   d. INDEX ('AND', 'HAND ME THE CUP AND SAUCER')

9.6 Examples of String Manipulation

In the previous sections, we introduced the FORTRAN string manipulation features and provided several examples of their use. We will now illustrate the application of these features in the solution of three sample problems. The first problem is a program for generating cryptograms; the second problem involves a subroutine for processing a DO loop header; the third problem is a text editor program.

Case Study: Generating Cryptograms

Problem

A cryptogram is a coded message formed by substituting a code character for each letter of an original message. The substitution is performed uniformly throughout the original message, that is, all A's might be replaced by Z, all B's by Y, and so on. We will assume that all punctuation (including blanks between words) remains unchanged.

Design Overview

The program must examine each character in a message, MESSAG, and insert the appropriate substitution for that character in the cryptogram, CRYPTO. This can be done by using the position of the original character in the alphabet string ALFBET as an index to the string of code symbols, CODE (e.g., the code symbol for the letter A should always be the first symbol in CODE; the code symbol for the letter B should be the second symbol in CODE, etc.).

Data Requirements

Program Parameter

the alphabet string (CHARACTER *26 ALFBET = 'ABC...Z')

Case Study: Generating Cryptograms, continued

Problem Inputs

replacement code (CHARACTER *26 CODE)
original message (CHARACTER *80 MESSAG)

Problem Output

the cryptogram (CHARACTER *80 CRYPTO)

Program Variables

position of original character in string ALFBET, used as an index to CODE
    (INTEGER POSCHR)
loop-control variable, which indicates next character in MESSAG to encode
    (INTEGER NEXT)

Initial Algorithm

1. Enter code string (CODE) and message (MESSAG).
2. Form cryptogram (CRYPTO) by replacing each letter in MESSAG with the corresponding code symbol.
3. Print CRYPTO.

Algorithm Refinements

Step 2 Refinement

2.1 DO for each character in MESSAG
     2.2 Locate position, POSCHR, of next message character in alphabet string, ALFBET.
     2.3 IF POSCHR is not equal to 0 THEN
         2.4 Insert corresponding code symbol into CRYPTO
     ELSE
         2.5 Insert the next message symbol into CRYPTO
     ENDIF
  CONTINUE

Coding

Figure 9.7 shows the program. In the figure, the statement

```
POSCHR = INDEX(ALFBET, MESSAG(NEXT : NEXT))
```

locates the current message symbol in the string ALFBET and the statement

```
CRYPTO(NEXT : NEXT) = CODE(POSCHR : POSCHR)
```

Case Study: Generating Cryptograms, continued

Figure 9.7. *Cryptogram Generator and Sample Cryptogram*

```
      PROGRAM CRYPTO
C Generates cryptograms

C Declarations
      CHARACTER *26 ALFBET
      PARAMETER (ALFBET = 'ABCDEFGHIJKLMNOPQRSTUVWXYZ')
      INTEGER POSCHR, NEXT
      CHARACTER *26 CODE
      CHARACTER *80 MESSAG, CRYPTO

C Enter code and message
      PRINT *, 'Enter the code symbol for each letter under that letter'
      PRINT *, ALFBET
      READ '(A)', CODE
      PRINT *
      PRINT *, 'Enter a message and I will display its cryptogram:'
      READ '(A)', MESSAG

C Substitute the code symbol for each letter in the message
      DO 10 NEXT = 1, LEN(MESSAG)
C         Locate the current message character in ALFBET
          POSCHR = INDEX(ALFBET, MESSAG(NEXT : NEXT))
          IF (POSCHR .NE. 0) THEN
C             Insert code for letter in CRYPTO
              CRYPTO(NEXT : NEXT) = CODE(POSCHR : POSCHR)
          ELSE
C             Insert non-letter in CRYPTO
              CRYPTO(NEXT : NEXT) = MESSAG(NEXT : NEXT)
          ENDIF
   10 CONTINUE

C Print the cryptogram
      PRINT *, CRYPTO

C Exit program
      STOP
      END

Enter the code symbol for each letter under that letter
ABCDEFGHIJKLMNOPQRSTUVWXYZ
ZYXWVUTSRQPONMLKJIHGFEDCBA

Enter a message and I will display its cryptogram:
ENCODE THIS *$?+ MESSAGE!
VMXLWV GSRH *$?+ NVHHZTV!
```

Case Study: Generating Cryptograms, continued

inserts the corresponding code symbol in the cryptogram. The statement

```
CRYPTO(NEXT : NEXT) = MESSAG(NEXT : NEXT)
```

inserts any message symbol that is not a letter directly into the cryptogram.

Testing

In the sample run, the code symbol for each letter is entered directly beneath that letter. The sample run ends with two lines of output: the first contains the message; the second contains its cryptogram. For a simple test, try using each letter as its own code symbol. In that case both lines should be the same. Remember, the program encodes only uppercase letters. Any lowercase letters and special symbols should not be changed.

The next problem involves scanning a character string and extracting substrings.

Case Study: Scanning a DO Loop Header

Problem

The DO loop header has the syntactic form

DO *label lcv = initial, limit, step*

For example,

```
DO 35 I = FIRST, LAST, 5
```

A compiler must determine whether a program line has this syntactic form. If it does, the compiler must separate the substrings representing the loop parameters *initial, limit,* and *step* from the rest of the string and save these substrings in separate character variables for later reference. We will write a program to perform this substring separation.

Design Overview

The task of our program is to identify and copy the DO loop parameters—*initial, limit,* and *step*—into the character variables INIT, LIMIT, and STEP, respectively.

The most difficult subtask for our program involves determining the starting and ending positions of the loop parameter strings. This, in turn, requires the identification of the positions in the header string of the equal sign

Case Study: Scanning a DO Loop Header, continued

(POSEQL) and the first and second commas (POS1CM and POS2CM) beyond the equal sign. If the second comma (and third parameter) in the header statement is missing, the string '1' is stored in STEP. If either the equal sign or the first comma is missing, an error message is printed and program execution is terminated. For simplicity, we will assume that the DO loop parameters contain no array element or function references.

Data Requirements

Program Parameters

the character '=' (EQUAL = '=')
the character ',' (COMMA = ',')
the character '1' (ONE = '1')

Problem Input

DO loop header (CHARACTER *80 HEADER)

Problem Outputs

initial value loop parameter (CHARACTER *80 INIT)
limit value loop parameter (CHARACTER *80 LIMIT)
step value loop parameter (CHARACTER *80 STEP)

Program Variables

position of '=' in HEADER (INTEGER POSEQL)
position of first ',' in HEADER beyond '=' (INTEGER POS1CM)
position of second ',' in HEADER beyond '=' (INTEGER POS2CM)

Initial Algorithm

1. Read HEADER.
2. Locate '=' and save its position in POSEQL. Print an error message and stop if '=' missing.
3. Locate first comma and save its position in POS1CM. Print error message and stop if ',' missing.
4. Locate second comma and save its position in POS2CM.
5. Save loop-parameter substrings and print results.

Algorithm Refinements

Step 5 Refinement

5.1 INIT is the substring between POSEQL and POS1CM.
5.2 IF the second comma is present THEN

Case Study: Scanning a DO Loop Header, continued

> 5.3 LIMIT is the substring between POS1CM and POS2CM and STEP is the substring after POS2CM
>
> ELSE
>
> 5.4 LIMIT is the substring after POS1CM and STEP is '1'
>
> ENDIF

Coding

Figure 9.8 shows the program. The statement

```
      POS1CM = INDEX(HEADER(POSEQL+1 : ), COMMA) + POSEQL
```

calls function INDEX to search for the first comma in the substring of HEADER following the equal sign. The position of this comma relative to the start of the string HEADER is obtained by adding POSEQL to the result of the substring search. To locate the second comma, the substring HEADER(POS1CM+1 :) must be searched.

Figure 9.8. *Program and Sample Output for Scanning a DO Loop Header*

```
      PROGRAM DOLOOP
C Separates and saves substrings of DO loop header

C Declarations
      CHARACTER *1 COMMA, EQUAL, ONE
      PARAMETER (COMMA = ',', EQUAL = '=', ONE = '1')
      CHARACTER *80 HEADER
      CHARACTER *80 INIT, LIMIT, STEP
      INTEGER POSEQL, POS1CM, POS2CM

C Enter data
      PRINT *, 'DO loop header:'
      READ '(A)', HEADER

C Search for equal sign - print error message if equal sign missing
      POSEQL = INDEX(HEADER, EQUAL)
      IF (POSEQL .EQ. 0) THEN
         PRINT *, ' = Sign missing'
         STOP
      ENDIF

C Search for first comma following = sign
C Print error message if comma is missing
      POS1CM = INDEX(HEADER(POSEQL+1 : ), COMMA) + POSEQL
      IF (POS1CM .EQ. POSEQL) THEN
         PRINT *, 'Comma is missing'
         STOP
      ENDIF
```

Case Study: Scanning a DO Loop Header, continued

```
C Search for second comma following first comma
      POS2CM = INDEX(HEADER(POS1CM+1 : ), COMMA) + POS1CM

C Save loop parameter substrings
      INIT = HEADER(POSEQL+1 : POS1CM-1)
      IF (POS2CM .NE. POS1CM) THEN
          LIMIT = HEADER(POS1CM+1 : POS2CM-1)
          STEP = HEADER(POS2CM+1 : )
      ELSE
          LIMIT = HEADER(POS1CM+1 : )
          STEP = ONE
      ENDIF

C Print results
      PRINT *
      PRINT *, 'Initial value expression: ', INIT
      PRINT *, 'Limit value expression: ', LIMIT
      PRINT *, 'Step value expression: ', STEP

C Exit program
      STOP
      END


DO Loop header:
DO 20 INDEX = FIRST, LAST-1, 10
Initial value expression:  FIRST
Limit value expression:  LAST-1
Step value expression:  10
```

Once the positions of the equal sign and the commas have been located (using the INDEX function), the substrings *delimited* by them (including all blanks) must be copied into INIT, LIMIT, and STEP. In each case, the copy can be performed using a simple character assignment statement such as

```
      INIT = HEADER(POSEQL+1 : POS1CM-1)
```

which assigns to INIT the substring delimited by the equal sign and the first comma.

Testing

Make sure that the DO loop program processes loop headers with and without a step parameter. The program should work regardless of whether blanks appear after the separator symbol ",". The program should also work prop-

Case Study: Scanning a DO Loop Header, continued

erly if the loop parameter expressions reference one-dimensional arrays or functions with a single argument. However, it will not be able to process expressions that reference multidimensional arrays or multiargument expressions.

Case Study: Text Editing Problem

Problem

There are many applications for which it is useful to have a computerized text editing program. For example, if you are preparing a laboratory report (or a textbook), it would be convenient to edit or modify sections of the report (improve sentence and paragraph structure, change words, correct spelling mistakes, etc.) at a computer terminal and then have a fresh, clean copy of the text typed at the terminal without erasures or mistakes.

Design Overview

A text editor system is a relatively sophisticated system of subprograms that can be used to instruct the computer to perform virtually any kind of text alteration. At the heart of such a system is a subprogram that replaces one substring in the text with another substring. As an example, consider the following sentence prepared by an overzealous member of the Addison-Wesley advertising group.

```
'THE BOOK BY KOFFMAN AND FRIEDMEN IN FRACTURED PROGRAMING IS GRREAT?'
```

To correct this sentence, we would want to specify the following edit operations:

1. Replace 'MEN' with 'MAN'
2. Replace 'IN' with 'ON'
3. Replace 'FRAC' with 'STRUC'
4. Replace 'AM' with 'AMM'
5. Replace 'RR' with 'R'
6. Replace '?' with '!'

The result is now at least grammatically correct.

```
'THE BOOK BY KOFFMAN AND FRIEDMAN ON STRUCTURED PROGRAMMING IS GREAT!'
```

We will write the replacement program module as the subroutine REPLAC. The data requirements are shown below.

Case Study: Text Editing Problem, continued

Data Requirements

Input Arguments

maximum length of TEXT (INTEGER MAXLEN)
character string to be replaced (CHARACTER *(*) OLD)
length of OLD (INTEGER OLDLEN)
character string to be inserted (CHARACTER *(*) NEW)
length of NEW (INTEGER NEWLEN)

Input/Output Arguments

character string being edited (CHARACTER *(*) TEXT)
current length of TEXT excluding blank padding (INTEGER CURLEN)

MAXLEN is a text editor system parameter that is defined to be equal to the maximum length of the text string. CURLEN would be defined when the string to be edited is first placed in TEXT (probably in the main program) and would be redefined each time a change was made to TEXT.

The first task to be performed by REPLAC is to locate the first occurrence in TEXT of the substring to be replaced, OLD (: OLDLEN). This can be accomplished using the function INDEX.

The additional data requirements for REPLAC are shown next. The algorithm follows.

Local Variables

the position of the first character of OLD in TEXT if OLD is found (INTEGER POSOLD)
length of edited text (INTEGER REVLEN)
temporary copy of the edited text (CHARACTER *1000 COPY)

Initial Algorithm

1. Search for OLD in TEXT.
2. If OLD is present, replace it with NEW; if not, print a "string missing" message.

Step 2 Refinement

2.1. IF OLD is found THEN
      2.2. Replace OLD with NEW
  ELSE
      2.3. Print OLD, "not found"
  ENDIF

Case Study: Text Editing Problem, continued

Algorithm Refinements

Before we can write the subroutine, a further refinement of step 2.2 is needed. If NEWLEN is larger than OLDLEN, it is possible that the length of the revised version of TEXT, REVLEN, would exceed MAXLEN. In this case, an error message should be printed and the replacement operation ignored; otherwise, a copy of TEXT can be made by concatenating the substring preceding OLD (the head of TEXT), NEW, and the substring following OLD (the tail of TEXT). The refinement of step 2.2 is shown next.

Step 2.2 Refinement

2.2.1 Set REVLEN to the length of the edited text.
2.2.2 IF REVLEN is greater than MAXLEN THEN
       2.2.3 Print "Revised text too long. Replacement ignored"
  ELSE
       2.2.4 Build COPY from NEW and the head and tail of TEXT. Redefine TEXT as COPY and CURLEN as REVLEN
  ENDIF

In forming COPY (step 2.2.4), the program must check for two special cases: TEXT starts with OLD or TEXT ends with OLD. In the former case, NEW becomes the head of COPY; in the latter case, NEW becomes the tail. The substring NEW (: NEWLEN) represents the actual character data in NEW, excluding blank padding.

Coding

Figure 9.9 shows subroutine REPLAC. A nested IF statement performs the text replacement. The innermost IF statement tests for the special cases mentioned above before building COPY from TEXT and NEW.

Testing

To test subroutine REPLAC, write a driver program that reads the three argument strings (TEXT, NEW, OLD), and their actual lengths. Next, your driver program should call the subroutine and display the value returned in TEXT. Make sure that you test the special cases discussed in the algorithm refinements. In any string substitution example, it is important to check that the program works for substrings at the beginning or the end of the string. Also, see what happens when the target string is not found in the original string. Finally, test REPLAC using the null string (length is 0) as a replacement string (NEW). In this case, the subroutine should simply delete string OLD from TEXT.

Case Study: Text Editing Problem, continued

Figure 9.9. *Subroutine REPLAC*

```
      SUBROUTINE REPLAC (TEXT, MAXLEN, CURLEN,
     +                   OLD, OLDLEN, NEW, NEWLEN)

C Replaces substring OLD with string NEW in TEXT

C Input Arguments
C    MAXLEN - maximum length of string TEXT
C    OLD - string to be replaced
C    OLDLEN - length of OLD
C    NEW - replacement string
C    NEWLEN - length of NEW
C    Input/Output Arguments
C    TEXT - string being edited
C    CURLEN - current length of TEXT

C Argument Declarations
      CHARACTER *(*) TEXT, OLD, NEW
      INTEGER MAXLEN, CURLEN, OLDLEN, NEWLEN

C Local Declarations
      INTEGER POSOLD, REVLEN
      CHARACTER *1000 COPY

C See if OLD is in TEXT. If so, replace it. If not, ignore request
      POSOLD = INDEX(TEXT, OLD( : OLDLEN))
      IF (POSOLD .NE. 0) THEN
C         Check revised length before replacement
          REVLEN = CURLEN + NEWLEN - OLDLEN
          IF (REVLEN .GT. MAXLEN) THEN
             PRINT *, ' Revised text too long, replacement ignored'
          ELSE
C            Build copy by replacing OLD with NEW in TEXT
             IF (POSOLD .EQ. 1) THEN
C               Replace head of TEXT with NEW
                COPY = NEW( : NEWLEN) // TEXT(POSOLD+OLDLEN : )
             ELSE IF (POSOLD + OLDLEN .EQ. CURLEN) THEN
C               Replace tail of TEXT with NEW
                COPY = TEXT( : POSOLD-1) // NEW( : NEWLEN)
             ELSE
C               Replace OLD in middle of TEXT with NEW
                COPY = TEXT( : POSOLD-1) // NEW( : NEWLEN) //
     +                 TEXT(POSOLD+OLDLEN : )
             ENDIF
             TEXT = COPY
             CURLEN = REVLEN
          ENDIF
      ELSE
          PRINT *, OLD, ' not found, replacement ignored'
      ENDIF
```

Case Study: Text Editing Problem, continued

```
C Exit subroutine
      RETURN
      END
```

1. Of what relevance is the assumption made in the discussion of the DO loop header that array element or function references should not appear in the DO loop control parameters?
2. Consider the subroutine in Fig. 9.9. Why is the character variable COPY needed in this program?
3. For each of the editing operations listed below, write a call statement to REPLAC.
   a. Replace 'FRAC' with 'STRUC'
   b. Replace the 'I' in 'IN' with an 'O'
   c. Insert an extra 'M' into 'PROGRAMING'
   d. Delete an 'R' from 'GRREAT'

9.7 Common Programming Errors

Now that we know how to manipulate different types of data, we must be careful not to misuse these data types in expressions. Character strings can be operands of the character operator (concatenation, //) and relational operators (.GT., .LE., etc.). Remember that character variables and character constants can be manipulated only with other character data.

Misspelling the name of a character variable (or neglecting to declare it) may result in compiler detection of syntax errors. This is because the type declaration intended for that variable will not be recognized if the variable name is spelled incorrectly. Consequently, the compiler will follow the implied type convention and assume that the variable is type INTEGER or REAL. Since arithmetic variables cannot be operands of character operators, diagnostic messages may be generated.

When writing substrings such as PRES(I : J), make sure that the constraints

$$1 \leq I \leq J \leq \text{LEN(PRES)}$$

are satisfied for all possible values of I and J. This means that the starting position, I, for the substring must be greater than or equal to 1 and the ending position, J, must be less than or equal to the length of string PRES. Also, the ending position must follow the starting position or at least be the same as the starting position. The latter constraint prevents the definition of substrings of length 0 or less. If these constraints are not satisfied, an execution error may occur.

The error described above may be caused by a loop that does not terminate properly or simply an incorrect subscript expression. Or if the value assigned to I (or J) is the result of a call to the string search function INDEX, it is possible for I (or J) to be set to zero. When in doubt, display the values of suspect substring expressions.

An additional source of error in character assignment statements has been mentioned earlier. That involves referencing the same character position on both sides of the assignment operator ("=" sign). The statement

```
PRES(1 : 5) = PRES(4 : 9)
```

is illegal, because positions 4 and 5 are both defined and referenced in this statement.

Remember that function LEN counts all characters stored in a character variable, including the blank padding. You will have to write your own function GETLEN (see Fig. 9.5) if you want to exclude the blank padding.

Table 9.1. *New FORTRAN Statements*

STATEMENT	EFFECT
Substring	
NEW (1 : NEWLEN)	Denotes the substring of NEW consisting of the first NEWLEN characters.
Concatenation	
NEW // OLD	Concatenates (joins) strings NEW and OLD
Functions with Character Arguments or Values	
LEN(NEW)	Returns the declared length of NEW
CHAR(0)	Returns the character in the first position (position zero) of the collating sequence for your compiler.
ICHAR('A')	Returns the position of A in the collating sequence
INDEX(SUBJCT, KEY)	Searches the string SUBJCT for the first occurrence of substring KEY. Returns the position of the first character of KEY in SUBJCT if found; otherwise, returns zero.

Chapter Review

In this chapter, we have described character string manipulation. We reviewed earlier work with character strings and introduced several new functions (LEN, INDEX, CHAR, and ICHAR) and a new operator for concatenation (//). We also discussed how to name and search for substrings. These new features are summarized in Table 9.1.

Many examples of these new features for manipulating character strings were presented. We have applied these features to generate cryptograms, to solve a problem that might arise in compiler design (processing a DO loop header), and in the design of a text editor replacement subroutine.

These kinds of problems are called nonnumerical problems and are among the most challenging in computer science. The techniques presented in this chapter should give you a better idea of how to use the computer to solve nonnumerical problems.

Quick-Check Exercises

1. The _____ _____ is used to join two strings. Its position in the precedence table is between the _____ and _____ operators.
2. Explain the difference between the terms "character set" and "collating sequence."
3. For each function below, explain its purpose, the type of its argument(s), and the type of its result.

   ```
   LEN, INDEX, ICHAR, CHAR
   ```

4. Which of the expressions below may return different results on different computers? Evaluate each expression for your computer.

   a. CHAR(32)   e. ICHAR('A')
   b. INDEX('ABC', 'A')   f. INDEX('A', 'ABC')
   c. '9' .LT. 'A'   g. 'A' .GT. 'Z'
   d. ICHAR('C') - ICHAR('A')   h. ' ' .LE. 'A'

   Answer questions 5–7 assuming the declarations

   ```
   CHARACTER STR1 *3, STR2 *5
   ```

5. What is the value of LEN(STR1 // STR2)?
6. Write a statement that changes the middle three characters of STR2 to 'ABC'.

7. If STR1 is 'ABC' and STR2 is 'VABCZ', what are the values of the following expressions?

a. INDEX(STR2, STR1)   d. INDEX(STR2, 'A')
b. INDEX(STR1, STR2)   e. INDEX(STR2(2 :), 'B')
c. INDEX(STR1, 'A')   f. INDEX(STR1 // STR2, 'CVA')

Answers to Quick-Check Exercises

1. concatenation operator (//); the relational operators and the arithmetic operators.
2. The character set is the set of characters that are recognized by the FORTRAN compiler, each with a unique character code. The collating sequence specifies the relative ordering of the characters in the character set.
3. LEN returns the length (an integer) of its string argument. INDEX returns the starting position (an integer) of the initial occurrence of its second argument (a string) in its first argument (a string). If its second argument is not found in its first argument, INDEX returns 0. ICHAR returns the character code (an integer) of its string argument. CHAR returns the character (a string) that has the character code specified by its integer argument.
4. If the results are computer dependent, we will assume the ASCII Code.

a. blank in ASCII   b. always 1   c. true in ASCII   d. 2 in ASCII
e. 65 in ASCII   f. always 0   g. always false   h. always true
5. 8
6. STR2(2 : 4) = 'ABC'
7. a. 2   b. 0   c. 1   d. 2   e. 2   f. 3

Review Questions

1. The function NOCCUR begins with the statements

```
INTEGER FUNCTION NOCCUR (SUBJCT, TARGET)
CHARACTER *(*) SUBJCT, TARGET
```

For each of the following references to the function NOCCUR, what are the lengths of the dummy arguments SUBJCT and TARGET?

Assume that TSTRNG and SSTRNG are character variables of size 10 and 20, respectively.

a. NOCCUR(SSTRNG, TSTRNG)
b. NOCCUR(TSTRNG, 'A')
c. NOCCUR(SSTRNG(4 : 12), 'EE')
d. NOCCUR('IS MISSY HERE', 'IS')
e. NOCCUR(SSTRNG // TSTRNG, TSTRNG // 'NO')

2. Given the declarations

```
CHARACTER *10 FLOWER
CHARACTER *24 DESCRP
DATA FLOWER / 'HEATHER' /
DATA DESCRP / 'HEATHER IS A WILD FLOWER' /
```

show the strings formed by the following expressions:

a. FLOWER // DESCRP(9 : 24)
b. DESCRP(1 : 11) // DESCRP(14 : 17)
c. DESCRP(:), DESCRP(1 :), DESCRP(: 24)
d. DESCRP(14 : 18) // 'AS A ROSE'
e. FLOWER(1 : 1) // FLOWER(4 : 5) // FLOWER(7 : 7)
f. FLOWER(7 : 12)

3. For each of the strings below, determine its length using the functions LEN and GETLEN. FLOWER and DESCRP are declared and initialized as in question 2.

a. FLOWER
b. DESCRP
c. FLOWER(1 : GETLEN(FLOWER))
d. 'MARIGOLD '
e. DESCRP(4 : 8) // FLOWER(3 : 3)
f. 'A' // 'B' // 'C'

4. Suppose ADDRES contains the string

```
'164 EILEEN DRIVE, ANYCITY, ANYSTATE 16444'
```

What value is returned for each of the following references to INDEX?

a. INDEX(ADDRES, 'ANYS')
b. INDEX(ADDRES, '164')
c. INDEX(ADDRES(2 :), '164')
d. INDEX(ADDRES(1 : 10) // ADDRES(11 : 17), 'END')
e. INDEX(ADDRES, 'CITIES')
f. INDEX(ADDRES(INDEX(ADDRES, ',') :), 'A')

Programming Problems

1. Write a program to read in a set of words (given below) represented as character strings of ten characters or less and determine whether each word falls between the words in FIRST and LAST (the words DINGBAT and WOMBAT, respectively). Print the words in FIRST and LAST and print each word read in along with the identifiers 'BETWEEN' or 'NOT BETWEEN', whichever applies. Use the following words as test data:

```
HELP        THE
ME          WOMBATS
STIFLE      BEFORE
THE         IT
DINGBAT     IS
AND         TOO
            LATE
```

2. Write a program to read a character string of length 20 into BUFFER and a character string into ITEM. Then search BUFFER for the string contained in ITEM. Print

   STRING FOUND

   if the string in ITEM is a substring of BUFFER. Print

   STRING NOT FOUND

   if the string in ITEM is not a substring of BUFFER. Test your program on the following strings:

   ```
   BUFFER: IS A MAN IN THE MOON
   ITEMS: MAN , NUT , N T , MEN  I

   BUFFER: IS DUST ON THE MOON
   ITEM: THEM, UST , DUST , IN , ON , O
   ```

   Hint: Use the function GETLEN (Fig. 9.5) to determine the length of each string.

3. Write a subroutine that will search a subject string for a specified target substring starting with a designated character position in the subject string (three input arguments). The subroutine will determine whether the substring is present and, if found, the position of its first occurrence.

4. Assume a set of data lines is to be processed. Each line contains a single character string that consists of a sequence of words, each separated by one or more blank spaces. Write a program that will read these lines and count the number of words with one letter, two letters, and so on, up to ten letters.

5. Write a subroutine that will scan a string TEXT of length N and replace all multiple occurrences of a blank with a single occurrence of a blank. You may assume that TEXT and N are input arguments. You should also have an output argument, COUNT, which will be used to return the number of occurrences of multiple blanks found in each call of the subroutine.

6. Write a program to read in a collection of data lines containing character strings of length less than or equal to eighty characters. For each line read, your program should do the following:
   a. Find and print the actual length of the string, excluding trailing blanks.
   b. Count the number of occurrences of four-letter words in each string.
   c. Replace each four-letter word with a string of four asterisks, ****.
   d. Print the new string.

7. Write a program that will process the employee record strings described in Table 9.2 and perform the following tasks:

a. For each employee compute the gross pay:

$$gross\ pay = hours\ worked * hourly\ pay +$$
$$overtime\ hours\ worked * hourly\ pay * 1.5$$

b. For each employee compute the net pay as follows:

$$net\ pay = gross\ pay - deductions$$

Deductions are computed as follows:

$$federal\ tax = (gross\ pay - 13 * no.\ of\ dependents) * .14$$
$$FICA = gross\ pay * .065$$

$$city\ tax = \begin{cases} \$0.00 \text{ if employee works in the suburbs} \\ 4\% \text{ of } gross\ pay \text{ if employee works in city} \end{cases}$$

$$union\ dues = \begin{cases} 0.00 \text{ if employee is not a union member} \\ 6.75\% \text{ of } gross\ pay \text{ otherwise} \end{cases}$$

Table 9.2. *Employee Record for Project 7*

COLUMNS	DATA DESCRIPTION
1–6	Employee number (an integer)
7–19	Employee last name
20–27	Employee first name
28–32	Number of hours worked (to the nearest 1/2 hour) for this employee
33–37	Hourly pay rate for this employee
38	Contains a C if employee works in the city office and an S for the suburban office
39	Contains an M if the employee is a union member
40–41	Number of dependents
42–46	Number of overtime hours worked (if any) (also to the nearest 1/2 hour)

For each employee, print a line of output containing

1. employee number
2. first and last name
3. number of hours worked
4. hourly pay rate
5. overtime hours
6. gross pay
7. federal tax
8. FICA
9. city wage tax (if any)
10. union dues (if any)
11. net pay

Also compute and print

1. number of employees processed
2. total gross pay
3. total federal tax withheld
4. total hours worked
5. total overtime hours worked

Use formats and provide appropriate column headings for employee output and labels for totals.

8. Shown below is the layout of a data string that the registrar uses as input for a program to print the end-of-the-semester final grade report for each student.

Columns	Data Description
1–6	Student number
7–18	Last name
20–26	First name
27	Middle initial
28–29	Academic year—FR, SO, JR, SR
30–32	First course—Department ID (3 letters)
33–35	First course—Number (3 digits)
36	First course—Grade A, B, C, D, or F
37	First course—Number of credits: 0–7
40–42	
43–45	Second course: data as described above
46	
47	
50–52	
53–55	Third course data
56	
57	
60–62	
63–65	Fourth course data
66	
67	
70–72	
73–75	Fifth course data
76	
77	

Write a program to print the following grade report sheet for each student.

Line	1	MAD RIVER COLLEGE
Line	2	YELLOW GULCH, OHIO
Line	3	
Line	4	GRADE REPORT, SPRING SEMESTER 1991
Line	5	

```
Line      6    (student number)   (year)    (student name)
               - - - - - - - - -  - - - -   - - - - - -
Line      7
Line      8                  GRADE SUMMARY
Line      9         COURSE
Line     10      DEPT   NMBR          CREDITS          GRADE
Line     11    1. - - -  - - -            -                -
Line     12    2. - - -  - - -            -                -
Line     13    3. - - -  - - -            -                -
Line     14    4. - - -  - - -            -                -
Line     15    5. - - -  - - -            -                -
Line     16
Line     17        SEMESTER GRADE POINT AVERAGE = - - -
```

Compute the grade-point average as follows:
1. Use 4 points for an A, 3 for a B, 2 for a C, 1 for a D, and 0 for an F.
2. Compute the product of points times credits for each course.
3. Add together the products computed in (2).
4. Add together the total number of course credits.
5. Divide (3) by (4) and print the result rounded off to two decimal places.
   Hint: Rounding is easy when formats are used for printing.
Use formats for all input and output. Your program should work for students taking anywhere from one to five courses. You will have to determine the number of courses taken by a student from the input data.

9. Write a program to read in a string up to ten characters representing a number in the form of a Roman numeral. Print the Roman numeral form and then convert to Arabic form (a standard FORTRAN integer). The character values for Roman numerals are

M	1000
D	500
C	100
L	50
X	10
V	5
I	1

Test your program on the following input.

```
LXXXVII      87
CCXIX       219
MCCCLIV    1354
MMDCLXXIII 2673
MDCDLXXXI   ?
```

Use formats for all input and output.

10. Write a program to read in an integer and print the integer and its Roman numeral representation.

11. A file of address labels consists of records that contain the three lines shown below.

    Line 1: ⟨Title⟩ ⟨First name⟩ ⟨Middle name⟩ ⟨Last name⟩
    Line 2: ⟨Street address⟩
    Line 3: ⟨City⟩, ⟨State⟩ ⟨Zipcode⟩

    Rewrite each label to a new file that consists of four lines for each record with the form:

    Zipcode
    State
    Title
    Last name

12. A number expressed in scientific notation is represented by its mantissa (a fraction) and its exponent. Write a subroutine that reads two character strings representing numbers in scientific notation. Write a subroutine that prints the contents of each record as a real value. Also, write a subroutine that computes the sum, product, difference, and quotient of the two numbers. *Hint:* The string −0.1234E20 represents a number in scientific notation. The fraction −0.1234 is the mantissa, and the number 20 is the exponent.

13. Write a program that generates the Morse code equivalent of a sentence. First, read the Morse code for each letter and punctuation character and save it in an array of strings. Next, read and convert the sentence. Your program should print the Morse code for each word on a separate line. The Morse code is as follows:

    A.-, B-..., C-.-., D-.., E., F..-., G--., H...., I.., J.---, K-.-, L.-.., M--, N-., O---,
    P.--., Q--.-, R.-., S..., T-, U..-, V...-, W.--, X-..-, Y-.--, Z--..

14. Write a set of subroutines to delete a substring from a source string, to insert a new string in a source string at a specified position, to indicate where a specified target string occurs in the source string, and to replace the first occurrence of a specified substring in a source string with another. Test these procedures by writing a text editor and performing several editing operations. The editor should be driven by the following menu.

    Enter the first letter of an edit operation described below:

    D—Delete a substring
    E—Enter a source string to be edited
    I—Insert a substring
    L—Locate a substring
    P—Print the source string
    R—Replace one substring with another
    S—Show the menu
    Q—Quit

15. Write a more complete text editor (see the previous project) that will edit a page of text. Store each line of the page in a separate element of an array of strings. Maintain a pointer (index) to the line currently being edited. In addition to the edit commands, include commands that move the index to the top of the page, the bottom of the page, or up or down a specified number of lines. Your program

should also be able to delete an entire line, insert a new line preceding the current line, and replace the current line with another. The first two of these new operations will require moving a portion of the array of strings up or down by one element.

16. An amusing program consists of a sentence generator that will read a series of four numbers and print out a sentence. Provide three arrays containing eight words each (maximum of ten characters to each word) called NOUN, VERB, and ADJECT. Fill each of these arrays with some appropriate words and then read four numbers (each in a range from 1–8). Write out a short sentence in which each number is the appropriate subscript from arrays in the following order:

    NOUN, VERB, ADJECT, NOUN

    An example would be to read 4, 5, 2, 6. This will print the strings NOUN(4), VERB(5), ADJECT(2), and NOUN(6). If their contents are:

    NOUN(4) is 'JOHN   '
    VERB(5) is 'LIKES   '
    ADJECT(2) is 'CRAZY   '
    NOUN(6) is 'BREAD   '

    The sentence

    JOHN LIKES CRAZY BREAD.

    would be printed. A trailing blank should not be printed; however, one blank between each word is needed and a period should be supplied at the end.

17. *Right-left justification of text:* Read in text that has arbitrary spacing between words (always at least one blank) and produce output lines that are X columns wide in which the first word in a line starts in column 1 and the last word ends in column X. Spacing between words should be even: the number of blanks separating any two words on a line should differ by no more than one. Note that this is not a one-line-in, one-line-out process: three input lines could, for instance, yield only one output line. Words must not be broken in the middle.

18. Redo the function plotting program (project 8, Chapter 8) using a string for LINE instead of an array.

19. Write an arithmetic expression translator that compiles fully-parenthesized arithmetic expressions involving the operators *, /, +, and −. For example, given the input string

    ((A+(B*C))−(D/E))

    the compiler would print out

    Z = (B*C)
    Y = (A+Z)
    X = (D/E)
    W = (Y−X)

Assume only the letters A through F can be used as variable names. *Hint:* Find the first right parenthesis. Remove it and the four characters preceding it and replace them with the next unused letter (G-Z) at the end of the alphabet. Print out the assignment statement used. For example, the following is a summary of the sequence of steps required to process the string above.

Expression Status	*Print*
((A+(B*C))–(D/E))	Z = (B*C)
((A+Z)–(D/E))	Y = (A+Z)
(Y–(D/E))	X = (D/E)
(Y–X)	W = (Y–X)

20. Write a subprogram BLNKSP that removes all blanks from a character string and "compacts" all nonblank characters in the string. Assume the last character of the input string is a dollar sign. You should have to scan the input string only once from left to right.

21. Write a program system (with appropriate documentation) that reads a FORTRAN program or subprogram and classifies each statement according to the following statement types:
    a. subroutine or function header
    b. type declaration (INTEGER, REAL, LOGICAL, or CHARACTER)
    c. data initialization statement
    d. comment statement
    e. assignment statement
    f. decision structure header IF (–) THEN
    g. loop structure header (DO loop or WHILE)
    h. structure terminator (CONTINUE, ENDIF, ENDWHILE)
    i. IF statement
    j. transfer statement (GOTO, RETURN, STOP)
    k. END statement
    l. decision structure alternative header (ELSE, ELSEIF(–) THEN)
    m. input/output statement (READ or PRINT)
    n. subroutine call
    o. none of the above (possible error)
    Assume that each statement fits on a single line. Print each statement and its type in a legible form. *Hint:* You may find the BLNKSP subroutine (project 20) helpful here.

10. Plotting Functions and Computer-Aided Design

IN THIS chapter, we will illustrate several different techniques for plotting functions in FORTRAN. We will show how to plot functions with one variable and how to plot parameteric equations. We will also show how to represent the graph of a function of two variables as a contour plot. Finally, we will provide a brief overview of computer facilities for engineering drawing and design.

10.1 ▬▬▬ Plotting Functions of One Variable

In this section and the next two, we will discuss several ways in which we can get the computer to plot the graphs of functions. In this section, we will discuss plotting functions of one variable. In the equation

$$y = F(x)$$

the function F describes a relationship between y, the *dependent variable*, and x, the *independent variable*.

Mapping a Function onto a Screen

The method we are about to describe is very general and will work for any function that has no singularities in the range of x values that we are plotting. A *singularity* exists at x_0 if $|F(x_0)|$ is too large to be represented in the computer. (*Warning:* This definition of singularity differs from the mathematical definition, which is that a singularity exists at x_0 if $F(x_0)$ is undefined at x_0.)

In order to plot a function of one variable, we compute $F(x)$ on a sequence of equally spaced x values. Our goal is to develop a program that will allow the user to specify the first and the last of these x values:

1. XINIT: the initial x value
2. XFINL: the final x value

The program will then plot $F(x)$ on the interval [XINIT, XFINL]. The number of points plotted will depend on the characteristics of the output device. We will assume the computer screen has twenty-four rows and eighty columns.

Plotting a function of one variable involves mapping a rectangular region of the x-y plane onto our computer screen. Since the x-y plane is a two-dimensional continuum and our computer screen is a two-dimensional arrangement of discrete cells, a considerable amount of information will be lost. Figure 10.1 depicts the function plotting problem. The region shaded in color in the x-y plane is to be mapped onto the computer screen causing the curve $y = F(x)$ to be represented as a finite sequence of characters.

Figure 10.1. *Mapping a Graph onto a Computer Screen*

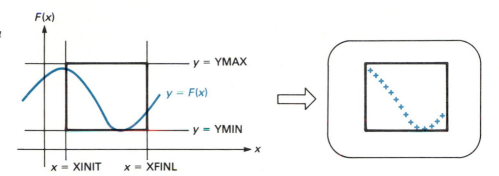

The region of the x-y plane that will be mapped onto the computer screen is bounded by four lines:

1. the line $x = $ XINIT on the left
2. the line $x = $ XFINL on the right
3. the line $y = $ YMIN, the minimum computed value for $F(x)$ on the interval [XINIT, XFINL]
4. the line $y = $ YMAX, the maximum computed value for $F(x)$ on the interval [XINIT, XFINL]

The maximum and minimum values of $F(x)$ will be relative to a finite number of tabulation points. We will discuss how these tabulation points are determined a little later in this section.

Plotting the continuous curve $y = F(x)$ requires imposing a grid structure upon the rectangular region of the x-y plane in Fig. 10.1. Suppose we plan to organize our computer screen, as shown in Fig. 10.2, so that twenty rows and seventy columns will be devoted to displaying the graph. The rest of the screen will be used to present labeling information. We can use a two-dimensional array, GRAPH, with twenty rows and seventy columns to represent our graph; each element in array GRAPH corresponds to a cell of our grid structure.

Figure 10.2. *Detail of Computer Screen Layout*

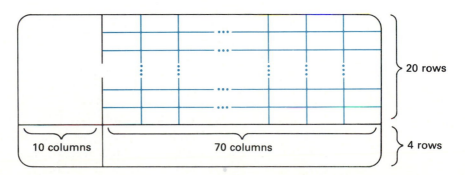

Figure 10.3 shows a portion of the screen in more detail. A ten-cell by ten-cell portion of our screen is superimposed on the corresponding portion of the x-y plane. The plotting program requires that the graph of the function, which is a continuous line, be represented by a finite number of characters, one for each column. (We will use the character '*' in plotting the function.) We will now discuss how to determine where each asterisk should be placed.

Figure 10.3. *Segment of Graph and Its Plot*

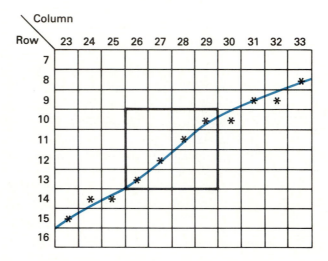

Figure 10.4 shows a part of Fig. 10.3, but with additional detail. Our plotting method progresses column by column. In each column, a row is marked with an asterisk. Figure 10.4 shows us at column 27. Columns 1–26 have already been marked. An important observation is that each column corre-

Figure 10.4. *Plotting the Point (XM, YV)*

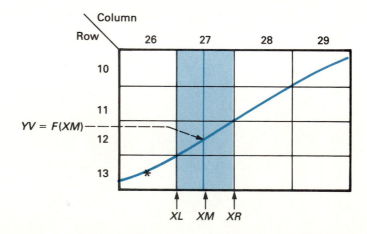

sponds to a particular interval of x values, say [XL, XR]. More significantly for our algorithm, these intervals have a midpoint XM. It is at this midpoint, XM, that we will evaluate the function, F, yielding a number, YV = F(XM). This y value, YV. will then be converted to a row number, and the corresponding cell in array GRAPH will be marked with an asterisk.

The Scaling Problem

The scaling problem is central to plotting functions with a computer. The *scaling problem* is to derive the mathematical relationships between columns and XM values on the one hand and rows and YV values on the other. In terms of Fig. 10.4, the scaling problem is to compute XM, given a particular column number, K, and to compute a row number, R, for a particular function value, YV. (See Section 6.6 for an introduction to scaling.)

Let us first consider how the midpoint, XM, is determined by the column number, K. Figure 10.5 illustrates the decision that XINIT will correspond to the midpoint of the first column and XFINL will correspond to the midpoint of the last column of the graph. (We are giving column numbers relative to the graph and not to the computer screen.) This decision completely determines the relationship between column number, K, and midpoint, XM. There are sixty-nine increments of size XINCR separating XINIT and XFINL. Therefore, the increment size is

        XINCR = (XFINL – XINIT) / 69.0

and the midpoint for column K is

        XM = XINIT + (K – 1) * XINCR

The above equation is the solution to the scaling problem along the x dimension of the graph. The divisor, 69.0 in this case, will change with the dimensions of the plot, but it will always be one less than the number of columns to be plotted.

Figure 10.5. *Scaling Problem in the x Dimension*

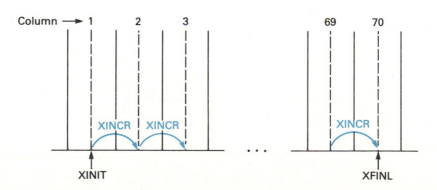

Along the y dimension, we want to be able to compute a row number, R, given the functional value, YV = F(XM). This problem is a little tricky. Figure 10.6 shows a decision to make the midpoint of row 1 correspond to the maximum value for $F(x)$, YMAX, and to make the midpoint of row 20 correspond to the minimum value for $F(x)$, YMIN. This determines that the distance between successive midpoints is

```
YINCR = (YMAX - YMIN) / 19.0
```

Figure 10.6. *Scaling Problem in the y Dimension*

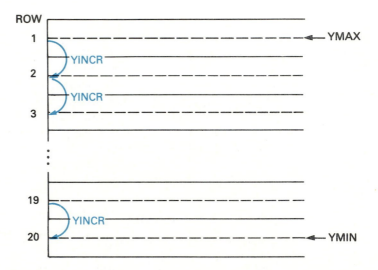

The row number, R, for a given y value, YV, depends upon the distance between YV and YMAX measured in terms of y increments, YINCR. This distance, YDIST, is computed as follows:

```
YDIST = (YMAX - YV) / YINCR
```

For example, YDIST is 1.0 means that YV is one y increment away from YMAX, so that YV belongs in row 2. If YDIST is 19.0, then YV is YMIN and belongs in row 20.

Using the FORTRAN intrinsic function NINT (nearest integer) we can express the relationship between row R and YDIST as

```
R = NINT(YDIST + 1.0)
```

Table 10.1 shows the relationship between YDIST and R imposed by this formula. This table covers all possibilities, since YDIST cannot be less than 0.0 nor greater than 19.0.

Having solved the scaling problem, we can now write a program that plots mathematical functions.

Table 10.1. *Relationship Between YDIST and R*

YDIST	R
YDIST < 0.0	impossible
0.0 ≤ YDIST < 0.5	1
0.5 ≤ YDIST < 1.5	2
1.5 ≤ YDIST < 2.5	3
2.5 ≤ YDIST < 3.5	4
3.5 ≤ YDIST < 4.5	5
. . .	. . .
17.5 ≤ YDIST < 18.5	19
18.5 ≤ YDIST < 19.5	20
YDIST ≥ 19.5	impossible

A Function Plotting Program

Figure 10.7 is a structure chart of a program system that plots a given function, $F(x)$, on a specified interval [XINIT, XFINL]. The user provides the values for XINIT and XFINL as input. The output consists of a discrete representation of the graph $y = F(x)$.

Figure 10.7. *Structure Chart for Plotting Program*

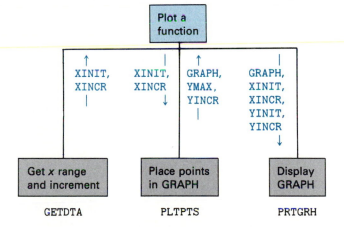

The main program variables include the two-dimensional array GRAPH. The array GRAPH is declared to be of type CHARACTER *1 and is initialized to all blanks by the statement

```
DATA GRAPH /NCELL * ' '/
```

The subroutine GETDTA reads in the initial and final x values: XINIT and XFINL. In addition, this subroutine computes and returns the value for XINCR, which is needed by two of the other subroutines. XFINL is a local variable since none of the other subroutines needs this value.

The subroutine PLTPTS does the actual plotting of the function by marking the appropriate row of each column of the array GRAPH with an asterisk. This is the heart of the plotting program. The subroutine PLTPTS contains the statement function

```
F(X) = 4.0 * (X - 0.5) ** 2
```

which defines the function we are plotting. To plot a different function, simply replace this one statement with another function statement. However, remember that the subroutine assumes a function that has no singularities on the interval [XINIT, XFINL].

There are two phases in the logic of PLTPTS. First, we must determine the maximum and minimum values for the function $F(x)$ at the seventy evaluation points, XM, given by:

```
XM = XINIT + (K - 1) * XINCR for K = 1, 2, . . . , NCOL
```

This involves seventy evaluations of the function $F(x)$. Since we will need these same seventy values during the second phase of our subroutine, we store them in an array YV declared:

```
REAL YV(NCOL)
```

This is a matter of saving time by the expenditure of space (or computer storage). Once the maximum and minimum values, YMAX and YMIN, are known, we can compute the increment value, YINCR.

During the second phase of the subroutine PLTPTS, we use the scaling formula derived earlier to convert each of the seventy functional values, YV(K), to a unique row value, R. The cell GRAPH(R,K) is then marked with an asterisk.

The subroutine PRTGRH prints the graph row by row along with appropriate labels. In order to get the x scale printed at the bottom of the graph, the subroutine uses array XSCALE to store the x values that will be printed.

The complete program system is shown in Fig. 10.8; the output generated by the program is given in Fig. 10.9.

Figure 10.8. *Plotting a Function $F(x)$*

```
      PROGRAM PLOT1
C Plots the function
C      F(X) = 4.0 * (X - 0.5) ** 2
C on a 20 row by 70 column grid

C Declarations
      INTEGER NROW, NCOL, NCELL
      PARAMETER (NROW = 20, NCOL = 70, NCELL = NCOL * NROW)
```

```
      REAL XINIT, XINCR, YMAX, YINCR
      CHARACTER *1 GRAPH(NROW,NCOL)
      DATA GRAPH /NCELL * ' '/

      CALL GETDTA (XINIT, XINCR)
      CALL PLTPTS (GRAPH, XINIT, XINCR, YMAX, YINCR)
      CALL PRTGRH (GRAPH, XINIT, XINCR, YMAX, YINCR)

C Exit program
      STOP
      END

C ----------------------------------------------------------------

      SUBROUTINE GETDTA (XINIT, XINCR)
C Asks the user for the initial and final X
C values and computes the X increment

C Output Arguments
C   XINIT - The initial X value
C   XINCR - The X increment

C Argument Declarations
      REAL XINIT, XINCR

C Local Declarations
      INTEGER NCOL
      PARAMETER (NCOL = 70)
      REAL XFINL

C Get initial and final X values from user:
      PRINT *, 'The function is plotted between the values you enter.'
      PRINT *
      PRINT *, 'Enter initial X value:'
      READ *, XINIT
      PRINT *, 'Enter final X value:'
      READ *, XFINL

C Compute X increment and return
      XINCR = (XFINL - XINIT) / REAL(NCOL - 1)
      RETURN
      END

C ----------------------------------------------------------------

      SUBROUTINE PLTPTS (GRAPH, XINIT, XINCR, YMAX, YINCR)

C Plots the function by marking appropriate
C cells of the array GRAPH with an asterisk

C Input Arguments
C   XINIT, XINCR - The initial X value and X increment
C Output Arguments
```

```
C   GRAPH - The grid of points on the X, Y plane
C   YMAX, YINCR - The largest Y value and Y increment
C Argument Declarations
      INTEGER NROW, NCOL
      PARAMETER (NROW = 20, NCOL = 70)
      CHARACTER * 1 GRAPH(NROW,NCOL)
      REAL XINIT, XINCR, YMAX, YINCR

C Local Declarations
      REAL YV(NCOL), YDIST, YMIN, XM
      INTEGER R, K

C Function definition:
      F(X) = 4.0 * (X - 0.5) ** 2

C PHASE ONE: Determine maximum and minimum
C            functional values
      YMAX = -10000.0
      YMIN =  10000.0
      DO 10 K = 1, NCOL
         XM = XINIT + (K - 1) * XINCR
         YV(K) = F(XM)
         IF (YV(K) .GT. YMAX) YMAX = YV(K)
         IF (YV(K) .LT. YMIN) YMIN = YV(K)
   10 CONTINUE

C Compute Y increment
      YINCR = (YMAX - YMIN) / REAL (NROW - 1)

C PHASE TWO: Mark graph column by column
C            using computed functional values
      DO 20 K = 1, NCOL
         YDIST = (YMAX - YV(K)) / YINCR
         R = NINT(YDIST + 1.0)
         GRAPH(R,K) = '*'
   20 CONTINUE

C Exit subroutine
      RETURN
      END


C -----------------------------------------------------------

      SUBROUTINE PRTGRH (GRAPH, XINIT, XINCR, YMAX, YINCR)
C Prints out the graph row by row

C Input Arguments
C   GRAPH - The grid of points on the X, Y plane
C   XINIT, XINCR - The initial X value and X increment
C   YMAX, YINCR - The largest Y value and Y increment
```

```
C Argument Declarations
      INTEGER NROW, NCOL
      PARAMETER (NROW = 20, NCOL = 70)
      CHARACTER *1 GRAPH(NROW,NCOL)
      REAL XINIT, XINCR, YMAX, YINCR

C Local Declarations
      INTEGER NXVAL
      PARAMETER (NXVAL = NCOL / 10)
      INTEGER R, K, L
      REAL YVAL, XVAL, XSCALE(NXVAL)

C Print out graph row by row with labels to the left
C of the first row and every fifth row
      PRINT *
      PRINT *, '    Y'
C     Print Row 1 (Y = YMAX)
      PRINT 15, YMAX, (GRAPH(1,K), K = 1, NCOL)
   15 FORMAT (1X, F6.1, 3X, 70A1)
C     Print the rest of the rows
      DO 10 R = 2, NROW
         IF (MOD(R, 5) .EQ. 0) THEN
            YVAL = YMAX - (R - 1) * YINCR
            PRINT 15, YVAL, (GRAPH(R,K), K = 1, NCOL)
         ELSE
            PRINT 25, (GRAPH(R,K), K = 1, NCOL)
   25       FORMAT (10X, 70A1)
         ENDIF
   10 CONTINUE

C Compute the X scale values (XSCALE)
      K = 10
      DO 20 L = 1, NXVAL
C        XVAL is X value for column K
         XVAL = XINIT + (K - 1) * XINCR
         XSCALE(L) = XVAL
         K = K + 10
   20 CONTINUE

C Print the X scale at the bottom of the graph
      PRINT 35, '|---------|', ('---------|', L = 1, NXVAL - 1)
   35 FORMAT (10X, 8A)
      PRINT 45, XINIT, (XSCALE(L), L = 1, NXVAL)
   45 FORMAT (1X, 8(4X, F6.1))
      PRINT 55, 'X -->'
   55 FORMAT (40X, A)

C Exit subroutine
      RETURN
      END
```

Figure 10.9. *Sample Function Plot*

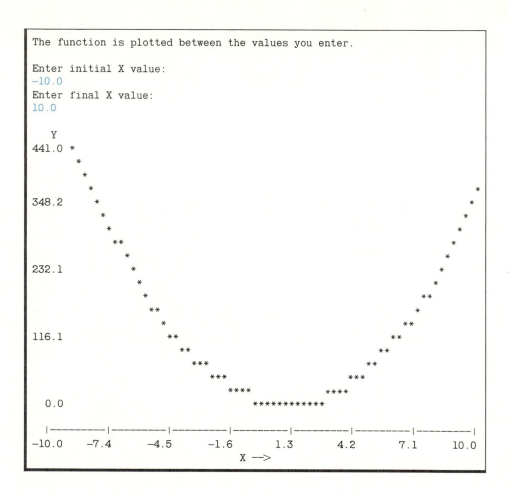

```
The function is plotted between the values you enter.

Enter initial X value:
-10.0
Enter final X value:
10.0

     Y
  441.0 *
          *
            *
              *
  348.2       *
               *
                *
                 **
                   *
  232.1           *
                 *
                *
              **
             *
  116.1    **
          **
         ***
        ***
       ****
    0.0          ************
```

10.2 ▬▬▬ Plotting Parametric Equations

Parametric equations express the values of a collection of variables as functions of a common parameter. For example, we might express the values of x and y in terms of some parameter t:

$$x = F(t)$$
$$y = G(t)$$

The parameter t is often viewed as a time parameter. The equations then express the evolution of x and y values in terms of time.

Parametric equations for two variables, such as the pair of equations given above, determine a curve in the *x-y* plane, assuming that the functions *F* and *G* are continuous. Parametric equations for three variables would determine a curve in three-dimensional space.

The techniques developed in the previous section can be modified easily to plot parametric equations. A two-dimensional array, GRAPH, should be used to store the points to be plotted. You must determine

- the range of values for *t* [TINIT, TFINL]
- the time interval, TINCR, between points

The algorithm for the subroutine that marks cells in GRAPH follows.

Algorithm for Marking Cells in GRAPH

1. DO for *t* starting at TINIT and increasing by TINCR
   2. Compute *x*(*t*)
   3. Compute *y*(*t*)
   4. Find the row number, R, corresponding to *x*(*t*)
   5. Find the column number, K, corresponding to *y*(*t*)
   6. Place an asterisk in GRAPH(R,K)
   CONTINUE

Steps 4 and 5 correspond to the scaling problem discussed in the previous section and should be solved in the same way. If the range of *x* and *y* values are known beforehand, then it is an easy matter to compute XINCR and YINCR and use these values in steps 4 and 5 (i.e., compute XDIST, YDIST, and then R and K). Otherwise, it will be necessary to first tabulate and store all values of *x*(*t*) and *y*(*t*) to find [XMIN, XMAX] and [YMIN, YMAX]. This should be done in a separate step before attempting to mark the cells in GRAPH.

10.3　Plotting Functions of Two Variables

As we continue our discussion of plotting functions using FORTRAN, we might consider plotting the graph of a function of two variables

$$z = F(x,y)$$

As in Section 10.1, the scaling problem is a central concern. You will be happy to learn that the scaling problem for functions of two variables is essentially solved in the same manner as for functions of one variable.

Many techniques exist to plot the graph of a function of two variables, but most of these techniques are beyond the scope of this text. (They involve issues of perspective and other sophisticated topics in computer graphics.) Two simple techniques, however, will be discussed here: displaying the graph plane by plane and the use of contour plots.

The Information Loss Problem

Graphing a function of two variables presents us with new problems insofar as information loss is concerned. We mentioned earlier that when we map a function of one variable onto the computer screen there is a loss of information because the computer representation is discrete, whereas the actual graph is a continuum. The same sort of consideration holds when we graph a function of two variables.

The graph of a function of one variable defines a curve in two-dimensional space (see Fig. 10.10). The graph of a function of two variables defines a surface in three-dimensional space (see Fig. 10.11). Since our computer screens and printouts are two-dimensional and the graph is three-dimensional, this presents us with a serious problem with respect to information loss. How can we map the three-dimensional graph onto the computer screen and yet retain enough information to make our computer representation useful?

Figure 10.10.

Graph of a Function of One Variable

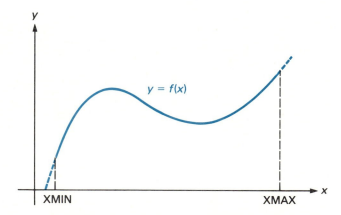

Plotting the Function Plane by Plane

One way of plotting the graph of a function of two variables is to project the graph plane by plane onto the computer screen. To do this, a sequence of N y values $(y_1, y_2, \ldots, y_N)$ is chosen. Each y value determines a plane, $y = y_j$. Each of these y values, when substituted into our original function of two variables, $F(x,y)$, will yield a function of one variable $f_j(x)$:

$$f_j(x) = F_j(x,y)$$

Figure 10.11.
Graph of a Function
of Two Variables

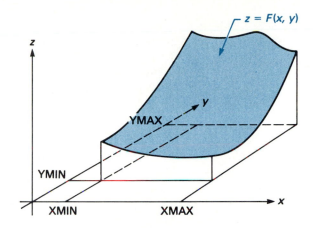

The graph of $z = f_j(x)$ is the intersection of the plane $y = y_j$ with the graph of the original function, $F(x,y)$. Each of these N functions, $f_j(x)$, $j = 1, 2, \ldots, N$, can be plotted using the technique described in Section 10.1. Figure 10.12 suggests what the output of such a program might look like. We can reconstruct the general contours of the original function, $z = F(x,y)$, in our mind's eye by examining these projections.

Figure 10.12. *Representing a Function Graph as a Set of Planes*

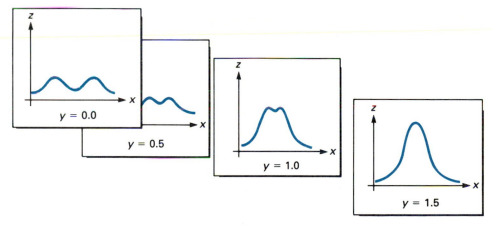

Contour Plots

Contour plots can be used to represent the graph of a function

$$z = F(x,y)$$

as a whole, not plane by plane. The idea of a contour plot is straightforward. If you have ever worked with a geographical map where heights above and below sea level are color coded, then you already have some familiarity with the basic concept. In a computer-generated contour plot for a function of two variables, the distance of the surface of the graph from the x-y plane is encoded using characters. All points on the surface of the graph within the same range of distances from the x-y plane are assigned the same character.

Figure 10.13 shows a small contour plot where the symbols +, –, and blank are used to code the value of z. The key to the contour plot is shown on the left. A grid structure consisting of fourteen rows and twenty columns has been imposed on a portion of the x-y plane.

Figure 10.13. *A Contour Plot and Its Key*

```
              KEY                              plot
     z value      symbol       -------------------------
                               -------------------------
     z ≥ 0.5         +         ---------   ---------
     z ≥ -0.5      blank       -------       -------
     z < -0.5        -         -----        +        -----
                               ---        +++          ---
                               -        +++++            -
                               -       +++++++           -
                               ---      +++++           --
                               -----     +++          ----
                               -------     +         -----
                               --------          -------
                               ----------    ---------
                               -------------------------
```

The function being plotted is evaluated at each of 14 * 20 = 280 grid points, and a symbol is chosen to represent the computed value. The plot in Fig. 10.13 shows a diamond-shaped hill (values of $z \geq 0.5$) rising above a valley (values of $z < -0.5$).

In general, a contour plot such as the one shown in Fig. 10.13 is generated by imposing a grid structure on a region of the x-y plane and evaluating the function at a point within each cell of the grid. This region is delimited by the lines $x =$ XMIN, $x =$ XMAX, $y =$ YMIN and $y =$ YMAX. This region is mapped onto our computer screen as shown in Fig. 10.14. We have decided to devote

Figure 10.14. *Mapping a Function of Two Variables onto a Screen*

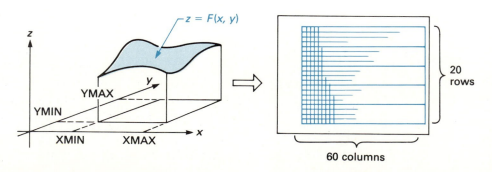

twenty rows and sixty columns to the plot. This will allow a key to be printed on the left side of the screen.

Each of the $20 * 60 = 1200$ cells on the screen corresponds to a definite region of the x-y plane. That region is a two-dimensional continuum of points. The constraints of our computer hardware dictate that the function be represented by only one character at each of these 1200 cells. This discrete sampling of the function is responsible for some of the information loss that occurs in contour plotting. The rest of the information loss is due to the fact that a continuum of possible functional values is reduced to one of a small collection of characters. The number of characters in the contour plot key is typically in the range of five to ten. If we incorporate too many characters in our key, hoping to counteract the information loss, the result is a plot that is visually confusing. Figure 10.15(a) shows a small section of the x-y plane. The grid is shown as well as the grid points at which the function will be evaluated. Functional values at these grid points are shown as blue lines that are perpendicular to the plane. Figure 10.15(b) shows the corresponding portion of our contour plot.

Figure 10.15. *Evaluation of F(x,y) at the Grid Points and Contour Plot for F(x,y)*

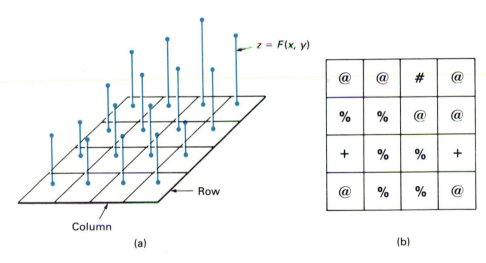

The Scaling Problem in the x and y Dimensions

Contour plotting involves three scaling problems, one in each of the three dimensions: x, y, and z. The scaling in the x dimension is solved once the decision is made that the midpoint of the first column of our plot will correspond to XMIN and the midpoint of the last column of our plot will correspond to XMAX. If there are NCOL columns (NCOL is 60 in Fig. 10.14), then the midpoints of successive columns are separated by the distance

    XINCR = (XMAX - XMIN) / (NCOL - 1)

Similarly, the scaling problem in the y dimension is solved once we decide to make the midpoint of the first row correspond to YMAX and the midpoint of the last row correspond to YMIN. Then the midpoints of successive rows will be a distance YINCR apart where

    YINCR = (YMAX - YMIN) / (NROW - 1)

and NROW is the number of rows in our contour plot (NROW is 20 in Fig. 10.14).

Our computational strategy is to compute $z = F(x,y)$ at the center point of each cell. The center point of the cell at the top left corner of our plot is (XMIN,YMAX). The nested DO loop below causes x and y to take on the appropriate values so that all grid points are "visited." The grid points will be visited row by row. Note that as we progress from row to row, y decreases, since the top of the contour plot corresponds to the maximum y value.

```
C Compute Z value for each point to be plotted
      Y = YMAX
      DO 10 R = 1, NROW
         X = XMIN
         DO 20 K = 1, NCOL
            Z = F(X,Y)                (X,Y) is a grid point
            ... Do what needs to be
                done with Z ...
C           Get next X value
            X = X + XINCR
   20    CONTINUE
C        Get next Y value
         Y = Y - YINCR
   10 CONTINUE
```

The Scaling Problem in the z Dimension

Let us now consider the scaling problem in the z dimension, which is to associate with every functional value, $z = F(x,y)$, an appropriate symbol based on the key of the contour map. There are two possibilities:

1. the key is known when we write the program
2. the key must be computed by the program itself

We will now discuss the first of these possibilities in detail. The second case will be discussed briefly at the end of this section.

In some cases, the key can be determined by mathematical analysis and therefore is known before we write the program. For example, in a contour plot of the function

    $z = \sin(a * x) + \cos(b * y)$

it is a simple matter of analysis to see that z must always lie within the range -2 to 2 since we are adding two sinusoidal functions (sin and cos) with amplitude 1. The scaling problem in the z dimension for the above function would require creating a table of correspondences between z values and characters. (See Table 10.2.) The symbols were chosen so that larger z values are represented by darker symbols. Furthermore, we want to highlight the details for positive z values, so we have decided to treat all negative values the same.

Table 10.2. *Sample Key for a Contour Plot*

CONDITION	SYMBOL
$z > 1.5$	#
$z \geq 1.0$	@
$z \geq 0.5$	%
$z \geq 0.0$	+
$z < 0.0$	.

It is a simple matter to save this table in a FORTRAN program and use it to convert a given z value to a plot symbol. This process is illustrated in the next section.

We will apply the theory that has been developed so far in the next problem, which deals with writing a computer program that generates a contour plot.

Case Study: Contour Plot for a Hemispherical Surface

Problem

We want to write a program that generates a contour plot of a function whose graph is a hemispherical surface.

Design Overview

The function that yields the hemispherical surface is

```
F(X,Y) = SQRT(1.0 - AMIN1(X ** 2 + Y ** 2, 1.0))
```

where AMIN1 is a FORTRAN library function that returns the minimum of the values in its argument list. We will plot this function for all x values between -1.0 and 1.0 and all y values between -1.0 and 1.0. Consequently, the values of $z = F(x,y)$ must lie between 0.0 and 1.0. We will use the key in Table 10.3 for the plot.

The boundary values for z and the plot symbols will be saved in arrays ZBOUND and SYMBOL, respectively. The values for XMIN, XMAX, YMIN, and YMAX are program parameters. We will draw the plot one row at a time, starting with the line $y = $ YMAX. The symbols to be printed in the current row will be stored in the character string RGRAPH (type CHARACTER *NCOL).

Case Study: Contour Plot for a Hemispherical Surface, continued

Table 10.3. *Key for Hemispherical Contour Plot*

CONDITION	SYMBOL
$z > 0.8$	#
$z \geq 0.6$	@
$z \geq 0.4$	%
$z \geq 0.2$	+
$z < 0.2$	.

Data Requirements

Program Parameters

the minimum x value (XMIN = -1.0)
the maximum x value (XMAX = 1.0)
the minimum y value (YMIN = -1.0)
the maximum y value (YMAX = 1.0)
the number of symbols in the key (KEYSIZ = 5)
the number of rows in the contour plot (NROW = 20)
the number of columns in the contour plot (NCOL = 60)

Problem Outputs

each row of the contour plot (CHARACTER *(NCOL) RGRAPH)

Additional Program Variables

the row being plotted (INTEGER R)
the x value for row R (REAL X)
the increment on the x-axis (REAL XINCR)
the column being defined (INTEGER K)
the y value for column K (REAL Y)
the increment on the y-axis (REAL YINCR)
the boundary values for the plot key (REAL ZBOUND(KEYSIZ))
the plot symbols (CHARACTER *1 SYMBOL(KEYSIZ))

Initial Algorithm

1. Compute XINCR and YINCR.
2. Define and display each row of the contor plot, starting with the row for which Y is YMAX.

Algorithm Refinements

We discussed the general approach to step 2 earlier. For a given Y value (a row of the plot), we must determine the appropriate plot symbol for each x value

Case Study: Contour Plot for a Hemispherical Surface, continued

along that row. To do this, we must first compute the value of F(X,Y) for each X and then convert this value to the corresponding plot symbol (a character). We will store the plot symbols as individual characters in the string variable RGRAPH.

Step 2 Refinement

2.1 Initialize Y to YMAX
2.2 DO for each row of the plot
    2.3 Set X to XMIN
    2.4 DO for each column, K, of the plot
        2.5 Compute Z = F(X,Y)
        2.6 Convert Z to a plot symbol
        2.7 Store the plot symbol as the
            Kth character in string RGRAPH
        2.8 Increment X by XINCR
    CONTINUE
    2.9 Display the string RGRAPH
    2.10 Decrement Y by YINCR
CONTINUE

Coding

Figure 10.16 shows the contour plot program. DO loop 20 corresponds to step 2.4 in the algorithm above. After the value of Z is computed, the IF statement compares Z to the boundary values saved in array ZBOUND to determine the corresponding plot symbol. The statement

```
RGRAPH(K:K) = SYMBOL(1)
```

executes when Z exceeds the largest boundary value. This statement sets the Kth character in string RGRAPH to the symbol that represents the largest Z values. This use of substring notation to define a single character in a string was covered in Section 9.2.

Testing

Figure 10.17 shows a sample contour plot generated for the test function F(X,Y) described earlier. To draw another contour plot, insert a different single-statement function definition for F(X,Y). Make sure that you also modify the DATA statement for ZBOUND if the range of function values changes. Alternatively, you could create a separate subroutine to initialize the array ZBOUND, as discussed next.

Case Study: Contour Plot for a Hemispherical Surface, continued

Figure 10.16. *Generating a Contour Plot for a Hemisphere*

```
       PROGRAM CONTOR
C Generates a contour plot of a hemispherical surface

C Declarations
       INTEGER NCOL, NROW, KEYSIZ
       PARAMETER (NCOL = 60, NROW = 20, KEYSIZ = 5)
       REAL XMIN, XMAX, YMIN, YMAX
       PARAMETER (XMIN = -1.0, XMAX = 1.0)
       PARAMETER (YMIN = -1.0, YMAX = 1.0)

       CHARACTER *(NCOL) RGRAPH
       REAL Z, XINCR, YINCR, ZBOUND(KEYSIZ)
       INTEGER R, K
       CHARACTER *1 SYMBOL(KEYSIZ)
       REAL F, X, Y

       DATA ZBOUND /0.80, 0.60, 0.40, 0.20, 0.20/
       DATA SYMBOL /'#', '@', '%', '+', '.'/

C Function definition
       F(X,Y) = SQRT(1.0 - AMIN1(X ** 2 + Y ** 2, 1.0))

C Compute X and Y increments
       XINCR = (XMAX - XMIN) / REAL (NCOL - 1)
       YINCR = (YMAX - YMIN) / REAL (NROW - 1)

C Generate contour plot row by row
       Y = YMAX
       DO 10 R = 1, NROW
          X = XMIN
          DO 20 K = 1, NCOL
C             Compute Z value at point (X,Y)
              Z = F(X,Y)
C             Place appropriate symbol in RGRAPH
              IF (Z .GT. ZBOUND(1)) THEN
                 RGRAPH(K:K) = SYMBOL(1)
              ELSE IF (Z .GE. ZBOUND(2)) THEN
                 RGRAPH(K:K) = SYMBOL(2)
              ELSE IF (Z .GE. ZBOUND(3)) THEN
                 RGRAPH(K:K) = SYMBOL(3)
              ELSE IF (Z .GE. ZBOUND(4)) THEN
                 RGRAPH(K:K) = SYMBOL(4)
              ELSE IF (Z .LT. ZBOUND(5)) THEN
                 RGRAPH(K:K) = SYMBOL(5)
              ENDIF

C             Get next X value
              X = X + XINCR
```

Case Study: Contour Plot for a Hemispherical Surface, continued

```
   20      CONTINUE
           PRINT 15, RGRAPH
   15      FORMAT (20X, A60)

C          Get next Y value
           Y = Y - YINCR
   10   CONTINUE

C Exit program
        STOP
        END
```

Figure 10.17.
Sample Contour Plot

Computing the Key at Execution Time

Suppose we have decided on a given collection of characters to use in our contour plot, but we do not know the range of *z* values that will correspond to a given character (see Table 10.4). The program can determine the desired *z* values once the maximum and minimum *z* values (ZMAX and ZMIN, respectively) are known. To determine these two values, the program must compute $z = F(x,y)$ at each grid point. This requires nested DO loops that take us row by row through the two-dimensional pattern of grid points. Once ZMAX and ZMIN have been found, we can assign *z* values for Table 10.4 that divide the *z* range into five regions.

Table 10.4. *Key for Unknown Range of z Values*

CONDITION	SYMBOL
$z > ?$	#
$z \geq ?$	@
$z \geq ?$	%
$z \geq ?$	+
$z < ?$	.

SELF-CHECK EXERCISE FOR SECTION 10.3

1. Write a subroutine that defines the values stored in the array ZBOUND for a function $F(x,y)$. *Hint:* The input arguments to the subroutine should be XMIN, XINCR, YMAX, YINCR, NUMCOL, NUMROW, and KEYSIZ; the output should be the array ZBOUND. Find ZMIN, ZMAX, and then ZINCR.

10.4 ▬▬ Introduction to Computer-Aided Design

Besides using the computer to plot functions, engineers frequently use the computer as a design tool. Computer graphics systems are widely available to help engineers make engineering drawings whose specifications are saved on disk. Later the engineer can modify the existing drawing or reuse parts of it in new drawings.

Early graphics systems provided a library of subroutines that the designer could call to draw standard objects such as circles, rectangles, and even polygons. The designer could specify the size and position of each individual object in an engineering drawing. The drawings were printed on line printers with graphics capability or drawn on special output devices called *plotters*.

Today, interactive menu-driven systems are available on personal computers and graphics workstations. The designer uses a mouse to position the cursor at the point where each new line or object is to be drawn. Next, the designer selects the desired object or line shape from a menu of available objects.

The engineer can also create three-dimensional drawings using a computer-aided design (CAD) system. To create a three-dimensional object, the engineer can rotate a two-dimensional object around a specified axis. Once an object has been designed, a CAD system can compute and display certain of its properties such as areas, volumes, and cross-sections.

When displaying a three-dimensional object, the engineer can rotate the object in space or request different views of the object. The engineer can use different colors to distinguish between parts of the drawing. For example, in a heating/air-conditioning diagram, components of the heating system can be drawn in one color, components of the cooling system in another color, and components used in both systems in still another color.

CAD systems are widely used in the following engineering fields:

- aerospace (design of aircraft and space vehicles)
- automotive (design of automobile bodies, engines, and other components)
- architecture (building design and room layout)
- electronics (circuit-board layout, integrated circuit fabrication, and wiring diagrams).

CAD systems can also be integrated with computer-aided manufacturing (CAD/CAM). In CAD/CAM, the specifications and dimensions created in the design phase are used as inputs in the manufacturing phase to control production tools, thereby automating the manufacturing process.

Computer-aided engineering (CAE) is another extension of CAD. A CAE system can complete an entire design by extrapolating from a few key sections provided by the engineer. It can also decompose an object into its component elements and perform mathematical computations to determine properties of individual elements such as stress and temperature.

10.5 ▬ Common Programming Errors

Since we did not introduce any new FORTRAN statements in this chapter, there are no new pitfalls to warn you about. However, this chapter does make extensive use of arrays and subprograms, so you should review the errors that are common with their use. To avoid argument list errors, you should continue to be careful about argument list length and the order of arguments. Also, check subscript boundary values in loops that process arrays to ensure that each array subscript remains in range for all values of the loop parameters. Finally, make sure you continue to declare the data types of all variables and user-defined functions so that errors are not introduced because of implicit (default) types.

▬ Chapter Review

This chapter discussed the use of the computer for plotting functions. Several kinds of function plots were described, including graphs of parametric equations and contour plots. We also introduced the topic of computer-aided design.

Quick-Check Exercises

1. What is a singularity?
2. In a plot of $y = F(x)$, _____ is the dependent variable and _____ is the independent variable.
3. What are parametric equations?
4. How many dimensions can be plotted in a contour plot?
5. Differentiate between CAD, CAD/CAM, and CAE.
6. Name two techniques for plotting a three-dimensional curve.

Answers to Quick-Check Exercises

1. A singularity is a point on a curve whose value is too large to be plotted.
2. y, x
3. Equations that express the values of a collection of variables as functions of a common parameter.
4. three dimensions
5. CAD is used for drawing or drafting. In CAD/CAM, the computer also controls the manufacturing process. In CAE, the computer analyzes properties of a drawing and assists in the engineering process.
6. Contour plots and plotting the function plane by plane.

Review Questions

1. Explain the scaling problem.
2. What is the scaling problem in a three-dimensional plot?
3. How can you use two-dimensional plots to represent a three-dimensional surface?
4. List three applications of computer-aided design in engineering.

Programming Projects

1. Plot each of the functions below over a suitable interval:
   a. $x^4 - 6x^3 - 5x^2 - 70x + 9$
   b. $3\cos(x) - x$
   c. $\sqrt{|\sin(x)| + |\cos(x)|}$
   d. $e^{-(x^2/2)}$

2. Write a program that will plot two functions on an interval [XINIT,XFINL], say

   ```
   Y = F(X)
   Y = G(X)
   ```

Use different symbols for the plot of *F* and *G*. Wherever the two functions intersect, use yet a third plotting symbol. Use your program to estimate the two points of intersection for

```
F(X) = SQRT(4.0 - X ** 2)
G(X) = 1.0 + X ** 2
```

3. Modify the program you wrote for project 2 so that the area between the two functions being plotted will appear shaded (i.e., filled with the symbol /; see Fig. 10.18). Try your program on the functions given in project 2 and any other functions you might want to try.

Figure 10.18.

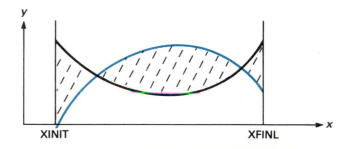

4. Write a parametric equation plotting program and plot the following parametric equations. Each curve must be considered separately. Choose an appropriate *x-y* scale and time increment in each case.
   a. $x = t^2$, $y = t^3$ $-1 \leq t \leq 2$
   b. $x = e^{-t}$, $y = e^t$ $0 \leq t \leq \ln 3$
   c. $x = e^t$, $y = e^{3t}$ $0 \leq t \leq \ln 2$
   d. $\left. \begin{array}{l} x = 3 + 2\sin(t) \\ y = 4\sin(t) \end{array} \right\}$ $-\pi/2 \leq t \leq \dfrac{\pi}{2}$
   e. $\left. \begin{array}{l} x = \cos(t) \\ y = \sin^2(t) \end{array} \right\}$ $0 \leq t \leq 2\pi$

5. Write a program to plot the trajectory of a golf ball for various initial velocities V and angles of elevation, θ. The user will be asked to enter the values for V (in feet/sec), THETA (in radians), and the distance, H, from the tee (at the origin) to the hole.

   The equations describing the ball's trajectory are

   $$X = (V \cos \theta)t$$
   $$Y = -\tfrac{1}{2}gt^2 + (V \sin \theta)t$$

   where g is the gravitational acceleration of 32 feet/sec².

   In your plot, show the location of the tee and the hole and the trajectory of the ball from the tee to where it first makes landfall (or, waterfall, as the case may be). (See Fig. 10.19).

Figure 10.19.

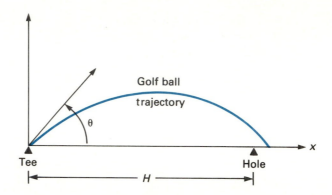

6. You are hidden from view of the golfer in project 5 at some point on the line between the tee and the hole. The distance between you and the golfer is D. You plan to deflect the golfer's ball by a shot of your own. You will hit your ball with an initial velocity, V_P, at an angle of elevation, θ_P.

   Write a program that will accept your opponent's initial velocity, V, and angle of elevation, THETA. The program will also be given the values of H (distance from tee to hole) and D (distance between you and your opponent). Once these values have been entered, the program will execute a loop in which it will accept a sequence of VP and THETAP values. For each VP and THETAP value, it will plot your ball's trajectory along with your opponent's. If both balls end up in the same cell of the array GRAPH at the same time, then both trajectories will be terminated at that point and that will be considered a hit. (See Fig. 10.20).

   Keep on entering VP and THETAP values until you hit your opponent's ball or get tired.

Figure 10.20.

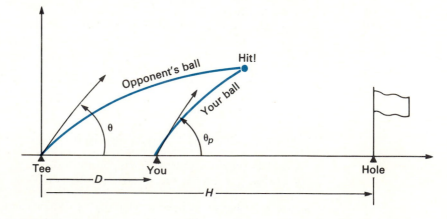

7. The problem of graphing equations given in polar coordinates duplicates several features of our program to plot parametric equations. An equation in polar coordi-

nates has the form

$R = F(\theta)$

where R is interpreted as the distance of a point from the origin and θ (THETA) is the angle (see Fig. 10.21).

Figure 10.21.

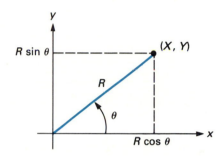

To plot equations given in polar coordinates, we let THETA take on a sequence of values, usually from 0 through $2 * \pi$. A small enough THETA increment must be chosen to get sufficient detail. For each THETA, we compute R = F(THETA). Then we transform the (R, THETA) pair to rectangular coordinates using the equations

```
X = R * COS(THETA)
Y = R * SIN(THETA)
```

These equations can be derived from a consideration of Fig. 10.21. Once we have the (X,Y) pair for the current values of R and THETA, we can mark the appropriate row and column of the array GRAPH.

Implement the technique described above to plot the following equations given in polar coordinates:

a. $R = \sin(\theta)$
b. $R = \cos(3 * \theta)$
c. $R = \sin(7 * \theta)$
d. $R = 3 - 3 * \sin(\theta)$
e. $R = \tan(\theta)$

8. Apply our contour-plotting technique to each of the following functions in an appropriate region near the origin. In some cases, the function $z = f(x,y)$ is not defined for certain (x,y) (parts a and b). In these cases, have your program print out a blank wherever the function is undefined.

a. $z = 9 - x^2 - y^2$
b. $z = 4 + x^2 - y^2$
c. $z = x^2 + y^2$
d. $z = \sin(x/2)\sin(y/2)$
e. $z = e^{-x}\sin(y)$

9. Write a program that generates a contour plot of the interference pattern produced by two sinusoidal wave generators operating in phase. The amplitude, z, of the disturbance at each point, (x,y), depends on the distance between (x,y) and the individual generators (or sources). The formula for z in terms of these distances, R1 and R2, is

```
Z = COS(R1) + COS(R2)
```

where R1 denotes the distance between the first generator and (x,y) and R2 denotes the distance between the second generator and (x,y).

Figure 10.22.

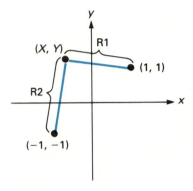

If the generators are at the points $(1,1)$ and $(-1,-1)$ (as shown in Fig. 10.22), then R1 and R2 are given by the formulae

```
R1 = SQRT((X-1.0) ** 2 + (Y-1.0) ** 2)
R2 = SQRT((X+1.0) ** 2 + (Y+1.0) ** 2).
```

Generate the contour plot for z delimited by the lines $x = 10$, $x = -10$, $y = 10$, $y = -10$.

11. Introduction to Numerical Methods

$\mathbf{I}$N THIS chapter, we will introduce the topic of numerical methods. We will discuss several computational techniques that are widely used in solving problems in engineering, economics, statistics, business, natural science, and social science. These techniques include finding roots of equations, matrix arithmetic, solving simultaneous equations, fitting a line to a data set, and numerical integration. We will also discuss FORTRAN features that are important in numerical computation such as double precision and complex numbers.

The sections in this chapter are fairly independent and may be studied in any order. Due to space limitations, we have generally presented only one method for performing a particular numerical operation. There are several different methods available for each of the operations discussed in this chapter. A list of references is provided for those wishing to delve deeper into the topic of numerical methods. There is also an extensive set of programming projects, many of which present alternative methods.

11.1　Finding Roots of Equations

A useful mathematical idea is to compute the roots of an equation

$$F(x) = 0$$

The roots of the above equation are the values for x that make this equation true. If we graph the function $F(x)$, as shown in Fig. 11.1, the roots of the equation are those points where the x-axis and the graph of the function intersect. The roots of the equation $F(x) = 0$ are also called the zeros of the function $F(x)$.

Figure 11.1. *Six Roots for the Equation $F(x) = 0$*

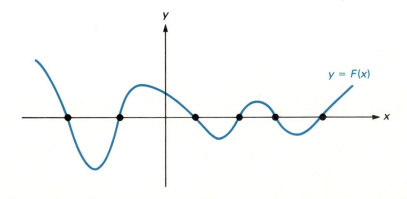

In this section, we will discuss two numerical methods for finding approximate real roots of an equation. When a numerical method is successful in finding a root, it is said to have *converged* to the root. When a numerical method fails, it is said to have *diverged*. Different root-finding methods have different properties in terms of convergence and divergence. Among the methods we will discuss, the bisection method converges relatively slowly (in general) as compared to Newton's method. The speed with which a method converges becomes an important issue when the function, $F(x)$, whose roots we are computing, requires costly computations. This is because finding roots of equations involves repeated evaluations of the function.

Despite its slow convergence properties, the bisection method will be discussed in detail because it does not require calculus, whereas Newton's method does. Newton's method is discussed at the end of this section, and its implementation is presented as an exercise for those students who have studied calculus.

Convergence Criteria

In general, root-finding methods generate a sequence of approximations to a root:

$$x_1, x_2, x_3, \dots, x_j, \dots$$

One problem is deciding when to terminate this generation process. In other words, when is a given x_j value "good enough" to be accepted as our answer?

There are three criteria for judging whether a given x_j is good enough. Since the satisfaction of one of these criteria causes the root-finding method to terminate, or converge, these are called convergence criteria. These criteria are given below. RT denotes the true root, EPSLON is some predetermined small number, x_j is the latest approximation, and x_{j-1} is the approximation before that.

Criteria for Convergence to the Root

1. $|F(x_j)| <$ EPSLON
2. $|x_j - \text{RT}| <$ EPSLON
3. $|x_j - x_{j-1}| <$ EPSLON

Criterion 1 states that x_j is considered a good enough approximation to the root if the value of $|F(x_j)|$ is very small. Criterion 2 states that x_j is considered a good enough approximation to the root if it is very close to the true root. Finally, criterion 3 states that x_j is considered a good enough approximation to the root if it is very close to the previous approximation, x_{j-1}. In other words, we do not expect to gain required accuracy by generating additional approximations.

One might wonder how criterion 2 can be applied in practice unless RT is already known. Actually, we do not need to know RT to claim that x_j is within EPSLON of RT, as the bisection method will demonstrate. It is sufficient to know that x_j and RT have been isolated to the same sufficiently small interval.

The convergence criteria are not equivalent. For example, Fig. 11.2(a) shows a situation in which x_j is within a distance EPSLON of RT, but $|F(x_j)|$ is greater than EPSLON. Figure 11.2(b) also shows a situation where $|F(x_j)| <$ EPSLON but the distance of x_j from RT is greater than EPSLON.

Figure 11.2. *Showing Nonequivalence of Convergence Criteria 1 and 2*

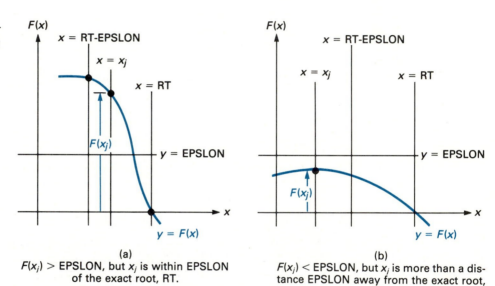

(a)
$F(x_j) >$ EPSLON, but x_j is within EPSLON of the exact root, RT.

(b)
$F(x_j) <$ EPSLON, but x_j is more than a distance EPSLON away from the exact root, RT.

The Bisection Method

The bisection method applies the second convergence criterion. We repeatedly generate approximate roots, x_j, until we have an approximation that is certain to be within a distance of EPSLON from the true root, RT. This can be done if we can isolate the true root and the approximate root within the same interval whose length is less than EPSLON. This is exactly what the bisection method does.

When using the bisection method, we first tabulate function values to identify intervals on which changes of sign occur. If a change of sign occurs on an interval, that interval must contain an odd number of roots. Figure 11.3 shows two such intervals. We keep on tabulating the function until we are certain we have isolated each root to a unique interval.

Let us assume that [XL,XR] is an interval on which a change of sign does occur and in which there is exactly one root. Furthermore, assume that the

Figure 11.3.
*Change of Sign
Implies an Odd
Number of Roots*

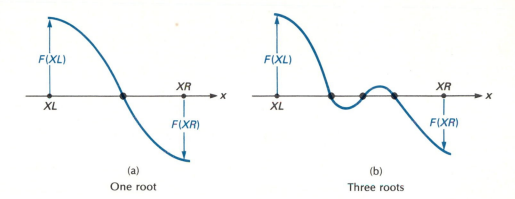

(a)
One root

(b)
Three roots

function $F(x)$ is continuous on this interval. If we bisect this interval by computing its midpoint, XM, using the formula

```
XM = (XL + XR) / 2.0
```

there are three possible outcomes: the root is in the left-half interval, [XL,XM]; the root is in the right-half interval, [XM,XR]; or F(XM) is zero. Figure 11.4 shows these three possibilities graphically.

If F(XM) is zero, there is no claim that XM is an exact root. In this case, we accept XM as an approximate root on the basis of convergence criterion 1 and the process terminates.

If the root is in one of the half intervals and the length of that interval is less than EPSLON, then the midpoint of that half interval must be within EPSLON of the true root. Thus, the midpoint of that half interval satisfies convergence criterion 2 and we are done. Otherwise, we make the half interval containing the root the new interval, and we continue by bisecting it. It should be obvious that under the assumptions we have given, if F(XM) never hits zero, then eventually the interval size will become less than EPSLON and the method will converge.

A Bisection Program

The FORTRAN program in Fig. 11.5 looks for an approximate root for the equation $F(x) = 0$ on the interval [XL, XR] using the bisection method. The endpoints, XL and XR, and the tolerance, EPSLON, are inputs from the user. The main program gets these three inputs, calls subroutine BISECT to perform the bisection procedure, and prints out the final results.

Computing the product F(XL) * F(XR) is the easiest way to detect a change of sign in the interval [XL,XR]. This product is negative when a change of sign occurs.

Figure 11.4. *Three Possibilities That Arise When the Interval [XL,XR] Is Bisected*

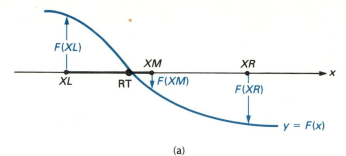

(a)
The root RT is in the half interval [*XL,XM*].

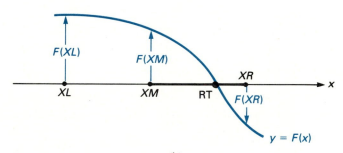

(b)
The root RT is in the half interval [*XM,XR*].

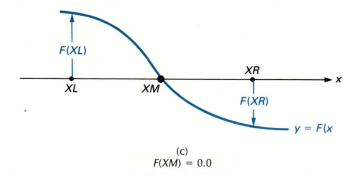

(c)
F(XM) = 0.0

A sample run of the program is shown in Fig. 11.6. Note that the intermediate values XL and XR are printed by BISECT, showing the convergence to the final answer.

Figure 11.5. *Finding a Root Using the Bisection Method*

```fortran
      PROGRAM ROOTS
C Finds a root of the equation
C          F(X) = 0
C on a specified interval [XL,XR] using the
C bisection method. The error tolerance is EPSLON.

C Declarations
      EXTERNAL F
      REAL XL, XR, EPSLON, ROOT
      LOGICAL ERR

C Get endpoints and error tolerance from user
      PRINT *, 'Enter left endpoint:'
      READ *, XL
      PRINT *, 'Enter right endpoint:'
      READ *, XR
      PRINT *, 'Enter tolerance:'
      READ *, EPSLON
      PRINT *

      CALL BISECT (XL, XR, EPSLON, F, ERR, ROOT)

C Report out results
      IF (ERR) THEN
C        No root found
         PRINT *, 'No root in this interval'
      ELSE
C        Root found
         PRINT *, 'Root found in this interval: ', ROOT
         PRINT *, 'Functional value at root:    ', F(ROOT)
      ENDIF

C Exit program
      STOP
      END

C -----------------------------------------------------------------

      REAL FUNCTION F(X)
C This is the function for which a root is being sought

C Argument Declarations
      REAL X

      F = 5 * X ** 3 - 2 * X ** 2 + 3

      RETURN
      END
```

```
C -----------------------------------------------------------------

      SUBROUTINE BISECT (XL, XR, EPSLON, F, ERR, ROOT)
C Implements the bisection method for finding a root of function F

C Input Arguments
C   [XL,XR] - The interval being examined
C   EPSLON - The error tolerance
C Output Arguments
C   ERR - Flag indicating whether or not there is an error
C   ROOT - The root being sought
C Functional Argument
C   F - The function

C Argument Declarations
      REAL XL, XR, EPSLON, F, ROOT
      LOGICAL ERR

C Local Declarations
      REAL XM, FM, FL, FR
      LOGICAL NTZERO

C Compute functional values at initial endpoints
      FL = F(XL)
      FR = F(XR)

C Look for root if change of sign occurs on interval.
C Otherwise, no root can be found.
      IF (FL * FR .GT. 0.0) THEN
          ERR = .TRUE.
      ELSE
C         Go for a root!
C         Compute initial midpoint
          XM = (XL + XR) / 2.0
          NTZERO = .TRUE.

C         Keep on searching so long as interval
C         size is too large and we didn't hit a 0
          DO WHILE (ABS(XR - XL) .GT. EPSLON          9 IF (...) THEN
                   .AND. NTZERO)
            FM = F(XM)
            IF (FM .EQ. 0.0) THEN
C               Zero hit
                NTZERO = .FALSE.
            ELSE IF (FL * FM .LT. 0.0) THEN
C               Zero in [XL,XM]
                XR = XM
            ELSE
C               Zero in [XM,XR]
                XL = XM
                FL = FM
            ENDIF
```

```
C            Print out new interval if there is one
             IF (NTZERO) PRINT *, 'New interval is ', XL, XR
C            New midpoint
             XM = (XL + XR) / 2.0
          ENDDO                                          GOTO 9
C                                                        ENDIF
C         Define result
C         Last value of XM is ROOT
          ROOT = XM
          ERR = .FALSE.
       ENDIF


C Exit subroutine
       RETURN
       END
```

Figure 11.6. *Sample Run of Bisection Method*

```
Enter left endpoint:
−1.0
Enter right endpoint:
1.0
Enter tolerance:
0.001

New interval is  −1.000000        0.0000000E+00
New interval is  −1.000000       −0.5000000
New interval is −0.7500000       −0.5000000
New interval is −0.7500000       −0.6250000
New interval is −0.7500000       −0.6875000
New interval is −0.7500000       −0.7187500
New interval is −0.7343750       −0.7187500
New interval is −0.7343750       −0.7265625
New interval is −0.7304688       −0.7265625
New interval is −0.7304688       −0.7285156
New interval is −0.7294922       −0.7285156
Root found in this interval: −0.7290039
Functional value at root:    −2.6941299E−05
```

Functions as Arguments

Note that the subroutine BISECT contains the function F as a dummy argument. This is the first time that we have seen a function used as an argument.

When a function is used as a dummy argument to a subroutine, you must remember to declare that function to be of the correct type within the subroutine. When a program unit passes a function (or subroutine) as an actual argument, that program unit must declare that function (or subroutine) as EXTERNAL. For example, the main program of our root-finding program contains the statement

```
EXTERNAL F
```

This allows the compiler to recognize F as a function and not as a variable or named constant. An important rule to remember, however, is that you cannot make a statement function EXTERNAL. Only functions and subroutines, which are independent program units, can be made EXTERNAL.

One final note about the program: the argument ERR of the subroutine BISECT will be used to tell the main program whether a root was found. If ERR is returned with the value .TRUE., then no root was found. This will happen if the user specifies an interval [XL,XR] on which no change of sign occurs. If the specified interval contains more than one root, only one of them will be found.

Program Style

Use of Function Arguments

The use of F as an argument for the subroutine BISECT is not necessary for program correctness. We could have written BISECT without this argument by including a statement function defining F within the subroutine. However, the use of F as an argument is preferred because it makes subroutine BISECT a more complete, self-contained entity. BISECT will find the root for any function passed as an argument without requiring the programmer to revise BISECT for each new function. The use of the function F as a dummy argument also makes the intent of the subroutine clearer. Conceptually, the function is more like an argument for the subroutine than an intrinsic part of the subroutine itself.

Newton's Method[M]

Newton's method for finding the roots of an equation starts with a guess, x_0, and then generates successive approximate roots $x_1, x_2, \ldots , x_j, x_{j+1}, \ldots$ using the iterative (or open) formula:

$$x_{j+1} = x_j - \frac{f(x_j)}{f'(x_j)}$$

where $f'(x_j)$ is the derivative of f evaluated at $x = x_j$. This open formula specifies an iteration by which new approximations are generated from previous ones. In particular, x_{j+1} is to be computed in terms of x_j, $f(x_j)$, and $f'(x_j)$. Figure 11.7 shows the geometric interpretation of Newton's method.

Newton's method uses convergence criterion 3. We will consider x_{j+1} the approximate root when two successive approximations are sufficiently close, that is, when

$$|x_{j+1} - x_j| < \text{EPSLON}$$

[M] Sections of this chapter marked with the superscript symbol[M] require calculus.

Figure 11.7. *Geometric Interpretation of Newton's Method*

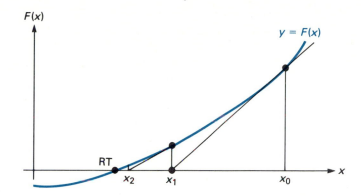

There are famous pathological cases where Newton's method cycles indefinitely. For example, this occurs in trying to find the root of

$$F(x) = x^3 - x$$

with an initial guess of $x = 1$ or $x = -1$. In general, Newton's method is more reliable and faster than the bisection method.

SELF-CHECK EXERCISE FOR SECTION 11.1

1. Write a subroutine NEWTON to replace subroutine BISECT in Fig. 11.5. *Hint:* Use an external function DF, which is the derivative of $F(x)$, as an argument.

11.2 ▬ Vectors and Matrixes

One- and two-dimensional arrays were introduced in Chapter 6. In many technical applications in science, engineering, economics, and business, arrays are used to represent mathematical objects called vectors and matrixes. In this section, we will learn how vectors and matrixes are represented in FORTRAN and how to write FORTRAN subroutines that perform basic operations on these objects.

Representing Vectors

A vector is a mathematical object consisting of a sequence of numbers (the components of the vector). A vector is said to be of dimension N if it consists of N components. We will use the notation $X(K)$ to denote the Kth component of the vector X. Unfortunately, the use of the word "dimension" in FORTRAN is not consistent with the standard mathematical usage. The FORTRAN array X in Fig. 11.8(a) is one-dimensional (in FORTRAN terms), whereas the vector it represents, shown in Fig. 11.8(b), is three-dimensional (in mathematical terms). An N-dimensional vector is represented in FORTRAN as a one-dimensional array plus an INTEGER variable that stores the value of N.

Figure 11.8. *FORTRAN Representation of a Vector*

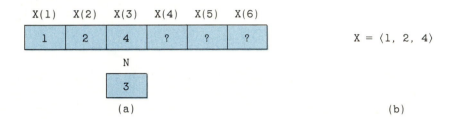

In general, if $X = \langle x_1, x_2, \ldots, x_N \rangle$ and $W = \langle w_1, w_2, \ldots, w_N \rangle$ are two vectors of dimension N, their scalar product is

The Scalar Product

Two vectors with the same number of components can be multiplied together forming the scalar (dot or inner) product. This is done by computing the sum of the product of corresponding components. Hence, if $X = \langle 1,2,4 \rangle$ and $W = \langle 2,3,1 \rangle$, their scalar product is

$$X \cdot W = \langle 1,2,4 \rangle \cdot \langle 2,3,1 \rangle = 1 * 2 + 2 * 3 + 4 * 1 = 12$$

In general, if $X = \langle x_1, x_2, \ldots, x_N \rangle$ and $W = \langle w_1, w_2, \ldots, w_N \rangle$ are two vectors of dimension N, their scalar product is

$$\sum_{i=1}^{N} x_i * w_i$$

where x_i and w_i denote the ith components of the vectors X and W, respectively.

Coding the computation of the scalar product of two N-dimensional vectors X and W is straightforward. A DO loop is required to traverse the vectors component by component. A variable SPROD is required to accumulate the sum. The FORTRAN code for doing this is shown next.

```
      SPROD = 0.0
      DO 10 K = 1, N
         SPROD = SPROD + X(K) * W(K)
   10 CONTINUE
```

Many of the subroutines we will develop in the rest of this chapter will require implementation of some sum, as was required in computing the scalar product. Translating from summation notation to FORTRAN is a fairly mechanical process. Figure 11.9 shows in some detail the correspondence between

Figure 11.9. *Summation Notation and DO Loop Parameters*

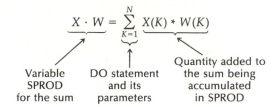

the mathematical expression of the scalar product and its implementation in FORTRAN.

Representing Matrixes

A matrix is a mathematical object that consists of a rectangular arrangement of numbers called the elements of the matrix. An *M*-by-*N* matrix consists of *M* rows and *N* columns. Each row is an *N*-dimensional vector, and each column is an *M*-dimensional vector. The element in the *I*th row and *J*th column is denoted by $A(I,J)$. Thus, an *M*-by-*N* matrix can be implemented in FORTRAN as a two-dimensional array with *M* rows and *N* columns.

Figure 11.10 shows a four-by-three matrix (a) and its implementation as a two-dimensional array (b). Note the necessity of the variables *M* and *N*, which specify the number of rows and the number of columns, respectively, in the matrix. The declared dimension of the array must be large enough to accommodate the largest matrix that we expect to use in our application. Thus, the array *A* of Fig. 11.10(b) has six rows and six columns, but only four rows and three columns are being used in representing the four-by-three matrix, *A*.

Figure 11.10.
Four-by-Three Matrix and Its Implementation as a Two-Dimensional Array

$$A = \begin{bmatrix} 1 & 1 & 1 \\ 2 & 3 & 1 \\ 1 & -1 & -1 \\ 0 & 1 & 2 \end{bmatrix}$$

M

$\boxed{4}$

N

$\boxed{3}$

A

	1	2	3	4	5	6
1	1	1	1	?	?	?
2	2	3	1	?	?	?
3	1	−1	−1	?	?	?
4	0	1	2	?	?	?
5	?	?	?	?	?	?
6	?	?	?	?	?	?

(a)   (b)

Multiplying a Matrix by a Vector

If A is an M-by-N matrix and X is an N-dimensional vector, then we can form the product of A and X, denoted by $A * X$, yielding an M-dimensional vector, Y. A matrix with M rows and N columns can only be multiplied on the right by a vector of dimension N. If A is an M-by-N matrix and W is an M-dimensional vector, then we can form the product of W and A, denoted by $W * A$, yielding an N-dimensional vector, Z. A matrix with M rows and N columns can only be multiplied on the left by a vector of dimension M. Figure 11.11 shows the multiplication of a four-by-three matrix, A, both on the right (a) and on the left (b). We will restrict our detailed discussion to Fig. 11.11(a).

Figure 11.11. *Multiplying a Matrix by a Vector*

$$
\begin{array}{ccc}
A & * \quad X \ = & Y
\end{array}
$$

$$
\begin{bmatrix} 1 & 1 & 1 \\ 2 & 3 & 1 \\ 1 & -1 & -1 \\ 0 & 1 & 2 \end{bmatrix} * \begin{bmatrix} 1 \\ 2 \\ 2 \end{bmatrix} = \begin{bmatrix} 5 \\ 10 \\ -3 \\ 6 \end{bmatrix}
$$

(a) Multiplication on the right

$$
\begin{array}{ccc}
W & * & A & = & Z
\end{array}
$$

$$
[2 \quad 0 \quad 1 \quad -1] * \begin{bmatrix} 1 & 1 & 1 \\ 2 & 3 & 1 \\ 1 & -1 & -1 \\ 0 & 1 & 2 \end{bmatrix} = [3 \quad 0 \quad -1]
$$

(b) Multiplication on the left

How were the components of the result vector in Fig. 11.11(a) computed? The answer is that the Ith component of Y, $Y(I)$ is the scalar product of the Ith row of the matrix A and the vector X. For example, $Y(2)$ is the scalar product of the second row of A (considered as a vector) and the vector X. These vectors are in color in Fig. 11.11(a). The relevant computation is

$$Y(2) = \langle 2, 3, 1 \rangle \cdot \langle 1, 2, 2 \rangle = 2 * 1 + 3 * 2 + 1 * 2 = 10$$

The mathematical formula for computing $Y(I)$ in the general case of the multiplication of an M-by-N matrix A and an N-dimensional vector X is

$$Y(I) = \sum_{K=1}^{N} A(I,K) * X(K)$$

Note that $A(I,K)$ denotes the Kth component of the Ith row of A and that $X(K)$ denotes the Kth component of the vector X. Translating mathematical summation notation into FORTRAN, we get the code below for computing $Y(I)$.

```
      Y(I) = 0.0
      DO 20 K = 1, N
         Y(I) = Y(I) + A(I,K) * X(K)
   20 CONTINUE
```

Once we have a description of how to compute a typical element of a vector, it is a simple matter to code the computation of the entire vector. All that we need to do is embed the computation of the typical element, $Y(I)$, in a DO loop where I is the loop index. The FORTRAN subroutine MVPROD in Fig. 11.12 uses this idea to compute the product of an M-by-N matrix A and an N-dimensional vector X. The result is an M-dimensional vector, Y.

Figure 11.12. *Subroutine MVPROD*

```
      SUBROUTINE MVPROD (M, N, A, X, Y)
C Computes the product of matrix A (M × N) and the
C N-dimensional vector X. The result is stored in vector Y.

C Input Arguments
C    M - row dimension for matrix A and dimension for vector Y
C    N - column dimension for matrix A and dimension for vector X
C    A - M by N matrix
C    X - N-dimensional vector
C Output Argument
C    Y - M-dimensional product vector

C Argument Declarations
      INTEGER M, N
      REAL A(M,N), X(N), Y(M)

C Local Declarations
      INTEGER I, K

C Compute each component, Y(I), in turn

      DO 10 I = 1, M
         Y(I) = 0.0
         DO 20 K = 1, N
            Y(I) = Y(I) + A(I,K) * X(K)
   20    CONTINUE
   10 CONTINUE

C Exit subroutine
      RETURN
      END
```

Matrix Multiplication

Multiplying a matrix by a vector is just a special case of multiplying a matrix by a matrix, since an N-dimensional vector can be viewed as either a matrix with N rows and 1 column or a matrix with 1 row and N columns. We will now develop a FORTRAN subroutine that will multiply any two matrixes, so long as they can be multiplied.

Two matrixes A and B can be multiplied together, yielding a new matrix, $C = A * B$, if the number of columns in A is equal to the number of rows in B.

In this case, the matrixes A and B are said to be "conformable" for multiplication. If A is an M-by-N matrix and if B is N by P, then the product matrix C will be M by P. This is consistent with our earlier discussion of multiplying a matrix (M by N) by a vector (N by 1). The result was a new vector (M by 1).

In analyzing the computation of the product of two matrixes, we first consider the computation of a typical element. For example, a typical element in the product matrix C is the element in the Ith row and Jth column. This element is denoted by $C(I,J)$. Once we know how to compute $C(I,J)$, it is a trivial matter to compute the rest of the matrix C. All we have to do is embed the computation of $C(I,J)$ in an appropriate looping mechanism, which allows I and J to take on all relevant values, as shown below.

```
        DO 10 I = 1, M
          DO 20 J = 1, P
              *** Compute C(I,J) ***
20          CONTINUE
10      CONTINUE
```

Let us now describe the computation of that typical element, $C(I,J)$, of the product matrix, $C = A * B$. $C(I,J)$ is just the scalar product of the Ith row of A and the Jth column of B. Figure 11.13 shows the computation of C when the square matrixes A and B are multiplied together. (A matrix is square if it has the same number of rows and columns.) For example, in computing $C(2,3)$, the second row of A (considered as a vector) is multiplied by the third column of B (considered as a vector). The elements involved are in color in Fig. 11.13.

Figure 11.13. *Multiplying Matrix A by Matrix B*

$$
\begin{array}{ccccccc}
A & * & B & = & C \\
\begin{bmatrix} 1 & 1 & 1 \\ 2 & 3 & 1 \\ 1 & -1 & -1 \end{bmatrix} & * & \begin{bmatrix} 2 & 0 & 1 \\ 1 & -1 & 0 \\ 3 & 1 & -1 \end{bmatrix} & = & \begin{bmatrix} 6 & 0 & 0 \\ 10 & -2 & 1 \\ -2 & 0 & 2 \end{bmatrix}
\end{array}
$$

The mathematical formula for this computation in the general case where A has N columns and B has N rows is

$$ C(I,J) = \sum_{K=1}^{N} A(I,K) * B(K,J) $$

Note that we are pairing the Kth component of the Ith row of A and the Kth component of the Jth column of B in forming this sum. Routinely translating the above sum into FORTRAN, we get the code shown below.

```
      C(I,J) = 0.0
      DO 30 K = 1, N
          C(I,J) = C(I,J) + A(I,K) * B(K,J)
30 CONTINUE
```

Embedding the above computation into the appropriate nested DO loop structure yields the computation of the entire product matrix. This is done in the subroutine MATMUL of Fig. 11.14. This is a general subroutine for multiplying any two conformable REAL matrixes.

Figure 11.14. *Subroutine MATMUL*

```
      SUBROUTINE MATMUL (M, N, P, A, B, C)
C Multiplies matrixes A and B yielding the product matrix C

C Input Arguments
C   M, N, P - dimensions for the matrixes A, B, and C
C   A - M by N matrix
C   B - N by P matrix
C Output Argument
C   C - M by P product matrix

C Argument Declarations
      INTEGER M, N, P
      REAL A(M,N), B(N,P), C(M,P)

C Local Declarations
      INTEGER I, J, K
      REAL CIJ

C Compute each C(I,J) in turn
      DO 10 I = 1, M
         DO 20 J = 1, P
            CIJ = 0.0
            DO 30 K = 1, N
               CIJ = CIJ + A(I,K) * B(K,J)
30          CONTINUE
            C(I,J) = CIJ
20       CONTINUE
10    CONTINUE

C Exit subroutine
      RETURN
      END
```

11.3 ▬ Solving Systems of Linear Equations

In the previous section, we saw that if we multiplied a matrix

$$A = \begin{bmatrix} 1 & 1 & 1 \\ 2 & 3 & 1 \\ 1 & -1 & -1 \end{bmatrix}$$

by a vector

$$X = \begin{bmatrix} 1 \\ 2 \\ 1 \end{bmatrix}$$

on the right, then the result is a vector

$$Y = \begin{bmatrix} 4 \\ 9 \\ -2 \end{bmatrix}$$

Now, let us consider another sort of problem. Suppose we know the matrix A and the vector Y, but we don't know the vector X. That is, we want to know which vector, X, when multiplied on the left by the matrix A will result in the vector Y. The problem is to find the three unknowns, $X(1)$, $X(2)$, and $X(3)$, in the equation:

$$
\begin{array}{ccccc}
A & * & X & = & Y \\
\begin{bmatrix} 1 & 1 & 1 \\ 2 & 3 & 1 \\ 1 & -1 & -1 \end{bmatrix} & * & \begin{bmatrix} X(1) \\ X(2) \\ X(3) \end{bmatrix} & = & \begin{bmatrix} 4 \\ 9 \\ -2 \end{bmatrix}
\end{array}
$$

To find the values of $X(1)$, $X(2)$, and $X(3)$, we must solve a system of three linear equations in three unknowns. We illustrate this by showing how each component of the vector Y is computed in terms of the matrix A and the vector of unknowns X. For example, $Y(1)$ is the scalar product of the first row of the matrix A and the vector X:

$$Y(1) = A(1,1) * X(1) + A(1,2) * X(2) + A(1,3) * X(3) = 4$$

Replacing the matrix elements $A(I,J)$ with their numerical values, we get the entire system of three linear equations in three unknowns, $X(1)$, $X(2)$, $X(3)$.

$$
\begin{array}{r}
X(1) + X(2) + X(3) = 4 \\
2 * X(1) + 3 * X(2) + X(3) = 9 \\
X(1) - X(2) - X(3) = -2
\end{array}
$$

We will use Gaussian elimination to solve these equations.

Gaussian Elimination

In Gaussian elimination, we attempt to reduce the original system of N linear equations to triangular form (also called upper triangular form). In *triangular form,* the coefficients below the diagonal in the matrix of coefficients are all 0 and the diagonal elements are all 1. Figure 11.15 shows the original system of equations in triangular form. The coefficients above the diagonal (in color) and the components of the constant vector Y no longer have their original values.

Figure 11.15.
Original System of Equations in Triangular Form

$$\begin{bmatrix} 1 & 1 & 1 \\ 0 & 1 & -1 \\ 0 & 0 & 1 \end{bmatrix} * \begin{bmatrix} X(1) \\ X(2) \\ X(3) \end{bmatrix} = \begin{bmatrix} 4 \\ 1 \\ 1 \end{bmatrix}$$

The three equations that correspond to Fig. 11.15 are shown below.

$$
\begin{aligned}
X(1) + X(2) + X(3) &= 4 \\
X(2) - X(3) &= 1 \\
X(3) &= 1
\end{aligned}
$$

This system can easily be solved for $X(1)$, $X(2)$, $X(3)$ by solving the last equation for $X(3)$ (i.e., $X(3)$ is 1), substituting this value in the next to last equation and solving for $X(2)$ (i.e., $X(2)$ is 2), and substituting these values in the first equation and solving for $X(1)$ (i.e., $X(1)$ is 1). This process is called *back substitution*. The algorithm for Gaussian elimination follows.

Algorithm for Gaussian Elimination

1. Transform the original system into triangular form.
2. Solve for the $X(i)$ by back substitution.

The Augmented Matrix

Before we can proceed further, we must decide upon appropriate data structures for representing a system of N linear equations in N unknowns. The preferred method of representation for such systems is the augmented matrix. This particular representation allows for the most concise coding of both triangularization and back substitution.

Figure 11.16 shows the form of an augmented matrix for a system of N linear equations in N unknowns. The augmented matrix will be represented by a two-dimensional array, AUG. Note that the augmented matrix has N rows and $N + 1$ columns. The last column of the augmented matrix (shown in color) contains the constant vector, Y (e.g., AUG(1,4) is $Y(1)$). The matrix of coefficients, A, is stored in the rest of the columns of the augmented matrix (e.g., AUG(1,1) is $A(1,1)$). Note that the vector of unknowns is nowhere to be seen. When a system of linear equations is represented as an augmented matrix the unknowns are implicit.

Figure 11.16.
Original Augmented Matrix AUG

$$\begin{bmatrix} A(1,1) & A(1,2) & A(1,3) & Y(1) \\ A(2,1) & A(2,2) & A(2,3) & Y(2) \\ A(3,1) & A(3,2) & A(3,3) & Y(3) \end{bmatrix} \qquad \begin{bmatrix} 1 & 1 & 1 & 4 \\ 2 & 3 & 1 & 9 \\ 1 & -1 & -1 & -2 \end{bmatrix}$$

(a) General form   (b) Our example

Our first goal is to triangularize the augmented matrix, that is, reduce it to a form in which AUG(1,1), AUG(2,2), and AUG(3,3) are 1 and AUG(2,1), AUG(3,1), and AUG(3,2) are zero, as shown in Fig. 11.17. All other values [shown in color in Fig. 11.17(a)] are written as symbols such as a'_{ij} and y'_i. The primes are used to emphasize that these values are not the same as the ones in the original system of equations.

Figure 11.17.
*Triangularized
Augmented Matrix*

$$\begin{bmatrix} 1 & a'_{12} & a'_{13} & y'_1 \\ 0 & 1 & a'_{23} & y'_2 \\ 0 & 0 & a_{13} & y'_3 \end{bmatrix}$$

(a) General form

$$\begin{bmatrix} 1 & 1 & 1 & 4 \\ 0 & 1 & -1 & 1 \\ 0 & 0 & 1 & 1 \end{bmatrix}$$

(b) Our example

**Triangularizing
the Augmented
Matrix**

Let us now turn our attention to the triangularization process, the process that transforms the original system of equations into a new system in upper triangular form. The rules of linear algebra guarantee that this new system will have the same solution as the original system if we confine ourselves to the following operations upon the augmented matrix, AUG:

- Multiply any row of AUG by a non-zero number.
- Add to any row of AUG a multiple of any other row.
- Swap any two rows.

If the system has a unique solution, we can get the system into triangular form by using just these three operations. (If not, our algorithm will detect this.)

We triangularize the augmented matrix by systematically moving down the diagonal, starting at AUG(1, 1). When we are working with a particular diagonal element, we call that element the pivot. When AUG(L,L) is the pivot, we have two goals:

1. normalize the pivot row, so that the pivot will take the desired value, 1
2. set all coefficients in the column below the pivot to zero, that is, give the elements AUG(L+1,L), AUG(L +2,L), ... , AUG(N,L) the value 0

The first goal is achieved by multiplying the pivot row (e.g., row L) by an appropriate constant (i.e., 1/AUG(L,L)), which is an application of operation 1. The second goal is achieved by applying operation 2 to the rows beneath the pivot row.

Experts recommend that to minimize computational round-off errors during the triangularization process, you should always place the largest possible coefficient (in absolute value) in the pivoting position. That is, when working with the Lth pivot, you should examine all the coefficients in the column beneath the pivot to find the coefficient that has the largest absolute value.

The pivot row and the row containing that largest coefficient should be swapped. This in no way changes the solution of the system of equations because swapping rows is one of the three permissible operations (operation 3). The process of switching the current row with the one containing the maximum pivot is called *pivoting*.

What if we encounter a maximum pivot element whose value is zero? This can happen only when all values beneath the pivot element are also zero. If a non-zero value cannot be found in the column beneath the pivot, the given system of equations does not have a unique solution.

The operations above are summarized in the algorithm that follows. The local variable OK indicates whether the system of equations has a solution.

Local Variables

the current row (INTEGER L)
a flag indicating whether the system has a solution (LOGICAL OK)

Algorithm for Subroutine GAUSS

1. Initially assume the system has a solution, OK = .TRUE
2. Start with the first row, L=1
3. DO WHILE (OK .AND. (L .LT. N))
    4. Pivot using the maximum pivot strategy
    5. IF (OK) THEN
            6. Normalize the pivot row
            7. Eliminate the coefficients beneath the pivot
        ENDIF
    8. Go on to the next row, L=L+1
    ENDDO
9. IF (OK) THEN
        10. Normalize row N
    END

Subroutine GAUSS is shown in Fig. 11.18. The code for steps 6, 7, and 10 are inserted directly in GAUSS. The loop that performs step 6 simply multiplies each coefficient in row L by 1/AUG(L,L) (stored in RCIPRL). The multiplication starts at column L+1, because the elements in columns 1, 2, ... , L−1 should all be zero. In step 10, only the elements in columns N and N+1 need to be changed.

In step 7, each row J beneath the pivot (J = L+1, L+2, ... , N) is modified so that the element in AUG(J,L) becomes zero. This is done by multiplying the pivot row (row L) by −AUG(J,L) (saved in XMULT) and then adding the pivot row to row J. The addition starts at column L+1 of row J because the elements in columns 1, 2, ... , L should all be zero.

Figure 11.18. *Subroutine GAUSS*

```
          SUBROUTINE GAUSS (AUG, N, OK)
C Triangularizes the augmented matrix AUG

C Input Argument
C    N – The number of equations
C Input/Output Argument
C    AUG – The system of equations as an augmented matrix
C Output Argument
C    OK – Flag indicating whether system is O.K. (nonsingular)

C Argument Declarations
          INTEGER N
          REAL AUG(N,*)
          LOGICAL OK

C Local Declarations
          INTEGER J, K, L
          REAL RCIPRL, XMULT

C System is assumed nonsingular; move down the diagonal
          OK = .TRUE.
          L = 1
          DO WHILE (OK .AND. (L .LT. N))              9 IF (...) THEN
C         Pivot
          CALL PIVOT (AUG, N, L, OK)
          IF (OK) THEN
C             Normalize pivot row
              RCIPRL = 1.0 / AUG(L,L)
              AUG(L,L) = 1.0
              DO 10 K = L+1, N+1
                  AUG(L,K) = AUG(L,K) * RCIPRL
  10          CONTINUE

C             Eliminate coefficients beneath pivot
              DO 20 J = L+1, N
                  XMULT = –AUG(J,L)
                  AUG(J,L) = 0.0
                  DO 30 K = L+1, N+1
                      AUG(J,K) = AUG(J,K) + XMULT * AUG(L,K)
  30              CONTINUE
  20          CONTINUE
          ENDIF
C         Next pivot
          L = L + 1
          ENDDO                                       GOTO 9
                                                      ENDIF

          IF (OK) THEN
C         Normalize N–th row
              RCIPRL = 1.0 / AUG(N,N)
              AUG(N,N) = 1.0
              AUG(N,N+1) = AUG(N,N+1) * RCIPRL
          ENDIF

C Exit subroutine
          RETURN
          END
```

548

Step 4 of GAUSS (the pivot step) is performed by subroutine PIVOT. The data requirements and algorithm for PIVOT follow Fig. 11.19; the subroutine is shown in Fig. 11.19.

Figure 11.19. *Subroutine PIVOT*

```
      SUBROUTINE PIVOT (AUG, N, L, OK)
C Performs pivoting with respect to the Lth row and the Lth column

C Input Arguments
C   N - The number of equations
C   L - The pivot row and column
C Input/Output Arguments
C   AUG - The augmented matrix
C   OK - Set to .FALSE. if search for non-zero pivot fails

C Argument Declarations
      INTEGER N, L
      REAL AUG(N,*)
      LOGICAL OK

C Local Declarations
      REAL XMAX, XTEMP
      INTEGER J, K, MAXROW

C Find maximum pivot
      XMAX = ABS(AUG(L,L))
      MAXROW = L
      DO 10 J = L+1, N
         IF (ABS(AUG(J,L)) .GT. XMAX) THEN
            XMAX = ABS(AUG(J,L))
            MAXROW = J
         ENDIF
  10  CONTINUE

C Swap rows if non-zero pivot was found
      IF (XMAX .EQ. 0.0) THEN
         OK = .FALSE.
      ELSE IF (MAXROW .NE. L) THEN
C        Swap rows
         DO 20 K = L, N+1
            XTEMP = AUG(L,K)
            AUG(L,K) = AUG(MAXROW,K)
            AUG(MAXROW,K) = XTEMP
  20     CONTINUE
      ENDIF

C Exit subroutine
      RETURN
      END
```

Input Arguments

the number of rows in the augmented matrix (INTEGER N)
the row being normalized (INTEGER L)

Input/Output Arguments

the augmented matrix (REAL AUG)
a flag indicating whether a non-zero pivot was found (LOGICAL OK)

Local Variables

the largest absolute value in column L (REAL XMAX)
the row containing the maximum value (INTEGER MAXROW)

Algorithm for PIVOT

1. Starting at row L, find the row, MAXROW, whose element in column L has the largest absolute value
2. IF the largest absolute value is zero THEN
       3. Set OK to .FALSE.
   ELSE IF MAXROW is not row L THEN
       4. Swap rows L and MAXROW
   ENDIF

Back Substitution

We can now derive the FORTRAN code for back substitution in terms of the augmented matrix, AUG. We will also need an array X to represent the vector of unknowns and an INTEGER variable N to store the number of unknowns (three).

The triangularized augmented matrix for our example system [see Fig. 11.17(b)] is rewritten below on the left with the corresponding storage locations in array AUG shown on the right (e.g., the contents of AUG(1,4) is 4).

$$
\begin{bmatrix} 1 & 1 & 1 & 4 \\ 0 & 1 & -1 & 1 \\ 0 & 0 & 1 & 1 \end{bmatrix}
\begin{bmatrix} \text{AUG(1,1)} & \text{AUG(1,2)} & \text{AUG(1,3)} & \text{AUG(1,4)} \\ \text{AUG(2,1)} & \text{AUG(2,2)} & \text{AUG(2,3)} & \text{AUG(2,4)} \\ \text{AUG(3,1)} & \text{AUG(3,2)} & \text{AUG(3,3)} & \text{AUG(3,4)} \end{bmatrix}
$$

The part of the matrix that is used in back substitution is shown in color. Applying the principle of back substitution to the diagram above, we can observe from the last row that

    X(3) = AUG(3,4) = 1

Next, we see from the second row that

    X(2) = AUG(2,4) - (AUG(2,3) * X(3)) = 1 - (-1 * 1) = 2

Finally, we see from the first row that

```
X(1) = AUG(1,4) - (AUG(1,2) * X(2) + AUG(1,3) * X(3))
     = 4 - (1 * 2 + 1 * 1) = 4 - (3) = 1
```

These observations lead to the algorithm for back substitution that follows.

Algorithm for Back Substitution Using the Augmented Matrix

1. Set X(N) to AUG(N,N+1).
2. For each L=N-1, N-2, ... , 2, 1 in turn compute

$$X(L) = AUG(L,N) - \sum_{J=L+1}^{N} AUG(L,J) * X(J)$$

This algorithm is implemented as subroutine BACK shown in Fig. 11.20.

Figure 11.20. *Subroutine BACK*

```
      SUBROUTINE BACK (AUG, N, X)
C Performs back substitution

C Input Arguments
C    AUG - The triangularized augmented matrix (N by N+1)
C    N - The number of equations
C Output Argument
C    X - The solution vector (X(1) through X(N))

C Argument Declarations
      INTEGER N
      REAL AUG(N,*), X(N)

C Local Declarations
      REAL SUM
      INTEGER L, J

      X(N) = AUG(N,N+1)
      DO 10 L = N-1, 1, -1
         SUM = 0.0
         DO 20 J = L+1, N
            SUM = SUM + AUG(L,J) * X(J)
 20      CONTINUE
         X(L) = AUG(L,N+1) - SUM
 10   CONTINUE

C Exit subroutine
      RETURN
      END
```

The final step in implementing the Gaussian elimination algorithm would be to write a main program. The algorithm for the main program follows.

Algorithm for Main Program

1. Store data in the augmented matrix, AUG
2. Call subroutine GAUSS to triangularize matrix AUG
3. IF a solution exists (OK is .TRUE.) THEN
     4. Call subroutine BACK to find the solution

Figure 11.21. *Main Program for Gaussian Elimination*

```
      PROGRAM LINSYS
C Solves a system of linear equations

C Declarations
      INTEGER N
      PARAMETER (N = 3, M = N + 1)
      REAL AUG(N, M), X(N)
      LOGICAL OK

C Store data in AUG

C        (1  1  1  4)
C  AUG = (2  3  1  9)
C        (1 -1 -1 -2)

      DATA AUG /1.0,2.0,1.0,  1.0,3.0,-1.0,
     +          1.0,1.0,-1.0,  4.0,9.0,-2.0/

C Call subroutine GAUSS to triangularize matrix AUG
      CALL GAUSS (AUG, N, OK)

C Call BACK and display solution if one exists
      IF (OK) THEN
          CALL BACK (AUG, N, X)
          PRINT *, 'The values of X are:'
          PRINT '(1X, 3F10.2)', X
      ELSE
          PRINT *, 'NO SOLUTION EXISTS'
      ENDIF

C Exit program
      STOP
      END


The values of X are:
      1.00      2.00      1.00
```

```
    5. Print out the solution
ELSE
    6. Print a message indicating there is no solution
ENDIF
```

Coding the Main Program

Figure 11.21 shows the main program. The DATA statement initializes AUG to the matrix shown earlier; the sample run displays the solution vector X.

Ill-Conditioned Systems

Unfortunately, not every system of N equations in N unknowns has a unique solution. The system may have no solution, in which case it is said to be singular, or it may have an infinite number of solutions, in which case it is said to be degenerate. The triangularization process will fail if the given system does not have a unique solution. A more serious danger is that our system of equations may be ill-conditioned. In the two-dimensional case (N is 2), this occurs when the two lines whose intersection we are trying to find are nearly parallel.

Another problem that arises in practice is that computational round-off errors can be significant when N is large. The larger N is, the more multiplying gets done in triangularizing the matrix. In large systems, these accumulating round-off errors may make the results obtained from Gaussian elimination useless. In these situations, iterative methods, such as Gauss-Seidel, are recommended. The Gauss-Seidel method is described at the end of this chapter in programming project 12.

11.4 ▬▬ Linear Regression and Correlation[M]

In this section, we will discuss how two important ideas from statistics, linear regression and correlation, are translated into FORTRAN code. Our discussion will be rather sketchy in that we do not have the space to develop the full rationale behind some of the formulae nor to elaborate upon certain issues. The interested reader is referred to the references at the end of the chapter.

The Concept of Regression

Regression is normally used for prediction. Suppose X and Y are two measurable quantities (or *observables*). For example, X might be the annual rainfall and Y might be annual tree ring growth, or X might be a professor's intelligence quotient and Y might be his or her salary. The concept of regression is to determine a relationship

$$Y = F(X)$$

on the basis of a finite sample of X and Y scores. This relationship is then used to predict Y values for given X values.

Regression might be linear or nonlinear, depending on whether the relationship, $F(X)$, is linear. Our discussion will be confined to linear regression, where the relationship $F(X)$ is linear. The linear relationship is then called the best fit line through the sample data. This line is of the form

$$Y = A + B * X$$

To determine the best fit line through sample data, we must make assumptions about X and Y. Different assumptions will yield different solutions for the coefficients A and B. We will assume that Y and not X is the random variable. This means that we can measure X exactly and that the Y values for a given X are assumed to be normally distributed about some mean.

Figure 11.22 shows three X values and the distributions of Y values for the populations they determine. The mean of the Y values for a given X value is denoted by $M_{Y|X}$. We will denote the standard deviation of the Y values for a given X by $S_{Y|X}$.

Figure 11.22. *Distribution of Y Values for Three X Values*

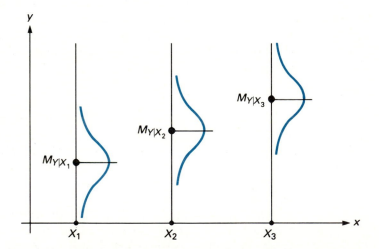

Figure 11.23 shows the distribution of Y values for the population associated with a given X value. The *mean*, $M_{Y|X}$, is a measure of central tendency for the Y values for this population, and the *standard deviation*, $S_{Y|X}$, is a measure of the dispersion (or spread) of the Y values for this population. For example, Fig. 11.23 might represent the distribution of intelligence quotients

for professors with a given income. The shaded region indicates all professors whose intelligence quotient is within one standard deviation of the mean for this population.

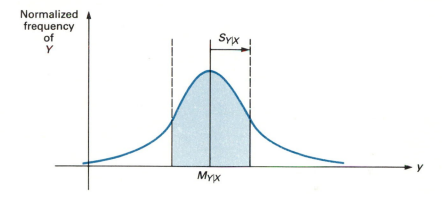

Figure 11.23. *Distribution of Y Values for a Given X with Mean $M_{Y|X}$ and Standard Deviation $S_{Y|X}$*

In linear regression, we assume that the means, $M_{Y|X}$, lie on some line

$$M_{Y|X} = \alpha + \beta * X$$

The problem is that we cannot determine this line exactly because we have only a finite amount of data relating to just some of the X values. On the basis of this finite sample, we must compute an estimate for the above linear relationship. That estimate is called the best fit line through the sample data. Its equation is:

$$Y = A + B * X$$

As you can see, A is a statistical estimate for α, and B is a statistical estimate for β. Depending upon the statistical properties of our finite sample, the estimates A and B will be more or less reliable. (This issue as to how confident we can be in the predictions we make with the computed coefficients A and B will not be discussed further. There are formulae for determining this, however.)

Figure 11.24 shows a scatter plot for some sample data. A *scatter plot* represents each observed pair of X-Y values in a sample as a point on a coordinate grid. Superimposed over the scatter plot are lines representing the actual linear relationship

$$M_{Y|X} = \alpha + \beta * X$$

and the best fit line

$$Y = A + B * X$$

based on the data available (eleven data points). As shown in Fig. 11.24, the best fit line (in color) is a statistical estimate for the relationship based on a finite sample of data.

Figure 11.24. *Scatter Plot Showing Best Fit and Actual Lines*

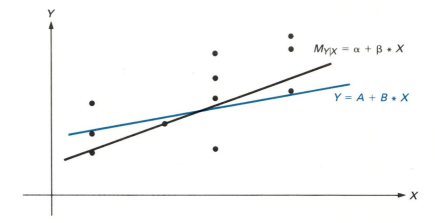

Computing the Linear Regression Coefficients, *A* and *B*

The values *A* and *B* are called *linear regression coefficients*. We will now discuss how these are computed on the basis of a finite sample.

Suppose we have a collection of *N* data points. Let us denote the *i*th data point by the pair (X_i, Y_i). That is, Y_i was observed in conjunction with X_i. The best fit line is defined as the unique line that minimizes the sum of the squares of the distances d_i, which are shown in Fig. 11.25. Each d_i is the distance, measured in parallel to the *Y* axis, between the point (X_i, Y_i) and the best fit

Figure 11.25. *Best Fit Line Minimizes the Sum of the Squares of the Distances d_i*

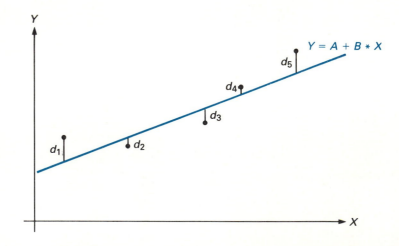

line. Thus,

$$d_i = Y_i - (B * X_i + A)$$

It is one of the marvels of calculus that we can discuss the distance d_i to the best fit line when it is the best fit line that we are trying to determine. The sum that we are trying to minimize

$$\sum_{i=1}^{N} d_i^2 = \sum_{i=1}^{N} (Y_i - (B * X_i - A))^2 = F(A,B)$$

is a function of the linear regression coefficients. We have called this function $F(A,B)$. By computing the partial derivatives of $F(A,B)$ with respect to A and B and setting these partial derivatives to 0, we get two linear equations in two unknowns A and B:

$$\frac{\partial F(A,B)}{\partial A} = 0$$

$$\frac{\partial F(A,B)}{\partial B} = 0$$

When we solve the resulting system of equations, we get

$$B = \frac{\sum_{i=1}^{N} (X_i - \overline{X})(Y_i - \overline{Y})}{\sum_{i=1}^{N} (X_i - \overline{X})^2}$$

$$A = \overline{Y} - B * \overline{X}$$

where $\overline{X}$ and $\overline{Y}$ denote the means of the observed X and Y values, respectively. That is,

$$\overline{X} = \frac{\sum_{i=1}^{N} X_i}{N}$$

$$\overline{Y} = \frac{\sum_{i=1}^{N} Y_i}{N}$$

The FORTRAN subroutine in Fig. 11.26 returns the linear regression coefficients A and B for a given collection of data points, (X_i, Y_i). XBAR and YBAR denote the means $\overline{X}$ and $\overline{Y}$, respectively. SUMXY is

$$\sum_{i=1}^{N} (X_i - \overline{X})(Y_i - \overline{Y})$$

and SUMXDS is

$$\sum_{i=1}^{N} (X_i - \overline{X})^2$$

XDIFF is introduced so that we do not have to compute (X(I) – XBAR) twice for every execution of DO loop 10.

Figure 11.26. *Computing the Linear Regression Coefficients A and B*

```
      SUBROUTINE LINREG (X, Y, N, XBAR, YBAR, A, B)
C Computes the linear regression coefficients, A and B
C for the N data points (X(I),Y(I)), given XBAR and YBAR.

C Input Arguments
C    X, Y – array of data points
C    N – number of points
C    XBAR, YBAR – the X and Y mean values
C Output Arguments
C    A, B – the linear regression coefficients

C Argument Declarations
      REAL X(*), Y(*), XBAR, YBAR, A, B
      INTEGER N

C Local Declarations
      REAL SUMXY, SUMXDS, XDIFF
      INTEGER I

      SUMXY = 0.0
      SUMXDS = 0.0
      DO 10 I = 1, N
         XDIFF = X(I) – XBAR
         SUMXY = SUMXY + XDIFF * (Y(I) – YBAR)
         SUMXDS = SUMXDS + XDIFF ** 2
  10  CONTINUE
      B = SUMXY / SUMXDS
      A = YBAR – B * XBAR

C Exit subroutine
      RETURN
      END
```

Correlation

Correlation differs from regression in that it measures the strength of a relationship rather than the actual parameters of that relationship. In computing the correlation between X and Y, we assume that both variables are random. In other words, we do not assume that the X values or Y values can be determined exactly.

Correlation is said to be high if there is a strong linear relationship between X and Y values. Otherwise, correlation is said to be low. Figure 11.27 shows four scatter plots along with a qualitative assessment of the correlation between X and Y. Note that in Fig. 11.27(d), although there is obviously a quadratic relationship between X and Y values, the correlation is low since correlation is a measure of the strength of linear relationships.

Figure 11.27. *Scatter Plots with Correlations*

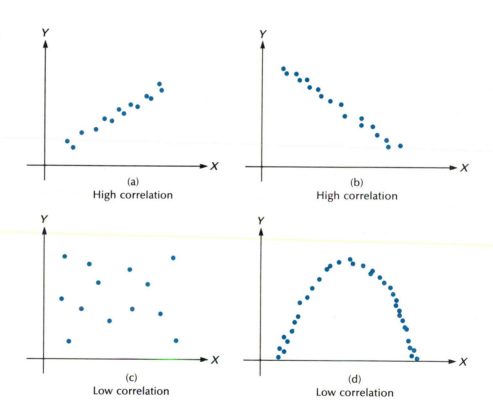

(a)
High correlation

(b)
High correlation

(c)
Low correlation

(d)
Low correlation

We will now give a formula for a statistic, r, that is a measure of correlation. This statistic is called the correlation coefficient.

We will present this statistic in terms of another statistic called *z-scores*. Z-scores are measured for the X and Y values independently. Again we assume a sample of N data points, (X_i, Y_i). The z-score for a given X_i is its distance from the sample mean, $\overline{X}$, measured in terms of the standard deviation, S_X:

$$Z_{X_i} = \frac{X_i - \overline{X}}{S_X}$$

An unbiased estimate of the standard deviation for our sample is

$$S_X = \sqrt{\frac{\sum\limits_{i=1}^{N} (X_i - \overline{X})^2}{N - 1}}$$

The z-score for a given Y_i value is

$$Z_{Y_i} = \frac{Y_i - \overline{Y}}{S_Y}$$

where $\overline{Y}$ is the mean and S_Y is the standard deviation for the observed Y values.

The correlation coefficient, r, is computed in terms of the z-scores as follows:

$$r = \sum_{i=1}^{N} \frac{(Z_{X_i} * Z_{Y_i})}{N - 1}$$

The values for r range between -1 and 1. If $|r| = 1$, then the given data points all lie on a line. If $r = 0$, then the X and Y values are said to be uncorrelated. (Again, this means there is absolutely no linear relationship observed between X and Y values.)

A FORTRAN function that computes the correlation coefficient, r, is given in Fig. 11.28. The arguments provided to the function are REAL arrays X and Y, which store the data points, and the INTEGER variable N, which denotes the number of data points in the sample. The variables XBAR and YBAR represent the means, and the variables SX and SY represent the standard deviations. ZXI denotes the z-score for X_i, and ZYI denotes the z-score for Y_i. PS is used to accumulate the sum of the products of ZXI and ZYI.

Figure 11.28.
Function for Computing the Correlation Coefficient

```
      REAL FUNCTION R (X, Y, N, XBAR, YBAR, SX, SY)
C Computes the correlation coefficient, R, using Z-scores
C for the N data points (X(I),Y(I))

C Input Arguments
C   X, Y - array of data points
C   N - number of data points
C   XBAR, YBAR - the X and Y mean values
C   SX, SY - the X and Y standard deviations

C Argument Declarations
      REAL X(*), Y(*), XBAR, YBAR, SX, SY
      INTEGER N
```

```
C Local Declarations
      REAL PS, ZXI, ZYI
      INTEGER I

      PS = 0.0
      DO 10 I = 1, N
          ZXI = (X(I) - XBAR) / SX
          ZYI = (Y(I) - YBAR) / SY
          PS = PS + ZXI * ZYI
  10  CONTINUE

C Define result and exit function
      R = PS / (N - 1)
      RETURN
      END
```

11.5　Numerical Integration[M]

The definite integral $\int_a^b f(z)\,dz$ denotes the area in the Euclidean plane bounded by the z-axis, the line $z = a$, the line $z = b$, and the curve $y = f(z)$. This area is shown in Fig. 11.29 for two different functions. Note that if the curve $y = f(z)$ dips below the z-axis, the part of the curve below the z-axis makes a negative contribution to the integral.

Figure 11.29. *Geometric Meaning of the Definite Integral*

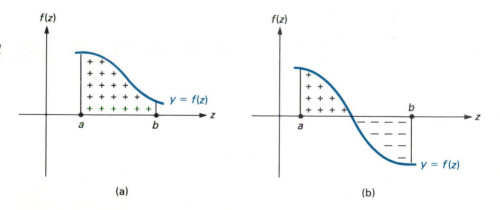

(a)　　　　　　　　(b)

There are two general classes of solutions to the problem of evaluating definite integrals by computer. Both classes involve evaluating the function $f(z)$, which we are integrating at a collection of sample points. The *quadrature methods* determine the sampling points by analysis of the function. Simpson's rule and members of its class choose the sampling points independently of the function being integrated. In practice, Simpson's rule is an effective and efficient method for doing numerical integration despite its simplicity.

Derivation of Simpson's Rule

Simpson's rule is derived from the following considerations. Suppose we want to integrate $f(z)$ over the interval $[a,b]$, as shown in Fig. 11.30. Clearly, if we divide the interval $[a,b]$ into an even number, N, of intervals, as shown in Fig. 11.30, then

$$\int_a^b f(z)\, dz = \sum_{\substack{i=2 \\ \text{Step 2}}}^{N} \int_{z_{i-2}}^{z_i} f(z)\, dz \qquad (1)$$

Our notation

$$\sum_{\substack{i=2 \\ \text{Step 2}}}^{N}$$

means that i takes on the values 2, 4, 6, ... , $N-2$, N. (Don't forget that N is assumed even.)

Figure 11.30. *Dividing the Interval of Integration into Subintervals*

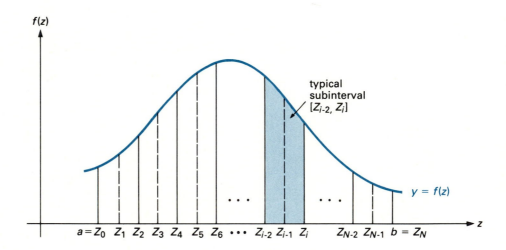

Equation (1) says that the original integral equals the sum of the $N/2$ integrals

$$\int_{z_{i-2}}^{z_i} f(z)\, dz$$

These $N/2$ integrals are computed over the subintervals $[z_{i-2}, z_i]$. Note that z_{i-1} is the midpoint of the subinterval $[z_{i-2}, z_i]$. Furthermore, the subscript, $i-1$, of a midpoint is always odd. The subscripts $i-2$ and i at the endpoints are always even.

A typical subinterval $[z_{i-2}, z_i]$ and the integral we are computing on that subinterval are shown in Fig. 11.31. The three points

point 1 $= (z_{i-2}, f(z_{i-2}))$
point 2 $= (z_{i-1}, f(z_{i-1}))$
point 3 $= (z_i, f(z_i))$

determine a unique quadratic polynomial. That is, there is a unique polynomial

$$P_i(z) = r * z^2 + s * z + t$$

that passes through the three given points. This polynomial is called an interpolating polynomial. In Fig. 11.31, the polynomial $P_i(z)$ is drawn as a black curve.

Figure 11.31. *Interpolating Polynomial $P_i(z)$*

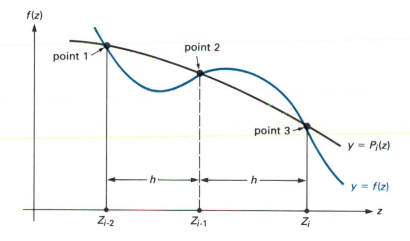

The fact that the polynomial $P_i(z)$ passes through three known points gives us enough information to solve for the coefficients r, s, and t. We know that $P_i(z) = f(z)$ when z is z_{i-2}, z_{i-1}, or z_i. This yields three equations in the three unknowns, r, s, and t. This system can be solved for r, s, and t (solution not shown).

Simpson's rule approximates

$$\int_{z_{i-2}}^{z_i} f(z)\ dz$$

as

$$\int_{z_{i-2}}^{z_i} P_i(z)\ dz$$

When we substitute the coefficients r, s, and t in $P_i(z)$ and integrate, we get

$$\int_{z_{i-2}}^{z_i} P_i(z)\, dz = \frac{h}{3}\left(f(z_{i-2}) + 4 \times f(z_{i-1}) + f(z_i)\right)$$

where $h = (b - a)/N$ is the size of one of the N intervals. The equation above approximates the integral of the original function, $f(z)$, over the interval $[z_{i-2}, z_i]$ in terms of the values of $f(z)$ at the endpoints and the midpoint of the interval.

Substituting the above equation into equation (1), we get Simpson's rule:

$$\int_a^b f(z)\, dz = \sum_{\substack{i=2 \\ \text{Step 2}}}^{N} \int_{z_{i-2}}^{z_i} f(z)\, dz$$

$$\approx \sum_{\substack{i=2 \\ \text{Step 2}}}^{N} \int_{z_{i-2}}^{z_i} P_i(z)\, dz$$

$$= \frac{h}{3} \sum_{\substack{i=2 \\ \text{Step 2}}}^{N} \left(f(z_{i-2}) + 4 \times f(z_{i-1}) + f(z_i)\right)$$

Recalling that $z_0 = a$ and $z_N = b$, we can rewrite the approximate integral as

$$\int_a^b f(z)\, dz \approx \frac{h}{3}\left(f(a) + 4 \times f(z_1) + f(z_2) + f(z_2) + 4 \times f(z_3) + f(z_4) + f(z_4)\right.$$
$$\left. + 4 \times f(z_5) + \cdots + f(z_{N-2}) + 4 \times f(z_{N-1}) + f(b)\right)$$

$$= \frac{h}{3}\left(f(a) + f(b) + 4 \times \sum_{\substack{i=2 \\ \text{Step 2}}}^{N} f(z_{i-1}) + 2 \times \sum_{\substack{i=2 \\ \text{Step 2}}}^{N} f(z_i)\right)$$

FORTRAN Implementation of Simpson's Rule

We will next implement Simpson's rule as expressed above in FORTRAN. Let us accumulate the sum

$$\sum_{\substack{i=2 \\ \text{Step 2}}}^{N} f(z_{i-1})$$

in the variable SUMODD and the sum

$$\sum_{\substack{i=2 \\ \text{Step 2}}}^{N} f(z_i)$$

in the variable SUMEVE. The approximate integral is then

$$\left(f(a) + f(b) + 4 * \text{SUMODD} + 2 * \text{SUMEVE}\right) * (h/3.0)$$

In an actual subroutine, f would be replaced by a function call or a statement function that evaluates the desired functional value. Very often, a statement function is adequate for accomplishing this.

Function SIMPSN in Fig. 11.32 computes an approximate value for

$$\int_a^b f(z) \, dz$$

using Simpson's rule for a given value of a, b, and N. For computational purposes, we rewrite the expressions for SUMODD and SUMEVE given above as follows:

$$\text{SUMODD} = \sum_{\substack{i=2 \\ \text{Step 2}}}^{N} f(z_{i-1}) = f(a + h) + f(a + 3 * h) + \cdots f(a + (N - 1) * h)$$

$$\text{SUMEVE} = \sum_{\substack{i=2 \\ \text{Step 2}}}^{N} f(z_i) = f(a + 2 * h) + f(a + 4 * h) + \cdots f(a + (N - 2) * h)$$

A variable z will denote the value of the current sample point. Each new value of z is determined by adding $2 * h$ to the previous value of z. Since $2 * h$ will be used over and over, we store it in a variable, DELTAZ.

Function SIMPSN in Fig. 11.32 computes the integral of the *standardized normal distribution function* (commonly known as the bell curve)

$$f(z) = \frac{e^{-(z^2/2)}}{\sqrt{2\pi}}$$

which is useful in statistics (see the discussion on correlation in Section 11.4). The FORTRAN expression

```
SIMPSN(0.0, 2.0, 2)
```

computes the value of this integral for $z = 0.0$ to $z = 2.0$ assuming the interval is divided into two subintervals. The actual value of this integral is 0.4772; the function result is 0.4736. When N is increased to 4, the function result is 0.4772. The dependence of the function result on N is discussed in the next section. To evaluate the definite integral of another function, it is only necessary to change the statement function definition in function SIMPSN.

Figure 11.32 *Computing a Definite Integral Using Simpson's Rule*

```
      REAL FUNCTION SIMPSN (A, B, N)
C Computes the area under the standard normal curve
C between A and B using Simpson's rule with N intervals

C Input Arguments
C   A, B - the end points of the integration region [A,B]
C   N - the number of intervals

C Argument Declarations
      REAL A, B
      INTEGER N

C Local Declarations
      REAL PI
      PARAMETER (PI = 3.14159)
      REAL H, DELTAZ, SUMODD, SUMEVE, Z
      INTEGER I

C Statement Function
      F(X) = EXP(-(X ** 2 / 2.0)) / SQRT(2.0 * PI)

C Compute required increments
      H = (B - A) / N
      DELTAZ = 2.0 * H

C Compute SUMODD
      SUMODD = 0.0
      Z = A + H
      DO 10 I = 2, N, 2
         SUMODD = SUMODD + F(Z)
         Z = Z + DELTAZ
   10 CONTINUE

C Compute SUMEVE
      SUMEVE = 0.0
      Z = A + DELTAZ
      DO 20 I = 2, N-2, 2
         SUMEVE = SUMEVE + F(Z)
         Z = Z + DELTAZ
   20 CONTINUE

C Compute integral and return
      SIMPSN = (F(A) + F(B) + 4.0 * SUMODD + 2.0 * SUMEVE) * (H / 3.0)
      RETURN
      END
```

Applying Simpson's Rule for a Sequence of *N* Values

As *N* increases, the approximate integral becomes closer to the actual integral. However, when using function SIMPSN, there is a point of diminishing returns, due to computational round-off errors. If you try to compute the integral for a sequence of increasing *N* values, say $N = 2, 4, 8, 16, 32,...$, that point of diminishing returns will become readily apparent. Before that point, successive approximations agree to more and more decimal places; beyond that point, the agreement becomes less and less.

In practice, we apply Simpson's rule for a sequence of *N* values to identify the point of diminishing returns. Usually the sequence of *N* values is such that *N* doubles for each iteration of Simpson's rule. A general rule of thumb is that if the integral we get when $N = 2 * k$ and the integral we get when $N = k$ agree to *D* decimal places, then the integral we got for $N = 2 * k$ is correct to $D + 1$ decimal places. There is a point, as mentioned above, where the agreement between successive approximations becomes worse and worse. If the number of correct digits we obtain in this manner is not adequate, then the use of double precision arithmetic is suggested. (See Section 11.7.)

SELF-CHECK EXERCISE FOR SECTION 11.5

1. Write a program that calls function SIMPSN in Fig. 11.32 for A = 0.0 and values of B starting at 0.5 and increasing to 5.0 in steps of 0.5. Compute each integral for values of *N* equal to 2, 4, 8, and 16. Print each result.

11.6 ▭ Using Numerical Methods Libraries

So far, we have introduced a number of subroutines for performing highly specialized numerical operations. Some subroutines came with a warning that they will not work in all cases, but there are other techniques that may work. We also saw that it would be fairly time-consuming for each individual engineer or scientist to implement his or her own library of subroutines. For all these reasons, several libraries of numerical subroutines hae been developed for use by engineers, scientists, and others who frequently perform numerical operations on data.

One of the most widely used collections of subroutines is the International Mathematics and Statistics Library (IMSL). The IMSL is a collection of thousands of subprograms available on most mainframes and minicomputers and even on some microcomputers.

The IMSL comprises three separate but coordinated libraries of subroutines:

    MATH/LIBRARY—subroutines for general applied mathematics
    STAT/LIBRARY—subroutines for statistics
    SFUN/LIBRARY—subroutines for special functions

Before using one of these libraries, you must first consult the manual for that library. The manual provides documentation for each subroutine along with instructions for using that subroutine and an example of its use. You will need to write a FORTRAN program that stores the data to be processed and correctly calls the subroutine you select. After the subroutine executes, your program should display the output arguments returned by the subroutine.

EXAMPLE 11.1

LSARG is an IMSL MATH/LIBRARY subroutine that solves a system of linear algebraic equations. Figure 11.33 shows part of the documentation for the subroutine. DLSARG is the double precision version of this subroutine. (Double precision is discussed in the next section.)

Figure 11.33. *Partial Documentation for LSARG*

LSARG/DLSARG (Single/Double precision)

PURPOSE: Solve a real general system of linear equations with iterative refinement.

USAGE: CALL LSARG (N, A, LDA, B, IPATH, X)

ARGUMENTS:

N	Number of equations (input)
A	N-by-N matrix containing the coefficients of the linear system (input)
LDA	Leading dimension of A exactly as specified in the dimension statement of the calling program (input)
B	Vector of length N containing the right-hand side of the linear system (input)
IPATH	Path indicator (input) IPATH = 1 means the system $A * X = B$ is solved. IPATH = 2 means the system *trans(a)* $* X = B$ is solved, where *trans(A)* is the transpose of A.
X	Vector of length N containing the solution to the linear system (output)

The line

 USAGE: CALL LSARG (N, A, LDA, B, IPATH, X)

in Fig. 11.33 shows the order of the arguments in a call to subroutine LSARG. The argument descriptions follow this line.

Figure 11.34 is a main program that uses function LSARG to solve the equation

 $A * X = B$

Figure 11.34. *Using Subroutine LSARG*

```
      PROGRAM USELSA
C Shows how to use subroutine LSARG

C Declarations
      INTEGER N, LDA, IPATH
      PARAMETER (N = 3, LDA = 3, IPATH = 1)
      REAL A(LDA,LDA), B(N), X(N)

C Set values for A and B

C           ( 33.0  16.0  72.0)          ( 129.0)
C      A = (-24.0 -10.0 -57.0)     B = ( -96.0)
C           ( 18.0 -11.0   7.0)          (   8.5)

      DATA A /33.0,-24.0,18.0,16.0,-10.0,-11.0,72.0,-57.0,7.0/
      DATA B /129.0, -96.0, 8.5/

C Call the subroutine to solve for X
      CALL LSARG (N, A, LDA, B, IPATH, X)

C Display results
      PRINT *, 'The values of X are:'
      PRINT '(1X, 3F10.2)', X

C Exit program
      STOP
      END


The values of X are:
     1.00      1.50      1.00
```

The PARAMETER statement

```
      PARAMETER (N = 3, LDA = 3, IPATH =1)
```

defines the subroutine input arguments that are not arrays; the DATA statements define the input argument arrays. The PRINT statements at the end display the output argument, vector X. ∎

11.7 ▬▬▬ **Double Precision and Complex Numbers**

In this section, we introduce two new data types: DOUBLE PRECISION and COMPLEX. The DOUBLE PRECISION type enables us to carry more significant digits in computations and, thus, to improve the accuracy of numerical algorithms.

Complex numbers are numbers of the form

$$x + i * y$$

where x and y are real numbers and i is the imaginary number $\sqrt{-1}$. Complex numbers have many important applications in science and engineering.

Double Precision

The programs presented in this chapter use type REAL (single precision) numbers to represent numeric quantities. A typical computer might provide seven-digit precision with the REAL data type. However, as we often pointed out in the previous sections, not all of these digits will be reliable due to round-off and truncation errors. Typically, only four or five of the seven digits will be accurate. The exact number of reliable digits varies from application to application.

The "double" in double precision refers to the amount of computer storage that is allocated to the representation of a double precision number as compared to a single precision number. A double precision number, such as DX in Fig. 11.35, occupies two words of computer memory, compared to the one word allocated for the single precision (REAL) variable X. All of this extra storage is devoted to extending the precision (mantissa) of the number. None of the extra bits are incorporated into the exponent. Therefore, double precision arithmetic increases only the accuracy, not the range, of computed results.

Figure 11.35. *Storage for REAL and DOUBLE PRECISION Numbers*

To use the DOUBLE PRECISION data type, the programmer must know

- how to declare double precision variables and arrays
- how to form double precision constants
- how to express operations in double precision arithmetic
- how double precision quantities are read and written
- how double precision functions are used and/or defined

Double precision variables and arrays are declared in the same way as variables of other FORTRAN types.

EXAMPLE 11.2

The statement

```
DOUBLE PRECISION DX, DARR(10)
```

declares a double precision variable, DX, and a double precision array, DARR, with ten elements.

Double precision two-dimensional arrays may also be declared. There is no automatic implicit typing of double precision variables. ∎

Double precision constants are distinguished from single precision (REAL) constants by the use of the special symbol D in lieu of the symbol E that is used in single precision constants. The symbol D is used in FORTRAN scientific notation to denote a double precision constant.

EXAMPLE 11.3

Assuming our computer allows seven-digits precision for REAL numbers, the following constants would be recognized as being DOUBLE PRECISION constants:

```
1.23456789D3
12.3456789D-5
8.219807654489D2
2.3D-12
0.1D0
```

The constant 2.3D-12 denotes the double precision representation of the number 2.3×10^{-12}. The constant 0.1D0 denotes the double precision representation of the number 0.1. It is important to realize that the FORTRAN constant 0.1 is not the same as the FORTRAN constant 0.1D0. The former is a single precision number, and the latter is a double precision number. Furthermore, they are not the same number, because the binary representation of 1/10 is not exact. This alerts us to a fundamental problem that arises in the use of double precision arithmetic. Unless double precision arithmetic is used correctly, it is no better than single precision arithmetic. ∎

Double Precision Arithmetic

Single precision and double precision arithmetic do not differ in terms of the operations that may be performed. Double precision numbers may be multiplied, divided, raised to powers, and so forth.

EXAMPLE 11.4

Assuming DX and DY are DOUBLE PRECISION variables, the assignment statement

```
DX = 2.0D0 * DY
```

will store twice the value of DY in DX. ∎

Although mixed-mode arithmetic involving type INTEGER, REAL, and DOUBLE PRECISION numbers is allowed, difficulties arise if an arithmetic expression mixes single precision and double precision quantities. In all mixed-mode expressions (except where a double precision number is being raised to an integer power), the non-double precision quantities are converted to double precision before the expression is evaluated. However, most compilers will do this conversion in a "stupid" way. That is, they will simply pad the mantissa of the single precision number with trailing zeros.

EXAMPLE 11.5 Assuming DX and DY are double precision variables, the assignment statements

```
DX = 0.1 * DY
DX = 0.1D0 * DY
```

are not equivalent. The first assignment statement contains a mixed-mode (single and double precision) expression on the right side of the assignment operator. As a result, the computation in the first assignment statement is no better than a single precision computation. (A chain is no stronger than its weakest link!) The second assignment statement is bona fide double precision arithmetic. The constant 0.1D0 denotes the double precision representation for the number 0.1. ∎

EXAMPLE 11.6 The condition

```
(0.1 .EQ. 0.1D0)
```

compares the single precision representation of 0.1 to its double precision representation. Because of the way the single precision number is converted to double precision before the comparison, the condition value is false, not true as we might expect. ∎

It is permissible to assign a double precision value to a type REAL variable. Most compilers simply truncate the extra digits in the mantissa of the double precision value.

Input and Output of Double Precision Numbers

Double precision values present no special problems in terms of input. A data value that uses the symbol D will be recognized as a double precision number. Double precision values should be read into double precision variables. Otherwise, a loss of precision will occur. In list-directed output, a double precision number is printed to the precision that the computer allows.

The F and D format codes can be used for formatted input and output of double precision quantities. The F$w.d$ format specification has the same significance whether it is being used with single precision or double precision quantities. The D$w.d$ format specification behaves just like the E$w.d$ specification, except that the exponential symbol E is replaced by D.

Using Functions with Double Precision Numbers

Many of the operations performed by the FORTRAN library functions can be applied to double precision numbers. For example, the functions DABS and IDINT, which require double precision arguments, correspond to the functions ABS and INT, which require type REAL arguments. The table of functions in Appendix A includes functions that require double precision arguments or return double precision results. Library functions that return double precision results always begin with the letter D.

Also listed in Appendix A is the function DPROD, which accepts two real arguments and computes their double precision product. DBLE is the type conversion function that converts from any numerical type (INTEGER, REAL, COMPLEX) to double precision.

The programmer may define double precision functions not provided by the FORTRAN library of functions. For example, the function header

```
DOUBLE PRECISION FUNCTION DF(DX, DY)
```

describes a function called DF that returns a double precision result. DF should be declared as type DOUBLE PRECISION in any program unit that calls it. The function result should be returned to a double precision variable. If the dummy arguments DX and DY are double precision, they must be declared as type DOUBLE PRECISION within the function definition.

Complex Numbers

The next data type to be discussed is type COMPLEX. Complex numbers are of great interest to scientists and engineers. In FORTRAN, complex numbers are represented using the data type COMPLEX.

EXAMPLE 11.7

The complex number

$$3.2 - i * 7.8$$

has a *real part* of 3.2 and an *imaginary part* of −7.8. It is written as the COMPLEX constant

```
(3.2, -7.8)
```

in FORTRAN. ∎

In general, the form of a COMPLEX constant in FORTRAN is two real or integer constants enclosed in parentheses and separated by a comma. Double precision values are not allowed. Hence, (3.2, 0.23D0) is not a legal COMPLEX constant, since the imaginary part is double precision.

COMPLEX variables and arrays are declared just like other variables and arrays.

EXAMPLE 11.8   The declaration

```
COMPLEX SEQ(10), Z
```

instructs the compiler to allocate storage for an array (SEQ) with ten elements and for a complex variable (Z). Each array element provides storage for two values representing the real and imaginary parts of a complex number. The real and imaginary parts of a complex number are single precision.   ∎

Complex Arithmetic

The rules governing COMPLEX arithmetic in FORTRAN are consistent with the rules of complex arithmetic, as described in Table 11.1. An integer or real operand used with a complex operand will be automatically converted to a complex number with an imaginary part of zero before the operation is performed.

Table 11.1. *Rules of Complex Arithmetic*

OPERATION	RESULT
$(a,b) + (c,d)$	$(a + c, b + d)$
$(a,b) - (c,d)$	$(a - c, b - d)$
$(a,b) * (c,d)$	$(a * c - b * d, a * d + b * c)$
$(a,b) / (c,d)$	$\left(\dfrac{a * c + b * d}{c^2 + d^2}, \dfrac{b * c - a * d}{c^2 + d^2} \right)$

The assignment of a COMPLEX value to a complex variable is allowed, as in

```
Z = (Z1 + Z2) / Z3
```

where Z, Z1, Z2, and Z3 are type COMPLEX. Mixed-mode assignments are also allowed, and the following rules apply. When a COMPLEX number is stored in an INTEGER or REAL variable, it loses its imaginary part. When an INTEGER or REAL number is stored in a COMPLEX variable, the imaginary part of the COMPLEX number will be 0.0, and the real part of the COMPLEX number will be the number being assigned (converted to REAL, if necessary).

Using Functions with Complex Numbers

Many of the operations performed by FORTRAN library functions can also be applied to COMPLEX numbers (see Appendix A). Library functions that return COMPLEX results begin with the letter C. There are certain library functions that are indispensable when we are working with COMPLEX arithmetic.

Other than .EQ. and .NE., the relational operators cannot be applied to

COMPLEX quantities. If Z is COMPLEX, then the following is not a valid LOGICAL expression:

```
(Z .LE. (2.3, 1.0))
```

We must compare the real and imaginary parts separately, as in

```
(REAL(Z) .LE. 2.3 .AND. AIMAG(Z) .LE. 1.0)
```

where the REAL and AIMAG functions extract the real and imaginary parts of a COMPLEX value, respectively.

Another useful built-in function is CMPLX, which takes two REAL numbers and constructs a complex number from them. The first argument of CMPLX becomes the real part of the result, and the second argument of CMPLX becomes the imaginary part of the result.

EXAMPLE 11.9   Assuming A and B are type REAL, the statement

```
Z = CMPLX(A, B)
```

stores the complex number $A + i * B$ in the COMPLEX variable Z. The type conversion function CMPLX is necessary, since expressions such as (A, B) are not allowed in FORTRAN.   ∎

The complex conjugate of a complex number

$$z = x + i * y$$

is defined to be the complex number

$$\bar{z} = x - i * y$$

The complex conjugate is important since many applications require computing the absolute value of a complex number, which is defined to be

$$z * \bar{z}$$

Note that $z * \bar{z}$ for $z = x + i * y$ is $x^2 + y^2$, which is a real number. The built-in function CONJ(Z) returns the complex conjugate of the COMPLEX number Z. The built-in function CABS(Z) returns the absolute value of a complex number Z.

COMPLEX function subprograms and statement functions do not differ from other types of functions that we have discussed. For example, the type COM-PLEX function F would begin with the header

```
COMPLEX FUNCTION F(Z)
```

If Z is a COMPLEX argument, it must be declared as such within the function. Also, it is important to declare F and the variable receiving the function result as type COMPLEX in all program units using F. Otherwise, the imaginary part of the result may be lost, because F would be type REAL by default in those program units.

Input and Output of Complex Numbers

In list-directed input, a complex data value is written as a complex constant (e.g., (2.31, 0.45E1)) where the parentheses and comma are required. When a COMPLEX value is displayed using list-directed output, the parentheses and the comma appear, as in

(0.231000000E 01, 0.450000000E 00)

Since no special format code is provided for the type COMPLEX, the F and E format codes are used to enter and display complex numbers. For each complex number to be read, two real number format codes must be provided, and two real numbers must be read from the input file. When a complex number is written using the F or E code, it is displayed as two real numbers. The comma and parentheses that denote a COMPLEX constant should not appear in the input file and will not appear in the output file when formatted output is used.

11.8 ▰▰ Common Programming Errors

The most common errors in programs that perform the numerical techniques discussed in this chapter are due to loss of accuracy in mathematical computations. A small round-off error is often magnified when computations are repeated, as is required by many of these algorithms. This loss of accuracy can cause programs to execute forever instead of converging to a result. If the programs do terminate, the results may be so inaccurate as to be useless.

Since these programs rely heavily on the use of subroutines and functions, be very careful when writing argument lists. Make sure each argument list has the correct number of arguments, and that the arguments are not misspelled or placed in the wrong position.

We recommend that you use double precision numbers to gain increased accuracy of representation, thereby reducing the effect of computational error. Make sure that you do not combine type REAL or type INTEGER operands with double precision operands, since this will negate the positive effect that otherwise would be realized.

Chapter Review

A number of different numerical techniques were discussed in this chapter, including manipulating vectors and matrixes, finding roots (bisection and Newton's method), solving simultaneous equations (Gaussian elimination), linear regression and correlation, and numerical integration (Simpson's rule). Two new data types, DOUBLE PRECISION and COMPLEX, were also introduced.

We have just scratched the surface in our discussion of numerical methods. There are dozens of good textbooks written on the subject. A small sample of these are listed below.

References on Numerical Methods

1. Carnahan, B., et al. *Applied Numerical Methods*. New York: John Wiley and Sons, Inc., 1964.
2. Conte, S. D., and de Boor, C. *Elementary Numerical Analysis*. 2nd ed. New York: McGraw-Hill, 1972.
3. McCracken, D., and Dorn, W. S. *Numerical Methods and FORTRAN Programming*. New York: John Wiley and Sons, Inc., 1964.
4. Dyck, V. A., et al. *Introduction to Computing: Structured Problem Solving Using WATFIV-S*. Reston, VA: Reston Publishing, 1979.
5. Lentner, Marvin. *Introduction to Applied Statistics*. Boston: Prindle, Weber and Schmidt, Inc., 1975.
6. User's Manual. *STAT/LIBRARY™ FORTRAN SUBROUTINES for Statistical Analysis, Version 1.0*. Houston: IMSL, Inc., April 1987.

Quick-Check Exercises

1. Name two methods for finding roots of a function.
2. List the three criteria for converging to a root.
3. What condition must hold to multiply matrix A by matrix B?
4. Write the complex number $3 - i \times 5$ as a complex constant in FORTRAN.
5. Can you represent larger numbers in FORTRAN using double precision variables?
6. Can you represent smaller (in absolute value) numbers in FORTRAN using double precision variables?
7. Can you declare arrays of double precision numbers?
8. What is a complex conjugate?
9. What property must a coefficient matrix have to be in triangular form?

Answers to Quick-Check Exercises

1. Newton's method and the bisection method
2. Assuming that EPSLON is a very small value, RT is the actual root, x_j is the current guess for a root, and x_{j-1} was the last guess:

    ABS(RT $- x_j$) < EPSLON
    ABS($F(x_j)$) < EPSLON
    ABS($x_j - x_{j-1}$) < EPSLON

3. The two matrixes must be conformable (i.e., matrix A must have the same number of rows as matrix B has columns).
4. (3.0, -5.0)
5. No, the exponent size is the same as for single precision.
6. Yes, there are more bits in the mantissa, so smaller decimal fractions can be represented more accurately.
7. yes
8. the complex number with the same real part as the original but whose imaginary part is the negative of the original number
9. All 1's must be along the major diagonal and all 0's below the diagonal.

Review Questions

1. Write the augmented matrix corresponding to the following system of equations:

$$2x_1 + 2x_2 - 4x_3 = 0$$
$$x_1 - 4x_2 + x_3 = 4$$
$$-x_1 + 3x_2 - 2x_3 = -5$$

2. Normalize column 1 of the augmented matrix for question 1.
3. What three operations can be performed on a system of linear equations?
4. How do you tell when you reach a point of diminishing returns in using Simpson's rule to compute an integral?
5. How do double precision numbers affect the range and accuracy of values that can be represented in computer memory?
6. Explain why you have to be careful when comparing double precision numbers and when comparing complex numbers.

Programming Projects

1. The polynomial

$$4x^3 - 12.3x^2 - x + 16.2$$

   has two zeros between 1 and 2. Use our bisection program to find them. You might want to tabulate the function values first to isolate the zeros in two intervals. Use a tolerance of 0.0005.

2. The polynomial

$$8x^3 + 2x^2 - 5x + 1$$

has three real zeros.

a. First, plot the function to determine appropriate intervals for the root-finding program.

b. Use the bisection program to find the three zeros to within a tolerance of 0.0005.

3. Repeat project 2 for the following functions:

a. $f(x) = x^4 + 3x^3 - 3x^2 - 6x + 1$

b. $f(x) = x^4 - 26x^3 + 131x^2 - 226x + 120$

4. If $x^n = c$, then $x^n - c = 0$ and the nth root of c is a zero of the second equation. Use this idea in conjunction with the bisection routine to compute

a. $\sqrt{2}$

b. $\sqrt[3]{7}$

to six decimal places.

5. Newton's method for finding the roots of an equation

$$f(x) = 0$$

starts with an initial guess, x_0, and then generates successive guesses $x_1, x_2, x_3, \ldots,$ $x_n, x_{n+1}, \ldots$ using the iterative formula:

$$x_{n+1} = x_n - \frac{f(x_n)}{f'(x_n)}$$

where x_{n+1} is the new guess generated from the previous guess, x_n. Figure 11.36 shows the geometric intuition behind Newton's method.

Figure 11.36.

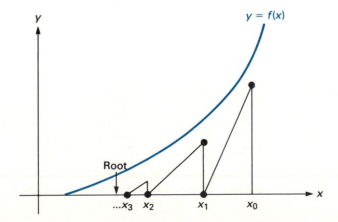

Write a program that will find roots of equations using Newton's method. The stopping criterion will be when successive guesses are very close, that is, $|x_{n+1} - x_n| <$ EPSLON.

6. In the Regula-Falsi method, the root is isolated to an interval $[XL, XR]$, just as in the bisection method. However, instead of breaking the interval into two subintervals at the midpoint, XM, of the interval, where

$$XM = \frac{XR - XL}{2}$$

we break the interval into two subintervals at the point XG defined by the formula

$$XG = XL - F(XL) * \frac{XR - XL}{F(XR) - F(XL)}$$

We then isolate the root to the subinterval (either $[XL, XG]$ or $[XG, XR]$) that has the change of signs. Figure 11.37 shows the intuition behind the Regula-Falsi method.

Write a program that will find roots of equations using Regula-Falsi.

Figure 11.37.

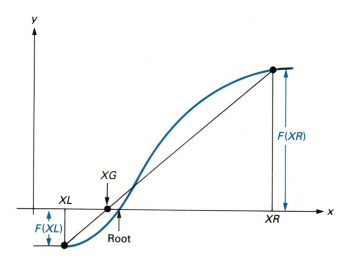

7. Write a program that will read in any two rectangular matrixes and multiply them if they are conformable. The program will print out either the product matrix or a message to the effect that the given matrixes are not conformable.

8. Write a program that will input a *square matrix* A (same number of rows and columns) and a nonnegative integer P and compute $A ** P$, the matrix A raised to the power P.

$A ** P$ is defined as follows:

$A ** 0 =$ the identity matrix, I
$A ** P = A * (A ** (P{-}1)), P \geq 1$

(*Note:* the identity matrix I is defined as follows:

$I(R,K) = 1$ if R equals K
       0 if R not equal to K)

9. Use Gaussian elimination to solve each of the following systems of equations:
   a. $x + 2y + z = 4$
        $2x + y - z = -1$
        $-x + y + z = 2$
   b. $x - y + 2z = 3$
        $2x + 3y - 6z = 1$
        $4x + y - 2z = 7$
   c. $3x - z = 7$
        $2x + y = 6$
        $3y - z = 7$

10. The inverse of a square matrix A is defined to be the matrix AINV that satisfies

    $A * \text{AINV} = I$ (the identity matrix—see project 8)

    If AINV exists, then A is said to be invertible. (If A is invertible, then so is AINV, and A is the inverse of AINV.) The inverse of a matrix A can be computed using Gaussian elimination. If A is not invertible, this technique will also tell us that.
       Let us describe how to set up the data to find the inverse of a matrix A. We will do this first with an example. Suppose we want to find the inverse of the following matrix:

    $$A = \begin{bmatrix} 1 & 2 & 1 \\ 2 & 1 & -1 \\ -1 & 1 & 1 \end{bmatrix}$$

    The problem solution is derived by setting up a work matrix, W, that has the original matrix, A, as its first three columns and the identity matrix as its last three columns:

    $$W = \begin{bmatrix} 1 & 2 & 1 & | & 1 & 0 & 0 \\ 2 & 1 & -1 & | & 0 & 1 & 0 \\ -1 & 1 & 1 & | & 0 & 0 & 1 \end{bmatrix}$$

    We now apply Gaussian elimination to the three leftmost columns. However, we modify Gaussian elimination as presented in the text, so that the three leftmost columns become the identity matrix. In other words, it is not sufficient to get the three leftmost columns in triangular form. This requires only a slight modification of the subroutine GAUSS. When we eliminate coefficients in the pivot column, we do so both above and beneath the pivot.

The key to this method is that as we apply Gaussian elimination to the left half of W, we apply all row operations throughout the matrix W. When the left side of W is diagonalized, the right side will contain the inverse of A. If Gaussian elimination fails because no non-zero pivot is found for a certain pivot element, then the original matrix A must be noninvertible.

Write a program that will input a square matrix and compute its inverse by this modification of Gaussian elimination.

11. A second class of solutions to systems of linear equations is by successive approximations (or iterative methods). In Jacobi's iteration, we solve the system

$$A * X = B$$

by first calculating a new matrix, D, where

$$D(I,J) = \begin{cases} -A(I,J) \,/\, A(I,I), & \text{when } I \neq J \\ 0 & \text{otherwise} \end{cases}$$

and a new vector, C, where

$$C(I) = B(I)/A(I,I) \qquad \text{for all } I$$

Clearly, a necessary condition for doing Jacobi's iteration is that all of the diagonal elements of the matrix A be non-zero.

The next step is to choose an initial approximate solution vector

$$X^{[0]}(I) = 0 \qquad \text{for all } I$$

We then compute subsequent solution vectors using the iterative formula

$$X^{[m]}(I) = \sum_{J \neq I} (D(I,J) * X^{[m-1]}(J)) + C(I)$$

That is, the Ith component of the mth solution vector is computed in terms of the components of the $(m-1)$st solution vector. We continue to do this until successive values of the solution vector become close enough together. In other words, the stopping criterion is

$$|X^{[m]}(I) - X^{[m-1]}(I)| < \text{EPSLON} \qquad \text{for all } I$$

Write a program that will solve systems of linear equations using Jacobi's iteration. Try your program on some of the systems given in project 9.

12. In Gauss-Seidel, we attempt to speed up convergence to the solution by feeding into the computation of the new solution vector elements

$$X^{[m]}(I)$$

the latest available values, which include

$$X^{[m]}(J) \,, J < I$$

Thus, the iterative formula for Gauss-Seidel is

$$X^{[m]}(I) = \sum_{J=1}^{I-1} D(I,J) * X^{[m]}(J)$$

$$+ \sum_{J=I+1}^{N} D(I,J) * X^{[m-1]} + C(I)$$

Write a program that will use this technique to solve systems of linear equations.

13. Find the best fit line and the correlation coefficient for the data set below.

Hours of TV Watched per Day, X	Student's Grade Point Average, Y
0.2	3.98
0.8	3.85
1.0	4.00
1.3	3.75
3.0	2.05
4.0	1.56
4.2	1.55
5.0	1.00
6.1	0.98
9.5	0.05

14. Compute the following definite integrals using Simpson's rule.

a. $\int_1^2 \sqrt{2 - (\sin x)^2} \, dx$

b. $\int_1^2 x \cos \frac{x}{2} \, dx$

c. $\int_1^2 (x^3 - 2x^2 + x + 5) \, dx$

d. $\int_{-3}^1 (1 + x^6) \, dx$

15. Write a program that does integration using Simpson's rule so N will take on the values 2, 4, 8, 16, and 32. For each $N > 2$, print out an error estimate using the formula

$$E_N = \frac{S_N - S_{N/2}}{15}$$

where E_N is the estimated error when the integral is computed with N intervals and this is given in terms of S_N, the integral for N intervals, and $S_{N/2}$, the integral for $N/2$ intervals.

Try your program on some of the integrals of project 14 and/or the standard normal distribution integral done in the text.

16. Write a program that will plot

    $$f(x) = x \cos \frac{x}{2}$$

    between $x = 0$ and $x = 2 * \pi$, shading in the region between the curve and the x-axis. The program will then print out the integral

    $$\int_0^{2\pi} x \cos \frac{x}{2} \, dx$$

17. Write one or more of the following programs using double precision arithmetic. Test your programs using relevant data.
    a. Newton's method, as described in project 5
    b. the bisection method in Fig. 11.5
    c. Gaussian elimination
    d. Gauss-Seidel, as described in project 12
    e. Simpson's rule, as implemented in Fig. 11.32

18. Write a program that will display the roots of a quadratic equation

    $$aX^2 + bX + C = 0$$

    and report whether they are real or complex. Use COMPLEX numbers to do this. The type REAL coefficients A, B, and C should be the inputs for your program.

Appendix A
FORTRAN Library Functions

The table that follows provides the generic and specific names for the FORTRAN library functions. You can use the generic name for a particular function (e.g., ABS) with arguments of any numeric type; the type of the result is determined by the type of the arguments. If you use the specific name (e.g., IABS), then the type of the function result and the required argument type are specified in the table below (e.g., INTEGER for IABS).

FUNCTION DESCRIPTION	GENERIC NAME	SPECIFIC NAME	NUMBER OF ARGUMENTS	TYPE OF ARGUMENTS	TYPE OF FUNCTION
Conversion of numeric to integer	INT	—	1	Integer	Integer
		INT		Real	Integer
		IFIX		Real	Integer
		IDINT		Double	Integer
		—		Complex	Integer
Conversion of numeric to real	REAL	REAL	1	Integer	Real
		FLOAT		Integer	Real
		—		Real	Real
		SNGL		Double	Real
		—		Complex	Real
Conversion of numeric to double precision	DBLE	—	1	Integer	Double
		—		Real	Double
		—		Double	Double
		—		Complex	Double
Conversion of numeric to complex	CMPLX	—	1 or 2	Integer	Complex
		—		Real	Complex
		—		Double	Complex
		—		Complex	Complex
Conversion of character to integer	—	ICHAR	1	Character	Integer
Conversion of integer to character	—	CHAR	1	Integer	Character
Truncation	AINT	AINT	1	Real	Real
		DINT		Double	Double
Rounding to nearest integer	ANINT	ANINT	1	Real	Real
		DNINT	1	Double	Double
Rounding to nearest integer	NINT	NINT	1	Real	Integer
		IDNINT	1	Double	Integer

585

FUNCTION DESCRIPTION	GENERIC NAME	SPECIFIC NAME	NUMBER OF ARGUMENTS	TYPE OF ARGUMENTS	TYPE OF FUNCTION
Absolute value	ABS	IABS	1	Integer	Integer
		ABS		Real	Real
		DABS		Double	Double
		CABS		Complex	Real
Remaindering	MOD	MOD	2	Integer	Integer
		AMOD		Real	Real
		DMOD		Double	Double
Transfer of sign	SIGN	ISIGN	2	Integer	Integer
		SIGN		Real	Real
		DSIGN		Double	Double
Positive difference	DIM	IDIM	2	Integer	Integer
		DIM		Real	Real
		DDIM		Double	Double
Double precision product	—	DPROD	2	Real	Double
Maximum value	MAX	MAX0	≥ 2	Integer	Integer
		AMAX1		Real	Real
		DMAX1		Double	Double
	—	AMAX0		Integer	Real
	—	MAX1		Real	Integer
Minimum value	MIN	MIN0	≥ 2	Integer	Integer
		AMIN1		Real	Real
		DMIN1		Double	Double
	—	AMIN0		Integer	Real
	—	MIN1		Real	Integer
Length of character item	—	LEN	1	Character	Integer
Index of a substring	—	INDEX	2	Character	Integer
Imaginary part of a complex value	—	AIMAG	1	Complex	Real
Conjugate of a complex value	—	CONJG	1	Complex	Complex
Square root	SQRT	SQRT	1	Real	Real
		DSQRT		Double	Double
		CSQRT		Complex	Complex
Exponential	EXP	EXP	1	Real	Real
		DEXP		Double	Double
		CEXP		Complex	Complex
Natural logarithm	LOG	ALOG	1	Real	Real
		DLOG		Double	Double
		CLOG		Complex	Complex
Common logarithm	LOG10	ALOG10	1	Real	Real
		DLOG10		Double	Double

FUNCTION DESCRIPTION	GENERIC NAME	SPECIFIC NAME	NUMBER OF ARGUMENTS	TYPE OF ARGUMENTS	TYPE OF FUNCTION
Sine	SIN	SIN	1	Real	Real
		DSIN		Double	Double
		CSIN		Complex	Complex
Cosine	COS	COS	1	Real	Real
		DCOS		Double	Double
		CCOS		Complex	Complex
Tangent	TAN	TAN	1	Real	Real
		DTAN		Double	Double
Arcsine	ASIN	ASIN	1	Real	Real
		DASIN		Double	Double
Arccosine	ACOS	ACOS	1	Real	Real
		DACOS		Double	Double
Arctangent	ATAN	ATAN	1	Real	Real
		DATAN		Double	Double
	ATAN2	ATAN2	2	Real	Real
		DATAN2		Double	Double
Hyperbolic sine	SINH	SINH	1	Real	Real
		DSINH		Double	Double
Hyperbolic cosine	COSH	COSH	1	Real	Real
		DCOSH		Double	Double
Hyperbolic tangent	TANH	TANH	1	Real	Real
		DTANH		Double	Double
Lexically greater than or equal to	—	LGE	2	Character	Logical
Lexically greater than	—	LGT	2	Character	Logical
Lexically less than or equal to	—	LLE	2	Character	Logical
Lexically less than	—	LLT	2	Character	Logical

Appendix B
Character Sets

The first chart shows the decimal code values in ASCII (American Standard Code for Information Interchange). Codes 0 through 31 and 126 and 127 represent nonprintable control characters. The code for a blank or space is 32. The next two charts show just the printable characters in EBCDIC (Extended Binary Coded Decimal Interchange Code) and in CDC (Control Data Corporation) Scientific. The code for a blank or space is 64 in EBCDIC and 45 in CDC Scientific.

ASCII Decimal Equivalence Chart

NUMBER	CHAR	NUMBER	CHAR	NUMBER	CHAR	NUMBER	CHAR
0	NUL	28	FS	56	8	84	T
1	SOH	29	GS	57	9	85	U
2	STX	30	RS	58	:	86	V
3	ETX	31	US	59	;	87	W
4	EOT	32	□	60	<	88	X
5	ENQ	33	!	61	=	89	Y
6	ACK	34	''	62	>	90	Z
7	BEL	35	#	63	?	91	[
8	BS	36	$	64	@	92	\
9	HT	37	%	65	A	93	]
10	LF	38	&	66	B	94	^
11	VT	39	'	67	C	95	_
12	FF	40	(	68	D	96	'
13	CR	41	)	69	E	97	a
14	SO	42	*	70	F	98	b
15	SI	43	+	71	G	99	c
16	DLE	44	,	72	H	100	d
17	DC1	45	—	73	I	101	e
18	DC2	46	.	74	J	102	f
19	DC3	47	/	75	K	103	g
20	DC4	48	0	76	L	104	h
21	NAK	49	1	77	M	105	i
22	SYN	50	2	78	N	106	j
23	ETB	51	3	79	O	107	k
24	CAN	52	4	80	P	108	l
25	EM	53	5	81	Q	109	m
26	SUB	54	6	82	R	110	n
27	ESC	55	7	83	S	111	o

ASCII Decimal Equivalence Chart

NUMBER	CHAR	NUMBER	CHAR	NUMBER	CHAR	NUMBER	CHAR
112	p	116	t	120	x	124	|
113	q	117	u	121	y	125	}
114	r	118	v	122	z	126	~
115	s	119	w	123	{	127	DEL

EBCDIC Code

Left digit(s) \ Right digit	0	1	2	3	4	5	6	7	8	9
6					□					
7					¢	.	<	(	+	|
8	&									
9	!	$	*	)	;	¬	–	/		
10							^	,	%	—
11	>	?								
12			:	#	@	'	=	"		a
13	b	c	d	e	f	g	h	i		
14							j	k	l	m	n
15	o	p	q	r						
16			s	t	u	v	w	x	y	z
17								\	{	}
18	[	]								
19				A	B	C	D	E	F	G
20	H	I								J
21	K	L	M	N	O	P	Q	R		
22								S	T	U	V
23	W	X	Y	Z						
24	0	1	2	3	4	5	6	7	8	9

Codes 00-63 and 250-255 are nonprintable control characters.

CDC Scientific Code

Left digit(s) \ Right digit	0	1	2	3	4	5	6	7	8	9
0	:	A	B	C	D	E	F	G	H	I
1	J	K	L	M	N	O	P	Q	R	S
2	T	U	V	W	X	Y	Z	0	1	2
3	3	4	5	6	7	8	9	+	–	*
4	/	(	)	$	=	□	,	.	≡	[
5	]	%	≠	↦	∨	∧	↑	↓	<	>
6	≤	≥	¬	;						

Appendix C
Introduction to MS-DOS and the Microsoft FORTRAN Compiler

The Microsoft FORTRAN compiler is designed to be used on an IBM PC computer or a compatible computer. To use this compiler, you must be familiar with the MS-DOS operating system (*MicroSoft Disk Operating System*). You must also be able to use an editor to create and modify source files and data files.

Introduction to MS-DOS

When you turn on, or *boot up*, a computer, the operating system is loaded into memory and begins execution. If your computer has a hard disk, the operating system will be on disk drive C (the hard disk) and will issue the prompt

```
C>
```

to inform you that it is ready. Most likely, you will be using a hard disk, and both the operating system and the FORTRAN compiler will be on disk drive C.

A principal function of an operating system is the maintenance of data files (including FORTRAN source files) on a floppy disk or a hard disk. In a class situation, you will probably be using a floppy disk for storage of your own FORTRAN source files and data files. If you are using a new floppy disk for file storage, you must *format* the disk before saving any files on it. If your new floppy disk is in disk drive B, the command

```
C>FORMAT B:
```

instructs MS-DOS to format the disk on drive B.

When you format a disk, you erase any data and files that may already be stored on it. So don't format a disk unless you are sure that it does not contain any important data. Do *not* attempt to format the hard disk, because that will erase your operating system and the FORTRAN compiler. If you are unsure whether the floppy disk you are using contains any important files, use the command

```
C>DIR B:
```

to display the directory for drive B. This directory shows the files currently on the floppy disk in drive B.

There are other MS-DOS commands for manipulating files. For example, you can delete a file that is no longer needed (using the ERASE command), duplicate a file (using the COPY command), list the contents of the file on the screen or the printer (using the TYPE command), change a file's name (using the RENAME command), or change the active disk directory. Table C.1 summarizes these commands.

Implementing the WHILE Loop in Microsoft FORTRAN

All the programs in the text except those that contain WHILE loops will run on Microsoft FORTRAN because it supports all the features of FORTRAN 77. We suggest you follow

Table C.1. *MS-DOS Commands*

COMMAND	EFFECT
`CD C:\F77EXAMP`	Makes subdirectory `F77EXAMP` on drive C the active directory
`DIR`	Displays the file names in the currently active disk directory
`DIR B:`	Displays the file names in the active directory for disk drive B
`FORMAT B:`	Formats the disk on drive B so it can be used for file storage; erases any existing files on the disk
`ERASE A:EXAMP1.EXE`	Deletes file `EXAMP1.EXE` from disk A
`COPY A:EXAMP1.FOR A:ME.FOR`	Makes a new copy of file `EXAMP1.FOR` on drive A; makes new file name `ME.FOR`
`RENAME A:ME.FOR PAY.FOR`	Changes the name of file `ME.FOR` on drive A to `PAY.FOR`

these steps to accommodate this exception:

1. Change the `DO WHILE` and `ENDDO` lines to comments.
2. Insert a labelled `IF` statement header that uses the *while condition*.
3. Insert the lines `GOTO` *label* and `ENDIF`.

These steps are demonstrated below.

```
      9 IF (while condition) THEN
C         DO WHILE (while condition)
          ...
          ... loop body
          ...
C         ENDDO
          GOTO 9
          ENDIF
```

Compiling and Running Microsoft FORTRAN Programs

The line below should be used to compile source file `EXAMP1.FOR`, which is saved on drive C.

```
C>FL EXAMP1.FOR
```

The Microsoft FORTRAN compiler displays the lines

```
Microsoft (R) FORTRAN Optimizing Compiler Version 4.10
Copyright (c) Microsoft Corp 1987, 1988. All rights reserved.

EXAMP1.FOR
```

If there are any syntax errors, error messages appear next, along with the number of the source file line containing the error. You should correct the errors and attempt to compile the source file again.

If there are no syntax errors, the system attempts to link the object file (EXAMP1.OBJ) created by the compilation step with any necessary library modules. The messages below then appear.

```
Microsoft (R) Segmented-Executable Linker  Version 5.01.20
Copyright (c) Microsoft Corp 1984-1988. All rights reserved.

Object Modules [.OBJ]: EXAMP1.OBJ
Run File [EXAMP1.EXE]: EXAMP1.EXE
List File [NUL.MAP]:NUL
Libraries[.LIB]:
Definitions File [NUL.DEF]: ;
```

If any errors are detected during linking, such as unresolved external references, these error messages appear next. You should go back to the source file, correct the lines in error, and recompile. If there are no errors, you can load and execute the *run file*, EXAMP1.EXE, as often as you wish using the command

```
C>EXAMP1
```

Creating a Listing File

If your program contains several syntax errors, it will be difficult to locate and correct the errors using the information displayed during compilation. You will probably want to obtain a listing file to help you debug the program. A listing file shows your source file with each line numbered and with error messages inserted following the line in error. The listing file must be obtained during the compilation step. To get a listing file, use the command below to compile your source file:

```
C>FL /Fs EXAMP1.FOR
```

Make sure the second letter F is in uppercase and the letter s is in lowercase.

The compiler then creates a listing file named EXAMP1.LST. You can use your word processor to examine this file and determine the cause of your errors. Make sure that you correct the source file, EXAMP1.FOR, and not the listing file. When you are ready to compile again, you should erase the listing file before compilation.

After running several FORTRAN programs, your disk may become filled. If you are not likely to rerun a program again, you can delete its object file (.OBJ) and its run file (.EXE) from your disk. However, it is a good idea to retain the source file for future reference.

Sending Output to the Printer

In Microsoft FORTRAN, you can easily send program output to the printer. In order to do this, you must insert the statement

```
OPEN (UNIT = 6, FILE = 'LPT1')
```

after the program declarations. To send a line of program output to the printer, use 6 as the unit number (the first symbol after the left parenthesis) in a WRITE statement:

```
WRITE (6, *) 'Hello ', USER
```

This statement prints the contents of variable USER after the string 'Hello'. The symbol * preceding the right parenthesis specifies list-directed output.

To send a line of output to the screen, list * as the unit number in a WRITE statement or use the PRINT statement. The next two statements display a string and the contents of USER on the screen.

```
WRITE (*, *) 'Hello ', USER
PRINT *, 'Hello again ', USER
```

The first symbol * in the WRITE statement denotes the standard system output device (the screen). The symbol * in the PRINT statement and the second symbol * in the WRITE statement specify list-directed output.

Appendix D
FORTRAN 8X

This appendix describes selected features of the new FORTRAN standard, currently called FORTRAN 8X.

Symbolic Names

The rules for symbolic names have been liberalized:

- Lowercase as well as uppercase letters may be used.
- The underscore character is allowed.
- The maximum length of a name is thirty-one characters.

The compiler does not distinguish between uppercase and lowercase letters appearing in a symbolic name. This means that HOURS_WORKED, Hours_Worked, and hours_worked are equivalent in a FORTRAN program.

Special Characters

The character set has been expanded to include many special characters. Some of these have special significance in FORTRAN, as listed in Table D.1.

Table D.1. *New Special Characters*

CHARACTER	USE
!	Indicates that the rest of the line is a comment
;	Separates multiple statements on the same line
"	Delimits a string (e.g., "Joe's hat")
<	Indicates less-than relation (e.g., X < Y); may be used with =, as in (X <= Y)
>	Indicates greater-than relation (e.g., X > Y); may be used with =, as in (X >= Y)

As indicated in Table D.1, the symbols < and > can be used in FORTRAN conditions instead of the symbol groups .LT. and .GT.. The symbol pairs <> and == mean the same as the symbols .NE. and .EQ., respectively.

Free-Form Statements

The new standard allows the programmer to specify that free-form rules are being used for statements instead of the fixed-form rules used so far (e.g., label in columns 1–5, statement in columns 7–72). If your compiler is set to recognize free-form statements, then each FORTRAN line can have up to 132 characters and you can begin a FORTRAN statement anywhere in the line. You can also place more than one statement on a line, provided you insert the symbol ; between statements on the same line.

Since column positions have no significance in free form, you can no longer use a C or a * in column 1 to indicate a comment. Instead, use the symbol ! anywhere in a line to indicate that what follows on that line is a comment.

In free form, blank characters must be used as separators between syntactic elements of a statement (e.g., between a label and a keyword). To indicate that a line is continued on the next line, place the symbol & as the last nonblank character on that line (or the last nonblank character before a ! indicating a comment).

Internal Subprograms

All subprograms in FORTRAN 77 are external subprograms that are compiled separately from the main program. The only data items defined in the main program that can be accessed by the subprogram are COMMON data items and data items passed as subprogram arguments. In the new standard, you can declare one or more internal subprograms before the END statement of the main program (usually between STOP and END). The first internal subprogram must be preceded by a CONTAINS statement. An internal subprogram is compiled as part of the main program, so it may access any main program variable or parameter that is not redeclared in the subprogram. An internal subprogram is called in the same way as an external subprogram.

Figure D.1 shows an internal subprogram for placing in numerical order two data items read into main program variables X and Y. Because X and Y are not passed as arguments, the subprogram cannot order any other pair of main program variables. The main program and subprogram are written in free form.

Array Operations

The features available for array manipulation have increased substantially. In FORTRAN 77, an array can appear without a subscript in an argument list, a DATA statement, a READ statement, or a PRINT statement. All other operators (e.g., +, *, .LT.) can manipulate only individual array elements. The new FORTRAN standard allows you to perform these operations on an entire array. For example, if X, Y, and Z are one-dimensional arrays with N elements, the statement

```
Z = 2.0 * X
```

multiplies each element of X by 2.0 (called scalar multiplication) and stores the result in Z (i.e., $Z(i) = 2.0 * X(i)$ for all i from 1 to N). In FORTRAN 77, we would need to write a loop to do this operation.

The statement

```
LessThan = (X > 25.0)
```

compares each element of array X with 25.0. If array LessThan is a LOGICAL array with N elements, the value of $X(i) > 25.0$ (.TRUE. or .FALSE.) is saved in LessThan(i).

```
PROGRAM INTERNAL
! Places two data values in numerical order

! Declarations
REAL X, Y              ! two input variables

! Enter data
PRINT *, 'Enter two numbers'
READ *, X, Y
CALL Order_Two         ! Order X and Y
PRINT *, 'Smaller is ', X, ', Larger is ', Y
STOP           ! main program


!**********************************
CONTAINS
SUBROUTINE Order_Two
! Switches the values of X and Y

! Local Declaration
REAL Temp              ! temporary memory cell

IF (X > Y) THEN    ! Switch values
   Temp = X
   X = Y
   Y = Temp
ENDIF

RETURN         ! Exit subprogram
END            ! of subprogram

!**********************************

END               ! of main program
```

We can also write expressions that involve two array operands. The statement

    Z = X + Y

stores $X(i) + Y(i)$ in $Z(i)$ for all i from 1 to N. We can use the arithmetic operators $-$, $*$, and $**$ in the same way.

We can perform similar operations on multidimensional arrays with the same dimensions. For the declared arrays

    INTEGER A(3, 5), B(3, 5), C(3, 5)

the statement

    C = A + B

stores the sum of arrays A and B in array C (i.e., $C(i, j) = A(i, j) + B(i, j)$).

Functions with Array Arguments

A number of new subroutines and functions manipulate array arguments. For example, the function MATMUL returns the product of two arrays. The statement

```
C = MATMUL(A, B)
```

stores the product of arrays A and B in array C. If A is an M × N array and B is an N × P array, then C should be an M × P array. The function DOTPRODUCT operates on two vectors (one-dimensional arrays) and returns their scalar product.

The *array reduction functions* SUM, PRODUCT, MAXVAL, MINVAL, and COUNT perform numerical or counting operations on an array and return a scalar result. SUM returns the sum of all elements in its array argument; PRODUCT returns the product of all elements in its array argument; MAXVAL and MINVAL return the largest and smallest value, respectively; and COUNT returns the number of elements in its array argument.

Structures

An array is a collection of data objects of the same type; a structure is a collection of one or more data objects of possibly different types. For example, the following statements declare a new data type (called a *derived type*) named Book and a structure named OneText, which has type Book.

```
TYPE Book
    CHARACTER *40 Title
    CHARACTER *25 Author_Name
    REAL Price
    INTEGER Number_on_Hand
END TYPE Book
TYPE (Book) :: OneText
```

OneText is a *parent structure* with the four *components*: Title, Author_Name, Price, and Number_on_Hand. Use the assignment statements

```
OneText%Title = 'The Old Man and the Sea'
OneText%Author_Name = 'Hemingway, Ernest'
OneText%Price = 6.95
OneText%Number_on_Hand = 35
```

to store the description of a book in structure OneText. Use the statement

```
BookValue = OneText%Price * OneText%Number_on_Hand
```

to compute the inventory value of the book.

CASE Decision Structure

The CASE control structure provides another way to specify decisions. Given the following price structure for concert tickets

Section	Ticket Price
100–140	25.00
200–240	25.00
300–340	20.00
340–390	15.00

the next CASE structure displays the cost of a ticket given the section number (Section).

```
SELECT CASE (Section)
CASE (100:140, 200:240)
   PRINT *, 'Ticket Price is 25.00'
CASE (300:340)
   PRINT *, 'Ticket Price is 20.00'
CASE (340:390)
   PRINT *, 'Ticket Price is 15.00'
CASE DEFAULT
   PRINT *, 'Invalid section number'
END SELECT
```

General DO Loop Structure

The DO loop has been generalized to allow exit from any point in the loop with the EXIT statement. You can use the new CYCLE statement at any point in a loop to suspend the current iteration and begin the next one. The DO loop below searches for the first occurrence of Key_Value, ignoring any element with a subscript that ends in 0. Loop exit occurs when Key_Value is found or all elements have been tested without finding Key_Value.

```
I = 0
DO
   I = I + 1                   ! Try next element
   IF (MOD(I, 10) = 0) THEN
      CYCLE                    ! Ignore subscripts 10, 20, etc.
   ELSE IF (SearchArray(I) = Key_Value) THEN
      Found = .TRUE.           ! Success — Key_Value found
      SearchIndex = I
      EXIT
   ELSE IF (I = MaxSize) THEN
      Found = .FALSE.          ! Failure — all elements examined
      EXIT
   ENDIF
ENDDO                          ! Repeat loop
```

Answers to Self-Check Exercises

Chapter 1

Section 1.2

1. −27.2 in cell 0, 75.62 in cell 999. Cell 998 contains the letter 'X', cell 2 contains 0.005.
2. *Main memory* stores information, including data and program instructions. The *central processing unit* manipulates the information in a computer. All information is processed by the CPU. A *disk* can hold information the same way main memory can. However, the disk usually can hold more information and can store it permanently. The *disk drive* controls the disk; it stores information on the disk and retrieves information from the disk.

Section 1.4

1. X = A + B + C means "add the values represented by A, B, and C together and save the result in X." X = Y / Z means "divide the value represented by Y by the value of Z and save the result in X." D = C − B + A means "subtract the value represented by B from that in C, then add the value of A, and save the result in D."

Section 1.5

1. The *source file* contains the program written in a high-level language, which is then translated by the compiler into the *object file*. The *linker* combines the *object file* with necessary program units from other object files to create the *load file*. The *loader* then places the *load file* in main memory.
2. The existence of a *syntax error* means that a part of the source code does not meet the syntax requirements of the high-level language. *Syntax errors* are found in the *source file*.

Section 1.6

1. END, READLN, BILL, RATE, START, BEGIN, CONST, XYZ123 are all legal symbolic names.
2. The corrected program is listed below:

```
REAL X, Y, Z
Y = 15.0
Z = -Y + 3.5
X = Y + Z
PRINT *, X, Y, Z
STOP
END
```

The first statement declares the three variables used in the program: X, Y, and Z. The next statement assigns the value of 15.0 to Y. The third statement adds the negative value of Y to 3.5, which means that it subtracts −15.0 from 3.5 and assigns the result, −11.5, to Z. The next statement adds the values of Y and Z (15 and −11.5) and assigns the result, 3.5, to X. The fifth statement prints out the values of the three variables, and the next statement stops the program. The last statement instructs the compiler to stop the translation of the source file. The numbers: 3.5, 15.0, and −11.5 are printed.

3. The correct PRINT statement is:

```
PRINT *, 'The value of X is ', X, ' pounds.'
```

4. c, e, f, h, j

Section 1.8

1. 15 is an *integer*
   'XYZ' is *character* data
   '*' is *character* data
   $25.12 is not valid
   15. is a *real* number
   −999 is an *integer*
   .TRUE. is a *logical* value
   'x' is *character* data
   "x" is not valid
   '9' is *character* data
   '−5' is *character* data

2. a. X = 4.0 * A * C
   b. A = A * C
   c. I = 2 * (−J)
   d. K = 3 * (I + J)
   e. X = (5 * A) / (B * C)
   f. I = 5 * J * 3

3. a. LOAD = ((PI ** 2) * A * E)/((L/R) ** 2)
       or
       LOAD = (PI ** 2 * A * E) / (L/R) ** 2

   b. HORSPW = (Q * W * TDH) / (550.0 * E)
   c. R = (12.0 * C) / (PI * D)

Section 1.9

1. The batch version of the trip program is listed below:

```
PROGRAM TRIPS
REAL SPEED, TIME, DISTNC, MILAGE, GALLON
OPEN (UNIT = 1, FILE = 'TRIPDATA', STATUS = 'OLD')
OPEN (UNIT = 2, FILE = 'TRIPRES', STATUS = 'NEW')
READ (1, *) DISTNC
WRITE (2, *) 'Distance in miles was ', DISTNC
READ (1, *) TIME
```

```
WRITE (2, *) 'Time of trip in hours was ', TIME
SPEED = DISTNC / TIME
WRITE (2, *) 'Average speed in MPH was ', SPEED
WRITE (2, *)
READ (1, *) GALLON
WRITE (2, *) 'Gallons used was ', GALLON
MILAGE = DISTNC / GALLON
WRITE (2, *) 'Miles per gallon was ', MILAGE
STOP
END
```

Chapter 2

Section 2.3

1. Data Requirements

   three numbers (REAL NUM1, NUM2, NUM3)

   ### Problem Outputs

   the sum of the three numbers (REAL SUM)
   the average of the three numbers (REAL AVERGE)

Algorithm

1. Read in the three numbers
2. Find the sum of the three numbers
3. Find the average of the three numbers
4. Print the values of the sum and the average

   ### Step 2 Refinement

   2.1 Add NUM1, NUM2, and NUM3 and store result in SUM

   ### Step 3 Refinement

   3.1 Divide SUM by 3.0 and store result in AVERGE

2. Data Requirements

   ### Problem Inputs

   list price of the item (REAL LIST)
   percentage of discount (REAL DISCNT)

   ### Problem Outputs

   reduced price (REAL PRICE)

Algorithm

1. Read in list price and percentage of discount
2. Find reduced price
3. Print the value of the reduced price

Step 2 Refinement

2.1 Subtract from the list price the product of the discount percentage and the list price

Section 2.5

1. true, false, true, true
2. a. Never   b. O.K.
3. a.
```
IF (ITEM .NE. 0) THEN
      PRODCT = PRODCT * ITEM
   ENDIF
   PRINT *, PRODCT
```
   b.
```
IF (X .GT. Y) THEN
      Z = X - Y
   ELSE
      Z = Y - X
   ENDIF
```
   c.
```
IF (X .EQ. 0) THEN
      ZROCNT = ZROCNT + 1
   ELSE
      IF (X .LT. 0) THEN
         MINSUM = MINSUM + X
      ELSE
         PLUSUM = PLUSUM + X
      ENDIF
   ENDIF
```

Section 2.6

1. a. 7.5   b. 30.0 when Y is 15.0
   a. 15.0   b. 50.0 when Y is 10.0
2.
```
      PROGRAM LARGE3
C Finds and prints the largest number

      INTEGER NUM1, NUM2, NUM3, MAXNUM

C Read three numbers
      PRINT *, 'Enter three integers separated by blanks:'
      READ *, NUM1, NUM2, NUM3

C Store the largest of NUM1 and NUM2 in MAXNUM
      IF (NUM1 .GT. NUM2) THEN
         MAXNUM = NUM1
```

```
          ELSE
             MAXNUM = NUM2
          ENDIF

C  Store the larger of NUM3 and MAXNUM in MAXNUM
          IF (NUM3 .GT. MAXNUM) THEN
             MAXNUM = NUM3
          ENDIF

C  Print result
          PRINT *, MAXNUM, ' is the largest number.'
          STOP
          END
```

3.
```
          PROGRAM SMALL4
C  Finds and prints the smallest number

          INTEGER NUM1, NUM2, NUM3, NUM4, MINNUM

C  Read four numbers
          PRINT *, 'Enter four integers separated by blanks:'
          READ *, NUM1, NUM2, NUM3, NUM4

C  Store the smallest of NUM1 and NUM2 in MINNUM
          IF (NUM1 .LT. NUM2) THEN
             MINNUM = NUM1
          ELSE
             MINNUM = NUM2
          ENDIF

C  Store the smaller of NUM3 and MINNUM in MINNUM
          IF (NUM3 .LT. MINNUM) THEN
             MINNUM = NUM3
          ENDIF

C  Store the smaller of NUM4 and MINNUM in MINNUM
          IF (NUM4 .LT. MINNUM) THEN
             MINNUM = NUM4
          ENDIF

C  Print result
          PRINT *, MINNUM, ' is the smallest number.'
          STOP
          END
```

Section 2.7

1. Case 2:

Program statement	NUM1	NUM2	NUM3	MINNUM	Effect
	?	?	?	?	
PRINT*, 'Enter three...'					Prints a prompt
READ*, NUM1, NUM2, NUM3	10	12	5		Reads the data
IF (NUM1 .LT. NUM2) THEN					Is 10 < 12?
					Value is true
MINNUM = NUM1				10	10 is smallest so far
IF (NUM3 .LT. MINNUM)...					Is 5 < 10?
					Value is true
MINNUM = NUM3					5 is smallest
PRINT*, MINNUM...					Prints 5 is the smallest number...

Case 3:

Program statement	NUM1	NUM2	NUM3	MINNUM	Effect
	?	?	?	?	
PRINT*, 'Enter three...'					Prints a prompt
READ*, NUM1, NUM2, NUM3	5	12	10		Reads the data
IF (NUM1 .LT. NUM2) THEN					Is 5 < 12?
					Value is true
MINNUM = NUM1				5	5 is smallest so far
IF (NUM3 .LT. MINNUM)...					Is 10 < 5?
					Value is false
PRINT*, MINNUM...					Prints 5 is the smallest number...

Case 4:

Program statement	NUM1	NUM2	NUM3	MINNUM	Effect
	?	?	?	?	
PRINT*, 'Enter three...'					Prints a prompt
READ*, NUM1, NUM2, NUM3	10	5	12		Reads the data
IF (NUM1 .LT. NUM2) THEN					Is 10 < 5?
					Value is false
MINNUM = NUM2				5	5 is smallest so far
IF (NUM3 .LT. MINNUM)...					Is 12 < 10?
					Value is false
PRINT*, MINNUM...					Prints 5 is the smallest number...

2. Case 1:

Program statement	HOURS ?	RATE ?	GROSS ?	NET ?	Effect
PRINT*, 'Enter hours...'					Prints a prompt
READ*, HOURS	30.0				Reads data
PRINT*, 'Enter hourly...'					Prints a prompt
READ*, RATE		5.00			Reads data
GROSS = HOURS * RATE			150.0		Calculates gross pay as 150.0
IF (GROSS .GT. TXBRAK)...					Is 150.0 > 100.0? Value is true
NET = GROSS — TAX				125.0	Net pay is 150 — 25, i.e., 125.0
PRINT*, 'Gross salary...'					Prints 150.0 as the gross salary
PRINT*, 'Net salary...'					Prints 125.0 as the net salary

Case 2:

Program statement	HOURS ?	RATE ?	GROSS ?	NET ?	Effect
PRINT*, 'Enter hours...'					Prints a prompt
READ*, HOURS	20.0				Reads data
PRINT*, 'Enter hourly...'					Prints a prompt
READ*, RATE		3.00			Reads data
GROSS = HOURS * RATE			60.0		Calculates gross pay as 60.0
IF (GROSS .GT. TXBRAK)...					Is 60.0 > 100.0? Value is false
NET = GROSS				60.0	Net pay is gross pay, i.e., 60.0
PRINT*, 'Gross salary...'					Prints 60.0 as the gross salary
PRINT*, 'Net salary...'					Prints 60.0 as the net salary

Section 2.8

1.
```
        PROGRAM TAXING
        REAL TXBRAK, TAX, MXHOUR
        PARAMETER (TXBRAK = 100.00)
        PARAMETER (TAX = 25.00)
        PARAMETER (MXHOUR = 40.0)
        REAL HOURS, RATE, GROSS, NET

C Enter HOURS and RATE
        PRINT *, 'Enter hours worked:'
        READ *, HOURS
```

```
            PRINT *, 'Enter hourly rate:'
            READ *, RATE

C Compute gross salary
            GROSS = HOURS * RATE

C Add overtime pay to GROSS
            IF (HOURS .GT. MXHOUR) THEN
                GROSS = GROSS + ((HOURS - MXHOUR) * RATE)
            ENDIF

C Compute net salary
            IF (GROSS .GT. TXBRAK) THEN
               NET = GROSS - TAX
            ELSE
               NET = GROSS
            ENDIF

C Print GROSS and NET
            PRINT *, 'Gross salary is $', GROSS
            PRINT *, 'Net salary is $', NET
            STOP
            END

2.          PROGRAM PAYING
            REAL TXBRAK, TAX, MXHOUR
            PARAMETER (TXBRAK = 100.00)
            PARAMETER (TAX = 25.00)
            PARAMETER (MXHOUR = 40.0)
            REAL HOURS, RATE, GROSS, NET

C Enter HOURS and RATE
            PRINT *, 'Enter hours worked:'
            READ *, HOURS
            PRINT *, 'Enter hourly rate:'
            READ *, RATE

C Compute gross salary
            IF (HOURS .GT. MXHOUR) THEN
               GROSS = (MXHOUR * RATE) + ((HOURS - MXHOUR) * 2 * RATE)
            ELSE
               GROSS = HOURS * RATE
            ENDIF
```

Section 2.9
```
1. IF (X .GT. Y) THEN
     LARGER = X
     SMALLR = Y
     PRINT *, 'X LARGER'
   ELSE
     LARGER = Y
```

```
      SMALLR = X
      PRINT *, 'Y LARGER'
   ENDIF
```

2. In the inner IF structure, the test for GPA less than 1.0 is made only if the GPA is not less than 2.0. Therefore, the test can never be true, and the case of GPA less than 1.0 (print "Flunked out") will never be handled.

3.

Program statement	SALARY	TAX	*Effect*
	13500.00	?	
IF (SALARY .LT. 0.0)...			Is 13500 < 0? Value is false
ELSE IF (SALARY .LT. 1500...			Is 13500 < 1500? Value is false
ELSE IF (SALARY .LT. 3000...			Is 13500 < 3000? Value is false
ELSE IF (SALARY .LT. 5000...			Is 13500 < 5000? Value is false
ELSE IF (SALARY .LT. 8000...			Is 13500 < 8000? Value is false
ELSE IF (SALARY .LT. 15000...			Is 13500 < 15000? Value is true
TAX = (SALARY - 8000) * ...			Assign 2800.0 to TAX

4. Negative values for SALARY would be calculated as legitimate values. Incorrect (negative) tax values would result.

5.
```
IF (SCORE .LT. 60) THEN
    PRINT *, 'F'
ELSE IF (SCORE .LT. 70) THEN
    PRINT *, 'D'
ELSE IF (SCORE .LT. 80) THEN
    PRINT *, 'C'
ELSE IF (SCORE .LT. 90) THEN
    PRINT *, 'B'
ELSE
    PRINT *, 'A'
ENDIF
```

6. Using a nested IF statement:
```
IF (GPA .LT. 3.0) THEN
    IF (GPA .LT. 1.0) THEN
        PRINT *, 'Failed semester - registration suspended'
    ELSE
        PRINT *, 'On probation for next semester'
    ENDIF
ELSE
    IF (GPA .LT. 3.5) THEN
        PRINT *, 'Deans list for semester'
```

```
     ELSE
        PRINT *, 'Highest honors for semester'
     ENDIF
  ENDIF
```

Section 3.1
1. Execute all the statements between the loop header and label 15 five times with the variable I5 increasing in value from 1 to 5.

2.
Program statement	COUNT	N	Effect
	?	?	
N = 5	?	5	Assigns 5 to N
DO COUNT = 1, N	1		Initializes COUNT to 1
PRINT*, '*****'			Prints a row of 5 stars
Increment and test COUNT	2		2 <= 5 is true
PRINT*, '*****'			Prints a row of 5 stars
Increment and test COUNT	3		3 <= 5 is true
PRINT*, '*****'			Prints a row of 5 stars
Increment and test COUNT	4		4 <= 5 is true
PRINT*, '*****'			Prints a row of 5 stars
Increment and test COUNT	5		5 <= 5 is true
PRINT*, '*****'			Prints a row of 5 stars
Increment and test COUNT	6		Exits loop

3.
Program statement	PROD	I	Effect
	?	?	
PROD = 1	1	?	Initializes PROD to 1
DO 20 I = 1, 5		1	Initializes I to 1
PROD = PROD * I	1		Multiplies PROD by 1
PRINT*, I, PROD			Prints values of I and PROD
Increment and test I		2	2 <= 5 is true
PROD = PROD * I	2		Multiplies PROD by 2
PRINT*, I, PROD			Prints values of I and PROD
Increment and test I		3	3 <= 5 is true
PROD = PROD * I	6		Multiplies PROD by 3
PRINT*, I, PROD			Prints values of I and PROD
Increment and test I		4	4 <= 5 is true
PROD = PROD * I	24		Multiplies PROD by 4
PRINT*, I, PROD			Prints values of I and PROD
Increment and test I		5	5 <= 5 is true
PROD = PROD * I	120		Multiplies PROD by 5

```
      PRINT*, I, PROD                              Prints values of I
                                                   and PROD
   Increment and test I                    6       Exits loop
```

4.
```
         PROGRAM COMP2
C Compares two methods for finding the sum of all integers
C from 1 to N inclusive

         INTEGER N, SUM1, SUM2, I

C Read the last integer (N)
         PRINT *, 'Enter the last integer in the sum:'
         READ *, N

C Find the sum (SUM) of all integers from 1 to N using a loop
         SUM1 = 0
         DO 10 I = 1, N
            SUM1 = SUM1 + I
   10 CONTINUE

C Find the sum (SUM2) of all integers from 1 to N using a formula
         SUM2 = N * (N + 1) / 2

C Print the results
         PRINT *, 'The result, using the loop method, is ', SUM1
         PRINT *, 'The result, using the formula, is ', SUM2

C Compare the results
         IF (SUM1 .EQ. SUM2) THEN
            PRINT *, 'Both methods yield the same result'
         ELSE
            PRINT *, 'The two methods yield different results'
         ENDIF

         STOP
         END
```

5.
```
         PROGRAM PRODN
C Finds and prints the product of all the integers from 1 to N

         INTEGER N, PRODCT, I

C Read the last integer (N)
         PRINT *, 'Enter the last integer in the product:'
         READ *, N

C Find the product (PRODCT) of all integers from 1 to N
         PRODCT = 1
         DO 10 I = 2, N
            PRODCT = PRODCT * I
   10 CONTINUE
```

```
C Print the product
      PRINT *, 'The product is ', PRODCT
      STOP
      END
```

Section 3.2
1.
```
      PROGRAM PROLIS
C Finds and prints the product of a list of data items

      INTEGER NMITEM, COUNT
      REAL ITEM, PRODCT

C Read the number of data items to be multiplied together
      PRINT *, 'Number of data items to be multiplied together?'
      READ *, NMITEM

C Find the product (PRODCT) of NMITEM data items
      PRODCT = 1.0
      DO 10 COUNT = 1, NMITEM
         PRINT *, 'Next item to be included in product?'
         READ *, ITEM
         IF (ITEM .NE. 0.0) THEN
            PRODCT = PRODCT * ITEM
         ENDIF
   10 CONTINUE

C Print the product
      PRINT *, 'The product is ', PRODCT
      STOP
      END
```

Section 3.3

1.
Program statement	N	SUM	I	NEXT	Effect
	?	?	?	?	
READ*, N	5				Reads in number of data items
SUM = 0		0			Initializes SUM to 0
DO 30 I = 1, N			1		Initializes I to 1
READ*, NEXT				3	Reads data item
IF (NEXT .GE. 0) THEN					Is 3 >= 0?
					Value is true
SUM = SUM + NEXT		3			Increments SUM by 3
Increment and test I			2		2 <= 5 is true
READ*, NEXT				−5	Reads data item
IF (NEXT .GE. 0) THEN					Is −5 >= 0?
					Value is false
SUM = SUM − NEXT		8			Increments SUM by 5
Increment and test I			3		3 <= 5 is true
READ*, NEXT				7	Reads data item

`IF (NEXT .GE. 0) THEN`				Is 7 >= 0?
				Value is true
`SUM = SUM + NEXT`	15			Increments SUM by 7
Increment and test I		4		4 <= 5 is true
`READ*, NEXT`			0	Reads data item
`IF (NEXT .GE. 0) THEN`				Is 0 >= 0?
				Value is true
`SUM = SUM + NEXT`	15			Increments SUM by 0
Increment and test I		5		5 <= 5 is true
`READ*, NEXT`			−9	Reads data item
`IF (NEXT .GE. 0) THEN`				Is −9 >= 0?
				Value is false
`SUM = SUM − NEXT`	24			Increments SUM by 9
Increment and test I		6		Exits loop
`PRINT*, SUM`				Prints the sum, 24

2.
```
    SUMPOS = 0.0
    SUMNEG = 0.0
    READ *, N
    DO 10 I = 1, N
        READ *, ITEM
        IF (ITEM .GE. 0.0) THEN
            SUMPOS = SUMPOS + 1
        ELSE
            SUMNEG = SUMNEG + 1
        ENDIF
10 CONTINUE
    PRINT *, 'The number of positive data items is ', SUMPOS
    PRINT *, 'The number of negative data items is ', SUMNEG
```

Section 3.4

1.
Program statement	N	SUM	ODD	*Effect*
	5	0	?	
`DO 10 ODD = 1, N, 2`			1	Initializes ODD to 1
`SUM = SUM + ODD`		1		Increments SUM by 1
Increment and test ODD			3	3 <= 5 is true
`SUM = SUM + ODD`		4		Increments SUM by 3
Increment and test ODD			5	5 <= 5 is true
`SUM = SUM + ODD`		9		Increments SUM by 5
Increment and test ODD			6	Exits loop

2. a. Nothing would be printed.
   b. −20, −15, −10, −5, 0, 5, 10, 15, 20
   c. −20
   d. 20, 0

3.
```
    PROGRAM ETOX
    INTEGER NUMTRM, FACT, I
    REAL X, EXPONT, XTERM
```

```
      PRINT *, 'Enter X and number of terms:'
      READ *, X, NUMTRM
      EXPONT = 1.0
      FACT = 1
      XTERM = 1.0
      DO 10 I = 1, NUMTRM
         FACT = FACT * I
         XTERM = XTERM * X
         EXPONT = EXPONT + XTERM / FACT
   10 CONTINUE
      PRINT *, EXPONT
      STOP
      END
```

Section 3.5

1. All powers of 2 from 2 through 1024 inclusive would be printed.
2.
```
      PROGRAM NPOWER
C Prints all powers of N less than 1000

      INTEGER MAXPOW
      PARAMETER (MAXPOW = 1000)
      INTEGER N, NEXPOW, POWER

C Read an integer N
      PRINT *, 'This program prints all powers < 1000 of an integer'
      PRINT *, 'Enter an integer:'
      READ *, N
      PRINT *

C Print each power of N less than MAXPOW
      NEXPOW = 1
      POWER = 1
      PRINT *, '          POWER     VALUE'
      DO WHILE (NEXPOW .LT. MAXPOW)
         PRINT *, POWER, NEXPOW
         NEXPOW = NEXPOW * N
         POWER = POWER + 1
      ENDDO
      STOP
      END
```

3. Displays 95, 90, 85, . . . , 5, 0, –5, . . . , –100, –105.

```
      DO 10 VAL = 95, -105, -5
         PRINT *, VAL
   10 CONTINUE
```

4.
```
      PROGRAM MAXMUL
      REAL MAXPRD
      PARAMETER (MAXPRD = 1000.0)
      REAL ITEM, PRODCT
```

```
   PRODCT = 1.0
   DO WHILE (PRODCT .LT. MAXPRD)
      READ *, ITEM
      IF (ITEM .NE. 0) THEN
         PRODCT = PRODCT * ITEM
      ENDIF
   ENDDO
   PRINT *, 'Product before exceeding limit is ', PRODCT / ITEM
   STOP
   END
```

5. Replace the corresponding step in the original program with

```
C Compute the next value of TERM and add it to the ...
      E = 1.0
      NEXT = 1
      TERM = 1.0
      DO WHILE (TERM .GE. 0.00005)
         E = E + TERM
         NEXT = NEXT + 1
         TERM = TERM / NEXT
      ENDDO
```

Section 3.6

1. a. 1 1
      2 1
      2 2
      3 1
      3 2
      3 3

      . . .

      5 5
   b. 1 5
      1 4
      1 3
      1 2
      1 1
      2 5
      2 4
      2 3
      2 2

      . . .

      4 5
      4 4
      5 5
   c. I =   1
            2
            1

```
I =        2
           4
           3
           2
I =        3
           6
           5
           4
           3
I =        4
           8
           7
           6
           5
           4
I =        5
          10
           9
           8
           7
           6
           5
```

Section 3.7

1.
```
IF (TYPE .EQ. 'D') THEN
     CURBAL = CURBAL + AMOUNT
     NUMCHK = NUMCHK + 1
  ELSE
     IF (TYPE .EQ. 'C') THEN
          CURBAL = CURBAL - AMOUNT
          NUMCHK = NUMCHK + 1
          IF (CURBAL .LT. 0.0) THEN
               PRINT *, 'Balance is below zero'
          ENDIF
     ELSE
          PRINT *, 'Illegal transaction'
     ENDIF
  ENDIF
```

2. Open an output file in the beginning and insert a WRITE statement to this file after every PRINT that is not a prompt. The WRITE statement should have the same output list as the PRINT statement.

3. Change .GT. in WHILE condition to .GE..

Chapter 4

Section 4.2

1. a. I = 12   c. I = −3   e. I = 0   g. X = 0.0
   b. I = −3   d. X = −3.14159   f. X = 0.0   h. Invalid

i. I = -30   l. A = 9   n. I = 1   p. I = 0
j. I = 3   m. X = -3.14159   o. I = 30   q. I = 30
k. X = -3.0

2. a. I = 10   f. X = 2.0   j. I = 2   n. I = 0
    b. I = -2   g. X = 10.0   k. X = 2.5   o. I = 50
    c. I = 10   h. Invalid   l. I = 15   p. I = 0
    d. X = 6.28318   i. I = -50   m. X = 1.570795   q. I = 50
    e. I = 2

3. a. WHITE = 1.666667   d. BLUE = - 3.0
    b. GREEN = 0.666667   e. LIME = 1
    c. ORANGE = 0   f. PURPLE = 0.0

Section 4.3
1.
```
PROGRAM EXPLOG
REAL SENVAL
PARAMETER (SENVAL = -1000)
REAL A, B
READ *, A, B
DO WHILE (A .NE. SENVAL)
    PRINT *, EXP(A * ALOG(B))
    READ *, A, B
ENDDO
STOP
END
```

The program listed above calculates B raised to the power of A.
2. ROUND = REAL(NINT (X * 100.0)) / 100.0
3. Introduce RLROOT and IMROOT (type REAL) to store the real and imaginary parts of the roots. Change the ELSE task as follows:

```
ELSE
    RLROOT = -B / (2.0 * A)
    IMROOT = SQRT(ABS(DISC))
    PRINT *, 'Root 1 is ', RLROOT, ' + i ', IMROOT
    PRINT *, 'Root 2 is ', RLROOT, ' - i ', IMROOT
ENDIF
```

Section 4.4

1.

```
                 .FALSE.      4.0  2.0     3.0  2.0
           .NOT. (FLAG .OR. ((Y + Z) .GE. (X - Z)))
```

2. a. BETWEN = (N .GE. -K) .AND. (N .LE. K)
   b. UPCASE = (CH .GE. 'A') .AND. (CH .LE. 'Z')
   c. DIVISR = (MOD(N, M) .EQ. 0)

Section 4.5

1. a.
   CITY

   | NEW□YORK |

   b.
   LASTNA

   | JACKSON□□□□□ |

   c.
   TRIP

   | HONEY |

   d.
   TEAM

   | ORIOLES□□ |

   e.
   FIRST   LAST

   | BILL□□ | | SMITH□ |

   f.
   TEAM

   | RED□STOCK |

2.
```
      CHARACTER *1 GRADE
      CHARACTER *6 CORSID
      CHARACTER *15 NAME, CLASS, MAJOR
      INTEGER CREDIT, IDNUM
      READ *, IDNUM, NAME, CLASS, MAJOR
      DO 10 I = 1, 3
          READ *, CORSID, CREDIT, GRADE
   10 CONTINUE
```

3. a. true   c. true   e. false   g. false   i. true
   b. false   d. false   f. true   h. true   j. false

Section 4.6

1. b. 4I is invalid, change to I4.
   c. F16.35X is invalid, change to F16.3, 5X.
   d. 2A and F3.3 are invalid, change to A2 and F6.3.

2. a. 1234   555.4567
   b. 1234   555.4567
   c. K = 1234
   d. ALPHA = 555.46
   e. K = 1234   ALPHA =   555.457

```
3.     INTEGER SSN01,SSN02, SSN03
       REAL HOURS, RATE, PAY
       CHARACTER * 3 LAST, FIRST

       PRINT 10, 'SOCIAL SECURITY NUMBER ', SSN01, '-', SSN02, '-',
      +          SSN03
10 FORMAT (1X, A, I3, A, I2, A, I4)
       PRINT 20, LAST, ', ', FIRST
20 FORMAT ('0', A, A, A)
       PRINT 30, 'HOURS RATE PAY'
30 FORMAT ('0', A)
       PRINT 40, HOURS, RATE, PAY
40 FORMAT (1X, F5.2, F5.2, F7.2)
```

Section 4.7
```
1. WEIGHT = AREA * 490.0
2. DO WHILE (STRNTH .LE. 0.0)
       PRINT *, 'Enter positive strength'
       READ *, STRNTH
   ENDDO
```

Chapter 5

Section 5.1
1. a. A and B are not declared in main program (inplicit REAL). X is declared as REAL (not INTEGER) in main program.
   b. MASSAG is a function, not a variable, so it cannot be an argument.
   f. Needs a third argument.
   h. Third argument is not type INTEGER.

```
2.     REAL FUNCTION LARGE2(X, Y)
       REAL X, Y
       IF (X .GE. Y) THEN
          LARGE2 = X
       ELSE
          LARGE2 = Y
       ENDIF
       RETURN
       END
```

To find the largest of A, B, C use the statement

```
       MAX = LARGE2(A, LARGE2(B, C))
```

```
3.     INTEGER FUNCTION POWER(N, K)
       INTEGER N, K
```

```
      INTEGER J, TEMPOW
      TEMPOW = 1
      DO 10 J = 1, K
          TEMPOW = TEMPOW * N
  10  CONTINUE
      POWER = TEMPOW
      RETURN
      END
```

4.
```
      REAL FUNCTION ALLPOW(N, K)
      INTEGER N, K, POWER
      IF (K .EQ. 0) THEN
          ALLPOW = 1.0
      ELSE IF (K .GT. 0) THEN
          ALLPOW = REAL(POWER(N, K))
      ELSE
          ALLPOW = 1.0 / (REAL(POWER(N, K))
      ENDIF
      RETURN
      END
```

5.
```
      ROUND (X, N) = REAL(NINT(X * 10.0 ** N)) / (10.0 ** N)
```

6.
```
      CONVRT(C) = 1.8 * C + 32.0
      DO 10 C = 0, 100
          F = CONVRT(C)
          PRINT *, F, C
  10  CONTINUE
```

7.
```
      DIST = HYPOT(SQUARE(X2 - X1) + SQUARE (Y2 - Y1))
```

Section 5.3
1. returns and displays the cube of its argument
2.
```
      SUBROUTINE SQURES (X, XSQUAR, XSQRT, POSFLG)
      REAL X, XSQUAR, XSQRT
      LOGICAL POSFLG
      XSQUAR = X * X
      XSQRT = SQRT(ABS(X))
      POSFLG = X .GE. 0.0
      RETURN
      END
```

Section 5.4

X	Y	Z
5	3	8
5	3	8
11	3	8
16	3	8
16	6	8

2.
```
INTEGER FUNCTION SUM (A, B)
INTEGER A, B
SUM = A + B
RETURN
END
```

Add declaration

```
INTEGER SUM
```

to main program. Use function calls

```
Z = SUM(X, Y)
Z = SUM(Y, X)
X = SUM(Z, Y)
Y = SUM(Y, Y)
```

3.
```
REAL X, Y, Z
LOGICAL FLAG
PRINT *, 'Enter a number: '
READ *, X
CALL SQRES (X, Y, Z, FLAG)
PRINT *, 'Square is ', Y, '   Square root is ', Z
IF (.NOT. FLAG) THEN
   PRINT *, 'Square root is imaginary'
ENDIF
STOP
END
```

Section 5.6

1. The values of NUM1 and NUM2 before the execution of ORDER are shown with a line through them.

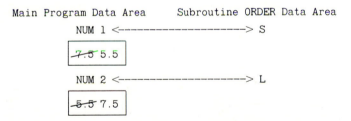

2. The three numbers would be stored in descending order (largest value first) in NUM1, NUM2, NUM3.

Chapter 6

Section 6.1

1. X3 is a simple variable; X(3) is an element of array X.
2. five memory cells that can each store 1 character

3. REAL SQROOT(10)
   INTEGER CUBE(−5 : 5)

4. REAL PRESUR(−10 : 10)

Section 6.2

1. X(5) and X(6) are changed; the rest of the values are the same.

X(1)	X(2)	X(3)	X(4)	X(5)	X(6)	X(7)	X(8)
16.0	12.0	6.0	8.0	12.0	14.0	14.0	−54.5

2. PRINT *, I, X(I)   displays 3 and 6.0
   PRINT *, X(I) + 1 displays 7.0
   PRINT *, X(I) + I displays 9.0
   PRINT *, X(I+1)   displays 8.0
   PRINT *, X(I+I)   displays 14.0
   PRINT *, X(2*I)   displays 14.0
   PRINT *, X(2*I−4) displays 12.0
   X(I−1) = X(I)   assigns 6.0 to X(2)
   X(I) = X(I+1)   assigns 8.0 to X(3)

Section 6.3

1.   DO 10 I = 1, 10
           SQROOT(I) = SQRT(REAL(I))
       10 CONTINUE

           DO 20 I = −5, 5
              CUBE(I) = I * I * I
       20 CONTINUE

Section 6.4

1.   DO 30 I = 1, 5
           PRINT *, I, SQROOT(I), CUBE(I)
       30 CONTINUE

2.   PRINT 35, (I, X(I), X(I)−AVERAG, I = 1, MAXITM)
       35 FORMAT (1X, I4, 3X, F8.1, 3X, F14.1)

Section 6.5

1.   SUBROUTINE NEGATE (LIST, N)
       INTEGER LIST(*), N
       INTEGER I
       DO 10 I = 1, N
          LIST(I) = −LIST(I)
       10 CONTINUE
       RETURN
       END

2. a. Invalid—A and B are not declared as arrays in the main program.
   b. Invalid—C(6) is only a single element of the array, not an array.
   c. Valid—stores the sum of arrays C and D in E.
   d. Valid but leads to an error—there is no seventh array element.
   e. Valid—adds only the first five array elements.
   f. Invalid—6 is not an array, and E is not an integer value.
   g. Valid—stores the sum of arrays D and C in E.
   h. Valid—doubles each element of array C.
   i. Invalid—C(1) is not an integer value.
   j. Valid but could lead to an error if C(1) is greater than 6.
   k. Valid—adds all elements of arrays C and D if C(1) is greater than 6; otherwise, adds only INT(ABS(C(1))) elements.

Section 6.6

1. ```
   INTEGER PRIME(10)
   DATA PRIME /2, 3, 5, 7, 11, 13, 17, 19, 23, 29/
   ```

2. When T is −5, the function value is −75. When T is 5, the function value is 75. Change the single statement function definition to

   ```
   F(T) = T ** 3 - 10 * T
   ```

   Change the line that prints the table heading (values of F(T)):

   ```
   PRINT 5, (I, I = -75, 75, 150 / 13)
   ```

   Change the DO loop body:

   ```
   FUNVAL = F(T)
   SCALED = NINT(65.0 * REAL(FUNVAL + 75) / 150.0)
   PLOT(SCALED) = '*'
   PRINT 25, 'T=', T, PLOT
   PLOT(SCALED) = ' '
   ```

Chapter 7

Section 7.1

1. a. The first solution requires the enrollment figures to be entered in a specified order; the second solution permits any order.

   ```
       DO 10 COURSE = 1, MAXCRS
           DO 20 CAMPUS = 1, 5
               DO 30 RANK = 1, 4
                   PRINT *, 'For course ', COURSE, ' enter # of students '
                   PRINT *, 'in year ', RANK, ' enrolled at campus ', CAMPUS
                   READ *, ENROLL(COURSE, CAMPUS, RANK)
   30          CONTINUE
   20      CONTINUE
   10 CONTINUE
   ```
   ```

```
        PRINT *, 'Enter course number or 0 to stop:'
        READ *, COURSE
        DO WHILE (COURSE .NE. SENVAL)
           PRINT *, 'Enter campus number (1-5):'
           READ *, CAMPUS
           PRINT *, 'Enter year (1-4):'
           READ *, RANK
           PRINT *, 'Enter number enrolled:'
           READ *, ENROLL(COURSE, CAMPUS, RANK)
           PRINT *, 'Enter course number or 0 to stop:'
        ENDDO

b.      JUNIOR = 0
        DO 10 COURSE = 1, 5
           DO 20 CAMPUS = 1, 5
              JUNIOR = JUNIOR + ENROLL(COURSE, CAMPUS, 3)
    20     CONTINUE
    10 CONTINUE
        PRINT *, 'The total enrollment of juniors is ', JUNIOR

c.      SOPHMR = 0
        DO 10 CAMPUS = 1, 5
           SOPHMR = SOPHMR + ENROLL(2, CAMPUS, 2)
    10 CONTINUE
        PRINT *, 'The total number of sophomores in course 2 is ', SOPHMR

d.      CAMSUM = 0
        DO 10 COURSE = 1, 5
           CRSSUM = 0
           DO 20 RANK = 1, 4
              CRSSUM = CRSSUM + ENROLL(COURSE, 1, RANK)
    10     CONTINUE
           PRINT *, 'Campus enrollment in course ', COURSE, ' is ', CRSSUM
           CAMSUM = CAMSUM + CRSSUM
    20 CONTINUE
        PRINT *, 'Total enrollment for main campus is ', CAMSUM

e.      UPRSUM = 0
        DO 10 CAMPUS = 1, 5
           CAMSUM = 0
           DO 20 COURSE = 1, 5
              DO 30 RANK = 3, 4
                 CAMSUM = CAMSUM + ENROLL(COURSE, CAMPUS, RANK)
    30        CONTINUE
    20     CONTINUE
           PRINT *, 'Upperclass enrollment for campus ', CAMPUS, ' is ',
     +        CAMSUM
           UPRSUM = UPRSUM + CAMSUM
    10 CONTINUE
        PRINT *, 'Total upperclass enrollment is ', UPRSUM
```

Section 7.3

1. The value 1 is returned. To return the last index value, delete the program flag and all references to it. Change the WHILE loop to a DO loop with a loop header

```
DO 10 I = 1, N
```

Initialize SEARCH to zero before the loop and reset SEARCH to I each time the TARGET is found. Delete the IF structure following the loop.

Section 7.4

1. To modify the BUBBLE subroutine to sort an array in descending order, change the IF–THEN statement condition from

```
IF (LIST(FIRST) .GT. LIST(FIRST+1)) THEN
```

to

```
IF (LIST(FIRST) .LT. LIST(FIRST+1)) THEN
```

Section 7.5

1.
```
    DO 30 I = 1, NUMCAT
        IF (GRADES(NXTGRD) .EQ. CATGRY(I)) THEN
            COUNTS(I) = COUNTS(I) + 1
        ENDIF
30 CONTINUE
```

2. Function GETMIN is similar to GETMAX. Subroutine DISPLY prints the student NAMES, SCORES, and GRADES if GRADES were assigned. Its body consists of the DO loop below.

```
        DO 10 I = 1, NUMSTU
            IF (GRADED) THEN
                PRINT *, NAMES(I), SCORES(I), GRADES(I)
            ELSE
                PRINT *, NAMES(I), SCORES(I)
            ENDIF
    10 CONTINUE
```

Subroutine ASSIGN assigns letter grades. Its body consists of a DO loop like the one below.

```
        DO 10 I = 1, NUMSTU
            IF (SCORES(I) .GE. BREAK(1)) THEN
                GRADES(I) = 'A'
            ELSE IF (SCORES(I) .GE. BREAK(2)) THEN
                GRADES(I) = 'B'
            .....

            ENDIF
    10 CONTINUE
```

The local array BREAK contains the scores at the boundaries for each grade category (e.g., BREAK(1) is 90, BREAK(2) is 80, etc.)

Subroutine SHOW displays a particular student's score. It first reads the student's name and then calls function SEARCH to locate the student's name (TARGET). If the name is found, the score is printed.

```
PRINT *, 'Enter the student''s name: '
READ *, TARGET
INDEX = SEARCH(NAMES, TARGET, NUMSTU)
IF (INDEX .NE. 0) THEN
   PRINT *, 'The score is ', SCORES(INDEX)
ELSE
   PRINT *, 'Student is not found'
ENDIF
```

Subroutine CHANGE is similar to SHOW, except that the IF structure changes a student's score (and grade if GRADED is true) rather than printing it. The IF structure becomes

```
IF (INDEX .NE. 0) THEN
   PRINT *, 'Enter new score: '
   READ *, SCORES(INDEX)
   IF (GRADED) THEN
      PRINT *, 'Enter new grade: '
      READ *, GRADES(INDEX)
   ENDIF
ELSE
   PRINT *, 'Student is not found'
ENDIF
```

Subroutines SORTNA and SORTSC are similar to subroutine BUBBLE. The NAMES are compared in SORTNA, and the SCORES are compared in SORTSC. If an out-of-order pair is found in either subroutine, the NAMES, SCORES, and GRADES for that pair must all be switched.

Section 7.7
1. 1.0, 2.0, 4.0
2. The original array NEXT is defined as 1, 3, 5, 7, 9; however, the calls to EXCH switch elements 1 and 4 and elements 2 and 3. The final array printed is 7, 5, 3, 1, 9. The two variables I are unconnected. Subroutine DEFINE is passed array NEXT as an argument so the subroutine cannot reference COMMON block WHAT.

Chapter 8

Section 8.2
1.
```
INTEGER AGE, YEAR, OCCODE
CHARACTER *11 SSNO
CHARACTER *1 INIT
CHARACTER *13 FIRST
CHARACTER *20 LAST
```

```
      READ 10, SSNO, LAST, FIRST, INIT, AGE, YEAR, OCCODE
   10 FORMAT(A11, A20, A13, A1, 3X, I2, 4X, I5, 4X, I3)
```

552-63-0179BROWN   JERRY   L 38   23   12

1 2 3 4 5 6 7 8 9 1011121314151 6   ···   32   ···   454647484950   ···   58596061626364656 6

2. Line layout:

Columns	Contents
1–6	account number
7–	not used
8–32	name of firm
33–	not used
34–41	previous account balance
42–	not used
43–48	charges for current month
49–	not used
50–55	credits for current month
56–	not used
57–63	total amount due
64–80	not used

Declarations, READ and FORMAT statements:

```
   INTEGER ACCNUM
   CHARACTER *25 FNAME
   REAL OLDBAL, CURCHG, CURCRD, TOTDUE

      READ 23, ACCNUM,FNAME,OLDBAL,CURCHG,CURCRD,TOTDUE
   23 FORMAT (I6,1X,A,1X,F8.2,1X,F6.2,1X,F6.2,1X,F7.2)
```

3. The FORTRAN statements for exercise 2 will still work. According to rule 6b, the decimal point need not be punched. If it is, the punched decimal point overrides the format descriptor. However, the data must be punched in the rightmost portion of the field. Zero entries need not be punched, because an F field with all blanks is read as a zero.

4. 30 FORMAT (F7.1 / I5, 2X, A / F6.1, I3)

5.   16312DAWN-321   49

1 2 3 4 5 6 7 8 9 101112131415161718l9

Section 8.3

1. There would be twelve lines of ten values each. Each value would be right-justified in a field of width 12 and three decimal places printed.
2. Each element of TEXT will contain the first character of the corresponding line of input followed by seventy-nine blanks. The first element of BUFFER will contain the character punched in column 1 of the data card. Then an error—"insufficient data"—will occur, because the next 79 card columns are ignored and the READ statement will try to enter a value for BUFFER(2) from the next data card.

3. | Variable Name | Contents |
    | --- | --- |
    | a. COLOR | 'BLUE' |
    | ID | 37288 |
    | COST | 672.25 |
    | b. NAME | 'DEB' |
    | FLIGHT | 698 |
    | AIRLIN | 'UNITED' |
    | DATE(1) | 6 |
    | DATE(2) | 13 |
    | DATE(3) | 75 |
    | c. NAME(1) | 'ELIE' |
    | NAME(2) | 'KOFF' |
    | AB | 624 |
    | RUNS | 126 |
    | HITS | 214 |
    | RBI | 42 |
    | AVE | .312 |

4. a.
```
    PRINT 47, TEMP, WCF
 47 FORMAT (I3,5X,12(I4,2X))
```
   b. No changes are required to either the PRINT or the FORMAT statement. The loop would print twenty-one lines, each containing a value for TEMP followed by the twelve values in WCF.

   c.
```
    PRINT 29
 29 FORMAT ('1 WIND CHILL FACTOR TABLE (DEGREES F)'
   +    'TEMPERATURE', 12X 'WIND VELOCITY (MILES PER HOUR)' /
   +    'READING (DEG F)',8X,'5',6X,'10',6X,'15 . . . 50')
```

5. a.
```
    PRINT 10, X
 10 FORMAT (5(1X, 4F8.2/)) or FORMAT (1X, 4F8.2)
```
   b.
```
    PRINT 20, N, (X(I), I = 1, N)
 20 FORMAT (1X, 'N = ', I2/5 (1X, 4F8.2/))
```
   c.
```
    PRINT 30, QUEUE
 30 FORMAT (170(1X, 6E15.6/)) or FORMAT (1X, 6E15.6)
```
   d.
```
    DO 40 I = 1, 120
       PRINT 50, ROOM(I), TEMP(I)
 40 CONTINUE
 50 FORMAT (1X, I3, 5X, F6.1)
```

Section 8.4

1.
```
 OPEN (UNIT = 3, FILE = 'TEXT', ACCESS = 'SEQUENTIAL',
   +    FORM = 'UNFORMATTED', STATUS = 'OLD')
```

2.
```
 SUBROUTINE GETREC (STOCK, AUTHOR, TITLE, PRICE, QUANT)
 INTEGER STOCK, QUANT
 REAL PRICE
 CHARACTER *20 AUTHOR, TITLE
 PRINT *, 'Stock number (enter 0 when done):'
```

```
READ *, STOCK
PRINT *, 'Author in quotes:'
READ *, AUTHOR
...
RETURN
END
```

Section 8.5

1. An additional alternative should be added to the IF structure shown in Fig. 8.6:

```
ELSE IF (OLDATA(1) .EQ. UPDATA(1)) THEN
    WRITE (UNIT = 3) UPDATA
    READ (UNIT = 1, END = 40) OLDATA
    READ (UNIT = 2, END = 40) UPDATA
```

2. If there are no sentinel records, it will be possible to reach the end of one file and still have records remaining to be processed on the other file. (This cannot happen when there are sentinel records because the main loop would execute until OLDATA and UPDATA both contained the sentinel record—the largest record in each file.) We will show how to modify the program to copy any remaining records from file UPDATE to file NEWMST after the end of file OLDMST is reached. First, initialize the character arrays OLDATA and UPDATA to all blanks using DATA statements. Next, change the statement in the main loop that reads file OLDMST to

```
READ (UNIT = 1, END = 94) OLDATA
```

   After the end of file 1 is reached, the code at label 94 should read the first record into UPDATA (if not read) and then copy any remaining records from file 2 (UPDATE) to NEWMST.

```
C Get first record from UPDATE if it was not read
   94 IF (UPDATA .EQ. '') THEN
          READ (UNIT = 2, END = 99) UPDATA
      ENDIF
C Copy any remaining records from UPDATE to NEWMST
      DO WHILE (.TRUE.)
          WRITE (UNIT = 3) UPDATA
          READ (UNIT = 2, END = 99) UPDATA
      ENDDO
```

   A branch to label 99 occurs when the end of file 2 is reached. At label 99, the files should be closed and the end-of-file record written to file NEWMST.

Section 8.7

1.
```
    DO 10 RECNUM = 1, MAXSTK
        READ (UNIT = 2, FMT = 21, REC = RECNUM)
    +       STOCK, AUTHOR, TITLE, PRICE, QUANT
        IF (STOCK .NE. 0) THEN
            PRINT *, STOCK, AUTHOR, TITLE, PRICE, QUANT
        ENDIF
 10 CONTINUE
```

2. Replace the ELSE task in Fig. 8.17 with:

```
      WRITE (UNIT = 2, FMT = 22, REC = RECNUM)
   22 FORMAT (A54)
      PRINT *, 'Record ', RECNUM, ' is deleted'
```

Chapter 9

Section 9.2

1. 042
   , JOHN QUINCY
   ADAMS,
   ADAMS, JOHN QUINCY

2. Change the first PRINT statement to

```
   PRINT *, SENTNC(FIRST+1 : NEXT-1) // SENTNC(FIRST :
   + FIRST) // 'AY'
```

Change the second PRINT statement to

```
   PRINT *, SENTNC(FIRST+1 : LENGTH-1) // SENTNC(FIRST :
   + FIRST) // 'AY'
```

3. Replace the statements FIRST = 1 through END with

```
          NEXT = 1
          DO WHILE (NEXT .LE. LENGTH)
             IF (SENTNC(NEXT : NEXT) .NE. BLANK) THEN
                FIRST = NEXT
                DO WHILE (SENTNC(NEXT : NEXT) .NE. BLANK .AND. NEXT
       +              .LT. LENGTH)
                   NEXT = NEXT + 1
                ENDDO
                PRINT *, SENTNC(FIRST : NEXT)
             ENDIF
             NEXT = NEXT + 1
          ENDDO
          STOP
          END
```

Section 9.3

1. JOHN ADAMS
   ADAMS J.Q.

2. a. 'ARE STRUCTURED PROGRAMS' is assigned to QUOTE.
   b. 'RAMS ARE STRUCTURED PROG' is assigned to QUOTE2.
   c. string in (b) is assigned to QUOTE.
   d. 'HIPS' is assigned to HIPPO.
   e. 'LARGE' is assigned to BIGGER.
   f. The blank string is assigned to BIGGER.
   g. The string 'ST' is inserted in positions 6 and 7 of BIGGER.

Section 9.5

1. Replace the statements DO 10 NEXT = LEN(STRING), 1, −1 through END with

```
      NEXT = LEN(STRING)
      DO WHILE (STRING(NEXT : NEXT) .EQ. BLANK .AND. NEXT .GT. 1)
         NEXT = NEXT − 1
      ENDDO

C set GETLEN
      IF (STRING(NEXT : NEXT) .EQ. ' ') THEN
         GETLEN = 0
      ELSE
         GETLEN = NEXT
      ENDIF
C
      RETURN
      END
```

2. a. 2   b. 0   c. 16   d. 0

Section 9.6

1. It is possible for a function reference to have commas in the argument list. Some array references may have commas as well.
2. It would be illegal to assign TEXT a new value by rearranging the substrings of the current TEXT.
3. a. CALL REPLAC (TEXT, MAXLEN, CURLEN, 'FRAC', 4, 'STRUC', 5)
   b. CALL REPLAC (TEXT, MAXLEN, CURLEN, 'IN', 2, 'ON', 2)
   c. CALL REPLAC (TEXT, MAXLEN, CURLEN, 'AMI', 3, 'AMMI', 4)
   d. CALL REPLAC (TEXT, MAXLEN, CURLEN, 'GRR', 3, 'GR', 2)

Chapter 10

Section 10.3

1.
```
          SUBROUTINE SETZ (ZBOUND, XMIN, XINCR, YMAX, YINCR,
         +                 NUMCOL, NUMROW, NUMSYM)

    C Sets the values in the array ZBOUND

          INTEGER NUMCOL, NUMROW, NUMSYM
          REAL ZBOUND(NUMSYM), XMIN, XINCR, YMAX, YINCR

          REAL ZMIN, ZMAX, ZINCR
          INTEGER R, K, L
          REAL X, Y, F
          F(X,Y) = SQRT (1.0 − MIN(X ** 2 = Y ** 2, 1.0))

    C Find ZMIN and ZMAX
          ZMIN = 1000.0
          ZMAX = −1000.0
          Y = YMAX
```

```
          DO 10 R = 1, NUMROW
            X = XMIN
            DO 20 K = 1, NUMCOL
               Z = F(X,Y)
               IF (Z .LT. ZMIN) ZMIN = Z
               IF (Z .GT. ZMAX) ZMAX = Z
               X = X + XINCR
 20         CONTINUE
            Y = Y - YINCR
 10      CONTINUE

C Set ZINCR and define ZBOUND
         ZINCR = (ZMAX - ZMIN) / REAL (NUMSYM)
         Z = ZMAX
         DO 30 L = 1, NUMSYM-1
            Z = Z - ZINCR
            ZBOUND(L) = Z
 30      CONTINUE
         ZBOUND(NUMSYM) = Z

         RETURN
         END
```

Chapter 11

Section 11.1

1. SUBROUTINE NEWTON (X0, EPSLN, F, DF, ERR, ROOT)

```
C Implements Newton's method for finding a root of the function F

C Input Arguments
C    X0 - The initial guess for the root
C    EPSLN - The error tolerance
C Output Arguments
C    ROOT - The root value
C    ERR - Flag indicating whether there is an error
C Functional Arguments
C    F - The function f(X) (an external function)
C    DF - f' (X) (an external function)

      REAL X0, EPSLN, ROOT, F, DF
      LOGICAL ERR

      REAL CORR, FPRIME, X1
      LOGICAL NTZERO

C Initialize the first guess and the loop-control variables
      X1 = X0
      CORR = 2 * EPSLN
      NTZERO = .TRUE.
```

```
C Repeat loop until convergence or zero derivative is found
      DO WHILE (ABS(CORR) .GT. EPSLN .AND. NTZERO)      9 IF (...) THEN
         FPRIME = DF(X1)
         IF (FPRIME .NE. 0.0) THEN
            CORR = F(X1) / FPRIME
            X1 = X1 - CORR
            PRINT *, 'X intercept is ', X1
         ELSE
            NTZERO = .FALSE.
         ENDIF
      ENDDO                                              GOTO 9
C                                                        ENDIF
C Define results
      IF (NTZERO) THEN
         ROOT = X1
         ERR = .FALSE.
      ELSE
         ERR = .TRUE.
      ENDIF

      RETURN
      END
```

Section 11.3

```
1.    PROGRAM GAUSS
C Solves a system of N linear equations in N unknowns
C by Gaussian elimination with pivoting. The system
C of equations is represented by an augmented matrix,
C AUG, and the solution is represented by the array, X.

      REAL AUG(10,11), X(10)
      INTEGER N
      LOGICAL OK

      CALL GETSYS (AUG, N)
      CALL GAUSS (AUG, N, OK)
      IF (OK) THEN
         CALL BACK (AUG, N, X)
         CALL REPORT (X, N)
      ELSE
         PRINT *
         PRINT *, 'This system is singular!'
      ENDIF
      STOP
      END

C -------------------------------------------

      SUBROUTINE GETSYS (AUG, N)
```

```
C Reads a system of N linear equations in N unknowns
C from the user in the form of an augmented matrix, AUG

      REAL AUG(10,*)
      INTEGER N

      INTEGER R, K

C Get number of equations, N
C and give user instructions
      PRINT *, 'Please enter number of equations:'
      READ *, N
      PRINT *
      PRINT *, 'Please enter system of equations'
      PRINT *, 'in form of augmented matrix, row'
      PRINT *, 'by row. You will be prompted to'
      PRINT *, 'enter each row in turn.'

C Get augmented matrix, row by row
      DO 10 R = 1, N
         PRINT *, 'Enter row # ', R
         READ *, (AUG(R,K), K = 1, N+1)
  10  CONTINUE
      RETURN
      END

C ------------------------------------------------

      SUBROUTINE REPORT (X, N)

C Reports out the solution vector, X

      REAL X(*)
      INTEGER N

      INTEGER I

      PRINT *
      PRINT *, 'The solution to this system is:'
      DO 10 I = 1, N
         PRINT *, 'X(', I, ') = ', X(I)
  10  CONTINUE
      RETURN
      END
```

Section 11.5

```
      PROGRAM NORMAL
C Computes areas under the standard normal curve using Simpson's rule

      REAL RESULT, Z, SIMPSN
      INTEGER N
```

```
C For each Z compute four approximations to the integral
      DO 10 Z = 0.5, 5.0, 0.5
          PRINT *, 'Approximate integrals for Z = ', Z, ' follows:'
          N = 2
          DO WHILE (N .LE. 16)                        19 IF (...) THEN
              RESULT = SIMPSN(0.0, Z, N)
              PRINT *, N, RESULT
              N = N * 2
          ENDDO                                           GOTO 19
C                                                         ENDIF
          PRINT *
   10 CONTINUE

      STOP
      END
```

Answers to Review Questions

Chapter 1

1. Three types of information stored on a computer are character data, real numbers, and integer numbers.
2. Two functions of the CPU are the performance of arithmetic operations and the control of all actions performed by the computer.
3. input devices: keyboard and mouse; output devices: screen and printer; secondary storage: floppy disk and hard disk
4. False. A computer cannot think.
5. The three categories of programming languages are machine language, assembly language, and high-level language.
6. High-level languages are easier to use, are portable, and resemble English.
7. Compilation and loading are needed to transform a high-level language to machine language.
8. A structured program is easier to read, understand, and maintain than an unstructured program. Also, a structured program is less likely to contain errors and is easier to debug (remove errors).
9. `INCOME, CONST, C3PO, R2DTWO` are all syntactically correct.
10. A memory cell is allocated to hold a real number identified by the name `CELL1`.
11. `CHARACTER *1 LET1, LET2, LET3, LET4, LET5`
    `PRINT *, 'Enter 5 letters of a name, separated by commas:'`
    `READ *, LET1, LET2, LET3, LET4, LET5`
    `PRINT *, LET5, LET4, LET3, LET2, LET1`
    `STOP`
    `END`

12. `PRINT *, 'The average size of a family is ', FAMSIZ`
13. The four standard data types in FORTRAN are integer data (type `INTEGER`), real data (type `REAL`), character data (type `CHARACTER`), and logical data (type `LOGICAL`).

Chapter 2

1. First, break the problem into a list of subproblems. Then describe the steps needed to solve each subproblem. Refine all the steps, providing greater detail, until the description can be translated directly into a program.
2. `LOGICAL`
3. The six relational operators described are `.LE.` (less than or equal to), `.LT.` (less than), `.GE.` (greater than or equal to), `.GT.` (greater than), `.EQ.` (equal to), and `.NE.` (not equal to).
4. The programmer should hand trace the program.
5.

Program statement	TEMP	Effect
	?	
PRINT *, 'Enter a...'	?	Prints a prompt
READ *, TEMP	27.34	Reads the data

```
      IF (TEMP .GT. 32.0) THEN

      PRINT *, 'Ice forming'
```

Is 27.34 > 32.0?
  Value is false
Print-message that temperature
is below freezing

```
6.  IF (HOURS .GT. 40.0) THEN
       GROSS = (40.0 * RATE) + ((HOURS - 40.0) * 1.5 * RATE)
    ELSE
       GROSS = RATE * HOURS
    ENDIF

7. IF (GENDER .EQ. 'FEMALE') THEN
      IF (AGE .GE. 18) THEN
         STATUS = 'ADULT'
      ELSE
         STATUS = 'CHILD'
      ENDIF
    ELSE
      IF (AGE .GE. 21) THEN
         STATUS = 'ADULT'
      ELSE
         STATUS = 'CHILD'
      ENDIF
    ENDIF

8. IF (GRADE .LE. 5) THEN
       PRINT *, 'Elementary school'
    ELSE IF (GRADE .LE. 8) THEN
       PRINT *, 'MIDDLE SCHOOL'
    ELSE IF (GRADE .LE. 12) THEN
       PRINT *, 'HIGH SCHOOL'
    ELSE IF (GRADE .GT. 12) THEN
       PRINT *, 'COLLEGE'
    ENDIF
```

Chapter 3

1. The IF structure will execute only once, but the WHILE loop body can execute a number of times.
2. For X = 8.0:

IF *Structure*	WHILE *Loop*
6.000000	6.000000
	4.000000
	2.000000
	0.000000

For X = 7.0:

5.000000	5.000000
	3.000000
	1.000000
	-1.000000

For X = 0.0, X = -7.0, and X = -8.0, nothing will be printed.

3. a. IF structure
   b. DO loop
   c. IF structure
   d. WHILE loop
   e. DO loop
   f. IF structure
   g. WHILE loop

4. a.
```
IF (AGE .GE. MINAGE) THEN
      PRINT *, 'Voting age'
   ELSE
      PRINT *, 'Under voting age'
   ENDIF
```

   b.
```
   DO 10 EMPLOY = 1, 5
         . . .
   10 CONTINUE
```

   c.
```
IF (GROSS .LT. RATE1) THEN
      . . .
   ELSE IF (GROSS .LT. RATE2) THEN
      . . .
   ELSE IF (GROSS .LT. RATE3) THEN
      . . .
   ELSE IF (GROSS .LT. RATE4) THEN
      . . .
   ELSE
      . . .
   ENDIF
```

   d.
```
READ *, ITEM
   DO WHILE (ITEM .NE. FINAL)
      IF (ITEM .EQ. 0.0) THEN
         NUMZER = NUMZER + 1
      ENDIF
      READ *, ITEM
   ENDDO
```

   e.
```
   DO 10 I = 1, 99, 2
         PRODCT = PRODCT * I
   10 CONTINUE
```

   f.
```
IF (SCORE .LT. 60) THEN
      GRADE = 'F'
   ELSE IF (SCORE .LT. 70) THEN
      GRADE = 'D'
   ELSE IF (SCORE .LT. 80) THEN
      GRADE = 'C'
   ELSE IF (SCORE .LT. 90) THEN
      GRADE = 'B'
   ELSE
      GRADE = 'A'
   ENDIF
```

```
    g. DO WHILE (VALUE .GE. 0.5)
           VALUE = VALUE / 2.0
           PRINT *, VALUE
       ENDDO
```

5. A DO loop is for counting; the loop-control variable progresses from one value to another changing by a certain increment. A WHILE loop is more general; it can be used for counting or for other purposes. It is used when the number of loop repetitions required cannot be determined before executing the program and reading the data.

6. A sentinel value is a value that, when read as input, indicates the end of the data.

7. The READ statements should appear before the WHILE loop and inside the WHILE loop, generally just before ENDDO.

8.
```
   SUM = 0.0
   PRINT *, 'ENTER PAY'
   READ *, PAY
   DO WHILE (PAY .NE. -1.0)
       SUM = SUM + PAY
       PRINT *, 'ENTER PAY'
       READ *, PAY
   ENDDO
```

9. For first data line, SLOPE is 0.5; for second data line, SLOPE is 3.0.

10. GOOD, GOOD, POOR, FAIR, POOR

11. The segment will print GOOD "forever."

Chapter 4

1. Values of type INTEGER take up less storage space in the computer's memory. Also, operations on INTEGER data are usually faster. Finally, calculations with INTEGER numbers are often more precise and more accurate than with REAL numbers.

2. 9.75

3.
```
   REAL, 14.0
   INTEGER, 14
   REAL, 3.5
   INTEGER, 3
   REAL, 3.5
   INTEGER, 2
```
   invalid arguments

4.
```
   MOD(11, 2)     = 1        ABS(-37.5 + 20)  = 17.5
   INT(-3.5)      = -3       SQRT(12 + 13)    =  5.0
   MAX0(-27,50,4) = 50       INT(-25.7)       = -25
   MIN0(-27,50,4) = -27      NINT(-18.7)      = -19
```

5. NUM1 = REAL(NINT(NUM1 * 100.0)) / 100.0

6. Cancellation error—When adding a very small number to a very large number, the effect of the small number may be lost.

   Arithmetic underflow—When a number is too small to be represented, it is stored as zero.

   Arithmetic overflow—A number becomes too large to be represented.

7.
```
IF (FLAG .OR. (COLOR .EQ. 'RED') .OR. ((MONEY .EQ. 'PLENTY')
+        .AND. (.NOT. TIMEUP))) THEN
    PRINT *, 'TRUE'
ELSE
    PRINT *, 'FALSE'
ENDIF
```

8.
```
OVRTIM = HOURS .GT. 40
```

9.
```
    PRINT 10, 'NAME', 'HOURS', 'RATE', 'PAY'
10 FORMAT (1X, A4, 11X, A5, 5X, A6, 5X, A8)

    PRINT 20, NAME, HOURS, RATE, PAY
20 FORMAT (1X, A10, 5X, F5.1, 5X, F6.2, 5X, F8.2)
```

Chapter 5

1.
```
INTEGER FUNCTION TOPENY (DOLLAR, CENTS)
INTEGER DOLLAR, CENTS
TOPENY = 100 * DOLLAR + CENTS
RETURN
END
```

2.
```
SUBROUTINE OUTGRD (SCORE)
INTEGER SCORE
IF (SCORE .GE. 90) THEN
    PRINT *, 'A'
ELSE IF (SCORE .GE. 80) THEN
    PRINT *, 'B'
ELSE IF (SCORE .GE. 70) THEN
    PRINT *, 'C'
ELSE IF (SCORE .GE. 60) THEN
    PRINT *, 'D'
ELSE
    PRINT *, 'F'
ENDIF
RETURN
END
```

3.
```
CHARACTER *1 OUTGRD (SCORE)
INTEGER SCORE
IF (SCORE .GE. 90) THEN
    OUTGRD = 'A'
...
ELSE
    OUTGRD = 'F'
ENDIF
RETURN
END
```

4. When a subprogram call occurs, all of the subprogram's local variables and parameters are allocated new memory cells (initially undefined). Each dummy argument is

associated with the memory cell(s) previously allocated to its corresponding actual argument.

5. A stub is a "dummy subprogram" substituted for an unwritten subprogram that allows the programmer to test the main program and the other completed subprograms.

6. A driver program is used to enter data and to call and test a single subprogram.

7. A structure chart shows the control hierarchy for program units (the main program and the subprograms) and also shows data flow between program units.

8. the structure chart

9. Even though the total number of program lines may increase, each program unit has a small number of lines, which are highly interrelated. Consequently, the program units are short, self-contained, and easier to test, debug, and reuse in new programs. Argument list errors become less likely as you gain more experience in using arguments.

Chapter 6

1. The DO loop references array element X(9), which does not exist. The error will be detected during program execution.

2. REAL SALES(0 : 6)

3. A real number is assigned to a CHARACTER array element—a syntax error.

4. The statement is syntactically correct; however, an execution error occurs if the integer read into COUNTS(1) is outside the range 1 to 5.

5. Two common ways of selecting an array element are as follows: using a DO loop-control variable as the array subscript so that the array elements are accessed in sequence; reading in the array subscript so that the elements are accessed in random order.

6. Assume MINSUB, MAXSUB, and I are type INTEGER variables.

```
      MINSUB = 1
      MAXSUB = 1
      DO 10 I = 2, 20
         IF (X(I) .LT. X(MINSUB)) MINSUB = I
         IF (X(I) .GT. X(MAXSUB)) MAXSUB = I
   10 CONTINUE
      PRINT *, 'The smallest value has subscript ', MINSUB
      PRINT *, 'The largest value has subscript ', MAXSUB
```

7.
```
      REAL X(100), Y(100)
      INTEGER I, N
      READ *, N
      DO 10 I = 1, N
         Y(I) = X(N-I+1)
   10 CONTINUE
```

Chapter 7

1. CHARACTER *20 TITLE(52, 10)
   The array element TITLE(3, 1) will contain the title of the number 1 song for week 3.

2. The array HOURS may be initialized as shown below:

```
REAL HOURS(5, 52, 7)
INTEGER SIZE
PARAMETER (SIZE = 5 * 52 * 7)
INTEGER EMPNO, WEEKNO, DAYNO
DATA HOURS /SIZE * 0.0/
```

or you can replace the DATA statement by the nested loops

```
    DO 10 EMPNO = 1, 5
        DO 20 WEEKNO = 1, 52
            DO 30 DAYNO = 1, 7
                HOURS(EMPNO,WEEKNO,DAYNO) = 0.0
30          CONTINUE
20      CONTINUE
10 CONTINUE
```

3. The nested loops below display five sums; each value displayed is the summation of three array elements.

```
    DO 10 ROW = 1, 5
        ROWSUM = 0.0
        DO 20 COL = 1, 3
            ROWSUM = ROWSUM + TABLE(ROW, COL)
20      CONTINUE
        PRINT *, ROWSUM
10 CONTINUE
```

4. The nested loops below display three sums; each value displayed is the summation of five array elements.

```
    DO 10 COL = 1, 3
        COLSUM = 0.0
        DO 20 ROW = 1, 5
            COLSUM = COLSUM + TABLE(ROW, COL)
20      CONTINUE
        PRINT *, COLSUM
10 CONTINUE
```

5. 20 30 25 80 40 60   Initial array
   20 25 30 40 60 80   Array after first pass
   20 25 30 40 60 80   Array after second and last pass

6.
```
    LIST(1) = LIST(6)
    DO 10 I = 5, 1, -1
        LIST(I+1) = LIST(I)
10 CONTINUE
```

7. Named common blocks can be used to separate different collections of COMMON data. Data that may be referenced by all or most of the subprograms in a program system are usually placed in blank COMMON rather than named COMMON.

8. a. CALL PSUM (A,MAXSIZ,1,MAXSIZ,VALID,SUM)
   b. CALL PSUM (A,MAXSIZ,FIRST,LAST,VALID,SUM)
   c. CALL PSUM (A,MAXSIZ,FIRST + 4,LAST,VALID,SUM)
   d. CALL PSUM (A,MAXSIZ,2,7,VALID,SUM)
   e. CALL PSUM (A,MAXSIZ,FIRST,LAST * 2,VALID,SUM)

9.   VALID   SUM
   a. .TRUE.   36.2
   b. .TRUE.   12.3
   c. .FALSE.   0.0
   d. .TRUE.   13.4
   e. .FALSE.   0.0

10. COMMON /EMPBLK/ NUMDEP(50), SALARY(100), N, FOUND, X, Y
    INTEGER NUMDEP, N, COUNT
    REAL SALARY, X, Y

11.

```
      SUBROUTINE PSUM (LIST,SIZE,I,J,LEGAL,SUM)

C Computes the sum of elements I through J of list

C Argument Definitions
C   Input Arguments
C     LIST - Array of items to be summed
C     SIZE - Size of the array
C     I - Index of first array element included in SUM
C     J - Index of last array element included in SUM
C   Output Arguments
C     LEGAL - Indicates whether an illegal index is
C             specified
C     SUM - Sum of the selected array elements

      INTEGER SIZE, I, J
      REAL LIST(SIZE), SUM
      LOGICAL LEGAL

C Local Variables
      INTEGER LCV

C Initialize SUM to zero
      SUM = 0.0

C Determine whether array indices are legal
      IF (I .LE. J .AND. J .LE. SIZE) THEN
         LEGAL = .TRUE.
      ELSE
         LEGAL = .FALSE.
         RETURN
      ENDIF

C Compute the sum
      DO 10 LCV = I, J
         SUM = SUM + LIST(LCV)
10    CONTINUE

      RETURN
      END
```

Chapter 8

1.
```
   READ 19, NAME, WKSAL, AGE, AUTHOR, NCHILD
19 FORMAT (A14, F5.2, I2, A8, I1)
```

2. The following lines are printed at the top of a new page:

```
BOB SOLOMON IS 84 YEARS OLD
HE EARNS 147.63 DOLLARS PER WEEK
HIS FAVORITE AUTHOR IS ARTHUR AND HE HAS 8 CHILDREN
```

3. a. Unit number is not specified.
   b. The Z format descriptor is illegal.
   c. There is no label on the FORMAT statement.

4.
```
IF (N .GT. 0 .AND. N .LE. MAXNUM) THEN
    READ (UNIT = 2, REC = N) INREC
ELSE
    PRINT*, N, ' IS OUT OF RANGE'
ENDIF
```

5.
```
PATRICIA    CHARLES    MARY       MEG
MARIE       CHUCK      RICHARD    SHEILA
IRENE       HOWARD     EDWARD     HELEN
```

Chapter 9

1.

	Length of SUBJCT	Length of TARGET
a.	20	10
b.	10	1
c.	9	2
d.	13	2
e.	30	12

2. a. 'HEATHER   IS A WILD FLOWER'
   b. 'HEATHER IS WILD'
   c. The same string is formed in all three cases,
      'HEATHER IS A WILD FLOWER'
   d. 'WILD AS A ROSE'
   e. 'HTHR'
   f. This substring name is illegal because it attempts to reference character positions that are outside the string FLOWER (i.e., character positions 11 and 12).

3.

	Using LEN	Using GETLEN
a.	10	7
b.	24	24
c.	7	7
d.	10	8
e.	5	5
f.	3	3

4. a. 34 b. 1 c. 26 d. 9 e. 0 f. 3

Chapter 10

1. The scaling problem consists of mapping the range of X and Y values into the screen width and height, respectively.
2. In a three-dimensional plot, the scaling problem consists of selecting different symbols to represent the range of values for Z.
3. You can use two-dimensional plots to represent a three-dimensional surface by plotting slices in two dimensions. Each slice should be plotted for a fixed value of the third variable. The values of the third variable should run from the minimum to the maximum in fixed increments.
4. Three applications of computer-aided design in engineering are: designing automobile bodies, drawing a wiring diagram for a building, integrated-circuit fabrication.

Chapter 11

1. $\begin{vmatrix} 2 & 2 & -4 & 0 \\ 1 & -4 & 1 & 4 \\ -1 & 3 & -2 & -5 \end{vmatrix}$

2. $\begin{vmatrix} 1 & 1 & -2 & 0 \\ 0 & -6 & 5 & 4 \\ 0 & 5 & -6 & -5 \end{vmatrix}$

3. multiplication of a row by a constant, adding or subtracting one row from another, swapping any two rows
4. If your computer can compute numerical results accurate to d significant digits, you have reached a point of diminishing returns if there is no change in the first d digits when the number of intervals is doubled.
5. Double precision improves the accuracy of numerical computations by increasing the number of significant digits in a result, but it does not affect the range of numbers that may be represented.
6. There is a possibility for error when the double precision representation of a number is compared to its floating point (type REAL) representation. When comparing complex numbers, be sure to compare the real and imaginary parts of the numbers separately.

Index

STATEMENT	EXAMPLE OF USE
Dummy arguments	`INTEGER NUMSTU, SCORE(*)`
	`INTEGER MAXSTU`
	`PARAMETER (MAXSTU = 120)`
COMMON statement	`COMMON STUDNT`
	`CHARACTER * 20 STUDNT(MAXSTU)`
Local variable	`CHARACTER * 20 NAME`
	`C Read each student name from file and score from user`
Assignment	`NUMSTU = 0`
WHILE statement	`DO WHILE (NUMSTU .LT. MAXSTU)`
File READ	`READ (UNIT = 1, FMT = 5, END = 99) NAME`
FORMAT statement	`5    FORMAT (A)`
Format-free PRINT	`PRINT *, 'Enter score for ', NAME`
Increment variable	`NUMSTU = NUMSTU + 1`
Format-free READ	`READ *, SCORE(NUMSTU)`
Array assignment	`STUDNT(NUMSTU) = NAME`
End of WHILE loop	`ENDDO`
	`C End of file reached`
CONTINUE	`99 CONTINUE`
RETURN	`RETURN`
END subroutine	`END`
	`C———————————————————————————————————————————`
Subroutine head	`SUBROUTINE DOGRAD(SCORE, NUMSTU, PASSED)`
	`C Assigns a grade, GRADE(I), to student I and resets`
	`C PASSED(I) to .FALSE. if student I has failed.`
Dummy arguments	`INTEGER NUMSTU, SCORE(*)`
	`LOGICAL PASSED(*)`
	`INTEGER MAXSTU`
	`PARAMETER (MAXSTU = 120)`
COMMON statement	`COMMON STUDNT`
	`CHARACTER * 20 STUDNT (MAXSTU)`
Named COMMON	`COMMON /GRD/ GRADE`
	`CHARACTER * 1 GRADE(MAXSTU)`
Local variable	`INTEGER I`
Function declaration	`LOGICAL FAILED`
	`C Assign grades and print results`